D1553777

Bruce J. MacLennan

The University of Tennessee, Knoxville

Functional Programming

Practice and Theory

ADDISON-WESLEY PUBLISHING COMPANY

Reading, Massachusetts • Menlo Park, California
New York • Don Mills, Ontario • Wokingham, England
Amsterdam • Bonn • Sydney • Singapore
Tokyo • Madrid • San Juan

To "the girls," Gail and Kimberly

Many of the designations used by manufacturers and sellers to distinguish their products are claimed as trademarks. Where those designations appear in this book, and Addison-Wesley was aware of a trademark claim, the designations have been printed in initial caps or all caps.

The programs and applications presented in this book have been included for their instructional value. They have been tested with care, but are not guaranteed for any particular purpose. The publisher does not offer any warranties or representations, nor does it accept any liabilities with respect to the programs or applications.

Library of Congress Cataloging-in-Publication Data

MacLennan, Bruce J.
    Functional programming : practice and theory / Bruce J. MacLennan.
       p.   cm.
    Bibliography: p.
    Includes index.
    ISBN 0-201-13744-5
    1. Functional programming languages. 2. Functional programming
(Computer Science)   I. Title.
QA76.73.F86M33   1989
005. 13--dc20
                                            89-31710
                                             CIP

ABCDEFGHIJ-MA-89

Preface

... for art and science are a single gift, called science inasmuch as art refashions the mind, and called art inasmuch as by science the world is refashioned.

Santayana, *Dialogues in Limbo*

Methodology Rather than Language

There is more to functional programming than simply programming in a functional language. As explained in Section 1.1, I view functional programming as a new *programming paradigm*, comparable in importance to structured programming. As such, it has value as a discipline of thought even in the absence of functional programming languages.

Throughout the book, functional programming is treated first as a means for reliably deriving programs and as a tool for analyzing programs and proving their correctness. Functional programming can be used this way even if the eventual implementation language is a conventional imperative language. In the process, the value of functional programming *languages* is naturally illustrated.

This broader view of functional programming, I hope, will make this book suitable as a text in courses on topics other than functional programming. For example, the emphasis on methodology rather than specific languages should make it suitable as an auxiliary text for courses in software engineering, software prototyping, formal specification, language systems (i.e., compilers and environments), data structures, and

algorithm analysis. The book could also be used as a disciplined introduction to programming in LISP, Scheme, or Prolog.

Scope and Organization

The subtitle of this book is *Practice and Theory*. I say "Practice and
Theory" rather than the usual "Theory and Practice" because this book
has an *inductive* organization—concretes are presented before abstractions. Thus readers can see the source and motivation for the abstractions
and, it is hoped, learn to form similar abstractions on their own. This
general skill is much more important than any of the particular abstractions discussed in this book. Additionally, the questions raised in the discussion of practical functional programming problems provide the
motivation for investigating the foundations of functional programming
later in the book.

The inductive principle also dictates the organization of the practice
portion of the book. In particular, the student will thoroughly investigate
first-order functions (functions that operate on data) before proceeding to
the more abstract higher-order functions (functions that operate on functions).

The theory portion of the book is also organized inductively: It deals
with concrete (string) transformations before discussing abstract (tree)
transformations, and introduces a specific calculus (the lambda calculus)
before discussing general calculi. The book also attempts to develop the
reader's skill in generalization by showing how the solution of various
problems for the case of arithmetic expressions can be extended to their
solution for a full functional programming language.

For several reasons, this book does not stress the implementation of
functional programming languages. First, on conventional architectures
functional languages are often implemented using the same techniques as
those used for functions in a conventional recursive, block-structured
language. These techniques are adequately covered in texts on programming language implementation. Second, the implementation of functional languages on unconventional architectures is changing so rapidly
that anything the reader would learn about them here soon would be
obsolete. I do, however, use Turner's bracket-abstraction algorithm and
SKI-reduction machine as examples of abstract transformations. Also, a
recursive interpreter for a functional language is developed in the context
of a discussion of universal functions—a starting point for developing
practical interpreters.

Choice of Language

In writing a book in a rapidly evolving area such as functional programming, one faces the problem of language choice: Which functional
language(s) should be used as a vehicle for presenting functional

programs? Most extant functional languages are experimental languages, which means that they are undergoing a process of evolution, and also means that the popular languages of today may be the forgotten languages of tomorrow. Therefore the use of such languages could lead to the premature obsolescence of this book.

The one exception is LISP. This quasi-functional language has been around for 30 years, and will likely be around for quite a few more. I have not used LISP in this book, however, for several reasons:

- LISP is not a purely functional language; it has a number of traditional imperative features. This tends to confuse students who are already familiar with LISP or who read LISP books on their own.

- By oversight or design, many of the most popular dialects of LISP are incapable of supporting full functional programming.[1] Thus students are misled into thinking that any LISP system is suitable for functional programming. It is hoped that the more widespread adoption in the future of Common LISP, which supports functional programming, will decrease the force of this argument.

- LISP has a number of undesirable semantic attributes that have only a historical justification, including dynamic scoping and the identification of "nonnull" and "false." These attributes complicate the discussion of important topics, such as the lambda calculus and the semantics of data types.

- The syntax of LISP is notoriously unreadable. It is hard to justify making the subject of functional programming more difficult by using, for example, the conditional syntax and opaque names such as 'car' and 'cdr' found in LISP. Some of the syntactic conventions even have semantic implications. For example, the LISP syntax for function application precludes treating argument lists as lists in fact, and complicates the discussion of important ideas such as "currying."

- Finally, the near identification of concrete and abstract syntax in LISP complicates the discussion of the important difference between them. This is because, in the case of LISP, the distinction is largely pointless.

On the other hand, I have adhered to LISP conventions whenever there would have been no distinct advantage in deviating from them. Also, Appendix C gives hints on doing functional programming in Common LISP (as well as Scheme).

What language have I used? Since the goal of the book is to teach functional programming *methodology* as opposed to functional programming

---

1. Specifically, their lack of support for "upward funargs" and lexical closures precludes the definition of higher-order functions.

languages, I have chosen a language that is likely to be understandable with little additional instruction: standard mathematical notation.[2] This selection has the additional advantage of more clearly separating the *mathematical methodology* of functional programming from the less interesting process of translating the functional design into a program in a (functional or imperative) programming language. Both processes, however, are illustrated.

Acknowledgments

I have drawn heavily from the work of the pioneers of functional programming, including the early papers by John McCarthy, Christopher Strachey, and Peter Landin, and the more recent books by William Burge and Peter Henderson. I have also made use of some of the work of John Backus, J. Barkley Rosser, Dana Scott, Dave Turner, and others. I am grateful to all of these computer scientists for the quality of their work and publications.

I'm especially grateful to Gyula Magó, who used this material in his class in 1987. His detailed and thoughtful criticisms have been very helpful in bringing this book to final form. I'm also grateful to Dan Friedman, Peter Greene, Guy Steele, and John Werth for their many useful comments on the manuscript. Of course, responsibility for the result must lie with me. I would also like to thank my students, who for nine years have tolerated the inadequacies of earlier versions of this manuscript. Finally, I'm delighted to be able to publicly thank my wife, Gail, for her patience during the time this book was "almost done."

Douglas Lake, Tennessee   B. J. M.

---

2. Despite my best intentions, I have been driven to give this notation a name (Φ) and specific syntax (see Appendix A), just as though it were a programming language. The major justification is that this permits me to discuss interpreters and language-processing problems in Chapters 11 and 12.

Contents

Chapter 9. Consistency of the Lambda Calculus   398

Chapter 10. Abstract Calculi   421

Chapter 11. Universal Functions   471

Appendix C: Functional Programming in Scheme and LISP 569

Index of Notation 576

Index 579

Part 1

Practice

Chapter 1

Functions

Why is the notation of arithmetic expressions of such benefit to the mathematician? The reason seems to be quite subtle and fundamental. It embodies the principles of structuring, which underlie all our attempts to master a complex problem or control a complex situation by analyzing it into simpler subproblems, with clean and narrow interfaces between them.

C. A. R. Hoare (1973, 15)

1.1 Introduction

The purpose of this book is to explain the theory and practice of an important new programming methodology: *functional programming*. This style of programming, also known as *applicative programming* and *value-oriented programming*, is important for six reasons.

First, functional programming dispenses with the ubiquitous assignment operation. As structured programming is often called "goto-less programming," so functional programming can be called "assignment-less programming." To discover how to program without assignment statements, let's pursue the analogy to structured programming. In structured programs the gotos are still there, but hidden inside higher-level, easier-to-use, *structured* control structures. As a result, structured programs are easier to reason about than those that use gotos.

The goal of functional programming is similar. It can be called "programming without assignments" since no assignments appear in functional programs. Just as the computer executing a structured program is in fact doing gotos, the computer executing a functional program is in fact doing assignments. In both cases, these constructs are hidden from the programmer—they are at a *lower level of abstraction*. The advantages of assignment-less programming are similar to those of goto-less programming: It is easier to understand programs, they can be derived more systematically, and it is easier to reason about them.

Even if you never write totally goto-less programs, the study of structured programming leads to a discipline that will improve your style. Similarly, even if you never write totally assignment-free programs, the experience gained from the study of functional programming will further improve your style.

The second reason that functional programming is important is that it encourages thinking at *higher levels of abstraction* by providing mechanisms (higher-order functions) for modifying the behavior of existing programs and combining existing programs. Thus functional programming encourages the programmer to work in units larger than the individual statements of a conventional programming language, a practice called *programming in the large* (DeRemer and Kron 1976). Functional programmers can use many of these ideas even when programming in a nonfunctional language.

The third reason for studying functional programming is that it provides a paradigm for programming *massively parallel computers*— computers with hundreds of thousands, perhaps millions of processors. As we begin to reach the speed of light and other limitations on computer speed, we can expect to see computers that achieve higher speed by greater parallelism. Further, VLSI technology permits massively parallel computers. How does one program such a computer? In functional programming, the absence of assignments, independence of evaluation order, and ability to operate on entire data structures provide paradigms for programming these machines.

The fourth reason for studying functional programming is its applications in artificial intelligence (AI). Currently most AI programming is done in LISP, a language that inspired much of the early work in functional programming. The study of functional programming is a good introduction to LISP programming and provides a good discipline for LISP programmers. PROLOG, the newest AI programming language, with many characteristics of a functional programming language, has been suggested as a successor to LISP. Further, as AI techniques are finding wider and wider applications, functional programming is becoming important to all programmers, not just AI programmers.

The fifth important reason for functional programming is that it is valuable in developing *executable specifications* and *prototype implementations*. The simple underlying semantics and rigorous mathematical foundations of functional programming, along with its high expressive ability, make it an ideal vehicle for specifying the intended behavior of programs. Functional programming can play this role even if no functional programming language system is available to execute the program. If such a system is available, however, we have something very valuable: an executable specification. This can be used as a prototype implementation to determine whether the specifications are correct, and as a benchmark against which to compare later implementations. Thus, even if you never intend to do functional programming, it can still be a valuable tool for formulating, expressing, and evaluating program specifications.

Finally, functional programming is important because it is connected to computer science theory. It provides a framework for viewing many of the decidability questions of programming and computers, a simpler framework than that provided by the usual approaches. Further, the study of functional programming is a good introduction to the denotational semantics of programming languages: The essence of denotational semantics is the translation of conventional programs into equivalent functional programs.

1.2 The World of Expressions and the World of Statements

Any programming language can be divided into two very different worlds: the world of *expressions* and the world of *statements* (Backus 1978). These two worlds are most easily explained by example. All higher-level languages have expressions of various *types*, including arithmetic expressions such as '$(a+b) \times c$',[1] relational expressions such as '$(a+b) = 0$', and Boolean expressions such as '$\neg (a \vee b)$'. As illustrated by these examples, expressions usually have a syntax patterned after everyday algebraic notation. Further, expressions usually appear on the right-hand sides of assignment statements, and in other contexts in which a *value* is required (such as in subscript expressions and parameters to procedures and functions). Thus the world of expressions includes all those programming language constructs whose purpose is to yield a *value* through the process of *evaluation*.

Higher-level languages also include *statements,* which are of two kinds. The first kind alters the control flow. These statements include conditionals, such as

if $x > 0$ **then** s := 1 **else** s := −1 **endif**

but also loops, gotos, and procedure invocations. The second kind of statements alters the *state* (memory) of the computer. Chief among these is the assignment statement

i := i + 1

---

1. Throughout this book we use single quotation marks ' ' to surround linguistic objects about which we are talking. Double quotation marks " " are used otherwise.

which alters the state of primary memory. There are also the input-output statements, which alter the state of secondary memory. The purpose of both kinds of statements is to *alter* something, either the flow of control or the state of the (primary or secondary) memory.

These two worlds have a number of important differences. For example, in the world of statements we know that the order in which things are done is very important. The statements

$$i := i + 1; \ a := a \times i;$$

have a very different effect from the following statements:

$$a := a \times i; \ i := i + 1;$$

In fact, many errors in programs are a result of doing things in the wrong order.[2]

Consider the following statement:

$$z := (2 \times a \times y + b) \times (2 \times a \times y + c);$$

The expression on the right of the assignment operation contains a *common subexpression*, '$2 \times a \times y$'. Many compilers eliminate the redundant evaluation of the common subexpression by replacing the one original assignment with these two:

$$t := 2 \times a \times y;$$
$$z := (t + b) \times (t + c);$$

In the world of expressions it is safe to do this optimization, since in an expression a given subexpression ('$2 \times a \times y$' in this case) will always have the same value.

Consider now a similar situation in the world of statements, the following two assignments:

$$y := 2 \times a \times y + b \ ; \ z := 2 \times a \times y + c;$$

Again we see a common subexpression. If we attempt to factor it out, however, we change the effect of the code:

---

2. In parallel programming, where many things can be happening at the same time, reasoning in the world of statements may become very difficult. As shown in Section 1.3, parallelism is not a problem in the world of expressions.

```
t := 2 × a × y;
y := t + b ;  z := t + c;
```

The problem is as follows: Because the value of 'y' has changed between the two occurrences of '2 × a × y', the values of these two occurrences are different. Of course, if the first assignment had been to a variable other than 'a' or 'y', then the common subexpression elimination would have been legal.

Although it is possible for a compiler to analyze a program to determine when common subexpressions can be eliminated from two or more statements, accomplishing this requires the sophisticated techniques of *global flow analysis*. Such analysis is usually expensive to perform and difficult to implement correctly. Thus common subexpression elimination is difficult in the world of statements but quite easy in the world of expressions. (People experience some of the same difficulties when they attempt to understand or reason about the effect of statements in a program.)

Here we have seen one advantage of expressions over statements, the ease of reasoning about programs; more advantages are presented later. The purpose of *functional programming* is the extension of the advantages of expressions to the entire programming language.

1.3 Evaluation Order Independence

To understand the properties of the world of expressions and the sources of its advantages, let's investigate the evaluation of arithmetic expressions. To *evaluate* something means to extract its value. Thus we can evaluate the arithmetic expression '$6 \times 2 + 2$' to yield its value, 14. Can we evaluate the expression '$(2ax + b)(2ax + c)$'? No, not unless we know the values of the names 'a', 'b', 'c', and 'x'. That is, the value of this expression is dependent on its *context of evaluation*. Therefore let's consider the evaluation of '$(2ax + b)(2ax + c)$', where $a = 3$, $b = 2$, $c = -1$, and $x = 2$. Since we are trying to understand expressions, we will follow the evaluation process in considerable detail.

In evaluating the preceding expression, there are many places where we can begin. For the sake of regularity, we work from left to right. Consider now the formula with all its operators made explicit:

$$(2 \times a \times x + b) \times (2 \times a \times x + c)$$

Before we can perform the first multiplication, '$2 \times a$', we must know the value of 'a' in the context of evaluation; it is 3. Therefore we substitute this value into the expression:

$$(2 \times 3 \times x + b) \times (2 \times a \times x + c)$$

We can now perform the multiplication '2×3', yielding

$$(6 \times x + b) \times (2 \times a \times x + c)$$

The remaining steps follow analogously and are shown in Fig. 1.1. We have used the *sign of transformation* '$\Rightarrow$' to indicate the successive steps in the evaluation.

In this example we reduced the left subexpression before the right subexpression. It is important to notice that, had we reduced the right subexpression first, we would have produced exactly the same value. Thus, again using '$\Rightarrow$' as a sign of transformation, we have

$$(2 \times a \times x + b) \times (2 \times a \times x + c) \;\Rightarrow\; (2 \times a \times x + b) \times (2 \times 3 \times x + c) \;\cdots$$
$$\Rightarrow\; (2 \times a \times x + b) \times 11 \;\Rightarrow\; \cdots \;\Rightarrow\; 154$$

In fact, every evaluation order will produce the same value, 154. This is because in the evaluation of pure expressions,[3] the evaluation of one subexpression cannot affect the value of any other subexpressions. Indeed, it would even be possible to do *parallel evaluation*, that is, evaluate several parts of the expression at the same time.

Exercise 1.1: Write out an evaluation of the expression in Fig. 1.1, but reduce the right subexpression to its value before the left.

Figure 1.1 Left-to-right evaluation of arithmetic expression.

$(2 \times 3 \times x + b) \times (2 \times a \times x + c)$
$\Rightarrow (6 \times x + b) \times (2 \times a \times x + c)$
$\Rightarrow (6 \times 2 + b) \times (2 \times a \times x + c)$
$\Rightarrow (12 + b) \times (2 \times a \times x + c)$
$\Rightarrow (12 + 2) \times (2 \times a \times x + c)$
$\Rightarrow 14 \times (2 \times a \times x + c)$
$\Rightarrow 14 \times (2 \times 3 \times x + c)$
$\Rightarrow 14 \times (6 \times x + c)$
$\Rightarrow 14 \times (6 \times 2 + c)$
$\Rightarrow 14 \times (12 + c)$
$\Rightarrow 14 \times (12 + -1)$
$\Rightarrow 14 \times 11$
$\Rightarrow 154$

---

3. A *pure expression* is an expression that does not perform any assignment operations, either explicitly or implicitly (e.g., through functions it calls). This is discussed in more detail later in this section.

It is easy to understand this independence of evaluation order if we draw the expression as a tree:

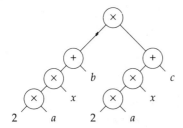

You can see that each operation depends only on those directly below it. The evaluation of a subtree can affect only that portion of the tree above itself; it cannot affect subtrees to either the right or the left. In evaluation we can begin at the leaves, and evaluate the nodes in any order (or in parallel) so long as the inputs to a node have been evaluated before we evaluate the node itself.

After we have attached values to a few of the leaves, the tree might look like this:

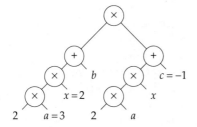

Whenever all the nodes below a given node are *decorated* with values, we can decorate the given node with the value resulting from applying the operation to the values below. For example, the lowest left × node can be decorated with the value 6:

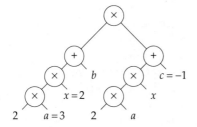

This permits the next '×' node up to be decorated with 12:

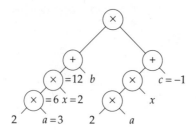

Before any further evaluation can take place, we must decorate some of the leaves. Hence the process of evaluation and decoration proceeds until the root is decorated, which gives the value of the entire expression tree:

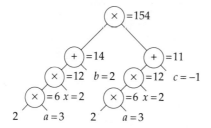

You can also see that several processes could work in parallel on decorating the tree. No matter what the order of decoration, as long as we obey the structure of the tree, we will always get the same answer.

This property of pure expressions—that is, independence of evaluation order—is called the *Church-Rosser property*, and is discussed at length in Chapters 9 and 10. The Church-Rosser property allows the construction of compilers that choose the evaluation order that makes the best use of machine resources. The ability to do parallel evaluation suggests one way to use multiprocessor computers.

Impure expressions do not in general have this property, as we can see by looking at an example from Pascal. Consider a Pascal expression such as 'a + 2*F(b)'. Is this pure or impure? To find out, we must look at the definition of F. Suppose it is

```
function F (x: integer): integer;
  begin
    F := x*x;
  end
```

Because F executes no assignment statements (except the pseudo-assignment to F to return the function value), it is a *pure* function. Clearly, in evaluating 'a + 2*F(b)', we could first evaluate either of the subexpressions 'a' and '2*F(b)' without affecting the value of the expression.

On the other hand, suppose that F were defined so that it assigns to a nonlocal variable:

```
function F (x: integer): integer;
  begin
    a := a + 1;
    F := x*x;
  end
```

In this case F is called a *pseudofunction* because it is not a pure function. Now suppose that the nonlocal variable 'a' is the same variable referred to in 'a + 2*F(b)'. Since F alters the value of 'a', the value of 'a + 2*F(b)' depends on which of 'a' and '2*F(b)' is evaluated first. In particular, if the initial value of 'a' is zero, then if 'a' is evaluated first the expression has the value $2b^2$, but if '2*F(b)' is evaluated first the expression has the value $2b^2 + 1$.

Exercise 1.2: Show in detail how the values $2b^2$ and $2b^2 + 1$ result from the different evaluation orders.

1.4 Referential Transparency

A person evaluating the expression '$(2ax + b)(2ax + c)$' would never go to the trouble of evaluating the subexpression '$2ax$' twice. Having once determined that $2ax = 12$, the human evaluator would substitute '12' for both occurrences of '$2ax$' and continue as follows:

$$(12 + b)(12 + c) \Rightarrow (12 + 2)(12 + c) \Rightarrow 14(12 + c) \Rightarrow$$
$$14(12 + -1) \Rightarrow 14(11) \Rightarrow 154$$

This is because a given arithmetic expression in a fixed context will always evaluate to the same value. Given the values $a = 3$ and $x = 2$, $2ax$ will *always* equal 12.

This is easy to see by looking at the tree form of the expression. Since the subexpression '$2 \times a \times x$' occurs twice, there is no reason to repeat the tree representing it; we can simply route both edges using the subexpression to the same subtree:

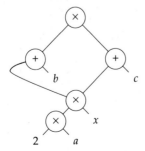

Strictly, we no longer have an expression *tree*, but rather an *acyclic graph*. Nevertheless, we can decorate the graph starting at the leaves in the same way as before:

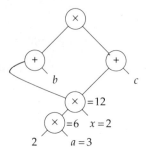

The only difference is that once the shared node is decorated, its value can be used by both the nodes above it.

The property just illustrated, called *referential transparency*,[4] means that in a fixed context the replacement of subexpression by its value is competely independent of the surrounding expression. Hence, having once evaluated an expression in a given context, we never again have to evaluate that expression in that context, because its value will never change. More generally, referential transparency can be defined as the universal ability to substitute equals for equals. In the context $a = 3$, $x = 2$ we can always substitute '12' for '2*ax*' and '2*ax*' for '12' without altering the value of the expression. Referential transparency results from the fact that the arithmetic operators have no memory, therefore every call of an operator with the same inputs produces the same result.

Why is referential transparency such a useful property? You know from mathematics how important it is to be able to substitute equals for equals. This lets you derive new equations from given equations, transform expressions into more useful forms, and prove things about expressions.

In the context of computer languages, referential transparency permits optimizations such as common subexpression elimination. For example, given the previous definition of the Pascal pseudofunction F, it is clear that, because F leaves a record in 'a' of the number of times it's been called, we could not eliminate the common subexpression from

(a + 2*F(b)) * (c + 2*F(b))

This is because changing the number of times that F is called might change the result of the program. In some languages this complicates

4. A term from logic; see (Quine 1960).

common subexpression elimination; other languages do not guarantee that a function will be called every time it's written!

1.5 Manifest Interfaces

Because mathematical notation has evolved over many hundreds of years, we expect it to exhibit a number of characteristics that increase its readability. One of these characteristics is *manifest interfaces*; that is, the input-output connections between a subexpression and its surrounding expression are visually obvious. Consider the expression '3 + 8'. The result of the addition depends only on the inputs to the operation (3 and 8), and these inputs are obvious in the written form of the expression— they sit immediately to the left and right of the operator. There are no hidden inputs to the plus operation.

Compare this with a procedure or function in a conventional programming language. There the result returned by the procedure or function can depend on nonlocal variables or local state variables; successive calls with the same inputs could produce different results. For example, if F is defined

```
function F (x: integer): integer;
   begin
     a := a + 1;
     F := a*x;
   end
```

there is no way to know the value of F(3) without first knowing the value of the nonlocal variable 'a'. Further, since the value of 'a' changes between calls of F, F(3) has a different value this time from its value last time. These *hidden interfaces* to the procedure make its behavior harder to understand.

Consider again the expression '$(2ax + b) \times (2ax + c)$'. As noted, the inputs to the first plus—'$2ax$' and 'b'—are manifest in the written form. Notice also that the role or function of the subexpression '$(2ax + b)$' within the entire expression is manifest: It constitutes the left argument of the multiplication. There are no hidden outputs or side effects of the addition. Therefore both the inputs and the outputs of this plus operator are easily determined: The inputs are the expressions '$2ax$' and 'b' on either side, and the output is delivered to the surrounding expression, '$\cdots \times (2ax + c)$'.

We can summarize the issue of manifest interfaces as follows. Expressions can be represented by trees, and the same tree represents both the syntactic structure of the expression and the way that data flows in the expression. Therefore subexpressions that communicate with each other can always be brought into contiguous positions in the tree, or in the written form of the expression. This does not hold in the world of statements; alterable variables permit nonlocal communication. In general the dataflow graph is not a tree, and it may have a very different structure from the syntax tree. Therefore it may not be possible to bring together communicating parts so that their interface is obvious. The structural identity of data dependencies and syntactic dependencies is certainly one of the principal advantages of pure expressions.

1.6 Hoare's Principles of Structuring

Hoare (1973, 16) says there "seem to be six fundamental principles of structuring,—transparency of meaning and purpose, independence of parts, recursive application, narrow interfaces, and manifestness of structure. In the case of arithmetic expressions these six principles are reconciled and achieved together with very high efficiency of implementation." We consider each principle in turn.

1. *Transparency of meaning* says that the meaning of the whole expression can be understood in terms of the meanings of its subexpressions. Thus the meaning of '$E + F$', where E and F may themselves be complicated subexpressions, depends wholly on the meanings of E and F (and of course '+').

2. *Transparency of purpose* means, as Hoare says, that "the purpose of each part consists solely in its contribution to the purpose of the whole." Thus, in '$E + F$' the only purpose of E is to compute the number that will become the left operand of '+'. Its purpose does not include any additional *side effects*.

3. *Independence of parts* says that the meanings of two nonoverlapping parts can be understood completely independently; E can be understood independently of F and vice versa. This is because the result computed by an operator depends only on the values of its inputs. It does not depend on the way these inputs are computed, nor on the use to which the value that it computes will be put.

4. *Recursive application* refers to the fact that arithmetic expressions are built up by the recursive application of uniform rules. Thus, if we know that 'E' and 'F' are expressions, then we know that '$E + F$' is an expression. And if we know that '$E + F$' and 'G' are expressions, then we also know that '$(E + F) \times G$' is an expression, and so on. Expressions of arbitrary complexity can be built up by applying the same rules over and over. Conversely, the same kind of analysis we applied to '$E + F$' can be applied recursively to each of its parts, E and F, until we reach the *atomic* (indivisible) constituents of expressions. As Hoare says, "the same structuring principle can be applied to the analysis of the parts as is applied to the understanding of the whole."

5. Arithmetic expressions have *narrow interfaces* because each arithmetic operation has only one output and only one or two inputs, and also because each of the inputs and outputs is a conceptually simple value (a number). That is, "the interface between the parts is clear, narrow, and well controlled."

6. *Manifestness of structure* refers to the fact that the structural relationships between parts of an arithmetic expression are obvious. One expression is a subexpression of another expression if the first is textually embedded in the second. Further, expressions are structurally unrelated if they do not overlap in any way. In Hoare's words, "the separation of the parts and their relation to the whole is clearly apparent from their written form."

Let's summarize the properties of pure expressions, as illustrated by conventional mathematical expressions:

- Value is independent of the evaluation order.
- Expressions can be evaluated in parallel.
- Referential transparency.
- No side effects.
- Inputs to an operation are obvious from the written form.
- Effects of an operation are obvious from the written form.

Our goal is to extend these advantages to all of programming.

1.7 Functions and Applicative Expressions

What is it about arithmetic expressions that gives them these desirable properties? First, they are structurally simple: They are uniformly constructed by the application of arithmetic operations to their arguments. Second, and most importantly, these operations are *pure functions,* that is, mathematical mappings from inputs to outputs. This means that the result of an operation depends only on its inputs. Also, if we construct a *pure expression* from these pure functions and constants, the value of this expression will always be the same.

For example, suppose we define[5] the pure function '*f*' as

$$f(u) \equiv (u + b)(u + c)$$

---

5. We use the identity sign '≡' to emphasize that we are defining something, as opposed to asserting an equation of two values.

where $b = 2$ and $c = -1$. (f is pure because it is defined in terms of pure functions, that is, the arithmetic operations addition and multiplication.) Now consider the evaluation of '$f(2ax)$' in a context in which $a = 3$ and $x = 2$. As for simple arithmetic expressions, the value is independent of evaluation order. We can evaluate the argument either before or after substitution, and get the same result. If we do it before,

$$f(2ax) \Rightarrow f(2 \times 3 \times 2) \Rightarrow f(12) \Rightarrow (12 + b)(12 + c) \Rightarrow$$
$$(12 + 2)(12 + -1) \Rightarrow 154$$

If we do it after,

$$f(2ax) \Rightarrow (2ax + b)(2ax + c) \Rightarrow (2 \times 3 \times 2 + b)(2ax + c) \Rightarrow \cdots \Rightarrow 154$$

These orders correspond to pass-by-value and pass-by-name in programming languages. Pass-by-value is often more efficient since the argument is evaluated only once. There is, however, a major difference from programming languages. Since we are dealing with pure expressions, whether we evaluate the parameter before or after substitution cannot affect the value of the expression.

Exercise 1.3: An exception to the preceding statement is considered at length in Chapters 7 and 12. Consider the evaluation of $f(1/a)$ in a context in which $a = 0$ and $f(x) \equiv 1$. That is, f is a constant function that always returns 1, no matter what its argument. Is there any difference between the two evaluation orders? Discuss.

Since our goal is to extend the advantages of arithmetic expressions to the entire programming language, let's investigate methods for programming with pure expressions. This kind of programming is variously referred to as *value-oriented programming*, *applicative programming*, and *functional programming*. Many people use these terms synonymously, although there are some subtle differences that we will make clear later.

Applicative programming is often distinguished from *imperative programming*, a programming style that makes use of *imperatives*, or orders. As we've seen, the world of statements is characterized by orders: change this, go there, replace that, and so forth. In contrast, the world of expressions involves the description of *values* (hence the term value-oriented programming). The next several chapters provide many opportunities to compare the applicative and imperative programming styles.

In *applicative programming* all our programs take the form of *applicative expressions*. Such an expression is either a constant (literal, e.g, '2', or named, e.g., 'π'), or an expression made up entirely of the *application* of pure functions to their arguments, which are also applicative expressions. In BNF notation,

<AE> ::= <id> (<AE> ,...) | <literal> | <id>

The applicative structure is most obvious if we write expressions in prefix form, that is,

sum {prod [prod (2, a), x], b}

rather than the usual '$2ax + b$'. (Following mathematical convention, we rotate through the brackets {[( )]} for readability.)

Applicative programming has only one fundamental built-in syntactic construct: the application of a function to its argument. In fact, this construct is so fundamental that it is usually represented implicitly, by juxtaposition, rather than explicitly, by some symbol. Thus 'sin θ' means the application of the function named 'sin' to the value named 'θ', and 'sum $(x, 1)$' means the application of the function named 'sum' to the pair composed of the value named 'x' and the number 1.

1.8 Function Definition

To program with functions, we must first consider the ways in which functions can be defined. Mathematically, a function is just a set of input-output pairs. Therefore, one way to define a function is to enumerate its pairs. We define 'not' as follows:

$$\text{not } \textbf{true} \equiv \textbf{false} \tag{1.1}$$
$$\text{not } \textbf{false} \equiv \textbf{true}$$

Similarly we can define 'or' as follows:

$$\text{or } \textbf{(true, true)} \equiv \textbf{true} \tag{1.2}$$
$$\text{or } \textbf{(true, false)} \equiv \textbf{true}$$
$$\text{or } \textbf{(false, true)} \equiv \textbf{true}$$
$$\text{or } \textbf{(false, false)} \equiv \textbf{false}$$

Obviously, *enumerative definition*—exhibiting the input-output correspondence for each possible input—is practical only when the function has a small, finite domain.

Exercise 1.4: Define the function and by enumerating its values for all legal inputs.

Not many functions can be defined by enumeration. Commonly functions are defined as *compositions* of already defined functions; this is called *definition by composition*. For example,

$$\text{implies } (x, y) \equiv \text{ or } (\text{not } x, y) \tag{1.3}$$

defines implication by the composition of negation and disjunction.

If we know how to apply the primitive functions, then all other function application is just substitution. For example, to evaluate 'implies (**true, false**)' we simply substitute the arguments into the definition of implies (Eq. 1.3), yielding

or (not **true, false**)

By our previous definitions of or (Eq. 1.2) and not (Eq. 1.1) we can evaluate this expression to **false**.

This substitution process is *domain-independent*—that is, the same regardless of whether we are dealing with functions of numbers, functions of characters, functions of trees, or whatever. In other words, given the definition

$$f[x] \equiv h\{x, g[x]\}$$

we know that

$$f[u(a)] = h\{u(a), g[u(a)]\}$$

regardless of the definitions of the functions g, h, u or of the constant a.

Often the definition of a function cannot be expressed simply as a composition of other functions. Rather, there are several different cases, each associated with a different composition. For example, the *signum* (algebraic sign) function could be defined *conditionally* as follows:

$$\text{sgn } x \equiv \begin{cases} 1, & \text{if } x > 0 \\ 0, & \text{if } x = 0 \\ -1, & \text{if } x < 0 \end{cases} \tag{1.4}$$

Similarly, a conditional definition of the absolute difference of x and y is as follows:

$$\text{absdif } (x, y) \equiv \begin{cases} x - y, & \text{if } x > y \\ y - x, & \text{if } x \leq y \end{cases} \tag{1.5}$$

So far we have seen ways to define a function as a fixed composition of other functions, or as one of a small, finite number of fixed compositions. Sometimes we wish to define a function in terms of an infinite number of compositions. For example, to define multiplication in terms of addition, we could write

$$m \times n \equiv \begin{cases} 0, & \text{if } m = 0 \\ n, & \text{if } m = 1 \\ n + n, & \text{if } m = 2 \\ n + n + n, & \text{if } m = 3 \\ \vdots & \vdots \end{cases} \qquad (1.6)$$

Because we cannot write down an infinite number of cases, this method of function definition is useful only if there is some regularity, some unifying principle, among the cases that allows us to generate the unwritten cases from the written ones. If such a unifying principle exists, it should be stated. This is the purpose of a *recursive definition,* one in which the thing defined is defined in terms of itself. For example, a recursive definition of multiplication is

$$m \times n \equiv \begin{cases} 0, & \text{if } m = 0 \\ n + (m - 1) \times n, & \text{if } m > 0 \end{cases} \qquad (1.7)$$

Then by successive substitution we can evaluate

$$2 \times 3 \Rightarrow 3 + (2 - 1) \times 3 \Rightarrow 3 + 1 \times 3 \Rightarrow 3 + 3 + (1 - 1) \times 3$$
$$\Rightarrow 3 + 3 + 0 \times 3 \Rightarrow 3 + 3 + 0 \Rightarrow 3 + 3 \Rightarrow 6$$

Recursion is the basic method for doing something iteratively, that is, over and over again.

Exercise 1.5: Evaluate the following expression, using the recursive definition of multiplication (Eq. 1.7): 3×5.

Exercise 1.6: Define recursively, in terms of multiplication, exponentiation to a nonnegative integer power.

Exercise 1.7: Define exponentiation (of nonnegative numbers) to an arbitrary integer power. *Hint:* Use conditional definition and the answer to the previous exercise.

Exercise 1.8: Define recursively, in terms of the successor and predecessor functions, addition to a nonnegative integer.

Exercise 1.9: Define addition for arbitrary integers.

Exercise 1.10: Define recursively, in terms of subtraction and less-than, division by a positive integer.

Finally, we must distinguish *explicit* and *implicit* definitions of functions. Consider definitions of numeric variables. In an explicit definition the variable appears on the left of an equation but not on its right. For example,

$$y \equiv 2ax$$

We use the sign of identity '≡' as a sign of *explicit definition*.

Explicit definitions have the advantage that they can be interpreted as *rewrite rules*—rules that tell us how to replace one class of expressions by another.[6] For example, this definition of y implies the rewrite rule

$$y \Rightarrow 2ax$$

This rule tells us how to eliminate the variable 'y' from any formula in which it occurs. For example, to eliminate 'y' from '$3y^2 + 5y + 1$' we apply the rewrite rule to obtain

$$3y^2 + 5y + 1 \Rightarrow 3(2ax)^2 + 5(2ax) + 1$$

The notion of explicit definition can be extended to sets of *simultaneous equations* as follows. A set of variables is explicitly defined by a set of equations provided that both (1) the equations are individually explicit and (2) they can be ordered so that no equation uses on its right-hand side a variable defined earlier in the list. For example,

$$y \equiv 2 \times a \times x$$
$$x \equiv 2$$
$$a \equiv 3$$

explicitly defines 'x', 'a', and 'y'. The preceding equations can be converted to the elimination rules:

$$y \Rightarrow 2 \times a \times x$$
$$x \Rightarrow 2$$
$$a \Rightarrow 3$$

These rules can be applied in order: The first can be applied until there are no more 'y's, the second until there are no more 'x's, and the third until there are no more 'a's. Thus we have the following reduction:

$$y \Rightarrow 2 \times a \times x \Rightarrow 2 \times a \times 2 \Rightarrow 2 \times 3 \times 2$$

---

6. Rewrite rules form much of the subject matter of Part 2 of this book.

We say a variable is defined *implicitly* if it is defined by an equation in which it appears on both sides. For example,

$$2a = a + 3$$

implicitly defines a to be 3. To find the value of a, it is necessary to *solve* the equation by using the rules of algebra. This solving process can be viewed as a way to convert an implicit definition into a more useful, explicit definition (the implicit definition cannot be directly converted into a rewrite rule). The equation

$$2a = a + 3$$

does not explicitly tell us what to substitute for 'a' in '$2 \times a \times x$'. Furthermore, the rewrite rules that result from explicit definitions *always terminate;* that is, repeated application of the rules will eventually eliminate all occurrences of the defined variable. On the other hand, it is possible to write implicit definitions that do not terminate—that do not define anything. Consider, for example, the implicit definition

$$a = a + 1$$

Although we can see that this equation has no solution, this fact might not be so obvious in more complicated cases. If we naively interpret the equation as a rewrite rule,

$$a \Rightarrow a + 1$$

then we can get nonterminating reductions such as the following:

$$2a \Rightarrow 2(a + 1) \Rightarrow 2((a + 1) + 1) \Rightarrow \cdots$$

As we see in Section 7.3, this phenomenon is closely related to Russell's Paradox.

Variables can also be defined implicitly by sets of *simultaneous equations.* For example,

$$2a = a + 3$$
$$d - 1 = 3d + a$$

implicitly defines $a = 3$ and $d = -2$. We can even have implicit definitions in which the variables do not appear on both sides of the equations. For example, in

$$2a = x$$
$$x + 1 = a + 4$$

neither 'a' nor 'x' appears on both sides of either equation. There is, however, no way to order the equations so that later equations make no use of variables defined in earlier equations. The implicitness can also be seen by combining the two equations into one:

$$2a + 1 = a + 4$$

In summary, an explicit definition tells us what a thing *is* (denoted by '≡'). An implicit definition states some properties that the thing must have (typically, satisfying an equation), with the implication that only one thing has those properties. Determining what the thing *is* requires a solving process.

Functions can also be defined either explicitly or implicitly. For example, these two equations implicitly define the implication function:

$$\text{and } [p, \text{ implies } (p, q)] = \text{and } (p, q) \tag{1.8}$$
$$\text{and } [\text{not } p, \text{ implies } (p, q)] = \text{or } [\text{not } p, \text{ and } (\text{not } p, q)]$$

These equations cannot be used explicitly to evaluate an expression such as 'implies (**true**, **false**)'. Using Boolean algebra, however, these equations can be solved to yield the following explicit definition:

$$\text{implies } (p, q) \equiv \text{or } (\text{not } p, q) \tag{1.3}$$

The explicit definition allows 'implies (**true**, **false**)' to be evaluated by simple substitution.

An advantage of functional programming is that, much like elementary algebra, it simplifies the transformation of implicit into explicit definitions. This is important because formal specifications of software systems often take the form of implicit definitions, whereas explicit definitions are usually easy to convert to programs. Thus functional programming provides a way to go from formal specifications to programs satisfying those specifications. We illustrate the process in the following chapters.

Exercise 1.11: Show that the explicit definition of implies (Eq. 1.3) satisfies the implicit definition (Eq. 1.8).

Exercise 1.12: (Advanced) Show that the explicit definition (Eq. 1.3) is the *unique* solution to the implicit definition (Eq. 1.8). That is, no other Boolean function satisfies these two equations, although there may be other ways of expressing this same function. *Hint:* Use truth tables.

Notice that recursive definitions are by their nature implicit. Nevertheless, since their left-hand side is simple (i.e., composed of only the name and formal parameters of the function), they can be easily converted to rewrite rules. For example, the following two equations constitute a recursive definition of factorial (for $n \geq 0$):

$$\text{fac } n \ \equiv \ n \times \text{fac } (n - 1), \ \text{if } n > 0$$
$$\text{fac } 0 \ \equiv \ 1$$

They can be converted to the rewrite rules:

$$\text{fac } n \ \Rightarrow \ n \times \text{fac } (n - 1), \ \text{if } n > 0$$
$$\text{fac } 0 \ \Rightarrow \ 1$$

These rewrite rules tell us how to transform a formula containing 'fac'. Performing the transformation, however, will not necessarily eliminate the function from the formula. For example,

$$2 + \text{fac } 3 \ \Rightarrow \ 2 + 3 \times \text{fac } (3 - 1)$$

On the other hand, if the computation is terminating, then repeated application of the rewrite rules will eventually eliminate 'fac' from the formula:

$$2 + 3 \times \text{fac } 2 \ \Rightarrow \ 2 + 3 \times 2 \times \text{fac } 1$$
$$\Rightarrow \ 2 + 3 \times 2 \times 1 \times \text{fac } 0$$
$$\Rightarrow \ 2 + 3 \times 2 \times 1 \times 1$$

These issues are discussed in more detail in Chapters 8 – 10.

1.9 History of Functional Programming

The history of functional programming actually begins before the invention of computers. In the early 20th century, many mathematicians were concerned about the foundations of mathematics. In particular they were worried about whether it made sense to talk about infinite sets and other infinite objects. Much of this concern was precipitated by Georg Cantor's (1845 – 1918) development in the late 19th century of a theory of infinities of higher and higher orders. Many mathematicians, such as Leopold Kronecker (1823 – 1891), questioned the legitimacy of these objects and condemned Cantor's theory as mere word spinning. These mathematicians insisted that a mathematical object could be said to exist only if, at least in principle, it could be constructed.

What does it mean for a number or other mathematical object to be *constructible*? This idea developed slowly over a number of years. In his *Formulaire de Mathématique* (1894 – 1908), Giuseppe Peano (1858 – 1932), a mathematician, logician, and linguist, had already shown how the natural numbers could be constructed by finitely many applications of the successor function (in just the way outlined in Exercises 1.8–1.10). Beginning in 1923, Thoralf Skolem (1887–1963) showed that almost all of the theory of natural numbers could be developed constructively by the extensive use of recursive definitions like that of Peano. Thus, by the first decades of the 20th century there was already considerable experience in the recursive definition of functions of the natural numbers.

These developments led mathematicians and logicians to ask what it means for an object to be constructible. To avoid questionable appeals to the infinite, it seemed reasonable to call an object constructible only if it could be constructed in a finite number of steps, each requiring only a finite amount of effort.[7]

In the 1930s there were many attempts to formalize the notion of constructibility (also known as *effective calculability* and *computability*). One of the most famous of these was Turing's definition of a class of abstract machines, since known as *Turing machines,* that perform simple reading and writing operations on a finite portion of a tape.[8] Another approach, based more directly on Skolem's and Peano's work, was Gödel's use in 1934 of *general recursive functions.*[9] A third approach, having a direct bearing on functional programming, was the *lambda calculus* developed by Church and Kleene in the early 1930s[10] (see Chapters 8 and 9). Many other notions of computability, such as *Markov algorithms* and *Post production systems,* were developed at about the same time.[11] It is remarkable that all these independently formulated notions of computability turned out to be equivalent (as was proved by Church, Kleene, Turing, and others in the late 1930s). This equivalence led Church (1936) to propose what has come to be known as *Church's Thesis,* that is, that the notion of a computable function should be identified with the notion of a general recursive function.

Thus, in the decades immediately preceding the invention of the electronic digital computer, a number of mathematicians and logicians had thoroughly investigated recursive functions, and shown that any computable function could be expressed (i.e., programmed) in terms of recursive functions.

The next major event in the history of functional programming was the

---

7. In this sense something is constructible only if it can be constructed with a finite amount of energy, a seemingly reasonable restriction.
8. Alan M. Turing (1912–1954), an English mathematician, logician, and early computer scientist. See Turing (1936) for a description of Turing machines. His proof of the undecidability of the halting problem is discussed in Section 9.9.
9. Kurt Gödel (1906–1978), a Czechoslovakian/American mathematician, logician, and computer scientist. Gödel attributed the idea of general recursive functions to the French mathematician Jacques Herbrand (1908–1931).
10. Alonzo Church (1903–), an American mathematician and logician; S. C. Kleene (1909–), an American mathematician and logician. See Church (1936) for a discussion of the lambda calculus.
11. Many of the fundamental papers can be found in Davis (1965).

publication of John McCarthy's (1960) seminal article on LISP.[12] In 1958 McCarthy investigated the use of linked-list operations to implement a symbolic differentiation program. Since differentiation is a recursive process, McCarthy was led to the use of recursive functions; he also found it convenient to be able to pass functions as arguments to other functions. The lambda calculus provides a notation that is very convenient for these purposes (see Chapters 8 and 9), and so McCarthy was led to Church's notation in his programming.

In 1958 a project was begun at MIT to implement a language incorporating these ideas. The result, known as LISP 1, was described in McCarthy's 1960 article, "Recursive Functions of Symbolic Expressions and Their Computation by Machine." The article, showing how a number of significant programs can be expressed as pure functions operating on list structures, can be viewed as the beginning of functional programming.[13]

In the late 1960s and early 1970s, a number of computer scientists investigated programming with pure functions—then called *applicative programming,* since the central operation was the *application* of a function to its argument. In particular, Peter Landin (1964, 1965, 1966) developed many of the central ideas of the use, notation, and implementation of applicative programming languages. An important side development was Landin's attempt to define a nonfunctional language—Algol-60—by translating it to the lambda calculus. This approach, as further developed by Strachey and Scott, led to the method of defining programming language semantics known as *denotational semantics.* In essence, denotational semantics defines the meaning of a program in terms of an equivalent functional program. Unfortunately, this method is beyond the scope of this book.[14]

Applicative programming, investigated by a small number of researchers throughout the 1960s and 1970s, has received increasing attention since 1978, when John Backus's Turing Award paper was published. In this paper Backus, the principal inventor of FORTRAN, severely criticized conventional programming languages, calling for the development of a new programming paradigm. He proposed a paradigm called *functional*

---

12. Historical information on LISP comes from McCarthy (1978).
13. LISP 1, often known as *pure* LISP, is a functional language; it has no assignment statement. Later versions of LISP, such as LISP 1.5 and the more recent Common LISP, are not purely functional because they include statements and assignment operations like conventional languages. Although it is possible to do functional programming in LISP, most LISP programs are not pure; they make extensive use of assignment. (The reasons are discussed in Section 3.10.) Thus, although the origins of functional programming can be found in LISP, its later development has been largely independent of the evolution of LISP.
14. For discussions of denotational semantics see Landin (1965, 1971), Scott (1970, 1971, 1972, 1973), Scott and Strachey (1971), Milne and Strachey (1976), Gordon (1979), and Stoy (1977).

programming, which is essentially applicative programming with an emphasis on the use of *functionals* (functions that operate on other functions—see Chapter 6). Many of Backus's functionals were inspired by the language APL,[15] an imperative language designed in the 1960s, which provided powerful assignmentless operators on data structures. Since Backus's paper the number of investigators working on functional programming languages and functional computer architectures has increased greatly.

Books discussing applicative and functional programming include Fox (1966), Foster (1967), Barron (1968), Burstall et al. (1971), Burge (1975), Henderson (1980), and Darlington et al. (1982). In this book we have drawn on the results of several of these investigators.

1.10 Functional Programming Languages

What does a functional program look like? A major portion of such a program would have to be the definitions of functions, but how are they organized?

Functional programming languages differ greatly in their syntactic styles, as can be seen in the sample programs in Figures 1.2–1.7. One reason for the lack of standard notation is that most functional programming languages are *experimental* languages, one of the purposes of which is to experiment with notation. On the other hand, underneath the syntactic idiosyncrasies most of these languages are basically the same—the lambda calculus. Landin invented the term *syntactic sugar* to refer to the abbreviations and syntactic conventions adopted by languages to make programming in the lambda calculus more convenient. The idea is that "a little bit of syntactic sugar helps you swallow the lambda calculus." As can be seen in the unsugared lambda calculus program in Figure 1.2, this sugar is very desirable!

Functional programs must be written in some functional programming language. In this book we use a language called Φ, which adheres closely

---

Figure 1.2 Functional program in unsugared lambda calculus.

$(\lambda xC.Cx\,6)$ (quo 192 24)

$((\lambda \text{fac}\ (\lambda nk.\ (\text{quo}\ (\text{fac}\ n)\ (\text{prod}\ (\text{fac}\ k)\ (\text{fac}\ (\text{dif}\ n\ k))\,)\,)\,)\,)\,)$

$Y(\lambda \text{fac}\ \lambda n\ (\text{if}\ (\text{equal}\ n\ 0)\ 1\ (\text{prod}\ n\ (\text{fac}\ (\text{dif}\ n\ 1))\,)\,)\,)\,)$

---

15. See Iverson (1962) for the original version of APL, and Pakin (1972) for a more recent version of the language. Iverson's 1979 Turing award lecture (Iverson 1980) discusses the importance of mathematical notation, using APL as an illustration.

to standard mathematical notation[16] and which therefore calls for little additional instruction to allow you to read programs in this language. In any case, since most functional languages are just sugared versions of the lambda calculus, it is usually easy to translate between them. Thus the functional programming techniques you learn here can easily be transferred to other functional languages. Our goal is methodology, not a particular language.

To acquaint you with the style of functional programming, let's walk through an (unrealistically trivial) session with the Φ functional programming system. Suppose that the system has been invoked and is waiting for a command, as indicated by the '$\rightarrow$' prompt:

$\rightarrow$

Like most functional programming systems, Φ is in a *read-evaluate-print loop*. That is, if we type in an expression, then the system will evaluate it and print out its value:

$\rightarrow 3 + 2 \times 3$
9
$\rightarrow$

We can conveniently evaluate more complicated expressions by using *auxiliary definitions* (introduced by the keyword **where**):

$\rightarrow (2 \times a \times x + b) \times (2 \times a \times x + c)$
    where $a \equiv 3$ **and** $b \equiv 2$ **and** $c \equiv -1$ **and** $x \equiv 2$
  154
$\rightarrow$

Note that the bindings ($a \equiv 3$, $b \equiv 2$, etc.) are completely *local* to the expression; they are forgotten as soon as the expression has been evaluated.

Next we consider another example, one involving function definition. Our goal is to compute $C(x, 6)$, the combinations of x things taken 6 at a time, where in this case $x \equiv 192 \div 24$. This will require us to define the function $C(n, k)$, which computes the number of combinations of n things taken k at a time:

$$C(n, k) \equiv \frac{n!}{k!(n-k)!} \tag{1.9}$$

16. 'Φ' (phi) stands for *functional* language. Although Φ is described in Appendix A, its use in this book should be self-explanatory.

To complete the definition, we must define an auxiliary function to compute the factorial of a number:

$$0! \equiv 1 \tag{1.10}$$
$$n! \equiv n(n-1)! \ \text{if} \ n > 0$$

The direct solution to this problem is to enter the expression whose value we want, '$C(x, 6)$', followed by auxiliary definitions of 'x' and 'C':

$\rightarrow$ $C(x, 6)$
    where $x \equiv 192 \div 24$
    and $C(n, k) \equiv$ fac n / [fac $k \times$ fac $(n - k)$]
      where fac $0 \equiv 1$
           fac $n \equiv n \times$ fac $(n - 1)$, if $n > 0$
   28
$\rightarrow$

Notice that the definition of C requires an auxiliary definition of fac. (Following mathematical convention, we use an italic typeface for single-letter identifiers, and a regular (roman) typeface for multi-letter identifiers. This permits us to distinguish the two-identifier expression 'fx' from the single identifier 'fx'.)

Now suppose that we wanted to compute $C(x, 4)$. Since the auxiliary definitions have been thrown away, we are starting with an empty environment, and must reenter the definitions of 'C' and 'fac':

$\rightarrow$ $C(x, 4)$
    where $x \equiv 192 \div 24$
    and $C(n, k) \equiv$ fac n / [fac $k \times$ fac $(n - k)$]
      where fac $0 \equiv 1$
           fac $n \equiv n \times$ fac $(n - 1)$, if $n > 0$
   70
$\rightarrow$

This is clearly unsatisfactory. Therefore Φ, like most functional programming systems, allows definitions to be entered that are retained over many expression evaluations. These are called *global definitions*.

We rework our example using global definitions. Working from the top down, our first step is to define C in terms of factorial:

$\rightarrow$ **let** $C(n, k) \equiv$ fac n / [fac $k \times$ fac $(n - k)$]
  C defined
$\rightarrow$

Next we enter a recursive definition of factorial:

$\rightarrow$ **let** fac 0 $\equiv$ 1
$\rightarrow$ fac n $\equiv$ $n \times$ fac $(n - 1)$, if $n > 0$
fac defined
$\rightarrow$

These two functions constitute our functional program, which we can now apply to input values. For example,

$\rightarrow$ fac 3
6
$\rightarrow$ C (8, 6)
28
$\rightarrow$

We have seen two instances of global *function* definitions; global *data* definitions are also permitted. For example, the following command gives the name x to the value of the expression '192 ÷ 24':

$\rightarrow$ **let** $x \equiv 192 \div 24$
x defined
$\rightarrow$

We can now use x in applications of the C function:

$\rightarrow$ C $(x, 6)$
28
$\rightarrow$ C $(x, 4)$
70
$\rightarrow$

And so forth.

The figures show the same programming session in several different functional programming languages. The session is shown in Φ (the notation we use) in Figure 1.3. Figure 1.4 shows our example in ISWIM ("if

---

Figure 1.3 Functional programming session in Φ.

let C (n, k) $\equiv$ fac n / [fac $k \times$ fac $(n - k)$]

let fac 0 $\equiv$ 1

    fac n $\equiv$ $n \times$ fac $(n - 1)$, if $n > 0$

let $x \equiv 192 \div 24$

C $(x, 6)$

Figure 1.4 Functional programming session in ISWIM.

---

let $C(n, k) = \text{fac}(n) / (\text{fac}(k) \, \text{fac}(n - k))$

    where rec $\text{fac}(n) = (n = 0) \to 1; \; n \, \text{fac}(n - 1);$

let $x = 192/24;$

  $C(x, 6)$

---

you see what I mean"), Landin's sugaring of the lambda calculus (Landin 1966). Many functional languages are based on Landin's notation. A language with a more equational style, Turner's Miranda, is shown in Figure 1.5 (Turner 1985b). Figure 1.6 shows the session in Scheme, which is very similar to Common LISP. Although neither of these languages is purely functional, they are perhaps the most available languages that support *higher-order functions* (required for "true" functional programming—see Chapter 6).[17] Finally, Figure 1.7 shows the session in an implementation of Backus's FP language (Backus 1978), a distinctive characteristic of which is the absence of any formal parameters.[18]

In summary, most functional programming systems accept commands of three kinds:

1. Function definitions, such as '**let** $C(n, k) \equiv \text{fac} \, n \, / \, [\text{fac} \, k \times \text{fac} \, (n - k)]$'.

2. Data definitions, such as '**let** $x \equiv 192 \div 24$'.

3. Expression evaluations, such as '$C(x, 6)$'.

What does a functional programming system do if we make an error? Suppose we had incorrectly defined C like this:

Figure 1.5 Functional programming session in Miranda.

```
C n k  =  fac n div (fac k * fac (n – k))
fac 0  =  1
fac n  =  n * fac (n – 1), n > 0
x  =  192 div 24
C x 6
```

---

17. See Rees and Clinger (1986) for the definition of Scheme and Abelson and Sussman (1985) for a good introduction to Scheme programming. See Steele (1984) for the definition of Common LISP. See Appendix C of this book for a guide to functional programming in Scheme and Common LISP.
18. FL is a more recent functional language designed by Backus and his colleagues (Backus, Williams, and Wimmers, 1986).

Figure 1.6 Functional programming session in Scheme.

```
(define (C n k)
  (/ (fac n) (* (fac k) (fac (– n k)) )) )
(define (fac n)
  (if (= 0 n) 1
      (* n (fac (– n 1)) )) )
(define x (/ 192 24))
(C x 6)
```

$\rightarrow$ **let** $C\,(n,\,k)\;\equiv\;$ fac $n\,/\,$[fac $k\,*\,$fac $(n-k)$]
C defined
$\rightarrow$

Then, if we tried the application '$C\,(8,\,4)$' we would get a zero-divide error:

$\rightarrow C\,(8,\,4)$
Division by zero
C broken

The Φ system, like most functional programming systems, has left the offending function suspended and entered a debugger, which is now prompting us for a debugging command.

When the source of the error is discovered, one or more functions must be *redefined* in order to correct it. In the simplest case we might reenter a corrected definition of the function:[19]

Figure 1.7 Functional programming session in FP.

Def $C \equiv \div\circ$ [! $\circ$ **1**, $\times\circ$ [! $\circ$ **2**, ! $\circ$ $-$]]

Def ! $\equiv$ eq0 $\rightarrow \overline{1}$; $\times\circ$ [id, ! $\circ$ sub1]

Def eq0 $\equiv$ eq $\circ$ [id, $\overline{0}$]

Def sub1 $\equiv\,-\circ$ [id, $\overline{1}$]

Def $x \equiv \div$:<192, 24>

C:<x, 6>

---

19. Typically, functional programming systems allow function definitions to be edited. Alternatively, a text file containing the definition could be edited, and the file reloaded.

$\rightarrow$ **let** $C\ (n,\ k) \equiv$ fac n / [fac $k \times$ fac $(n-k)$]
   C redefined

$\rightarrow$

Similarly, names of data values can be redefined:

$\rightarrow$ **let** $x \equiv 192 \div 24$
   x defined
$\rightarrow x$
  8
$\rightarrow$ **let** $x \equiv 27 \times (8 + 96)$
   x redefined
$\rightarrow x$
  2808

What's going on here? We said that a major characteristic of functional programming is that it dispenses with variables and the assignment operation. Yet these redefinitions look remarkably like assignments. What is the difference between a global (re)definition and an assignment? Is our language basically imperative after all?

Almost every functional language is embedded inside an imperative *shell*.[20] This is necessary for the reasons just illustrated: permitting the redefinition of functions and data when they are incorrect or when they must be modified for other reasons, such as enhancement. Indeed, it can be claimed that a programming environment is an *appropriate* use of imperative language constructs (MacLennan 1985).

The fact that every practical functional language is embedded in an imperative shell does not negate the advantages of functional programming. The use of imperative features is highly restricted: Redefinition is allowed only at the global level under the direct control of the interactive user. Programs are not allowed to redefine names; for example, we could not execute '**let** $i \equiv i + 1$' under the control of a loop. That is, *programmers* can define and redefine names, but *programs* cannot. Thus *within* the definitions of functions, where programming is hard, we are in the dependable world of expressions. We are in the world of statements only when we are outside the program, in the relatively simpler world of program modification.

1.11 The Structure of Functional Programs

You have seen how function and data definitions may be typed into a functional programming system, and how functions can be interactively

---

20. Although purely functional shells have been proposed; see (O'Donnell 1985) and (Hall and O'Donnell 1985) for an example. Some of the relevant ideas are discussed in Chapter 7.

applied to data. On the other hand, you may be asking, "This is all very well for 'toy' programs, but how can real programs be done this way?" To convince you that functional languages are useful for practical programming and can support the development of large software systems, let us present some features of a typical functional programming system (that is, Φ). *These details have no importance in their own right!*

First we consider the matter of program entry. It is obviously impractical to type in function and data definitions afresh in every terminal session. Therefore most functional programming systems allow a file to be loaded that contains function and data definitions. A large functional program, like large programs in conventional languages, is generally structured as one or more files containing function and data definitions. Once loaded, these definitions can be invoked interactively from the terminal. For example, suppose the file 'combinations' contains the source commands shown here:

> **let** $C(n, k) \equiv$ **fac** n / [**fac** $k \times$ **fac** $(n - k)$]
> **let fac** $0 \equiv 1$
>   **fac** $n \equiv n \times$ **fac** $(n - 1)$, if $n > 0$

(Of course a real program file might contain hundreds of function definitions such as these.) We can command the Φ system to read this file by typing

> → **do** 'combinations'
> combinations done
> →

The system interprets the commands in the file just as though they were typed in from the terminal.

What about data files? Many programs process large data sets; we certainly don't want to have to type these in interactively. One solution is to write input files in the form of data definition commands. For example, a file called input might look like this:

> **let** input $\equiv$ <
> (1234,   ('Smith',   'John'),   24.2),
> (8754,   ('Jones',   'Susan'),   39.5),
>
>   ⋮   ⋮   ⋮   ⋮
>
> (5632,   ('Brown',   'Donald'), 42.5)>

This file can be loaded in the usual way:

> → **do** 'input'
> input done.
> →

This approach requires that the file be in the form of a legal data definition, which may be inconvenient; a solution is discussed later. This approach also does not address the problem of *writing* files so that they can be used by other programs.

A more general approach to the problem of files is to include a construct in the language that allows external file names to be treated as global names for sequences.[21] Thus, wherever we make use of the expression **file** 'OldMaster' we are referring to the contents of the file called OldMaster. For example, the application

process_updates (file 'OldMaster', file 'Updates')

passes the files OldMaster and Updates to the function process_updates (which is assumed to produce a new master file). The result of this application can be stored into the file system by using an external file name on the left of a data definition:

$\rightarrow$ **let file** 'NewMaster' $\equiv$ process_updates (**file** 'OldMaster', **file** 'Updates')
NewMaster defined
$\rightarrow$

This *defines* the file NewMaster to be the result of applying process_updates to the files OldMaster and Updates. For another example, suppose we have a Pascal compiler on a file called Pascal and a Pascal program on a file called prog.pas. We might compile it, producing object code prog.exe and listing prog.lst, as follows:

$\rightarrow$ **do** 'Pascal'
Pascal done
$\rightarrow$ **let** (**file** 'prog.exe', **file** 'prog.lst') $\equiv$ Pascal (**file** 'prog.pas')

Here we have assumed that Pascal is also the name of the compiler function defined by the file Pascal.

Finally, it is often convenient to compile a program so that it can be invoked from the operating system, with file names provided as parameters. To accomplish this we compile the functional program as a batch program—a file containing a collection of function and data declarations followed by a single expression to be evaluated. The structure of the batch-program file might be like this:

---

21. Sequences are data structures similar to both arrays and files; they are also similar to LISP lists. Functional sequence processing is discussed at length in Chapters 2 and 3.

let process_updates (x, y) ≡ ... body of process_updates ...
let summarize S ≡ ... body of an auxiliary function ...

$\vdots$

other function and data definitions

$\vdots$

process_updates (input1, input2)

Here 'input1' and 'input2' are predefined names that are automatically bound to the input file(s) passed to the program by the operating system. The value of the expression 'process_updates (input1, input2)' is used to supply the values of the output file(s) whose names were passed to the program by the operating system. Again, the details are not important. What is important is that you see how it's possible to construct significant functional programs. Although you may not yet see how anything useful can be done without assignment statements, you should at least understand the structure of large functional programs.

Chapter 2

Applicative Languages

2.1 Language Frameworks

This chapter introduces the data types and operations used throughout the book. The data types (particularly sequences) are typical of those in applicative languages. Although applicative languages differ in their built-in types, the fundamentals of applicative programming are independent of the types provided.

Because our goal is to teach applicative programming *methodology*, not a particular applicative programming *language*, we do not want to be concerned with either the syntax or the semantics of particular languages. On the other hand, because we must write our programs in *some* language, we must make certain syntactic and semantic commitments. In the case of syntax, as already noted we will adhere as closely as possible to standard mathematical notation. The case of semantics seems harder however: How can we write programs without knowing the available data types and operators?

This problem can be solved by observing that all programming languages comprise two parts, one independent of the intended application domain, and the other dependent on the application domain (Landin 1966, Backus 1978). The domain-independent part, often called the *frame-*

work, includes the basic linguistic mechanisms that are used to construct programs. For an imperative language the framework typically includes the control structures, the procedure mechanism, and the assignment operation. For an applicative language the framework includes the function definition and function application mechanisms. Other constructs, such as the conditional (if-expression), can often be subsumed under either function definition or function application.[1]

The domain-dependent part of a language is a set of *components* that are useful in that domain. For example, the components useful for numerical programming include the floating-point numbers, operations (+, −, etc.), and relations (=, ≤, etc.). Thus the framework provides the form, and the components the content, from which programs are constructed. The choice of framework determines the *kind* of language we have, such as applicative or imperative. The choice of components orients the language toward a class of problems, such as numeric or symbolic.

Now we can understand how it is possible to learn applicative programming *methodology* without learning a particular applicative programming *language*. On one hand, most applicative languages have the same framework (the possible ways of constructing applicative programs are relatively few). Basically, we need the ability to *define* functions, including both conditional and recursive definitions,[2] and the ability to *invoke* functions.

On the other hand, most applicative languages provide similar components, which can be understood as follows. The components of an applicative language are just the intrinsic (built-in) data types and the operations defined on values belonging to these types, and the intrinsic data types can be classified as either *atomic* (indivisible data items) or *composite* (data structures). We use the atomic data values found in almost all languages, whether applicative or imperative: numbers, Boolean values, and strings. The data structure (composite data type) that we use is the *sequence*, found in almost all applicative languages and almost no imperative languages. Thus sequences are characteristically applicative data structures. Taking numbers, Booleans, strings, and sequences as the components from which applicative programs are constructed, permits learning applicative programming methodology without becoming enmeshed in the details of a particular language; what you learn is useful for *any* applicative language, and even for applicative programming in imperative languages.

---

1. For an example of subsumption under definition, see the definitions of factorial in Figures 1.3 and 1.5. For an example of subsumption under function application, see Figure 1.6 and Section 2.2.
2. Explicit enumeration of the input-output pairs of a function can be considered a special case of conditional definition.

2.2 Atomic Data Types

As just noted, the atomic data values we use are numbers, Booleans, and strings. The values belonging to these types are collectively referred to as *atoms* because they are noncomposite (i.e., indivisible) data values. For arithmetic we have both integers

$$\cdots, -3, -2, -1, 0, 1, 2, 3, \cdots$$

and floating-point numbers

$$3.14159, 2.71828, 6.02 \times 10^{23}, -0.01, \cdots$$

together with the well-known operations[3]

$$+, -, \times, \div, /, =, \neq, <, >, \leq, \geq$$

Following mathematical convention, we use the symbol $\mathbb{Z}$ for the integer type and the symbol $\mathbb{R}$ for the type that includes both integers and floating-point numbers.

Notice that we have described both a set of *data values* and a set of *primitive operations* on those values. These operations are primitive in the sense that they are intrinsic (built-in), and that any other operations we wish to perform on the data values must be constructed from the primitive operations. For example, squaring could be defined in terms of multiplication:

square $n \equiv n \times n$

By requiring all operations on the data values to be expressed in terms of the primitives, we improve the portability and maintainability of our programs. A data type is called *abstract* when it is specified in terms of a set of (abstract) values and operations, rather than in terms of a (concrete) implementation. In this book all data types are abstract unless specified otherwise.

Let us now describe the abstract type **string**. String values are written as sequences of zero or more characters surrounded by quotation marks:

'a', 'dog', 'call', 'var', "

For the time being, the only operations we permit on strings are tests of equality and inequality: '=' and '≠'. Later there will be occasion to define operations for converting strings to sequences, and vice versa.

---

3. We use '÷' for integer (truncating) division and '/' for general division.

Finally, the Boolean abstract data type, $\mathbb{B}$, is composed of the Boolean values

true, false

together with the primitive operations on these values:

$\neg, \wedge, \vee, \text{if}, =, \neq$

The 'if' operation takes three arguments; the second and third must be of the same type. The application if (B,T,F) returns T if B is **true** and F if B is **false**. Thus if $(x > y, x - y, y - x)$ can be read "if x is greater than y then $x - y$ else $y - x$." The behavior of if is expressed by the following equations:

$$\text{if } (\textbf{true}, T, E) = T \tag{2.1}$$
$$\text{if } (\textbf{false}, T, E) = E$$

As you probably know, if has a special property: It evaluates either T or F, but not both. The intent is to avoid evaluating an expression that may be undefined.

Since conditional definitions are so common, we introduce a special notation for them. For simple conditionals, such as if (B, T, E), we write

if B **then** T **else** E **endif**

as in many programming languages. For nested conditionals, such as if $[B_1, T_1, \text{if} (B_2, T_2, E)]$, we write

if B_1 **then** T_1 **elsif** B_2 **then** T_2 **else** E **endif**

and so forth. Using this notation, the definition of the factorial function can be written

fac $n \equiv$ **if** $n = 0$ **then** 1 **else** $n \times$ fac $(n - 1)$ **endif**

Usually it is more convenient to stack the alternatives, as follows:

$$\text{fac } n \equiv \begin{cases} 1, & \text{if } n = 0 \\ \textbf{else } n \times \text{fac } (n - 1) \end{cases}$$

This is a compromise between common programming notations and conventional mathematical notation:

$$\text{fac } n \equiv \begin{cases} 1, & \text{if } n = 0 \\ n \times \text{fac } (n - 1), & \text{otherwise} \end{cases}$$

Since one goal of applicative programming is to facilitate manipulating and reasoning about programs, we always investigate the properties of any functions or data types we define. For example, it is useful to know when a function can be factored out of an expression. In this case we investigate whether functional application can be factored out of a conditional:

$$\text{if } [B,\ F(T),\ F(E)] = F\ [\text{if } (B,\ T,\ E)]$$

Or, using the special **if** syntax,

$$\textbf{if } B \textbf{ then } F(T) \textbf{ else } F(E) \textbf{ endif} \ = \ F\ (\textbf{if } B \textbf{ then } T \textbf{ else } E \textbf{ endif}) \qquad (2.2)$$

This equation tells us that, for example,

$$\textbf{if } x > y \textbf{ then } \sin x \textbf{ else } \sin y \textbf{ endif}$$

can be (slightly) simplified to

$$\sin\ (\textbf{if } x > y \textbf{ then } x \textbf{ else } y \textbf{ endif})$$

The proof of Eq. (2.2) is simple. Suppose that $B = \textbf{true}$. Then, by the definition of if (Eq. 2.1), the left-hand side of (2.2) is equal to $F(T)$. Similarly, the conditional on the right-hand side equals T, so that the entire right-hand side equals $F(T)$. Since $F(T) = F(T)$ we know Eq. (2.2) holds when $B = \textbf{true}$. The case for $B = \textbf{false}$ is exactly analogous.

Have we covered all the cases? What if B is neither **true** nor **false**? For example, B could be a non-Boolean value—or, if the computation B does not terminate, no value at all. Observe that in both cases the left side of Eq. (2.2) is undefined. On the right side the conditional is undefined, but whether F applied to an undefined value is undefined or not is a subtle problem, discussed in Chapters 7 and 12. For now, we need observe only that if both sides of the equation are defined, then they are equal. Whenever we prove things about applicative expressions we must pay careful attention to the domain over which they are defined.

Exercise 2.1: Prove Eq. (2.2) for the case $B = \textbf{false}$.

Exercise 2.2: Prove the following identity:

$$\textbf{if } P \textbf{ then if } Q \textbf{ then } X \textbf{ else } Y \textbf{ endif else } Z \textbf{ endif} =$$
$$\textbf{if } P \wedge Q \textbf{ then } X \textbf{ elsif } P \textbf{ then } Y \textbf{ else } Z \textbf{ endif}$$

Compare the behavior of the two sides of the equation when Q is undefined.

2.3 Sequences

All the data types discussed so far are atomic because all the values belonging to them are indivisible. In the rest of this chapter we define a composite abstract type, the *sequence*, called composite because its values are divisible into smaller values.

Since an abstract data type includes both *values* and *primitive operations* defined on those values, we must consider both sequence values and sequence operations. Hence our first task must be to define sequence values, which we do very informally, essentially by example. The data values, called *sequences*, are written as finite sequences of values, all of the same type, surrounded by angle brackets. For instance, <5,8,16> is a sequence containing the integers 5, 8, and 16, in that order. Also

$$<\text{'cat', 'dog', 'bird'}>$$

is a sequence of three strings. Sequences of sequences, such as

$$< <3, 6>, <2>, <4, 1, 5> >$$

are permitted if the subsequences are the same type. This nesting can be continued to any depth.

Unlike sets, sequences can have duplicate elements; <0,0,0> is a sequence of three zeros. Sequences can have any number of elements, including one. Thus <32> is the sequence containing only the integer 32; it is *not* the same as the number 32. Sequences can also be empty, that is, have no elements: <>. This is called the *null sequence* and is often named *nil*. ('Null' is the adjective; 'nil' is the noun. Thus we speak of a sequence being null or nonnull, but say that nil has no elements. That is, nil is null.)

Notice that there is not just one type "sequences," but rather a *family* of abstract types such as "sequences of integers," "sequences of strings," "sequences of sequences of integers"—in general, "sequences of τs" for each type τ. We call "sequence" a *generic*[4] type, and call "sequence of integer," "sequence of string," and so on *particular* types. Properly speaking, "sequence" is not a type at all; think of it as a function that can be passed various particular types as parameters: sequence($\mathbb{Z}$), sequence(**string**), sequence[sequence($\mathbb{Z}$)], and so on. The function then returns a particular type as its value.

Following conventional notation, we write τ^* instead of sequence(τ); this notation is read "τ-sequences." Thus we have types $\mathbb{Z}^*$, **string***, $(\mathbb{Z}^*)^*$, and so forth.

Our next task is to define informally the primitive operations defined

---

4. Generic (from the Latin *genus* (race, kind)) means pertaining to an entire group or class. These types are also called *polymorphic* because they have many (from the Greek *poly*) forms (from the Greek *morphe*).

on sequences.[5] Since all applicative languages provide essentially the same primitive sequence operations, there is no problem deciding which operations to use. On the other hand, it is instructive to discover for ourselves the operations we need, acquiring techniques that will be useful when we invent other data types for which, unlike sequences, these commonly accepted conventions do not exist.

To determine the primitive operations on sequences systematically so that we will have confidence that we have enough primitive operations (without undue redundancy) to do useful programming, let us first consider the fundamental requirements on the primitive operations:

- We must be able to construct any sequence from its components in a finite number of steps. The operations required for this are called *constructors*.

- Since there is not much point to putting something into a sequence unless you can get it out, we must have a way to select any element from the sequence. The operations that accomplish this are called *selectors*.

- We must be able to distinguish among different classes of sequences, such as null sequences and one-element sequences; otherwise we won't know from which locations it is possible to select. The operations that accomplish this are called *discriminators*.

Furthermore, for simplicity and economy, it is important to have a small, finite number of constructors, selectors, and discriminators.

What constructors, selectors, and discriminators are required for sequences? We can avoid an infinite number of constructors by observing that any n-element sequence can be obtained by adding the appropriate element to an $n-1$-element sequence. For example, <5,8,16> can be obtained by prefixing 5 onto <8,16> (or, of course, by postfixing 16 onto <5,8>). Similarly, we can get <8,16> from <16> by prefixing 8, and <16> from <> by prefixing 16. Thus any sequence can be built up from <> by prefixing the appropriate values. The result is that two constructors are sufficient: nil, which creates an empty sequence, and prefix, which prefixes an arbitrary value onto an arbitrary sequence.[6] (Of course there may be other sufficient sets of constructors; see Exercises 2.3 and 2.4).

It is natural that there be a discriminator that distinguishes between the two classes of sequences generated by the two constructors. Thus we

---

5. These operations derive ultimately from those in the LISP language; see (McCarthy 1960), (McCarthy et al. 1969), and (Steele 1984).
6. We use nil for a constant function and < > for the value it returns; this is an extremely subtle distinction that can be largely ignored. In Section 2.8 you will see that nil is defined without mention of < >, and that in fact < > is just syntactic sugar for nil.

Table 2.1 Primitive operations on sequences.

Kind of Sequence	Null	Nonnull
Discriminators	null	($\neg$ null)
Constructors	nil	prefix
Selectors	—	first, rest

have the discriminator null, which determines whether its argument is null (i.e., generated by the constructor nil).

There are also only two classes of sequences from which the selectors must be able to retrieve components. Since the null sequence contains no components, it has no associated selectors. On the other hand, the prefixing operation takes two objects, an element and a sequence, and combines them into a composite structure. Thus it is natural that corresponding to this constructor there be two selectors: first, which retrieves the first element of the sequence, and rest, which retrieves the remaining elements of the sequence.

Thus it turns out that for sequences just five operations—two selectors, two constructors, and one discriminator—will suffice for all the functions on sequences we might want to program. The primitive sequence operations are summarized in Table 2.1.

Exercise 2.3: Suppose we had taken *postfixing* rather than *prefixing* as the second sequence constructor. What then would be the natural selectors and discriminators for sequences?

Exercise 2.4: Consider the following three operations:

1. Creation of empty sequence:

   nil = < >

2. Creation of singleton sequence:

   singl x = $< x >$

3. Catenation of sequences:

   cat $(<x_1, \ldots, x_m>, <y_1, \ldots, y_n>) = <x_1, \ldots, x_m, y_1, \ldots, y_n>$

Is this a sufficient set of constructor operations for sequences? What are the associated discriminators and selectors? Discuss any difficulties in this set of sequence primitives.

Exercise 2.5: *(Advanced)* Show that τ^* is the free monoid generated by the type τ. *Hint:* Consider the operations described in the preceding exercise.

2.4 Exploration of Sequence Primitives

Here we explore informally the properties of the primitive operations on sequences,[7] a prelude to the formal definition of the operations in Section 2.5. (If you're already familiar with these sequence-processing operations, skip to that section.)

First let us characterize sequence values. We will write $x \in \tau$ to mean that x is a member of type τ. How can we specify the members of the sequence type τ^*? Clearly, sequence denotations belong to τ^* provided their elements belong to τ:

$$<x_1, \ldots, x_n> \in \tau^* \text{ if and only if } x_1, \ldots, x_n \in \tau$$

Since there are only two ways to get a sequence, from nil or from prefix, we can define τ^* more carefully as follows:

$$\begin{aligned} &\text{nil} \in \tau^* \\ &\text{prefix } (x, S) \in \tau^*, \text{ if } x \in \tau \text{ and } S \in \tau^* \\ &z \notin \tau^*, \text{otherwise} \end{aligned} \qquad (2.3)$$

Notice that '$\in$' is not an operator that belongs to these abstract types, but a *meta-operator* for talking *about* the types.

The function first returns the first element of a sequence; for example,

```
first <5,8,16> = 5
first <<1,2>, <3,4>> = <1,2>
```

Notice in the second example that the first element of $<<1,2>, <3,4>>$ is the sequence $<1,2>$. It makes no sense to apply first to the null sequence or to an atom (null sequences and atoms don't have a first element). Thus first of the null sequence, first $<>$, and first of the atom 18, first 18, are both undefined.

The complementary operation to first is rest, which returns all of a sequence *except* the first element; for example,

```
rest <5,8,16> = <8,16>
rest <<1,2>, <3,4>> = <<3,4>>
rest <3> = <>
```

---

7. The operations we call 'first', 'rest', 'prefix', and 'null' correspond to the LISP and Scheme operations 'car', 'cdr', 'cons', and 'null'. Common LISP permits 'first' and 'rest' with essentially the same meanings as ours. Appendix C contains a general discussion of applicative programming in LISP and Scheme.

Because it makes no sense to apply rest to null sequences or atoms, rest <> and rest 18 are undefined.

The first and rest operations can be combined to perform other selection operations; for instance,

first (rest <5,8,16>) ⇒ first <8,16> ⇒ 8

Hence first (rest S) reduces to the second element of S. Since it is useful, we give it a name:

second S ≡ first (rest S)   (2.4)

Similarly, it is easy to see that first [rest (rest S)] is the third element of S, and so forth.

Exercise 2.6: Show that first [rest (rest S)] is the third element of S. That is, based on the informal definitions of the sequence operations, show that

first [rest (rest $<S_1, S_2, S_3, \ldots, S_n>$)] = S_3

What are the requirements on S for the expression to be defined?

Exercise 2.7: Evaluate this expression:

first {rest [first (rest <<1,2,3>, <2,4,6>, <3,6,9>>)]}

State in words the effect of

first {rest [first (rest S)]}

The operation prefix (x, y) creates a sequence whose first element is x and the rest of whose elements come from y. For instance,

```
prefix (5, <8,16>) = <5,8,16>
prefix (<1,2>, <<3,4>>) = <<1,2>, <3,4>>
prefix (<5>, <<8>,<16>>) = <<5>, <8>, <16>>
prefix (5, <>) = <5>
```

In an application such as prefix (5, <8,16>) it is best *not* to think of the sequence <8,16> as being modified; we do not modify things in applicative programming. Rather, think of a new sequence being computed that contains the elements 5, 8, and 16, with the 8 and 16 *copied* from the sequence <8,16>.

Notice that the first argument to prefix need not be an atom, although it must agree in type with the elements of the second argument. On the other hand, its second argument must be a sequence; thus prefix (5, 8) is undefined.

Since prefix is such a common operation, let us use the following infix abbreviation:[8]

$$x : y \;\Rightarrow\; \text{prefix } (x, y)$$

This is read "x prefix y." Thus we can write

$$5 : <8,16> \;=\; <5,8,16>$$

and so forth.

Note that although the symbol ':' is symmetric, the prefixing operation is not commutative, $x : y \neq y : x$. Furthermore, the types of its arguments are different: The second argument must be a sequence, and the first must be of the same type as the elements of this sequence. An asymmetric symbol would be preferable, but ':' is quite common in the applicative programming literature.

Exercise 2.8: Evaluate the following expressions, or explain why they cannot be evaluated:

a. $7 : <8,2,6>$

b. $<6,5> : <4,4,7,2>$

c. $<12> : <2,6,5>$

d. $5 : <8>$

e. $<8> : 5$

f. nil : 5

g. 5 : nil

h. nil : nil

i. $<<>> : <<<>>>$

Parts (g)–(i) are really trick questions. What is the ambiguity in them?

---

8. We use infix operators only when they are well-established in mathematical notation, or when they substantially improve readability and occur frequently.

Exercise 2.9:   Evaluate this expression:

3 : nil

In general, what is the effect of x : nil?

Exercise 2.10:   Evaluate this expression:

3 : (7 : nil)

In general, what is the effect of x : (y : nil)? What would be a good (descriptive) name for the function $f(x, y) \equiv x : (y : \text{nil})$?

The meanings of first, rest, and ':' are summarized in the following informal equations, in which, $x_0, x_1, \ldots, x_n$ represent any data values of the same type (sequence or atom).

$$\text{first} <x_0, x_1, \ldots, x_n> = x_0 \tag{2.5}$$
$$\text{rest} <x_0, x_1, \ldots, x_n> = <x_1, \ldots, x_n>$$
$$x_0 : <x_1, \ldots, x_n> = <x_0, x_1, \ldots, x_n>$$

The ':' operation is the inverse of first and rest. For example, since

$$\text{first} <5,8,16> = 5$$
$$\text{rest} <5,8,16> = <8,16>$$

and

$$5 : <8,16> = <5,8,16>$$

we see that

$$(\text{first} <5,8,16>) : (\text{rest} <5,8,16>) \Rightarrow 5 : <8,16> \Rightarrow <5,8,16>$$

The first and rest operations also invert ':'. For example,

$$\text{first} (5 : <8,16>) = \text{first} <5,8,16> = 5$$
$$\text{rest} (5 : <8,16>) = \text{rest} <5,8,16> = <8,16>$$

Thus it is easy to see that the following equations hold (where S and T are sequences and x is any value compatible with S):

$$\text{first} (x : S) = x \tag{2.6}$$
$$\text{rest} (x : S) = S$$
$$\text{first} \, T : \text{rest} \, T = T \ \ (\text{if } T \text{ is nonnull})$$

These equations say that the selectors and the prefix constructor invert each other. We will see later that the same equations indirectly define the operations first, rest, and ':'. They are summarized in Fig. 2.1.

We turn now to the discriminator null, which asks whether a sequence is empty. For instance,

    null <> = **true**
    null <5,8,16> = **false**
    null <<>> = **false**

The sequence <<>> is not null because it contains a single element—that is, the null sequence, <>. This is more apparent if we write it in the equivalent form <nil>. Also observe that

    first <<>> = <>

The null function is not defined for atoms; thus null 5 is undefined.

The null discriminator is defined informally by the following equations, in which x is any value:

    null <> = **true**   (2.7)
    null <x, · · · > = **false**

Although this is quite clear, in the long term it will be better to express the behavior of null *algebraically*. This means that we must show how null interacts with the other operators, as we did in Eq. (2.6) for first, rest, and ':'. Therefore we consider the result of applying null to each sequence-valued operation, leading to the following equations:

    null nil = **true**   (2.8)
    null $(x : S)$ = **false**

Figure 2.1 Relation of sequence constructor and selectors.

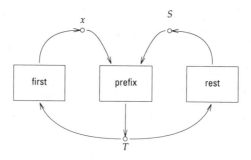

Figure 2.2 Informal summary of properties of sequence types.

$$(\text{first } T) : (\text{rest } T) = T, \quad \text{if } \neg \text{null } T$$

first $(x : S) = x$ rest $(x : S) = S$

null nil = **true**   null $(x : S)$ = **false**

nil $\in \tau^*$ $x : S \in \tau^*$

$$z \notin \tau^*, \text{otherwise}$$

Undefined expressions (*a* an atom, *x* anything):

first nil	rest nil
first *a*	rest *a*
null *a*	$x : a$

Figure 2.2 summarizes the properties of sequence types at which we have arrived in our informal analysis.

Exercise 2.11:   Say whether each of the following is true, and explain why.

a. $5 \in \mathbb{Z}^*$

b. $\langle 5,8,16 \rangle \in \mathbb{Z}^*$

c. $\langle 5,8,16 \rangle \in$ **string***

d. $\langle 5 \rangle \in \mathbb{Z}^*$

e. $\langle \rangle \in \mathbb{Z}^*$

f. **true** $\in \mathbb{Z}^*$

g. 'cat' $\in$ **string***

2.5 Engineering Specifications

Based on some intuitive ideas about the nature of sequences, and some reasoning about the operations necessary to construct sequences and select their components, so far we have postulated a number of primitive sequence-processing functions. We've also reached some conclusions about their domains (e.g., that first is undefined on nil), and derived some algebraic properties from their expected behavior (e.g., that first $(x : S) = x$). Unfortunately, this is not an adequate definition of the sequence data type.

Ordinary language, although well-suited to ordinary affairs, leaves too many details to context and understanding. This is intolerable in engineering, where the consequences of misunderstanding may be disastrous. In engineering, clarity and precision of expression are crucial—the reason that all engineering disciplines (and most of the arts) have developed specialized technical languages and notations, such as blue-prints, musical scores, engineering drawings, circuit diagrams, and especially mathematics.

For engineering purposes we must state our meaning more precisely than is convenient in ordinary language. On the other hand, mathematics demands more rigor than is necessary in engineering. Thus we steer a middle course, using mathematics as a language of clear thinking, while avoiding getting mired in mathematical subtleties.

In *software* engineering the result of the engineering process is software. Since, in functional programming, software takes the form of either a function or an abstract data type, in this book we limit our attention to the mathematical specification of functions and abstract data types. Furthermore, since the specification of abstract data types includes the specification of their primitive operations, we can concentrate on just the abstract type problem.

In the remainder of this chapter we discuss a way of mathematically specifying an abstract data type—that is, a way of stating mathematically the values that belong to that type, the legal formulas that can be written of that type, and the values of these formulas. We use a method called *algebraic specification* because it defines the values and primitive operations in terms of their abstract algebraic properties.[9] We will present our algebraic specification in a particular form, which we call an *archetype*, a term used in engineering design to refer a mathematical model of the behavior of the thing being designed (Asimow 1962).[10] Thus the following sections explain archetypes for abstract data types.

2.6 Archetypes for Abstract Data Types

The definition of an abstract data type should tell us all we must know to use the type effectively. What sort of information is required? First, it is necessary to know the *syntax* of the data type: the constants and primitive operations of the data type and the legal ways of combining them into formulas. Second, it is necessary to describe the *semantics* of the data type: the meanings of the primitive operations, that is, the values they compute when given legal inputs. Finally, it is necessary to describe the *pragmatics* of the data type: the purposes, effects, and implications of the actual use of the primitive operations.[11] Notice that each part of the

---

9. Representative examples of the large literature on algebraic specification are (Goguen, Thatcher, and Wagner 1978), (Guttag 1977, 1980), (Scott 1974), (Cartwright 1980), and (Kamin 1983).

10. The chief (Greek *arche*) model (Gr. *typos*) of a thing.

11. The terms *syntax, semantics,* and *pragmatics* are borrowed from the names of the three primary divisions of *semiotics,* the theory of signs (Morris 1938). Also note that semantics refers to the meaning of an expression *to some interpreter.* For computer languages the interpreter may be either a person (e.g., a programmer) or a computer (e.g., that will

specifications builds upon, presupposes, and refines the preceding parts. Thus the syntax is only the first part of the story; it tells us what it is for a formula to be well-formed, but does not specify its value. Similarly, the semantics specifies the value of a formula, but not what will be the practical effects of its use. Conversely, it makes sense to talk of the value of a formula only if we know it is well-formed, and it makes sense to talk of the practical effects of evaluating a formula only if we know it has a value.

Thus archetypes for abstract data types have three components whose purposes are to define the syntax, semantics, and pragmatics of the data type. We illustrate these ideas by developing an archetype for the sequence data types (see Fig. 2.3).

Figure 2.3 Archetype for sequence types (first version).

Syntax:

$\tau^* \in$ **type**, for all $\tau \in$ **type**

$\text{nil} \in \tau^*$

$\text{null}: \tau^* \to \mathbb{B}$

$\text{first}: \tau^* \to \tau$

$\text{rest}: \tau^* \to \tau^*$

$\text{prefix}: \tau \times \tau^* \to \tau^*$

$x : S \Rightarrow \text{prefix}\,(x,\,S)$

$<> \Rightarrow \text{nil}$

$<x_1, x_2, \ldots, x_n> \Rightarrow x_1 : <x_2, \ldots, x_n>$

Semantics:

$\text{nil} \in \tau^*$	$x : S \in \tau^*$
$z \notin \tau^*$, otherwise	
$\text{null nil} = \textbf{true}$	$\text{null}\,(x{:}S) = \textbf{false}$
$\text{first nil} \neq x$	$\text{first}\,(x{:}S) = x$
$\text{rest nil} \neq S$	$\text{rest}\,(x{:}S) = S$

Pragmatics:

The first, rest, prefix, and null operations all take constant time.
The prefix operation is significantly slower than the others.

---

execute the program). These may be quite different; Gorn (1961) distinguishes *human semantics* and *mechanical semantics*. The semantics part of an archetype specifies the mechanical semantics; the human semantics is left unspecified (it is simply the semantics of a first-order theory with equality). Thus the archetype specifies the formal symbol structures (values) generated by a computational process, but not necessarily their mathematical interpretation (which is what logicians usually mean by semantics). In other words, we distinguish a *semantic specification* (of a computation) from the *semantics of a specification*. See also (Zemanek 1966).

2.7 Syntax

The first component of the sequence archetype, labeled 'Syntax', is intended to describe the legal ways in which expressions involving sequences can be constructed. In an applicative language the specification of syntax is relatively simple; it is merely necessary to describe the legal ways that functions and arguments can be put together. This is because of the uniformity of applicative languages: An expression of type τ can be used anywhere an argument of type τ is expected, and a function expecting an argument of type τ can be called with any expression of type τ. Thus, except for some occasional syntactic sugar, the syntax can be completely specified by listing for each primitive operation (1) the name of the operation, (2) the types of the arguments (i.e., the *domain* of the operation), and (3) the type of value returned (i.e., the *range* of the operation). This information is called the *signature* of the operation.

Look now at the sequence archetype (Fig. 2.3). The first line,

$$\tau^* \in \textbf{type}, \text{ for all } \tau \in \textbf{type} \tag{2.9}$$

says that if τ is any type (such as $\mathbb{Z}$, or **string**) then τ^* is also a type. Hence $\mathbb{Z}^*$, **string***, and so forth are all legal sequence types. Also notice that we are guaranteed the existence of types such as $(\mathbb{Z}^*)^*$, the type of all sequences of sequences of integers. The effect of the declaration (Eq. 2.9) is to require that there be a type τ^* for any type τ.

The next five lines are the signatures for the primitive operations. For example, the signature

$$\text{null: } \tau^* \to \mathbb{B} \tag{2.10}$$

means that the operation called null takes a τ-sequence as its argument and returns a Boolean result. Similarly,

$$\text{prefix: } \tau \times \tau^* \to \tau^* \tag{2.11}$$

means that the operation called prefix takes a pair of values of type τ and τ-sequence as input, and returns a τ-sequence as result. Such a signature is analogous to a function heading in a language like Ada or, as here, Pascal:

```
function prefix (x: T; y: Tsequence): Tsequence;
```

A minor difference is that a procedure heading also names the formal parameters used in the body of the function.

The major difference is that the preceding Pascal function works for only a single type T. Thus, if we want several different kinds of sequences in our Pascal program, we must define several different sequence types:

type
   integerSeq = $\cdots$;
   charSeq = $\cdots$;

We must also define different prefix functions to go with them:

function integerPrefix (x: **integer**; y: integerSeq): integerSeq;
   . . .

function charPrefix (x: **char**; y: charSeq): charSeq;
   . . .

Pascal cannot define a *generic* sequence type, although some languages, such as Ada, do have this ability. These languages also permit the definition of generic *functions*—functions that work on values of various types. Since our sequence type is also generic, we will likewise take the primitive sequence operations to be generic.

Thus, for each particular type τ, we take τ^* to be a type "containing" its own (particular) first, rest, prefix, null, and nil operations. If F is a generic operation (i.e., an operation in a generic type), then we use the notation F_τ to denote the operation F particularized to the type τ. Thus, for $\mathbb{Z}^*$, the type "sequence" parameterized by $\mathbb{Z}$, we have the particular operations $\text{first}_\mathbb{Z}$, $\text{rest}_\mathbb{Z}$, and so on. Similarly, for **string*** we have particular operations $\text{first}_\textbf{string}$, $\text{rest}_\textbf{string}$, and so on. From the generic signature

$$\text{first: } \tau^* \to \tau \qquad\qquad (2.12)$$

we can get the particular signatures by substitution:

$$\text{first}_\mathbb{Z}: \mathbb{Z}^* \to \mathbb{Z}$$
$$\text{first}_\textbf{string}: \textbf{string}^* \to \textbf{string}$$

We normally omit the subscript when the type parameter is clear from context. For example, if S is a sequence of integers, then we write first S instead of $\text{first}_\mathbb{Z}$ S. Because generally the type can be determined from context, it is omitted.

Exercise 2.12: Determine whether each of the following formulas is syntactically correct. If so, evaluate it (or explain why you can't).

a. $3 : \text{nil}_\mathbb{Z}$

b. $\text{first}_\textbf{string}$ <2, 3, 5>

c. $5 : (7 : \text{nil}_\mathbb{B})$

d. $\text{nil}_\mathbb{Z} : \text{nil}_\mathbb{Z}$

e. $\text{nil}_{\mathbb{Z}}$: <<4, 3>, < >, <2>>

f. $\text{first}_{\mathbb{Z}}$ $\text{nil}_{\mathbb{Z}}$

g. $\text{rest}_{\mathbb{Z}}$ <4, 7, –1>

The signatures of the various operators can be summarized in a *type signature* such as shown in Fig. 2.4. Type signatures present the syntax of an entire type in graphical form; we provide them for most types.

The signature of a function should not be interpreted as implying that the function is defined on all members of its domain. For example, consider the signatures for first and rest:

$$\text{first: } \tau^* \to \tau \qquad (2.13)$$
$$\text{rest: } \tau^* \to \tau^*$$

These signatures say that τ^* is the domain of both first and rest. We know, however, that neither function is defined on null sequences. Thus we say that first and rest are *partial* functions on the type τ^*. In contrast to standard mathematical notation, the signatures should not be interpreted as implying that functions are *total* on their domains (i.e., defined on all members of the domain).[12]

After the operator signatures we find a rewrite rule in the Syntax part:

$$x : S \implies \text{prefix } (x, S) \qquad (2.14)$$

This means that formulas of the form '$x : S$' are syntactic sugar for corresponding formulas of the form 'prefix (x, S)'. The last two lines of

---

Figure 2.4 Signature for sequence types (first version).

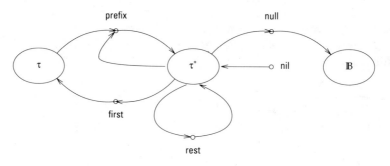

---

12. For now we ignore some important issues related to the specification of partial functions; see Chapter 4.

Syntax introduce the angle-bracket notation as syntactic sugar for nested prefix calls:

$$<> \Rightarrow \text{nil}$$

$$<x_1, x_2, \ldots, x_n> \Rightarrow x_1 : <x_2, \ldots, x_n>$$

(2.15)

Taken together, these rewrite rules say that a *sequence denotation* (a sequence of items separated by commas and surrounded by angle brackets) is an abbreviation for a series of prefix applications:

$$<x_1, x_2, \ldots, x_{n-1}, x_n> \Rightarrow x_1 : (x_2 : \cdots : (x_{n-1} : (x_n : \text{nil})) \cdots)$$

Indeed, since we take ':' to be right associative, we can write

$$<x_1, x_2, \ldots, x_{n-1}, x_n> \Rightarrow x_1 : x_2 : \cdots : x_{n-1} : x_n : \text{nil}$$

(2.16)

Thus the formula <5, 8, 16> is considered an abbreviation for the formula

$$5 : 8 : 16 : \text{nil}$$

We can see this by applying the rewrite rules (2.15):

$$<5, 8, 16> \Rightarrow 5 : <8, 16>$$
$$\Rightarrow 5 : 8 : <16>$$
$$\Rightarrow 5 : 8 : 16 : <>$$
$$\Rightarrow 5 : 8 : 16 : \text{nil}$$

This in turn is an abbreviation for

prefix {5, prefix [8, prefix (16, nil)]}

Exercise 2.13:   Based on the rewrite rules (2.15), show that these formulas are equal:

$$<<1,2>, <3,4>> = (1 : 2 : \text{nil}) : (3 : 4 : \text{nil}) : \text{nil}$$

2.8 Semantics

Next we consider the specification of semantics: how well-formed formulas are interpreted by the computer. In an applicative language we must specify the values that belong to the data type and the values that are computed by the syntactically correct formulas. One way of doing this is to implement the data type in some programming language. A better way is to give a set of mathematical axioms that specify the values belonging to the type and that determine the values of formulas; then we can use mathematical techniques for reasoning about the formulas. Thus our semantic specifications usually consist of two parts: an existence axiom and a set of equations.

The existence axioms tell us what values belong to the data type. For example, look at the existence axiom from Fig. 2.3:

$$\text{nil} \in \tau^*$$
$$x : S \in \tau^*$$
$$z \notin \tau^*, \text{otherwise}$$

This tells us that members of the type include nil as well as every result of a prefix operation $x : S$. Furthermore, the exclusionary phrase, '$z \notin \tau^*$, otherwise', tells us that these are the only members of the type. This means that if we must prove something about all sequences, it suffices to prove it about nil and about arbitrary sequences of the form $x : S$. Chapter 3 includes many examples of this method.

The equations specify the values of the operations indirectly, telling when we can replace one formula by another. For example,

$$\text{rest}\,(x : S) = S \tag{2.17}$$

tells us that a (well-formed) formula of the form 'rest $(x : S)$' can always be replaced by S, and vice versa. In effect we define an *equivalence relation* on the well-formed formulas: two formulas are equivalent if and only if we intend them to have the same value.

How can you tell whether you have the right equations? Basically we want a set of equations that determine the values of the operators on all legal arguments—that is, equations that will define exactly one value for each well-formed formula. In other words, our semantic specification should make every equation between formulas either true or false.

The semantic equations are called *complete* if they are sufficient to either prove or disprove every (well-formed) equation between formulas. This means that the specification attaches at least one value to every well-formed formula. For example, if we omitted

$$\text{null nil} = \textbf{true} \tag{2.18}$$

then the remaining equations would be insufficient to prove either null nil = **true** or null nil ≠ **true**; our specification would be incomplete.

We also want our specification to be *consistent*, which means that we cannot prove both S and not-S for any statement S. This implies that our specification does not attach more than one value to a formula. For example, suppose we accidently had the following two equations in our specification:

$$\text{null nil} = \textbf{true} \qquad\qquad (2.19)$$
$$\text{null nil} = \textbf{false}$$

To see how this leads to a contradiction, start with the true equation

$$\text{null nil} = \text{null nil}$$

Applying the first equation in (2.19) to the left and the second to the right, we obtain

$$\textbf{true} = \textbf{false}$$

This contradicts the Boolean archetype (see Appendix B), which states the (obvious) requirement that **true** ≠ **false**.[13] Hence our goal is a set of equations that is both complete and consistent. We can establish the consistency of a specification by implementing it correctly—since an inconsistent specification cannot be implemented, the existence of à correct implementation proves the consistency of the specification.[14] Because there are implementations of sequences that satisfy our archetype (e.g., in correct LISP systems), we know that it is consistent (see Chapter 4).

Although it may be quite difficult to establish the completeness of a specification,[15] we can convince ourselves that our equations for the primitive operations are complete (and consistent) by ensuring that they define a unique output for each allowable input. Observe that every sequence is either nil or can be written in a unique way in the form $x : S$. That every sequence can be represented in these forms *at least* one way is guaranteed by the existence axiom (Eq. 2.3). That it can be so represented in *exactly* one way can be proved; see Exercises 2.15–2.18. Since these representations are unique, stating the result of an operator on formulas in each of these forms will ensure a complete and consistent specification of the operator; we will have defined a unique result for every possible input.

For example, Eq. (2.8), repeated here, tells us how to compute a result for null T for every sequence T; we simply interpret the equations as rewrite rules:

$$\text{null nil} \Rightarrow \textbf{true} \qquad\qquad (2.8)$$
$$\text{null } (x{:}S) \Rightarrow \textbf{false}$$

---

13. We have used two properties of '=' that follow from referential transparency: (1) if $x = y$, then one may be replaced by the other in any proposition without changing its truth, and (2) $x = x$, which follows from (1).
14. Here we appeal to a well-known theorem of logic that a system of axioms is consistent if and only if it is satisfiable (i.e., has at least one model).
15. In fact, the best we can hope for is to establish the *relative completeness* of the specification for a data type. That is, propositions concerning the data type are decidable *provided* that propositions concerning the other data types are decidable.

The result of an application of null can then be determined in any particular case. For example,

$$null <5,8,16> \Rightarrow null\ (5:<8,16>) \Rightarrow \textbf{false}$$

We know that Eq. (2.8) determines a *unique* result since nil $\neq x{:}S$, for all x and S (Exercise 2.15).

Similarly, since a nonnull sequence T can be written in the form $T = x{:}S$ in exactly one way, Eq. (2.6) determines exactly one value for rest T. To see this, interpret the equation as a rewrite rule:

$$rest\ (x{:}S) \Rightarrow S \tag{2.20}$$

The result of any particular application of rest can be computed by this rule. For example,

$$rest <5,8,16> \Rightarrow rest\ (5:<8,16>) \Rightarrow <8,16>$$

Notice that all the equations in Fig. 2.3 can be interpreted as rewrite rules; thus we know how to compute a unique value for any particular application of the primitive operations. In this way we can convince ourselves of the consistency and completeness of the equations.

To ensure completeness we must specify the behavior of the operations on every sequence, even those that are not legal inputs to the operation. Notice, however, that first nil and rest nil are specified in an odd way, by the following *inequations:*

$$
\begin{aligned}
&first\ nil \neq x \\
&rest\ nil \neq S
\end{aligned}
\tag{2.21}
$$

The intent, of course, is that these formulas are undefined. Why have we expressed this fact in this way?

There are several senses of 'undefined', with corresponding reasons for specifying that a formula be undefined. For example, we might want to leave certain decisions to the implementor of the data type. In this case 'undefined' means 'undefined by this specification'; we only hope that implementors will tell us what they decide. Thus, if we didn't want to specify the results of first nil and rest nil, we could put these statements in the archetype:

first nil is undefined

rest nil is undefined

In this case our specification is *intentionally incomplete.* We cannot derive $x = rest\ nil$ for any value x, but neither can we derive $x \neq rest\ nil$; the axioms leave all such issues undecided. Thus the implementor can decide to make rest nil = nil, to make it an error, or to do anything else with this formula.

Leaving issues such as this undecided tends to impede portability; different implementors may make different choices. To avoid this we may wish to be more assertive, stating that these formulas are errors in accordance with the mathematical sense of undefined: A formula is undefined if it has no value. One common way of expressing this is by equations such as these:

$$\text{first nil} = \perp \tag{2.22}$$
$$\text{rest nil} = \perp$$

Here the symbol '$\perp$' denotes the "undefined value."[16] The only problem with this manner of expression is that it requires the machinery of domain theory for its proper interpretation. Without this, we might naively apply the equations in the usual way and, for example, conclude from Eq. (2.22) and $1/0 = \perp$ that first nil = 1/0. This was probably not the intent of the specification.

How then do we specify that the formulas first nil and rest nil have *no value*? This can be directly expressed by the inequations

$$\text{first nil} \neq x \tag{2.21}$$
$$\text{rest nil} \neq S$$

For example, the first of these says that for every value x, first nil $\neq x$. In other words, first nil is not equal to anything; it has no value. (Of course, the names we use, x and S, have no special significance.) The requirements of this specification are quite specific. For example, we are allowed to derive rest nil $\neq$ nil, so implementors are not allowed to implement rest this way. Further, since the specification does not allow implementors to return *any* value, they have no choice but to abort the program (or go into an infinite loop!).

Once a complete and consistent set of equations has been developed, it is customary to try to reduce the set of equations to the smallest number from which all the rest can be derived. For example, the equation

$$(\text{first } T) : (\text{rest } T) = T, \text{ if } \neg \text{null } T \tag{2.23}$$

is not necessary since it can be derived from the definitions of first, rest, and null (see Exercise 2.19). Reducing the set of equations simplifies consistency proofs since fewer equations must be shown to be satisfiable.

---

16. Actually, $\perp$ denotes the bottom of a lattice, but this theory is beyond the scope of this book. See, for example, (Scott 1970–1977) or (Milne and Strachey 1976, Section 2.2.1).

A large body of computer science theory is devoted to the study of equational and similar methods of specifying semantics, including (Goguen, Thatcher, and Wagner 1978), (Guttag 1977, 1980), (Scott 1974), (Cartwright 1980), and (Kamin 1983). Applying abstract algebra and category theory to these specification problems, this theory tries to find ways to determine whether particular sets of equations have desirable properties such as consistency and completeness. For the time being we take an engineering rather than a mathematical approach. Thus we permit specifications that are not completely formal, so long as they specify clearly the intended syntax, semantics, and pragmatics of the data type. Unfortunately, the axioms in Fig. 2.3 leave certain crucial issues undecided (see Section 2.10).

Exercise 2.14: Explain why it is important that each sequence can be represented *in a unique way* in one of the forms nil or $x:S$. *Hint:* Suppose a certain sequence T could be represented in two distinct ways, $x:S = T = y:S$, where $x \neq y$. Apply first to both sides of the equation $T = T$ and show how this leads to a contradiction.

Exercise 2.15: Prove that

$$\text{nil} \neq x:S \tag{2.24}$$

for all x, S. *Hint:* Assume the converse and apply null to both sides. What reasonable assumption must you make about the Boolean data type? Can you find it in the Boolean archetype (see Appendix B)?

Exercise 2.16: Prove that $x \neq y$ implies that $x:S \neq y:T$ for all S, T. *Hint:* Consider the contrapositive.

Exercise 2.17: Prove that $S \neq T$ implies that $x:S \neq y:T$ for all x, y.

Exercise 2.18: Use the preceding three exercises to prove that every sequence has a unique representation in one of the forms nil or $x:S$.

Exercise 2.19: Show that Eq. (2.23) can be derived from the properties in Fig. 2.3.

Exercise 2.20: Prove that

$$x:y:S \neq y:x:S \tag{2.25}$$

for all x, y, S such that $x \neq y$. This shows that order of elements is significant for sequences.

Exercise 2.21:   Prove from the archetype that

$$\text{first } <S_1, S_2, \ldots, S_n> = S_1 \tag{2.26}$$

for $n > 0$. This equation shows that first has the expected property listed in Eq. (2.5). *Hint:* Use Eqs. (2.6) and (2.15).

Exercise 2.22:   Prove from the archetype that

$$\text{rest } <S_1, S_2, \ldots, S_n> = <S_2, \ldots, S_n> \tag{2.27}$$

for $n > 0$.

Exercise 2.23:   Prove from the archetype that

$$S_0 : <S_1, \ldots, S_n> = <S_0, S_1, \ldots, S_n> \tag{2.28}$$

for $n \geq 0$.

2.9 Pragmatics

The 'Pragmatics' section of an archetype deals with the purposes, effects, and implications of the actual use of the functions and data values belonging to the type. For our purposes the pragmatics is usually performance information—for example, that a certain operation takes constant time, or that a certain operation takes significantly more time than another operation. This performance information is important in algorithm analysis (see Chapter 3).

The performance information may be either empirical generalizations drawn from knowledge of typical implementations, or performance requirements that any acceptable implementation must meet. In practice the two are related, since stating feasible requirements requires some knowledge of typical implementation techniques.

In the case of the sequence archetype (Fig. 2.3), the Pragmatics section tells us that first, rest, prefix, and null all take constant time. It also tells us that prefix takes significantly longer than the others; hence for some purposes we can count just the prefix operations, ignoring the others. These performance requirements reflect the most common, LISP-style, implementation of sequences.

The Pragmatics section may also discuss permissible limitations on implementations of the data type. For example, an archetype for integers (see Appendix B) will probably specify an infinite range of integers, whereas we probably want to permit implementations that restrict integers to some finite range (typically -2^n through $2^n - 1$, for some reasonable n). It is also appropriate to state in the Pragmatics section minimum capabilities that an acceptable implementation must meet—for example, that an implementation of integers includes at least the range -2^{32} through $2^{32}-1$.

Finally, the Pragmatics section may discuss semantic issues that are left unresolved in the Semantics section. Indeed, the Pragmatics section is something of a catchall for anything that is important to state in the archetype, but that doesn't fall clearly into the Syntax or Semantics sections.

Appendix B collects the archetypes for all abstract types used in this book.

Exercise 2.24:   In Pascal or some other language with which you are familiar, define the sequence data type $\mathbb{Z}^*$, including the sequence-processing primitives (first, rest, prefix, null).

2.10 The Problem of Infinite Sequences

Since we have defined the meaning of each of the sequence operators on every kind of sequence, it would seem that our archetype is complete. Unfortunately, the axioms in Fig. 2.3 are not sufficient. As you probably know, sequences are often represented in memory by records linked by pointers. For example, <5, 8, 16, 3> would be represented as follows:

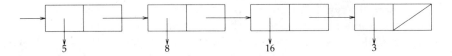

Consider now a structure such as the following, in which a later record points back to an earlier record:

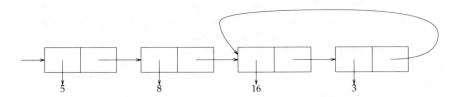

As we follow through the records in the sequence, we see the elements in the order

$$5, 8, 16, 3, 16, 3, 16, 3, \ \cdots$$

Therefore it is reasonable to interpret this circular structure as the *infinite sequence*

$$<5, 8, 16, 3, 16, 3, 16, \ \cdots >$$

Are such infinite (or circular) sequences allowed? We have seen that they can be easily implemented by pointers. Also, they turn out to be very useful in some applications (see Chapter 7). On the other hand, they can make storage management significantly more difficult (since they preclude reference-counting schemes). More importantly, they make inductive proofs of program correctness much harder (as will become apparent in Chapter 3). Therefore, whether infinite sequences are permitted or not is an important language-design issue.

The problem is that our semantic axioms in Fig. 2.3 neither require nor exclude infinite sequences. That they do not require them can be seen by the fact that our informal *finite* sequences satisfy the axioms. That they do not exclude them can be seen by considering the infinite sequence of zeroes $C = <0, 0, \cdots>$, which can be represented as follows:

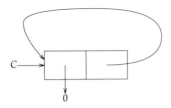

The archetype does not permit us to decide whether or not C is a sequence. The existence axiom states

$$\text{nil} \in \tau^*$$
$$x : S \in \tau^*$$
$$z \notin \tau^*, \text{ otherwise}$$

Applying this to the case $C = 0 : C$ yields

$$C \in \mathbb{Z}^*, \text{ if } 0 \in \mathbb{Z} \text{ and } C \in \mathbb{Z}^* \qquad (2.29)$$
$$C \notin \mathbb{Z}^*, \text{ otherwise}$$

Since $0 \in \mathbb{Z}$ is true, we find $C \in \mathbb{Z}^*$ if and only if $C \in \mathbb{Z}^*$! We can consistently assume either $C \in \mathbb{Z}^*$ or $C \notin \mathbb{Z}^*$; neither assumption lands us in a contradiction. Thus the archetype (Fig. 2.3) is incomplete after all. Our reasoning about the possible forms of sequences ensured that the primitive operators were completely specified, but not that the existence of values was completely specified.

If we assume that C is a legitimate sequence, then we find that the other axioms give it perfectly reasonable properties. For example, the selectors and prefix constructor apply to it:

$$\text{first } C = 0, \text{ rest } C = C \text{ and } 0 : C = C$$

Since C can be written in the form '$0 : C$' it is, by the equations in Fig. 2.3, a nonnull sequence of integers:

null C = null $(0 : C)$ = **false**

Furthermore, the usual sequence properties hold:

first $(0 : C) = 0$ and rest $(0 : C) = C$
(first C) : (rest C) $= C$

We are forced to conclude that the archetype in Fig. 2.3 does not exclude C from sequencehood. Indeed, the archetype permits many other infinite sequences, some of which are not circular, such as the natural number sequence

$$N = <0, 1, 2, 3, 4, \cdots >$$

Even though there is no simple way to implement this as a linked structure, it is permitted by the archetype.

Exercise 2.25:   Show that the assumption $N \in \mathbb{Z}^*$ does not lead to a contradiction in Fig. 2.3 and that from this assumption one can conclude that N is in fact a nonnull sequence.

We face an important issue: Are we going to have infinite sequences? There are really two versions of this question: Should infinite sequences be *permitted*? Should infinite sequences be *required*? As mentioned earlier, the answers to these questions can affect our language profoundly.

For the time being we answer both questions in the negative. There are several reasons. First, we never intended to have infinite sequences; our informal development earlier in this chapter was entirely motivated by considerations of finite sequences. In particular we assumed that any sequence could be written as a finite enumeration of the form $<x_1, x_2, \ldots, x_n>$. Second, permitting infinite sequences complicates inductive proofs of programs, as will become clear in Chapter 3; see also (Cartwright and Donahue 1982). Third, most of the applicative programs we develop in this book work on arbitrary finite sequences, but don't work on arbitrary infinite sequences. This suggests that infinite sequences are fundamentally different from finite sequences. Finally, some infinite sequences have unintuitive properties (such as rest $C = C$) that don't apply to finite sequences. Infinite data structures are important and useful in functional programming, however, as you will see in Chapter 7 and occasionally thereafter.

It is clear now that the axioms in Fig. 2.3 are not complete since they allow infinite sequences in addition to the intended finite sequences.

Figure 2.5 Archetype for sequence types (final version).

Syntax:

$\tau^* \in$ **type**, for all $\tau \in$ **type**

nil $\in \tau^*$
null: $\tau^* \to \mathbb{B}$
first: $\tau^* \to \tau$
rest: $\tau^* \to \tau^*$
prefix: $\tau \times \tau^* \to \tau^*$
length: $\tau^* \to \mathbb{N}$

$x{:}S \Rightarrow$ prefix (x, S)
$<> \Rightarrow$ nil
$<x_1, x_2, \ldots, x_n> \Rightarrow x_1 : <x_2, \ldots, x_n>$

Semantics:

nil $\in \tau^*$ $\qquad\qquad\qquad\qquad$ $x : S \in \tau^*$

$\qquad\qquad$ $z \notin \tau^*$, otherwise

null nil $=$ **true** $\qquad\qquad\qquad$ null $(x{:}S) =$ **false**
first nil $\neq x$ $\qquad\qquad\qquad\quad$ first $(x{:}S) = x$
rest nil $\neq S$ $\qquad\qquad\qquad\quad$ rest $(x{:}S) = S$
length nil $= 0$ $\qquad\qquad\qquad$ length $(x{:}S) = 1 +$ length S

$\qquad\qquad$ length is a total function on τ^*

Pragmatics:

The first, rest, prefix, and null operations all take constant time.
The prefix operation is significantly slower than the others.
The length operation takes time at most proportional to the length of
its argument.

How can we add additional axioms to guarantee that our sequences are
finite?

A solution that suggests itself immediately is to add a *finiteness axiom*
that requires the length of a sequence to be a finite natural number:

For any sequence S, length (S) is a finite natural number. $\qquad$ (2.30)

If we take $\mathbb{N}$, the set of natural numbers,[17] to include only finite numbers,
then it is sufficient to say that

length: $\tau^* \to \mathbb{N}$ $\qquad\qquad\qquad\qquad\qquad\qquad\qquad\qquad$ (2.31)
length is a total function on τ^*

---

17. The term "natural number" is sometimes used to refer to the set of positive integers {1,
2, 3, ...} (Iyanaga and Kawada 1977), and sometimes used to refer to the set of nonnegative integers {0, 1, 2, ...} (MacLane and Birkhoff 1967). We take $\mathbb{N}$ to include 0.

Of course, we haven't defined length, but it is easy to add equations to do so:

$$\text{length nil} = 0$$
$$\text{length } (x{:}S) = 1 + \text{length } S \tag{2.32}$$

Figure 2.5 displays a revised archetype for sequence types; its signature is shown in Fig. 2.6.

Exercise 2.26: Prove inductively that the preceding definition of length agrees with our intuitive notion of length. That is,

$$\text{length } <x_1, \ldots, x_n> = n \tag{2.33}$$

Exercise 2.27: Explain in detail why some finite number of applications of rest must eventually reach nil.

Exercise 2.28: Prove that

$$x{:}S \neq x{:}x{:}S \tag{2.34}$$

for all x, S. This shows that multiplicity of elements is significant for sequences. Why does this property hold for the Fig. 2.5 archetype, but not for the Fig. 2.3 archetype? Give a counterexample to this property that is permitted by Fig. 2.3 sequences.

Figure 2.6 Signature for sequence types.

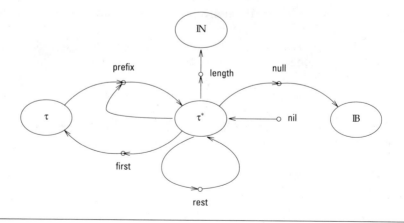

Chapter 3

Applicative Sequence Processing

3.1 Goals

In this chapter we demonstrate that applicative programming is possible—not an obvious property, since applicative programming dispenses with two of the most useful tools of conventional imperative programming: the variable and the assignment operation. We work through a number of simple programming problems to acquaint you with the applicative style.

We also demonstrate that applicative programming, beyond being just possible, is actually preferable to imperative programming for many problems. In particular, we show that applicative programs are often simpler than the corresponding imperative programs, and that it is often easier to prove applicative programs correct, as well as to analyze them (e.g., for performance). Thus, for comparison, we program certain problems both imperatively and applicatively. Also, we often prove or analyze programs.

Finally, this chapter will develop your *skill* in applicative programming, which like any skill must be improved by practice. We have included a large number of exercises in programming, proof, and analysis, some of them very easy and some of them harder. We strongly suggest you try *all* the exercises: When they *all* seem easy, you will know you have a good handle on applicative programming.

3.2 Element Selection

To help you understand sequence processing, we present a number of examples. First we define a useful utility function elt[1] such that elt (S, i) is the ith element of the sequence S. For instance,

> elt (<5, 8, 16, 25>, 3) = 16
> elt (<<5, 6>, <9, 32>, <7, 16>>, 2) = <9, 32>

since 16 is the third element of <5, 8, 16, 25> and <9, 32> is the second element of <<5, 6>, <9, 32>, <7, 16>>.

In general, elt takes a sequence of any type and a (nonzero) natural number, and returns a value belonging to the base type of the sequence. That is, if elt is applied to a τ sequence and a natural number, it returns a value of type τ. Thus its signature is

> elt: $\tau^* \times \mathbb{N} \to \tau$, for all $\tau \in$ **type**

Since there is an elt function for each type τ, it is a *generic* or *polymorphic* function, just like first, rest, and prefix.

It's a good idea to write down a signature for every function you define. Not only is this good documentation, but it helps you to be clear in your own mind about the arguments the function is expected to accept. In this case observe that elt is a *partial function* on $\tau^* \times \mathbb{N}$, since it is not defined on all pairs of τ-sequences and natural numbers. In particular, it is defined only on those pairs for which the natural number is between 1 and the length of the sequence (inclusive). There are some subtleties involved with the specification of partial functions that we ignore for now (see Chapter 4).

How should we program this function? First we must ask which subcases can be solved directly. In the case of elt this is fairly easy, since by definition elt $(S, 1)$ is just the first element of S. That is,

> elt $(S, 1)$ = first S $\hspace{4em}$ (3.1)

The next step in solving a problem such as this is to find some way to reduce the general problem to the subcases that are already solved. Notice that

---

1. We name functions by nouns, such as 'element', rather than verbs, such as 'select', to reflect the descriptive, rather than imperative, import of expressions in an applicative language: *Form follows function.*

$$\text{elt} (<5, 8, 16, 25>, 3) = 16$$
$$\text{elt} (<8, 16, 25>, 2) = 16$$
$$\text{elt} (<16, 25>, 1) = 16$$

In general,

$$\text{elt} (S, i) = \text{elt} (\text{rest } S, i - 1) \qquad (3.2)$$

We have reduced the original problem, elt (S, i), to one that is closer to the solved problem, elt $(S, 1)$, since $i-1$ is closer to 1 than is i. We now have two cases:

$$\text{elt} (S, i) = \text{first } S, \qquad\qquad \text{if } i = 1 \qquad (3.3)$$
$$\text{elt} (S, i) = \text{elt} (\text{rest } S, i - 1), \quad \text{if } i > 1$$

These two equations define elt completely; they could be entered as is into applicative programming systems that permit "equational" definitions. For systems that don't allow this style of definition, the equations must combined into an if-then-else-style conditional definition:

$$\text{elt} (S, i) \equiv \begin{cases} \text{first } S, \text{ if } i = 1 \\ \textbf{else } \text{elt} (\text{rest } S, i - 1) \end{cases} \qquad (3.4)$$

We usually show both the equational definition and the conditional definition. The equational definition is usually more readable, but the conditional is more explicit and easier to translate into imperative languages. (Their pros and cons are discussed further in Chapter 5.)

We can gain insight into the execution of elt by tracing the evaluation of a particular expression, such as elt $(<A, B, C, D>, 3)$:

$$\text{elt} (<A, B, C, D>, 3) \Rightarrow \begin{cases} \text{first } <A, B, C, D>, \text{ if } 3 = 1 \\ \textbf{else } \text{elt} (\text{rest } <A, B, C, D>, 3 - 1) \end{cases}$$

$$\Rightarrow \text{elt} (<B, C, D>, 2)$$

$$\Rightarrow \begin{cases} \text{first } <B, C, D>, \text{ if } 2 = 1 \\ \textbf{else } \text{elt} (\text{rest } <B, C, D>, 2 - 1) \end{cases}$$

$$\Rightarrow \text{elt} (<C, D>, 1)$$

$$\Rightarrow \begin{cases} \text{first } <C, D>, \text{ if } 1 = 1 \\ \textbf{else } \text{elt} (\text{rest } <C, D>, 1 - 1) \end{cases}$$

$$\Rightarrow \text{first } <C, D>$$

$$\Rightarrow C$$

Such traces—really very simple forms of *algebraic manipulation*—are one example of a situation in which applicative programs are easier to manipulate than imperative programs.[2]

Exercise 3.1:   Trace 'elt (<'dog', 'cat', 'goat', 'duck', 'bird'>, 4)'.

Exercise 3.2:   Trace 'elt (<<2, 4>, <3, 9>, <4, 16>>, 3)'.

Exercise 3.3:   Trace 'elt (19 : <3, 5, 23, 8>, 4)'.

Exercise 3.4:   Simplify the formula 'elt $(x : S, i)$' given that you know that $i > 1$ and that prefixing is more expensive than arithmetic.

Exercise 3.5:   Simplify the formula 'elt $(x : y : S, n + 2)$' given that you know that $n > 0$.

The trace shows that elt works in a particular case, giving us some confidence that our definition is correct. Therefore a trace is usually the first thing you should do to check a definition. A trace, however, shows that the definition is correct only in a particular case, not that it works in general. To show that it works for all cases, we must decide what we *mean* by the function's working. A reasonable choice for elt follows:

$$\text{elt} (<S_1, \ldots, S_n>, i) = S_i, \text{ for } 1 \le i \le n \qquad (3.5)$$

It is particularly easy to reason inductively about recursively defined functions such as elt. Therefore let's develop an inductive proof that Eq. (3.5) holds.

Consider first the case $i = 1$. Mimicking the evaluation of the function in an algebraic derivation, we have the following:

$$\begin{aligned}
\text{elt} (<S_1, \ldots, S_n>, i) &= \text{elt} (<S_1, \ldots, S_n>, 1), \text{ since } i = 1 \\
&= \text{first} <S_1, \ldots, S_n>, \text{ by Eq. (3.1)} \\
&= S_1, \text{ by Eq. (2.26)}
\end{aligned}$$

Hence Eq. (3.5) is true for the case $i = 1$.

For the inductive step, suppose that Eq. (3.5) is true for all $j < i$, where $1 < i \le n$; we want to show that it's true for i. By Eq. (2.27),

$$\text{elt} (<S_1, \ldots, S_n>, i) = \text{elt} (\text{rest} <S_1, \ldots, S_n>, i - 1) \qquad (3.6)$$

---

2. Of course, traces don't have to be done manually; many applicative programming systems will trace expressions for you.

By Eq. (2.27), since $n \geq 1$,

$$\text{rest} <S_1, \ldots, S_n> = <S_2, \ldots, S_n>$$

Thus the right-hand side of Eq. (3.6) reduces to

$$\text{elt} (<S_2, \ldots, S_n>, i - 1)$$

Since $1 < i \leq n$ we know that $n > 1$ and therefore $n - 1 \geq 1$. Hence it is legitimate to apply the inductive hypothesis—that Eq. (3.5) is true for $j < i$. Since $i - 1 < i$ and the $i - 1$ element of $<S_2, \ldots, S_n>$ is S_i, by the inductive hypothesis we know that the preceding expression is equal to S_i.[3] This proves that elt satisfies Eq. (3.5):

$$\text{elt} (<S_1, \ldots, S_n>, i) = S_i, \text{ for } 1 \leq i \leq n \qquad (3.5)$$

We pause to make a very important observation. Notice that the structure of the inductive proof is the same as the structure of the recursive program. In the base of the induction we utilized Eq. (3.1), the base of the recursion; in the inductive step we utilized Eq. (3.2), the recursive step. This is no coincidence: Recursion and induction are really two sides of the same coin. This means that if we want to prove something inductively about a recursive program, then the program itself provides the structure of the proof. As we will see, this even extends to the case structure: Where the program has a conditional with several arms, there the proof will have several cases. Therefore your best guide in attacking an inductive proof is the recursive structure of the program. In fact, the two are so closely related, that perhaps the best strategy is to develop the program and its correctness proof in tandem.[4] We state this as a principle:

Induction recapitulates recursion.

Having developed a definition of elt and proved that it's correct, our next step is to translate the definition into a programming language. In Common LISP[5] elt is defined as follows:

3. If you find this step insufficiently rigorous, let $S'_k = S_{k-1}$, $n' = n - 1$ and $i' = i - 1$. Then apply the inductive hypothesis to elt (S', i').
4. See also the book *Recursion, Induction, and Programming* (Wand 1980).
5. Common LISP and Interlisp both have 'elt' built in, although the Common LISP function is not compatible with our function, since it indexes from 0. We follow the Interlisp convention and index from 1 because this is more in accord with mathematical convention. Note also that we use the Common LISP 'if' in preference to the older (and less readable) 'cond'.

```
(defun elt (S i)
  (if (= i 1) (first S)
      (elt (rest S) (– i 1)))))
```

It is not even difficult to translate the definition into an imperative language, provided the language supports recursive procedures and the ability to define a sequence data type. For example, in Pascal we have the following:

```
function elt (S: tausequence; i: integer): tau;
  begin
    if i = 1 then elt := first (S)
    else elt := elt (rest (S), i – 1)
  end {elt}
```

We have omitted the definitions of the data types 'tau' and 'tausequence' and also the definitions of the 'first' and 'rest' functions. (Also, the function works only for a particular sequence type.)

The elt function is sufficiently useful that we adopt a special "array subscripting" notation for it:

$$A_i \Rightarrow \text{elt}(A, i)$$

Thus 'A_1' and 'first A' are the same. This notation is justified by Eq. (3.5), which says that elt (A, i) returns A_i, the ith element of A.

If M is a sequence of sequences, often we must compose element-selection operations. Since a sequence of sequences can be thought of as a matrix, we use the following notation for compound selection:

$$M_{i,j} \Rightarrow (M_i)_j \Rightarrow \text{elt}[\text{elt}(M, i), j]$$

If M is of type $(\tau^*)^*$, then M_i is of type τ^* and $M_{i,j}$ is of type τ. Of course, we extend this convention to any number of subscripts.

Exercise 3.6:   Evaluate the expression

$$<<2, 4>, <3, 9>, <4, 16>>_{3,1}$$

Exercise 3.7:   Define conditionally the function length defined equationally in Fig. 2.5.

Exercise 3.8:   Translate your conditional definition of length into a programming language such as LISP or Pascal.

3.3 Catenation

Next let us define a function cat such that cat (S, T) is the concatenation of the sequences S and T. Its signature is

$$\text{cat: } \tau^* \times \tau^* \to \tau^*$$

since it operates on sequences of any type. For example,

cat (<1, 2>, <3, 4, 5>) = <1, 2, 3, 4, 5>
cat (<'cat', 'dog', 'horse'>, <'goose', 'duck'>) =
   <'cat', 'dog', 'horse', 'goose', 'duck'>

Note that cat (<1, 2>, <3, 4, 5>) is different from <1, 2> : <3, 4, 5>. The latter is in fact syntactically incorrect since we cannot prefix integer sequences onto integer sequences (we can prefix only integers onto integer sequences).

Exercise 3.9: Explain the difference between prefix and cat in terms of their signatures.

Let's use the same problem-solving technique that we used with elt, asking, What cases of cat are immediately solvable? The answer is, those in which one of the sequences to be catenated is null—for instance,

cat (<>, <4, 5, 6>) = <4, 5, 6>

In general,

cat (<>, T) = T
cat (S, <>) = S

Next we must investigate how the general problem can be reduced to either of these two cases. For instance, since we know that

$$\text{cat }(<>, T) = T \tag{3.7}$$

we can work on reducing the first argument to an empty sequence. Therefore let's explore a case in which the first argument to cat is nonnull, and see whether we can reduce it to an invocation in which the first argument is null:

cat (<2>, <3, 4, 5>)

Because we know that cat $(<>, <3, 4, 5>) = <3, 4, 5>$ and also that $2{:}<3, 4, 5> = <2, 3, 4, 5>$, we can use the first equation to substitute for $<3, 4, 5>$ in the second, yielding

$$2 : \text{cat} (<>, <3, 4, 5>) = <2, 3, 4, 5>$$

The right-hand side of this equation is the intended value of cat $(<2>, <3, 4, 5>)$, however, so we see the equation

$$\text{cat} (<2>, <3, 4, 5>) = 2 : \text{cat} (<>, <3, 4, 5>)$$

Thus we can apply cat to a one-element sequence and an arbitrary sequence by prefixing the first (and only) element of the first sequence to the result of catenating nil with the second sequence:

$$\text{cat} (<S_1>, T) = S_1 : \text{cat} (<>, T)$$

Now let's consider a more complicated example, a sequence of length two:

$$\text{cat} (<1, 2>, <3, 4, 5>)$$

We already know how to do

$$\text{cat} (<2>, <3, 4, 5>) \Rightarrow <2, 3, 4, 5>$$

so all we need do is reduce the new case to the preceding case:

$$\begin{aligned} \text{cat} (<1, 2>, <3, 4, 5>) &= 1 : <2, 3, 4, 5> \\ &= 1 : \text{cat} (<2>, <3, 4, 5>) \end{aligned}$$

Thus we get the catenation of a length-two sequence with an arbitrary sequence by prefixing the first element of the first sequence to the catenation of the rest of the first sequence with the second sequence:

$$\text{cat} (<S_1, S_2>, T) = S_1 : \text{cat} (<S_2>, T)$$

Summarizing, we have

$$\begin{aligned} \text{cat} (<1, 2>, <3, 4, 5>) &= 1 : \text{cat} (<2>, <3, 4, 5>) \\ \text{cat} (<2>, <3, 4, 5>) &= 2 : \text{cat} (<>, <3, 4, 5>) \\ \text{cat} (<>, <3, 4, 5>) &= <3, 4, 5> \end{aligned}$$

Performing the same derivation for an arbitrary (nonnull) sequence, we get

$$\begin{aligned}
\text{cat}(S, T) &= <S_1, \ldots, S_m, T_1, \ldots, T_n> \\
&= S_1 : <S_2, \ldots, S_m, T_1, \ldots, T_n> \\
&= S_1 : \text{cat}(<S_2, \ldots, S_m>, <T_1, \ldots, T_n>) \\
&= S_1 : \text{cat}(\text{rest } S, T)
\end{aligned}$$

Therefore, for any nonnull sequence S,[6]

$$\text{cat}(S, T) = \text{first } S : \text{cat}(\text{rest } S, T) \tag{3.8}$$

Summarizing, we have two simultaneous equations that together define cat:

$$\begin{aligned}
\text{cat}(S, T) &= T, && \text{if null } S \\
\text{cat}(S, T) &= \text{first } S : \text{cat}(\text{rest } S, T), && \text{if } \neg \text{ null } S
\end{aligned}$$

These can be easily transformed into the conditional definition:

$$\text{cat}(S, T) \equiv \begin{cases} T, & \text{if null } S \\ \textbf{else } \text{first } S : \text{cat}(\text{rest } S, T) \end{cases} \tag{3.9}$$

It is now but a small step to translate to a programming language such as LISP:

```
(defun cat (S T)
  (if (null S) T
    (cons (first S) (cat (rest S) T)))))
```

or Pascal (in which case we must have a separate version for each sequence type 'tausequence'):

```
function cat (S, T: tausequence): tausequence;
begin
  if null (S) then cat := T
  else cat := prefix (first (S), cat (rest (S), T))
end {cat}
```

We will find that many recursive definitions fit this pattern: (1) a *stopping condition* that forms the *base* of the recursion and (2) a recursive invocation of the function in which the problem is reduced to a simpler problem. In sequence processing the stopping condition often takes the form 'null $(\cdots)$', just as in numerical functions it often takes the form '$\cdots = 0$'. You should again note the similarity between recursive function

6. We take application to have higher precedence than any binary operator. Hence 'first $S : X$' means '(first $S) : X$'.

definitions and mathematical proofs by induction. Later you'll see how this similarity simplifies proving things about recursive functions.

It should be mentioned that if we had decided to reduce the *second* argument rather than the first to the null sequence, we would have found the going much tougher. How did we know to avoid this approach? The sequence-processing primitives favor working on the beginning of a sequence (hence the first argument of cat). This sort of intuition comes from practice with using the primitives.

Although it is relatively easy to prove that cat is correct, we will first convince ourselves by tracing the evaluation of cat $(<1,2>, <3,4,5>)$:

Trace	Justification
cat $(<1, 2>, <3, 4, 5>) \Rightarrow$ first $<1, 2> :$ cat (rest $<1, 2>, <3, 4, 5>)$	Eq. (3.8)
$\Rightarrow 1 :$ cat $(<2>, <3, 4, 5>)$	Eqs. (2.26) and (2.27)
$\Rightarrow 1 :$ first $<2> :$ cat (rest $<2>, <3, 4, 5>)$	Eq. (3.8)
$\Rightarrow 1 : [2 :$ cat $(<>, <3, 4, 5>)]$	Eqs. (2.26) and (2.27)
$\Rightarrow 1 : (2 : <3, 4, 5>)$	Eq. (3.7)
$\Rightarrow 1 : <2, 3, 4, 5>$	Eq. (2.15)
$\Rightarrow <1, 2, 3, 4, 5>$	Eq. (2.15)

Exercise 3.10: Trace 'cat $(<\text{'dog'}, \text{'cat'}, \text{'goat'}>, <\text{'duck'}, \text{'bird'}>)$'.

Exercise 3.11: Trace 'cat $(<7, 12, 4, 0>, <>)$'.

Exercise 3.12: Trace 'cat $(<<2, 4>, <3, 9>>, <<4, 16>>)$'.

Exercise 3.13: Trace 'cat $(0, <1, 2, 3>)$'. *Hint:* Be careful!

How can we prove that this definition of cat is correct? First we must decide what we mean by its correctness. As a start we know that cat must satisfy the equation

$$\text{cat} (<S_1, \ldots, S_m>, <T_1, \ldots, T_n>) = <S_1, \ldots, S_m, T_1, \ldots, T_n> \qquad (3.10)$$

for all $m, n \geq 0$. Since the definition of cat is recursive on its first argument, and induction recapitulates recursion, the obvious approach is an inductive proof on m. Therefore consider the case $m = 0$; we want to show that

$$\text{cat} (<>, <T_1, \ldots, T_n>) = <T_1, \ldots, T_n>$$

Since <> is the null sequence, this follows directly from Eq. (3.7), which is in effect the first clause in the definition of cat.

Now consider the case $m > 0$. This means that S is nonnull, so Eq. (3.8)—the second clause in the definition of cat—applies:

$$\text{cat}\,(<S_1, \ldots, S_m>, <T_1, \ldots, T_n>) =$$
$$\text{first} <S_1, \ldots, S_m> : \text{cat}\,(\text{rest} <S_1, \ldots, S_m>, <T_1, \ldots, T_n>)$$

Since $m > 0$ the first and rest operations are defined on S, and we can apply Eqs. (2.26) and (2.27). Hence the right-hand side of the preceding equation equals

$$S_1 : \text{cat}\,(<S_2, \ldots, S_m>, <T_1, \ldots, T_n>)$$

By the inductive hypothesis, cat satisfies Eq. (3.10) for sequences of length less than m. In the preceding expression the first argument to cat has length $m - 1$ (by Eq. 2.32), so we can write the preceding expression

$$S_1 : <S_2, \ldots, S_m, T_1, \ldots, T_n>$$

By Eq. (2.28) this is

$$<S_1, S_2, \ldots, S_m, T_1, \ldots, T_n>$$

which proves the case $m > 0$. Hence Eq. (3.10) is proved and we know that cat works for all $m \geq 0$.

Since the cat function is so common, we introduce an infix notation for it:

$$S {\char`\^} T \;\Rightarrow\; \text{cat}\,(S, T)$$

Hence $<1, 2> {\char`\^} <3, 4, 5> = <1, 2, 3, 4, 5>$. The symbol '$\wedge$' is called a tie bar, and '$S {\char`\^} T$' is read "S catenate T."

Exercise 3.14: Show that

$$S {\char`\^} T = S_1 : S_2 : \cdots : S_n : T$$

As usual we have assumed that ':' is right-associative, that is, that $S{:}T{:}U = S{:}(T{:}U)$. *Hint:* Induction recapitulates recursion.

Exercise 3.15: Prove the following properties of cat:

$$<> {\char`\^} S = S {\char`\^} <> = S$$
$$S {\char`\^} (T {\char`\^} U) = (S {\char`\^} T) {\char`\^} U$$

The first says that <> is the identity of the '$\wedge$' operation; the second, that '$\wedge$' is associative. Hence a sequence type is a *monoid* with respect to this operation.

Exercise 3.16: Prove the following properties of cat:

a. length $(S \wedge T)$ = length S + length T

b. $(S \wedge T)_i = S_i$, if $1 \le i \le$ length S

c. $(S \wedge T)_{(\text{length } S) + i} = T_i$, if $1 \le i \le$ length T

Exercise 3.17: Define the function member: $\tau \times \tau^* \to \mathbb{B}$ such that member (x, S) is **true** if and only if x is an element of the sequence S. That is, member $(C, <A, B, C, D>)$ = **true**, but member $(C, <E, F, G, H>)$ = **false**. To test your definition, trace the evaluation of member $(7, <3,5,7,9>)$. (This is essentially the LISP 'member' function.)

Exercise 3.18: Prove inductively that

member $(x, <S_1, S_2, \ldots, S_n>)$ = **true** if and only if for some i, $1 \le i \le n$, $x = S_i$.

$$(3.11)$$

Exercise 3.19: Prove that

member $(x, S \wedge T)$ = member $(x, S) \vee$ member (x, T)

Exercise 3.20: Suppose S is a sequence of pairs, that is, has the form

$<<a_1, b_1>, <a_2, b_2>, \ldots, <a_n, b_n>>$

where all the a_i and b_i are of the same type. Define the function assoc (x, S) to be the first b_i for which $x = a_i$. For instance,

assoc ('CA', <<'FL', 'Tallahassee'>, <'CA', 'Sacramento'>, <'NJ', 'Trenton'>>) =
  'Sacramento'
assoc $(7, <<1, 0>, <7, 9>, <2, 6>, <7, 3>>)$ = 9

(This function is similar to Common LISP 'assoc', except that the LISP function returns the entire (dotted) pair whose first element is x.) What is the signature of assoc? What are some ways that assoc could behave if $x \ne a_i$ for all i? Discuss the tradeoffs between these behaviors.

Exercise 3.21: Suppose S and T are τ sequences of the same length. For instance,

$S = <S_1, S_2, \ldots, S_m>$
$T = <T_1, T_2, \ldots, T_m>$

Define trans2 (S, T) to be the sequence containing the pairs $<S_i, T_i>$; that is,

$$<<S_1, T_1>, \ldots, <S_m, T_m>>$$

(This is essentially the 'pairlis' function of LISP.) What is the signature of trans2? Prove that your definition is correct, that is, satisfies the following:

$$\text{trans2 } (S, T) = <<S_1, T_1>, \ldots, <S_m, T_m>>$$

Exercise 3.22: Suppose that all the elements of S are distinct. What is assoc $[S_i, \text{trans2 } (S, T)]$ equal to? Prove your answer.

Exercise 3.23: Define a function indsubst,

$$\text{indsubst: } \tau \times \mathbb{N} \times \tau^* \to \tau^*$$

so that indsubst (x, i, A) is "the indexed substitution of x for the ith element of A." That is, indsubst (x, i, A) is a sequence exactly like A except that its ith element has been replaced by x:

$$\text{indsubst } (x, i, <A_1, \ldots, A_{i-1}, A_i, A_{i+1}, \ldots, A_n>) \Rightarrow$$
$$<A_1, \ldots, A_{i-1}, x, A_{i+1}, \ldots, A_n>$$

How should indsubst (x, i, A) behave if $i > $ length A?

Exercise 3.24: Translate your definition of indsubst into LISP.

Exercise 3.25: Translate your definition of indsubst into Pascal or some other imperative language with which you are familiar.

Exercise 3.26: Prove inductively that

$$\text{elt } [\text{indsubst } (x, j, A), j] = x, \text{ for } 1 \leq j \leq \text{length } A$$
$$\text{elt } [\text{indsubst } (x, i, A), j] = A_j, \text{ for } i \neq j, \ 1 \leq i, \ j \leq \text{length } A$$

These two equations specify that indsubst does what we expect it to do—that is, change the ith element to x, but leave the rest alone.

Exercise 3.27: Prove the following properties of indsubst:

a. length $[\text{indsubst } (x, i, A)] = $ length A

b. indsubst $[y, i, \text{indsubst } (x, i, A)] = $ indsubst (y, i, A)

c. indsubst $[y, j, \text{indsubst } (x, i, A)] = $ indsubst $[x, i, \text{indsubst } (y, j, A)]$, if $i \neq j$

d. indsubst $(x, i, S \wedge T)$ = indsubst $(x, i, S) \wedge T$, if $1 \le i \le$ length S

e. indsubst $(x, i, S \wedge T)$ = $S \wedge$ indsubst $(x, i -$ length $S, T)$,
    if length $S < i \le$ length $(S \wedge T)$

For these proofs you will have to appeal to previously established properties of the elt function.

Exercise 3.28: Define the function subst1st: $\tau \times \tau \times \tau^* \to \tau^*$ so that subst1st (x, y, S) is a sequence like S, except that the *first* (leftmost) occurrence of y has been replaced by x. For example,

subst1st (23, 0, <2, 16, 0, 45, 3, 0, 12>) = <2, 16, 23, 45, 3, 0, 12>

Exercise 3.29: Define the function subst: $\tau \times \tau \times \tau^* \to \tau^*$ so that subst (x, y, S) is a sequence like S, except that *all* (top-level) occurrences of y have been replaced by x. For example,

subst ('cat', 'animal', <'the', 'animal', 'likes', 'animal', 'food'>) =
    <'the', 'cat', 'likes', 'cat', 'food'>

(This is a subset of the meaning of 'subst' in LISP.)

Exercise 3.30: State and prove some useful properties of subst.

Exercise 3.31: Define the function lsubst: $\tau^* \times \tau \times \tau^* \to \tau^*$ so that lsubst (S', y, S) is a sequence like S except the sequence S' becomes a segment replacing all occurrences of y. For example,

lsubst (<'c', 'o', 'u', 'n', 't'>, 'x', <'x', '=', 'x', '+', '1'>) =
    <'c', 'o', 'u', 'n', 't', '=', 'c', 'o', 'u', 'n', 't', '+', '1'>

(This is the function of the 'lsubst' function in Interlisp.)

3.4 Reductions

The elt operation deals with individual elements of an array (sequence). As you know from previous programming experience, however, we often want to do something to *all* elements of an array—for example, add all the elements of an array together, or apply the sine function to every element of an array. In a conventional programming language these operations are accomplished by writing a loop. How do we accomplish them in applicative programming, where there are no loops?

Consider as an example the function sum: $\mathbb{R}^* \to \mathbb{R}$, which adds all the elements of a sequence:

$$\text{sum } <S_1, S_2, \ldots, S_n> = S_1 + S_2 + \cdots + S_n \qquad (3.12)$$

This operation is called the *sum reduction* of a sequence. What is the simple case? An obvious choice is a one-element sequence, since

$$\text{sum } <S_1> = S_1 \qquad (3.13)$$

One way to reduce the $n > 1$ case to the $n-1$ case is the *method of differences*, in which we reason as follows. Since all sequences are built up from nil by prefixing, we ask ourselves how the output of the function changes when a new element is prefixed onto its input. For example, if we change T to $x:T$, how does the value of sum T change in going to sum $(x:T)$? The answer, of course, is

$$\text{sum } (x:T) = x + \text{sum } T \qquad (3.14)$$

Since any nonnull S can be written in the form $x:T$, we have

$$\text{sum } S = \text{first } S + \text{sum } (\text{rest } S) \qquad (3.15)$$

Eqs. (3.13) and (3.15) lead immediately to a recursive definition of the sum function:

$$\text{sum } S \equiv \begin{cases} \text{first } S, & \text{if length } S = 1 \\ \textbf{else } \text{first } S + \text{sum } (\text{rest } S) \end{cases} \qquad (3.16)$$

Can this definition be improved? Our original informal description of sum (Eq. 3.12) did not specify whether or not sum was expected to operate correctly on the null sequence. What should be the value of sum $<>$? Notice that sum currently satisfies Eq. (3.14) for all *nonnull* sequences T. If we generalize this to apply to *all* sequences, what is implied about the sum of the null sequence? Substituting nil for T in Eq. (3.14) yields

$$\text{sum } (x:\text{nil}) = x + \text{sum } <>$$

We know by Eq. (3.13), however, that sum $<x> = x$, so $x = x + \text{sum } <>$ and therefore sum $<> = 0$. This seems intuitively plausible: The sum of the elements in the empty sequence is 0. The resulting revised definition of sum is

$$\text{sum } S = \begin{cases} 0, & \text{if null } S \\ \textbf{else } \text{first } S + \text{sum } (\text{rest } S) \end{cases} \qquad (3.17)$$

Note that the definition of sum is a little simpler and that the sum function is more general—that is, works correctly on a wider range of arguments. This version of the sum function may seem slightly less efficient since it takes an additional iteration to sum a nonnull sequence, but it is actually much more efficient since it does not call the length function on each iteration. Also notice that part of the motivation for our generalization was that it would widen the applicability of the algebraic laws characterizing sum—in this case,

$$\text{sum } (x : S) = x + \text{sum } S, \text{ for all } x \in \mathbb{R}, S \in \mathbb{R}^* \qquad (3.18)$$

With our original definition of sum, we would have had to add the condition that S is nonnull. Such "algebra-motivated" generalization, quite common in applicative programming, often leads to more regular and more easily interfaced functions.[7]

Exercise 3.32: Analyze the performance of the sum function in Eq. (3.16). How can the effect of the length test be achieved more efficiently?

Exercise 3.33: Translate sum into LISP, Pascal, or another programming language.

Exercise 3.34: Define the function prod: $\mathbb{R}^* \to \mathbb{R}$, which computes the *product reduction* of a sequence, that is, multiplies all the elements of a sequence. What should be the value of prod <>? Justify your answer. Prove that your definition works correctly, i.e., satisfies

$$\text{prod } S = S_1 \times S_2 \times \cdots \times S_n$$

(The '*' function in Common LISP and the 'times' function in Interlisp are similar to this function.)

Exercise 3.35: Prove from Eq. (3.17) the following properties of sum:

a. sum (rest S) = sum $S - S_1$

b. sum $(x{:}S)$ = x + sum S

c. sum $(S {^\wedge} T)$ = sum S + sum T

d. sum [indsubst (x, i, A)] = sum $A - A_i + x$

Prove analogous properties for prod. Are there any exceptions or limitations on these identities?

---

7. The '+' function in Common LISP and the 'plus' function in Interlisp are similar to our sum function. Thus (+ 3 1 8 –5) ⇒ 7.

Exercise 3.36: Define append: $(\tau^*)^* \to \tau^*$ to be the cat reduction of a sequence of sequences, that is,

append $<S_1, S_2, \ldots, S_n> = S_1 {\wedge} S_2 {\wedge} \cdots {\wedge} S_n$

What should be the value of append $<>$? Prove that your definition works correctly. What identities does append satisfy? (The 'append' function in LISP works in this way.)

Exercise 3.37: Do the same for the *and reduction*:

and $S = S_1 \wedge S_2 \wedge \cdots \wedge S_n$

What is the signature of and? (The 'and' function in LISP works in this way.)

Exercise 3.38: Specify, define, and prove the correctness of the *or reduction*. (This is the meaning of 'or' in LISP.)

Exercise 3.39: Using the same pattern, define dif to be the *difference reduction* of a sequence. Show why this leads to the following result:

dif $<S_1, S_2, S_3, \ldots, S_n> = S_1 - S_2 + S_3 - \cdots \pm S_n$

That is, dif computes *alternating* differences.

Exercise 3.40: Define min to return the minimum of a sequence of numbers. Can min be considered some kind of reduction? Explain. What should be the value of min $<>$? Justify. (LISP has 'min' and 'max' functions with this meaning.)

Exercise 3.41: Define sublis: $(\tau^*)^* \times \tau^* \to \tau^*$ so that sublis (P, S) is the result of performing on S the substitution pairs in the sequence P. For example, if $S = <\text{'the'}, \text{'X'}, \text{'in'}, \text{'the'}, \text{'Y'}>$, then

sublis $(<<\text{'X'}, \text{'mouse'}>, <\text{'Y'}, \text{'house'}>>, S) =$
  $<\text{'the'}, \text{'mouse'}, \text{'in'}, \text{'the'}, \text{'house'}>$
sublis $(<<\text{'X'}, \text{'cat'}>, <\text{'Y'}, \text{'hat'}>>, S) = <\text{'the'}, \text{'cat'}, \text{'in'}, \text{'the'}, \text{'hat'}>$

(This is a subset of the 'sublis' function of LISP.) *Hint:* sublis is closely related to a subst reduction of P (Ex. 3.29). To see this, consider the function

$f(P, S) \equiv$ subst (second P, first P, S)

What is the effect of an f-reduction? Once you see this you can eliminate the definition of f from the definition of sublis.

Exercise 3.42: Define subpair: $\tau^* \times \tau^* \times \tau^* \to \tau^*$ so that, if X and Y are sequences of values, then subpair (X, Y, S) is a sequence like S except that values in X have been replaced by corresponding values in Y. For example,

subpair (<'a', 'b', 'c'>, <'12', '−2', '5'>, <'2', 'a', 'x', '+', 'b', '+', 'c', '−', 'a'>) =
<'2', '12', 'x', '+', '−2', '+', '5', '−', '12'>

(This is a subset of the 'subpair' function of Interlisp.)

3.5 Mappings

We have seen how to use a two-argument function (e.g., '+', '×') to reduce a sequence to a single value. Another common operation is to apply a one-argument function to every element of a sequence. For example, if S is a sequence of numbers representing angles, we might wish to compute the sines of the corresponding angles. This operation is called *mapping* the sine function across the sequence S, so we will call our function map_sin:

$$\text{map\_sin} <S_1, S_2, \ldots, S_n> = <\sin S_1, \sin S_2, \ldots, \sin S_n> \qquad (3.19)$$

Its signature is map_sin: $\mathbb{R}^* \to \mathbb{R}^*$.

What is the simple case? Based on our previous experience, it is natural to try the null sequence. The result of applying sine to every element in the null sequence is—the null sequence:

$$\text{map\_sin} <> = <> \qquad (3.20)$$

To recursively reduce the general case toward the null case, we apply the Method of Differences, changing T to $\theta{:}T$ and observing the change in map_sin:

$$\text{map\_sin } T = <\sin T_1, \ldots, \sin T_n>$$
$$\text{map\_sin } (\theta : T) = <\sin \theta, \sin T_1, \ldots, \sin T_n>$$

We get the second right-hand side from the first by prefixing sin θ. Therefore

$$\text{map\_sin } (\theta : T) = \sin \theta : \text{map\_sin } T \qquad (3.21)$$

Or, in a form more useful for our purposes,

$$\text{map\_sin } S = \sin (\text{first } S) : \text{map\_sin } (\text{rest } S), \text{ for nonnull } S$$

This leads directly to the recursive definition

$$\text{map\_sin } S \equiv \begin{cases} <>, \text{ if null } S \\ \textbf{else } \sin (\text{first } S) : \text{map\_sin (rest } S) \end{cases} \tag{3.22}$$

Exercise 3.43: Translate map_sin into LISP, Pascal, or another programming language.

Exercise 3.44: Prove that the definition of map_sin (Eq. 3.22) satisfies Eqs. (3.20) and (3.21).

Exercise 3.45: Prove that map_sin satisfies Eq. (3.19).

Exercise 3.46: Prove the following algebraic law:

map_sin $(S \wedge T)$ = map_sin S $\wedge$ map_sin T

(This, with map_sin $<>$ = $<>$, says that map_sin preserves the identity and operation of the monoid $\mathbb{R}^*$. Therefore map_sin is a *monoid homomorphism* on $\mathbb{R}^*$.)

Exercise 3.47: Prove the following identities:

a. first (map_sin S) = sin (first S)

b. rest (map_sin S) = map_sin (rest S)

c. length (map_sin S) = length S

d. (map_sin $S)_i$ = sin S_i

e. indsubst (sin x, i, map_sin A) = map_sin [indsubst (x, i, A)]

Exercise 3.48: Suppose that square $x \equiv x^2$. Define the function map_square: $\mathbb{R}^* \to \mathbb{R}^*$, which applies square to every element of its argument.

Exercise 3.49: Define a function that takes the square root of every element of a sequence. Consider equations analogous to those in Exercise 3.47. In each equation for this new operation, the expression on the right is defined for some arguments for which the expression on the left is undefined. Explain.

Exercise 3.50: Define a function map_prod: $(\mathbb{R}^*)^* \to \mathbb{R}^*$ to map the product reduction across a sequence of sequences. For example,

map_prod $<<2, 3>, <1, 4, 6>, <3>, <>, <5, 5>>$ = $<2 \times 3, 1 \times 4 \times 6, 3, 1, 5 \times 5>$
$$= <6, 24, 3, 1, 25>$$

Show that your definition is correct, that is, that

$$\text{map\_prod } S = <\text{prod } S_1, \text{prod } S_2, \ldots, \text{prod } S_n>$$

Exercise 3.51: The vector_prod function computes the element-wise product of two vectors (sequences). For example,

$$\text{vector\_prod } (<2, 4, 1>, <3, 2, 0>) = <2 \times 3, 4 \times 2, 1 \times 0> = <6, 8, 0>$$

Its signature is vector_prod: $\mathbb{R}^* \times \mathbb{R}^* \to \mathbb{R}^*$. Show that the following is a correct definition of vector_prod:

$$\text{vector\_prod } (S, T) \equiv \text{map\_prod } [\text{trans2 } (S, T)]$$

where trans2 is as defined in Exercise 3.21. You can use previously proved properties of map_prod and trans2. What purpose does the application of trans2 serve?

Exercise 3.52: Translate the preceding definition of vector_prod into LISP, Pascal, or another language. Note that to do this you must define a prod function that expects a sequence of two numbers, and a trans2 function that expects two sequences. You must also define map_prod.

Exercise 3.53: Show that sum [vector_prod (U, V)] computes the inner product of the vectors (sequences) U and V.

Exercise 3.54: Define a difference mapping. For example,

$$\text{map\_dif } <<2, 3>, <1, 4, 6>, <3>, <>, <5, 5>> = <2-3, 1-4+6, 3, 0, 5-5>$$
$$= <-1, 3, 3, 0, 0>$$

Show that your definition is correct:

$$\text{map\_dif } S = <\text{dif } S_1, \text{dif } S_2, \ldots, \text{dif } S_n>$$

What is the signature of map_dif?

Exercise 3.55: Define the function vector_dif, which computes the element-wise difference of two vectors (sequences).

Exercise 3.56: Show that the following expression computes the sum of the squares of the differences between corresponding elements of the two vectors U and V:

$$\text{sum } \{\text{map\_square } [\text{vector\_dif } (U, V)]\}$$

This is an important component of the least-squares algorithm.

3.6 Sequence Generation

We have seen how to reduce a sequence to a single value and how to map a sequence into another of the same size. This suggests that we should consider ways to expand a single value into a sequence. Since we are going from a single value to a multitude of values, this multitude must be generated in some regular fashion from the given value. For example, suppose we wish to generate a sequence of the sines of the angles from $0°$ to $89°$. If we had the sequence <0, 1, 2, . . . , 89>, then we could get the desired result by applying map_sin:

$$\text{map\_sin } <0, 1, 2, \ldots, 89> = <\sin 0, \sin 1, \sin 2, \ldots, \sin 89>$$

It would be very tedious (and error-prone) to write out the sequence <0, 1, 2, . . . , 89> explicitly, and the sequence is so regular that it should to be easy to generate. Therefore we define a function interval: $\mathbb{Z} \times \mathbb{Z} \to \mathbb{Z}^*$ such that

$$\text{interval } (m, n) = <m, m + 1, m + 2, \ldots, n - 1> \tag{3.23}$$

Then our sequence of sines will be map_sin [interval (0, 90)].
   It might seem more natural to have specified

$$\text{interval } (m, n) = <m, m + 1, m + 2, \ldots, n> \tag{3.24}$$

As will be seen in Exercise 3.61, however, the version in Eq. (3.23) has nicer algebraic properties.
   How can we define interval? First observe the identity

$$\text{interval } (m, n) = m : \text{interval } (m + 1, n), \text{ for } m < n$$

This essentially gives us the recursive step. An obvious choice for the base of the recursion is interval $(m, m + 1) = <m>$, but our definition is more regular and more general if we take interval $(m, m) = <>$. Then interval will satisfy a number of useful algebraic properties; for example, for all integers l, m, n (whether positive or negative),

$$\text{interval } (l, m) \frown \text{interval } (m, n) = \text{interval } (l, n), \text{ for } l \le m \le n$$
$$\text{interval } (m, n) = m : \text{interval } (m+1, n), \text{ for } m < n$$

The definition of interval follows easily:

$$\text{interval } (m, n) \equiv \begin{cases} <>, \text{ if } m \ge n \\ \textbf{else } m : \text{interval } (m + 1, n) \end{cases} \tag{3.25}$$

Other sequence-generation operators are discussed in Chapter 6.

Exercise 3.57: Show that the definition of Eq. (3.25) satisfies the following algebraic properties (for l, m, n integers):

a. length [interval (m, n)] $= n - m$, for $m \leq n$

b. first [interval (m, n)] $= m$, for $m < n$

c. rest [interval (m, n)] $=$ interval $(m + 1, n)$, for $m < n$

d. m : interval $(m + 1, n)$ $=$ interval (m, n), for $m < n$

e. [interval (m, n)]$_i$ $= m + i - 1$, for $1 \leq i \leq n - m$

f. interval (l, m) ⌢ interval (m, n) $=$ interval (l, n), for $l \leq m \leq n$

g. null [interval (m, n)] $= m \geq n$

Exercise 3.58: Translate the recursive definition (Eq. 3.25) of interval into LISP, Pascal, or another programming language.

Exercise 3.59: Show that, if $m \neq n$ then

$$\text{interval } (m, n) \frown \text{interval } (n, m) = \text{interval } (n, m) \frown \text{interval } (m, n)$$

Suggest a use for the formula interval (m, n) ⌢ interval (n, m).

Exercise 3.60: Prove that the following are true for all positive integers m, n:

a. sum [interval $(1, n)$] $= n(n - 1)/2$

b. sum {map_square [interval $(1, n)$]} $= n(n - 1)(2n - 1)/6$

c. prod [interval $(1, n)$] $= (n - 1)!$

d. prod [interval (m, n)] $= (n - 1)! \,/\, (m - 1)!$

Exercise 3.61: Consider the interval function specified in Eq. (3.24); define this function recursively. Compare the identities satisfied by this function with those proved in Exercise 3.57. Which version do you prefer? Defend your choice.

Exercise 3.62: There is an alternate interpretation of interval (m, n) where $m > n$, that is,

$$\text{interval } (m, n) = <m - 1, m - 2, m - 3, \ldots, n>, \text{ if } m > n$$

Define interval to work in this fashion, and discuss the relative merits of the two definitions. Which definition do you prefer?

Exercise 3.63: Define the function subseq: $\tau^* \times \mathbb{N} \times \mathbb{N} \to \tau^*$ so that subseq (S, m, n) is a subsequence formed from the mth through the nth elements of S. What should be the result of this function if $m > n$? Can you think of useful interpretations for the cases when $n > $ length S or $m < 0$? (This is similar to the 'subseq' function of Common LISP, except that the latter indexes from 0.)

Exercise 3.64: Consider the function collation: $\mathbb{R}^* \times \mathbb{R}^* \to \mathbb{R}^*$, which merges two sorted sequences into a sorted sequence; for instance,

collation (<2, 5, 6, 8, 12>, <3, 3, 6, 7, 9, 10>) = <2, 3, 3, 5, 6, 6, 7, 8, 9, 10, 12>

Show that the following definition accomplishes this:

$$\text{collation } (S, T) \equiv \begin{cases} T, & \text{if null } S & (3.26) \\ S, & \text{if null } T \\ S_1 : \text{collation (rest } S, T), & \text{if } S_1 \leq T_1 \\ T_1 : \text{collation } (S, \text{rest } T), & \text{if } S_1 > T_1 \end{cases}$$

What algebraic properties do you think collation satisfies? For example, is it associative, commutative, or distributive over other operations? Prove at least three identities satisfied by collation.

Exercise 3.65: The definition of collation in Eq. (3.26) preserves duplicate elements in its input sequences. Define a different version of collation that eliminates duplicates (provided there are no duplicates in either of its input sequences). For example,

collation (<2, 5, 6, 8, 12>, <3, 6, 7, 9, 10>) = <2, 3, 5, 6, 7, 8, 9, 10, 12>

Explore the properties of this version of collation.

Exercise 3.66: Translate the definition of collation in Eq. (3.26) into LISP, Pascal, or another programming language.

Exercise 3.67: Define a function that performs a *collation reduction* on a sequence of sequences. What is its signature?

Exercise 3.68: Define a function that eliminates duplicates from a sorted sequence. Does it matter whether the sequence is sorted in ascending or descending order?

The following exercises define and investigate some of the sequence processing operations proposed by Backus (1978) in his Turing Award paper.

Exercise 3.69: Define the *distribute left* function:

$$\text{distl } (x, <S_1, S_2, \ldots, S_n>) = <<x, S_1>, <x, S_2>, \ldots, <x, S_n>> \qquad (3.27)$$

What is its signature? Define the analogous *distribute right* function. Show that your definitions are correct (i.e., satisfy Eq. (3.27) and the analogous equation for right distribution).

Exercise 3.70: The first, rest, and prefix functions operate on the front of sequences. In terms of first, rest, and prefix, define analogous functions, last, butlast, and postfix, that operate on the ends of sequences. For example,

$$\text{last } <S_1, \ldots, S_{n-1}, S_n> = S_n$$
$$\text{butlast } <S_1, \ldots, S_{n-1}, S_n> = <S_1, \ldots, S_{n-1}>$$
$$\text{postfix } (<S_1, \ldots, S_n>, x) = <S_1, \ldots, S_n, x>$$

State the signatures. Derive a number of identities relating the functions to each other and to the other functions we have defined. (Backus calls these functions '1r', 'tlr', and 'apndr'. Common LISP has 'last' and 'butlast', except that its 'last' returns the last dotted pair rather then the last element.)

Exercise 3.71: Define the *rotate left* and *rotate right* functions so that

$$\text{rotl } <S_1, S_2, \ldots, S_n> = <S_2, \ldots, S_n, S_1>$$
$$\text{rotr } <S_1, \ldots, S_{n-1}, S_n> = <S_n, S_1, \ldots, S_{n-1}>$$

These can be defined nonrecursively by making use of already defined functions. Prove several identities involving these functions.

Exercise 3.72: Define the *transpose* operation:

$$\text{trans } <<S_{1,1}, S_{1,2}, \ldots, S_{1,n}>, \ldots, <S_{m,1}, S_{m,2}, \ldots, S_{m,n}>>$$
$$= <<S_{1,1}, \ldots, S_{m,1}>, <S_{1,2}, \ldots, S_{m,2}>, \ldots, <S_{1,n}, \ldots, S_{m,n}>>$$

Hint: Note that trans2 (Exercise 3.21) is like a special case of trans. What is the signature of trans?

Exercise 3.73: The *forward difference* of a sequence S is the sequence

$$\Delta S = <S_2 - S_1, S_3 - S_2, \ldots, S_n - S_{n-1}>$$

The forward differences are useful in many numerical problems as an approximation of the derivative. Show that the following expression computes the forward differences of the numbers in the sequence S:

$$\Delta S \equiv \mathsf{map\_dif}\,(\mathsf{trans}\,<\mathsf{rest}\,S,\,\mathsf{butlast}\,S>)$$

The function butlast was defined in Exercise 3.70.

3.7 Sequence Equality

In this section we define a function equal: $\tau^* \times \tau^* \to \mathbb{B}$ for testing the equality of sequences. For example

> equal (<2, 4, 17>, <9, 7, –4>) = **false**
> equal (<2, 4, 17>, <2, 4, 17>) = **true**
> equal (<2, 4, 17>, <2, 4, 17, 7>) = **false**

Until now we have written '$S = T$', where S and T are sequence-valued expressions. The symbol '=', however, is not the sequence-equality operation we need. Rather, '=' is a *metasymbol* used for talking *about* formulas in the functional programming language. The assertion '$S = T$' means that the formulas S and T are always interchangeable: One can always be replaced by the other (provided, as usual, that they're both defined). For instance, the equation

> cat $(x : S, T) = x : \mathsf{cat}\,(S, T)$

means that a (well-formed) formula of the form 'cat $(x : S, T)$' can always be replaced by the corresponding formula of the form '$x : \mathsf{cat}\,(S, T)$', and vice versa. It is a statement *about* the two formulas (programs) 'cat $(x : S, T)$' and '$x : \mathsf{cat}\,(S, T)$'.

On the other hand, '=' is not an *object symbol*—that is, not an operator in the abstract data type of sequences. We can see this by looking in the archetype (Fig. 2.5): The only operators listed in the Syntax part are nil, null, first, rest, and prefix; no '=' operation is listed. Thus a formula such as 'cat $(x : S, T) = x : \mathsf{cat}\,(S, T)$' is not well-formed (not a program) since it contains the undefined symbol '='.

An equality operation on sequences is certainly useful, so we should have it.[8] We didn't include it in the sequence archetype because this allowed us to bring up the important distinction between metasymbols and object symbols just discussed. Also, equal is very easy to define in terms of the primitive operations in Fig. 2.5. Finally, not including an equality operation in the archetype allows us to further investigate *referential transparency,* in particular the relation between equality on the object level and interchangeability on the metalevel. First, let's define equal.

---

8. In fact, we adopt the policy of specifying an equality operation on every data type for which it makes sense and is computable.

Intuitively, two sequences are equal if they have the same number of elements and corresponding elements are equal. That is,

$$\text{equal } (<S_1, S_2, \ldots, S_m>, <T_1, T_2, \ldots, T_n>) = \textbf{true}$$

if and only if $m = n$ and for each i, $S_i = T_i$. The obvious base for the recursion is $m = n = 0$:

$$\text{equal } (<>, <>) = \textbf{true}$$

If either m or n is zero and the other is nonzero, then equal returns **false**. The only remaining case is that both m and n are nonzero; that is, both S and T are nonnull. Here it is easy to see that we must compare the first elements of both S and T (using the '=' operation on the base type of the sequence type), and then compare the rest of the two sequences by a recursive application of equal.[9] This is summarized in the following equation:

$$\text{equal } (S, T) = (\text{first } S = \text{first } T) \wedge \text{equal } (\text{rest } S, \text{rest } T), \text{ if } S \text{ and } T \text{ nonnull}$$

We check to make sure we've covered all the cases:

null S	null T	equal (S, T)
true	true	true
true	false	false
false	true	false
false	false	first $S = $ first $T \wedge$ equal (rest S, rest T)

To convert this into a conditional definition, observe that, in the first three rows of the table, either S or T is null, and that in these cases we return **true** just when they are *both* null. The direct definition then follows:

$$\text{equal } (S, T) \equiv \begin{cases} \text{null } S \wedge \text{null } T, \text{ if null } S \vee \text{null } T \\ \textbf{else } \text{first } S = \text{first } T \wedge \text{equal } (\text{rest } S, \text{rest } T) \end{cases} \quad (3.28)$$

Can we prove that definition (3.28) is correct? We want equal to return **true** when the sequences are equal, and **false** when they're not. Thus the archetype for equal is

---

9. There are some hidden difficulties if the elements of the sequences are themselves sequences. The definition of equal is correct despite these problems (see p. 94).

equal $(S, T) =$ **true**, if $S = T$ $\hspace{4cm}$ (3.29)

equal $(S, T) =$ **false**, if $S \neq T$

It is routine to prove that the definition of equal (Eq. 3.28) satisfies its archetype (Eq. 3.29); you are taken through the steps in Exercises 3.75–3.81.

Exercise 3.74: With most implementations of the '$\wedge$' operator, the preceding definition will compare all of the elements of S and T, even if their first elements are unequal. This is because '$\wedge$' usually evaluates both its arguments before it decides whether to return **true** or **false**. Define equal in such a way that it stops comparing as soon as it finds unequal elements, regardless of the way '$\wedge$' works.

In the following exercises you prove that Eq. (3.28) satisfies Eqs. (3.29).

Exercise 3.75: Suppose that length $S = 0$; show that equal $(S, S) =$ **true**. This is the base of the induction.

Exercise 3.76: Assume that equal $(U, U) =$ **true** for all U such that $0 \leq$ length $U <$ length S. Show that equal $(S, S) =$ **true**. This is the inductive step.

Exercise 3.77: Assemble the preceding two exercises into a proof that $S = T$ implies that equal $(S, T) =$ **true**. *Hint:* Recall that $S = T$ means that S and T are interchangeable.

Exercise 3.78: Suppose that length $S = 0$; prove that equal $(S, T) =$ **true** implies that $S = T$. *Hint:* Recall that in Exercise 2.18 you showed that every sequence has a unique representation in one of the forms nil and $a : U$.

Exercise 3.79: Suppose that for all U such that $0 \leq$ length $U <$ length S we know that equal $(U, V) =$ **true** implies $U = V$. Prove that if length $S > 0$ then equal $(S, T) =$ **true** implies $S = T$. *Hint:* First show that T is nonnull and then apply the hypothesis.

Exercise 3.80: Assemble the preceding two exercises into an inductive proof that equal $(S, T) =$ **true** implies $S = T$.

Exercise 3.81: Combine the preceding exercise with Exercise 3.77 to show that the definition of equal (Eq. 3.28) satisfies its archetype (Eq. 3.29).

Having proved that equal $(S, T) =$ **true** just when $S = T$, there is no harm in writing '$S = T$' for 'equal (S, T)'. That is, we introduce the syntactic sugar:

$$S = T \;\Rightarrow\; \text{equal } (S, T)$$
$$S \neq T \;\Rightarrow\; \neg (S = T)$$

Henceforth we can write '$S = T$' for sequences just as we do for the atomic data types (integers, Booleans, etc.).

We adopt the general policy that whenever an abstract data type has an '$=$' operator, that operator will return **true** just when its arguments are equal (i.e., interchangeable), and **false** when they're not equal. That is, we will always have the property

$$(X = Y) \;=\; \textbf{true}, \; \text{if } X = Y \tag{3.30}$$
$$(X = Y) \;=\; \textbf{false}, \; \text{if } X \neq Y$$

where the leftmost '$=$' signs are object symbols and the other occurrences are metasymbols. In effect this policy guarantees that the object and meta uses of '$=$' always correspond. Although we have introduced a *systematic ambiguity* between the object and metalevels, Eqs. (3.30) ensure that the ambiguity is benign.

3.8 Performance Analysis and Optimization

To illustrate the performance analysis and optimization of applicative programs, we consider the reverse function, which reverses a sequence. That is,

$$\text{reverse } <S_1, S_2, \ldots, S_n> \;=\; <S_n, \ldots, S_2, S_1>$$

To define this we note that the base of the recursion is obviously the null sequence since reverse $<> = <>$. Applying the Method of Differences, we next ask, How can we reverse $x:S$? One way is to use the postfix function (defined in Exercise 3.70) to append x to the right end of reverse S. That is, the recursive step is based on the identity

$$\text{reverse } [\text{prefix } (x, S)] \;=\; \text{postfix (reverse } S, x)$$

which reflects the symmetry between prefix and postfix. The resulting definition is

$$\text{reverse } S \;\equiv\; \begin{cases} <>, \; \text{if null } S \\ \textbf{else } \text{postfix [reverse (rest } S), \text{first } S] \end{cases} \tag{3.31}$$

Exercise 3.82: Translate this definition of reverse into LISP. Note that you must also define postfix.

Exercise 3.83: Translate this definition of reverse into Pascal or another imperative language.

Exercise 3.84: Prove the following identities:

a. length (reverse S) = length S

b. reverse [postfix (S, x)] = x : reverse S

c. reverse (reverse S) = S

d. first (reverse S) = last S

e. rest (reverse S) = reverse (butlast S)

f. (reverse S)$_i$ = $S_{\text{length}(S)-i+1}$

f. reverse [prefix (x, S)] = postfix (reverse S, x)

h. reverse $(S\char94 T)$ = reverse T $\char94$ reverse S

i. sum (reverse S) = sum S

j. map_sin (reverse S) = reverse (map_sin S)

You must appeal to previously proved properties of postfix.

Let's estimate the performance of this reverse definition—that is, determine how many steps it takes to reverse an n-element sequence. Clearly the reverse function invokes itself n times, and during each of those invocations calls postfix, rest, and first. The first and rest operations are primitives, whose archetype (Fig. 2.5) specifies that they take a constant amount of time. As you discovered in defining postfix, however, the postfix operation must skip to the end of its first argument to append its second argument. Thus the postfix operation itself requires time proportional to the length of its first argument. Since postfix is called during each invocation of reverse, the total time for reverse is the product of a constant and

$$(n-1) + (n-2) + (n-3) + \cdots + 2 + 1 + 0 = \sum_{i=0}^{n-1} i = \frac{n(n-1)}{2} = O(n^2)$$

Thus reverse takes time approximately proportional to the square of the length of its argument sequence. Can we find a faster algorithm? Is it even possible to reverse a sequence in linear time (i.e., time proportional to the length of the sequence)? Think about how you invert a stack of books, moving one book at a time. (The stack of books is like a sequence because you can operate only on the top/front.) You take the book on the top and place it beside the stack. Then you take the next book from the old stack and put it on top of the new stack. By the time the old stack is empty, the new stack is the reverse (i.e., the inversion) of the old stack. Observe that we have operated only on the tops of the stacks; it seems plausible that this approach can be implemented using our primitive functions, which operate only on the front of sequences (and which take constant time).

Since we have no variables in our applicative language, we must use formal parameters to represent the two stacks. Let's define a function revaux (reverse auxiliary) such that revaux (S, T) reverses the sequence S onto the front of the sequence T. That is, if S represents the old stack and T the new, then revaux completes the inversion process. The process begins with the old stack containing the sequence to be reversed and the new stack containing nothing:

$$\text{reverse } S \equiv \text{revaux } (S, <>) \tag{3.32}$$

One recursive step of revaux must move an element from the front (top) of S to the front (top) of T:

$$\text{revaux } (S, T) = \text{revaux } (\text{rest } S, \text{first } S : T)$$

What terminates the process? Clearly, the emptiness of the old stack, in which case the new stack is the reversed sequence:

$$\text{revaux } (<>, T) = T$$

Thus the complete definition of revaux is

$$\text{revaux } (S, T) \equiv \begin{cases} T, & \text{if null } S \\ \textbf{else } \text{revaux } (\text{rest } S, \text{first } S : T) \end{cases} \tag{3.33}$$

This definition illustrates a common trick of applicative programming: using formal parameters to simulate variables. If this approach is carried too far, however, the resulting programs are even less readable than the corresponding imperative programs—which defeats the purpose of applicative programming.

Exercise 3.85: Translate the improved version of reverse (Eqs. 3.32 and 3.33) into LISP.

Exercise 3.86: Translate the improved version of reverse into Pascal.

Exercise 3.87: Prove for the improved definition of reverse the properties in Exercise 3.84. Compare the complexities of the proofs for the original (Eq. 3.31) and improved versions.

Now that we have a better algorithm for reverse, we may wish to perform a more detailed performance analysis.[10] Let's write out the program without syntactic sugar, so that all the functions are visible. Equation (3.32) becomes

$$\text{reverse } S = \text{revaux } (S, \text{nil}) \tag{3.34}$$

and Eq. (3.33) becomes

$$\text{revaux } (S, T) \equiv \text{if } \{\text{null } S, T, \text{revaux } [\text{rest } S, \text{prefix (first } S, T)]\} \tag{3.35}$$

It is also helpful to use the notation $\mathbf{T}[\![E]\!]$ to represent the time it takes to evaluate the expression E.[11] Our goal is to derive a formula for T_n, the time required by this program to reverse an n element sequence. Therefore we begin by writing

$$T_n \equiv \mathbf{T}[\![\text{reverse } S]\!] \tag{3.36}$$

where length $S = n$. We derive the formula for T_n by simulating (algebraically!) the execution of the formula 'reverse S'. For example, Eq. (3.34) tells us that reverse S leads to the application revaux $(S, <>)$, leading to another equation:

$$\mathbf{T}[\![\text{reverse } S]\!] = C_{\text{call}} + \mathbf{T}[\![\text{revaux } (S, <>)]\!] \tag{3.37}$$

where C_{call} is the time (assumed constant) to call and return from a function (reverse in this case). Our informal analysis tells us that the time required to execute revaux $(S, <>)$ depends on the length of S. Therefore we define R_n to be this time:

$$R_n = \mathbf{T}[\![\text{revaux } (S, T)]\!] \tag{3.38}$$

---

10. There was not much point in doing this before; it was sufficient to know that the algorithm was quadratic. Finding a better algorithm is generally more profitable than tuning a poorer one.
11. This presumes some knowledge of the implementation of the applicative language. To illustrate the technique we here assume a conventional, sequential implementation on a conventional (so-called von Neumann) computer. (We explain later the reason for the unusual brackets, $[\![\ ]\!]$.)

where length $S = n$. (We know that the length of T does not affect the time. Why?) Combining Eqs. (3.36), (3.37), and (3.38) tells us that $T_n = R_n + C_{call}$, so our goal must be to find a formula for R_n.

Equation (3.35) tells us that the action taken by revaux depends on whether S is null. Therefore we will have two cases, R_0 and R_n, for $n > 0$. To compute R_0 we must ask, What actions must revaux perform in this case? First, it must do the null test, which we are assuming returns **true**. Next it must do the conditional test. Finally, it must execute the consequent (true branch) of the conditional, which simply returns T. We can write this as follows:

$$R_0 = \mathbf{T}[\![\text{revaux } (<>, T)]\!] \qquad\qquad\qquad (3.39)$$
$$= C_{call} + \mathbf{T}[\![\text{null } S]\!] + \mathbf{T}[\![\text{if } (, ,)]\!] + \mathbf{T}[\![T]\!]$$

The sequence archetype (in Appendix B) tells us that the time to execute a null test is constant; let C_{null} be this time. Similarly, the Boolean archetype (in Appendix B) tells us that a conditional takes constant time (call it C_{if}), and we can assume that fetching the value of a variable takes no time. Substituting into Eq. (3.39) gives the following formula for $\mathbf{T}[\![\text{revaux } (<>, T)]\!]$:

$$R_0 = C_{call} + C_{null} + C_{if} \equiv C_1 \qquad\qquad\qquad (3.40)$$

For convenience, the three constants are combined into one, C_1.

Next we consider R_n for $n > 0$. Looking at Eq. (3.35), we see that we still must do the null test and the conditional, which take time C_{null} and C_{if}. We can also see that we must do a first, a rest, and a prefix, all of which take constant time, according to their archetype. Finally we return the result of invoking revaux with rest S, a sequence with $n-1$ elements; this invocation takes time R_{n-1}. Adding these together yields

$$R_n = C_{call} + \mathbf{T}[\![\text{if } \{\text{null } S, T, \text{revaux } [\text{rest } S, \text{prefix } (\text{first } S, T)]\}]\!],$$
$$\text{where null } S = \mathbf{false}$$
$$= C_{call} + C_{null} + C_{if} + C_{rest} + C_{first} + C_{prefix} + R_{n-1}, \text{ for } n > 0$$

Hence,

$$R_n = C_2 + R_{n-1} \qquad\qquad\qquad (3.41)$$

where again all the constants are lumped into one. Equation (3.41) is a *recurrence relation* that, together with the *boundary condition* (Eq. 3.40), defines R_n for all $n \geq 0$. The recurrence is easily solved (in this case) to yield

$$T_n = nC_2 + C_1 + C_{\text{call}} \qquad (3.42)$$
$$\textbf{where} \quad C_1 \equiv C_{\text{call}} + C_{\text{null}} + C_{\text{if}}$$
$$\textbf{and} \quad C_2 \equiv C_{\text{call}} + C_{\text{null}} + C_{\text{if}} + C_{\text{rest}} + C_{\text{first}} + C_{\text{prefix}}$$

Notice the similarity of the form of the recurrence equations (3.40 and 3.41) and the definition of the function (3.31). Earlier we saw that the form of definition shows us the form of the inductive proof; here we see it also shows the form of the performance equation.

We can now calculate T_n, the time to reverse an n-element sequence— provided we know the times for the primitive operations (C_{null}, C_{if}, etc.). We could calculate these times *analytically* from their implementations, much as we just did for reverse. For the primitive operations, however, this approach may not be a good idea; there are too many variables (instruction caching, memory-bank conflicts, etc.). A better approach is to determine the times *empirically*, measuring the time the functions take in a variety of contexts.[12]

Given timings for the primitive operations, whatever their source, we can then use Eq. (3.42) to estimate the execution time of applications of reverse. Remember, however, that this is still an estimate; we made many approximations in deriving Eq. (3.42). For example, we ignored variations in the function-invocation overhead for revaux, as well as the fact that taking the false branch of a conditional may require different time from taking the true branch. We also ignored the fact that prefix operations are not really constant-time, since they may take much longer if they require a preceding garbage-collection step.

Are we justified in ignoring these factors? Are our assumptions reasonable? It is difficult to say *a priori*. Instead, as good engineers, we should back up our analytical performance evaluation with empirical performance measurement, thus discovering whether our assumptions are reasonable. After many analytical/empirical comparisons, we will build up a good intuition about what can be safely ignored and what cannot.

Before leaving the topic of performance evaluation, we must make several important observations. First, the process by which we derive the recurrence relation (Eq. 3.41) and its boundary condition (Eq. 3.40) is very mechanical, and in fact can be largely automated. The basic rule is

$$\mathbf{T}[\![f(E_1, \ldots, E_n)]\!] = \mathbf{T}[\![E_1]\!] + \cdots + \mathbf{T}[\![E_n]\!] + \mathbf{T}[\![f(\, , \ldots, \,)]\!] \qquad (3.43)$$

which must be applied recursively to a formula until its time is expressed in terms of the times for primitive operations.[13] This process is a kind of

---

12. Some knowledge of the implementation will help in designing an accurate measurement procedure.
13. Of course, some functions, such as if, must be handled specially since they may not evaluate all their arguments. Such *lenient* functions are discussed in Chapters 7 and 12. In this analysis we assume all parameters are passed by value.

symbolic evaluation, since we are symbolically going through the evaluation of the expression to get something other than its value. In this case the result is a set of recurrence equations for the execution time of the expression. Simplifying and solving the recurrence equations is more difficult, but computerized algebra systems can help.

Finally we discuss the unusual brackets $[\![\ ]\!]$. We didn't surround the argument of **T** with the usual brackets, ( ), [ ], or { }, because expressions within $[\![\ ]\!]$ must be treated specially. To appreciate this, observe the following "derivation." It is certainly the case that

$$\mathbf{T}[\![\text{rest } S]\!] = C_{\text{rest}} \tag{3.44}$$

Now note that by Eq. (3.43) we have

$$\mathbf{T}[\![\text{rest } [\text{rest } (a{:}S)]]\!] = 2C_{\text{rest}} + C_{\text{prefix}} \tag{3.45}$$

We also know that $\text{rest } (a : S) = S$. Therefore, substituting equals for equals in Eq. (3.45) we have

$$\mathbf{T}[\![\text{rest } S]\!] = 2C_{\text{rest}} + C_{\text{prefix}} \tag{3.46}$$

Things equal to the same thing are equal to each other, however, so from Eqs. (3.44) and (3.46) we can conclude that $C_{\text{rest}} + C_{\text{prefix}} = 0$. This is ridiculous. Where did we go wrong?

Looking back, we see that our error was in replacing $\text{rest } (a{:}S)$ by S in Eq. (3.45). Just because the *value* of $\text{rest } (a{:}S)$ is the same as the *value* of S does not mean that the *execution times* of these two formulas are the same. On the other hand, this step seems justified by referential transparency, which says that we can always substitute equals for equals.

Clearly we must be more careful; equals cannot always be substituted for equals. Therefore we distinguish *referentially transparent contexts,* in which they can, from *referentially opaque contexts,* in which they cannot. Of course, this distinction doesn't do us much good unless we have some independent way of telling the two contexts apart, as fortunately there is.

Any statement whose truth depends only on the value of a formula and not on the way it's written is a referentially transparent context. Since most of the time we are concerned with the *functional* properties of our programs—that is, with the values they return—most of our statements are referentially transparent, and we can safely substitute equals for equals. Sometimes, however, we are concerned with other properties of our programs; statements concerning them may be referentially opaque. In these we cannot safely substitute equals for equals. Referentially opaque contexts are usually easy to spot since their truth depends on the *written* form of the expression. Therefore, statements dealing with the *performance* properties of programs are referentially opaque, as are statements dealing with their *physical* properties (such as length).

Needless to say, we must be very careful when reasoning in referentially opaque contexts. This is the purpose of the brackets ⟦ ⟧; they surround a referentially opaque expression, and warn us that we cannot assume that equals can be substituted for equals. Outside these brackets, we can reason as usual.[14]

Exercise 3.88: Perform a detailed time-performance analysis of the original version of reverse (Eq. 3.31).

Exercise 3.89: Perform a detailed time-performance analysis of cat, as defined in Eq. (3.9).

Exercise 3.90: Perform detailed time-performance analyses of other functions previously defined in the text or in your answers to exercises.

Exercise 3.91: Use techniques similar to those in this section to perform detailed *space*-performance analyses of both versions of reverse (Eq. 3.31 and Eqs. 3.34 and 3.35).

Exercise 3.92: Perform a detailed space-performance analysis of cat (Eq. 3.9).

3.9 Tail Recursion and Iteration

Our definition of elt (Eq. 3.4) is recursive, as is the Pascal function definition of elt we derived from it. The same holds for the cat function (Eq. 3.9). In general, whenever we want to do something repetitively in applicative programming we do it recursively; recursion is the principle means of repetition in applicative programming. Thus what would be accomplished by an *iterative statement* (such as a **for**, **while**, or **repeat** loop) in an imperative language is accomplished by recursion in an applicative language. On the other hand, you are probably aware that on most computers iterative statements are more efficient than recursive-function invocations.[15] It seems then that applicative programming could be criticized because it encourages—even forces—us to program recursively jobs

---

14. Quine (1960) introduces the referential transparency/opacity distinction in the general context of language and logic.
15. This observation applies only to conventional (von Neumann) computers. Computers specially designed for applicative languages implement recursive functions very efficiently. Also, architectural features can be included in conventional computers that significantly increase the speed of recursive-function invocations.

that could be programmed iteratively.[16] Thus it would seem that applicative programming is inherently inefficient. In this section we show how to avoid this inefficiency.

What allows a function such as elt to be programmed iteratively in an imperative language? First consider an abbreviated trace of an invocation of cat:

$$
\begin{aligned}
\mathsf{cat}\,(<0,\,1,\,2>,\,<3,\,4,\,5>) &\Rightarrow 0:\mathsf{cat}\,(<1,\,2>,\,<3,\,4,\,5>)\\
&\Rightarrow 0:1:\mathsf{cat}\,(<2>,\,<3,\,4,\,5>)\\
&\Rightarrow 0:1:2:\mathsf{cat}\,(<>,\,<3,\,4,\,5>)\\
&\Rightarrow 0:1:2:<3,\,4,\,5>\\
&\Rightarrow 0:1:<2,\,3,\,4,\,5>\\
&\Rightarrow 0:<1,\,2,\,3,\,4,\,5>\\
&\Rightarrow <0,\,1,\,2,\,3,\,4,\,5>
\end{aligned}
$$

The recursive invocation is described by the following equation:

$$
\mathsf{cat}\,(S,\,T)\,=\,\mathsf{first}\,S:\mathsf{cat}\,(\mathsf{rest}\,S,\,T) \tag{3.8}
$$

We can see that cat does something (i.e., rest S) before calling itself, and something else (i.e., first $S : \cdots$) to the result returned by the recursive application. These "postprocessing operations" can be seen stacking up on the left in the preceding trace; their execution remains pending as long as the recursive calls of cat continue. As you are probably aware, on a conventional computer a stack keeps track of these pending operations; this stack makes recursive calls relatively inefficient. More specifically, the information necessary to resume the pending operations is stored in activation records, one for each pending function. These activation records occupy space proportional to the depth of the recursion. Hence recursion is space-inefficient. Further, because it takes time to manage the stack—to create and dispose of the activation records—recursion is time-inefficient. Can we avoid the need to stack activation records for iterative programs?

In general a recursive invocation of a function f is described by an equation such as

$$
fx\,=\,A_x[f(B_x x)]
$$

Here B represents the operations performed *before* the recursive invocation of f, and A represents the operations performed *after* the recursive

---

16. In investigating higher-order functions in Chapter 6, we'll see that the recursion can often be hidden in primitive functions that are programmed iteratively. By using these functions we can often avoid explicit recursion and hence are not forced to program recursively.

invocation. A trace of an application of f will look like this (we omit parentheses for clarity):

$$fx = A_1 f B_1 x$$
$$= A_1 A_2 f B_2 B_1 x$$
$$= A_1 A_2 A_3 f B_3 B_2 B_1 x$$
$$\vdots$$
$$= A_1 A_2 A_3 \cdots A_{n-2} A_{n-1} A_n f B_n B_{n-1} B_{n-2} \cdots B_3 B_2 B_1 x$$
$$= A_1 A_2 A_3 \cdots A_{n-2} A_{n-1} A_n B_n B_{n-1} B_{n-2} \cdots B_3 B_3 B_1 x$$

Here it is clear we do the B operations on the way into the recursion and the A operations on the way out (as usual, we read function applications from right to left).

When can a recursive function be programmed iteratively? Suppose that f performs no operations on the value returned by the recursive call; that is, $A_x\, y = y$. Then a trace looks like this:

$$fx = f B_1 x$$
$$= f B_2 B_1 x$$
$$= f B_3 B_2 B_1 x$$
$$\vdots$$
$$= f B_n B_{n-1} B_{n-2} \cdots B_3 B_2 B_1 x$$
$$= B_n B_{n-1} B_{n-2} \cdots B_3 B_2 B_1 x$$

Since there is nothing to be done on return, no operations A are being stacked up. For a concrete example, consider the following abbreviated trace of an invocation of elt:

$$\text{elt}\,(<A,\ B,\ C,\ D,\ E>,\ 4) \Rightarrow \text{elt}\,(<B,\ C,\ D,\ E>,\ 3)$$
$$\Rightarrow \text{elt}\,(<C,\ D,\ E>,\ 2)$$
$$\Rightarrow \text{elt}\,(<D,\ E>,\ 1)$$
$$\Rightarrow D$$

Once we "reach the bottom" of the elt calls we are done; no operations have to be done "on the way out." This is different from the cat example, in which, once we reach the bottom of the cat calls, we must work our way up through the ':' operations.

A function such as elt that doesn't do anything after the recursive return is called *tail-recursive* because the last thing it must do is recursively call itself. Since there is nothing to do "on the way out" of the recursion, there is no reason to stack up pending operations. This suggests that the power of recursion is not needed for tail-recursive functions. Indeed, a tail-recursive call can be implemented by updating the parameters and branching back to the entry point of the function. For example, consider this tail-recursive Pascal definition of elt:

```
function elt (S: tausequence; i: integer): tau;
begin
  if i=1 then elt := first (S)
  else elt := elt (rest (S), i − 1)
end {elt}
```

Since no operations are performed after recursive return, there is no reason to make the recursive call. Instead we update the values of the parameters 'S' and 'i' and branch back to the entry point:

```
function elt (S: tausequence; i: integer): tau;
label 1;
begin
1: if i = 1 then elt := first (S)
  else begin  S := rest (S);
              i := i − 1;
              goto 1 end
end {elt};
```

Notice that this definition of elt is not recursive; it will not incur the overhead of a recursive invocation. Of course, it would be more readable to express the iteration using the **while** loop of Pascal:

```
function elt (S: tausequence; i: integer): tau;
begin
  while i≠1 do
    begin S := rest (S); i := i − 1 end;
  elt := first (S)
end {elt}
```

This function definition is not applicative; we have made significant use of assignments and **goto**s (or their equivalents). By deriving the program applicatively, however, we have proved its correctness and established some algebraic properties of the function. If we convert the tail recursion to iteration carefully, this optimization will not introduce bugs. Deriving the imperative version directly, and proving its correctness, would be considerably more complicated. It is especially difficult to prove algebraic properties of the imperative version, although C. A. R. Hoare (1969) and others (Dijkstra 1976, Reynolds 1981) have developed methods for doing so.

Fortunately, we usually need not worry about performing this *tail-*

recursion optimization since the compilers for many applicative languages (including most LISP compilers) do it automatically. That is, these compilers recognize cases in which the last thing a function must do is call itself, and in these cases compile assignments and a jump instead of a recursive invocation. Thus we have both the manageability of applicative programming and the efficiency of imperative programming. We henceforth call tail-recursive functions *iterative* on the assumption that this optimization is done automatically. Tail recursion in applicative languages is as efficient as iteration in imperative languages.

Exercise 3.93: Suppose that no operations are done before the recursive call; that is, $B_x \, x = x$. Explain why this isn't an interesting situation.

Exercise 3.94: Determine whether your definition of length in Exercise 3.7 is tail-recursive.

Suppose a function is not defined iteratively. What can we do to improve its efficiency? For example, recall our definition of cat, which is not iterative:

$$\text{cat}\,(S,\,T) = \begin{cases} T, & \text{if null } S \\ \textbf{else } \text{first } S : \text{cat (rest } S,\, T) \end{cases} \tag{3.9}$$

Also recall that a trace looks like this:

$$
\begin{aligned}
\text{cat}\,(<0,\,1,\,2>,\,<3,\,4,\,5>) &\Rightarrow 0 : \text{cat}\,(<1,\,2>,\,<3,\,4,\,5>) \\
&\Rightarrow 0 : 1 : \text{cat}\,(<2>,\,<3,\,4,\,5>) \\
&\Rightarrow 0 : 1 : 2 : \text{cat}\,(<\,>,\,<3,\,4,\,5>) \\
&\Rightarrow 0 : 1 : 2 : <3,\,4,\,5> \\
&\Rightarrow 0 : 1 : <2,\,3,\,4,\,5> \\
&\Rightarrow 0 : <1,\,2,\,3,\,4,\,5> \\
&\Rightarrow <0,\,1,\,2,\,3,\,4,\,5>
\end{aligned}
$$

Thus the elements of the first sequence—<0, 1, 2>—are held until the bottom of the recursion is reached, at which point they are prefixed in reverse order to <3, 4, 5>. That is, 2 is prefixed first, yielding <2, 3, 4, 5>; 1 is prefixed next, yielding <1, 2, 3, 4, 5>; and 0 is prefixed last, yielding <0, 1, 2, 3, 4, 5>.

To avoid the recursive call (i.e., to program cat iteratively) we must find a way to hold the elements of the first sequence in reverse order. The linear-time version of reverse suggests how this can be done: Use an additional parameter R to hold a stack (sequence) of the reversed elements of the first sequence. Thus our new cat works as shown in Table 3.1. It's easy to see that the algorithm falls into two phases: building up R from S, and moving R onto T. The general step in the first phase is described by the following transformation:

$$R, \ S, \ T \ \Rightarrow \ \text{first } S : R, \ \text{rest } S, \ T$$

This process begins with R null and is completed when S is null. The general step in the second phase is described by this transformation:

$$R, \ T \ \Rightarrow \ \text{rest } R, \ \text{first } R : T$$

This process is finished when R is null, at which point T is the desired result.

This algorithm is easy to implement applicatively if we use two auxiliary functions, cataux1 and cataux2, representing the two iterative phases. Thus we have the following equational definition:

$$\text{cat }(S, \ T) \ = \ \text{cataux1 }(<>, \ S, \ T) \tag{3.47}$$

cataux1 $(R, \ S, \ T) \ = \ $ cataux1 (first $S : R$, rest $S, \ T$), if $S \neq <>$
cataux1 $(R, \ <>, \ T) \ = \ $ cataux2 $(R, \ T)$

cataux2 $(R, \ T) \ = \ $ cataux2 (rest R, first $R : T$), if $R \neq <>$
cataux2 $(<>, \ T) \ = \ T$

It is easy to translate these equations into a conditional definition of an iterative cat:

Table 3.1. Trace of iterative catenation.

R	S	T
$<>$	$<S_1, S_2, S_3, \ldots, S_m>$	$<T_1, \ldots, T_n>$
$<S_1>$	$<S_2, S_3, \ldots, S_m>$	$<T_1, \ldots, T_n>$
$<S_2, S_1>$	$<S_3, \ldots, S_m>$	$<T_1, \ldots, T_n>$
$\vdots$	$\vdots$	$\vdots$
$<S_m, S_{m-1}, \ldots, S_3, S_2, S_1>$	$<>$	$<T_1, \ldots, T_n>$
$<S_{m-1}, \ldots, S_3, S_2, S_1>$	$<>$	$<S_m, T_1, \ldots, T_n>$
$\vdots$	$\vdots$	$\vdots$
$<S_2, S_1>$	$<>$	$<S_3, \ldots, S_m, T_1, \ldots, T_n>$
$<S_1>$	$<>$	$<S_2, S_3, \ldots, S_m, T_1, \ldots, T_n>$
$<>$	$<>$	$<S_1, S_2, S_3, \ldots, S_m, T_1, \ldots, T_n>$

$$\text{cat}\,(S,\ T) \equiv \text{cataux1}\,(<>,\ S,\ T) \tag{3.48}$$

$$\textbf{where}\ \ \text{cataux1}\,(R,\ S,\ T) \equiv \begin{cases} \text{cataux2}\,(R,\ T),\ \text{if null } S \\ \textbf{else}\ \text{cataux1}\,(\text{first } S : R,\ \text{rest } S,\ T) \end{cases}$$

$$\textbf{where}\ \ \text{cataux2}\,(R,\ T) \equiv \begin{cases} T,\ \text{if null } R \\ \textbf{else}\ \text{cataux2}\,(\text{rest } R,\ \text{first } R : T) \end{cases}$$

Because all these functions are defined iteratively, they are easy to translate to an iterative imperative program (see Fig. 3.1). We must, however, be careful about the order of the assignments to 'T' and 'R' in the definition of cataux2—a typical difficulty in imperative programming. This is one reason that it's better to let the compiler do the tail-recursion optimization rather than doing it manually.

Exercise 3.95: Explain why it was necessary to reverse the order of the assignments to 'T' and 'R' in the imperative definition of cataux2 (Fig. 3.1).

Exercise 3.96: Improve the readability of the Pascal implementation of cat by using **while** loops instead of **gotos**.

Figure 3.1 Imperative implementation of catenation.

```
function cat (S, T: tausequence): tausequence;

  function cataux1 (R, S, T: tausequence): tausequence;
  label 1;
  begin
1:  if null (S) then cataux1 := cataux2 (R, T)
      else begin  R := prefix (first (S), R); S := rest (S); goto 1 end
  end {cataux1};

  function cataux2 (R, T: tausequence): tausequence;
  label 1;
  begin
1:  if null (R) then cataux2 := T
      else begin  T := prefix (first (R), T); R := rest (R); goto 1 end
  end {cataux2};

begin
  cat := cataux1 (nil, S, T)
end {cat};
```

Exercise 3.97: Improve your Pascal implementation in the previous exercise by eliminating the auxiliary functions.

Exercise 3.98: Translate the improved version of reverse (Eqs. 3.32 and 3.33) into Pascal and perform the tail-recursion optimization (i.e., make your definition iterative).

We pause to compare the time performance of the recursive and iterative versions of cat informally. We consider only the time necessary for prefixing, call/return, and simple jumps. Look again at the recursive definition:

$$\text{cat } (S,\ T) \equiv \begin{cases} T, & \text{if null } S \\ \textbf{else } \text{first } S : \text{cat (rest } S,\ T) \end{cases} \qquad (3.9)$$

This implementation performs n = length S calls, n prefix operations, and no jumps. Thus the time performance of the recursive implementation is approximately

$$T_r = nC + nP$$

where C is the time for a call/return and P is the time for a prefix operation (both times are assumed constant).

Next we consider the performance of the iterative implementation of cat. In the first phase (cataux1) we perform n jumps and n prefix operations as S is moved to R. In the second phase (cataux2) we perform n jumps and n prefix operations as R is moved to T. In addition three calls are needed: cat, cataux1, and cataux2. Hence the time for the iterative implementation of cat is approximately

$$T_i = 2nJ + 2nP + 3C$$

where J is the time for a jump. Now the tail-recursion optimization will improve the performance of cat by $T_r - T_i$, which is

$$\begin{aligned} T_r - T_i &= nC + nP - (2nJ + 2nP + 3C) \\ &= (n - 3)C - 2nJ - nP \end{aligned}$$

Thus we are saving $n - 3$ calls at the expense of $2n$ jumps and n prefix operations. The tail-recursion optimization will improve performance if this amount is positive, that is, if $n - 3$ calls take more time than $2n$ jumps and n prefix calls. Since prefix is relatively expensive, it is not at all clear whether this will be the case. It's also informative to consider the relative times:

$$T_i / T_r = \frac{2nJ + 2nP + 3C}{nC + nP} = 2\frac{J + P}{C + P} + \frac{3C}{nC + nP} \rightarrow 2\frac{J + P}{C + P}, \text{ as } n \rightarrow \infty$$

If $C \approx P \approx 10J$, then $T_i / T_r \approx 1.1$ as $n \rightarrow \infty$; thus the imperative version actually takes *more* time. The moral is: *Don't go to the trouble to optimize unless you have determined that this will be worthwhile in the environment of use.*

Exercise 3.99: Suppose that $C \approx P \approx 2J$; compute T_i / T_j as $n \rightarrow \infty$. Now try $100J$. Next try $C \approx 10P$ and $P \approx 10J$. Can you draw any general (qualitative) conclusions?

Exercise 3.100: Analyze the *space* performance of the recursive and iterative versions of cat. For this purpose, let A be the average size of an activation record and S the average size of a sequence element (i.e., a record in a linked list). Compare the performances under a variety of assumptions about the relative size of A and S. What conclusions can you draw?

We have compared the recursive and iterative cats with respect to performance; now we compare them with respect to *understandability*. The recursive definition (Eq. 3.9) is short, easy to understand, and easy to manipulate mathematically. For example, it's easy (even trivial) to show that it satisfies the following identities:

cat (nil, T) = T
cat ($a : S, T$) = a : cat (S, T)

It's also easy to prove properties such as

length [cat (S, T)] = length S + length T

Unfortunately, the definition is (nontail) recursive, which means that on many computers it's less efficient than an iterative definition.

We have seen that we can improve the efficiency of cat by defining it iteratively:

cat (S, T) $\equiv$ cataux1 (<>, S, T)   (3.48)

where cataux1 (R, S, T) $\equiv \begin{cases} \text{cataux2 } (R, T), \text{ if null } S \\ \textbf{else } \text{cataux1 (first } S : R, \text{ rest } S, T) \end{cases}$

where cataux2 (R, T) $\equiv \begin{cases} T, \text{ if null } R \\ \textbf{else } \text{cataux2 (rest } R, \text{ first } R : T) \end{cases}$

This definition, however, is more than twice as long as the original recursive definition and much less amenable to mathematical treatment. Thus, to prove that the iterative definition satisfies even the simple identity cat (nil, T) = T requires the following steps:

$$\begin{aligned} \text{cat (nil, } T) &= \text{cataux1} (<>, \text{nil}, T) \\ &= \text{cataux2} (<>, T) \\ &= T \end{aligned}$$

To prove the only sightly more complicated identity a : cat (S, T) = cat $(a : S, T)$ requires an inductive proof, as can be seen by the following derivation:

$$\begin{aligned} \text{cat } (a : S, T) &= \text{cataux1} (<>, a : S, T) \\ &= \text{cataux1 (first } [a : S] : <>, \text{rest } [a : S], T) \\ &= \text{cataux1} (<a>, S, T) \end{aligned}$$

At this point we have nowhere to go without resorting to inductive proofs about the properties of cataux1 (which will lead us to inductive proof of the properties of cataux2). Indeed, our iterative definition of cat, although written in an applicative language, is just as unmanageable as if programmed imperatively.

Exercise 3.101: Prove that

a : cat (S, T) = cat $(a : S, T)$

for the iterative definition of cat.

Exercise 3.102: Prove for the iterative definition of cat that

length [cat (S, T)] = length S + length T

Let's summarize. It's possible to program applicatively in an imperative language, as demonstrated repeatedly in translating our applicative programs into Pascal. This is possible because applicative programming (but *not* functional programming—see Chapter 6) is a subset of imperative programming; to program applicatively in an imperative language we simply avoid using variables, assignment statements, and all control structures except for **if** statements and recursive-function calls. Superficially the programs may be imperative (e.g., may use assignments for returning function values and creating record values), but in spirit they're applicative.

On the other hand, the iterative definitions of reverse and cat demonstrate that it's also possible to program imperatively in an applicative language. These programs are superficially applicative (they use no assignments, variables, or loops), but in spirit they're imperative. Thus the ways that the *parameters R, S,* and *T* are passed around among cat, cataux1, and cataux2 are exactly analogous to the ways that the *variables R, S,* and *T* would be assigned in an imperative implementation of cat (see Fig. 3.1). In effect we're doing imperative programming in an applicative language.

There are, however, real differences between applicative and imperative programming; as we've seen, the recursive definitions of reverse and cat are simpler and more manageable than the iterative versions. These differences apply regardless of whether these definitions are expressed in an applicative or imperative *language.* It is the applicative programming *style* that is preferable to the imperative programming *style.* Thus there is little point programming in an applicative *language* if you use an imperative *style.* In this book we attempt to adopt the applicative idiom completely, allowing us to see clearly its strengths and weaknesses.

One weakness is apparent already: A simple recursive definition of a function may be significantly less efficient than a more complicated iterative definition. We would like both the simplicity of the recursive definition and the efficiency of the iterative definition. One way to accomplish this—an active research area—is to find ways to implement applicative languages more efficiently. One example has already been shown: Tail-recursive definitions can be implemented iteratively. Since the compiler does this automatically, we can have both the simplicity of the recursive definition and the efficiency of the iterative definition. This example should indicate some of the possibilities for efficient applicative language implementations on conventional computers. Another possibility being actively pursued is the development of unconventional architectures designed specifically to execute applicative programs efficiently. This topic is beyond the scope of this book, although one approach is discussed in Section 10.9.

Exercise 3.103: Instead of trying to directly prove properties of the iterative definition of cat, we might adopt the following strategy. First we prove that the iterative definition always returns the same result as the recursive definition. Then we can prove properties such as

length [cat (S, T)] = length S + length T

for the recursive definition and safely assume that they hold for the iterative version. Do the following:

1. Prove that the recursive and iterative definitions of cat always return the same result.

2. Discuss which properties can be proved in this way and which cannot. *Hint:* In what way is the iterative definition of cat *intended* to be different from the recursive definition? Also recall the discussion at the end of Section 3.8.

Exercise 3.104: Prove that the recursive and iterative definitions of reverse always return the same result.

3.10 Copying in Applicative Languages

We have encouraged you to think of the sequence-processing primitives as making new copies of their argument sequences, rather than as modifying them—the simplest way to understand the effect of these operations, which also helps us shed imperative habits of thought. For example, we do not think of cat (*S, T*) as joining *S* and *T*, but as creating a new sequence with copies of the elements of *S* and *T* in order. Similarly, the various substitution operations should not be thought of as modifying their argument sequences. For example, indsubst (*x, i, A*) (see Exercises 3.23–3.27) does not assign a new value to the *i*th element of *A*, but rather it creates a new sequence just like *A*, except in the *i*th position, which has the value *x*. In this section we briefly discuss ways to avoid the inefficiency of actually doing this copying.

Although copying is a useful way to *understand* operations on sequences, it is not necessarily a useful way to *implement* them. For example, on most sequential computers sequences are implemented as linked record structures. This technique permits the sequence primitives to be implemented without copying the argument sequences and without altering their structure.[17] This technique also results in the sharing of records among many different sequences, which tends to decrease storage use. On the other hand, sharing records between sequences means that a modification to a shared record may affect many different sequences—often a cause of difficult-to-find bugs in programs written in languages that permit the modification of sequence structures, such as LISP.

Thus with the usual implementation of sequences we find ourselves in the following situation. In general, it is *not* safe to implement substitution operations by a destructive assignment to a sequence record, since that record might be shared by other sequences. In these cases we must make a fresh copy of some or all of the sequence in which the substitution is to be made. On the other hand, empirical observations show that in fact many sequences are not shared. Thus it would be perfectly safe to do a destructive substitution on these sequences if only we *knew* they were unshared.

---

17. For a discussion of sequence implementation, see (MacLennan 1987b, Chapter 9), or any book on data structures.

The goal is now clear. For an application such as indsubst (x, i, A) we need to know whether or not A (or a part of A) is shared. If it is not shared, then A can be destructively altered by the indsubst operation, which is both efficient and safe. If it is shared, then the only safe thing to do is to create a fresh copy of A (actually, just the part of A up to the modified element).

There are several ways to accomplish this goal. The simplest is *reference counting*, a method of keeping track of the number of pointers to a record in memory (MacLennan 1987b, Chapter 11). Reference counting is often used to reclaim storage automatically; thus the basic mechanism for keeping track of sharing may already be available. On the other hand, because reference counting is relatively expensive (since every access to a record must update its reference count), it's probably not worthwhile to include it just for the sake of optimizing indsubst and similar functions.

A better approach is, to the extent possible, to determine at compile time which sequences have shared components and which do not. This permits a very simplified form of reference counting to be used in just those cases that cannot be decided at compile time; many programs do not require reference counting at all. For example, Hudak and Bloss (1985) describe static data flow analysis algorithms that allow many updates to unshared arrays to be identified. In cases where this analysis fails, they alter the execution order to avoid copying. In this Hudak and Bloss utilize the evaluation order independence of applicative languages (see Chapter 1); in an imperative language this optimization would be much more difficult. If all else fails they resort to a simplified form of reference counting. This combination of methods seems to eliminate almost all unnecessary copying in practical applicative programs.

Exercise 3.105:   Consider the formula:

cat [indsubst (x, i, A), subseq $(A, 1, j)$]

In what order should the arguments to cat be evaluated so as to avoid copying (assuming these are the only two uses of A)? Explain. (subseq was defined in Exercise 3.63.)

Exercise 3.106:   Define a destructive indsubst function in LISP, Pascal, or another imperative language.

Exercise 3.107:   Write cat [indsubst (x, i, A), subseq $(A, 1, j)$] in Pascal in such a way that a destructive indsubst can be safely used.

Chapter 4

Applicative Set Processing

4.1 Archetypes and Prototypes

In this chapter we use sequences to construct *prototype implementations* of two abstract data types: finite sets and finite functions. What is the difference between an archetype and a prototype? According to the definition of 'ideal' in the *American Heritage Dictionary,*

> *Prototype* and *archetype* both denote original models of things subsequently reproduced. What develops from a *prototype* may represent significant modifications from the original. An *archetype*, in contrast, is usually construed as an ideal form that establishes an unchanging pattern for all things of its kind.

Another dictionary says,

> The *archetype* is the primal form, actual or imaginary, according to which any existing thing is constructed; the *prototype* has or has had actual existence. . . .

These definitions of *archetype* are consistent with our previous use of the term. In our case an archetype is a mathematical description of the properties of something, usually an abstract data type. It tells us *what* we want the operators to do but gives us no hint *how* we will implement them, or even if it's possible to implement them. Thus the requirements defined by an archetype are possibly noncomputable and perhaps even inconsistent.

The consistency and computability of the archetype—the *chief* model—can be established by the *prototype*—the *first* model. A prototype implementation demonstrates the feasibility of the archetype by exhibiting an implementation of the specified operations in terms of operations already known to be feasible. Since an inconsistent archetype cannot be implemented, a correct prototype implementation proves the consistency of the archetype. (We appeal here to a theorem of logic: A set of axioms is consistent if and only if it is satisfiable.) Furthermore, since the prototype is a program, it proves the *computational* feasibility of the axioms—that is, that the axioms can be satisfied by *computable* functions. This is important because it is possible to write perfectly consistent specifications that nevertheless cannot be implemented on a computer (specifications for so-called *undecidable* problems—see Section 9.9). In summary,

- An archetype says what you want,

- A prototype proves you haven't asked for the impossible.

Since a prototype is intended only to show feasibility, it need not be an efficient implementation of the archetype. More importantly, the prototype should be simple, allowing us to see that it correctly implements the archetype.

In Chapter 2 we investigated an archetype for the sequence data type; Appendix B contains archetypes for the other primitive data types of our applicative language. In investigating the foundations of functional programming in Chapter 8, we develop prototypes for these data types. In this chapter we develop both archetypes and prototypes for two useful abstract data types: finite sets and finite functions.

4.2 Archetype for Finite Sets

"It is a matter of practical expediency to construct an archetype in the abstract before constructing a prototype in the material" (Asimow, 1962, 73). Our first task in developing an archetype for finite sets must be to consider the operations we want to be part of this data type and determine the properties of these operations. Clearly we would like to permit the traditional operations $\in$, $\cap$, $\cup$, and $\setminus$ (set difference). We would also like to be able to compare finite sets—$\subset$, $\subseteq$, $=$, and $\neq$—and we should have a name for the empty set, $\emptyset$. Finally, we must be able to construct arbitrary finite sets. (The resulting type signature is shown in Fig. 4.1.)

What is the difference between finite sets and sequences? Recall that for sets the order and multiplicity of the elements is not significant; the following are all considered the same set:

$$\{2, 4, 5\}, \quad \{5, 2, 4\}, \quad \{4, 5, 2, 4\}, \quad \{2, 4, 5, 4, 4, 2\}$$

On the other hand, for sequences both order and multiplicity *are* significant; the following are different sequences:

$$<2, 4, 5>, \quad <5, 2, 4>, \quad <4, 5, 2, 4>, \quad <2, 4, 5, 4, 4, 2>$$

Thus we have two *aggregate* data types: one recognizing both order and multiplicity, the other recognizing neither order nor multiplicity. This classification suggests two other possibilities: aggregates recognizing multiplicity but not order, and aggregates recognizing order but not multiplicity. In fact, the first possibility is useful in many applications; aggregates with multiplicity but not order are called *multisets* or *bags*.

Exercise 4.1: Discuss the remaining possibility: aggregate structures recognizing order but not multiplicity.

Sets are similar to sequences in that they can be constructed inductively—an $n + 1$ element set can be created by adding one element to an n-element set. This operation, combined with a means for creating

---

Figure 4.1 Signature for finite set types.

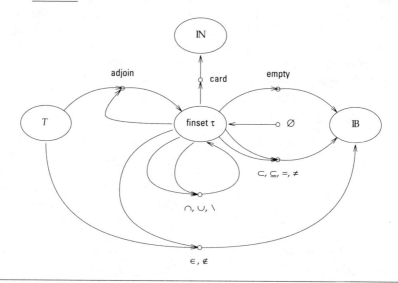

empty sets, allows the construction of any finite set. Thus we will have two constructors: one for creating empty sets and one for adding an element to an arbitrary finite set. For a complete and coherent set of operations we should require these constructors to have associated discriminators and selectors.

How do we create empty sets? For this we postulate the niladic (parameterless) operation $\varnothing$, whose value is the empty set, $\varnothing = \{\}$. For an associated discriminator we postulate empty with the intuitive meaning that empty S = **true** if and only if S is the empty set. No selectors are associated with $\varnothing$ since the empty set has no components.

To construct nonempty sets, we postulate the operation adjoin, which adds one element to a set, adjoin $(x, S) = \{x\} \cup S$. For example,

$$\text{adjoin } (2, \{3, 6, 1\}) = \{2, 3, 6, 1\}$$
$$\text{adjoin } (2, \{3, 2, 7\}) = \{2, 3, 2, 7\} = \{3, 2, 7\}$$

If we let finset τ be the name of the data type of all finite sets whose members are of type τ, then the signature of adjoin is

$$\text{adjoin: } \tau \times \text{finset } \tau \rightarrow \text{finset } \tau$$

For convenience we introduce the conventional curly brace notation as syntactic sugar for nested adjoins:

$$\{\} \Rightarrow \varnothing \tag{4.1}$$
$$\{x_1, x_2, \ldots, x_n\} \Rightarrow \text{adjoin } (x_1, \{x_2, \ldots, x_n\})$$

For example, $\{3, 2, 7\}$ is an abbreviation for[1]

$$\text{adjoin } \{3, \text{adjoin } [2, \text{adjoin } (7, \varnothing)]\}$$

A list of zero or more values in curly braces is called a *set denotation*.

No special discriminator is needed to test for nonempty sets; $\neg$ empty S will do the job. We can specify the empty discriminator more carefully by considering its result for each kind of set:

$$\text{empty } \varnothing = \textbf{true}$$
$$\text{empty } [\text{adjoin } (x, S)] = \textbf{false} \tag{4.2}$$

These equations, which form our archetype for empty, can be interpreted as rewrite rules that allow us to compute the output of empty for any legal input:

$$\text{empty } \varnothing \Rightarrow \textbf{true}$$
$$\text{empty } [\text{adjoin } (x, S)] \Rightarrow \textbf{false}$$

---

1. Notice that, following mathematical convention, curly braces have two uses: surrounding set denotations and surrounding argument lists. The resulting ambiguities are few and easily resolved.

Exercise 4.2: Prove that

$$\emptyset \neq \text{adjoin } (x, S) \text{ for all } x, S$$

Hint: Assume the contrary and use the archetype for empty (Eq. 4.2). What fact do you need from the Boolean archetype (see Appendix B)?

Our next task is to formalize in an archetype our requirements for $\in$. To characterize the behavior of $\in$ we must consider its interaction with each of the two kinds of sets: empty sets and nonempty sets. Clearly, what we mean by an empty set is that it has no members, so $x \in \emptyset$ is always **false**:

$$x \in \emptyset = \textbf{false} \qquad (4.3)$$

On the other hand, adjoin (y, S) is intended to be a set whose members are y and all the members of S. Therefore we surely know that $y \in \text{adjoin } (y, S)$. We also know that $x \in \text{adjoin } (y, S)$ whenever $x \in S$. These properties are combined in the following axiom:

$$x \in \text{adjoin } (y, S) = (x = y \lor x \in S) \qquad (4.4)$$

Equation (4.4) characterizes $\in$ on nonempty sets, but it reciprocally characterizes adjoin, since it says that the only members of adjoin (y, S) are y and the members of S.

Since any finite set can be expressed as a finite number of adjoins to the empty set, Eqs. (4.3) and (4.4) define the $\in$ function for all finite sets.[2] To see this, observe that they can be interpreted as rewrite rules that tell us how to compute the output of $\in$ for any legal input:

$$\begin{aligned} x \in \emptyset &\Rightarrow \textbf{false} \\ x \in \text{adjoin } (y, S) &\Rightarrow x = y \lor x \in S \end{aligned} \qquad (4.5)$$

Repeated application of the second rule will eventually reduce the set to $\emptyset$. Hence any membership test can be computed in a finite number of steps.

Note that Eq. (4.4) makes use (on the right) of an '=' operation defined on τ, the base type of the finite set type. Thus we make the important assumption that type τ has a computable equality relation; without this

---

2. Whether they define it *consistently* is another issue, taken up later in this section.

assumption there is no computable way of determining whether or not an object is a member of a set. Since it is our intention to define an '=' operator on any type for which it is computable, we will have finite set types whenever they are computationally feasible.[3]

Exercise 4.3: Use the reduction rules for ∈ (Eqs. 4.5) to compute the value of this expression:

$$3 \in \{5, 8, 7\}$$

Note that you must first use Eqs. 4.1 to eliminate syntactic sugar.

We have considered the constructors and discriminators of finite sets; it remains to consider the selectors. Since the empty set has no members, it has no selectors. Therefore we turn to the selectors associated with nonempty sets. First note that since sets are unordered, we can't think of adjoin (x, S) as making x the first element of the set; we must think of it as putting x *somewhere* in the set. Thus

$$\text{adjoin } (1, \{2, 3\}) = \{1, 2, 3\} = \{2, 1, 3\} = \{2, 3, 1\} = \cdots$$

Hence many ways exist to construct the same abstract set:

$$\text{adjoin } (1, \{2, 3\}) = \text{adjoin } (2, \{1, 3\}) = \text{adjoin } (3, \{1, 2\}) = \{1, 2, 3\}$$

We say that sets have *multiple abstract representations*. For example, adjoin $(1, \{2, 3\})$ and adjoin $(2, \{1, 3\})$ are two abstract representations of the same set.

The relevance of this to selectors is that, unlike the prefix operation, the adjoin operation is not one to one. That is, since there are many element/set pairs that can be adjoined to yield a given set, there is no unique element/set pair to which a given set can be decomposed. This precludes the provision of a selector function for finite sets; the full reasons are somewhat complicated and discussed later (p. 126 and Section 4.8).

We have a very odd situation: a data structure into which we can put things (with the constructor), but out of which we can't get anything (since there are no selectors). What saves the finite set data type from

---

3. The major types for which equality is not computable are the function types $D \to R$ and the "infinite" types discussed in Chapter 7. Thus we cannot have finite sets of these things.

being useless is that the ∈ operator functions in some ways like a selector, since it allows us to find out what's in the structure. We call it an *interrogator* since it asks a question about the components of a structure.

The constructors, discriminators, and interrogators for finite sets are summarized in the following table:

Kind of Set	Empty	Nonempty
Discriminator	empty	(¬ empty)
Constructor	∅	adjoin
Interrogator	—	∈

Exercise 4.4:   An alternative to the adjoin operation is to provide an operation singl x that creates a singleton set containing x, singl $x = \{x\}$. In combination with ∅ and the union operation, singl permits the construction of any finite set. What else is needed in a complete and coherent finite set data type designed around singl?

Now that we have decided on the constructors for finite sets, we can state our existence axiom. Since we want no other members of finset τ other than empty sets and nonempty sets, the axiom says that all members of finset τ must result from either ∅ or adjoin:

$$\varnothing \in \text{finset } \tau \tag{4.6}$$
$$\text{adjoin } (x,\ S) \in \text{finset } \tau$$
$$z \notin \text{finset } \tau \text{ otherwise}$$

Note that we are using ∈ in two different ways: as a metasymbol and an object-symbol. In Eq. (4.6) ∈ is used to express *type* membership and thus is a metasymbol for talking *about* the type finset τ. ∈ is also an operator *in* the abstract data type finset τ and is thus an object-symbol that can be used in programs dealing with finite sets. Although two different symbols for the two different ideas would be convenient, both uses are conventional, and confusion is unlikely.[4]

Do the properties we've derived so far adequately characterize finite sets? Unfortunately they're incomplete, since they leave critical issues undecided. For example, we have not prohibited infinite sets. One way to do this is to require that every set be expressible as a set denotation, $\{x_1, \ldots, x_n\}$. A more rigorous solution is analogous to the one we used

---

4. You saw a similar dual use of '=' in Section 3.7.

for sequences: We specify a card (cardinality) function that must be defined for all members of the type:

> card: finset τ → IN
> card is total on finset τ.

This is our *finiteness axiom.*

We can specify card by considering its behavior on each of the kinds of sets specified in Eq. (4.6). Clearly, the cardinality of the empty set is 0:

$$\text{card } \varnothing = 0 \tag{4.7}$$

The cardinality of adjoin (x, S) depends on whether or not x is in S:

$$\text{card } [\text{adjoin } (x, S)] = \text{card } S, \text{ if } x \in S \tag{4.8}$$
$$\text{card } [\text{adjoin } (x, S)] = 1 + \text{card } S, \text{ if } x \notin S$$

Equations (4.7) and (4.8), which completely specify card since they determine its value on every class of sets, also provide a basis for inductive proofs about finite sets because they guarantee that all sets can be built up from $\varnothing$ by a finite number of adjoins.

Exercise 4.5: Convert Eqs. (4.7) and (4.8) to rewrite rules and use them to compute the value of card $\{5, 8, 7\}$.

So far, except for their names, there is little difference between prefix and adjoin (and nil and $\varnothing$, and null and empty). How do we express the fact that adjoin constructs sets whereas prefix constructs sequences? The principal difference between sets and sequences is that sequences preserve order and multiplicity, whereas sets do not. That prefix preserves these properties is expressed in the inequations (Eqs. 2.25 and 2.34):

$$x : y : S \neq y : x : S, \text{ for } x \neq y$$
$$x : S \neq x : x : S$$

These inequations also show us how we can express the fact that adjoin does not preserve these properties:

$$\text{adjoin } [x, \text{adjoin } (y, S)] = \text{adjoin } [y, \text{adjoin } (x, S)] \tag{4.9}$$
$$\text{adjoin } (x, S) = \text{adjoin } [x, \text{adjoin } (x, S)]$$

We cannot show that finite sets obey these equations. Therefore, as it stands, our archetype is still incomplete because it does not allow us to prove the properties that we expect of finite sets.

One solution is simply to add Eqs. (4.9) to the archetype, but we would still be unsure about whether we had covered all the cases. A better approach is to fall back on the most general characterization of sets of which we can think: Two sets are equal just when they have the same members. This so-called *Axiom of Extensionality* is easily stated mathematically:

$$S = T \text{ if and only if for all } x, \ x \in S \ = \ x \in T \qquad\qquad (4.10)$$

The *extension* of a set is its members; this axiom says that two sets are the same if they have the same extension—that is, the same members—regardless of how the set is written. There is another way to look at it: Since $\in$ is the only interrogator—the only way to find out about a set's members—Eq. (4.10) says that two sets are interchangeable if there are no *observable differences* between them. Specifically, the axiom says that S is interchangeable with T in all (referentially transparent) contexts if $x \in S$ is interchangeable with $x \in T$ in all (referentially transparent) contexts. The Axiom of Extensionality allows us to prove Eqs. (4.9).

Exercise 4.6:   Show that Eqs. (4.9) are implied by Eq. (4.10) (together with the archetype for $\in$ and well-known properties of Boolean values).

Exercise 4.7:   Show that sequences do not satisfy the Axiom of Extensionality. That is, it is not true that

$$S = T \text{ if and only if for all } x, \ \text{member } (x, S) \ = \ \text{member } (x, T)$$

Exhibiting a counterexample is sufficient.

The archetypes for the intersection, union, and difference operations follow directly from their intuitive meanings. For example, since $S \cap T$ is the set containing all those elements that are in both S and T, we can write its archetype:

$$x \in (S \cap T) \ = \ (x \in S) \wedge (x \in T) \qquad\qquad (4.11)$$

Because of the Axiom of Extensionality (Eq. 4.10), we know that this rule completely characterizes $S \cap T$. The specifications of union and set difference are similar (see Fig. 4.2).

The (improper) subset operation ($\subseteq$) can be specified in a number of ways. Since its intended meaning is that all the members of S are also in T, we can see that $S \subseteq T$ is true just when $S \setminus T$ is empty. Hence

$$S \subseteq T \ = \ \text{empty } (S \setminus T) \qquad\qquad (4.12)$$

On the other hand, we can specify $\subseteq$ more constructively by observing its behavior on the two kinds of sets: empty and nonempty. For empty sets we know that $\varnothing \subseteq S$ is always true. For an arbitrary nonempty set $S' = \text{adjoin}\,(x, S)$ we know that $S' \subseteq T$ just when $x \in T$ and $S \subseteq T$. The archetype for $\subseteq$ follows directly:

Figure 4.2 Archetype for finite set types.

Syntax:

finset $\tau \in$ **type**, for all $\tau \in$ **type**

$\varnothing \in$ finset τ

adjoin: $\tau \times$ finset $\tau \rightarrow$ finset τ

empty: finset $\tau \rightarrow \mathbb{B}$

$\in, \notin : \tau \times$ finset $\tau \rightarrow \mathbb{B}$

card: finset $\tau \rightarrow \mathbb{N}$

$\cap, \cup, \setminus$: finset $\tau \times$ finset $\tau \rightarrow$ finset τ

$\subset, \subseteq, =, \neq$: finset $\tau \times$ finset $\tau \rightarrow \mathbb{B}$

$\{\} \Rightarrow \varnothing$

$\{x_1, x_2, \ldots, x_n\} \Rightarrow \text{adjoin}\,(x_1, \{x_2, \ldots, x_n\})$

Semantics:

$\varnothing \in$ finset τ

adjoin $(x, S) \in$ finset τ

$z \notin$ finset τ otherwise

empty $\varnothing = $ **true**

empty $[\text{adjoin}\,(x, S)] = $ **false**

$x \in \varnothing = $ **false**

$x \in \text{adjoin}\,(y, S) = (x = y \;\vee\; x \in S)$

$\varnothing \subseteq S = $ **true**

adjoin $(x, S) \subseteq T = x \in T \;\wedge\; S \subseteq T$

card $\varnothing = 0$

card $[\text{adjoin}\,(x, S)] = \text{card}\,S,\;$ if $x \in S$

card $[\text{adjoin}\,(x, S)] = 1 + \text{card}\,S,\;$ if $x \notin S$

card is a total function on finset τ

$S = T$ if and only if for all $x, x \in S = x \in T$

$x \in S \cap T = x \in S \wedge x \in T$

$x \in S \cup T = x \in S \vee x \in T$

$x \in S \setminus T = x \in S \wedge x \notin T$

$x \notin S = \neg (x \in S)$

$S = T = S \subseteq T \wedge T \subseteq S$

$S \neq T = \neg (S = T)$

$S \subset T = S \subseteq T \wedge S \neq T$

$$\varnothing \subseteq S = \textbf{true} \qquad\qquad (4.13)$$
$$\text{adjoin}\,(x,\,S) \subseteq T = x \in T \wedge S \subseteq T$$

These equations are easily converted into rewrite rules that permit the computation of $\subseteq$ on any inputs.

Exercise 4.8: Convert Eqs. (4.13) into rewrite rules, and use them, together with Eqs. (4.5) and (4.1), to evaluate the following:

$$\{3, 7, 2\} \subseteq \{7, 3\}$$

Notice that we have specified an equality operator (=) on finite sets:

$$(S = T) = S \subseteq T \wedge T \subseteq S \qquad\qquad (4.14)$$

As for sequences, we use the '=' symbol, ambiguously, as both an object symbol and a metasymbol.[5] As an object symbol the set equality operation $S = T$ returns **true** when S and T have the same elements and **false** when they do not. On the other hand, we cannot simply *assume* that this operator specified in Eq. (4.14) returns **true** just when its arguments are interchangeable as sets. Although we *want* this property to be true of our data type, without proof we cannot be sure that our archetype guarantees it. Indeed, if our archetype does not guarantee this consistency between the object and metalevel uses of '=', then we must conclude that it does not adequately capture our intuitive idea of finite sets. We will produce such a proof when discussing the consistency and completeness of the archetype. For now, we suppose that Eq. (4.14) is adequate.

An advantage of developing an archetype before a prototype is that this permits us to prove things about our data type before it is implemented. For example, just on the basis of the archetypes for finite sets and well-known properties of Boolean values we can show that $S \cap T = T \cap S$. First observe that

$$
\begin{aligned}
x \in S \cap T &= x \in S \wedge x \in T &&\text{Eq. (4.11)}\\
&= x \in T \wedge x \in S &&\text{commutativity of } \wedge\\
&= x \in T \cap S &&\text{Eq. (4.11)}
\end{aligned}
$$

Since for all x, $x \in S \cap T = x \in T \cap S$, by the Axiom of Extensionality we know that $S \cap T = T \cap S$. Many other properties are just as easy to prove.

---

5. Note that in Eq. (4.14) the first occurrence of '=' is an object use; the second is a meta-use.

Exercise 4.9: Show that finset τ is a *distributive lattice* over $\cap$ and $\cup$. That is, show that the $\cap$ and $\cup$ operations are idempotent, commutative, associative, absorptive, and distributive over one another:

a. $S \cap S = S \cup S = S$ (idempotent)

b. $S \cup T = T \cup S,\ S \cap T = T \cap S$ (commutative)

c. $S \cap (T \cap U) = (S \cap T) \cap U$ (associative)
   $S \cup (T \cup U) = (S \cup T) \cup U$

d. $S \cap (S \cup T) = S \cup (S \cap T) = S$ (absorptive)

e. $S \cup (T \cap U) = (S \cup T) \cap (S \cup U)$ (distributive)
   $S \cap (T \cup U) = (S \cap T) \cup (S \cap U)$

Note: You must use well-known properties of the Booleans.

Exercise 4.10: Prove the following properties of finite sets:

a. $S \setminus S = \emptyset$

b. $\emptyset \cap S = \emptyset \setminus S = \emptyset$

c. $\emptyset \cup S = S \setminus \emptyset = S$

d. $S \setminus (T \cap U) = (S \setminus T) \cup (S \setminus U)$

e. $S \setminus (T \cup U) = (S \setminus T) \setminus U$

f. $S \cap (T \setminus U) = (S \cap T) \setminus U$

g. $(S \cup T) \setminus U = (S \setminus U) \cup (T \setminus U)$

h. $(S \cap T) \setminus U = (S \setminus U) \cap (T \setminus U)$

Exercise 4.11: Prove the following:

adjoin $(x, S) \cup T$ = adjoin $(x, S \cup T)$

Exercise 4.12: Prove the following:

adjoin $(x, S) \cap T = S \cap T$, if $x \notin T$
adjoin $(x, S) \cap T$ = adjoin $(x, S \cap T)$, if $x \in T$

Exercise 4.13: Prove the following:

adjoin (x, S) = adjoin $[x, S \setminus$ adjoin $(x, \emptyset)]$

Exercise 4.14: Prove that if $S \neq \emptyset$, then for some x and T such that $x \notin T$, $S = \text{adjoin}(x, T)$.

Exercise 4.15: Prove that if $S \neq \emptyset$ then there are x and T such that $S = \text{adjoin}(x, T)$ and $\text{card } S = 1 + \text{card } T$. (This is a basis for inductive proofs about finite sets.)

Exercise 4.16: Prove Eq. (4.12), given the definition of $\subseteq$ in Eqs. (4.13). *Hint:* Use induction on card S.

Exercise 4.17: An alternative characterization of $\subseteq$ is

$$S \subseteq T = \textbf{true, if } S \cap T = S$$
$$S \subseteq T = \textbf{false, if } S \cap T \neq S$$

Show that these conditions are equivalent to either Eq. (4.12) or Eqs. (4.13).

Exercise 4.18: Prove that $S \cup T = T$ is also equivalent any of the preceding characterizations of $\subseteq$.

Exercise 4.19: Prove the following:

$$\text{card}(S \cup T) + \text{card}(S \cap T) = \text{card } S + \text{card } T$$

Exercise 4.20: Develop an archetype for multisets.

We now discuss an important problem caused by sets having multiple abstract representations. In Section 2.8 we assured ourselves of the consistency and completeness of our axioms by considering the behavior of each operation on the two kinds of sequences, nil and $x{:}S$. Since every nonnull sequence can be written in a unique way in the form $x{:}S$, defining a function on an input in such a form led to its having a unique output. In fact, in Exercise 2.14 you investigated the reasons this uniqueness is critical.

Now we are faced with a data type in which the values do not have unique representations in terms of the constructors. In algebraic terms, the sequence data type is *free* because every constructor expression yields a different value. The finite set data type is *unfree* or *constrained* because properties such as Eqs. (4.9) force certain constructor expressions to have the same values.

To see the problems to which an unfree types can lead, suppose we include in our archetype the following axiom:

$$\text{any}[\text{adjoin}(x, S)] = x \tag{4.15}$$

The intent is to define an operation any: finset $\tau \to \tau$ that picks an element out of a set; it might be the selector we said earlier that we couldn't have.[6] We can't have this operation because Eq. (4.15) makes our archetype inconsistent. To see this, first note, as proved in Exercise 4.6, that

$$\text{adjoin } [1, \text{adjoin } (2, \varnothing)] \ = \ \text{adjoin } [2, \text{adjoin } (1, \varnothing)] \tag{4.16}$$

Hence we have two abstract representations of the same set. Now apply any to both sides of Eq. (4.16) and conclude that $1 = 2$—a contradiction. To be able to implement our archetype, we must reject Eq. (4.15).

Although Eq. (4.15) makes our archetype inconsistent, eliminating the equation does not guarantee that the archetype is consistent; there may be other inconsistencies in the axioms. To satisfy ourselves that our archetype is consistent, we could prove that all the functions are single valued by showing that their values are equal—as sets—no matter how their inputs are represented as adjoins. In effect we would prove that the truth of propositions about sets does not depend on the order of the elements between the curly braces. In Section 4.6 you will see (in a slightly different context) the effort required to accomplish this. Here we use an approach discussed in Section 4.1: establishing the consistency of the archetype by showing that it has at least one correct implementation (see Sections 4.4 through 4.6).

4.3 Applications of Finite Sets

Let's consider some simple applications of finite sets. First we develop a function for constructing finite sets from sequences, finset←seqn:[7]

$$\text{finset←seqn: } \tau^* \ \to \ \text{finset } \tau$$

For example

$$\text{finset←seqn } <3, 5, 8> \ = \ \{3, 5, 8\}$$

This operation provides a bridge between finite sets and the sequence manipulation functions we have already developed. Our intention is that if L is a sequence and $S = \text{finset←seqn } L$, then

$$x \in S \ = \ \text{member } (x, L)$$

---

6. Functions such as any that select an unspecified element of data structure are called *choice* functions.
7. The arrow in finset←seqn is not an operator but is just part of the name of the function; it should be read, "finite set from sequence."

(You defined the member function in Exercise 3.17.) Thus we have the following identity:

$$x \in \text{finset}\leftarrow\text{seqn } L \ = \ \text{member } (x, L) \tag{4.17}$$

This operation is easy to implement; it is simply an **adjoin**-reduction of the sequence of elements:

$$\text{finset}\leftarrow\text{seqn } L \ \equiv \ \begin{cases} \varnothing, \text{ if null } L \\ \textbf{else adjoin } [\text{first } L, \text{ finset}\leftarrow\text{seqn } (\text{rest } L)] \end{cases}$$

Exercise 4.21: Prove that the definition of finset←seqn satisfies Eq. (4.17).

Next we consider some uses of sets involving texts represented as sequences of words (strings). For example, the text "to be or not to be" is represented by the sequence

$$T \ = \ <\text{'to', 'be', 'or', 'not', 'to', 'be'}>$$

In general, suppose $T \in \textbf{string}^*$ is any such text; it might represent a literary work. We can obtain a finite set representing the vocabulary of T by the expression finset←seqn T. Then the vocabulary size of T is card (finset←seqn T).

Now suppose we have two texts, $T, U \in \textbf{string}^*$, and that we want to find their common vocabulary. We simply take the intersection of the two sets:

$$\text{finset}\leftarrow\text{seqn } T \ \cap \ \text{finset}\leftarrow\text{seqn } U$$

If we want to know the proportion of words in T that also occur in U, we write

$$\frac{\text{card } (T' \cap U')}{\text{card } T'} \quad \begin{array}{l} \textbf{where} \ \ T' \equiv \text{finset}\leftarrow\text{seqn } T \\ \textbf{and} \ \ U' \equiv \text{finset}\leftarrow\text{seqn } U \end{array}$$

Suppose that $L \in (\textbf{string}^*)^*$ is a sequence of texts (i.e., a sequence of word sequences) and for each text we want to know the size of its vocabulary relative to the total vocabulary of all the texts. That is, we want to compute a sequence $M \in \mathbb{R}^*$ such that M_i is the proportion of words used in L_i, relative to the words used in all the texts.

Our first step is to convert the sequence of texts into a sequence of the vocabularies of those texts. If we call the latter sequence S, we can see that

$S \in$ (finset **string**)*

S is computed by mapping finset←seqn across L:

$S \equiv$ map_set L

$\qquad$ **where** map_set $L \equiv \begin{cases} \text{nil, if null } L \\ \textbf{else } \text{finset←seqn (first } L) \text{ : map\_set (rest } L) \end{cases}$

The total vocabulary, $V \in$ finset **string**, used in the texts is just the union reduction of S:

$V \equiv$ union S

$\qquad$ **where** union $S \equiv \begin{cases} \varnothing, \text{ if null } S \\ \textbf{else } \text{first } S \cup \text{union (rest } S) \end{cases}$ $\qquad$ (4.18)

Therefore the total vocabulary size v is just the cardinality of the total vocabulary:

$v \equiv$ card V

To get the relative size of the vocabularies, we compute our proportions relative to v. Now, for each of the text vocabularies S_i we want to compute the proportion of the total vocabulary in S_i, or (card S_i)/v. Further, we want to do this for each text vocabulary S_i, so we must map this function across the sequence S. Therefore the solution is

$M \equiv$ map_relcard S

$\qquad$ **where** map_relcard $S \equiv \begin{cases} \text{nil, if null } S \\ \textbf{else } [\text{card (first } S) \ / \ v] : \text{map\_relcard (rest } S) \end{cases}$

Exercise 4.22:   Think of a useful application for finite sets and program it.

Exercise 4.23:   Compare and contrast this finite set data type with finite sets in Pascal.

4.4 Development of a Prototype for Finite Sets

How can we implement finite sets? Although there are many possibilities (e.g., arrays, hash tables, bit vectors, sorted arrays, B-trees), the purposes of a prototype are best served by a simple implementation. The obvious choice in our case is to represent a finite set by a sequence containing its elements. Since order and multiplicity of elements are preserved by sequences but are ignored by sets, however, we will have many sequences representing the same set. For example, the set {1, 2, 3} may be represented by any of these sequences:

$$<1, 2, 3>, <1, 3, 2>, <2, 1, 3>, <2, 3, 1>, <3, 1, 2>,$$
$$<3, 2, 1>, <1, 1, 2, 3>, <1, 2, 3, 1>, \cdots$$

We say that there are many *physical* or *concrete* representations for the same *abstract* value.

Compare this with our earlier observation that sets also have multiple *abstract* representations. A value has multiple abstract representations when several constructor expressions have that value. For example, every nonnull sequence has a unique abstract representation as a composition of prefix applications, but any set (with at least two members) has multiple abstract representations as compositions of adjoins.[8] Notice that the issue of multiple abstract representation makes no reference to the implementation of the data type; that is the meaning of *abstract*. In fact, whether a data type has multiple abstract representations is completely independent of whether it is implemented with multiple concrete representations. For example, even though sets have multiple abstract representations, we could implement them in a way that assigns a unique concrete representation to every set (say, by sorting the elements and eliminating duplicates). Conversely, even though sequences have unique abstract representations, we could implement them in a way that permitted one abstract sequence to be represented by a variety of different data structures (say, by permitting links to be omitted between elements in contiguous memory locations). The relationship between multiple representations at the abstract and concrete levels can be visualized as in Fig. 4.3.

The nonunique concrete representation of sets carries both costs and benefits. For example, we could ensure that there is exactly one representation of each set by requiring the sequence to be sorted and duplicate-free. There are two difficulties. First, this requires the base type τ to have a total order relation (which it may not).[9] Second, it requires the operations (such as union) to maintain the order, which complicates their definition and makes the prototype difficult to prove.

On the other hand, one cost of nonunique concrete representation is that we must ensure that the implementations of the set operations hide the fact that there may be many distinct sequences representing the same

---

8. Recall (p. 126) that the sequence data type is *free*, but the set data type is *constrained*.
9. For example, finite sets have a partial order ($\subseteq$) but not a total order. Another example is the finite function type discussed later in this chapter.

Figure 4.3 Multiple representation at abstract and concrete levels.

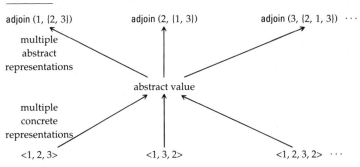

abstract set. For example, we cannot implement set equality by the equality test on the sequences,

$$S = T \equiv \text{equal } (S, T)$$

since <1, 2> and <2, 1, 1> are different sequences that represent the same set. We want to hide from the user of the finset abstract type the details of the implementation (such as nonunique concrete representation), which permits the implementation of finset to be changed without affecting programs that use the abstract type.

Let's consider how each finite set operation can be implemented in terms of sequence operations. The implementations of empty and adjoined sets are obvious:

$$\emptyset \equiv <> \tag{4.19}$$
$$\text{adjoin } (x, S) \equiv x : S$$

Note that adjoin may introduce duplicates into the set, as permitted by our representation.[10] The empty test is just the null test:

$$\text{empty } S \equiv \text{null } S \tag{4.20}$$

Also, given our representation scheme, the membership operation on sets is just the membership operation on sequences:

$$x \in S \equiv \text{member } (x, S) \tag{4.21}$$

Next consider the dyadic (binary) set operators. Union is easy since we can simply catenate the sequences representing the sets:

---

10. By 'representation' we mean the concrete representation unless otherwise specified.

Figure 4.4 Partial prototype for finite set types.

---

abstract type finset $\tau \equiv \tau^*$

$\varnothing \equiv$ nil

adjoin $(x, S) \equiv x : S$

empty $S \equiv$ null S

$x \in S \equiv$ member (x, S)

card $S \equiv$ *exercise*

$S \cup T \equiv S \wedge T$

$$S \cap T \equiv \begin{cases} \varnothing, \text{ if empty } S \\ \textbf{else} \text{ adjoin (first } S, \text{ rest } S \cap T), \text{ if first } S \in T \\ \textbf{else} \text{ rest } S \cap T \end{cases}$$

$S \setminus T \equiv$ *exercise*

$S \subseteq T \equiv$ empty $(S \setminus T)$

$x \notin S \equiv \neg (x \in S)$

$S = T \equiv S \subseteq T \wedge T \subseteq S$

$S \neq T \equiv \neg (S = T)$

$S \subset T \equiv S \subseteq T \wedge S \neq T$

$$S \cup T \equiv S \wedge T \tag{4.22}$$

This too may introduce duplicates. For example, to compute the union $\{1, 2, 3\} \cup \{2, 3, 4\}$ we form the catenation

$$<1, 2, 3> \wedge <2, 3, 4> = <1, 2, 3, 2, 3, 4>$$

which represents the set $\{1, 2, 3, 4\}$, albeit with some redundancy.

Now consider intersection. We want the elements of $S \cap T$ to be just those elements of S that are also in T. Consider the simple case first: If S is empty, then so is $S \cap T$. This gives us the base for our recursion. Now suppose that S has at least one element x. If x is in T, then we want it to be in the intersection; if it's not in T, then it shouldn't be in the intersection. The recursive implementation follows immediately:[11]

$$S \cap T \equiv \begin{cases} \varnothing, \text{ if empty } S \\ \textbf{else} \text{ adjoin (first } S, \text{ rest } S \cap T), \text{ if first } S \in T \\ \textbf{else} \text{ rest } S \cap T \end{cases} \tag{4.23}$$

---

11. You may be confused to see set and sequence operators used together. This is permitted only when we are implementing the finite set data type because, from the viewpoint of the implementor, sets *are* sequences. Elsewhere, sets and sequences are considered different types (see Section 4.5).

This definition also follows from the following three equations, as proved in Exercises 4.10(b) and 4.12:

$$\varnothing \cap T = \varnothing \tag{4.24}$$
$$\mathsf{adjoin}\,(x,\,S) \cap T = \mathsf{adjoin}\,(x,\,S \cap T),\ \text{if}\ x \in T$$
$$\mathsf{adjoin}\,(x,\,S) \cap T = S \cap T,\ \text{if}\ x \notin T$$

Set difference is analogous to intersection, except that we include a member of S in the result only if it's *not* a member of T. Clearly most of the prototype implementations of the other operations follow the same pattern: They are either simple recursive definitions or definitions in terms of already defined operations (see Fig. 4.4). Some issues relating to the type finset τ itself as discussed in the next section.

Exercise 4.24: Write a recursive definition of card. *Hint:* Recall Eqs. (4.7) and (4.8).

Exercise 4.25: Write a recursive definition of \.

Exercise 4.26: Write a definition of $\cup$ that eliminates duplicates (assuming there are none in the input sequences). *Hint:* You can do this nonrecursively by using functions you've already defined.

Exercise 4.27: Write a recursive definition of $\subseteq$. *Hint:* Look at the archetype.

Exercise 4.28: Translate the definitions of $\cap$, \, and $\subseteq$ into LISP or some other language.

Exercise 4.29: Develop a prototype implementation of finite sets based on sequences with no duplicates.

4.5 Typing in Applicative Languages

In this section we consider two orthogonal issues in the type system of a language: (1) *strong typing* versus *weak typing* and (2) *dynamic typing* versus *static typing*. A language is strongly typed if it enforces type abstractions, and weakly typed otherwise. All applicative languages (and almost all modern languages) have strong *primitive* types. That is, users are not permitted to violate the *built-in* type abstractions. For example, they cannot add the integer value 17 to the Boolean value **true**, even though **true** might be represented by the same bit pattern as the integer value 1. Strong typing interprets the type's archetype as a specification of the *most* the user can do: If an operation is not specified in the archetype, it is not allowed.[12]

Weak typing is more flexible than strong typing. For example, if we know that the Boolean values **false** and **true** are represented by the same bit patterns as the integers 0 and 1, then weak typing permits us to "add" the Boolean value $m > 0$ to the integer n. Thus interpreting $n + (m > 0)$ as an integer yields n if $(m > 0) = $ **false** and $n + 1$ if $(m > 0) = $ **true**. With strong typing one would have to write

$$n + \text{if } (m > 0, 0, 1)$$

to get the same effect. Being able to write $n + (m > 0)$ is convenient and flexible, but requires one to know the concrete representations of **true** and **false**.

Strong typing trades off its *security* and *portability* against the *flexibility* of weak typing. Since security is essential for reliable programming and since portability helps preserve the software investment, it is hardly surprising that modern programming languages opt for strong typing. In this book we assume that all primitive types are strong.

So far we have discussed strong typing only in conjunction with the primitive types. We turn now to user-defined types, where the tradeoffs are much less clear. To see the issues, suppose that we intend to define a new data type, finset τ, and that we intend to represent finite sets by sequences of type τ.

Is finset τ a strong type or a weak type? If weak, then every set is really just a sequence that we are thinking of, for the moment, as a set. Thus, whenever convenient, we can choose to think of a set as a sequence and write, for example, rest $(S \cap T)$. This is in fact exactly the approach taken by LISP, in which an expression such as

(rest (intersection S T))

is perfectly legal.[13] As is usual with weak typing, its less constrained nature permits flexibility that is often useful. Further, so long as the *primitive* types are strongly typed, weak typing of *user-defined* types does not impede portability. Weak typing, however, does prevent *representation independence*.

What is the value of representation independence? Lehman's (1980, 1981) First Law of Software Engineering says, "Programs that are used

---

12. Of course, operations that are defined *in terms* of those in the archetype are permitted.
13. Common LISP permits 'rest' in addition to the older 'cdr'.

will evolve or decay into uselessness." Software often evolves by changing (concrete) representation. For example, we might initially implement finite sets as sequences without duplicates, but later decide that sequences with duplicates are better (perhaps because we are doing a lot of unions and duplicates arise rarely). When the representation of a data type is changed, it is necessary to investigate every module in the program that depends on the representation. To minimize the number of modules impacted by a change of representation, it is usually worthwhile to restrict representation dependence to the module that *implements* the type abstraction. All the other modules—the ones that *use* the type abstraction—should be representation independent. Thus representation independence facilitates program evolution, which helps preserve the software investment. In summary, fundamental economic (and hence engineering) considerations suggest that primitive types should *always* be strong and that user-defined type abstractions should *usually* be strong.

In engineering, however, nothing is ever this simple. Certainly type abstractions exist that are of such local use in a program that it is not worthwhile to make them strong; such abstractions exist only in the programmer's mind. Why isn't strong typing always preferable? There are costs that must be traded off against the benefits. First is flexibility: It might be very convenient to think of a sequence as a set of some times and as a sequence at other times. Thus notice that weak typing would permit all the operations of sequences to be automatically extended to work on sets. This applies not only to primitives, such as first and rest, but also to user-defined functions. For example, if we've defined a map_sin function that operates on sequences, then we have for free a map_sin that works on sets.

There is a danger: We may generate things that we think are sets but that really aren't. This may happen by accidently violating the invariants that the representation is assumed to obey, such as a requirement that there be no duplicates in the sequences representing sets. This could be caused, for example, by doing a prefix operation on a set, thereby directly introducing a duplicate. You would never do such a thing, you say? Unfortunately, you might do it accidentally. For example, since sin θ = sin (θ + 360°), applying map_sin to a sequence with no duplicates may generate a sequence that has duplicates. There is no guarantee that the invariants of the type abstraction are preserved.

Another cost of strong typing is *verbosity*. To see this, suppose that strings were represented as sequences of characters and that they were weakly typed. Then we could use rest *s* to return all of a character string except the first character. On the other hand, if strings are strongly typed, then either we must depend on the type designer to provide a "rest for strings" (say, string_rest *s*), or we must get its effect by a circumlocution such as this:

string←seqn [rest (seqn←string s)]

This of course presumes that the type designer has had the foresight to provide us with the string←seqn and seqn←string conversion functions.

The preceding verbose expression could be improved by using shorter names for the conversion functions. Also, we could define a new function string_rest if we intended to use it often enough:

string_rest s ≡ string←seqn [rest (seqn←string s)]

In either case we've complicated the program.

A different way to look at this issue is that the strongly typed example is more *explicit*. We've said exactly what we intend: Take this string, convert it to a sequence, take the rest of it, and convert the result back to a string. Verbosity and explicitness are really two sides of the same coin. They both mean "more words"; the difference is that "verbosity" suggests that the additional words are bad, whereas "explicitness" suggests they are good.

Nowadays, with increased concern for making programs understandable, we tend to focus on the good aspects of "more words" and choose explicitness at the expense of verbosity. Therefore, in this book most of our type abstractions are strong.[14] The pros and cons of strong versus weak typing of user-defined data types are summarized in Table 4.1.

Granted that we want the ability to have strong user-defined types, how can we accomplish this in an applicative language? Let us note that although most applicative languages have strong primitive types, few

Table 4.1. Strong versus weak user-defined types.

Strong	Weak
Data abstraction and information hiding enforced (pro)	Data abstraction and information hiding not enforced (con)
Operations defined on concrete type not automatically extended to abstract type (con)	Operations defined on concrete type automatically extended to abstract type (pro)
More explicit (pro)	Less explicit (con)
More verbose (con)	Less verbose (pro)
Facilitate multiple concrete representation (pro)	Do not facilitate multiple concrete representation (con)

14. Exceptions are the arithmetic expression trees (see Chapter 5) and the infinite types (see Chapter 7).

protect the programmer's type abstractions.[15] Thus we cannot present the *usual* construct for the definition of strong types; instead we present an approach based on Turner's (1985b) Miranda language.

The basic problem is that to some functions finset τ is a strong type whereas to others it's a weak type. In particular, our policy of strong typing tells us that the functions that *use* finset τ should see it as a different type from τ^* and every other type. On the other hand, the functions that *implement* finset τ must see this type as just another name for τ^* since they must apply sequence operations to the sequences representing sets.

How can we distinguish contexts in which finset τ must be interpreted strongly from those in which it must be interpreted weakly? For our purposes we can say that a type is interpreted strongly everywhere *except* in the implementations of the primitive functions of the abstract type, in which it is interpreted weakly according to the type definition

type finset $\tau \equiv \tau^*$

We know which functions these are; they are listed in the Syntax part of the archetype. This strictly limits the region of the program over which an abstract type is interpreted weakly.

Let's briefly turn to the issue of static versus dynamic typing, which is commonly confused with that of strong versus weak typing. A language is *statically typed* if all or most of its type checking can be accomplished at compile time; it is *dynamically typed* if its type checking must be performed at run time. Notice that this issue is completely orthogonal to that of strong versus weak typing (although a language that uses weak typing throughout will have little or no type checking at any time). Strong typing means that the type abstractions are enforced. Whether that enforcement takes place at run time or compile time is an independent issue.

What about applicative languages? Is their typing static or dynamic? Traditionally, applicative languages have been dynamically typed, one of the many characteristics that applicative programming has inherited from LISP. Dynamic typing is very flexible and adds relatively little overhead to the interpreters often used to execute applicative programs. When performance is important, however, programs are usually compiled rather than interpreted, and run-time type checking significantly slows down the execution speed of compiled code. This is one reason for a trend in recent years toward statically typed applicative languages.

What about convenience? Although it's a bother to have to state the types of things, many consider this worthwhile. Stating the signature of a function is good documentation, providing useful information to all pro-

---

15. Exceptions are LCF (Gordon, Milner, and Wadsworth 1979), ML (MacQueen 1984), and Miranda (Turner 1985).

gram readers, computers as well as human beings. Whether a type signature is stated in a comment, for human consumption, or as a declaration, for human and machine consumption, seems to entail little difference in convenience. Furthermore, powerful *type-inference systems* are now available that can deduce at compile time the types of most expressions in a program. Thus type declarations are almost always optional.

What about flexibility? Static typing does not necessarily lose the ability to have functions that work on things belonging to many different types. A sufficiently rich static type system has most of the *useful* flexibility of dynamic typing. In particular, if the language supports parameterized types (such as finset) and polymorphic procedures (such as elt), then little is lost.

On the other hand, static typing facilitates proving things about programs. In fact, knowing the type of a thing is often just what we need to crack a proof. You have already seen cases where we made use of the fact that something was of type finset τ, and therefore could be written as either $\varnothing$ or adjoin (x, S). By limiting the kinds of things that can pass across function interfaces, types break up the program into units that can be proved individually. (See the following section for more examples, especially the proof that the prototype implementation satisfies the Axiom of Extensionality.)

To be able to view applicative programming as a widely applicable *methodology*, we must have programs that can be implemented in many different languages. Since it is much easier to adapt a statically typed program to a dynamically typed language than vice versa, static typing forms a better basis for a methodology. Furthermore, a methodology should support *reliable* programming. Since static typing aids reliable programming by both facilitating proofs and permitting compile-time checking of type interfaces, we assume static typing throughout this book.

4.6 Proof of Finite Set Prototype

Although a prototype implementation is supposed to prove the consistency and computational feasibility of the archetype, it proves nothing unless it is known to be a correct implementation of the archetype. Thus our next task is to prove that the prototype in Fig. 4.4 satisfies the archetype in Fig. 4.2.

The first item in the Semantics part of the archetype is the existence axiom, which says that every set can be written either as the empty set or as an adjoin:

$$\varnothing \in \text{finset } \tau \qquad\qquad (4.6)$$
$$\text{adjoin } (x, S) \in \text{finset } \tau$$
$$z \notin \text{finset } \tau \text{ otherwise}$$

But by our prototype $\varnothing \equiv$ <> and adjoin $(x, S) \equiv x:S$. When these substitutions are made in Eq. (4.6) we obtain the existence axiom for sequences (Eq. 2.3). Therefore we know Eq. (4.6) holds.

The next axioms in the archetype specify empty:

$$\text{empty } \varnothing = \textbf{true} \tag{4.2}$$
$$\text{empty } [\text{adjoin } (x, S)] = \textbf{false}$$

To prove that the prototype implementation satisfies these properties is a simple matter of substitution:

$$\text{empty } \varnothing = \text{empty nil} = \text{null nil} = \textbf{true}$$

The last equality follows by the sequence archetype.

Exercise 4.30:   Prove that the prototype satisfies

$$\text{empty } [\text{adjoin } (x, S)] = \textbf{false}$$

Exercise 4.31:   Prove that the prototype satisfies

$$x \in \varnothing = \textbf{false} \tag{4.3}$$

Exercise 4.32:   Prove that the prototype satisfies

$$x \in \text{adjoin } (y, S) = (x = y \lor x \in S) \tag{4.4}$$

Hint: Use induction on the length of the sequence representing S.

Exercise 4.33:   Prove that your prototype definition of card (Exercise 4.24) satisfies the archetype (Eqs. 4.7 and 4.8).

Next consider union; the property we must satisfy is

$$x \in S \cup T = x \in S \lor x \in T \tag{4.25}$$

We substitute the prototype definitions of union and membership into the left-hand side of this equation:

$$x \in S \cup T = x \in (S \wedge T) = \text{member } (x, S \wedge T)$$

Similarly, the right-hand side of Eq. (4.25) yields

$$\text{member } (x, S) \lor \text{member } (x, T)$$

Therefore we must show that

$$\text{member}\,(x,\,S\mathbin{^}T) = \text{member}\,(x,\,S) \lor \text{member}\,(x,\,T)$$

But you proved this in Exercise 3.19.

Next we prove that the prototype implementation of intersection (Eq. 4.23) satisfies the defining axiom of intersection:

$$x \in S \cap T = x \in S \land x \in T \qquad\qquad (4.11)$$

Induction recapitulates recursion. Therefore, since the definition of intersection is recursive on its first argument, we should try a proof that uses induction on S. For the base of the recursion take $S = \emptyset$. By Eq. (4.23) we have $S \cap T = \emptyset$, so the left side of Eq. (4.11) is $x \in \emptyset = \textbf{false}$. Since $S = \emptyset$ we can transform the right side of Eq. (4.11) as follows:

$$x \in S \land x \in T = x \in \emptyset \land x \in T = \textbf{false} \land x \in T = \textbf{false}$$

Therefore the base of the induction is established.

For the inductive step assume that S has at least one element, so it can be written $S = y : Z$. As our inductive hypothesis we assume the desired result for all sequences shorter than S, in particular, for Z,

$$x \in Z \cap T = x \in Z \land x \in T \qquad\qquad (4.26)$$

Since $y \in T$ is either **false** or **true**, we first suppose that $y \in T = \textbf{false}$. In this case Eq. (4.23) reduces to

$$y{:}Z \cap T = Z \cap T \qquad\qquad (4.27)$$

First simplify the left-hand side of Eq. (4.11):

$$
\begin{aligned}
x \in (S \cap T) \;&=\; x \in (y{:}Z \cap T) &&\text{since } S = y{:}Z\\
&=\; x \in Z \cap T &&\text{by Eq. (4.27)}\\
&=\; x \in Z \land x \in T &&\text{by Eq. (4.26)}
\end{aligned}
$$

Now consider the right-hand side:

$$
\begin{aligned}
x \in S \land x \in T \;&=\; x \in y{:}Z \land x \in T &&\text{since } S = y{:}Z\\
&=\; (x = y \lor x \in Z) \land x \in T &&\text{Eq. (4.4)}\\
&=\; (x = y \land x \in T) \lor (x \in Z \land x \in T) &&\text{Boolean algebra}\\
&=\; x \in Z \land x \in T &&\text{since } (x{=}y \land x{\in}T) = \textbf{false}
\end{aligned}
$$

To understand the last step in this derivation, recall that $y \in T = \textbf{false}$. Therefore, if $x = y$ is **true**, then $x \in T$ is also **false**.

We have shown that Eq. (4.11) holds when $y \in T$ is **false**. The proof when it is **true** is analogous (see Exercise 4.34). Therefore we know that the prototype implementation of intersection (Eq. 4.23) satisfies its archetype (Eq. 4.11). The inductive proofs of correctness for \ and $\subseteq$ recapitulate their recursive implementations. For $\notin$, $=$, $\neq$, and $\subset$ the correctness proof is immediate because the prototype definition *is* the archetype.

Exercise 4.34: Complete the inductive proof that Eq. (4.23) satisfies Eq. (4.11) by showing that (4.11) holds when $S = y{:}Z$ and $y \in T$ is **true**.

Exercise 4.35: Prove that your prototype implementation of set difference satisfies the archetype

$$x \in S \backslash T = x \in S \wedge x \notin T$$

Exercise 4.36: Prove that your prototype definition of subset satisfies the archetype (Eqs. 4.13).

The most important property in the archetype, the *Axiom of Extensionality*, is left to prove:

$$S = S' \text{ if and only if for all } x, x \in S = x \in S' \qquad (4.10)$$

Since the axiom is an "if and only if," there are two steps to the proof.

First we must show that $S = S'$ implies that for all x, $x \in S = x \in S'$. That is, interchangeable sets have the same extension. Therefore let's suppose that $S = S'$, which means that S and S' are interchangeable in all (referentially transparent) contexts. In particular, S can be replaced by S' on the right-hand side of the equation:

$$x \in S = x \in S$$

This gives us $x \in S = x \in S'$, which it was our object to prove.

Now we turn to the second half of our proof, which is to show that if $x \in S = x \in S'$ for all x, then $S = S'$. This is more subtle since we must show that S is interchangeable with S' in all (referentially transparent) contexts. To see the subtlety, consider the sequences $S = <1, 2>$ and $S' = <2, 1, 1>$; both represent the set $\{1, 2\}$. Further, notice that $x \in S = x \in S'$ for all x (i.e., the two sequences have the same members, albeit not in the same order). On the other hand, it is easy to find contexts in which S and S' are not interchangeable. For example, first $S = 1$ and first $S' = 2$, so first $S \neq$ first S'. What's happened?

We have just shown that S and S' are not interchangeable *as sequences*, but it was never our intention to show that they be so. What we want to show is that S and S' are interchangeable *as finite sets*. That is, we must show that if $E(\cdot)$ is any context in which a *finite set* is expected, then $E(S)$ and $E(S')$ are interchangeable. We call a context $E(\cdot)$ *extensional* when the value of $E(S)$ depends only on the extension of S. If $E(\cdot)$ is an extensional context, then $E(S) = E(S')$ whenever S and S' have the same members. Therefore our task is to prove that all finite set contexts are extensional.

On the face it seems impossible to prove something about *any* context in which a set can occur. Here the notion of an abstract data type can help: Since any operation on finite sets must ultimately be defined in terms of the primitive operations of the finite set data type, we need consider only the primitive operations as potential contexts.

Let's put the proof in the form of a challenge: Suppose that S and S' are two sets with the same extension (i.e., $x \in S = x \in S'$). Can we come up with a formula (constructed from primitive operations) that can tell S and S' apart? It is easy to convince ourselves that the extensionally specified operators ($\cap$, $\cup$, $\setminus$, adjoin) cannot make this distinction. For example, as shown in Exercise 4.35, the implementation of set difference satisfies

$$x \in S \setminus T = x \in S \wedge x \notin T \tag{4.28}$$

Therefore we can derive the following:

$$
\begin{aligned}
x \in S \setminus T &= x \in S \wedge x \notin T && \text{by Eq. (4.28)} \\
&= x \in S' \wedge x \notin T && \text{since } x \in S = x \in S' \\
&= x \in S' \setminus T && \text{by Eq. (4.28)}
\end{aligned}
$$

Hence, if S and S' have the same extension, then so do $S \setminus T$ and $S' \setminus T$. The proof that $T \setminus S = T \setminus S'$ is analogous. Therefore set difference will not allow us to distinguish extensionally identical sets.

All the extensionally specified operators pass on the property of extensional identity. Therefore, if there is a way to distinguish S and S', it must use a nonextensionally specified operator ($\in$, empty, card, $\subset$, $\subseteq$, or $=$). To prove our prototype satisfies the Axiom of Extensionality, we must prove that each of these operators is an extensional context. That is, if $E(\cdot)$ is one of these operators, then $E(S) = E(S')$.

For $\in$ there's nothing to be proved, since we assume that $x \in S = x \in S'$. Next consider empty; we must show that empty S = empty S'. We know that either $S = \varnothing$ or, for some x and T, $S = $ adjoin (x, T). Suppose $S = \varnothing$; we know that empty S = **true** and $x \notin S$ for all x, and hence that $x \notin S'$ for all x. From this we can conclude that $S' = \varnothing$—if not, we could write it in the form adjoin (a, S''). But then, since $a \in$ adjoin (a, S'') always, we could conclude $a \in S'$, contradicting the fact that $x \notin S'$ for all x. On the other hand, suppose that empty S = **false**; then S can be written in the form adjoin (a, T). This tells us that $a \in S$ and therefore that $a \in S'$. We conclude that $S' \neq \emptyset$, since if it's empty $a \notin S'$. Hence empty S' is also **false**. Therefore we have proved that empty $(\cdot)$ is an extensional context.

The proof that card $(\cdot)$ is an extensional context is a straightforward induction on the length of the sequence representing S; it is left to the reader (Exercise 4.37).

Since the subset operator has two set arguments, there are two parts to the extensionality proof for it: We must show both that $S \subseteq T = S' \subseteq T$ and that $T \subseteq S = T \subseteq S'$. Consider first $S \subseteq T = S' \subseteq T$. Here we appeal to the definition $S \subseteq T = $ empty $(S \setminus T)$. But we proved earlier that set difference passes on extensional identity. Hence, for all x, $x \in S\setminus T = x \in S'\setminus T$. Now we appeal to the previously proved fact that empty $(\cdot)$ is an extensional context, concluding that empty $(S \setminus T) = $ empty $(S' \setminus T)$. Therefore $S \subseteq T = S' \subseteq T$. The proof that $T \subseteq S = T \subseteq S'$ is exactly analogous. Thus we conclude that $\subseteq$ is an extensional context for sequences representing finite sets.

The proofs for $=$ and $\subset$ follow easily. Therefore, since all the primitive operations are extensional contexts for sequences representing finite sets, we can conclude that all finite set contexts are extensional. Hence our prototype satisfies the Axiom of Extensionality.

Exercise 4.37: Prove that card $(\cdot)$ is an extensional context for sequences representing finite sets.

Exercise 4.38: Show that if S and S' have the same extension then $T \subseteq S = T \subseteq S'$.

Exercise 4.39: Prove that '$=$' is an extensional context for sequences representing finite sets. *Hint:* Simplify your proof by showing $(S = T) = (T = S)$.

Exercise 4.40: Prove that '$\subset$' is an extensional context for sequences representing finite sets.

4.7 Performance Analysis of Finite Set Prototype

Although correctness and understandability rather than efficiency were the primary criteria in designing the prototype, it is nevertheless good practice to evaluate its performance. After all, the prototype might be adequate for our purposes, and, in any case, the performance of the prototype is a good benchmark against which other implementations can be compared.

First consider the membership test $x \in S$. In the worst case x is not a member of S, so we search to the end of S, which requires $|S| + 1$ steps, where $|S|$ is the length of the sequence representing S. In the best case

x is the first element of S, so only one step is required. It is reasonable to expect that if x is in S then, on the average, about $|S|/2$ steps are required.

Let's now do the analysis more carefully. To compute the average case it's necessary to consider equally likely situations. In the absence of any information to the contrary, it's reasonable to assume that if $x \in S$ then it's equally likely to be in any of the $n = |S|$ positions of S. Hence the average time to find x will be

$$\frac{1}{n}\left[1+2+3+ \cdots +(n-1)+n\right] = \frac{1}{n}\frac{n(n+1)}{2} = \frac{n+1}{2}$$

On the other hand, if $x \notin S$, then $n+1$ steps are required. If we *assume* that there's a 50-50 chance that x is in S, then the average time under all circumstances is

$$\tfrac{1}{2}\left[\frac{n+1}{2}+n+1\right] = \tfrac{1}{2}\left[\frac{3(n+1)}{2}\right] \approx \frac{3}{4}|S|$$

This assumption is highly questionable, but the most parsimonious in the absence of any additional information.

Next consider $S \cap T$. Here the analysis is a little more complicated, so let $m = |S|$ and $n = |T|$. The definition of intersection recurs on S, so the outer loop will execute m times. Each step, however, includes a membership test on T, which may take from 1 to $n+1$ steps. In the worst case S and T are disjoint, and each membership test takes $n+1$ steps. Thus in the worst case $S \cap T$ takes $m(n+1)$ steps; that is, it's $O(mn)$.

Consider now the best case and suppose $m \le n$. In the best case each of the m elements of S will be found in T, which (if we assume the members of S are distinct) will require membership tests taking $1, 2, \ldots, m$ steps (although not necessarily in that order). Thus if $m \le n$ the total steps required are

$$1+2+3+ \cdots +m = \frac{m(m+1)}{2}$$

Exercise 4.41: Complete the best-case analysis for $m > n$.

Exercise 4.42: Describe the situation that is the worst case for $S \setminus T$ and estimate the performance of the function in this situation. Do the same for the best case.

Exercise 4.43: Describe the best-case situation for $S \subseteq T$, given $n = |S| > 0$. Analyze the best-case performance. Do the same for the worst case.

Exercise 4.44: Estimate the best- and worst-case performances of $S = T$.

Exercise 4.45: If we define $\subset$ in the following straight forward way,

$$S \subset T \equiv (S \subseteq T) \wedge (S \neq T)$$

then the operation requires us to perform three subset tests. Explain why. Design a more efficient implementation.

Exercise 4.46: Estimate the performance of the union operation (Eq. 4.18).

Exercise 4.47: Perform a *detailed* time-performance analysis (using the $T[\![\ ]\!]$ notation) of $\in$.

Exercise 4.48: Perform detailed time-performance analyses of the other finite set operations ($\cap$, \, card, $\subseteq$, =, $\subset$).

Exercise 4.49: Analyze the performance of the set implementation based on sequences without duplicates (developed in Exercise 4.29).

4.8 Choice Functions and Multiple Representations

As noted in Section 4.2, we cannot have a selector function for finite sets that reverses the adjoin operation because no unique element/set pair is adjoined to yield a given set. Later we showed that the attempt to provide a *choice function*, through the axiom

$$\text{any } [\text{adjoin } (x, S)] = x \qquad\qquad (4.15)$$

led to an inconsistent specification. The reason is that the result returned by any depends on the abstract representation of the set; sets have multiple abstract representations. Perhaps, however, there is a way to specify any that doesn't depend on the abstract representation. Before addressing this possibility, let's try to justify all the fuss over any by showing that it's quite useful.

The any function is very convenient since it permits us to break down sets in much the same way first and rest permit us to break down sequences. The ability to process the elements of a set one at a time permits many functions on finite sets to be defined in a representation-independent way. For example, the cardinality function can be defined directly by

$$\text{card } S \equiv \begin{cases} 0, & \text{if empty } S \\ \textbf{else } 1 + \text{card } (S \setminus \text{any } S) \end{cases}$$

Because any S returns an unspecified element of S, we know that $S \setminus$ any S has one fewer elements than S. In fact, the combination $S \setminus$ any S is so common, that we call it the *remainder* of the set:

$$\text{rem } S \equiv S \setminus \text{any } S \tag{4.29}$$

Similarly, any simplifies the definition of the intersection of two sets:

$$S \cap T \equiv \begin{cases} \varnothing, \text{ if empty } S \\ \textbf{else} \text{ adjoin (any } S, \text{ rem } S \cap T), \text{ if any } S \in T \\ \textbf{else} \text{ rem } S \cap T \end{cases} \tag{4.30}$$

Notice that both definitions are independent of the concrete representation of sets: It does not matter whether the sets are represented by sequences with duplicates or without duplicates, or even whether they are represented by sequences at all. This independence is desirable—it means that less of our software must be changed if the concrete representation is changed. The any function also permits $\in$, $\cup$, and $\subseteq$ to be defined independent of representation.

As a further justification of the utility of any, notice that it permits the definition of a function that converts a finite set to a sequence. This is necessary to print and display sets, and also permits the application of sequence operations such as mappings and reductions.

Exercise 4.50: Use any to define $\in$, $\cup$, and $\subseteq$.

Exercise 4.51: Use any (and rem) to define a function seqn←finset: finset $\tau \to \tau^*$ that converts a finite set to a sequence with the same members.

You can now see the usefulness of any; it's therefore worthwhile to try harder to provide it. Our previous attempt (Eq. 4.15) failed because it specified the result of any S to depend on the abstract representation of S. This was not our intention; we simply want any S to be *any* member of S. Therefore, trying to state exactly what we want, no more and no less, we postulate that

$$\text{any } S \in S = \textbf{true}, \text{ if } S \neq \varnothing \tag{4.31}$$

Let's see what we can do with this axiom. Consider the formula

$$\text{any } \{1, 2\}$$

Expanding the set denotation and applying Eqs. (4.31) and (4.4) we discover that

$$\text{any } \{1, 2\} = 1 \lor \text{any } \{1, 2\} = 2 \qquad (4.32)$$

is **true**. This seems to be just what we want: any $\{1, 2\}$ returns either 1 or 2.

Unfortunately, Eq. (4.32) is not just what we want. It must be interpreted to mean that, in a given execution of a program, either any $\{1, 2\} = 1$ or any $\{1, 2\} = 2$, but that the same choice must be made throughout the execution. We cannot interpret Eq. (4.32) to mean that each invocation of any $\{1, 2\}$ returns either 1 or 2. To see why, recall that the reflexive property of equality says that $A = A$, always. Now consider the true proposition

$$\text{any } \{1, 2\} = \text{any } \{1, 2\}$$

Taking one occurrence of any $\{1, 2\}$ to be 1 and the other to be 2 would allow us to conclude that $1 = 2$. The only way to allow this indeterminacy in any and avoid contradictions is to give up referential transparency, the ability to substitute equals—too high a cost.

More practically, recall the definition of intersection using any (Eq. 4.30). The second clause is

$$S \cap T = \text{adjoin (any } S, \text{ rem } S \cap T), \text{ if any } S \in T$$

Clearly, for this to work correctly, both invocations of any S must return the same member of S. It does no good to test one member and then adjoin another. Further, the same member must be returned by the invocation of any hidden inside the definition of rem:

$$\text{rem } S \equiv S \setminus \text{any } S \qquad (4.29)$$

In practice, the only way any can be implemented is by putting the concrete representation of the set in some standard form from which a determinate element can be selected—for example, sorting the members and then taking the first.

Let's summarize. To have both consistency and referential transparency, every function must have at most one output for a given abstract input. Therefore, even if the abstract input may have multiple abstract representations or multiple concrete representations, the value returned cannot depend on these representations. Since we want consistency and referential transparency, we cannot have an any function that simply grabs a convenient member from the set. The same argument applies to any *choice function*, that is, to any function that selects an unspecified element from a structure.

One solution is to give up any, as in Section 4.2, but the usefulness of any leads us to look for alternative solutions. As you saw, there is no problem if any is made to return the same value for all representations of the same abstract set.[16] One way to accomplish this is to guarantee that there is a unique (or *canonical*) concrete representation for each abstract set; then any can always return the same member for the same abstract set. A common canonical representation for finite sets is sorted sequences. Since we allow any values (including other sets) to be the members of a set, however, the sorting could be done only if we require the base type for every finite set type to have a total order. This could restrict the allowable finite set types. In addition, requiring the sequence elements to be sorted makes some of the set operations, such as adjoin, slower (although most will be faster), as well as more difficult to prove. Another solution is to permit multiple concrete representations of the same set, but to require that any always return the same value from any of those representations. In practice this also requires every base type to have a total order, as explained later in this section.

Thus we are permitted the following choices: (1) give up referential transparency, (2) give up any, (3) restrict ourselves to implementations that have a unique concrete representation for each abstract value, or (4) require every permissible base type to have a total order. Choice (2), giving up any, which seems simplest, has been presented so far in this chapter.

Giving up any does have costs; without any there is no general mechanism for iterating through the elements of a set—in particular, we have no way to print a finite set. Therefore let's now consider choice (4), which is predicated on the existence of a total order for each permissible base type.

First observe that most types have a natural total order. Integer and real numbers are ordered by less than; strings can be ordered lexicographically, given an ordering on the character set; Booleans can be ordered arbitrarily: **false** < **true**. Sequences can be ordered provided that their elements can be ordered. Therefore for all these types we take the total order to be denoted by the '<' symbol.

Exercise 4.52:   Define an operation $<: \tau^* \times \tau^* \to \mathbb{B}$ that compares two sequences lexicographically, based on the the < relation on their elements. For example,

$$<1, 8, 0> \ < \ <3, 0, 1> \ = \ \textbf{true}$$
$$<5, 5, 0> \ < \ <5, 4, 9> \ = \ \textbf{false}$$
$$<4, 9> \ < \ <4, 9, 0> \ = \ \textbf{true}$$

---

16. The solution adopted by Manna and Waldinger (1985) for their *choice* and *rest* functions.

Now consider types τ that do not have a natural total order. For example, there is no natural total order on finite sets. For these we simply define a total order, picking a useful, efficient order if possible. You will see later how this can be done for sets.

If we assume that the elements of finite sets can be totally ordered, there are several ways to select elements from sets. For example, we could define an operator min, which returns the minimum element of a set, specified as follows:

$$\text{min } S \in S \tag{4.33}$$
$$\text{for all } x \in S, \text{min } S \leq x$$

A more constructive definition is

$$\text{min } [\text{adjoin } (x, \varnothing)] = x \tag{4.34}$$
$$\text{min } [\text{adjoin } (x, S)] = x, \text{ if } x < \text{min } S$$
$$\text{min } [\text{adjoin } (x, S)] = \text{min } S, \text{ otherwise}$$

Since a finite set has a unique minimum, this solution does not create the difficulties that arose with any.

Exercise 4.53: Prove that Eqs. (4.33) are equivalent to Eqs. (4.34).

Exercise 4.54: Develop a prototype implementation of min and prove that is satisfies either Eqs. (4.33) or Eqs. (4.34).

Exercise 4.55: Neither Eq. (4.33) nor Eqs. (4.34) state the meaning of min $\varnothing$. Write an axiom to do this and justify your answer.

For many purposes it may be more useful to provide a function that converts a finite set into an ordered sequence:

$$\text{sort: finset } \tau \to \tau^*$$

This can be specified by the following axioms:

$$\text{member } (x, \text{sort } S) = x \in S \tag{4.35}$$
$$(\text{sort } S)_i < (\text{sort } S)_j, \text{ if } i < j$$

More constructively,

$$\text{sort } \varnothing = <> \tag{4.36}$$
$$\text{sort } [\text{adjoin } (x, \varnothing)] = <x>$$
$$\text{sort } [\text{adjoin } (x, S)] = x : \text{sort } S, \text{ if } x < \text{first } (\text{sort } S)$$

It is easy to define min if we are given sort:

$$\text{min } S \equiv \text{first (sort } S) \tag{4.37}$$

It is also quite easy to define an inefficient sort, if we're given min (see Exercise 4.58). Notice, however, that the archetype in Fig. 4.2 provides neither operation, and that sort and min can't be implemented in terms of the operations provided. Therefore, if we want them, one or the other must be put into the archetype and implemented in the prototype.

Finally, we return to the issue of total orders, which, as noted, can be provided for most types even if they don't have a natural total order. So far we have encountered only one type that does not have a natural total order: finite sets. Nevertheless we can easily define a reasonable total order on them:

$$S < T \equiv \text{sort } S < \text{sort } T$$

The ordering on sets depends on the ordering on sequences, which we've said is lexicographic. Therefore, min and sort even make sense on sets of sets, sets of sets of sets, and so forth.[17]

Exercise 4.56: Prove that the implementation of min in Eq. (4.37) satisfies either Eqs. (4.33) or Eqs. (4.34).

Exercise 4.57: Prove that Eqs. (4.35) and (4.36) are equivalent.

Exercise 4.58: Use the min function to implement sort. Prove your implementation satisfies either Eqs. (4.35) or Eqs. (4.36). What is the name of the sort you have implemented?

Exercise 4.59: Develop a prototype implementation of sort and prove that it satisfies either Eqs. (4.35) or Eqs. (4.36).

Exercise 4.60: Write a formula that returns a sorted sequence of the common vocabulary of texts (string sequences) S and T.

Exercise 4.61: Define a function max that returns the maximum element of a set.

Exercise 4.62: Write a formula that returns the elements of a set in *ascending* order.

---

17. In Section 4.9 you meet another type without a natural total order, finite functions, for which a reasonable order can also be defined.

Exercise 4.63: Define a function img_sin: finset $\mathbb{R} \to$ finset $\mathbb{R}$ so that img_sin S is the image of the set S under the sine function. That is, $\sin \theta \in$ img_sin S if and only if $\theta \in S$. *Hint:* Use sort and map_sin.

Exercise 4.64: Define a function cart: (finset τ) $\times$ (finset τ') $\to$ finset ($\tau \times \tau'$) that computes the Cartesian product of two sets. That is,[18]

$$(x, y) \in \text{cart}\,(S, T) = x \in S \wedge y \in T$$

Prove that your definition is correct and estimate its performance. *Hint:* Use min or sort.

Exercise 4.65: Compare the performance of two implementations of cart, one using min, the other using sort. Assume that the sort function works in $O(n \log n)$ time.

4.9 Archetype for Finite Functions

The *table* is one of the most common data structures, especially in systems programs such as compilers, editors, and operating systems. A table T is composed of a number of *entries,* with each of which a *key* is associated. When the table T is presented with the key k—an operation we write fapply (T, k)—the table returns the entry having that key if such an entry exists. We require that each key have at most one associated entry; thus the table is *single-valued.*

Mathematically a table can be viewed as a finite set of ordered pairs (k, e) in which k is a key and e is the corresponding entry. This set is also required to be single valued; that is, for each k there is at most one pair (k, e) in the set. Now recall that mathematically a function is just a single-valued set of ordered pairs. Therefore a table can be thought of as a finite function (i.e., a function with a finite domain), and table lookup fapply (T, k) can be thought of as function application, $T(k)$. For this reason we use $T(k)$ and Tk as abbreviations for fapply (T, k).

We write finfunc $(D \to R)$ for the type of finite functions with domain (input) type D and range (output) type R. Hence the signature of fapply is

fapply: finfunc $(D \to R) \times D \to R$

In this section we develop an archetype and a prototype for finite functions. The notation and operators are based on (MacLennan 1973, 1975).

How can we create finite functions? Since a finite function is math-

---

18. Pairs are defined formally in Chapter 5. For now it is sufficient to know that the pair (x, y) is like the sequence $<x, y>$, except that the types of the elements need not be the same.

ematically a single-valued set of ordered pairs, we could define an operation finfunc←finset that converts a single-valued set of pairs into the equivalent finite function.

A more constructive approach is to build up a table one entry at a time by inserting entries into an initially empty table; this is the inductive approach used on all our composite data types so far. For this purpose let's name the empty table nihil. Thus fapply (nihil, k) is undefined for all k. Alternatively, we can say that the domain of nihil is the empty set.

We also need a way to add entries to tables. Although we do not actually update things in applicative languages, we can define analogous pure functions that return new tables. We can construct a table containing the pairs

$$(x_1, y_1), (x_2, y_2), \ldots, (x_n, y_n)$$

by successive applications of the *extension* function, exten:

$$\text{exten} \{ \cdots \text{exten} [\text{exten} (\text{nihil}, x_1, y_1), x_2, y_2], \ldots, x_n, y_n \} \qquad (4.38)$$

We define exten (T, k, e) to add the pair (k, e) to T only if k is not in the domain of T. Otherwise the application exten (T, k, e) is illegal. Its signature is

$$\text{exten:} \ \text{finfunc} (D \to R) \times D \times R \ \to \ \text{finfunc} (D \to R)$$

It is error-prone to write particular finite functions as large compositions of exten (e.g., Eq. 4.38). Therefore we introduce some syntactic sugar, allowing Eq. (4.38) to be written as a *finite function denotation*:

$$[x_1 \mapsto y_1, x_2 \mapsto y_2, \ldots, x_n \mapsto y_n] \qquad (4.39)$$

The arrow '$\mapsto$' should be read "maps to." Since Eq. (4.39) is defined in terms of exten, and exten is legal only if there is not already an entry for the given key, you can see that the denotation (4.39) is legal only if all the x_i are distinct.

Exercise 4.66: Without looking at the archetype, write the rewrite rules that define finite function denotations in terms of nihil and exten.

Exercise 4.67: Explain why your rewrite rules imply that all the x_i in Eq. (4.39) must be distinct.

It is also very useful to be able to delete entries from tables. We define the *restriction* of T, restr (T, k), to be a finite function just like T except that the pair whose key is k, $k \mapsto T(k)$, has been deleted. We define this operation to be *tolerant;* that is, it returns T if k is not in the domain of T.

We also define a tolerant table-updating operation:

$$\text{overl: finfunc}\, (D \rightarrow R) \times D \times R \;\rightarrow\; \text{finfunc}\, (D \rightarrow R)$$

The effect of overl (T, k, e) is the same as exten (T, k, e), except that if T already contains a pair $k \mapsto T(k)$, then this is deleted before the insertion of the new entry. Hence the overl operation can be simply defined in terms of exten:

$$\text{overl}\, (T, k, e) \;=\; \text{exten}\, [\text{restr}\, (T, k), k, e] \qquad\qquad (4.40)$$

The name for this operation, overl (overlay), reflects its tolerant nature.

Notice that because of the tolerant definition of overl, restr does not invert overl. In particular, if k is in the domain of T and $T(k) \neq e$, then

$$\text{restr}\, [\text{overl}\, (T, k, e), k] \neq T$$

The reason is that overl may throw away a previous entry for k in T. On the other hand, restr does invert the less tolerant exten operation:

$$\text{restr}\, [\text{exten}\, (T, k, e), k] = T$$

The reason is that the left-hand side is defined only if k is not in the domain of T. Hence restr throws away exactly what the exten added.

Several other operations are useful on finite functions. For example, since it is an error to write fapply (T, k) when k is not in the domain of T, it is useful to be able to determine whether a given value is in the domain of a finite function. One way to do this is to define a Boolean-valued function in_dom (T, k) that returns **true** when k is in the domain of T. An alternative approach is to define an operation dom T that returns a finite set representing the domain of T. Given dom, we can easily define in_dom:

$$\text{in\_dom}\, (T, k) \equiv k \in \text{dom}\, T$$

We cannot define dom in terms of in_dom because we would have to try all potential domain elements k to see whether in_dom (T, k) is true. Therefore we take dom as the primitive operation.

The dom operator has two other purposes. First, by requiring it to be total on finfunc $(D \rightarrow R)$, we guarantee that finite functions are indeed finite. Second, it permits us to express the *Axiom of Extensionality* for finite functions:

$$F = G \text{ if and only if } \text{dom}\, F = \text{dom}\, G \text{ and,} \qquad\qquad (4.41)$$
$$\text{for all } x \in \text{dom}\, F, F(x) = G(x)$$

This says that two finite functions are interchangeable if and only if they have the same input-output pairs. In stating this axiom, we utilize the two principal *interrogators* of the finite function type: dom and fapply. In other words, two finite functions are considered identical if the interrogators cannot discover a difference between them. This is analogous to finite sets, where $\in$ is the principal interrogator.

Figure 4.5 Archetype for finite function types.

Syntax:

finfunc $(D \to R) \in$ **type** for all $D, R \in$ **type**

nihil $\in$ finfunc $(D \to R)$
fapply: finfunc $(D \to R) \times D \to R$
dom: finfunc $(D \to R) \to$ finset D
restr: finfunc $(D \to R) \times D \to$ finfunc $(D \to R)$
exten: finfunc $(D \to R) \times D \times R \to$ finfunc $(D \to R)$
overl: finfunc $(D \to R) \times D \times R \to$ finfunc $(D \to R)$
=, $\neq$: finfunc $(D \to R) \times$ finfunc $(D \to R) \to \mathbb{B}$

$Fx \Rightarrow$ fapply (F, x)
$[\,] \Rightarrow$ nihil
$[x_1 \mapsto y_1, x_2 \mapsto y_2, \ldots, x_n \mapsto y_n] \Rightarrow$ exten $([x_2 \mapsto y_2, \ldots, x_n \mapsto y_n], x_1, y_1)$

Semantics:

nihil $\in$ finfunc $(D \to R)$
exten $(F, x, y) \in$ finfunc $(D \to R)$, if $x \notin$ dom F
$z \notin$ finfunc $(D \to R)$ otherwise

fapply (nihil, x) $\neq y$
fapply [exten $(F, x, y), x$] $= y$
fapply [exten $(F, x, y), z$] $=$ fapply (F, z), if $x \neq z$

restr (nihil, x) $=$ nihil
restr [exten $(F, x, y), x$] $= F$
restr [exten $(F, x, y), z$] $=$ exten [restr $(F, z), x, y$], if $x \neq z$

dom nihil $= \varnothing$
dom [exten (F, x, y)] $=$ dom $F \cup \{x\}$
dom is a total function on finfunc $(D \to R)$

overl $(F, x, y) =$ exten [restr $(F, x), x, y$]

$F = G$ if and only if dom $F =$ dom G,
  and for all $x \in$ dom $F, Fx = Gx$

$(F = G) =$ **true**, if $F = G$
$(F = G) =$ **false**, if $F \neq G$
$(F \neq F) = \neg (F = G)$

Pragmatics:

The fapply, dom, exten, restr, and overl operations take time at most proportional to the number of pairs in the finite function.

We have specified that the object-level equality and inequality operators are consistent with the metalevel operators by

$$(F = G) = \textbf{true}, \ \text{if} \ F = G$$
$$(F = G) = \textbf{false}, \ \text{if} \ F \neq G$$

The left occurrence of '=' in each case is object level; the right, metalevel.

The archetype for finite functions appears in Fig. 4.5. As usual, we show the effect of each operator on each of the classes of finite functions (nihil and non-nihil). This ensures us of the completeness of our axioms; consistency will be established by the prototype.

Exercise 4.68: Summarize in words each of the properties in the archetype for finite functions.

Exercise 4.69: Prove or disprove that, for all finite functions F,

exten [restr $(F, x), x, y$] $= F$

That is, exten inverts restr.

Exercise 4.70: Prove the following:

a. fapply [overl $(F, x, y), x$] $= y$

b. fapply [overl $(F, x, y), z$] $=$ fapply (F, z), if $x \neq z$

c. restr [overl $(F, x, y), x$] $= F$, if $x \notin$ dom F

d. restr [overl $(F, x, y), z$] $=$ overl [restr $(F, z), x, y$], if $x \neq z$

e. dom [overl (F, x, y)] $=$ dom $F \cup \{x\}$

f. exten [restr $(F, x), x, F(x)$] $= F$

g. fapply [restr $(F, x), x$] $\neq y$

h. fapply [restr $(F, x), z$] $=$ fapply (F, z), for $x \neq z$

Exercise 4.71: Write a recursive function finfunc←seqn that converts a sequence of pairs into a corresponding finite function. Earlier pairs should take precedence over later pairs with the same first element. Prove that your definition satisfies the following identities:

finfunc←seqn nil $=$ nihil
finfunc←seqn [$(x, y) : S$] $=$ overl (finfunc←seqn S, x, y)

Exercise 4.72: Prove the following:

a. exten [exten $(F, x, y), x', y'$] = exten [exten $(F, x', y'), x, y$]

b. overl [overl $(F, x, y), x, y'$] = overl (F, x, y')

Exercise 4.73: Prove the following:

a. exten $([x_1 \mapsto y_1, \ldots, x_n \mapsto y_n], x, y) = [x \mapsto y, x_1 \mapsto y_1, \ldots, x_n \mapsto y_n]$

b. fapply $([x_1 \mapsto y_1, \ldots, x_k \mapsto y_k, \ldots, x_n \mapsto y_n], x_k) = y_k$

c. restr $([x_1 \mapsto y_1, \ldots, x_k \mapsto y_k, \ldots, x_n \mapsto y_n], x_k)$
   $= [x_1 \mapsto y_1, \ldots, x_{k-1} \mapsto y_{k-1}, x_{k+1} \mapsto y_{k+1}, \ldots, x_n \mapsto y_n]$

d. overl $([x_1 \mapsto y_1, \ldots, x_k \mapsto y_k, \ldots, x_n \mapsto y_n], x_k, y)$
   $= [x_1 \mapsto y_1, \ldots, x_k \mapsto y, \ldots, x_n \mapsto y_n]$

e. dom $[x_1 \mapsto y_1, \ldots, x_n \mapsto y_n] = \{x_1, \ldots, x_n\}$

f. $[\ldots, x_i \mapsto y_i, \ldots, x_j \mapsto y_j, \ldots] = [\ldots, x_j \mapsto y_j, \ldots, x_i \mapsto y_i, \ldots]$

These properties show that function denotations work in the expected way.

Exercise 4.74: Write axioms to specify a function rng that returns the range of a finite function. That is, rng F is the set of all y such that for some $x \in$ dom $F, y = F(x)$. Implement rng. *Hint:* Look at the axioms for dom; use sort for your implementation.

Exercise 4.75: Prove that

$$\text{rng } [x_1 \mapsto y_1, \ldots, x_n \mapsto y_n] = \{y_1, \ldots, y_n\}$$

Exercise 4.76: The following axioms define a different restriction operation. res (F, S) is a table containing just those pairs from F whose keys are in the finite set S. It is specified

> fapply [res $(F, S), x$] = Fx, if $x \in S$
> fapply [res $(F, S), x$] $\neq y$, otherwise

Or, more constructively,

> res: finfunc $(D \to R) \times$ finset $D \to$ finfunc $(D \to R)$
> res (nihil, S) = nihil
> res [exten $(F, x, y), S$] = exten [res $(F, S), x, y$], if $x \in S$
> res [exten $(F, x, y), S$] = res (F, S), if $x \notin S$

Implement this operation and prove that your implementation is correct. *Hint:* Use sort.

Exercise 4.77:   Implement restr in terms of res and prove that your implementation is correct.

Exercise 4.78:   Prove that

$$\text{res} ([x_1 \mapsto y_1, \ldots, x_k \mapsto y_k, \ldots, x_n \mapsto y_n], \{x_1, \ldots, x_k\}) = [x_1 \mapsto y_1, \ldots, x_k \mapsto y_k]$$

Exercise 4.79:   Define a function that overlays one finite function on another:

$$\text{ovl: finfunc} (D \to R) \times \text{finfunc} (D \to R) \to \text{finfunc} (D \to R)$$

The result of ovl (F, G) is as follows. Let $H = \text{ovl} (F, G)$; then dom H = dom $F \cup$ dom G, if $x \in$ dom F, then $Hx = Fx$. If $x \in$ dom $G \setminus$ dom F, then $Hx = Gx$. Write axioms to specify this function, implement it, and prove that your implementation is correct.

Exercise 4.80:   What are the algebraic properties of ovl (see Exercise 4.79)? Is it commutative? Associative? What is the result of an overlay with nihil?

4.10 Applications of Finite Functions

Let's consider a simple application of finite functions. We are given a text (a sequence of words) $S \in$ **string*** and wish to compute from it a frequency table $F \in$ finfunc (**string** $\to$ IN). That is, for each word $w \in S$ we want $F(w)$ to be the number of occurrences of w in S. Clearly we must iterate through the sequence S and, for each word w, add the pair $w \mapsto 1$ to the table if w was not already in it, or replace the pair $w \mapsto n$ by $w \mapsto n+1$ if it was. To be more precise, we define a function

$$\text{frequency: } \textbf{string}^* \to \text{finfunc} (\textbf{string} \to \text{IN})$$

so that $F = \text{frequency } S$. If S is null, then F is the empty table:

$$\text{frequency nil} = \text{nihil}$$

This is the base of our recursion.

Now we apply the method of differences. Suppose that we have already computed $F' \equiv \text{frequency } S$. How can we get from this to $F = \text{frequency } (w:S)$? Either $w \in$ dom F' or not; that is, either there is already an entry for w in the table or not. If not, then

$$F = \text{exten} (F', w, 1)$$

If there is, then

$$F = \text{overl} [F', w, F'(w) + 1]$$

Notice that we used the overlay operation because we want to replace the previous entry for w with the new one. Therefore we have the following recursive definition of frequency:

$$\text{frequency } S \equiv \begin{cases} \text{nihil, if null } S \\ \textbf{else } \text{freqaux [first } S, \text{ frequency (rest } S)] \end{cases}$$

$$\textbf{where } \text{freqaux } (w, F') \equiv \begin{cases} \text{exten } (F', w, 1), \text{ if } w \notin \text{dom } F' \\ \textbf{else } \text{overl } (F', w, F'w + 1) \end{cases}$$

We have defined the auxiliary function freqaux as a convenient way of naming F'.

Can this definition be simplified? Whenever we process a word w we want to increase the number of occurrences of that word by one, where a word that does not occur at all is taken to have a default occurrence count of zero. Thus we define a function

$$\text{default: finfunc } (D \to R) \times R \times D \to R$$

which allows us to provide a default value for any key not in the domain:

$$\text{default } (F, d, w) \equiv \begin{cases} Fw, \text{ if } w \in \text{dom } F \\ \textbf{else } d \end{cases}$$

Then we can express F in terms of F' as follows:

$$F = \text{overl } [F', w, \text{default } (F', 0, w) + 1]$$

Recall that the overl operation will work regardless of whether there was already an entry for w in F'. This leads to the following recursive definition of frequency:

$$\text{frequency } S \equiv \begin{cases} \text{nihil, if null } S \\ \textbf{else } \text{overl } [F', \text{first } S, \text{default } (F', 0, \text{first } S) + 1] \end{cases}$$

$$\textbf{where } F' \equiv \text{frequency (rest } S)$$

Exercise 4.81: Estimate the performance of default (F, d, x), assuming that dom F and fapply (F, x) each take time proportional to the number of pairs in F.

Exercise 4.82: Estimate the performance of the frequency function assuming that overl takes time proportional to the number of pairs in the table. What if overl is constant time?

Exercise 4.83:   Write a function image such that image (F, S) is the image of the finite set S under the finite function F. That is, $x \in S$ if and only if $Fx \in$ image (F, S). In other words, image (F, S) is the set of all Fx for x in the set S. *Hint:* Use min or sort. What will you do if some $x \in S$ is not in dom F? Discuss the alternatives and the reasons for preferring one over the others.

Exercise 4.84:   Define an operation that computes the *composition* of two finite functions, comp (F, G). That is,

fapply [comp (F, G), x] $=$ fapply [F, fapply (G, x)]

What will you do about values that are in the range of G but not in the domain of F?

Exercise 4.85:   Define an operation that computes the *inverse* of a finite function, inv F. That is, $y =$ fapply (F, x) if and only if $x =$ fapply (inv F, y). Note that inv F should be defined only if F is one-to-one. Explain.

Exercise 4.86:   Prove the following for any one-to-one finite functions F and G:

inv (inv F) $= F$
inv [comp (F, G)] $=$ comp (inv G, inv F)

Does this say anything about the meaning of composition when the range of G is not a subset of the domain of F?

4.11 Prototype for Finite Functions

Next we turn to a prototype implementation of finite functions. Since mathematically functions are just sets of pairs, and we have already introduced the type finset, the obvious implementation represents a finite function as a finite set of pairs. Unfortunately, for the reasons discussed in Section 4.8, it is difficult to process the elements of a finite set; sequences are much more convenient. Therefore we declare the abstract type finfunc

abstract type finfunc $(D \rightarrow R) \equiv (D \times R)^*$

and consider the definition of the operators. We have used '$D \times R$' for the *type* of ordered pairs whose left elements are of type D and whose right elements are of type R. Ordered pairs are discussed in detail in the next chapter; for now we need know only that the ordered pair (x, y) is very much like the two-element sequence $<x, y>$. The principal difference is that in a pair the types of x and y may differ. The left and right operations are analogous to first and second; if $P = (x, y)$, then left $P = x$ and right $P = y$.

To extend the finite function F with the pair (x, y), we simply add it to the sequence that represents the function:

$$\text{exten}\ (F,\ x,\ y)\ \equiv\ (x,\ y):F,\ \text{ if } x \notin \text{dom}\ F \tag{4.42}$$

Notice that Eq. (4.42) applies only if x is not already in the domain of the function. Since this is the only situation in which exten is defined, our prototype need not implement the case where $x \in \text{dom}\ F$. Also notice that the time for exten is a constant.

We turn next to the domain extraction operation, dom F. We would like to take each element of the sequence of pairs, extract the left element of each pair, and form a set of the results—that is, to map the left operation across the sequence of pairs. Thus the definition of dom is

$$\text{dom}\ F\ \equiv\ \text{finset} \leftarrow \text{seqn}\ (\text{map\_left}\ F)$$

The map_left operation is defined as usual (see Fig. 4.6). The performance of this implementation of dom is obviously linear in the number of entries in F.

To restrict the finite function F by eliminating x from its domain, we must delete the pair (x, Fx) from its representing sequence. This is easily done recursively; the relevant equations are

$$\text{restr}\ [(k, e):F,\ k]\ =\ F$$
$$\text{restr}\ [(k', e):F,\ k]\ =\ (k', e):\text{restr}\ (F, k),\ \text{ for } k' \neq k$$
$$\text{restr}\ (\text{nihil}, k)\ =\ \text{nihil}\ (\text{so that restr is tolerant})$$

The prototype implementation of overl follows directly from its axiom in the archetype.

Exercise 4.87: Complete the recursive definition of restr.

Exercise 4.88: Estimate the performance of this implementation of the restr operation.

We next turn to the lookup operation, fapply (F, x). We must search the sequence representing F for a pair whose first element is x. In Exercise (3.20) you defined a function assoc, which searches a sequence for a pair with a given first element:

$$\text{assoc}\ (x, S)\ \equiv\ \begin{cases} \text{second (first } S),\ \text{if } x = \text{first (first } S) \\ \textbf{else}\ \text{assoc}\ (x,\ \text{rest}\ S) \end{cases}$$

This is the basis for the prototype definition of the lookup operation:

$$\text{fapply } (F, x) \equiv \begin{cases} \text{right (first } S), \text{ if } x = \text{left (first } S) & (4.43) \\ \textbf{else } \text{fapply (rest } F, x) \end{cases}$$

The number of steps necessary to perform fapply (F, x) is the same as the number necessary to do the assoc—on the average, half the number of elements in the sequence. Therefore the number of steps for a table lookup is generally proportional to the number of entries in the table. Of course, there are more efficient ways to implement tables that still satisfy the archetype, but the purpose of the prototype is clarity, not efficiency. The prototype implementation of finite functions is summarized in Fig. 4.6.

Exercise 4.89: Prove that the prototype implementation in Fig. 4.6 satisfies the archetype in Fig. 4.5. Don't forget to prove that the Axiom of Extensionality is satisfied.

Exercise 4.90: Given the prototype implementation of fapply in Eq. (4.43), suggest a constant-time implementation of overl.

Exercise 4.91: Design an implementation of finite functions that uses hashing techniques and the elt function. Assuming that elt takes constant time, estimate the performance of the finite function operations.

Exercise 4.92: Develop an archetype and prototype for *finite relations*. See (MacLennan 1988) for some useful relational operators.

Figure 4.6 Prototype for finite functions.

abstract type finfunc $(D \rightarrow R) \equiv (D \times R)^*$

nihil $\equiv$ nil

dom $F \equiv$ finset$\leftarrow$seqn (map_left F)

$$\textbf{where } \text{map\_left } S \equiv \begin{cases} \text{nil, if null } S \\ \textbf{else } \text{left (first } S) : \text{map\_left (rest } S) \end{cases}$$

restr $(S, x) \equiv exercise$

exten $(F, x, y) \equiv (x, y) : F$

overl $(F, x, y) \equiv$ exten [restr $(F, x), x, y$]

$$\text{fapply } (F, x) \equiv \begin{cases} \text{right (first } S), \text{ if } x = \text{left (first } S) \\ \textbf{else } \text{fapply (rest } S, x) \end{cases}$$

Chapter 5

Applicative Tree Processing

5.1 Direct Products of Types

In previous chapters we investigated sequences as a way to group together data of the same type. As you know from your experience with conventional languages, however, we must often group together data of differing types. For example, Pascal and Ada provide *arrays* as a way to group *homogeneous* data, and *records* as a way to group *heterogeneous* data. As you've seen, although more flexible, our sequence data types are very similar to arrays. In this section we introduce a data type analogous to records.

For an example of a heterogeneous data structure, consider a personnel record consisting of an employee's name n (of type **string**) and hourly rate r (of type $\mathbb{R}$). We cannot represent this record as a sequence $<n, r>$ since our archetype requires the elements of a sequence to be of the same type. Why not simply eliminate this restriction and permit heterogeneous sequences? Many applicative languages do in fact do this. Unfortunately, there are problems with this simple solution. In particular, if S is a heterogeneous sequence, then we do not know the type of elt (S, i) unless we know the value of i. Thus elt $(<n, s>, i)$ is of type **string** if $i = 1$

and of type $\mathbb{R}$ if $i = 2$. Since i might be computed at run time, we cannot in general know the type of expressions such as elt (S, i) until run time. Thus permitting heterogeneous sequences would preclude most compile-time type checking and hence require dynamic typing. As discussed in Section 4.5, there are a number of reasons to prefer static typing. Therefore we require sequences to be homogeneous.

The need for heterogeneous data structures, however, remains. We will provide them, but in a way compatible with static typing. Since we want to be able to determine most types at compile time, we must give up the ability to compute selectors at run time (as with elt). This is, of course, exactly what conventional languages do. In Pascal or Ada it is permissible to compute an array selector (i.e., subscript) at run time, since all the elements of the array are of the same type. On the other hand, record selectors (i.e., field names) are fixed in the text of the program.

The data type we need has already been introduced, albeit informally. The type $T \times U$ is the type of all pairs (x, y) for which x is of type T and y is of type U. We call $T \times U$ the *direct product* of the types T and U. For example, the direct product **string** $\times \mathbb{R}$ is just the type we need for our personnel records since it is the type of all pairs (n, r), where $n \in$ **string** and $r \in \mathbb{R}$. Thus we could define a type pers_recd of personnel records

$$\textbf{type } \text{pers\_recd} \equiv \textbf{string} \times \mathbb{R} \tag{5.1}$$

and a type pers_file of sequences of personnel records

$$\textbf{type } \text{pers\_file} \equiv \text{pers\_recd}^* \tag{5.2}$$

An example of a personnel file (i.e., a value of type pers_file) is

$$<(\text{'John'}, 35.00), (\text{'Debby'}, 38.25), (\text{'Hank'}, 17.10)>$$

By replacing pers_recd by its value (Eq. 5.1), we see that the type of this file is pers_file $=$ (**string** $\times \mathbb{R})^*$.

We have described the *values* associated with the type $T \times U$—that is, the pairs (x, y) for which $x \in T$ and $y \in U$. But you know that this is an incomplete description of an *abstract data type*. To complete the description we must also specify the *primitive operators* defined on these data values. It is clear that in this case we need a *constructor* for making pairs (x, y) from their components x and y, and *selectors* for extracting the left and right components of such a pair.

For the constructor we take the comma itself. Thus, if $x \in T$ and $y \in U$, then $(x, y) \in T \times U$. For clarity we always surround applications of the comma operator with parentheses.

For selectors we define two functions left and right that extract the components of a pair:

$$\text{left } (x, y) = x \tag{5.3}$$
$$\text{right } (x, y) = y$$

The signatures of these functions, depicted in Fig. 5.1, are apparent:

left: $T \times U \to T$
right: $T \times U \dashrightarrow U$

Pairs are interchangeable just when their components are interchangeable, which leads to the following simple extensionality axiom:

$$(x, y) = (x', y') \text{ if and only if } x = x' \text{ and } y = y' \tag{5.4}$$

This is the metalevel meaning of '='. Notice that, following the policy stated in Section 4.2 (p. 119) we have also defined an object level '=' operation on pairs; $p = p'$ returns **true** when p and p' are the same pair, and **false** otherwise:

$$(p = p') = \textbf{true}, \text{ if } p = p' \tag{5.5}$$
$$(p = p') = \textbf{false}, \text{ if } p \neq p'$$

If the component types T and U have '=' operators that are consistent with the metalevel use of '=', then from Eqs. (5.4) and (5.5) we can show that

---

Figure 5.1 Signature for direct product types.

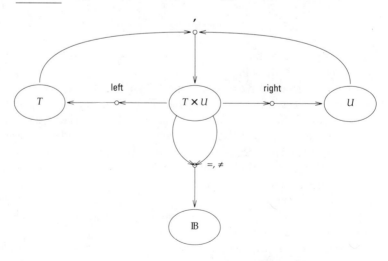

$$[(x, y) = (x', y')] \quad = \quad (x = x' \wedge y = y') \tag{5.6}$$

(See Exercise 5.2.) Thus you can see that the object-level '=' is defined (computable) on $T \times U$ if and only if there are '=' operators defined on T and U.

Exercise 5.1: Define a function

pairs: $T^* \times U^* \rightarrow (T \times U)^*$

that pairs up corresponding elements of two sequences:

pairs $(S, T) \; = \; <(S_1, T_1), (S_2, T_2), \ldots, (S_n, T_n)>$

How does this function differ from the trans2 function defined in Exercise 3.21?

Exercise 5.2: Suppose that types T and U have object-level '=' operators that are consistent with their metalevel '='. Prove that Eq. (5.6) follows from axioms (5.4) and (5.5).

So far we've considered only pairs of values. What about triples, quadruples, and, in general, n-tuples of values? For example, suppose our personnel records must include the employee's name n (of type **string**), hourly rate r (of type $\mathbb{R}$), and employee number e (of type $\mathbb{N}$). We can accomplish this by representing an employee record as a pair $(n, (r, e))$ in which the right member is itself a pair (r, e). Thus personnel records are of type **string** $\times (\mathbb{R} \times \mathbb{N})$, which we abbreviate **string** $\times \mathbb{R} \times \mathbb{N}$. That is, we take '$\times$' to be right associative. If we similarly take the comma to be right associative, then we have a very convenient notation for triples and longer tuples:

$$(n, r, e) = (n, (r, e))$$

Expressions of the form $(x_1, x_2, \ldots, x_n)$ will generally be referred to as *tuples* or *lists*. These conventions are summarized in the archetype in Fig. 5.2. Note that we have also defined T^n to be the n-fold product of T with itself. For example, since '=' takes two arguments of type $T \times U$, we can write

$$=: (T \times U)^2 \rightarrow \mathbb{B}$$

as an abbreviation for

$$=: [(T \times U) \times (T \times U)] \rightarrow \mathbb{B}$$

Figure 5.2 Archetype for direct product types.

Syntax:

$T \times U \in$ **type**, for all $T, U \in$ **type**

left: $T \times U \to T$

right: $T \times U \to U$

$=, \neq: (T \times U)^2 \to \mathbb{B}$

$T_1 \times T_2 \times \cdots \times T_n \Rightarrow T_1 \times (T_2 \times \cdots \times T_n)$

$T^1 \Rightarrow T$

$T^n \Rightarrow T \times T^{n-1}$, for $n > 1$

$(x_1, x_2, \ldots, x_n) \Rightarrow (x_1, (x_2, \ldots, x_n))$

Semantics:

$(x, y) \in T \times U$

$z \notin T \times U$ otherwise

left $(x, y) = x$

right $(x, y) = y$

$(x, y) = (x', y')$ if and only if $x = x'$ and $y = y'$

$(p = p') =$ **true**, if $p = p'$

$(p = p') =$ **false**, if $p \neq p'$

$p \neq p' = \neg (p = p')$

Pragmatics:

All operations except '=' and '$\neq$' take constant time.

The time complexity of '=' and '$\neq$' depends on that of the '=' operations of the base types.

Exercise 5.3: Define a function

total_rate: (**string** $\times \mathbb{R}$)* $\to \mathbb{R}$

such that total_rate S is the total of the hourly rates of all the personnel described in the sequence S of personnel records.

Exercise 5.4: *(Advanced)* Define a function

elt: $T^n \times \mathbb{N} \to T$

such that elt (X, i) is the ith element of the n-tuple $X \in T^n$. Note that the obvious definition will not work when $i = n$; discuss. Explain why the existence of such a function does not contradict our earlier remark that static typing does not permit the computation of selectors into heterogeneous structures.

Exercise 5.5: Consider the following function definition:

$$\text{choose } (x,\, i) \equiv \begin{cases} \text{left } x, \text{ if } i = 0 \\ \text{else right } x \end{cases}$$

If this definition were legal, it would permit the following expression, which violates static typing: choose [(**true**, 2), i]. First explain why this expression violates static typing. Then, show that the preceding definition is in fact *not* permitted since it violates the Boolean archetype (Appendix B).

Exercise 5.6: Prove by induction that

$$[(x_1, x_2, \ldots, x_n) = (y_1, y_2, \ldots, y_n)] = (x_1 = y_1 \land x_2 = y_2 \land \cdots \land x_n = y_n)$$

Next we introduce some syntactic sugar for direct product types.[1] The desirability of this sugar can be seen by extending our previous example. Suppose that in addition to name, hourly rate, and employee number, we also want to keep track of the hours worked (a real number) by each employee. The type of personnel records is then

type pers_recd $\equiv$ **string** $\times$ $\mathbb{R}$ $\times$ $\mathbb{N}$ $\times$ $\mathbb{R}$

A typical personnel record looks like this:

$p = (\text{'Harry'}, 45.15, 2049, 36.25)$

How can we access the hours worked from a personnel record such as p? Recall that the comma is right associative, so the preceding quadruple is really the nested pairs

$p = (\text{'Harry'}, (45.15, (2049, 36.25)))$

Hence Harry's hours worked is right [right (right p)], as can be seen from the following:

right p = $(45.15, (2049, 36.25))$
right (right p) = $(2049, 36.25)$
right [right (right p)] = 36.25

Similarly, Harry's employee number is left [right (right p)]. In effect, the applications of left and right are taking us through the binary tree representing p:

---

1. This notation ultimately derives from (Landin 1966). Variants of it are found in several applicative languages such as Miranda (Turner 1985b). See also (Hoare 1972).

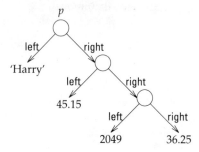

This is an unsatisfactory way to access the components of a tuple; it is too error-prone to count to the position of the desired component and assemble the correct lefts and rights. One solution is to count just once and then define *selector functions:*

$$\text{name } p \equiv \text{left } p \tag{5.7}$$
$$\text{hr\_rate } p \equiv \text{left (right } p)$$
$$\text{emp\_no } p \equiv \text{left [right (right } p)]$$
$$\text{hrs\_worked } p \equiv \text{right [right (right } p)]$$

Since we will want to define selector functions such as these for any tuple but the simplest, we introduce some syntactic sugar to make their definition more convenient and reliable. In particular, we take the declaration

structure pers_recd ≡   (5.8)
    empl (name ∈ **string**, hr_rate ∈ $\mathbb{R}$, emp_no ∈ $\mathbb{N}$, hrs_worked ∈ $\mathbb{R}$)

to define the selector functions (Eqs. 5.7) in addition to the (weak) type

    type pers_recd ≡ **string** $\times$ $\mathbb{R}$ $\times$ $\mathbb{N}$ $\times$ $\mathbb{R}$

and the *constructor function*

    empl $(n, r, e, h) \equiv (n, r, e, h)$

The value of the constructor function is explained later (p. 170); for now think of it as a documentation aid. Declaration (5.8) is analogous to the following Pascal record-type declaration:

```
type pers_recd = record
    name: string;
    hr_rate: real;
    emp_no: integer;
    hrs_worked: real
  end;
```

Pascal, like most imperative languages, permits the values of fields to be altered by assignment. In applicative languages, although we don't alter data, it is often useful to create a new tuple that is just like another, except in one field. For example, to create a record like p, but with an hourly rate 10% higher, we can write

$$\text{empl (name } p, 1.1 \times \text{hr\_rate } p, \text{ emp\_no } p, \text{ hrs\_worked } p) \qquad (5.9)$$

This solution, however, is not very readable; we must look closely to see exactly what is being done. It looks as though we're computing an entire new record, although we're simply changing one field. Also, the solution is error-prone to write; we must remember the names of all the fields in their proper order. If we happen to reverse two fields of the same type, the resulting record will be garbled. To avoid these problems we need a notation that is like an assignment in that it mentions only what is being changed. We can accomplish this by defining *substitutions* for each field. For example, let's define

$$\text{hr\_rate! } (v, p) \equiv \text{empl (name } p, v, \text{ emp\_no } p, \text{ hrs\_worked } p)$$

Then hr_rate! (v, p) is the "hourly rate substitution of v in p." Equation (5.9) is now more readable:

$$\text{hr\_rate! } (1.1 \times \text{hr\_rate } p, p)$$

Hence we assume that declaration (5.8) defines a substitution function for each field.

In general a *structure declaration* has the form

$$\textbf{structure } T \equiv C\,(\phi_1 \in T_1, \ldots, \phi_n \in T_n)$$

where T is the name of the defined type (equal to $T_1 \times \cdots \times T_n$), C is the name of the constructor function, $\phi_1, \ldots, \phi_n$ are the names of the selector functions, and $\phi_1!, \ldots, \phi_n!$ are the names of the substitution functions.

Note that the selectors and constructors together satisfy identities such as the following:

$$\text{name [empl } (n, s, k, h)] = n$$

In general,

$$\phi_i[C(x_1, x_2, \ldots, x_n)] = x_i$$

On the other hand, since $T = T_1 \times \cdots \times T_n$, such tuples also satisfy all the usual properties of tuples, such as

$$\text{right [empl } (n, s, k, h)] = (s, k, h)$$

Figure 5.3 Archetype generated by structure declarations for direct products.

Declaration:

  abstract structure $T \equiv C\,(\phi_1 \in T_1, \phi_2 \in T_2, \ldots, \phi_n \in T_n)$

Syntax:

  $T \in \textbf{type}$
  $C\colon T_1 \times T_2 \times \cdots \times T_n \to T$
  $\phi_i\colon T \to T_i$
  $\phi_i!\colon T_i \times T \to T$
  $=, \neq\colon T^2 \to \mathbb{B}$

Semantics:

  $C(x_1, \ldots, x_n) \in T$
  $z \notin T$ otherwise
  $\phi_i[C(x_1, x_2, \ldots, x_n)] = x_i$
  $\phi_i[\phi_i!\,(x, t)] = x$
  $\phi_i[\phi_j!\,(x, t)] = \phi_i t$, if $i \neq j$
  $C(x_1, \ldots, x_n) = C(y_1, \ldots, y_n)$ if and only if $x_1 = y_1, \ldots, x_n = y_n$
  $(t = t') = \textbf{true}$, if $t = t'$
  $(t = t') = \textbf{false}$, if $t \neq t'$
  $t \neq t' \;=\; \neg\,(t = t')$

Pragmatics:

  All operations except '=' and '≠' take constant time.
  The time complexity of '=' and '≠' depends on that of the '=' operations of the base types.

In many cases we would like a direct product type to be *strong;* that is, the only primitive functions defined on it should be the constructor, selectors, and substitutions listed in the structure declaration (MacLennan 1987b, 202–204, 270–272). In this case we put the word **abstract** in front of the structure declaration:

  abstract structure $T \equiv C\,(\phi_1 \in T_1, \ldots, \phi_n \in T_n)$ \hfill (5.10)

The result is that $\phi_1, \ldots, \phi_n$ and $\phi_1!, \ldots, \phi_n!$ are the *only* operations defined on things of type T, and C is the *only* operation for creating something of type T. In effect declaration (5.10) generates the archetype shown in Fig. 5.3. Note also that the archetype of Fig. 5.2 is generated by the structure declaration

  abstract structure $T \times U \equiv (\text{left} \in T, \text{right} \in U)$

Notice that an abstract structure declaration generates a *free algebra:* Objects are equal just when they're constructed in the same way. This is because there are no additional laws constraining differently constructed objects to be the same. Another way to look at this is that the equivalence relation defined by '=' is just equality of construction.[2]

Exercise 5.7: What other identities are satisfied by tuples of type pers_recd?

Exercise 5.8: Prove from the archetype in Fig. 5.3 that

$$\phi_i![x, C(x_1, \ldots, x_i, \ldots, x_n)] = C(x_1, \ldots, x, \ldots, x_n)$$

Exercise 5.9: Suppose the type of rational numbers is defined by the structure

abstract structure rational $\equiv$ ratio (numer $\in \mathbb{Z}$, denom $\in \mathbb{N}$)

It is assumed that the numerator and denominator have been reduced to lowest terms.

a. Define a function to create a rational number from two integers (i.e., reduce them to lowest terms with a positive denominator).

b. Define functions to add, subtract, multiply, divide, and negate rational numbers.

Hint: Define an auxiliary function for the greatest common divisor of two integers.

5.2 Direct Sums of Types

Sometimes it is useful to represent the members of what is intuitively one abstract type by values drawn from two or more concrete types. For example, suppose we wish to manipulate a file (sequence) of personnel records of past and present employees. For present employees we want the records to contain the employee's name, employee number, and hourly rate. For past employees we want the employee's name, an indi-

---

2. Recall that in Section 4.2 we contrasted sequences, which are free types, with sets, which are unfree.

cator of whether he or she is alive, and the year of separation. The information required is expressed in the type declarations:

structure present_empl ≡
    present(pr_name ∈ **string**, emp_no ∈ IN, hr_rate ∈ IR)
structure past_empl ≡ past(pa_name ∈ **string**, alive ∈ IB, sep_year ∈ IN)

Now we would like to say that the file is a sequence of records of *either* of the preceding types. Unfortunately this violates our requirement that sequences be homogeneous.

We need a type whose members comprise both of the preceding types. If we think of types as sets of values, then one obvious solution is to take the union of the two types. Thus, the type of our file would be

type pers_file ≡ (present_empl ∪ past_empl)*

There are problems with this solution. Suppose S ∈ pers_file is a personnel file. Then first S is of type present_empl ∪ past_empl. Unfortunately we have no functions that operate on members of union types. For example, the type of the selector hr_rate is

hr_rate: present_empl → IR

This is not compatible with the type of first S, so we cannot write hr_rate (first S). This incompatibility reflects the fact that hr_rate makes sense only for present employees; we don't know whether first S is the record of a present or past employee. Clearly we need some way to *tag* each member of the file so that we can determine whether it is of type present_empl or past_empl. This problem is common enough that it's worthwhile to develop a general solution.

Let's outline the requirements. First, we need a way to combine two types T and U into a type that contains the union of their members, but in such a way that we can determine for each member whether it came from T or U. Such a type, called the *direct sum* of the types T and U, is denoted by a boldface plus sign, $T + U$. It is also called a *discriminated union* because it discriminates between the elements that came from T and U.

The need to discriminate between the members of T and U leads to our second requirement, for operations that determine whether a given value in $T + U$ came from T or U. Thus we postulate two *discriminators*

1st?: $(T + U)$ → IB,   2nd?: $(T + U)$ → IB

such that 1st? x is **true** when x came from T and **false** when it came from U. Similarly, 2nd? x tests whether x came from U; although not necessary, it's convenient and symmetrical. We call T and U the two *variants* of the type $T + U$.

Our third requirement is for operations that convert values of type T or U to corresponding values of type $T + U$. These operations are responsible for tagging their inputs in such a way that the tags can be tested by 1st? and 2nd?. Thus we postulate two *injectors*

$$\text{1st: } T \to (T + U), \quad \text{2nd: } U \to (T + U)$$

with the intended meaning that 1st x takes a value of type T and converts it into a value of type $T + U$—specifically, a value belonging to the first variant of $T + U$.

It is also essential that there are *only* two variants of $T + U$. That is, every value $z \in (T + U)$ is either equal to 1st x for some $x \in T$, or equal to 2nd y for some $y \in U$. Hence we can completely characterize the behavior of 1st? by the equations

$$\text{1st? (1st } x) = \textbf{true}, \quad \text{1st? (2nd } y) = \textbf{false}$$

The equations for 2nd? are exactly analogous.

Finally, just as we need functions for converting from T or U to $T + U$, we also need functions for converting in the opposite directions:

$$\text{1st}^{-1}\text{: } (T + U) \to T, \quad \text{2nd}^{-1}\text{: } (T + U) \to U$$

Clearly, 1st^{-1}, when applied to an object belonging to the first variant, has the effect of removing the tag:

$$\text{1st}^{-1} \text{ (1st } x) = x$$

As suggested by the notation, 1st^{-1} forces an object belonging to the first variant of $T + U$ back to being of type T. What happens if we apply 1st^{-1} to an value belonging to the second variant? The result is undefined:

$$\text{1st}^{-1} \text{ (2nd } x) \neq z$$

The 1st^{-1} and 2nd^{-1} operations are called *filters*—they allow only those values belonging to a particular variant to pass.

The preceding operations are all we need to deal with direct sum types. Following the policy stated in Section 4.2, however, we include '=' and '≠' operations because they are computable. Figure 5.4 is the signature for direct sum types; the archetype is in Fig. 5.5.

Figure 5.4 Signature for direct sum types.

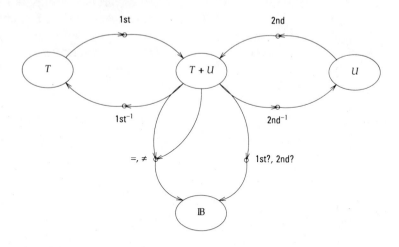

Figure 5.5 Archetype for direct sum types.

Syntax:

$$T + U \in \textbf{type}, \text{ for all } T, U \in \textbf{type}$$

1st: $T \to T + U$	2nd: $U \to T + U$
1st^{-1}: $T + U \to T$	2nd^{-1}: $T + U \to U$
1st?: $T + U \to \mathbb{B}$	2nd?: $T + U \to \mathbb{B}$

$$=, \neq: (T + U)^2 \to \mathbb{B}$$

$$T_1 + T_2 + \cdots T_n \implies T_1 + (T_2 + \cdots + T_n)$$

Semantics:

1st $x \in T + U$ 2nd $x \in T + U$

$z \notin T + U$ otherwise

1st^{-1} (1st x) $= x$	2nd^{-1} (2nd x) $= x$
1st^{-1} (2nd x) $\neq y$	2nd^{-1} (1st x) $\neq y$
1st? (1st x) $=$ **true**	2nd? (2nd x) $=$ **true**
1st? (2nd x) $=$ **false**	2nd? (1st x) $=$ **false**
1st x $=$ 1st y if and only if $x = y$	2nd x $=$ 2nd y if and only if $x = y$

$$1\text{st } x \neq 2\text{nd } y$$

$(x = y) =$ **true**, if $x = y$ $(x = y) =$ **false**, if $x \neq y$

$$(x \neq y) = \neg (x = y)$$

Pragmatics:

All operations except '=' and '$\neq$' take constant time. The time complexity of '=' and '$\neq$' depends on that of the '=' operations of the base types.

Exercise 5.10: Explain the archetype for the metalevel '=' (Fig. 5.5).

The names 1st and 2nd are not very descriptive. Therefore, as we did for direct product types, we introduce some syntactic sugar for defining direct sums. The declaration

structure $T \equiv v_1: T_1 + v_2: T_2 + \cdots + v_n: T_n$

defines T to be the direct sum $T_1 + T_2 + \cdots + T_n$, but in addition makes $v_1, v_2,..., v_n$ the names of the variants. This defines the discriminators $v_i?$, injectors v_i, and filters v_i^{-1}; see Fig. 5.6 for an archetype. Again, the resulting type is free.

Let's illustrate these structure declarations for direct sums. Suppose

---

Figure 5.6 Archetype generated by structure declarations for direct sums.

Declaration:
    abstract structure $T \equiv v_1: T_1 + v_2: T_2 + \cdots + v_n: T_n$

Syntax:
    $T \in$ **type**

    $v_i: T_i \to T$
    $v_i^{-1}: T \to T_i$
    $v_i?: T \to \mathbb{B}$
    $=, \neq: T^2 \to \mathbb{B}$

Semantics:
    $v_i x \in T$
    $z \notin T$ otherwise

    $v_i^{-1} (v_i\, x) = x$
    $v_i^{-1} (v_j\, x) \neq y$, if $i \neq j$

    $v_i? (v_i\, x) =$ **true**
    $v_i? (v_j\, x) =$ **false**, if $i \neq j$

    $v_i\, x = v_i\, y$ if and only if $x = y$
    $v_i\, x \neq v_j\, y$, if $i \neq j$

    $(x = y) =$ **true**, if $x = y$
    $(x = y) =$ **false**, if $x \neq y$
    $(x \neq y) = \neg (x = y)$

Pragmatics:
    All operations except '=' and '≠' take constant time.
    The time complexity of '=' and '≠' depends on that of the '=' operations of the base types.

we need a function to return either an integer, if it works correctly, or an error message, if something goes wrong. We define the type:

structure int_or_msg $\equiv$ int: $\mathbb{Z}$ + msg: **string**

This declaration defines the appropriate injectors, discriminators, and filters:

int: $\mathbb{Z} \rightarrow$ int_or_msg,	msg: **string** $\rightarrow$ int_or_msg
int?: int_or_msg $\rightarrow \mathbb{B}$,	msg?: int_or_msg $\rightarrow \mathbb{B}$
int^{-1}: int_or_msg $\rightarrow \mathbb{Z}$,	msg^{-1}: int_or_msg $\rightarrow$ **string**

An example use of this type is a division function that returns an error message for divisions by zero:

$$\text{quotient } (x, y) \equiv \begin{cases} \text{msg 'division by zero', if } y = 0 \\ \textbf{else } \text{int } (x \div y) \end{cases}$$

Exercise 5.11: How would you determine whether the value returned by quotient is an integer or a message? Give examples.

The preceding example illustrates an important use of direct sums: augmenting types with special values indicating error conditions. Frequently it isn't important to indicate the precise cause of the error. In such cases the variant tag itself bears the information; we could use any type as the base type of the error variant. This is called a *degenerate variant*. For example, if we cared only that an integer operation produced an error, not what the error was, we could define an "augmented" integer type by

structure augint $\equiv$ error_int: **string** + legal_int: $\mathbb{Z}$

and then use

error_int "

(i.e., a tagged empty string) to indicate an error.

Since the value to be tagged is irrelevant, it is misleading to suggest that it is relevant. Therefore for these purposes we provide a special "trivial type" that contains exactly one value, the "trivial value." There are no operations defined on the trivial value except '=', which is always **true**, and '$\neq$', which is always **false**. Since it has exactly one member, the trivial type is conventionally symbolized by '**1**'; its one and only value is represented (for reasons that will become apparent later) by '()' (the archetype is in Fig. 5.7).

Figure 5.7 Archetype for trivial type.

Syntax:

$1 \in$ **type**

$() \in \mathbf{1}$

$=, \neq: \mathbf{1}^2 \to \mathbb{B}$

Semantics:

$() \in \mathbf{1}$

$z \notin \mathbf{1}$ otherwise

$[() = ()]$ = **true**

$[() \neq ()]$ = **false**

Pragmatics:

Both operations take constant time.

The trivial type permits a less misleading way of defining augint:

structure augint $\equiv$ error_int: **1** + legal_int: $\mathbb{Z}$

Here it is explicit that the value underlying the error_int variant is irrelevant. To create the (one and only) object belonging to this variant, we write 'error_int ()', which can be used just like msg in quotient:

$$\text{quotient } (x, y) \equiv \begin{cases} \text{error\_int } (), \text{if } y = 0 \\ \textbf{else } \text{legal\_int } (x \div y) \end{cases}$$

Since the signature of this function is

quotient: $\mathbb{Z}^2 \to$ augint

the filters error_int^{-1} and legal_int^{-1} and the discriminators error_int? and legal_int? must be used to test or further process the values returned. In the next section you will see other uses of degenerate variants.

Exercise 5.12: Define a function

augsum: augint$^2 \to$ augint

such that augsum (x, y) returns $x + y$ as a legal_int if x and y are both legal_ints, but returns error_int if either (or both) x and y are error_ints.

It is frequently useful to have a direct sum type *all* of whose variants are degenerate. For example, the type

$$\textbf{structure}\ \text{color} \equiv \text{red: } \textbf{1} + \text{blue: } \textbf{1} + \text{green: } \textbf{1} \qquad (5.12)$$

has three variants, red, blue, and green, all degenerate. By expanding the archetype (Fig. 5.6) you can see that there are exactly three values of type color: red (), blue (), and green (). These values have the expected properties, such as red () = red () and red () ≠ blue (). Declaration (5.12) should remind you of the *enumeration types* found in languages such as Pascal:

> **type** color = (red, blue, green);

These are just sugarings of declarations such as (5.12). In fact, there is no reason not to write declaration (5.12)

> **structure** color ≡ red + blue + green

and not to write the values belonging to color as red, blue, and green.

Exercise 5.13: Expand declaration (5.12) according to Fig. 5.6 and simplify the resulting equations. For example,

> red () = red () since () = () (always: reflexivity).

Exercise 5.14: Define the data type **2** ≡ **1** + **1**. To what familiar data type is **2** similar? Discuss the similarities and differences.

In many cases the variants of a direct *sum* type are direct *product* types. In these cases we let the name of the product type also serve as the name of the variant. For example, if we write

$$\textbf{structure}\ \text{pers\_recd} \equiv \text{present}(\text{pr\_name} \in \textbf{string}, \text{emp\_no} \in \mathbb{N}, \text{hr\_rate} \in \mathbb{R})$$
$$+ \text{past}(\text{pa\_name} \in \textbf{string}, \text{alive} \in \mathbb{B}, \text{sep\_year} \in \mathbb{N})$$
$$(5.13)$$

then we have defined the variants present and past, including their discriminators, injectors, and filters. For example, we have

> present: $\textbf{string} \times \mathbb{N} \times \mathbb{R} \to \text{pers\_recd}$
> present?: $\text{pers\_recd} \to \mathbb{B}$
> present^{-1}: $\text{pers\_recd} \to \textbf{string} \times \mathbb{N} \times \mathbb{R}$

In addition, the selectors are defined directly on the sum type:

> hr_rate: $\text{pers\_recd} \to \mathbb{R}$

Of course hr_rate p is defined only if p belongs to the proper variant. Thus it satisfies the archetype:

hr_rate [present (n, e, r)] $= r$
hr_rate [past (n, a, s)] $\neq y$

In effect, hr_rate acts as both a filter and a selector.

Notice that both variants of pers_recd have a field representing the employee's name. These fields are named (rather arbitrarily) pr_name and pa_name, allowing all the selectors to be distinct. Since these fields intuitively represent the same attribute, it would be better to factor them out into a single attribute 'name'.[3] This leads to the type declaration

structure pers_recd $\equiv$ empl (name $\in$ **string**,   (5.14)
data $\in$ present (emp_no $\in$ IN, hr_rate $\in$ IR)
+ past (alive $\in$ IB, sep_year $\in$ IN))

(The variable part of the record is called 'data'.) A constructor for a present employee then looks like this:

empl ['Harry', present (2049, 45.15)]

The preceding structure declaration is essentially equivalent to the following Pascal variant record declaration:

```
type pers_recd = record
  name: string;
  case variant: (present, past) of
    present: (emp_no: integer; hr_rate: real);
    past: (alive: Boolean; sep_year: integer)
  end {record}
```

You can see that structure declarations are easy to translate into conventional languages.

We have introduced two new data types: direct products and direct sums. Can we provide prototype implementations of either? In the remainder of this section, we develop a prototype implementation of direct sums; in the next section we reduce sequences to direct products.

To implement the direct sum $T + U$ we need a kind of value that can hold either a value x of type T or a value y of type U. Now we know that each member (x, y) of the direct product $T \times U$ contains both a value x of

---

3. In Exercise (5.16) you are asked to prove that the type $T \times U + T \times V$ is "essentially the same as" $T \times (U + V)$.

type T and a value y of type U. This suggests a way to represent direct sums by direct products. Values belonging to the first variant of $T + U$ can be represented by pairs (x, y) in which we ignore the y component; values belonging to the second variant are pairs (x, y) in which we ignore the x component. Further, we must be able to distinguish between values belonging to the two variants. Therefore we represent each value in the sum type by a triple (v, x, y) in which v is a Boolean value specifying whether we should pay attention to the x or y component. Hence values belonging to the first variant will have the representation (**true**, x, ω_U), where ω_U is an irrelevant value of type U. Values belonging to the second variant have the representation (**false**, ω_T, y), where ω_T is an irrelevant value of type T. In summary, we represent the direct sum $T + U$ by the direct product $\mathbb{B} \times T \times U$. This is analogous to taking a Pascal variant record type such as the following:

```
type pers_recd = record
  name: string;
  case variant: (present, past) of
    present: (emp_no: integer; hr_rate: real);
    past: (alive: Boolean; sep_year: integer)
  end {record}
```

and "flattening" it to a nonvariant record type:

```
type pers_recd = record
  name: string;
  variant: (present, past);
  present: record emp_no: integer; hr_rate: real end;
  past: record alive: Boolean; sep_year: integer end
  end {record}
```

Given this prototype representation of direct sums, it is routine to produce prototype implementations for the injector, discriminator, and filter functions.

Exercise 5.15: Complete the prototype implementation of direct sum types (Fig. 5.5) in terms of direct product types (Fig. 5.2).

5.3 Recursively Defined Types

There is an apparent similarity between sequences such as <5, 9, 7, 32> and tuples such as (5, 8, 7, 32). In this section we explore in more depth the relation between sequences and tuples. In the process we will develop a powerful new way of defining data types.

Suppose that x, y, and z are values belonging to some type T. What can we say about the difference between $<x, y, z>$ and (x, y, z)? First consider their types. The three-tuple (x, y, z) is of type T^3, which is the type of all triples of Ts. On the other hand, the sequence $<x, y, z>$ is of type T^*, the type of all (finite) sequences of Ts, no matter what their length. This suggests that T^* is somehow the union of all the product types T^n. Thus we will investigate the possibility that

$$T^* = T^0 \cup T^1 \cup T^2 \cup T^3 \cup \cdots$$

One problem is immediate: We have assigned no meaning to the *zero-fold product* T^0. Clearly this should correspond to the type containing just the null sequence, but our direct product archetype (Fig. 5.2) defines no such thing as a zero tuple. We defer consideration of this problem.

The second problem is that, as shown in the previous section, union types violate static typing. Therefore, we replace the unions with direct sums

$$T^* = T^0 + T^1 + T^2 + T^3 + \cdots$$

and continue.

Yet another problem is that it seems impossible that these two things can be equal *as abstract types* since the operations defined on sequences are different from those defined on direct sums of direct products. For example, first and rest are defined on members of T^*, whereas 1st? and 2nd? are defined on the direct sum. Thus we must use a looser notion of equality. We intend that every sequence $<x_1, \ldots, x_n> \in T^*$ *correspond* to a tuple $(x_1, \ldots, x_n) \in T^n$, and vice versa. We say that there is an *isomorphism* (i.e., a one-to-one correspondence) between T^* and the sum of all the T^n:

$$T^* \cong T^0 + T^1 + T^2 + T^3 + \cdots \tag{5.15}$$

Here we use '$\cong$' as a sign of isomorphism.

Now we face the fundamental problem. We have nowhere said that infinite sums, such as Eq. (5.15), are defined. You know from your mathematical experience that infinite sums of numbers may not be defined; the limit may not exist. What makes us think that infinite direct sums of *types* exist?

The existence of the sum (5.15) is not obvious. Nevertheless, let's suppose for the time being that it does exist, and see what we can learn about its properties. This investigation will give us the insight needed to convince ourselves that the sum does in fact exist.

Equation (5.15) says that the type T^* of sequences of Ts has an infinite number of variants, including T^0, the type of zero-tuples of Ts; T^1, the type of one-tuples of Ts; T^2, the type of two-tuples of Ts; etc. Since we don't know what to make of T^0, we consider first the type T^+ of *nonnull* sequences of Ts. Then $T^* \cong T^0 + T^+$. The (alleged) equation corresponding to Eq. (5.15) is

$$T^+ \cong T^1 + T^2 + T^3 + T^4 + \cdots \qquad (5.16)$$

Since we are uncertain of the legitimacy of the infinite sum, our first goal is to rewrite (5.16) in finite form. Now what do we know about T^n? By the archetype for product types (Fig. 5.2), $T^n = T \times T^{n-1}$. Therefore Eq. (5.16) can be written

$$T^+ \cong T + (T \times T^1) + (T \times T^2) + (T \times T^3) + \cdots$$

Note that each term after the first contains the factor '$T \times$'. Going boldly forward, we factor this out, which yields

$$T^+ \cong T + T \times (T^1 + T^2 + T^3 + \cdots) \qquad (5.17)$$

The factoring is legitimate in the sense that the types $T \times (U + V)$ and $(T \times U) + (T \times V)$ are isomorphic. That is, every element of $T \times (U + V)$ can be mapped into a unique element of $(T \times U) + (T \times V)$ and vice versa.[4]

Exercise 5.16: Show

$$T \times (U + V) \cong (T \times U) + (T \times V)$$

by exhibiting total, one-to-one functions from each type to the other. That is, exhibit total, one-to-one functions

$$f: T \times (U + V) \to (T \times U) + (T \times V)$$
$$g: (T \times U) + (T \times V) \to T \times (U + V)$$

Hint: Begin by completing '$f(t, \text{1st } u) =$'.

Now notice that the parenthesized expression in Eq. (5.17) is just the right-hand side of Eq. (5.16). Therefore we substitute the left-hand side of (5.16) into (5.17) to get

$$T^+ \cong T + (T \times T^+) \qquad (5.18)$$

---

4. For a concrete example, compare the unfactored type declared in Eq. (5.13) with its factored equivalent in Eq. (5.14).

This is the finite equation we sought. Note, however, that we have made it finite at the expense of making it *recursive*. Often recursion is just a way to express an infinite formula in a finite way. On the other hand, just because we can write down a recursive equation doesn't mean that it has a solution. We must still convince ourselves that a solution exists.

Let's now switch back to the original problem, the relation between T^* and tuple types. Consider the infinite sum

$$T^* \cong T^0 + T^1 + T^2 + T^3 + \cdots \qquad (5.15)$$

To write this in finite form by using recursion, we must factor T out of all the terms of degree one or greater. If we write $T^1 \cong T \times T^0$, then we can write Eq. (5.15) as

$$T^* \cong T^0 + (T \times T^0) + (T \times T^1) + (T \times T^2) + \cdots \qquad (5.19)$$

It is not immediately obvious that T^0 has this property; we continue to defer this issue. Now we factor out T on the right-hand side of Eq. (5.19) to get

$$T^* \cong T^0 + T \times (T^0 + T^1 + T^2 + \cdots)$$

In the parentheses we see the right-hand side of Eq. (5.15), which we replace by the left-hand side to get

$$T^* \cong T^0 + T \times T^* \qquad (5.20)$$

Once again we have succeeded (albeit by rather dubious mathematics) in reducing the infinite sum (5.15) to a finite recursive equation. We can read Eq. (5.20) as follows: The type of T-sequences corresponds to the direct sum of the zero-tuples of Ts and of the pairs composed of a T and a sequence of Ts.

To convince ourselves of the meaningfulness of Eq. (5.20) let's investigate the values belonging to T^*. The archetype for direct sums (Fig. 5.5) tells us that every member z of T^* belongs to one of two variants:

1st x, for some $x \in T^0$
2nd (x, y), for some $x \in T, y \in T^*$

Since intuitively T^0 represents the type of zero-tuples of Ts, and it seems reasonable to assume there is just one such zero-tuple (just as there is just one null sequence), we identify T^0 with the trivial type **1**:

$$T^0 \cong \mathbf{1}$$

Does this satisfy $T \cong T \times T^0$, which we used in deriving Eq. (5.19)? In the following exercise you will show that T is "essentially the same as" (i.e., isomorphic to) $T \times \mathbf{1}$.

Exercise 5.17: Show that $T \cong T \times \mathbf{1}$; that is, T is isomorphic to $T \times \mathbf{1}$. *Hint:* Show that there is a total, one-to-one function $T \to T \times \mathbf{1}$ and a total, one-to-one function $T \times \mathbf{1} \to T$.

Given our identification of T^0 and $\mathbf{1}$, we can now enumerate the kinds of values that belong to T^*, as given by Eq. (5.20),

$$1\text{st } ()$$
$$2\text{nd } [x_1, 1\text{st } ()]$$
$$2\text{nd } \{x_1, 2\text{nd } [x_2, 1\text{st } ()]\}$$
$$2\text{nd } (x_1, 2\text{nd } \{x_2, 2\text{nd } [x_3, 1\text{st } ()]\})$$
$$\vdots$$

where the x_i are of type T. These are the trees:

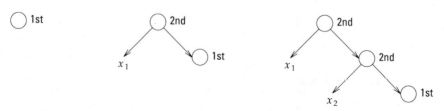

They should look familiar since they are just sequences in their usual linked implementation:

We can make them more familiar by using the structure declaration

> **abstract structure** $T^* \equiv$ nil $+$ prefix (first $\in T$, rest $\in T^*$) (5.21)

in which 'nil' is equivalent to 'nil: $\mathbf{1}$'. According to this declaration, the values of type T^* are just

```
nil
prefix (x₁, nil)
prefix [x₁, prefix (x₂, nil)]
prefix {x₁, prefix [x₂, prefix (x₃, nil)]}
```
$$\vdots$$

for $x_i \in T$. It is clear now that Eq. 5.21 (like 5.20) does in fact define T^*. In fact, the definition of Eq. (5.21) corresponds to the usual data structure representing sequences. For example, in Pascal we can write:[5]

```
type Tsequence = record
  case variant: (nil, prefix) of
    nil: ();
    prefix: (first: T; rest: ↑Tsequence)
  end;
```

The only difference is that Pascal requires the recursion to be broken by a pointer type.

By the archetype for structure declarations (Figs. 5.2 and 5.6), the type declaration (Eq. 5.21) gives T^* the archetype in Fig. 5.8. If we compare this archetype with the sequence archetype presented in Chapter 2 (Fig. 2.5), we see some differences. For example, the test for a null sequence is called null in Fig. 2.5, but nil? in Fig. 5.8; clearly they are the same function. Also, Eq. (5.21) does not define a length function, nor does it require it to be total. On the other hand, finiteness is implicit in our structure declarations (as explained later), so length is not needed for this purpose. Finally, Eq. (5.21) does define an '=' operator, which we omitted from the archetype in Fig. 2.5, but defined recursively in Section 3.7. Thus the type defined by Eq. (5.21) and that defined by Fig. 2.5 differ in only minor respects. In effect Eq. (5.21) is a *one-line* prototype implementation of sequence types!

Although Fig. 5.8 contains some useless operations (such as nil^{-1}), it also contains some new useful ones. For example, prefix^{-1} takes a nonnull sequence and decomposes it into a pair containing its first and rest components. Also, first! replaces the first element of a sequence. We will continue to use the sequence operations with which we are familiar, but will feel free to use the operations of Fig. 5.8 when convenient.

We have seen that the recursive structure declaration (Eq. 5.21) makes sense and is in fact equivalent to the usual record-based implementation of sequences. Thus, if we permit recursive structure declarations, then we do not have to build sequences into our language as a primitive type; we

5. This is not quite legal standard Pascal. We leave it for the reader to make the necessary but uninteresting changes.

Figure 5.8 Archetype generated by recursive definition of sequences.

Declaration:

    abstract structure T^* ≡ nil + prefix (first ∈ T, rest ∈ T^*), for all T ∈ **type**

Syntax:

    T^* ∈ **type**, for all T ∈ **type**

    nil ∈ T^*
    nil^{-1}: $T^* \to \mathbf{1}$
    nil?: $T^* \to \mathbb{B}$

    prefix: $T \times T^* \to T^*$
    prefix^{-1}: $T^* \to T \times T^*$
    prefix?: $T^* \to \mathbb{B}$

    first: $T^* \to T$
    rest: $T^* \to T^*$

    first!: $T \times T^* \to T^*$
    rest!: $T^* \times T^* \to T^*$

    =, ≠: $(T^*)^2 \to \mathbb{B}$

Semantics:

    nil ∈ T^* prefix (x, y) ∈ T^*

                        $z \notin T^*$ otherwise

    nil? nil = **true**,   nil? [prefix (x, S)] = **false**
    nil^{-1} nil = (), nil^{-1} [prefix (x, S)] ≠ z

    prefix? [prefix (x, S)] = **true**,   pretix? nil = **false**
    prefix^{-1} [prefix (x, S)] = (x, S), prefix^{-1} nil ≠ z

    first [prefix (x, S)] = x,   rest [prefix (x, S)] = S
    first nil ≠ z,   rest nil ≠ z

    first [first! (x, S)] = x rest [rest! (S', S)] = S'
    rest [first! (x, S)] = rest S first [rest! (S', S)] = first S
    first! $(x,$ nil$)$ ≠ z rest! $(S,$ nil$)$ ≠ z

    prefix (x, S) = prefix (x', S') if and only if $x = x'$ and $S = S'$
    prefix (x, S) ≠ nil

    $(S = S')$ = **true**, if $S = S'$
    $(S = S')$ = **false**, if $S \neq S'$
    $S \neq S'$ = $\neg(S = S')$

Pragmatics:

    All operations except '=' and '≠' take constant time. The '=' and '≠' operations take time proportional to the product of the length of the list and the complexity of '=' on the base type.

can define them as in Eq. (5.21). This suggests, as we will see in the following sections, that recursive structure declaration is a useful way of defining data structures. It is thus all the more important that we determine whether this use of recursion is legitimate; that is, if equations like (5.21) can always be solved. Scott (1974) showed that recursive structure declarations always have a unique minimum solution. There may be other, nonminimal solutions: Adding all the infinite sequences to T^* will still permit it to satisfy Eq. (5.21).[6] We do not present Scott's proof here, but merely observe that the values belonging to the minimum solution are just finite trees such as we exhibited for T^*.

Exercise 5.18: Show that the following is a correct implementation of cat:

$$\text{cat}(S,\ T) \equiv \begin{cases} T, \text{ if nil? } S \\ \textbf{else} \text{ rest! } [\text{cat (rest } S,\ T),\ S] \end{cases}$$

Exercise 5.19: Implement indsubst using first! and rest!.

Exercise 5.20: Show some typical values in the recursively structured type

abstract structure $T \equiv$ int: $\mathbb{Z}$ + box: T

Write out an archetype for this type.

Exercise 5.21: Write out the archetype generated by the recursive structure declaration

abstract structure $N \equiv Z + S\,(P \in N)$

Show that this type can be interpreted as a concrete representation for natural numbers. To what natural number does Z correspond? If $n \in N$, how would you interpret Sn? How would you interpret Pn, for $n \neq Z$?

Exercise 5.22: Write a recursive structure declaration for binary trees with integers at their leaves.

Exercise 5.23: Write a recursive structure declaration for well-formed formulas in the propositional calculus. Use strings for atomic propositions.

---

6. Recall our discussion of infinite sequences in Section 2.10; see also Section 7.6.

5.4 Formal Patterns and Equational Definitions

Since Chapter 2, we have used the '$\times$' symbol in signatures such as

$$\text{elt}: T^* \times \text{IN} \to T \tag{5.22}$$

to indicate that the function in question has more than one argument. By no coincidence, we use the same symbol for direct product types. Signature (5.22) is to be interpreted literally: The elt operation takes as its argument a tuple of type $T^* \times \text{IN}$. In this sense all functions are unary; some, however, take their one argument from a direct product type. This way of looking at multiple-argument functions is sometimes useful; the argument list can be treated as a bona fide data value. For example, the following formula calls alloc with $m - n$ and $x \div$ blocksize if $m > n$, and with $n - m$ and 0 otherwise:

$$\text{alloc [if } m > n \text{ then } (m - n, x \div \text{blocksize}) \text{ else } (n - m, 0) \text{ endif]}$$

Notice that the value returned by the conditional expression is the actual parameter list to be passed to alloc. By interpreting parameter lists as members of direct product types, we give them the status of *first-class citizens* in the language. Aside from increased regularity and flexibility, this will have many other benefits, especially when we turn to higher-order functions in Chapter 6.[7]

There are some further important consequences of interpreting multiple-argument functions as single-argument functions on direct product types. For example, since elt is really a single argument function, the definition we derived in Chapter 3

$$\text{elt } (S, i) \equiv \begin{cases} \text{first } S, \text{ if } i = 1 \\ \textbf{else } \text{elt (rest } S, i - 1) \end{cases} \tag{3.4}$$

can be seen to be an abbreviation for the more basic definition

$$\text{elt } P \equiv \begin{cases} \text{first (left } P), \text{ if right } P = 1 \\ \textbf{else } \text{elt [rest (left } P), \text{ right } P - 1] \end{cases} \tag{5.23}$$

Here we have used the archetype (Fig. 5.2), which tells us that if the argument $P = (S, i)$, then $S = \text{left } P$ and $i = \text{right } P$. Definition (5.23) is more basic than (3.4) because it shows explicitly that elt is a function that takes a pair P as its argument.

---

7. Note that when a tuple is used as an argument list, we permit the use of alternative brackets, [ ] and { }, for readability.

In general, if $F: T \times U \to V$ is any dyadic (two-argument) function, then we take the definition

$$F(x, y) \equiv \cdots x \cdots y \cdots$$

where '$\cdots x \cdots y \cdots$' is any expression involving 'x' and 'y', to be an abbreviation for

$$FP \equiv \cdots \text{left } P \cdots \text{right } P \cdots$$

where by '$\cdots \text{left } P \cdots \text{right } P \cdots$' we mean the result of substituting 'left P'' for 'x' and 'right P'' for 'y' throughout '$\cdots x \cdots y \cdots$'. We extend this convention in the obvious way to any number of arguments. For example,

$$F(x, y, z) \equiv \cdots x \cdots y \cdots z \cdots$$

is an abbreviation for

$$FT \equiv \cdots \text{left } T \cdots \text{left (right } T) \cdots \text{right (right } T) \cdots$$

in which T represents the argument *triple*.

These abbreviations are quite valuable. They allow us to define multiple-argument functions in the familiar way. Also, they express in a very graphic form the type of input the function expects. A definition such as

$$\text{elt } (S, i) \equiv \cdots$$

says that elt expects a value *of the form* (S, i), that is, a value P such that $P = (S, i)$ for some S and i. The archetype for direct products guarantees that there are *unique* values S and i that are combined to form the pair P. Thus the *formal* parameter list '(S, i)' can be thought of as a kind of *pattern* that is matched against the input to elt, which must be an *actual* parameter list. For example, in the call elt $(<5, 7, 0>, 2)$ we match the pair $(<5, 7, 0>, 2)$ against the formal pattern (S, i), which results in binding S to $<5, 7, 0>$ and i to 2. We use the term *formal pattern* to refer to a construction expression used in a name-binding context, such as the left-hand side of a function definition.

We can extend this pattern-matching idea to any context in which names are defined. For example, if the expression 'find k' returns a pair in **string** $\times \mathbb{R}$, then we take

$$\text{'hourly rate of'} \;\;\hat{}\;\; \text{name} \;\;\hat{}\;\; \text{'='} \;\;\hat{}\;\; \text{string}\leftarrow\text{number rate}$$
$$\textbf{where } (\text{name, rate}) \equiv \text{find } k$$

to be an abbreviation for

'hourly rate of' ∧ left (find k) ∧ '=' ∧ string←number [right (find k)]

Here we are matching the pattern (name, rate) against the pair returned by find k. Thus, if find k = ('Debby', 38.25), then we bind

name = left ('Debby', 38.25) = 'Debby'
rate = right ('Debby', 38.25) = 38.25

In general, if '··· x ··· y ···' is an expression involving the identifiers x and y, and P is an expression that returns a pair, then we take

··· x ··· y ··· **where** $(x, y) \equiv P$

to be an abbreviation for

··· left P ··· right P ···

We make the obvious extension for longer tuples.

Declarations like '**where** $(x, y) \equiv P$' are called *deconstructors* because they decompose (or deconstruct) the value P according to the constructor expression (x, y). Since there are unique x and y from which P is constructed, the deconstructor is well-defined. Deconstructors add no new power to the language; they are merely syntactic sugar that can be eliminated by putting in the necessary left and right calls.

Exercise 5.24: Show that the function definition

$F(x_1, x_2, \ldots, x_n) \equiv E$

where E is any expression, is equivalent to the function definition

$FT \equiv [E$ **where** $(x_1, x_2, \ldots, x_n) \equiv T]$

Deconstructors provide a convenient way to bind several names in one declaration. For example, if we want to compute the product of both roots of a quadratic equation we can write

root1 × root2
   where (root1, root2) $\equiv$ $((-b + d) / (2 \times a), (-b - d) / (2 \times a))$
      where $d \equiv$ sqrt $(b^2 - 4 \times a \times c)$

Here we construct a pair containing the two roots, which is then deconstructed by '**where** (root1, root2) $\equiv$'. Since this construction/deconstruction process is fairly common, many applicative languages provide *compound declarations,* to accomplish the same thing more conveniently. For example, the preceding expression could be written

$$\begin{aligned} &\text{root1} \times \text{root2} \\ &\quad \textbf{where} \;\; \text{root1} \;\equiv\; (-b + d) \,/\, (2 \times a) \\ &\quad \textbf{and} \quad\;\; \text{root2} \;\equiv\; (-b - d) \,/\, (2 \times a) \\ &\qquad\qquad\qquad \textbf{where} \;\; d \;\equiv\; \text{sqrt}\,(b^2 - 4 \times a \times c) \end{aligned}$$

This may be more efficient since the system will not actually construct the pair. In general we have

$$E \;\; \textbf{where} \;\; v_1 \equiv E_1 \;\; \textbf{and} \;\; v_2 \equiv E_2 \;\; \textbf{and} \cdots \textbf{and} \;\; v_n \equiv E_n$$

as syntactic sugar for

$$E \;\; \textbf{where} \;\; (v_1, v_2, \ldots, v_n) \equiv (E_1, E_2, \ldots, E_n)$$

Everything we've said about formal patterns applies naturally to direct product types defined by structure declarations. For example, suppose we've defined the strong type pers_recd as in Eq. (5.8). To define a function wages p that computes the wages for personnel record p, we can write

$$\text{wages } p \;\equiv\; \text{hr\_rate } p \times \text{hrs\_worked } p \tag{5.24}$$

This is exactly analogous to the Pascal function

```
function wages (p: pers_recd): real;
  begin wages := p.hr_rate * p.hrs_worked end
```

On the other hand, we could use a formal pattern and write

$$\text{wages } p \;\equiv\; r \times h \quad \textbf{where} \;\; \text{empl}\,(n, r, e, h) \equiv p \tag{5.25}$$

Or we could use the pattern as the formal parameter and write

$$\text{wages } [\text{empl}\,(n, r, e, h)] \;\equiv\; r \times h \tag{5.26}$$

This version makes it obvious that wages expects a record constructed by empl. In effect the formal pattern 'empl (n, r, e, h)' is matched against the input record, which results in binding r to the hourly rate and h to the hours worked. Which of the three definitions (5.24, 5.25, or 5.26) is used is largely a matter of taste, although later you will see some circumstances in which one may be preferable.

The pattern-matching interpretation of formal parameters is also useful for taking apart *nested* constructors. For an example, suppose the employee's name is represented as a tuple:

structure name_recd ≡ full_name (1st ∈ **string**, mid ∈ **string**, last ∈ **string**)
structure pers_recd ≡
    empl (name ∈ name_recd, hr_rate ∈ ℝ, emp_no ∈ ℕ, hrs_worked ∈ ℝ)

To compute a string containing the employee's name, last name first, we could write:

revname {empl [full_name $(F, M, L), r, e, h$]} ≡ $L \wedge$ ',' $\wedge F \wedge$ ' ' $\wedge M$

The alternative is to use selectors:

$$\text{revname } p \equiv \text{last nm} \wedge \text{',' } \wedge \text{ 1st nm} \wedge \text{' '} \wedge \text{ mid nm}$$
$$\textbf{where } \text{nm} \equiv \text{name } p$$

In the first case we must know the exact format of the records; in the second, the names of the selector functions. Again, the choice is largely a matter of taste.

Because constructors are one-to-one, formal patterns can use construction expressions to apply selectors implicitly. This suggests that we can also use formal patterns to apply implicitly *filters* from direct sum types, since the corresponding injectors are one-to-one. For example, if we have defined

structure pers_recd ≡
    empl (name ∈ **string**,
        data ∈ present (hr_rate ∈ ℝ, emp_no ∈ ℕ, hrs_worked ∈ ℝ)
        + past (· · ·))

then we can use

$$\text{wages } \{\text{empl } [n, \text{present } (r, e, h)]\} \equiv r \times h$$

instead of

$$\text{wages } p \equiv \text{hr\_rate } p \times \text{hrs\_worked } p$$

Finally, it's convenient to extend the preceding conventions to implicit discriminators. For example, suppose we want the function rate: pers_recd → **string** × ℝ to return an employee's name and hourly rate, where the rate is taken to be 0 for past employees. This is simply defined by the following two equations:

$$\text{rate } \{\text{empl } [n, \text{ present } (r, e, h)]\} \equiv (n, r) \qquad (5.27)$$
$$\text{rate } \{\text{empl } [n, \text{ past } (a, s)]\} \equiv (n, 0)$$

The discriminators (past? and present?) are supplied automatically (see Exercise 5.25).

An advantage of this equational style of definition is that the compiler can check to ensure that you've covered all the cases, and warn you if you haven't. Another common use of equational definitions is illustrated by our structure declaration for sequences:

abstract structure $T^* \equiv$ nil $+$ prefix (first $\in T$, rest $\in T^*$) $\qquad (5.21)$

We can define cat by giving a clause for each variant of the type:

$$\text{cat } (\text{nil}, T) \equiv T$$
$$\text{cat } [\text{prefix } (x, S), T] \equiv \text{prefix } [x, \text{ cat } (S, T)]$$

With the usual syntactic sugar this is just

$$\text{cat } (\text{nil}, T) \equiv T$$
$$\text{cat } (x : S, T) \equiv x : \text{cat } (S, T)$$

Notice how well structure declarations and the equational style mesh with the Method of Differences. The structure declaration tells you how the values of the type are constructed, and hence how to alter the input to the function. The resulting equation derived by the Method of Differences is exactly the clause required for the recursive step. You'll see many examples of equational definitions in the following sections.

Exercise 5.25: Turn Eqs. (5.27) into an explicit conditional definition by putting in the implicit discriminators, injectors and selectors.

Exercise 5.26: Use formal patterns to define a function sum_legal: augint$^2 \to \mathbb{Z}$ such that sum_legal (x, y) takes two legal_ints x and y and returns $x + y$. The function is undefined if either x or y (or both) is an error_int.

Exercise 5.27: Extend your answer to the preceding exercise to return an error_int whenever either (or both) of its arguments is an error_int.

Exercise 5.28: Repeat Exercise 5.9 using formal patterns to simplify your definitions.

5.5 Arithmetic Expression Notations

We next consider a number of examples of applicative programming drawn from the implementation of language systems (e.g., compilers and interpreters). To limit the discussion to essentials, we restrict our attention to a very simple language: arithmetic expressions. Thus the language we are considering could be described by the following BNF grammar:

$$
\begin{aligned}
expr &= expr\ addop\ term\ |\ term \\
addop &= +\ |\ - \\
term &= term\ mulop\ factor\ |\ factor \\
mulop &= \times\ |\ / \\
factor &= monad\ factor\ |\ primary \\
monad &= sqrt\ |\ log\ |\ ln\ |\ sin \\
primary &= identifier\ |\ number\ |\ (\,expr\,)
\end{aligned}
$$

For example, one expression in this language is

$$(2 \times a \times y + b) \times (2 \times a \times y + c) \tag{5.28}$$

This is called the *infix* form of an expression because the operator is written between the operands. Although people usually write expressions this way, it is not necessarily the most convenient form for computer processing.

You may be familiar with several other ways of writing expression that are particularly convenient in computer applications. For example, the *postfix* or *reverse Polish* form of an expression positions an operator after its operands:

$$2\, a \times y \times b + 2\, a \times y \times c + \times$$

This representation of expressions is widely known because of its use on RPN (Reverse Polish Notation) calculators. The virtue of this notation is that it is *parenthesis free;* that is, parentheses are never necessary to group the operands of an operator.

The usual infix notation in not parenthesis free. For example, if we rewrite Eq. (5.28) without parentheses,

$$2 \times a \times y + b \times 2 \times a \times y + c$$

then it has quite a different meaning (i.e., value). The usual notation also depends on *precedence relations (priorities)* to allow parentheses to be eliminated. For example, multiplication is of higher precedence than addition, so $'a + b \times c'$ means $'a + (b \times c)'$. Postfix notation is simpler in that it

Figure 5.9 Postfix code for arithmetic expression.

```
LDC 2
LOD a
MUL
LOD y
MUL
LOD b
ADD
LDC 2
LOD a
MUL
LOD y
MUL
LOD c
ADD
MUL
```

requires neither precedence relations nor parentheses to associate an operator unambiguously with its operands.

One reason that language implementors are interested in postfix notation is that it corresponds to the usual order in which operations are done on a computer. For example, the code generated from the postfix sequence

$$2\,a \times y \times b + 2\,a \times y \times c + \times$$

might be that shown in Fig. 5.9. Thus a compiler often puts arithmetic expressions (and perhaps the whole program) in postfix form just before code generation.

Another expression representation widely used in language systems is *prefix* or *Polish* notation, named for the Polish logician Jan Łukasiewicz (1878–1956). Another parenthesis-free notation, it differs from postfix notation only in that it places the operator before its operands:

$$\times + \times \times 2\,a\,y\,b + \times \times 2\,a\,y\,c$$

Prefix notation is essentially the notation of function application, as we can see by adding parentheses and commas:

$$\times \left[\,+ \{\times [\times (2,a), y], b\}, + \{\times [\times (2,a), y], c\} \right]$$

Another useful way to represent expressions is as trees:

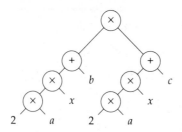

The virtue of this representation is that it makes manifest the structure of the expressions, showing how the inputs and outputs of the operators are connected. In Chapter 10 we explore at considerable length the manipulation of trees.

5.6 Representing Arithmetic Expressions

Since we will write applicative programs to manipulate expressions in these various forms, we must design a representation for each in terms of the available data types. Since the prefix and postfix notations are linear, expressions in these forms can be conveniently represented as sequences. For example, the preceding prefix expression can be represented by the sequence

<'×', '+', '×', '×', '2', 'a', 'y', 'b', '+', '×', '×', '2', 'a', 'y', 'c'>

Here we have represented identifiers, operators, and constants by strings. Similarly, the corresponding postfix expression can be represented by the string sequence

<'2', 'a', '×', 'y', '×', 'b', '+', '2', 'a', '×', 'y', '×', 'c', '+', '×'>

Unfortunately, representing arithmetic expressions as values in **string*** makes it difficult to determine whether a particular element represents a constant, identifier, or operator. Therefore a better solution is to define a direct sum type:

> **structure** element ≡ con: ℝ + id: **string** + mop: monad + dop: dyad
> **structure** monad ≡ sqrt + log + ln + sin
> **structure** dyad ≡ plus + minus + times + divide

(mop and dop stand for "monadic operator" and "dyadic operator.") Then we can represent postfix expressions by values of type element*. Our previous example is now

> <con 2, id 'a', dop times, id 'y', dop times, id 'b', dop plus,
>   con 2, id 'a', dop times, id 'y', dop times, id 'c', dop plus, dop times>

Note that every element of the sequence bears a tag.

How can trees be represented? Consider a tree such as this, in which T and U represent subtrees; that is, we have a '+' node with two descendents, T and U.

The natural way to represent this node is as a three-tuple, (plus, T', U'), in which 'plus' represents the label of the node and T' and U' are the tuples representing the subtrees T and U. Identifiers and constants are represented by themselves. Thus the tuple representation of the tree form of our example expression is

> (times, (plus, (times, (times, 2, 'a'), 'y'), 'b'),
>   (plus, (times, (times, 2, 'a'), 'y'), 'c'))

Indeed this is essentially the way programs are represented in LISP; a LISP expression corresponding to our example is

> (times (plus (times (times 2 a) y) b)
>   (plus (times (times 2 a) y) c))

That is, LISP programmers program in trees (albeit written in a linear form).

Why did we put the node label first and its descendants second and third in our tuple representation of trees? We could have used other arrangements, such as (T', plus, U'). Putting the node label (operator) first in the sequence, however, makes it more accessible; also, n-adic operators can be represented uniformly as $n+1$-tuples in which the first element is the node label. In different circumstances some other arrangement might be more convenient; the issues remain the same.

There are some obvious similarities between the representations of the prefix and tree forms of expressions. Indeed, as written, they contain exactly the same atoms in order from left to right:

> <dop times, dop plus, dop times, dop times, con 2, id 'a', id 'y', id 'b',
>   dop plus, dop times, dop times, con 2, id 'a', id 'y', id 'c'>
> (times, (plus, (times, (times, 2, 'a'), 'y'), 'b'),
>   (plus, (times, (times, 2, 'a'), 'y'), 'c'))

Notice, however, that the tree form is more structured than the prefix sequence. The prefix sequence is "flat," that is, all at a single level of structure. As a result a nontrivial algorithm is required to extract the sub-parts of the expressions, such as the operands of an operator. To identify the second argument of the first multiplication we must use a sort of parsing process to find the end of the first operand since this is not marked in the prefix sequence in any way. As we'll see later, this can be done; but it's awkward.

The tree representation does not have this difficulty. If T is a tuple representing a dyadic application in tree form, then left T is the operator (node label), left (right T) is its first operand, and right (right T) is its second operand. Because the tree form is more structured, structural components of the expression are directly accessible. The advantages of trees are discussed further in Chapter 10.

5.7 Descriptions of Expression Representations

What constitutes a legal postfix sequence? Or a legal tree? Although we have given several examples, we have not specified very precisely what is to be allowed. The type declaration

type postfix ≡ element*
    where structure element ≡
        con: $\mathbb{R}$ + id: **string** + mop: monad + dop: dyad

places some limits on postfix sequences, but leaves many questions unanswered. For example, is the null sequence a legal postfix sequence? How about the sequence <con 3, dop plus>? We are missing a specification of the allowable forms for each of these ways of representing expressions.

You have already seen a BNF grammar describing the legal infix arithmetic expressions. We will use a similar approach to defining the legal postfix expressions. One method is to write a BNF grammar describing legal expressions for generating postfix sequences.[8] We begin with the simplest postfix sequences, which contain a single identifier or constant:

    postfix = <id string> | <con number> | $\cdots$

What are the other kinds of postfix sequence? We can have a monadic operator preceded by one legal postfix sequence, or a dyadic operator preceded by two legal postfix sequence. Thus, if P and Q are legal postfix sequences, then so is $P \wedge Q \wedge$<dop dyop>, where dyop represents any

---

8. Note that the BNF grammars are not part of the Φ language, but are mathematical notation used to talk about sequences.

dyadic operator. For example, if P is <con 2, id 'a', dop times> and Q is <id 'y'>, then

$$P \wedge Q \wedge <\text{dop times}> = <\text{con 2, id 'a', dop times, id 'y', dop times}>$$

is a legal postfix sequence. This allows us to complete our grammar for sequences representing legal postfix expressions:

        postfix = <id string> | <con number>
              | postfix ∧ <mop monad>
              | postfix ∧ postfix ∧ <dop dyad>

To complete the definition of the allowable structures, of course, we must specify the allowable monadic operators and dyadic operators. The operators can be defined by enumeration:

        monad = sqrt | log | ln | sin
        dyad = plus | minus | times | divide

   Next we consider a grammar to specify all the structures representing legal expression trees. The simplest trees are just individual identifiers and constants:

   structure tree = ident: **string** + const: ℝ + · · ·

The only other kinds of trees are nodes representing monadic and dyadic applications. Thus, if m is a monadic operator and T is a tuple representing a tree, then (m, T) is a tuple representing the application of m to T. Similarly, if d is a dyadic operator and T and U represent trees, then (d, T, U) represents the application of d to T and U. This leads directly to a structural description of trees:

   structure tree ≡ ident: **string**   (5.29)
              + const: ℝ
              + monadic (monop ∈ monad, arg ∈ tree)
              + dyadic (dyop ∈ dyad, arg1 ∈ tree, arg2 ∈ tree)

Exercise 5.29:   Write a grammar for prefix sequences.

Exercise 5.30:   Translate the preceding definition of tree (Eq. 5.29) into a Pascal or Ada type declaration.

Exercise 5.31:   Explain in detail how values of type tree could be represented in LISP.

5.8 Tree-to-Postfix Conversion

A typical problem in implementating language systems is the conversion
of programs from one representation to another. To illustrate the use of
applicative programming methods to solve these problems, let's develop
a function for converting trees to postfix expressions (actually, the tuples
representing trees to the sequences representing postfix expressions).

Since we have already defined the classes of structures representing
trees and postfix expressions, it is easy to specify the domain and range of
the conversion function:

post←tree: tree → postfix

Thus post←tree must accept any legal tree and compute the corresponding postfix expression.

We can develop our intuition for the problem by considering a few
examples. The simplest trees, individual constants and identifiers,
correspond to single-element postfix expressions:

post←tree (const 2) = <con 2>
post←tree (ident 'a') = <id 'a'>

Next we consider a slightly more complicated tree:

(Here 'c' represents const and 'i' represents ident.) The desired result for
this tree is

post←tree [dyadic (times, const 2, ident 'a')] = <con 2, id 'a', dop times>

To relate this to the simpler cases, note that the right-hand side can be
rewritten

<con 2, id 'a', dop times>
   = <con 2> ∧ <id 'a'> ∧ <dop times>
   = post←tree (const 2) ∧ post←tree (ident 'a') ∧ <dop times>

We can begin to see the recursive pattern that will be used to convert
trees in terms of the conversion of their subtrees. To bolster our intuition
let's try a more complicated example:

post←tree {dyadic [times, dyadic (times, const 2, ident 'a'), ident 'y']}
= <con 2, id 'a', dop times, id 'y', dop times>

The right-hand side of this equation can be expressed in terms of the simpler cases in the same way as before:

<con 2, id 'a', dop times, id 'y', dop times>
= <con 2, id 'a', dop times> ∧ <id 'y'> ∧ <dop times>
= post←tree [dyadic (times, const 2, ident 'a')]
∧ post←tree (ident 'y') ∧ <dop times>

Having developed our intuitive understanding of the problem, we can now turn to a more systematic development of the post←tree function. We can develop the function by considering each variant of tree. This is aided by comparing the structural descriptions of trees and postfix expressions side by side:

tree ≡ const: ℝ	postfix = <con number>
+ ident: **string**	| <id identifier>
+ monadic (monop ∈ monad, arg ∈ tree)	| postfix ∧ <mop monad>
+ dyadic (dyop ∈ dyad, arg1 ∈ tree, arg2 ∈ tree)	| postfix ∧ postfix ∧ <dop dyad>

The simplest trees, represented by constants and identifiers, are converted into single-element sequences:

$$\text{post←tree (const } n) \equiv <\text{con } n> \tag{5.30}$$
$$\text{post←tree (ident } x) \equiv <\text{id } x>$$

Trees of the form monadic (m, T), representing monadic applications, are converted into sequences of the form $T' ∧ <\text{mop } m>$, where T' is the conversion of T. Thus

$$\text{post←tree [monadic } (m, T)] \equiv \text{post←tree } T ∧ <\text{mop } m> \tag{5.31}$$

Similarly, trees of the form dyadic (d, T, U), representing dyadic applications, are converted to sequences of the form $T' ∧ U' ∧ <\text{dop } d>$, where T' and U' are the conversions of T and U. Thus

$$\text{post←tree [dyadic } (d, T, U)] \equiv \tag{5.32}$$
$$\text{post←tree } T ∧ \text{post←tree } U ∧ <\text{dop } d>$$

Equations (5.30–5.32) define post←tree, which is trivial to convert into a conditional definition:

$$\text{post}\leftarrow\text{tree } E \equiv \tag{5.33}$$

$$
\begin{cases}
<\text{con (const}^{-1} E)>, \text{ if const? } E \\
<\text{id (ident}^{-1} E)>, \text{ if ident? } E \\
\text{post}\leftarrow\text{tree (arg } E) \wedge <\text{mop (monop } E)>, \text{ if monadic? } E \\
\text{post}\leftarrow\text{tree (arg1 } E) \wedge \text{post}\leftarrow\text{tree (arg2 } E) \wedge <\text{dop (dyop } E)>, \text{ if dyadic? } E
\end{cases}
$$

As noted before, equational languages (such as Φ) do this conversion automatically.

Notice that the clauses in the definition of post←tree exactly correspond to the clauses in the structural description of trees: The function must handle every kind of tree, and the structure declaration describes the kinds of trees. Allowing the domain structure to dictate the function structure in this way helps ensure that no cases are overlooked.[9]

We summarize the foregoing observations in a programming principle:

> The Domain Structure Principle: *The structure of a function is determined by the structure of its domain.*

You already saw a special case of this, the Method of Differences. Since the structure of a sequence domain is

$$\text{nil } + \text{ prefix (first } \in T, \text{ rest } \in T^*)$$

the definitions of functions on this domain generally have the following clauses:

$$F \text{ nil} \equiv \cdots$$
$$F[\text{prefix } (x, S)] \equiv \cdots FS \cdots$$

The second clause is exactly what you derive when you apply the Method of Differences. That is, you ask, What do I do to FS to get $F[\text{prefix } (x, S)]$?

Also notice how the Domain Structure Principle relates to our observation that induction recapitulates recursion. As we have seen, recursively structured domains, such as sequences, tend to lead to recursively structured functions. Since inductive proofs about these functions tend to recapitulate their recursion, you can see that the domain structure also determines the proof structure. For example, in proofs about functions over sequences, the base is typically nil, and the inductive step goes from S to prefix (x, S). In summary, the structure of the domain of a function is critical information for both defining the function and proving things about it.

---

9. Programming systems often aid programmers by warning them if there are variants without corresponding equations.

Exercise 5.32: Compare for readability the equational definition of post←tree (Eqs. 5.30 – 5.32) and the conditional definition (Eq. 5.33).

Exercise 5.33: Trace the execution of

post←tree {dyadic [times, dyadic (times, const 2, ident 'a'), ident 'y']}

Exercise 5.34: Translate post←tree into LISP, Pascal, or some other programming language.

Exercise 5.35: Define a function pre←tree that converts a tree into a prefix expression.

Exercise 5.36: Define a function that returns the *size* of a tree, where the size is defined to be the total number of constants, identifiers, and operators.

Exercise 5.37: Define a function that returns the *height* of a tree, where its height is defined to be the maximum distance from the root to a leaf. Trees consisting of a single identifier or constant node are defined to have a height of zero.

Exercise 5.38: Define a *flattening* function that converts a tree into a fully parenthesized infix expression sequence.

Exercise 5.39: Modify your answer to Exercise (5.38) to produce a *minimally parenthesized* infix expression (i.e., a sequence containing only those parentheses required to override the precedence of the operators).

5.9 Tree Evaluation

In this section we develop a simple interpreter for arithmetic expressions in tree form. To simplify the development we begin by designing a function to evaluate *constant trees,* that is, trees that do not contain any identifiers:

```
structure const_tree
    ≡ const: ℝ
    + monadic (monop ∈ monad, arg ∈ const_tree)
    + dyadic (dyop ∈ dyad, arg1 ∈ const_tree, arg2 ∈ const_tree)
```

Thus const_trees are a proper subclass of the trees defined previously, that is, those having only constants at the leaves.

Our goal will be to define a function value←ctree for evaluating constant trees. For example, evaluating the tree

yields

value←ctree {dyadic [plus, dyadic (times, const 2, const 3), const 5]} = 11

Thus the type signature of value←ctree is

value←ctree: const_tree → ℝ

How can we go about defining value←ctree? Since the structure of the function is determined by structure of its domain, we observe that there are three kinds of const_trees:

1. const n, for $n \in$ ℝ

2. monadic (m, x), for $m \in$ monad, $x \in$ const_tree

3. dyadic (d, x, y), for $d \in$ dyad, $x \in$ const_tree, $y \in$ const_tree

We expect three corresponding cases in our definition; let's consider each kind of const_tree in turn.

The simplest kind of const_tree is a single leaf, represented by an constant. Clearly the value of the tree const 3 is simply 3:

value←ctree (const 3) = 3

More generally, we have the case for const nodes:

$$value←ctree\ (const\ n) \equiv n \qquad\qquad (5.34)$$

Next we consider a monadic operation such as sqrt (square root):

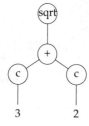

Part of the process of evaluating this expression must be the application of the square root function to some number. But what number? The square root function is to be applied to the number that is the value of the expression represented by dyadic (plus, const 2, const 3). Therefore, before we can apply the square root operation we must evaluate its argument. That is,

value←ctree {monadic [sqrt, dyadic (plus, const 2, const 3)]}
= √ {value←ctree [dyadic (plus, const 2, const 3)]}

Don't confuse the variant name 'sqrt' on the left of this equation with the function name '√' on the right. The degenerate variant sqrt denotes the square root operation in the *interpreted* language (i.e., the language of constant trees). On the other hand, '√' denotes the square root operation in the *interpreting* language—Φ, in which value←ctree is written. That is, const_tree is the *object language* and Φ is the *metalanguage*.

With the foregoing discussion in mind, it can be seen that the general equation for the evaluation of monadic nodes is

$$\text{value←ctree [monadic } (m, x)] \equiv f \text{ (value←ctree } x) \qquad (5.35)$$

where m is a monadic operator and f is the function denoted by m.

Clearly, for a dyadic node we must evaluate both arguments before performing the indicated operation. Thus, if d is a dyadic operator and f is the function denoted by d, then[10]

$$\text{value←ctree [dyadic } (d, x, y)] \equiv f \text{ (value←ctree } x, \text{value←ctree } y) \qquad (5.36)$$

The only remaining task is the conversion from an operator symbol such as plus or minus to the function to execute it, such as + or −. One solution is to break Eqs. (5.35) and (5.36) into subcases for each operation

value←ctree [dyadic (plus, x, y)] ≡ value←ctree x + value←ctree y
value←ctree [dyadic (minus, x, y)] ≡ value←ctree x − value←ctree y

and so forth. Perhaps a better solution is to delegate this conversion to auxiliary functions ev_monad and ev_dyad:

value←ctree [monadic (m, x)] ≡ ev_monad (m, value←ctree x)
value←ctree [dyadic (d, x, y)] ≡ ev_dyad (d, value←ctree x, value←ctree y)

---

10. Note that Eqs. (5.34–5.36) imply that value←ctree is a homomorphism of the free algebra const_tree into $\mathbb{Z}$.

Here ev_monad (m, x) performs on x the monadic operation denoted by m, and ev_dyad (d, x, y) performs on x and y the dyadic operation denoted by d. Each is simply defined by a series of cases:

ev_monad (sqrt, x) $\equiv \sqrt{x}$
ev_monad (log, x) $\equiv \log x$
ev_monad (ln, x) $\equiv \log x \; / \log e$
ev_monad (sin, x) $\equiv \sin x$

ev_dyad (plus, x, y) $\equiv x + y$
ev_dyad (minus, x, y) $\equiv x - y$
ev_dyad (times, x, y) $\equiv x \times y$
ev_dyad (divide, x, y) $\equiv x / y$

Notice that the *particular* operations allowed in expressions are contained in the definitions of the types monad and dyad and the functions ev_monad and ev_dyad. Thus we have separated the *domain-independent language framework*, reflected in the value←ctree function, from the *domain-dependent components*, reflected in the ev_monad and ev_dyad functions. (Recall the discussion of language frameworks and components in Section 2.1.) The value←ctree function could be used to evaluate any constant tree constructed of monadic and dyadic operators, simply by supplying the appropriate functions for handling those operators.

Exercise 5.40: Trace the execution of

value←ctree (dyadic [plus, const 3, dyadic (times, const 2, const 3)])

Assume the usual meanings for plus and times.

Exercise 5.41: Translate value←ctree into LISP, Pascal, or some other programming language.

We have seen how to evaluate the trees corresponding to expressions like

$$3 + 2 \times 3$$

Next we generalize our previous interpreter so it can handle arbitrary expression trees—trees with identifiers for leaves. That is, we want to be able to handle the trees corresponding to expressions like

$$2 \times a \times y + b$$

Our previous interpreter was called value←ctree because it evaluated things of type const_tree (constant tree); our new interpreter is called value←tree because it evaluates things of type tree (arbitrary arithmetic expression trees). To design this evaluator, we must first consider in more detail the nature of evaluation.

To *evaluate* something is to extract its value; to evaluate an expression such as '$2 \times a \times y + b$' we must find its value. There is a hidden assumption: that this expression, as it stands, has a value. We must ask whether '$2 \times a \times y + b$' indeed has a value. The answer, of course, is no; we cannot specify a value for this expression until we have specified values for the identifiers 'a', 'y', and 'b'.

Let's consider this issue in more general terms. An expression is called *open* if it contains any identifiers that are not defined or otherwise given meanings within that expression. Thus '$2 \times a \times y + b$' is an open expression because the identifiers 'a', 'y' and 'b' are not defined within that expression.

An expression is called *closed* if it is not open, that is, contains no undefined identifiers. Expressions can be closed in two ways: Either they contain no identifiers at all, such as '$3 + 2 \times 3$', or they contain identifiers that are defined within the expression. Thus

$$(a + 1) \times (a - 1) \textbf{ where } a \equiv 3 + 2 \times 3$$

is closed because the identifier 'a' is defined (given a value, namely, 9) within the expression. Open and closed expressions are discussed further in Sections 11.2 and 11.3.

It is clear that if E is an open expression, then it makes no sense to ask, What is the value of E? The hidden assumption, that E has a value, is false under these circumstances. For the hidden assumption to be true, for E to have a value, usually all its subparts must have values; in particular, all its identifiers must have values. Thus E has a value only if we specify some *context* that specifies the meanings of the identifiers in E. If E is open it makes sense to ask the value of E in C, but not, the value of E. An open expression is incomplete in the sense that it doesn't have a value until we specify a context for its interpretation.

We can now see that our general value←tree function, which must be able to evaluate both open and closed expressions, must have an additional parameter representing the context of evaluation. Thus its signature must be

$$\text{value←tree: tree} \times \text{context} \to \mathbb{R} \qquad (5.37)$$

where context is an (as yet undefined) type representing a context of evaluation.

We know how to represent trees as tuples; how shall we represent contexts? The key requirement is that we be able to determine the value of any identifier in the expression. Thus a context must be represented as some kind of table (a *symbol table*) mapping identifiers into their values. There are many ways to represent such a table, but we already defined a data type convenient for the purpose: finite functions. Thus the type context is defined

type context ≡ finfunc (**string** → $\mathbb{R}$)

For example, the context defining $a = 3$, $b = 2$, $c = -1$, and $y = 2$ can be represented by the finite function

$$C \equiv ['a' \mapsto 3, 'b' \mapsto 2, 'c' \mapsto -1, 'y' \mapsto 2]$$

The value of an identifier can then be retrieved from this table by applying it to the string representing the name of the identifier:

$C('a') = 3$, $C('b') = 2$, etc.

We now are prepared to define our general tree evaluator.

Consider the result of value←tree (E, C), where E is an expression represented as a tree and C is a context represented as a finite function. Since function structure is determined by domain structure, we recall the definition of general expression trees:

> **structure** tree ≡ const: $\mathbb{R}$ (5.29)
>   + ident: **string**
>   + monadic (monop ∈ monad, arg ∈ tree)
>   + dyadic (dyop ∈ dyad, arg1 ∈ tree, arg2 ∈ tree)

We can expect our definition to include a case to handle each kind of tree. The only case really different from the corresponding one in constant trees is the one to handle identifiers. What should be the result of value←tree (ident 'a', C)? Clearly, we must look up the value of 'a' in the context C:

value←tree (ident 'a', C) = $C('a')$

It is then simple to write the equations that define value←tree:

value←tree (const n, C) ≡ n (5.38)
value←tree (ident x, C) ≡ Cx
value←tree [monadic (m, x), C] ≡ ev_monad [m, value←tree (x, C)]
value←tree [dyadic (d, x, y), C] ≡
    ev_dyad [d, value←tree (x, C), value←tree (y, C)]

Notice that we can use the same ev_monad and ev_dyad functions as in the definition of value←ctree.

Exercise 5.42: Translate Eqs. (5.38) into a conditional definition of value←tree.

Exercise 5.43: Translate your definition of value←tree into LISP, Pascal, or another programming language.

Exercise 5.44: Trace the evaluation of

value←tree (dyadic [times, dyadic (times, const 2, ident 'a'), ident 'y'], C}
where $C \equiv$ ['a' $\mapsto$ 3, 'b' $\mapsto$ 2, 'c' $\mapsto$ −1, 'y' $\mapsto$ 2]

Exercise 5.45: Define a function tree←post: postfix → tree that converts a postfix expression into the corresponding tree. *Hint:* How you would evaluate a postfix expression using a stack? Recall our simulation of the stacks in the tail-recursive version of cat in Section 3.9.[11]

Exercise 5.46: Define a function tree←pre that converts a prefix expression into a tree.

Exercise 5.47: Based on our definition of a tree evaluator, and using a postfix-to-tree converter, define a postfix evaluator.

Exercise 5.48: *(Advanced)* Use the usual precedence algorithm to convert an infix expression to tree form. *Hint:* Use sequences to simulate the operator and operand stacks.

5.10 Unification

We turn next to the unification of two formulas so they are equal (Robinson 1965), a tree-processing problem that is very important in artificial intelligence and the implementation of logic programming languages like Prolog. Consider these two arithmetic expressions:

$$2 \times u, \quad a \times (x + 1)$$

Unification tries to answer the question, Is there some substitution of formulas for the variables that will make these two formulas identical? For example, if in the first formula we let $u \Rightarrow (x + 1)$ we get

$$2 \times (x + 1)$$

---

11. This is known as "pseudo-interpretation" (MacLennan 1975) or "evaluation on a non-standard domain" (Sintzoff 1972).

If in the second we let $a \Rightarrow 2$, then we also get

$$2 \times (x + 1)$$

Therefore these two formulas can be unified by the substitutions

$$u \Rightarrow (x + 1), \quad a \Rightarrow 2$$

The substitutions resulting from unification can be used for substitution in other formulas or as a context for evaluation. For example, consider an algebraic simplification rule such as

$$u + u \Rightarrow 2 \times u \tag{5.39}$$

The left-hand side can be unified with the formula

$$(x + 1) + (x + 1) \tag{5.40}$$

by the substitution $u \Rightarrow (x + 1)$. Performing this substitution on $2 \times u$, the right-hand side of rule (5.39), yields

$$2 \times (x + 1)$$

which is the result of applying simplification rule (5.39) to formula (5.40).

Notice that unification attempts to make its arguments *formally* equal, that is, equal as trees. It is not sensitive to the values of the formulas. Thus these two formulas

$$(x - x) \times 2, \quad 0 \times y$$

cannot be unified because there is no substitution for the variables that will make '$(x - x)$' *formally* equivalent to '0', although the two are obviously equivalent numerically.

How can we go about developing a unification function? The goal of unifying trees T and U is to find a substitution Σ that when applied to T and U yields equal trees. We call such a substitution the *unifier* of T and U. To state this more precisely, we first must define the type of substitutions. Since these substitutions are mappings of identifiers to their values, it is natural to represent them by finite functions. For example, the substitution

$$u \Rightarrow (x + 1), \quad a \Rightarrow 2$$

is represented by the finite function Σ:

$$\Sigma \equiv [\,'u' \mapsto \text{dyadic (plus, ident } 'x', \text{const } 1), \; 'a' \mapsto \text{const } 2] \tag{5.41}$$

It is easy to see that the type of substitutions is

$$\text{substitution} \equiv \text{finfunc}\,(\textbf{string} \to \text{tree}) \qquad (5.42)$$

To make use of substitutions, we suppose the existence of a function

$$\text{subst: substitution} \times \text{tree} \to \text{tree} \qquad (5.43)$$

such that subst (Σ, T) is the tree resulting from performing on T the substitutions represented by Σ. For example, if Σ is as defined in Eq. (5.41), then

subst [Σ, dyadic (times, const 2, ident 'u')]
= dyadic [times, const 2, dyadic (plus, ident 'x', const 1)]

The subst function is straightforward to define, as you'll discover in Exercise 5.49.

Exercise 5.49:   Define the subst function as just described. *Hint:* The structure of the function is determined by its domain.

We can now state more precisely the goal of unification. The goal of unifying T and U is to find a $\Sigma \in$ substitution such that

$$\text{subst}\,(\Sigma, T) = \text{subst}\,(\Sigma, U), \quad \text{if } \Sigma = \text{unifier}\,(T, U)$$

Also, we want Σ to be the smallest such function; that is, it should not contain any useless substitutions.

What if the trees T and U cannot be unified? In that case unifier should return some special value. Therefore we define unifier to return a value belonging to a direct sum type unification that indicates whether the unification was successful and, if so, what substitution unifies the trees.

$$\textbf{structure}\ \text{unification} \equiv \text{failure} + \text{success: substitution} \qquad (5.44)$$

The signature for unifier is then

$$\text{unifier: tree}^2 \to \text{unification}$$

Its specification is

If unifier $(T, U) = $ success Σ, $\qquad (5.45)$
then Σ is minimum finite function in finfunc (**string** $\to$ tree)
such that subst $(\Sigma, T) = $ subst (Σ, U);

If unifier $(T, U) = $ failure,
then there is no Σ such that subst $(\Sigma, T) = $ subst (Σ, U).

By "minimum" we mean that Σ defines no substitutions beyond those required to unify T and U. Note that there may be several minimal substitutions. For example, $x + 1$ and $y + 1$ may be unified by either the substitution $x \Rightarrow y$ or the substitution $y \Rightarrow x$.

How can we go about defining unifier? Clearly it must go in parallel through the trees T and U, building up the unifying substitution as it goes. That is, at any given point during the unification we have a value $\Upsilon \in$ unification indicating the result of the unification so far.[12] If $\Upsilon =$ failure then the unification has already failed, so there's no point in continuing to try. If $\Upsilon =$ success Σ, for some substitution Σ, then we know that Σ has unified the formulas so far, and that we must try to extend Σ into a substitution that unifies T and U.

To accomplish the preceding, it is convenient that unifier call an auxiliary function unaux:

$$\text{unaux: tree} \times \text{tree} \times \text{unification} \rightarrow \text{unification}$$

The application unaux (T, U, Υ) takes the result Υ of the unification so far, attempting to extend it to unify T and U. Given this auxiliary, the result of unifier (T, U) is computed by finding the extension of nihil that unifies T and U:

$$\text{unifier } (T, U) \equiv \text{unaux } (T, U, \text{success nihil})$$

Notice that we have "tagged" nihil with the injector success to indicate the unification has initially succeeded.

Now let's turn to the definition of unaux; as usual the structure of the function is determined by the structure of its domain. In this case we have two trees as inputs; we must make sure we've covered all the possible combinations. First, however, are a few simple cases that are independent of the structures of the trees. The simplest case occurs when the unification has already failed; unaux simply returns the failure code:

$$\text{unaux } (T, U, \text{failure}) \equiv \text{failure} \tag{5.46}$$

Since we have handled the case in which $\Upsilon =$ failure, in the following we assume $\Upsilon =$ success Σ for some substitution Σ.

The next simplest case occurs when T and U are the same trees since then they are already equal and no additional substitutions are needed:

$$\text{unaux } (T, T, \Upsilon) \equiv \Upsilon \tag{5.47}$$

If T and U are not the same tree, it is necessary to consider their structure.

---

12. 'Υ' (upsilon) stands for the *unification*.

We must be careful to ensure that we have considered all the cases. T and U can each be identifiers, constants, monadic applications, or dyadic applications. This suggests that 16 cases must be handled! Since in most of these combinations unification is impossible, however, we can simplify our analysis by restricting our attention to those cases in which T and U are potentially unifiable. The remaining cases, where unification is impossible, can be handled with an **else** clause. The possibility (•) and impossibility (blank) of unification is indicated in the following table:

$T\downarrow$ $U\rightarrow$	ident	const	monadic	dyadic
ident	•	•	•	•
const	•	•		
monadic	•		•	
dyadic	•			•

Note that formulas are generally potentially unifiable only with formulas of their own kind (except for identifiers, which are potentially unifiable with anything). This suggests that we must treat identifiers as a special case.

Either T or U (or both) might be identifiers. First consider the case where T is an identifier; that is, $T = \text{ident } x$ for some string x. This corresponds to the first row of the table, in which an identifier potentially unifies with any formula. If the identifier is already bound, however, it can be unified only if the value to which it is bound can be unified in its place. For example, if x is already bound, say to (2×3), then $(x + 1)$ can be unified with $((2 \times a) + 1)$ only if the value of x, (2×3), is unifiable with $(2 \times a)$. In this case it is, by the substitution $a \Rightarrow 3$. Thus, if $x \in \text{dom } \Sigma$, then unaux returns the result of unifying with U the formula bound by x:

$$\text{unaux (ident } x, U, \text{ success } \Sigma) \equiv \qquad\qquad (5.48)$$
$$\text{unaux } (\Sigma x, U, \text{ success } \Sigma), \text{ if } x \in \text{dom } \Sigma$$

This result will be success or failure depending on whether or not Σx unifies with U.

If, on the other hand, x is unbound, we can sometimes simply add the substitution $x \Rightarrow U$ to Σ. For example, $(x + 1)$ unifies with $((2 \times a) + 1)$ by the substitution $x \Rightarrow (2 \times a)$. Unfortunately this doesn't always work. To see this suppose that U is the identifier y and that $y \Rightarrow x$ is already in Σ. In this case we do not want to add $x \Rightarrow U$ to Σ—this would result in the circular substitutions $x \Rightarrow y$, $y \Rightarrow x$. Although x is not bound, y is, so we must unify with the tree to which y is bound.

Therefore we next consider the case in which $U = \text{ident } y$, corresponding to the first column of the table. Since unaux is symmetric in T and U, clearly the case where y is bound is analogous to Eq. (5.48). Hence

$$\begin{aligned} \text{unaux } (T, \text{ ident } y, \text{ success } \Sigma) &\equiv \\ \text{unaux } (T, \Sigma y, \text{ success } \Sigma), &\text{ if } y \in \text{dom } \Sigma \end{aligned} \qquad (5.49)$$

We have covered the cases in which either T or U (or both) are bound identifiers. The remaining cases are those in which either T or U (or both) are unbound identifiers. If $T = \text{ident } x$ is unbound, then we simply add $x \Rightarrow U$ to Σ. Since the unification succeeds in this case, its equation is

$$\begin{aligned} \textbf{else } \text{ unaux } (\text{ident } x, \, U, \text{ success } \Sigma) &\equiv \\ \text{success } [\text{exten } (\Sigma, x, U)], &\text{ if } x \notin \text{dom } \Sigma \end{aligned} \qquad (5.50)$$

On the other hand, if $U = \text{ident } y$ is unbound, then we add $y \Rightarrow T$ to Σ:

$$\begin{aligned} \textbf{else } \text{ unaux } (T, \text{ ident } y, \text{ success } \Sigma) &\equiv \\ \text{success } [\text{exten } (\Sigma, y, T)], &\text{ if } y \notin \text{dom } \Sigma \end{aligned} \qquad (5.51)$$

If both T and U are unbound, then either of these extensions will work (and there is not a unique minimal Σ).

We have handled the first row and the first column of the table. The remaining cases are where T and U are not identifiers. Thus unification is possible only if they are the same variant of tree. The case where they are both constants has already been handled, so we proceed to the monadic and dyadic applications.

Exercise 5.50:   Explain why the case of constants has already been handled.   That is,   show   that   the   already   derived   equations   specify   that unaux (const k, const k, Υ) returns Υ.

Suppose that T and U are monadic applications. Under what conditions can they be unified? At very least they must have the same operator. Thus we can assume

$$T = \text{monadic } (m, X) \text{ and } U = \text{monadic } (m, Y)$$

These formulas are formally equal if and only if there is a substitution that makes X formally equal to Y. Furthermore, the substitution that makes T equal to U is just that which makes X equal to Y. Thus this case is handled by the equation

$$\text{unaux } [\text{monadic } (m, X), \text{ monadic } (m, Y), \Upsilon] \equiv \text{unaux } (X, Y, \Upsilon) \qquad (5.52)$$

For dyadic applications, the job is slightly more complicated. First suppose that T and U have the forms

T = dyadic (d, X, X') and U = dyadic (d, Y, Y')

Clearly T and U are unifiable only if there is a *single* substitution that unifies X with Y and X' with Y'. We can proceed in two steps. First we find a substitution Σ', extending Σ, that unifies X and Y:

success Σ' = unaux $(X, Y,$ success $\Sigma)$

Then we find a substitution Σ'', extending Σ', that unifies X' and Y':

success Σ'' = unaux $(X', Y',$ success $\Sigma')$

This is the substitution needed to unify T and U. The resulting equation is immediate:

unaux [dyadic (d, X, X'), dyadic (d, Y, Y'), Υ] $\equiv \Upsilon''$ (5.53)
    where $\Upsilon'' \equiv$ unaux (X', Y', Υ')
      where $\Upsilon' \equiv$ unaux (X, Y, Υ)

We have covered all the cases in which unification is possible, so if none of these hold unaux must return failure:

else   unaux $(T, U, \Upsilon) \equiv$ failure   (5.54)

The resulting definition of unifier appears in Fig. 5.10. Why is the word **else** before the clauses corresponding to Eqs. (5.50) and (5.51) is critical?

Figure 5.10 Unification for arithmetic expressions.

unifier $(T, U) \equiv$ unaux $(T, U,$ success nihil)
  where   unaux: tree $\times$ tree $\times$ unification $\rightarrow$ unification
        unaux $(T, U,$ failure) $\equiv$ failure
        unaux $(T, T, \Upsilon) \equiv \Upsilon$
        unaux (ident $x, U,$ success $\Sigma) \equiv$ unaux $(\Sigma x, U,$ success $\Sigma)$, if $x \in$ dom Σ
        unaux $(T,$ ident $y,$ success $\Sigma) \equiv$ unaux $(T, \Sigma y,$ success $\Sigma)$, if $y \in$ dom Σ
        unaux [monadic (s, X), monadic (s, Y), Υ] $\equiv$ unaux (X, Y, Υ)
        unaux [dyadic (s, X, X'), dyadic (s, Y, Y'), Υ] $\equiv \Upsilon''$
           where $\Upsilon'' \equiv$ unaux (X', Y', Υ')
             where $\Upsilon' \equiv$ unaux (X, Y, Υ)

      else   unaux (ident $x, U,$ success $\Sigma) \equiv$ success [exten (Σ, x, U)], if $x \notin$ dom Σ
           unaux $(T,$ ident $y,$ success $\Sigma) \equiv$ success [exten (Σ, y, T)], if $y \notin$ dom Σ
           else   unaux $(T, U, \Upsilon) \equiv$ failure

Exercise 5.51: Equation (5.53) attempts to unify X and Y before trying to unify X' and Y'; that is, it works from left to right in T and U. Could we work from right to left instead? Write the equation corresponding to Eq. (5.53) that attempts to unify X' and Y' before attempting X and Y.

Exercise 5.52: How could the dyadic case, Eq. (5.53), be specified more independent of order? Suppose that we unified separately X with Y and X' with Y'. What operation on finite functions is needed to combine these separate unifications into a unification of T and U? Develop an archetype and prototype for this operation. Compare the efficiency of the original version of unifier with your new version, *assuming that the unification (X, X') can be done in parallel with the unification (Y, Y').*

Exercise 5.53: Translate the unification algorithm in Fig. 5.10 into LISP, Pascal, or some other programming language.

Exercise 5.54: Define a function that returns a table containing the number of occurrences for each identifier in a tree. Thus processing the tree corresponding to

$$(2 \times a \times x + b) \times (2 \times a \times x + c)$$

returns the table

$$['a' \mapsto 2, 'x' \mapsto 2, 'b' \mapsto 1, 'c' \mapsto 1]$$

Exercise 5.55: Define a function transform: $\text{tree}^3 \rightarrow \text{tree} + \text{failure}$ that attempts to apply a transformation rule to a formula by unification. That is,

transform (F, L, R)

attempts to transform F by the rule $L \Rightarrow R$; it does this by unifying F with L and performing the resulting substitutions on R. The function should return either the transformed formula or an indication that unification was impossible. (Transformation rules are the subject of Chapter 10.)

To prove that our definition of unifier is correct, we must show that the definition in Fig. 5.10 satisfies the archetype (Eq. 5.45). Because the archetype is defined in terms of subst, we must first define this function (the archetype and prototype are identical).

Since the structure of subst is determined by the structure of its domain, tree, we consider each kind of tree. The result of performing a substitution on a monadic application results from performing the substitution on its operand:

$$\text{subst } [\Sigma, \text{monadic } (m, T)] = \text{monadic } [m, \text{subst } (\Sigma, T)] \qquad (5.55)$$

For dyadic applications both operands must be processed:

$$\text{subst } [\Sigma, \text{ dyadic } (d, T, U)] = \text{dyadic } [d, \text{ subst } (\Sigma, T), \text{ subst } (\Sigma, U)] \qquad (5.56)$$

The result of performing a substitution on a constant is just that constant:

$$\text{subst } (\Sigma, \text{ const } k) = \text{const } a \qquad (5.57)$$

The result of performing a substitution on an identifier depends on whether or not that identifier is in the domain of the substitution. If not, then it remains:

$$\text{subst } (\Sigma, \text{ ident } x) = \text{ident } x, \text{ if } x \notin \text{dom } \Sigma \qquad (5.58)$$

If so, then it must be replaced:

$$\text{subst } (\Sigma, \text{ ident } x) = \text{subst } (\Sigma, \Sigma x), \text{ if } x \in \text{dom } \Sigma \qquad (5.59)$$

Notice that we perform the Σ substitution on the tree Σx that has replaced ident x; this is necessary because Σx may contain identifiers that need replacing themselves. For example, performing the substitutions

$$x \Rightarrow y + a, \; y \Rightarrow b \times 2$$

on the expression '$x + 1$' should result in

$$x + 1 \Rightarrow y + a + 1 \Rightarrow b \times 2 + a + 1$$

Although this repeated substitution process is required, it should worry us—it may cause a tree to be passed to the inner subst that is larger than that passed to the outer one. This means that the size of the argument does not decrease on each step—the property we usually use to convince ourselves of termination.

Does subst always terminate? A little thought shows that, if Σ contains the substitution $x \Rightarrow x$, then subst $(\Sigma, \text{ ident } x)$ will never terminate. This problem is not too serious since the substitution $x \Rightarrow x$ can never arise from our unification process. Why? We are forced, however, to recognize that subst is not total on its domain substitution $\times$ tree since there are certain combinations for which it doesn't terminate. This counterexample also encourages us to look for nonterminating substitutions that *could* arise from unification.

The trouble with $x \Rightarrow x$ is that the substitution does not eliminate x and thus gets no closer to termination. The reason this situation cannot arise is that the two trees are identical, and the unification of identical trees does not extend the substitution. This suggests that a nonterminating substitution could result from an identifier that is replaced by a (different) tree containing that same identifier, for example, $x \Rightarrow 1 + x$. It is easy to see that if Σ contains this substitution rule, then subst may not terminate:

$$x \Rightarrow 1 + x \Rightarrow 1 + 1 + x \Rightarrow 1 + 1 + 1 + x \Rightarrow \cdots$$

Can a substitution rule such as $x \Rightarrow 1 + x$ arise from unification? It doesn't take long to see that such a rule results from unifying x and $1 + x$, so nonterminating substitutions are a serious issue that cannot be ignored.

You may think that the possibility of these nonterminating substitutions has simply proved that unifier is incorrect, but the problem is much deeper. Recall that the purpose of unification is to find a substitution that makes two expressions formally identical. Thus in the preceding example we asked whether there is any substitution for x that will make 'x' and '$1 + x$' the same formulas. Now, if you imagine replacing x by the infinite sequence of '1 +'s, you will see that this substitution does in fact unify the formulas:

$$x \Rightarrow 1 + 1 + 1 + 1 + 1 + 1 + 1 + \cdots$$
$$1 + x \Rightarrow 1 + (1 + 1 + 1 + 1 + 1 + 1 + \cdots)$$
$$\Rightarrow 1 + 1 + 1 + 1 + 1 + 1 + 1 + \cdots$$

One more than infinity is still infinity. In this sense the result returned by unifier is correct. Since it forces subst into nontermination, however, it is problematic.

To guarantee that subst terminates, we must guarantee that unifier never produces a substitution rule that produces its own left-hand side. It is insufficient to prevent rules that *directly* produce their left-hand sides; we must also prevent sets of rules that do so indirectly, such as $x \Rightarrow y + 1$, $y \Rightarrow x + 1$. Thus preventing nonterminating substitutions is complicated, since every time we introduce a new rule, we must ensure that it hasn't created any cycles. Because this so-called "occurs check" is quite expensive, many logic programming systems do not perform it, and as a result may produce nonterminating substitutions. Whether such *cyclic* substitutions should be permitted, and if not, whether the "occurs check" is worth performing, are open issues in the design of logic programming languages.

Exercise 5.56: Exhibit two formulas that are unified by the substitution $x \Rightarrow y + 1, y \Rightarrow x + 1$.

Exercise 5.57: Modify unifier to perform the "occurs check."

We have taken a long digression since we set about proving unifier correct. We've discovered that we must be much more careful in specifying its behavior. We revise specification (5.45) as follows:

If unifier (T, U) = success Σ,   (5.60)
and subst (Σ, T) and subst (Σ, U) terminate,
then Σ is minimum finite function in finfunc (**string** $\rightarrow$ tree)
such that subst (Σ, T) = subst (Σ, U);

If unifier (T, U) = failure,
then there is no Σ such that subst (Σ, T) = subst (Σ, U).

You are taken through the steps of the correctness proof in the following exercises.

It is often easier to prove a more general proposition than the one we're interested in. That is the case here, so we'll prove the correctness of unaux, from which the correctness of unifier will follow as an easy corollary. To this end we specify unaux:

1. If unaux $(T, U, \text{success } \Sigma')$ = success Σ, and subst (Σ, T) and subst (Σ, U) terminate, then Σ is a minimal extension of Σ' such that subst (Σ, T) = subst (Σ, U).

2. If unaux $(T, U, \text{success } \Sigma')$ = failure, then there is no Σ extending Σ' such that subst (Σ, T) = subst (Σ, U).

First we show that the definition in Fig. 5.10 satisfies property (1). The tricky part is discovering how to do the inductive proof. Induction recapitulates recursion, but which recursion? Since, by hypothesis, we know that subst (Σ, T) and subst (Σ, U) both terminate, one choice is to do induction on N, the number of times subst is invoked by subst (Σ, T) and subst (Σ, U) together. Notice that since the subst invocations must walk the trees T and U, N is at least as big as the combined sizes of (number of nonleaf nodes in) T and U.

Exercise 5.58: Show that property (1) holds for the case $N = 0$ (i.e., subst is not invoked). (*Hint:* If $N = 0$, then T and U are either both constants, or both identifiers not in the domain of Σ.)

For the inductive part of the proof assume $N > 0$. The inductive hypothesis is as follows:

If unaux $(T, U, \text{success } \Sigma')$ = success Σ, and subst (Σ, T) and subst (Σ, U) together terminate in $k < N$ subst invocations, then Σ is a minimal extension of Σ' such that subst (Σ, T) = subst (Σ, U).

The inductive part of the proof breaks down into a number of cases according to the structure of the program.

Exercise 5.59:   Prove the case $T = \text{ident } x$ where $x \in \text{dom } \Sigma$ and $x \in \text{dom } \Sigma'$. *Hint:* Apply Eq. (5.48).

Exercise 5.60:   Prove the case $T = \text{ident } x$ where $x \in \text{dom } \Sigma$ and $x \notin \text{dom } \Sigma'$. *Hint:* Apply Eq. (5.50).

The cases in which $U = \text{ident } y$ are like the preceding two exercises; apply Eqs. (5.49) and (5.51).

Exercise 5.61:   Show that the remaining cases in which T or U is an identifier ($T = \text{ident } x$, $U = \text{ident } y$, $x \notin \text{dom } \Sigma$, $y \notin \text{dom } \Sigma$) cannot occur. *Hint:* In this case only Eq. (5.47) would apply, but it would imply that $N = 0$.

The preceding exercises handle all cases in which T or U is an identifier. In the remaining cases we can assume that since unaux is successful, T and U must be the same variant.

Exercise 5.62:   Show that the case $T = \text{const } x$, $U = \text{const } y$ cannot occur since it would imply that $N = 0$. *Hint:* Apply Eq. (5.47).

Exercise 5.63:   Prove the inductive step for the case $T = \text{monadic } (m, T')$, $U = \text{monadic } (m, U')$. *Hint:* Apply Eq. (5.52).

Exercise 5.64:   Prove the inductive step for the case $T = \text{dyadic } (d, T', T'')$, $U = \text{dyadic } (d, U', U'')$. *Hint:* Apply Eq. (5.53).

Exercise 5.65:   Assemble Exercises (5.58–5.64) into the proof that unaux satisfies property (1).

Exercise 5.66: Prove property (2), which states that, if unaux $(T, U, \text{success } \Sigma')$ = failure, then there is no Σ extending Σ' such that subst (Σ, T) = subst (Σ, U). *Hint:* This can be established by proving the contrapositive:

If there is a Σ extending Σ' such that subst (Σ, T) = subst (Σ, U), then unaux $(T, U, \text{success } \Sigma') \neq$ failure.

The proof—again by induction on N, the total number of subst invocations in subst (Σ, T) and subst (Σ, U)—requires a case analysis similar to that for property (1).

Chapter 6

Higher-Order Functions

6.1 Functional Mapping

In Section 3.5 we saw several functions that perform the same operation on every element of a sequence. For example, map_sin applies sin to every element of a sequence, returning a sequence of the results:

$$\text{map\_sin } S = <\sin S_1, \sin S_2, \ldots, \sin S_n>$$

Similarly, map_square applies square to every element of a sequence, returning a sequence of the results:

$$\text{map\_square } S = <\text{square } S_1, \text{square } S_2, \ldots, \text{square } S_n>$$

(In each case we assume $n = \text{length } S$.) A related function, map_length, applies length to each element of a sequence of sequences, returning a sequence of the lengths of those sequences:

$$\text{map\_length } <S_1, \ldots, S_n> = <\text{length } S_1, \ldots, \text{length } S_n>$$

In general, if 'map_f' is any one of these functions, then

$$\text{map\_}f\ S\ =\ <fS_1,\ fS_2,\ \ldots,\ fS_n>$$

Let's review the definitions of these functions:

$$\text{map\_sin}\ S\ \equiv\ \begin{cases} \text{nil, if null } S \\ \textbf{else } \sin\ (\text{first } S)\ :\ \text{map\_sin (rest } S) \end{cases}$$

$$\text{map\_square}\ S\ \equiv\ \begin{cases} \text{nil, if null } S \\ \textbf{else } \text{square (first } S)\ :\ \text{map\_square (rest } S) \end{cases}$$

$$\text{map\_length}\ S\ \equiv\ \begin{cases} \text{nil, if null } S \\ \textbf{else } \text{length (first } S)\ :\ \text{map\_length (rest } S) \end{cases}$$

Notice that all follow exactly the same pattern, differing only in the function applied to the elements of the sequence. Using 'f' to represent this function, the general pattern can be written

$$\text{map\_}f\ S\ \equiv\ \begin{cases} \text{nil, if null } S \\ \textbf{else } f(\text{first } S)\ :\ \text{map\_}f\ (\text{rest } S) \end{cases}$$

It is tedious to have to reconstruct this pattern every time we need to map a function on a sequence. Also, although the pattern is simple, eventually we are likely to make an error, such as forgetting the rest or first operation on S. A better solution is to *abstract* the common pattern and give it a name, following the *Abstraction Principle*: Avoid requiring something to be stated more than once; factor out the recurring pattern. The pattern then can be used repeatedly by invoking its name.

To accomplish this abstraction, we need a general pattern—let's call it map—that can be used to create the functions map_sin, map_square, and map_length. As you have seen many times, general patterns are usually represented by functions; particular instances result from applying these functions to particular arguments. In this case, we create the map_sin instance by applying the general pattern map to sin: 'map (sin)'. Similarly, map_square = map (square) and map_length = map (length).

After defining map, we can get the effect of 'map_sin S' by applying 'map (sin)' to S, which we can write '[map (sin)] S'. As usual, the juxtaposition of [map (sin)] and S means that the function [map (sin)] is to be applied to S. Note, however, that the function to be applied is itself the result of applying map to sin, as indicated by 'map (sin)'. Because the parentheses are not necessary, we can write '[map sin] S' for '[map (sin)] S'. Furthermore, adopting the convention that function application associates to the left, we can eliminate the brackets:

$$\text{map sin } S\ =\ [\text{map sin}]\ S$$

In general, '*fxy*' means '(*fx*)*y*'—that is, the application to *y* of the result of applying *f* to *x* (presuming, of course, that the value of *fx* is a function).

Figure 6.1 is a *data-flow diagram* for mapping, it shows how a typical input is processed. In addition, it shows how the data-flow diagram for map *f* is constructed from the data-flow diagram for *f* (i.e., by replicating it as many times as there are elements in the input sequence). Many of the functions we investigate in this chapter can be thought of as ways to combine data-flow diagrams and are thus ways to construct larger programs from smaller ones—a kind of *programming in the large* (DeRemer and Kron 1976).

What is the signature of map? Since sin: $\mathbb{R} \to \mathbb{R}$ and map_sin: $\mathbb{R}^* \to \mathbb{R}^*$, the function returned by map sin must have the signature

$$(\text{map sin}): \ \mathbb{R}^* \to \mathbb{R}^*$$

Therefore, since map takes a function of type $\mathbb{R} \to \mathbb{R}$ and returns a function of type $\mathbb{R}^* \to \mathbb{R}^*$, it must in this application have the type

$$(\mathbb{R} \to \mathbb{R}) \ \to \ (\mathbb{R}^* \to \mathbb{R}^*)$$

That is, when map is applied to a function from reals into reals it returns a function from real sequences into real sequences. This, however, is not the type of map. Consider map length. Since length: $T^* \to \mathbb{N}$, for all T (i.e., length is polymorphic), it is easy to see that in this application map length has type $(T^*)^* \to \mathbb{N}^*$. Hence in this application the type of map is

$$(T^* \to \mathbb{N}) \ \to \ [(T^*)^* \to \mathbb{N}^*]$$

That is, if map is given a function $T^* \to \mathbb{N}$, it returns a function of type

---

Figure 6.1 Data-flow diagram for mapping.

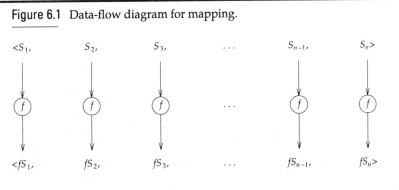

map *f* S

$(T^*)^* \to \mathbb{N}^*$. In general, if $f: D \to R$, then map f has type $D^* \to R^*$. Hence, the signature of map is

$$\text{map}: (D \to R) \to (D^* \to R^*), \text{ for all } D, R \in \textbf{type} \tag{6.1}$$

That is, for any types D and R, if map is applied to a function of type $D \to R$, then it returns a function of type $D^* \to R^*$.

To complete an archetype for map, we must specify its semantics. First let's use the equation

$$\text{map } f\ S\ =\ <fS_1, fS_2, \ldots, fS_n> \tag{6.2}$$

although it is a little imprecise because of the use of the '$\cdots$' notation. To make it more precise, recall that every sequence can be written in one of two forms, nil or $x : y$. This gives us two cases to handle: either $n = 0$ or $n > 0$. Substituting the case $n = 0$ in Eq. (6.2), we get

$$\text{map } f\ \text{nil}\ =\ \text{nil} \tag{6.3}$$

This is obvious: Mapping any function across the empty sequence returns the empty sequence. For the $n > 0$ case we have

$$\text{map } f\ (x : S)\ =\ fx\ :\ \text{map } f\ S \tag{6.4}$$

Equations (6.3) and (6.4) constitute the archetype for the map operation (a prototype implementation is shown in Section 6.3).

Since map is a general-purpose operator for generating mapping functions, we need never again define a mapping function explicitly. For example, since

$$\text{interval } (0, 90)\ =\ <0, 1, 2, \ldots, 88, 89>$$

we can get a sequence of the sines of the angles from $0°$ to $89°$ by map sin [interval (0, 90)]. Using map, sequences of the cosines or tangents are just as easy:

$$\text{map cos [interval (0, 90)]}, \quad \text{map tan [interval (0, 90)]}$$

Similarly, if M is a matrix (sequence of number sequences), then map (map square) will square every element of the matrix:

map (map square) M
= map (map square) $<<M_{1,1}, \ldots, M_{1,n}>, \ldots, <M_{m,1}, \ldots, M_{m,n}>>$
= $<\text{map square } <M_{1,1}, \ldots, M_{1,n}>, \ldots, \text{map square } <M_{m,1}, \ldots, M_{m,n}>>$
= $<<\text{square } M_{1,1}, \ldots, \text{square } M_{1,n}>, \ldots,$
   $<\text{square } M_{m,1}, \ldots, \text{square } M_{m,n}>>$

Finally, suppose E is a sequence representing a file of employee records; each personnel record in E is represented by the following structure:

structure pers_recd $\equiv$
    empl (name $\in$ **string**, hr_rate $\in$ $\mathbb{R}$, dept $\in$ $\mathbb{N}$, emp_no $\in$ $\mathbb{N}$)

For example, if r is an element of E , then hr_rate r and name r would return the hourly rate and name of the employee described by record r. To generate a sequence N of all the employees' names, we must map across E a function to select the name field from each record:

$N \equiv$ map name E

Exercise 6.1: Using map, write a formula that applies the sin function to every element of a (two-dimensional) matrix M.

Exercise 6.2: Using map write a formula that applies the square function to every element of a three-dimensional array A.

Exercise 6.3: Using map, write a formula that returns a sequence of the first elements of a sequence of sequences Q.

Exercise 6.4: Using map, write a formula that converts a sequence of sequences S into a sequence of the corresponding finite sets.

Exercise 6.5: Using map, write a formula that negates every member of a (two-dimensional) Boolean matrix M.

Exercise 6.6: Write a formula that reverses every sequence in the sequence of sequences S.

Exercise 6.7: Write a formula that takes the factorial of every number in the sequence V.

Exercise 6.8: Write a formula that takes a sequence of sets S and returns a sequence of the cardinalities of the sets.

Exercise 6.9: Write a formula that takes a sequence of arithmetic expression trees T and returns a Boolean sequence that tells whether or not each tree is a constant node.

Exercise 6.10: Write a formula that takes a sequence of constant trees (Section 5.9) and returns a sequence of their values.

Exercise 6.11: Write a formula that extracts the employee numbers from the file (sequence) E of employee records.

Exercise 6.12: Prove the following properties of map from its archetype (Eqs. 6.3 and 6.4):

null (map f S) = null S
length (map f S) = length S
map f (S ∧ T) = map f S ∧ map f T

Exercise 6.13: For each of the following identities, determine the conditions under which each side is defined, and show that when both sides are defined they have the same value:

first (map f S) = f(first S)
(map f S)$_i$ = $f(S_i)$
rest (map f S) = map f (rest S)
indsubst (fx, i, map f S) = map f [indsubst (x, i, S)]

We have seen that the map operator is useful; can be implemented? To help derive a prototype definition of map, let's look again at a particular instance, say map_sin:

$$\text{map\_sin } S \equiv \begin{cases} \text{nil, if null } S \\ \textbf{else } \text{sin (first } S) : \text{map\_sin (rest } S) \end{cases}$$

We want map to be defined so that map sin = map_sin, map square = map_square, and so on—in general, that map f = map_f. (Notice the difference: 'map f' is an application of map to f; 'map_f' is just the name of a function.) The simple approach is to take a correct definition of map_f

$$\text{map\_}f \ S \equiv \begin{cases} \text{nil, if null } S \\ \textbf{else } f(\text{first } S) : \text{map\_}f \text{ (rest } S) \end{cases}$$

and substitute 'map f' for every occurrence of 'map_f':

$$\text{map } f \ S \equiv \begin{cases} \text{nil, if null } S \\ \textbf{else } f(\text{first } S) : \text{map } f \text{ (rest } S) \end{cases} \tag{6.5}$$

This is apparently a recursive definition of map; we seem to have succeeded. Closer inspection reveals, however, that this definition differs from those we are used to. In particular, there are two formal parameters on the left, 'f' and 'S', but they are not in a parameter list in the usual way.

In effect Eq. (6.5) implicitly defines the map operation; it says that for all f and S, if map is applied to f, and the result is applied to S, then that result is equal to the right-hand side. Can we be sure that this equation has a solution? In other words, is there a function map that satisfies it? To answer this question we must investigate the solution of equations in which the unknowns are functions, such as Eq. (6.5).

6.2 Definition of Functional Programming

The map function differs from the functions considered earlier. Those functions operated on *data*, that is, numbers, strings, sequences, and so forth. As seen from their signatures, functions such as sin, first, and prefix accept data as arguments and return data as results:

$$\text{sin: } \mathbb{R} \to \mathbb{R}, \text{ first: } T^* \to T, \text{ prefix: } T \times T^* \to T^*$$

The argument of the map function, however, is another function, such as sin, square, or length, and the value it returns is a mapping function, such as map_sin, map_square, or map_length. This fact is reflected in the functional equations that map satisfies, such as map sin = map_sin, map square = map_square, and map length = map_length. It is also apparent in its signature:

$$\text{map: } (D \to R) \to (D^* \to R^*), \text{ for all } D, R \in \textbf{type}$$

Functions like map that operate on functions are called *higher-order* to contrast them with the more usual *first-order* functions, which operate on data.[1] Higher-order functions are characterized by an arrow '→' in the denotations of their domain and/or range types.

We have seen that higher-order functions arise naturally from attempts to abstract common patterns of function definition. Such functions are quite common in mathematics, where they are usually called *operators* or *functionals*. Since computer scientists often apply the term 'operator' to first-order functions, such as '+', '−', '×', and '/', let's instead use the terms 'higher-order function' and 'functional' to refer to functions that accept functions as arguments or return them as results.

We can now define *functional programming* as that style of applicative programming that makes extensive use of functionals.[2] By allowing

---

1. Data objects can be considered *zeroth-order* functions since they return a value even when given *no* input; that is, data and constant functions are equivalent. First-order functions then operate on zeroth-order functions (data), second-order on first-order, and so on. Since our higher-order functions are usually polymorphic (generic), they can operate on functions of any order, so long as the types are correct.
2. This is the way Backus (1978) used the term. Other writers use 'functional programming' as a synonym for 'applicative programming'—needless duplication of terminology that leaves an important concept unnamed.

programs to be written at a higher level of abstraction, functional programming attempts to simplify the programming process. The source of this simplification can be seen in the map example: By finding common patterns of function definition and naming them, we save ourselves the trouble of rediscovering them. We avoid reinventing the wheel.

Functional programming is both more secure and more efficient than applicative programming without functionals. Since we reproduce the repeating pattern by computer rather than manually, we decrease the chance that the pattern will be copied incorrectly. Also, although the prototype implementations of many functionals are recursive (e.g., Eq. 6.5), they need not be implemented this way. If built into the language or recast in a tail-recursive form, they can be very efficient. Therefore the use of functionals such as map avoids needless recursion and improves the efficiency of functional languages, even on conventional computer architectures.

Functional programming can be viewed as just one more step in the process of abstraction that has characterized the evolution of programming languages. The designers of the first programming languages identified useful, frequently recurring patterns of machine instructions, abstracting these patterns into the statements of programming languages, and similarly abstracted useful, frequently recurring patterns of data into the data structures of programming languages. This process has continued. For example, early developers of structured programming identified useful, frequently recurring patterns of **goto**s and conditionals, and abstracted them into higher-level control structures such as **if–then–else**, **while–do**, and **repeat–until**. Functional programming can be viewed as the next step in this process. Useful, frequently recurring patterns of recursive definitions (or assignment statements and loops in imperative languages) are identified and then abstracted and made into functionals.

6.3 Functional Abstraction

Does the expression 'map sin' have any meaning, or is it incomplete without an argument, such as in 'map sin S'? There are two ways to convince ourselves that 'map sin' is meaningful without an argument. First, we intend that 'map sin' have a meaning—the function we previously called map_sin, which was defined explicitly. Second, because we plan to use formulas such as 'map sin' as arguments themselves, such as in map (map sin), they must be meaningful in their own right. We expect the actual parameter to a function to denote a value and hence expect 'map sin' to denote a value. To solve Eq. (6.5) to get an explicit expression for 'map sin', we must be able to write the definition of map in the form

$$\text{map } f \equiv \cdots$$

We don't know, however, what to put on the right of this equation. That is, we don't know how to eliminate the S from the left-hand side of the defining equation for map (Eq. 6.5). In this section we discuss a way to do this.

Since we will study functions in considerable depth, we must have a clear, precise notation for describing functions. To explain the notation, let's use a simpler function than map. Suppose we want to define the function Δ so that Δf applied to any a is $f(a+1) - f(a)$. (This is, of course, the *first difference* of f.) That is, Δ satisfies the equation

$$\Delta fa = f(a+1) - f(a)$$

For example, Δ square is the function $2n+1$ since

$$\Delta \text{ square } n = (n+1)^2 - n^2 = 2n+1$$

Notice that Δ is a function that takes a real function (such as square) as its argument and returns a real function as its result (in this case the function of n that returns $2n+1$). Hence the signature of Δ is

$$\Delta \colon (\mathbb{R} \rightarrow \mathbb{R}) \rightarrow (\mathbb{R} \rightarrow \mathbb{R})$$

To write the value returned by the application Δf, an apparent answer is

$$\Delta f \equiv f(x+1) - f(x)$$

By the right-hand side of this equation we mean the (anonymous) function that takes x into $f(x+1) - f(x)$—that is, the function that takes 0 into $f(1) - f(0)$, 1 into $f(2) - f(1)$, and so forth:

$$0 \mapsto f(1) - f(0), \; 1 \mapsto f(2) - f(1), \; 2 \mapsto f(3) - f(2), \ldots$$

Thus by 'Δf' we mean some function g such that $g(x) = f(x+1) - f(x)$.

Notice that the usual mathematical notation is not very clear on this point. Whether '$x^2 + x - 1$' denotes a particular number or a function depends to a large extent on context; if we had previously defined a value for x or treated it as a constant, then this expression would be taken as denoting a particular number. If we had not previously specified the value of x, then the expression would be interpreted as a function of x. Our interpretation might also be influenced by the fact that 'x', 'y', 'z' are conventionally used as unspecified *variables*, while 'a', 'b', and so on are conventionally used as *constants*. Such ambiguity and context sensitivity is not acceptable in a programming language.

Consider the "function" '$x^2 + y - z$'. To apply it to arguments, such as

4, 18, and 3, we must know which formal parameters go with which actuals. Should the result be $4^2 + 18 - 3$, or $18^2 + 4 - 3$, or something else? Depending on whether the identifiers 'x', 'y', and 'z' are constants or variables, this formula could be interpreted either as a particular number or as any one of the following functions:

$$f(x) \equiv x^2 + y - z$$
$$f(y) \equiv x^2 + y - z$$
$$f(z) \equiv x^2 + y - z$$
$$f(x, y) \equiv x^2 + y - z$$
$$f(y, x) \equiv x^2 + y - z$$
$$f(x, y, z) \equiv x^2 + y - z$$
$$f(y, x, z) \equiv x^2 + y - z$$
$$f(z, y, x) \equiv x^2 + y - z$$

and so forth. The formula could even be interpreted as a function such as $f(w, x) \equiv x^2 + y - z$! The problem is that we don't know which identifiers are to be interpreted as constants and which are to be interpreted as formal parameters to the function. Therefore when the function $x^2 + y - z$ is applied to actual parameters, such as $(\pi, 1)$, we don't know how to establish the correspondence between the actuals and the formals.

When we name a function, we have an opportunity to distinguish the formal parameters from other identifiers in the definition of the function. For example, in

$$f(x) \equiv x^2 - 3a$$

'x' is the formal parameter and 'a' is a *free* (nonlocal) identifier (presumably it was defined elsewhere).

The function returned by Δ square is not explicitly defined and given a name, however, so there is nowhere to put its formal parameters. This is what's missing from

$$\Delta f \equiv f(x + 1) - f(x)$$

One way to denote a function so that its formal parameters are clearly identified is to give this otherwise anonymous function a name—for instance, by an auxiliary definition:

$$\Delta f \equiv g \quad \textbf{where} \quad g(x) \equiv f(x + 1) - f(x)$$

The **where** declaration gives us a place to specify that x is the formal parameter of g. Although adequate for many purposes, it will in the long run be useful if we attack the problem head on and develop a precise denotation for anonymous functions.

One simple solution would be to eliminate the name of the function, 'f', from a definition such as

$$f(x) \equiv x^2 - 3a$$

Thus '$(x) \equiv x^2 - 3a$' could be used to denote the function that takes any x into $x^2 - 3a$. In fact, mathematicians use the similar notation '$x \mapsto x^2 - 3a$' with exactly this interpretation. We'll use this more readable notation even though in computer science it's more common to use the *lambda notation*, '$\lambda x(x^2 - 3a)$'. The *functional abstraction* '$x \mapsto (x^2 - 3a)$' can be read "the function that takes x into $x^2 - 3a$."

We can use this notation to solve some functional equations, such as the following:

$$f(x) = x^2 - 3x$$

It says that f is a function that, when applied to any x, yields $x^2 - 3x$. We can solve this equation for f by using the functional abstraction to move the x from the left to the right:

$$f \equiv x \mapsto (x^2 - 3x)$$

To check this solution, we ask the value of $f(5)$, substituting '5' for 'x' throughout its scope. More specifically, we start with

$$f(5)$$

Since $f \equiv x \mapsto (x^2 - 3x)$, we substitute '$x \mapsto (x^2 - 3x)$' for '$f$' and get

$$x \mapsto (x^2 - 3x)(5)$$

Now we replace this expression by a copy of the *body* of the abstraction (i.e., '$x^2 - 3x$'), in which all the 'x's are replaced by '(5)':

$$(5)^2 - 3(5) = 25 - 15 = 10$$

This is called the *copy rule* for function evaluation because the invocation '$f(5)$' is actually replaced by a copy of the body of the function with its parameter textually substituted—that is, '$(5)^2 - 3(5)$'. In general, whenever we see a function $x \mapsto E$ applied to an actual parameter A, we can replace the entire application by a copy of E in which every occurrence of x is replaced by A. Chapters 8 and 9 discuss the lambda calculus, a mathematical theory that describes this process very precisely; it is the fundamental theory of applicative programming.

Functional abstraction permits us to solve functional equations that have arbitrary variables on the left-hand side. For example, we had the equation

$$\Delta f x \;=\; f(x+1) - f(x)$$

We can cancel 'x' from the left and move it to the right by converting the right side to a functional abstraction:

$$\Delta f \;=\; x \mapsto [f(x+1) - f(x)]$$

This gives us an explicit formula for Δf, which we can read, "Δf is the function that takes any x into the difference of $f(x+1)$ and $f(x)$."

To arrive at an explicit formula for Δ, we cancel the 'f' from the left and move it to the right:

$$\Delta \;=\; f \mapsto \{x \mapsto [f(x+1) - f(x)]\}$$

This is read, "Δ is the function that takes any f into the function that takes any x into the difference of $f(x+1)$ and $f(x)$." We can check this result by evaluating a specific application, such as 'Δ square 2', by substitution and the copy rule:

$$
\begin{aligned}
\Delta \text{ square } 2 &= f \mapsto \{x \mapsto [f(x+1) - f(x)]\} \text{ square } 2 \\
&= x \mapsto [\text{square}(x+1) - \text{square}(x)]\, 2 \\
&= \text{square}(2+1) - \text{square}(2) = 3^2 - 2^2 = 5
\end{aligned}
$$

We get the second line by replacing 'f' by 'square' (and dropping the '$f \mapsto$'); the third, by replacing 'x' by '2' (and dropping the '$x \mapsto$').

To generalize the preceding example, if we have any functional equation

$$Fx \;=\; E$$

in which x is arbitrary and does not occur in F, then we can solve for F by canceling x from the left side and moving it to the right:

$$F \;=\; x \mapsto E$$

This process, called "solving a functional equation *by abstraction*," is the functional analog of the familiar process of solving an algebraic equation by dividing both sides by the same quantity:

$$Ax \;=\; E \quad \Rightarrow \quad A \;=\; E/x$$

How do we know that solving an equation by functional abstraction works? Consider the analogous algebraic process, solving an equation by division. This process is based on an identity, $Ax/x = A$ (or, if you prefer, on two identities, $x/x = 1$ and $A1 = A$). That is, if we know $Ax = E$, then by referential transparency we also know $Ax/x = E/x$. Hence, by the identity $Ax/x = A$, we have $A = E/x$. Solving by functional abstraction is also based on an identity:

$$x \mapsto Fx \ = \ F \tag{6.6}$$

Although this looks unfamiliar, it's easy to understand through a couple of examples. All Eq. (6.6) says is that the function that takes any x into sin x is the sin function, that the function that takes any x into square x is the square function, and so forth. In effect, it tells us that, for an arbitrary x, abstraction by x inverts application to x.

Although Eq. (6.6) is quite obviously true, it can be proved in a simple way. Two functions F and G are equal if and only if, for all a, $Fa = Ga$. Therefore let $G = x \mapsto Fx$. Observe that for any a the copy rule gives us

$$Ga \ = \ (x \mapsto Fx)a \ = \ Fa$$

Hence, for all a, $Fa = Ga$, so $F = G = x \mapsto Fx$. Much of the power of functional programming derives from its ability to manipulate programs algebraically by means of identities such as Eq (6.6).

Exercise 6.14: Prove the related cancellation rule, that application to x inverts abstraction by x:

$$(x \mapsto E)x \ = \ E$$

Here E represents any formula, which may or may not include occurrences of x.

We can now answer the question of whether the formula 'map sin' has meaning on its own. Substituting sin for f in Eq. (6.5), we obtain

$$\text{map sin } S \ = \ \begin{cases} \text{nil, if null } S \\ \textbf{else } \sin (\text{first } S) \ : \ \text{map sin (rest } S) \end{cases}$$

Now we can use functional abstraction to move S from the left to the right:

$$\text{map sin } = \ S \mapsto \begin{cases} \text{nil, if null } S \\ \textbf{else } \sin (\text{first } S) \ : \ \text{map sin (rest } S) \end{cases}$$

This can be read, "map sin is the function that takes any S into nil if S is null, otherwise the result of prefixing the sine of the first element of S onto the result of mapping sine across the rest of S."

Indeed, functional abstraction can be applied to Eq. (6.5) to yield a direct definition of map:

$$\text{map } f \equiv S \mapsto \begin{cases} \text{nil, if null } S \\ \textbf{else } f \text{ (first } S) : \text{map } f \text{ (rest } S) \end{cases} \tag{6.7}$$

This definition fits our usual syntax for a function definition and explicitly depicts the fact that map returns a function. Furthermore, it can be directly translated into some programming languages. For example, in Scheme[3] we would write

```
(define (map f)
  (lambda (S)
    (if (null? S) nil
      (cons (f (car S)) ((map f) (cdr S)) )) ))
```

An invocation of map would be written

```
((map sin) (interval 0 90))
```

(Note, however, that the Scheme and LISP sine functions expect their arguments to be in radians.) The functional structure is less clear in Common LISP, which does not permit a formal parameter or the result of a function call to be directly used as a function. That is, instead of '(f (first S))' and '((map f) (rest S))' we must write '(funcall f (first S))' and '(funcall (map f) (rest S))' The operation '(funcall F A)' applies function F to actual parameter A. The Common LISP definition of map is

```
(defun map (f)
  #'(lambda (S)
    (if (null S) nil
      (cons (funcall f (first S))
            (funcall (map f) (rest S)) )) )) )
```

Similarly, an invocation of map would be written

```
(funcall (map #'sin) (interval 0 90))
```

Note that the definition of map (Eq. 6.7) cannot be translated into Pascal, Ada, or any other language that prohibits functions from being the results

---

3. An overview of functional programming in both Scheme and Common LISP is found in Appendix C. See (Abelson and Sussman 1985) for a detailed account of Scheme programming and (Rees and Clinger 1986) for the language definition.

Figure 6.2 Archetype and prototype for map functional.

Archetype

Syntax:
map: $(T \to U) \to (T^* \to U^*)$, for all $T, U \in$ **type**

Semantics:
map f nil = nil
map $f (x : S) = fx :$ map $f S$

Pragmatics:
With sequential implementations map $f S$ takes linear time; on some parallel implementations it takes constant time.

Prototype

$$\text{map } f \equiv S \mapsto \begin{cases} \text{nil, if null } S \\ \textbf{else } f(\text{first } S) : \text{map } f \text{ (rest } S) \end{cases}$$

---

of functions. This is our first example of a functional programming *technique* that requires a functional programming *language*. Nonfunctional languages do not permit as high a degree of abstraction as do functional languages.

The archetype and prototype for map appear in Fig. 6.2. Note that construction of a mapping function, map f, takes constant time. Since the construction of a function by a functional is always in constant time, this fact is not mentioned in any of the archetypes.

Exercise 6.15: Use functional abstraction to obtain an explicit formula for map. How would you read this formula?

Exercise 6.16: Trace the execution of map square <1, 2, 3>.

Exercise 6.17: Prove that the prototype implementation of map satisfies its archetype.

Exercise 6.18: Write a Common LISP or Scheme expression that computes each of the following:

a. The square of every element of a matrix (sequence of sequences of numbers) M.

b. The first element of each element of a sequence of sequences L.

c. The negation of each element of a Boolean matrix (sequence of sequences) M.

d. The lengths of each sequence in a sequence of sequences L.

And so forth, as in Exercises 6.1–6.10. Note that in Common LISP you must use funcall. (See Appendix C for hints on functional programming in Common LISP and Scheme.)

Exercise 6.19: Suppose that F is defined as follows:

$F \equiv$ map map <I, sin, cos, tan, sec, csc>

(I is the identity function, $Ix = x$.)

a. What is the value of F?

b. To see how F might be used, trace the evaluation of the following expression:

map $f \mapsto \{f[\text{interval}\,(0,\,90)]\}\;F$

c. What are the requirements on S so that 'map map S' is legal?

d. What is the signature of 'map map'?

Hint: Remember that function application is left-associative.

Exercise 6.20: Define a functional rev that exchanges the paramaters of its argument. Thus rev $f\,(x,\,y) = f\,(y,\,x)$. Assume that its argument is a binary function.

Let's briefly consider the performance of the map operator. Clearly the prototype definition we have shown will take n steps, where n is the length of the argument sequence. Can we do better? Since applications of the argument function to sequence elements are independent of each other, they could be performed in parallel. That is, map $f\,S$ could be performed in constant time if the number of processors were at least the number of elements in S. Recall that one advantage we claimed for applicative programming was that it provides paradigms for utilizing highly parallel computers, the map function is an example.

Exercise 6.21: Implement map iteratively in LISP or Scheme. Try to use tail recursion rather than the imperative constructs in these languages.

6.4 Functional Abstraction and Mapping

In this section we use map and functional abstraction to introduce the techniques of functional programming. Suppose we wished to define the sequence M to be the result of doubling every member of the sequence S.

This is clearly an application of the map functional, so we could define

$$\text{double } n \equiv 2 \times n$$
$$M \equiv \text{map double } S$$

Similarly, to multiply each member of S by π, we would write

$$\text{pi\_times } x \equiv \pi \times x$$
$$N \equiv \text{map pi\_times } S$$

Finally, to add one to every element of a sequence S, we write

$$\text{succ } x \equiv 1 + x$$
$$Q \equiv \text{map succ } S$$

Although one could argue that the double and succ functions are generally useful, pi_times is not likely to find many applications. Here we have violated the Abstraction Principle in a different way: We have named patterns that are *not* useful and *not* frequently recurring.

To avoid this proliferation of named functions that are only used once or twice, instead of naming them, we can describe them *anonymously* as functional abstractions. For example,

$$M \equiv \text{map } n \mapsto (2 \times n) \, S$$
$$N \equiv \text{map } x \mapsto (\pi \times x) \, S$$
$$Q \equiv \text{map } x \mapsto (1 + x) \, S$$

To see that these functional abstractions work, consider this evaluation of map $x \mapsto (2 \times x)$ <3, 4, 5>:

$$\text{map } x \mapsto (2 \times x) \, <3, 4, 5>$$
$$= <x \mapsto (2 \times x) \, 3, \ x \mapsto (2 \times x) \, 4, \ x \mapsto (2 \times x) \, 5 >$$
$$= <2 \times 3, 2 \times 4, 2 \times 5>$$
$$= <6, 8, 10>$$

For another example, take map $x \mapsto (1 + x)$ <3, 5, 6, 5>:

$$\text{map } x \mapsto (1 + x) \, <3, 5, 6, 5>$$
$$= <x \mapsto (1 + x) \, 3, \ x \mapsto (1 + x) \, 5, \ x \mapsto (1 + x) \, 6, \ x \mapsto (1 + x) \, 5>$$
$$= <1 + 3, 1 + 5, 1 + 6, 1 + 5>$$
$$= <4, 6, 7, 6>$$

Exercise 6.22: Trace the evaluation (as we just did) of the following expressions:

map $n \mapsto (n + 1)$ <1, 2, 3>
map $n \mapsto (1 - n)$ <3, -5, -6, 5>
map $x \mapsto (1 / x)$ <1, 2, 3>
map $x \mapsto (x = 0)$ <2, 0, 1, 3, 0, 0, 5>
map $S \mapsto (0 : S)$ <<3, 4>, <2, 6, 6>, <2>, <3, 4, 5>, < >, <5>>

Exercise 6.23: Trace the evaluation of the following expressions:

map $x \mapsto (x / 2)$ <2, 4, 8>
map $n \mapsto (n - 1)$ <1, 2, 3, 4>
map $a \mapsto (a < 0)$ <5, -2, 0, 4, -1>
map $a \mapsto (a : \text{nil})$ <3, 4, 6>

Consider a simple application. Suppose we have a sequence of characters C, and that for each character we wish to determine whether or not that character belongs to a given finite set S. For example, S might be the letters of the alphabet, and we might wish to characterize each character in C as alphabetic or nonalphabetic. Since we want to perform the same operation on each element of a sequence and return a sequence of the results, let's use the map functional. That is, we want to map some function P across C:

$$\text{map } P \ C \ = \ <PC_1, PC_2, \ldots, PC_n>$$

where Px returns **true** if x is in S and **false** otherwise. Hence P is defined by the equation

$$Px \ = \ x \in S$$

Solving this equation for P by functional abstraction yields

$$P \equiv x \mapsto (x \in S)$$

Therefore, to classify all the members of the sequence C on the basis of whether they are elements of S, and to return a sequence of the results, we write

$$\text{map } x \mapsto (x \in S) \ C$$

Thus we are mapping across the sequence C the function that asks whether its argument is a member of S.

In general, note that $x \mapsto (x \in S)$ is the function that asks whether its argument is a member of S. Thus $x \mapsto (x \in S)$ is the *characteristic function* corresponding to the set S.[4] Familiarity with such functional programming idioms is useful.

Exercise 6.24: Using map and functional abstraction, write formulas to perform the following operations on every element of a sequence and return a sequence of the results:

a. Add 0.5 to the element.

b. Convert each element from degrees to radians.

c. Convert each element x to a pair $<x, x>$.

d. Test to see whether the element is nonnegative.

e. Convert each element x into a singleton set.

f. Delete a fixed value a from each element (assumed to be a finite set).

Exercise 6.25: Using map and functional abstraction, write a formula that takes the reciprocal of each element of a matrix (sequence of real sequences).

Exercise 6.26: Using map and functional abstraction, write a formula that takes a matrix of characters and returns a Boolean matrix with **true** for each blank character and **false** for any nonblank character.

Exercise 6.27: Using map and functional abstraction, define Backus's "distribute left" function:

distl $(x, S) = <<x, S_1>, <x, S_2>, \ldots, <x, S_n>>$

Also define the "distribute right" function distr (S, x).

Exercise 6.28: Suppose $S \in (T^*)^*$ is a sequence of sequences and $i \in$ IN is a fixed positive number. What would be the effect of map $s \mapsto [\text{elt} (s, i)] S$?

Exercise 6.29: Suppose that $S \in [\text{finfunc} (D \to R)]^*$ is a sequence of tables represented as finite functions. Write an expression that looks up k in each of these tables and returns a sequence of the results. That is, the result returned should be

$<S_1 k \; S_2 k, \ldots, \; S_n k>$

where each $S_i k$ is the result of applying finite function S_i to k.

---

4. The characteristic function of a set returns **true** for base type values that are in the set, and **false** for values that aren't.

Exercise 6.30: Suppose that $F \in$ finfunc $(D \to R)$ and that $S \in D^*$. Write a formula to return a sequence of the results of applying F to each member of S:

$$<FS_1, FS_2, \ldots, FS_n>$$

Note that map $F\ S$ will not do it since the map operator works only on the usual (infinite) functions, not on finite functions. *Hint:* How can you turn a finite function of type finfunc $(D \to R)$ into an equivalent function of type $D \to R$?

Exercise 6.31: Define a functional

fmap: finfunc $(D \to R) \to (D^* \to R^*)$

which does for *finite* functions what map does for infinite functions. That is, for a finite function F,

fmap $F\ S\ =\ <FS_1, FS_2, \ldots, FS_n>$

Note that instead of defining a new functional fmap we could simply overload the definition of map.

Exercise 6.32: Define a functional

smap: $T^* \to (\mathbb{N}^* \to T^*)$

with the following property for all sequences $S \in T^*, P \in \mathbb{N}^*$:

smap $S\ P\ =\ <S_{P_1}, S_{P_2}, \ldots, S_{P_n}>$

In what sense is smap similar to map and fmap? *Hint:* Think of the sequence S as a function $S(k) = S_k$. Suggest a possible use for the smap functional. Also note, as remarked in Exercise 6.31 with regard to fmap, that map could be overloaded to accomplish smap.

6.5 Sections of Binary Operators

Many of the functional abstractions discussed in the preceding section have intuitively obvious meanings. For example, $n \mapsto (n + 1)$ is the successor function, $x \mapsto (1 / x)$ is the reciprocal function, $x \mapsto (x = 0)$ is a zero test, $n \mapsto (n - 1)$ is the predecessor function, and $x \mapsto (x / 2)$ is the halving function. Other examples appear in Table 6.1.

Since these abstractions are so useful we adopt a special abbreviation for them, derived from (Wile 1973). If '$\bigcirc$' represents any infix binary

operator, we will allow the *presection* or *left section* '$[x\bigcirc]$' as an abbreviation for '$y \mapsto (x \bigcirc y)$'. Then, since $y \mapsto (x \bigcirc y)\, y = x \bigcirc y$, we have the
simple identity

$$[x \bigcirc]\, y \;=\; x \bigcirc y$$

Notice how the notation suggests the algebraic identity, a strong argument in favor of this abbreviation.

　　We consider some examples. Note that $[2\times]\, x = 2 \times x$ and $[\pi\times]\, x = \pi \times x$. Thus to double every element of S we write map $[2\times]\, S$, and to multiply every element by π we write map $[\pi\times]\, S$. For example,

$$
\begin{aligned}
\text{map } [2\times] <1,\,2,\,3> \;&=\; <[2\times]\,1,\, [2\times]\,2,\, [2\times]\,3> \\
&=\; <2\times1,\, 2\times2,\, 2\times3> \\
&=\; <2,\,4,\,6>
\end{aligned}
$$

Similarly, to take the successor of every element in a sequence we use
map $[1+]\, S$, to take the reciprocal of every element we use map $[1\,/]\, S$, and
to prefix x onto every element we use map $[x\,:]\, S$.

Table 6.1. Example uses of operator sections.

Abstraction	Meaning	Abbreviation
$x \mapsto (1 + x)$	Successor	$1+$
$x \mapsto (0 - x)$	Negate	$0-$
$x \mapsto (2 \times x)$	Double	$2\times$
$x \mapsto (1\,/\,x)$	Reciprocal	$1/$
$x \mapsto (0 = x)$	Zero test	$0=$
$x \mapsto (0 \neq x)$	Nonzero test	$0\neq$
$x \mapsto (a : x)$	Prefix a	$a:$
$x \mapsto (a \in x)$	Contains a?	$a\in$
$x \mapsto (a,\, x)$	Prepair with a	$a,$
$x \mapsto (x - 1)$	Predecessor	-1
$x \mapsto (x\,/\,2)$	Halve	$/2$
$x \mapsto (x < 0)$	Negative test	<0
$x \mapsto (x > 0)$	Positive test	>0
$x \mapsto (x \leq 0)$	Nonpositive test	≤ 0
$x \mapsto (x \geq 0)$	Nonnegative test	≥ 0
$x \mapsto (x : \text{nil})$	Convert to unit sequence	$:\text{nil}$
$x \mapsto (x \in s)$	Convert set to characteristic function	$\in s$
$x \mapsto (x,\, a)$	Postpair with a	$,\,a$

Exercise 6.33:   Trace the evaluation of the following expressions:

map [1 +] <3, 6, 0, 4, 4>
map [1 /] <1, 2, 3>
map [0 :] <<2, 3>, <6, 2, 4>, <2>, < >, <0, 0>>
map [0 ∈] <{2, 3}, {6, 0, 2}, {0, 0}>

Analogously, we allow the *postsection* or *right section* '[○ y]' as an abbreviation for '$x \mapsto (x \bigcirc y)$'. Then, since $x \mapsto (x \bigcirc y) x = x \bigcirc y$, we have the identity

$$[\bigcirc y] x = x \bigcirc y$$

For example, $[/2] x = x/2$, $[-1] x = x-1$, and $[:nil] x = x{:}nil$. Thus, to halve every element of S we write map [/2] S, to decrement every element we write map [−1] S, and to prefix every element onto nil (thus converting the elements into sequences) we write map [:nil] S. For example,

$$\begin{aligned} \text{map } [/2] <6, 8, 2> &= <[/2] 6, [/2] 8, [/2] 2> \\ &= <6/2, 8/2, 2/2> \\ &= <3, 4, 1> \end{aligned}$$

Let's consider several examples of this notation. Recall our previous example, in which we classified the elements of a sequence C on the basis of whether they belonged to a finite set S. Using a right section, this can be written

map [∈ S] C

This expresses our intention quite clearly: to return a sequence of the results of testing whether a given element of C is a member of S. It also shows how functional programming techniques factor out and name common control-flow patterns, thus saving us the bother (and potential mistakes) of repeating these patterns over and over.

Table 6.1 shows the abbreviated forms for the functions discussed previously. The effect of these functional abstractions is depicted in the data-flow diagram in Figure 6.3.

We introduce one last bit of notation. Infix operators such as + and × represent functions just like prefix operators (first, ¬). A potential ambiguity, however, results from using infix operators as actual parameters. For example, the expression

map + S

Figure 6.3 Data-flow diagram for left section.

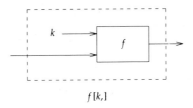

$f[k,]$

is intended to represent the result of mapping the + operator across the sequence of pairs S. Also, however, it could be interpreted to mean the sum of map and S. Although most of these ambiguities could be resolved by typing, it is better notation to avoid the confusion altogether. Therefore, when an infix operator is being used as a functional argument, we write it in brackets; for example,

map [+] S

Exercise 6.34: Trace the evaluation of the following expressions:

map [−1] <1, 2, 3>
map [<0] <5, −3, 6, 0, −2>
map [:nil] <2, 3, 6>
map [+] <(2, 3), (−6, 1), (4, 0)>

Exercise 6.35: Justify informally the meaning of each operation listed in Table 6.1. For example, to show that [+1] is the successor function, derive

$[+1] x = x + 1$

Exercise 6.36: Using map and left and right sections, redo Exercises 6.24 – 6.32 (or state that this can't be done with sections).

6.6 Currying

The map function is often used in expressions of the form 'map f S', which suggests that it has two arguments: f, the function to be mapped, and S, the sequence across which to map it. On the other hand, we've seen that expressions of the form 'map f' are also meaningful, which suggests that map has one argument. Finally, if map does have two arguments, then why don't we write applications in the form 'map (f, S)', as customary for two-argument functions?

To unravel these problems, we begin by considering a simpler function, prf, which is defined

$$\text{prf } x \equiv [x{:}] \equiv y \mapsto (x:y)$$

Thus prf a S prefixes a on sequence S; for example,

$$\text{prf } 3 <5, 8, 7> = <3, 5, 8, 7>$$

The prf function is obviously closely related to the prefix function; in fact they satisfy the identity

$$\text{prf } x \ y = \text{prefix } (x, y)$$

Thus if we have either function we can define the other.

Is the difference between these functions only notational, or more fundamental? First consider their signatures. We know the signature for prefix:

$$\text{prefix: } (T \times T^*) \rightarrow T^*$$

Thus prefix takes a *tuple*, of type $T \times T^*$, and returns a sequence of type T^*.

To determine the signature for prf, note that prf x is a function that takes any sequence y into the sequence $x : y$. Hence prf x has type

$$(\text{prf } x): T^* \rightarrow T^*$$

Therefore it's easy to see that prf itself has type

$$\text{prf: } T \rightarrow (T^* \rightarrow T^*)$$

Thus prf is a function that takes something of type T, and returns a *function* that takes and returns something of type T^*.

Although prefix and prf have quite different signatures, they are still seen to be closely related. Furthermore, this pair of functions is not unique in this relationship. For any function f defined on a tuple type $D_1 \times D_2$,

$$f: (D_1 \times D_2) \rightarrow R$$

there is a corresponding function F defined on the first domain that returns a function defined on the second domain:

$$F: D_1 \rightarrow (D_2 \rightarrow R)$$

The second function is called the *curried* version of the first function;[5] the first function, the *uncurried* form of the second. For example, prefix and prf are the uncurried and curried forms of each other.

Note that at a deep level our language has only *monadic* (single-argument) functions. There are two ways to get the effect of more than one argument. First, the single argument can be a tuple, which allows us to combine several data values into one. Second, we can use a curried function, which takes the first argument and returns a function that takes the second argument, and so forth. Do we need two ways to accomplish the same thing? Is one approach better than the other?

Some applicative languages do in fact focus on one approach. Perhaps the most intuitive approach is to treat argument lists as tuples—the usual approach in mathematics, and the convention used in preceding chapters. Unfortunately this simple solution is not convenient when we begin to program with higher-order functions. Although we could define an uncurried version of map,

$$\text{map}: [(D \rightarrow R) \times D^*] \rightarrow R^*$$

the necessity of providing both of the agrguments of map, as in map (f, S), prevents us from using map f as a function.[6] Perhaps for this reason, some specifically functional languages have adopted the convention of currying *all* functions with more than one argument.[7] Thus instead of 'prefix (x, S)' we write 'prefix x S'; instead of 'member (x, S)', 'member x S'; and so forth. One advantage of this approach is that no special left-section notation is required to bind the first argument of a function. For example, 'prefix x' is the function that prefixes x (which we write '[x:]'), and 'member x' is the function that tests x for membership (which we write as '[$x \in$]').

There are, however, several disadvantages to currying all functions. First, although this allows binding the initial arguments of a function, it does not permit binding the other arguments. For example, we cannot bind the second argument of a function, as in [:S] or [$\in S$], without some

---

5. Such functions are named after Haskell Curry, an American mathematician and logician (1900–1982) who popularized this way of thinking about dyadic (two-argument) functions. Curry helped lay the foundation of functional programming through his development of *combinatory logic* (Curry, Feys and Craig, 1958). Currying itself was invented by Moses Schönfinkel (Schönfinkel 1924).
6. This is exactly the situation in LISP, where this operation is written (mapcar f S).
7. Such languages include KRC (Turner 1981) and Miranda (Turner 1985b).

additional devices.[8] Thus we cannot generalize the curried approach to argument binding. The second problem is that higher-order functions, especially function-valued functions, may be less efficient than first-order functions under some implementation strategies. Therefore it would be unwise to combine these strategies with widespread currying. Finally, as will be seen shortly, it is often convenient to be able to treat a parameter list as a first-class value, which then can be manipulated like any other value (see also Section 5.4). This convenience is lost if all functions are curried.

The preceding considerations have led us to use both curried and uncurried functions in this book. Which do we use in any given case? In agreement with common mathematical practice, first-order functions are generally uncurried. Thus [+] is a function $\mathbb{R} \times \mathbb{R} \to \mathbb{R}$. For higher-order functions we let the abstraction suggest the organization of the parameters. Thus, since map f is a meaningful unit on its own, we have curried the parameters of map. Although in a few cases the choices were not clear, we hope that they are at least natural. In any case you should be aware that this is one area of difference among functional languages.

Exercise 6.37: Define a functional curry that curries a binary function:

curry $f\ x\ y\ =\ f(x, y)$

Write a signature for curry.

Exercise 6.38: Define a functional uncurry that uncurries a binary function:

uncurry $f(x, y)\ =\ fxy$

Write a signature for uncurry.

6.7 Filtering

Suppose we wish to extract from a sequence S of numbers all those numbers that are positive. That is, we want

positives <3, −2, 6, −1, −5, 8, 9> = <3, 6, 8, 9>

We can't use map since it always gives an output sequence the same

---

8. Such as operator sections, or a functional similar to rev (see Exercise 6.20) for reversing the order of a function's arguments.

length as the input sequence, and the output of positives may be shorter than the input. Of course, we can always use explicit recursion:

$$\text{positives } S \equiv \begin{cases} \text{nil, if null } S \\ \text{first } S : \text{positives (rest } S), \text{ if first } S > 0 \\ \textbf{else} \text{ positives (rest } S) \end{cases}$$

It is apparent, however, that *filtering* a sequence to remove those elements that don't have a given property is a common, useful operation. Therefore let's define the functional fil so that fil P is a function to filter a sequence by the predicate (Boolean-valued function) P. The definition is an easy generalization of positives:

$$\text{fil } P \equiv S \mapsto \begin{cases} \text{nil, if null } S \\ \text{first } S : \text{fil } P \text{ (rest } S), \text{ if } P(\text{first } S) \\ \textbf{else} \text{ fil } P \text{ (rest } S) \end{cases}$$

Thus, for example, fil $[> 0]$ S is a sequence of all positive elements of S. This definition is easily translated into a functional language such as Common LISP or Scheme. In Scheme,

```
(define (fil P)
  (lambda (S)
    (cond ((null S) nil)
          ((P (car S)) (cons (car S) ((fil P) (cdr S)) ))
          (else ((fil P) (cdr S)) )) ))
```

We used cond instead of if because it's more convenient for expressing three-way conditionals. Also recall that car = **first** and cdr = **rest**.

To arrive at the definition of fil directly, we must first specify its behavior precisely. Clearly, filtering the null sequence by any predicate returns the null sequence:

fil $P <> = <>$

Now, proceeding by the Method of Differences, suppose we are filtering a nonnull sequence, $S = x : T$. If Px is **true**, then we want x to be in the filtered result; otherwise we don't. Therefore, it is easy to see that we have three cases:

$$\text{fil } P <> = <> \tag{6.8}$$
$$\text{fil } P \ (x : T) = x : (\text{fil } P \ T), \text{ if } Px$$
$$\text{fil } P \ (x : T) = \text{fil } P \ T, \text{ if } \neg Px$$

Figure 6.4 Archetype and prototype for filter functional.

Archetype

Syntax:
 fil: $(T \rightarrow \mathbb{B}) \rightarrow (T^* \rightarrow T^*)$, for all $T \in$ **type**

Semantics:
 fil P nil $=$ nil
 fil P $(x : S) = x :$ fil P S, if $Px =$ **true**
 fil P $(x : S) =$ fil P S, if $Px =$ **false**

Pragmatics:
 With a sequential implementation fil P S takes linear time; with some parallel implementations it takes constant time.

Prototype

$$
\text{fil } P \equiv S \mapsto \begin{cases} \text{nil, if null } S \\ \text{first } S : \text{fil } P \text{ (rest } S), \text{ if } P(\text{first } S) \\ \textbf{else } \text{fil } P \text{ (rest } S) \end{cases}
$$

Equation (6.8) constitutes an archetype for the fil functional; both the archetype and prototype are summarized in Fig. 6.4. Note that the archetype and prototype are identical if the functional language permits equational definitions.

Now let's prove an important property of fil, that is,

$$x \in \text{fil } P \text{ } S = Px \wedge x \in S \tag{6.9}$$

For convenience we use '$\in$' to denote membership in a sequence (i.e., the member function). Property (6.9) follows easily from three lemmas:

Lemma 1: If x is a member of fil P S, then it is an element of S:

$$x \in \text{fil } P \text{ } S \rightarrow x \in S$$

That is, fil doesn't add any elements that weren't in S. To prove this, observe the recursive definition of fil (Eq. 6.8), noting that only one of the clauses of the conditional contributes any elements to the result sequence:

$$\text{first } S : \text{fil } P \text{ (rest } S), \text{ if } P(\text{first } S) \tag{6.10}$$

The element placed in the result is first S, which is obviously an element of S. Therefore the lemma is proved.

Lemma 2: If x is a member of fil P S, then it satisfies the predicate P:

$$x \in \text{fil } P \ S \ \rightarrow \ Px$$

To prove this, observe again the only clause that contributes to the result is Eq. (6.10), which contributes first S, but only if $P(\text{first } S)$ is true. Therefore all the elements of the result satisfy P, and the lemma is proved.

Lemma 3: If x is a member of S and satisfies P, then it is also a member of fil P S:

$$x \in S \wedge Px \ \rightarrow \ x \in \text{fil } P \ S$$

That is, fil captures *all* members of S that satisfy P.

Exercise 6.39: Prove Lemma 3.

Let's consider a few applications of fil. Since $[\in S]$ is a predicate that tests for membership in S, fil $[\in S]$ T is a sequence of all those elements of the sequence T that are also members of the sequence S (i.e., the intersection of S and T). This leads to convenient (nonrecursive) definitions of the sequence-intersection function used to implement finite sets (see Fig. 4.3):

$$S \cap T \equiv \text{fil } [\in S] \ T$$

Its correctness is defined by the following property:

$$x \in (S \cap T) = x \in S \wedge x \in T \tag{4.11}$$

This follows easily from the properties of fil (Eq. 6.9):

$$
\begin{aligned}
x \in (S \cap T) &= x \in \text{fil } [\in S] \ T \\
&= [\in S] \, x \wedge x \in T \\
&= x \in S \wedge x \in T
\end{aligned}
$$

This proof—which is certainly simpler than the inductive proof of this property (see Section 4.6)—illustrates another advantage of functionals: Once we have proved a property of a functional (such as Eq. 6.9), we can use it again and again, thus simplifying the proof of every program in which the functional is used.

The membership test $x \in S$ can be implemented by extracting all the members of S equal to x and seeing whether the resulting sequence is nonnull:

$$x \in S \equiv \neg \, \text{null (fil } [= x] \, S) \hspace{5em} (6.11)$$

Although this implementation of membership is a little inefficient on a sequential computer (Why?), it may execute in constant time on a parallel computer.

Consider a data processing example. Suppose E is the employee database defined in Section 6.1 and that we want to extract a subfile D containing all the employees of department 52. First define a predicate for testing whether an employee is in department 52:

$$\text{in\_dept\_52 } r \equiv (52 = \text{dept } r)$$

D results by filtering with this predicate:

$$D \equiv \text{fil in\_dept\_52 } E.$$

Exercise 6.40: Show that the definition of $\in$ in Eq. (6.11) is correct.

Exercise 6.41: Write a nonrecursive expression to find all nonnull elements of a sequence of sequences; for example,

$$f<<1, 2>, < >, <3, 5, 6>, <4>> \; = \; <<1, 2>, <3, 5, 6>, <4>>$$

Exercise 6.42: Write a nonrecursive expression to determine the number of zeros in a sequence; for example,

$$f<4, 0, 3, 2, 0, 0, 9, 1, 1, 0, 6> \; = \; 4$$

Exercise 6.43: Write a formula for a function that returns a sequence of just the nonempty members of a sequence of finite sets.

6.8 Composition

As already noted, an important goal of functional programming is to find the frequently occurring, useful ways to combine functions, and then to abstract the common patterns and name them. Therefore in the next few sections we discuss some functionals already identified as useful and frequently recurring; in each case we give several applications.

Because the function in_dept_52 defined in Section 6.7 is not generally useful, we probably should not clutter the program with its definition. To avoid this, we can use functional abstraction:

$$D \equiv \text{fil } r \mapsto (52 = \text{dept } r) \, E$$

Figure 6.5 Data-flow diagram for composition.

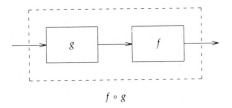

$$f \circ g$$

Alternatively, we can use a local declaration:

$$D \equiv \text{fil } P\ E \quad \textbf{where}\ \ Pr \equiv (52 = \text{dept } r)$$

Yet another approach is to try to identify functionals that allow us to conveniently construct functions such as in_dept_52. Observe that in_dept_52 does two things: (1) selects the department field of a record and (2) compares the resulting department number to 52. The first operation is accomplished by dept; the second can be written [52=]. We need a functional that connects the functions dept and [52=] end to end—that is, that feeds the output of dept into the input of [52=]. This functional is just the mathematician's composition operator:

$$(f \circ g)\,x = f(gx)$$

That is, $f \circ g$ is a function that feeds its argument through g and f, in that order. It can be visualized as the data-flow diagram in Fig 6.5; the archetype and prototype are in Fig. 6.6.

Figure 6.6 Archetype and prototype for composition.

Archetype

Syntax:
$\circ : [(S \to T) \times (R \to S)] \to (R \to T)$, for all $R,\ S,\ T \in$ **type**

That is, $(f \circ g) : R \to T$ for $f : S \to T$ and $g : R \to S$

Semantics:
$(f \circ g)\,x = f(gx)$

Pragmatics:
Composition takes the same time as the composed functions.

Prototype
$f \circ g \equiv x \mapsto f(g\,x)$

Therefore in_dept_52 ≡ [52=] ∘ dept, and we can write the definition of D:

$$D ≡ \text{fil} ([52=] ∘ \text{dept}) E$$

We can immediately see how to do many similar operations. For example, to define a subfile containing all employees who earn more than $100 an hour, we can write

$$\text{fil} ([> 100] ∘ \text{hr\_rate}) E$$

To find the employees who earn more than $100 an hour in department 52, we can do a double filter:

$$\text{fil} ([> 100] ∘ \text{hr\_rate}) \{\text{fil} ([52=] ∘ \text{dept}) E\}$$

E can be eliminated from this formula to yield a formula for the function to extract all the employees satisfying these criteria:

$$\text{fil} ([>100] ∘ \text{hr\_rate}) ∘ \text{fil} ([52=] ∘ \text{dept})$$

It then becomes much clearer that we are running two successive filters, the first to find departments equal to 52 and the second to find rates greater than 100. Thus the general form for filtering by the predicates p and q is fil p ∘ fil q.

Exercise 6.44: Define the composition operator (comp f g) in LISP or Scheme.

Exercise 6.45: To allow us to write '$f ∘ g ∘ h$' without ambiguity, prove that composition is associative: $f ∘ (g ∘ h) = (f ∘ g) ∘ h$.

Exercise 6.46: Write a formula for a function that eliminates from a sequence of numbers all elements less than 0 or greater than 99.

Exercise 6.47: Write a formula for a function to compute the square root of all the nonnegative elements of a sequence.

Exercise 6.48: Write a formula for a function to return the first nonblank element of a sequence of characters.

Exercise 6.49: Suppose E is a sequence of the employee records defined in Eq. (5.13). Write a formula to return a sequence of all present employees whose hourly rate is greater than 100.

Exercise 6.50: Show that

distl (x, S) = map $([x:] \circ [:nil])$ S

Exercise 6.51: Define distr using map, composition, and operator sections.

Exercise 6.52: The assoc function is defined so that

assoc $[a, <(a_1, b_1), (a_2, b_2), \ldots, (a_n, b_n)>]$ = b_k

where k is the first index for which $a = a_k$. Show that the following is a correct definition of assoc:

assoc (a, S) ≡ $[\text{right} \circ \text{first} \circ \text{fil} ([a =] \circ \text{left})]$ S

Explain why this definition may be less efficient than the obvious recursive definition.

Exercise 6.53: Using map, [×], and pairs, define vector_prod, the element-wise product of two vectors.

Exercise 6.54: The Euclidean distance between two n-dimensional points p and q is defined as follows:

$$\delta(p, q) = \sqrt{(p_1 - q_1)^2 + \cdots + (p_n - q_n)^2}$$

Show that the following is a correct definition of this function:

δ ≡ sqrt $\circ$ sum $\circ$ map (square $\circ$ [−]) $\circ$ pairs

Exercise 6.55: The inner product of two vectors U and V is defined as follows:

ip (U, V) = $U_1 V_1 + U_2 V_2 + \cdots + U_n V_n$

Implement ip nonrecursively by using sum, vector_prod, and composition.

Exercise 6.56: Show that

map $f \circ$ map g = map $(f \circ g)$

Discuss any limitations on the domains of definitions of the two sides of the equation. Discuss how this equation might be useful for optimizing functional programs.

Exercise 6.57: Extend composition to finite functions. That is, "overload" the composition operator so that compositions between finite and infinite functions are permitted. Let $f: S \rightarrow T$ and $g: R \rightarrow S$ be infinite functions and let $F \in \text{finfunc}\,(S \rightarrow T)$ and $G \in \text{finfunc}\,(R \rightarrow S)$ be finite functions. The following combinations should be permitted, with the indicated type:

$$f \circ G, \; F \circ g, \; F \circ G : R \rightarrow T$$

6.9 Construction

Suppose we want to construct from the employee file E a sequence composed of pairs, in which each pair contains an employee's name and hourly rate (this is called a *vertical* subfile of the given file). That is, we need a function F such that

$$F: \text{pers\_recd}^* \rightarrow (\textbf{string} \times \mathbb{R})^*$$

Since F performs the same operation on every element of a sequence, it can be implemented as a mapping, $F \equiv \text{map } G$, for some as yet undetermined function

$$G: \text{pers\_recd} \rightarrow (\textbf{string} \times \mathbb{R})$$

G, the function that takes any personnel record r and returns its name-rate pair, is

$$r \mapsto (\text{name } r, \text{ hr\_rate } r)$$

Therefore one simple way to get the sequence of name-rate pairs is by

$$\text{map } r \mapsto (\text{name } r, \text{ hr\_rate } r) \; E$$

Let's reflect on this solution. Recall that the goal of functional programming is to identify common patterns in applicative programs and to define higher-order functions that implement those patterns. In particular, any time we write a functional abstraction such as

$$r \mapsto (\text{name } r, \text{ hr\_rate } r)$$

we should ask ourselves whether this represents a common pattern that should be captured in a functional.

The pattern in this case is to apply two functions (here name and hr_rate) to one piece of data and to form a tuple of the results. In general, from x we are computing (fx, gx). Let's call the function $x \mapsto (fx, gx)$ that accomplishes this the *functional construction*[9] of f and g, and write it '$(f ; g)$'. It is defined by the equation

$$(f ; g)\, x \;=\; (fx,\, gx) \tag{6.12}$$

The semicolon is intended to suggest the comma in the tuple notation.

   With functional construction, the sequence of name-rate pairs can be computed by

> map (name; hr_rate) E

Although this may not seem like much of an improvement, by incorporating the pattern into a functional we open the way for identifying algebraic laws obeyed by the pattern. For example, the following identity is easy to show:

> left $\circ (f ; g) = f$

Note, however, that the right-hand side may be defined in some circumstances in which the left is undefined.

   The type signature for functional construction is depicted in Fig. 6.7. An archetype and prototype appear in Fig. 6.8.

   Just as n-tuples are defined in terms of $(n-1)$-tuples (Section 5.1), we define general functional constructions as follows:

$$(f_1; f_2; \cdots ; f_{n-1}; f_n) \;\Rightarrow\; (f_1; (f_2; (\cdots (f_{n-1}; f_n) \cdots)))$$

Figure 6.7 Type signature for functional construction.

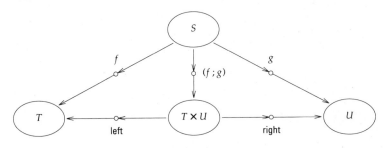

---

9. Introduced, with slightly different notation, in (Backus 1978).

Figure 6.8 Archetype and prototype for functional construction.

Archetype

Syntax:

$[;]: [(S \rightarrow T) \times (S \rightarrow U)] \rightarrow [S \rightarrow (T \times U)]$, for all $S, T, U \in$ **type**

That is, $(f ; g): S \rightarrow (T \times U)$, for $f: S \rightarrow T$ and $g: S \rightarrow U$.

$(f_1; f_2; \cdots ; f_{n-1}; f_n) \Rightarrow (f_1; (f_2; \cdots ; f_{n-1}; f_n))$

Semantics:

$(f ; g) x = (fx, gx)$

Pragmatics:

With sequential implementations, n-ary construction takes the sum of the times of the constructed functions. With some parallel implementations it takes the time of the slowest function.

Prototype

$(f ; g) \equiv x \mapsto (fx, gx)$

The intuitive meaning of $(f_1; \cdots ; f_n)$ is "construct a tuple by applying the functions $f_1, \ldots, f_n$ to the argument." That is,

$(f_1; \cdots ; f_n) x = (f_1x, \ldots, f_nx)$

Let's consider an example from scientific programming; a table of the angles from 0° to 89° with their sines, cosines, and tangents. Notice that for any angle θ,

(I; sin; cos; tan) θ = (θ, sin θ, cos θ, tan θ)

Here I is the identity function, $I x \equiv x$. Therefore the table is

map (I; sin; cos; tan) [interval (0, 90)]

Exercise 6.58: Show that

(map I; map sin; map cos; map tan) [interval (0, 90)]

produces a table that is the "transpose" of the previous example.

Exercise 6.59: Define the functional construction operation (constr $f g$) in LISP or Scheme.

Exercise 6.60: Show that the following function averages a sequence of numbers:

$$avg \equiv [/] \circ (sum; length)$$

Exercise 6.61: The first difference of a sequence is defined as follows:

$$\Delta S = <S_2 - S_1, S_3 - S_2, \ldots, S_n - S_{n-1}>$$

Show that the following is a correct definition of Δ:

$$\Delta \equiv map\ [-] \circ pairs \circ (rest;\ butlast)$$

Exercise 6.62: Prove the following:

$$(f_1; f_2; \cdots ; f_n) \circ g = (f_1 \circ g; f_2 \circ g; \cdots ; f_n \circ g)$$

Exercise 6.63: Prove the following identities:

$$left \circ (f; g) = f$$ (6.13)
$$right \circ (f; g) = g$$

Exercise 6.64: Suppose we have the following structure declaration for a direct product type:

structure $T \equiv C (\phi_1 \in T_1, \phi_2 \in T_2, \ldots, \phi_n \in T_n)$

Show the following identities:

a. $C \circ (\phi_1; \phi_2; \cdots ; \phi_n) = \mathbf{I}$

b. $(\phi_1; \phi_2; \cdots ; \phi_n) \circ C = \mathbf{I}$

c. $\phi_i \circ \phi_j! = \phi_i \circ right$, for $i \neq j$

d. $\phi_i \circ \phi_i! = left$

e. $\phi_i! \circ (\phi_i; \mathbf{I}) = \mathbf{I}$

f. $\phi_k \circ C = left \circ right^{k-1}$

Exercise 6.65: Suppose we have the following structure declaration:

structure $T \equiv C (\phi_1 \in T_1, \ldots, \phi_m \in T_m) + D (\psi_1 \in U_1, \ldots, \psi_n \in U_n)$

Show the following identities:

a. $C^{-1} = (\phi_1; \cdots ; \phi_m)$
(Of course, the analogous result holds for D.)

b. $C \circ C^{-1} = \mathbf{I}, \quad C^{-1} \circ C = \mathbf{I}$
In effect this identity shows that the notation C^{-1} is accurate, that C^{-1} is indeed the inverse of C.

c. $\phi_k = \text{left} \circ \text{right}^{k-1} \circ C^{-1}$

Exercise 6.66: Show that the following function will determine whether its argument is greater than 2 and less than 100:

$$[\wedge] \circ (\ [> 2]; [< 100]\ )$$

Exercise 6.67: Use functional construction to define a function that tests whether its argument is equal to 28, 29, 30, or 31.

Sometimes the *functional direct product* is more useful than functional construction. The direct product $f \times g$ of two functions is defined by the following equation:

$$(f \times g)(x, y) = (fx, gy) \tag{6.14}$$

The type signature of the functional direct product appears in Fig. 6.9; you will investigate it in Exercises 6.68–6.74.

Exercise 6.68: Develop archetypes and prototypes for the functional direct product. Draw a data-flow diagram.

Exercise 6.69: Define the functional direct product (dprod $f g$) in LISP or Scheme.

Exercise 6.70: Implement functional direct product (Eq. 6.14) in terms of functional construction.

Exercise 6.71: Implement functional construction in terms of functional direct product (Eq. 6.14). *Hint:* Define the *diagonal* function $\Delta x \equiv (x, x)$.

Exercise 6.72: Prove the following:

$$(f_1 \times f_2) \circ (g_1 \times g_2) = (f_1 \circ g_1) \times (f_2 \circ g_2)$$

Exercise 6.73: Prove the following:

$$(f_1 \times f_2) \circ (g_1 ; g_2) = (f_1 \circ g_1) ; (f_2 \circ g_2)$$

Exercise 6.74: Show the following identities:

$$\text{left} \circ (f \times g) = f \circ \text{left} \qquad\qquad (6.15)$$
$$\text{right} \circ (f \times g) = g \circ \text{right}$$

Discuss limitations on the identities, that is, situations in which one side is defined but the other isn't. Note that these identities are equivalent to Fig. 6.9.

We further illustrate the use of functionals by way of several more examples. A common operation performed on a database is *indexing* it on a particular field that is to be used as a *key*. For example, if we index the employee database E on the employee number field, it becomes easy to access an employee's record given his or her employee number. The simplest way to represent an indexed database is as a finite function. For example, if $X \in \text{finfunc}\,(\mathbb{N} \rightarrow \text{pers\_recd})$ is the database indexed on employee number, then Xn is the employee record for employee number n. Such an indexed database can be thought of as a two-column table:

Employee Number	Employee Record
25	Record for employee number 25
16	Record for employee number 16
842	Record for employee number 842
3	Record for employee number 3
7065	Record for employee number 7065
⋮	⋮

Let's now generate the indexed database X from the unindexed database E. Recall that finfunc←seqn S will convert a sequence of pairs into a finite function, giving us:

$$X = \text{finfunc}\leftarrow\text{seqn} \,<(n_1, r_1), \ldots, (n_m, r_m)>$$

Figure 6.9 Type signature for functional direct product.

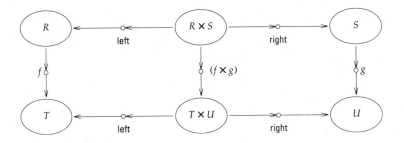

where r_i is the employee record for employee number n_i. This sequence is constructed by mapping a function across E which, for each record r_i, generates the pair (n_i, r_i). We want to write this pair as a function of r_i. Therefore, since $n_i = \text{emp\_no } r_i$, we have

$$(n_i, r_i) = (\text{emp\_no } r_i, \mathbf{I} \, r_i)$$
$$= (\text{emp\_no}; \mathbf{I}) \, r_i$$

Therefore we can generate the indexed file X from E by

$$X \equiv \text{finfunc}{\leftarrow}\text{seqn } [\text{map (emp\_no; I)} \, E\,]$$

Let's generalize this process and define a function index that will index a database on a given field, for example

$$X \equiv \text{index emp\_no } E$$

The type of index is

$$\text{index}: (\text{pers\_recd} \rightarrow T) \rightarrow [\text{pers\_recd}^* \rightarrow \text{finfunc} \, (T \rightarrow \text{pers\_recd})]$$

That is, index takes a selector function $\phi: \text{pers\_recd} \rightarrow T$ on personnel records, and returns a function that takes employee files (of type pers_recd*) into indexed employee files of type finfunc $(T \rightarrow \text{pers\_recd})$. It is easy to see that

$$\text{index } \phi \, E \equiv \text{finfunc}{\leftarrow}\text{seqn } [\text{map } (\phi; \mathbf{I}) \, E\,]$$

Finally, we can use composition to eliminate the particular database E:

$$\text{index } \phi \equiv \text{finfunc}{\leftarrow}\text{seqn} \circ \text{map } (\phi; \mathbf{I})$$

Now, if S is a sequence of employee numbers, we can obtain a sub-database containing the corresponding employee records by fmap X S.[10]

Now let's consider payroll computation, a very common data processing application. We are given a file $W \in (\mathbb{N} \times \mathbb{R})^*$ that contains a pair for each employee who worked this week. Each pair is of the form (n, h), where n is the employee's number and h is the hours he or she worked this week. We want the payroll file $P \in (\textbf{string} \times \mathbb{R})^*$ to be a sequence of pairs (m, w), where m is the employee's name and w is this week's wages. Let's work top down, so suppose for a moment that we have a function payroll_comp defined so that payroll_comp $(n, h) = (m, w)$. Then P is generated by mapping payroll_comp across W:

$$P \equiv \text{map payroll\_comp } W$$

10. The fmap functional was defined in Exercise 6.31; it permits extracting a *horizontal* subfile of the given file.

Continuing top down, suppose that wages (n, h) is the wages earned by employee number n for h hours of work. Then we can define payroll_comp:

$$\text{payroll\_comp } (n, h) = (m, w)$$
$$= (\text{name } [Xn], \text{wages } [n, h])$$

This is because Xn is the employee record for employee number n, and therefore name $[Xn]$ is the name field of this employee record.

Using composition on finite functions as defined in Exercise 6.57, we can eliminate the auxiliary definition of payroll_comp as follows:

$$\text{payroll\_comp } (n, h) = (\text{name } [Xn], \text{wages } (n, h))$$
$$= ([\text{name} \circ X] \, n, \text{wages } (n, h))$$
$$= ([\text{name} \circ X \circ \text{left}] \, (n, h), \text{wages } (n, h))$$
$$= (\text{name} \circ X \circ \text{left; wages}) \, (n, h)$$

Therefore

$$\text{payroll\_comp} \equiv (\text{name} \circ X \circ \text{left ; wages})$$

and we can do the mapping directly:

$$P \equiv \text{map } (\text{name} \circ X \circ \text{left ; wages}) \, W \qquad\qquad (6.16)$$

Thus, for each element of W, we construct a pair. The data-flow diagram in Fig. 6.10 shows how this pair is constructed.

Next let's derive wages. Let $s \equiv \text{hr\_rate } (Xn)$ be the employee's hourly rate. We assume that the employee earns time-and-a-half for any hours

---

Figure 6.10 Data-flow diagram for payroll computation.

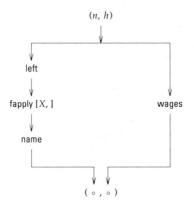

over 40 in a week. Thus the hourly rate for the first 40 hours or less is s; the hourly rate for any hours over 40 is $1.5s$. Now notice that min $(h, 40)$ is the number of hours up to a maximum of 40, and that max $(h - 40, 0)$ is the hours over 40, if any. Therefore the wages earned are

$$w = s \times \min(h, 40) + 1.5s \times \max(h - 40, 0)$$

We can factor s out of this to yield the definition of wages:

$$\text{wages }(n, h) \equiv \text{hr\_rate }(Xn) \times [\min(h, 40) + 1.5 \times \max(h - 40, 0)] \qquad (6.17)$$

If we wish, we can factor (n, h) out of this definition to obtain

$$\text{wages} \equiv \qquad\qquad\qquad\qquad\qquad\qquad\qquad\qquad\qquad (6.18)$$
$$[\times] \circ \{(\text{hr\_rate} \circ X) \ \boldsymbol{\times} \ [+] \circ (\min \circ [,40]; [1.5\times] \circ \max \circ [,0] \circ [-40])\}$$

Exercise 6.75: Show that Eq. (6.18) is equivalent to Eq. (6.17). Discuss the relative merits of the two definitions of **wages**.

Exercise 6.76: Suppose that S is a sequence of personnel records. Write a formula that computes a sequence of personnel records like S, except that every employee has been given a 10% raise.

6.10 Function-Level Definitions and Multilevel Functions

Functions can be defined at either the *object level* or the *function level* (these terms are due to Backus (1981)). For example, if we define the average of a sequence as

$$\text{avg } S \equiv \text{sum } S \text{ / length } S \qquad\qquad\qquad (6.19)$$

then we have defined it at the object level, since its behavior is described in terms of a general domain object S. On the other hand, if we define it as:

$$\text{avg} \equiv [/] \circ (\text{sum}; \text{length}) \qquad\qquad\qquad (6.20)$$

then we have defined it at the function level, since we've shown how it's composed of other functions ([/], sum, and length in this case). Similarly, the function that tests whether its argument is greater than 2 and less than 100 can be defined at either the object level

$$x \mapsto (x > 2 \ \wedge \ x < 100) \qquad\qquad\qquad (6.21)$$

or the function level

$$[\wedge] \circ ([>2]; [<100]) \hspace{4cm} (6.22)$$

Recall also Eqs. (6.17) and (6.18).

Should functions be defined at the object level or the function level? The object-level definitions probably seem more readable, since they show exactly what is done to the function's arguments. Further, function-level definitions tend to be unreadable when the function's body is complicated; compare Eq. (6.18) with its object-level equivalent (Eq. 6.17). This may, however, be partly an issue of familiarity; most programmers are not used to thinking at the function-level. Also, function-level definitions can be made clearer by thinking of them as descriptions of data flow. For example, Eq. (6.20) says that the input is to be routed through sum and length, and those results are to be combined by division; Eq. (6.22) says that the input is to be passed through the [>2] and [<100] tests, and the results combined by [∧].

Object- and function-level definitions also differ in their mathematical tractability. Function-level definitions are more amenable to algebraic proofs. For example, applying Eqs. (6.13) and (6.15):

$$\text{left} \circ (\log \times \text{sum}) \circ (\text{length}; \text{map log}) = \log \circ \text{left} \circ (\text{length}; \text{map log})$$
$$= \log \circ \text{length}$$

On the other hand, object-level definitions seem more useful for object-level proofs, such as the inductive proofs of Chapter 3.

You can see that many tradeoffs are involved in choosing between object-level and function-level definitions. Since this is a stylistic issue that the functional programmer must face, you must develop your own sense of the pros and cons.

Before leaving the topic of object and function level definitions, let's discuss a third option provided by some functional languages:[11] *multilevel functions*. This is an attempt to have function-level definitions with the readability of object-level definitions. Object-level definitions obtain much of their readability from the use of infix operators; compare the infix use of '/' in 'sum S / length S' with its less readable occurrence in '[/] ∘ (sum; length)'. If we use function-level definitions extensively, however, the infix notation is not used much; the most readable notation will be wasted. Multilevel functions solve this problem by overloading the infix operators so that, in addition to their usual object-level meanings, they also can be used as higher-order functions. For example, if f and g are two real-valued functions over a domain D, then f / g is permitted as an abbreviation for $[/] \circ (f; g)$. We say that / has been *lifted* so that it

---

11. For example, Backus's language FL (Backus, Williams, and Wimmers, 1986). Multilevel functions were used extensively in Menger's innovative (and unjustly neglected) notation for the integral and differential calculi; see (Menger 1944–1959).

works on higher-order objects (functions rather than data). Lifted division satisfies the identity

$$(f \mathbin{/} g)x = fx \mathbin{/} gx \qquad (6.23)$$

and has the signature $[/]\colon (D \to \mathbb{R})^2 \to (D \to \mathbb{R})$. There is no ambiguity in the multilevel use of '/' since the arguments in the two cases are of different types ($\mathbb{R}$ or $D \to \mathbb{R}$); that is, '/' is a generic operator.

Multilevel operators make function-level definitions much easier to understand. For example, the definition of avg in Eq. (6.20) becomes

$$\mathsf{avg} \equiv \mathsf{sum} \mathbin{/} \mathsf{length} \qquad (6.24)$$

This is quite readable: "The average is the sum divided by the length." Similarly, the function to test whether its argument is greater than 2 and less than 100 (Eq. 6.22) becomes

$$[{>}2] \wedge [{<}100] \qquad (6.25)$$

The argument must be "greater than 2 and less than 100."

A further improvement results from *mixed*-level functions. For example, we can permit any combination of object- and function-level arguments to '>' by these equations (x and y are numbers; f and g, functions):

$$
\begin{aligned}
x > y &= \text{the usual greater-than test} \\
(x > g)y &= x > gy \\
(f > y)x &= fx > y \\
(f > g)x &= fx > gx
\end{aligned}
$$

This permits an alternative to the use of sections, since $(\mathbf{I} > 2)x = (x > 2)$, where $\mathbf{I}$ is the identity function, $\mathbf{I}x = x$. For example, Eq. (6.25) can be written

$$\mathbf{I} > 2 \;\wedge\; \mathbf{I} < 100 \qquad (6.26)$$

A more significant use of mixed-level functions occurs in the following function-level definition of wages:

$$\mathsf{wages} \equiv \mathsf{hr\_rate} \circ X \circ \mathsf{left} \times [\mathsf{min} \circ (\mathsf{right};\, 40) + 1.5 \times \mathsf{max} \circ (\mathsf{right} - 40;\, 0)] \qquad (6.27)$$

Notice the mixed-level use of multiplication and subtraction. The mixed-level use of construction (;) requires comment since construction is just the lifted pairing operator (,). We have not made ',' multilevel—this would prevent us from forming tuples that contain functions. Instead we've made ';' multilevel, allowing constructions that include data as well as functions.

Observe that in Eq. (6.26) **I**, the identity function, can be thought of as meaning "the input." Similarly, in (6.27) left and right can be thought of as meaning "the left argument" and the "right argument." In both cases functions take the place of formal parameters. In particular, in (6.27) left and right are the selector functions that select the individual arguments from the argument list. Of course, any selector functions appropriate to the argument may be used; hrs_worked × hr_rate is the function that multiplies an employee's hours worked by his or her hourly rate.

We again leave it to you to decide the value of multilevel definitions. To help you make up your mind, we often show both object- and function-level definitions; from here on, we assume that all object-level infix operators (except ',') are multilevel.

Exercise 6.77: Show that Eqs. (6.25) and (6.26) are equivalent to Eq. (6.22).

Exercise 6.78: Show that Eq. (6.27) is equivalent to Eq. (6.18).

Exercise 6.79: Show that the following is a correct definition of distl:

distl $(x, S) \equiv$ map $(x : \mathbf{I} : $ nil$)$ S

Exercise 6.80: Use multilevel functions to improve the readability of

fil $([> 100] \circ$ hr_rate$) \circ$ fil $([52=] \circ$ dept$)$

Exercise 6.81: Define a higher-order function lift that "lifts" its argument, assumed to be a binary function. Thus

lift $f (g, h) = f \circ (g; h)$

Then the function f can be made multilevel by overloading its definition with $f \equiv$ lift f. Thus, to define lifted division, $[/] \equiv$ lift $[/]$. What is the signature of lift?

6.11 The Reduction Functionals

We have seen how the map functional can be used to transform a sequence into another sequence of the same length and how the fil functional can be used to select certain elements from a sequence. Are any other functionals useful for sequence processing? Recall that in Chapter 3 we defined several *reduction* functions that computed a result by applying a binary operation between adjacent sequence elements. In particular we defined

$$\text{sum } S = S_1 + S_2 + \cdots + S_{n-1} + S_n$$
$$\text{prod } S = S_1 \times S_2 \times \cdots \times S_{n-1} \times S_n$$
$$\text{append } S = S_1 \wedge S_2 \wedge \cdots \wedge S_{n-1} \wedge S_n$$
$$\text{and } S = S_1 \wedge S_2 \wedge \cdots \wedge S_{n-1} \wedge S_n$$
$$\text{or } S = S_1 \vee S_2 \vee \cdots \vee S_{n-1} \vee S_n$$
$$\text{dif } S = S_1 - (S_2 - (S_3 - \cdots - (S_{n-1} - S_n) \cdots))$$

The similar meanings of these functions suggest that reduction is a useful, recurring pattern that can be incorporated into a functional. Thus our goal is to define redr ("reduce from the right") so that sum = redr [+], prod = redr [×], append = redr [^], and so forth. For a general binary function f we want

$$\text{redr } f\, S = f(S_1, f(S_2, \cdots f(S_{n-1}, S_n) \cdots)) \tag{6.28}$$

Notice that the results are accumulated from right to left. This definition can be expressed more precisely by the following equations:

$$\text{redr } f <x> = x$$
$$\text{redr } f (x : S) = f(x, \text{redr } f\, S)$$

These equations in turn lead directly to a recursive definition of redr:

$$\text{redr } f\, S \equiv \begin{cases} \text{first } S, \text{ if null (rest } S) \\ \textbf{else } f\, [\text{first } S, \text{redr } f\, (\text{rest } S)] \end{cases}$$

Exercise 6.82: Define redr in LISP or Scheme.

Let's summarize the meaning and use of redr by a *simplification rule:* Whenever we see a formula of the form

$$f(S_1, f(S_2, \ldots, f(S_{n-1}, S_n) \ldots))$$

or can transform a formula into this form, we can simplify the formula by rewriting it

redr $f\, S$

Similarly, if $\bigcirc$ is any infix operator, then we can simplify the formula

$$S_1 \bigcirc (S_2 \bigcirc (S_3 \bigcirc \cdots \bigcirc (S_{n-1} \bigcirc S_n) \cdots))$$

by rewriting it

redr $[\bigcirc]\, S$

For example, to compute

$$S_1 - S_2 + S_3 - \cdots \pm S_n$$

we rewrite it in the form

$$S_1 - (S_2 - (S_3 - \cdots - (S_{n-1} - S_n) \cdots))$$

and then simplify it to

redr [−] S

Figure 6.11 is a data-flow diagram for redr.

The redr functional suggests a redl functional that performs a reduction from the left. That is, for a infix operator O,

redl [O] S $= (\cdots ((S_1 O S_2) O S_3) O \cdots O S_{n-1}) O S_n$

or for a prefix function f,

Figure 6.11   Data-flow diagram for redr.

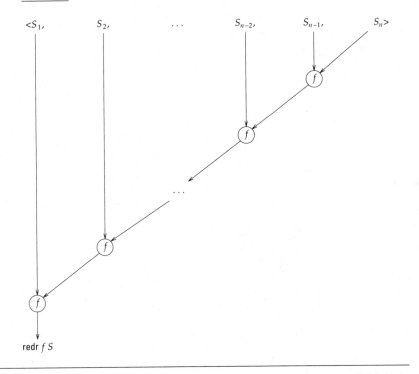

redr f S

$$\text{redl } f\ S\ =\ f\,(f\,(\ldots f\,(f\,(S_1,\,S_2),\,S_3),\,\ldots,\,S_{n-1}),\,S_n)$$

The data-flow diagram for redl is in Fig. 6.12.

Of course, we could define redl recursively as we did for redr, but, more instructively, let's make use of redr rather than beginning from scratch. This will show us the relation between the functionals. Hence we transform an application of redl into a form that can be simplified by redr. We are given

$$\text{redl } f\ S\ =\ f\,(f\,(\ldots f\,(f\,(S_1,\,S_2),\,S_3),\,\ldots,\,S_{n-1}),\,S_n)$$

and we want to transform it into a formula of the form

$$g\,(T_1,\,g\,(T_2,\,g\,(T_3,\,\ldots,\,g\,(T_{n-1},\,T_n)\ldots)))$$

Notice that the first form nests to the left (see Fig. 6.12)—that is, in the first argument of f—while the second form nests to the right (see Fig. 6.11)—that is, in the second argument of g. Hence we can begin by writing $g = \text{rev } f$ (see Exercise 6.20) which gives us

$$\text{redl } f\ S\ =\ g\,(S_n,\,g\,(S_{n-1},\,\ldots,\,g\,(S_3,\,g\,(S_2,\,S_1))\ldots))$$

Figure 6.12 Data-flow diagram for redl.

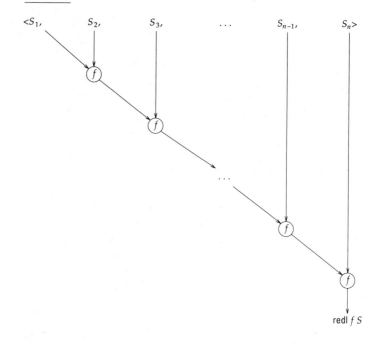

Although this is closer, the subscripts on S run down, while those on T run up. If we let $T = \text{reverse } S$, however, then $T_i = S_{n-i+1}$ and we have

$$\text{redl } f\ S\ =\ g\ (T_1, g\ (T_2, \ldots, g\ (T_{n-2}, g\ (T_{n-1}, T_n))\cdots))$$

The right-hand side of this equation can be simplified to redr $g\ T$, so we have shown that

$$\text{redl } f\ S\ =\ \text{redr } g\ T$$

where $g = \text{rev } f$ and $T = \text{reverse } S$. Hence

$$\text{redl } f\ S\ =\ \text{redr (rev } f)\ (\text{reverse } S)$$

Hence

$$\text{redl } f = \text{redr (rev } f)\circ\text{reverse}$$

Of course, this is an inefficient implementation of redl; it would be better to implement it directly. The following definition avoids the reverse:

$$\text{redl } f\ (x{:}S)\ =\ \text{redlaux } (f, x, S) \tag{6.29}$$
$$\textbf{where } \text{redlaux } (f, y, \text{nil}) \equiv y$$
$$\text{redlaux } (f, y, x{:}S) \equiv \text{redlaux } [f, f\ (y, x), S]$$

Notice that this definition is also tail-recursive, and hence as efficient as an iterative reduction. A translation into Scheme is straightforward:

```
(define (redl f)
  (define (redlaux f y S)
    (if (null S) y
        (redlaux f (f y (car S)) (cdr S)) ))
  (lambda (S) (redlaux f (car S) (cdr S)) ))
```

Exercise 6.83: Show that definition (6.29) is correct.

We have defined redl, which reduces from the left, and redr, which reduces from the right. For associative operators such as +, ×, ∧, ∧, and ∨, the order in which we reduce is unimportant, suggesting that we define an *order-independent* reduction operator, red. There are several reasons: (1) Because order-independent reduction is less constrained, it can be more easily transformed into other forms; (2) An order-independent reduction is potentially more efficient because the redl and redr functionals require a minimum of n steps to reduce an n-element sequence, whereas red can reduce an n-element sequence in $\log_2 n$ steps (see Fig. 6.13).

Figure 6.13 Data-flow diagram for red.

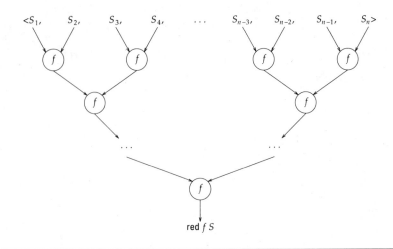

The archetype for order-independent reduction is

> red f $<x>$ $= x$, if f is associative
> red f $(S \char94 T) = f$ (red f S, red f T), if f is associative
> red f $S \ne y$, if f isn't associative

This reflects the fact that the reductions can be done in any order, as long as the operator is associative. The simplification rule for red is as follows. For any associative infix operator O, the pattern

> $S_1 O S_2 O \cdots O S_{n-1} O S_n$

can be simplified to

> red $[O]$ S

It is easy to produce an implementation of red that operates in $\log_2 n$ time if we assume a constant-time function split that divides a sequence into two sequence of equal size (or nearly equal, for sequences of odd length). For example,

> split $<2, 3, 1, 7, 3, 6>$ = $(<2, 3, 1>, <7, 3, 6>)$

The resulting recursive step is

> red f S $= f\{$red f [left (split S)], red f [right (split S)]$\}$, if $\neg$ null (rest S)

Figure 6.14 Archetype and prototype for reductions.

Archetype

Syntax:

    redr, redl, red: $(T \times T \to T) \to (T^* \to T)$, for all $T \in$ **type**

Semantics:

    redr $f <x> = x$
    redr $f (x : S) = f (x, \text{redr } f S)$,

    redl $f <x> = x$
    redl $f [\text{postfix } (S, x)] = f (\text{redl } f S, x)$

    red $f <x> = x$, if f is associative
    red $f (S \wedge T) = f (\text{red } f S, \text{red } f T)$, if f is associative
    red $f S \neq y$, if f isn't associative

Pragmatics:

    With sequential implementations redr $f S$, redl $f S$, and red $f S$ all take
    linear time.
    With some parallel implementations red $f S$ takes logarithmic time.

Prototype

$$\text{redr } f \equiv x \mapsto \begin{cases} \text{first } S, & \text{if null (rest } S) \\ \textbf{else } f [\text{first } S, \text{redr } f (\text{rest } S)] \end{cases}$$

    redl $f \equiv$ redr (rev f) $\circ$ reverse
    red $f \equiv$ redr f

It can be simplified by the use of functional direct product, as in the following prototype implemention of red:

    red $f <x> \equiv x$ (6.30)
    red $f S \equiv [f \circ (\text{red } f \times \text{red } f)] (\text{split } S)$, if $\neg$ null (rest S)

The reduction functionals are summarized in Fig. 6.14.

Exercise 6.84: Show that the function defined in Eq. (6.30) executes in $\log_2 n$ time (assuming that split operates in constant time).

Exercise 6.85: Implement split. (Don't, however, try to make it operate in constant time.)

Exercise 6.86: Prove that the definition of red in Eq. (6.30) satisfies

    red $f (S \wedge T) = f (\text{red } f S, \text{red } f T)$

for S, T nonnull, and f associative.

Exercise 6.87: Show the following identities:

sum = red [+] ∘ [0:]
prod = red [×] ∘ [1:]
and = red [∧] ∘ [**true:**]
or = red [∨] ∘ [**false:**]
append = red [⌃] ∘ [nil:]
$S \subseteq T$ = red [∧] (**true** : map [∈ T] S)

Exercise 6.88: Write an expression for the union of all the elements of a nonnull sequence of finite sets S. How would you modify the expression to correctly handle the possibility of S being null?

Exercise 6.89: Show that

ip ≡ red [+] ∘ map [×] ∘ pairs

is a correct implementation of inner product for nonnull vectors.

6.12 The Accumulation Functionals

We do not yet have sum = redr [+], prod = redr [×], and so forth, for these functions are defined on the null sequence, whereas redr [+], redr [×], and so forth are not. Recall that we defined sum <> = 0, prod <> = 1, and <> = **true**, and so forth. The problem with making redr work correctly on null sequences is that the value to be returned depends on the function being used for reduction. One way around this problem is to give redr an additional parameter, the "initial value" of the reduction. Call this alternative version accr (accumulate from the right):

accr (f, i) nil ≡ i
accr (f, i) $(x : S)$ ≡ $f [x,$ accr (f, i) $S]$

It is characterized by the following simplification rule:

$$\text{accr} (f, i) S = f (S_1, f (S_2, \cdots f (S_{n-1}, f (S_n, i)) \cdots)) \qquad (6.31)$$

Compare this carefully with the simplification rule for redr (Eq. 6.28). Given accr we have sum = accr ([+], 0), prod = accr ([×], 1), append = accr ([⌃], nil), and = accr ([∧], **true**), and so on. Alternatively, we can get the same result from redr by supplying the initial value explicitly:

sum S = redr [+] [postfix $(S, 0)$]
prod S = redr [×] [postfix $(S, 1)$]
append S = redr [⌃] [postfix $(S,$ nil)]
and S = redr [∧] [postfix $(S,$ **true**)]

Then we have

$$\mathsf{sum} <> = \mathsf{redr}\ [+]\ [\mathsf{postfix}\ (<>, 0)] = \mathsf{redr}\ [+]\ <0> = 0$$

as expected. In general, if $f : T \times T \to T$, then

$$\mathsf{accr}\ (f, i)\ S = \mathsf{redr}\ f\ [\mathsf{postfix}\ (S, i)]$$

That is, $\mathsf{accr}\ (f, i) = \mathsf{redr}\ f \circ \mathsf{postfix} \circ [,i]$. Note, however, that accr is also meaningful for functions with the signature $f : S \times T \to T$ in which $S \neq T$. For example,

$$S \wedge T \equiv \mathsf{accr}\ (\mathsf{prefix}, T)\ S \tag{6.32}$$

Thus accumulation can be used for many purposes for which reduction would not work at all; another example appears later in this section.

Which of these reduction functionals is preferable? We use both because for some functions—those without a right identity—the initial value may have no meaning. For these functions redr should be used. Also, accumulation is more general than reduction, since it may apply to functions whose arguments are not of the same type.

We also define accumulation from the left with the simplification rule:

$$\mathsf{accl}\ (f, i) = f\ (f\ (\ldots f\ (f\ (i, S_1), S_2), \ldots S_{n-1}), S_n) \tag{6.33}$$

The archetypes and prototypes for accumulation are in Fig. 6.15.

Figure 6.15 Archetype and prototype for accumulations.

Archetype

Syntax:
  $\mathsf{accr}: \{[(S \times T) \to T] \times T\} \to (S^* \to T)$, for all $S,\ T \in$ **type**
  $\mathsf{accl}: \{[(S \times T) \to S] \times S\} \to (T^* \to S)$, for all $S,\ T \in$ **type**

Semantics:
  $\mathsf{accr}\ (f, z)\ \mathsf{nil} = z$
  $\mathsf{accr}\ (f, z)\ (x : Y) = f\ [x, \mathsf{accr}\ (f, z)\ Y]$

  $\mathsf{accl}\ (f, z)\ \mathsf{nil} = z$
  $\mathsf{accl}\ (f, z)\ [\mathsf{postfix}\ (X, y)] = f\ [\mathsf{accl}\ (f, z)\ X, y]$

Pragmatics:
  Accumulations take linear time.

Prototype
  $\mathsf{accr}\ (f, i)\ \mathsf{nil} \equiv i$
  $\mathsf{accr}\ (f, i)\ (x : Y) \equiv f\ [x, \mathsf{accr}\ (f, i)\ Y]$
  $\mathsf{accl}\ (f, z) \equiv \mathsf{accr}\ (\mathsf{rev}\ f, z) \circ \mathsf{reverse}$

Exercise 6.90: Show that

sum = accr ([+], 0)
dif = accr ([−], 0)
prod = accr ([×], 1)
and = accr ([∧], **true**)
or = accr ([∨], **false**)
append = accr ([⌢], nil)
reverse = accl (rev [:], nil)
$S \wedge T$ = accr ([:], T) S
$S \subseteq T$ = and ∘ map [∈ T] S

Exercise 6.91: Define accl and accr in LISP or Scheme.

Exercise 6.92: accl and accr correspond to redl and redr. Explain why there is no accumulation functional corresponding to red.

Exercise 6.93: Prove that the prototype definition of accl satisfies the archetype (Fig. 6.15).

Exercise 6.94: Use accumulation to define the partial sums of a sequence:

$$\text{psum } S = <0, S_1, S_1 + S_2, S_1 + S_2 + S_3, \ldots, S_1 + S_2 + S_3 + \cdots + S_n>$$

Modify your solution to compute the partial sums from the right.

Exercise 6.95: Write a formula to adjoin all the elements of a sequence L to a set S.

Exercise 6.96: Given two sequences S and T, use accumulation to compute

$$S_n : S_{n-1} : \cdots : S_2 : S_1 : T$$

Exercise 6.97: Define map as an accumulation from the right.

We now consider a simple data processing example. Suppose we have a file Updates ∈ $(\mathbb{N} \times \text{pers\_recd})^*$ represented as a sequence of pairs:

$$\text{Updates} = <(n_1, r_1), (n_2, r_2), \ldots, (n_k, r_k)>$$

In each pair n_i is an employee number and r_i is a new employee record for that employee. We have an old employee database

OldMaster ∈ finfunc $(\mathbb{N} \rightarrow \text{pers\_recd})$

represented as a finite function indexed on the employee numbers. We wish to generate a new employee database NewMaster in which the records in Updates replace those in OldMaster. Furthermore, if a record in Updates does not have a corresponding record in OldMaster, then we want it to be added.

In a conventional language we would read the file Updates sequentially and, for each record (n_i, r_i), update the file by either adding or replacing the record in OldMaster. Recall that overl (Fig. 4.5) is defined so that overl (f, x, y) adds the pair (x, y) to the finite function f, possibly replacing the previous pair for x. Since, by the definition of tuples (Fig. 5.2), $(f, x, y) = (f, (x, y))$, the result of processing the first pair in Updates is

$$F_1 \equiv \text{overl (OldMaster, Updates}_1)$$

The result of processing the second record is

$$F_2 \equiv \text{overl } (F_1, \text{Updates}_2)$$

In general, the result of processing the ith record is

$$F_i \equiv \text{overl } (F_{i-1}, \text{Updates}_i)$$

and the desired final result, NewMaster, is the result of processing all k records:

$$\text{NewMaster} \equiv F_k$$

Putting these together yields the following nested equation:

NewMaster =
  overl (. . . overl (overl (OldMaster, Updates$_1$), Updates$_2$), . . . , Updates$_k$)

This can be simplified using left accumulation (Eq. 6.33):

$$\text{NewMaster} = \text{accl (overl, OldMaster) Updates}$$

We can summarize this in the following definition of a general function to perform the updating operation on given old master and update files to yield a new master file:

$$\text{perform\_updates } (F, U) \equiv \text{accl (overl, } F) \, U$$

Exercise 6.98: Suppose that $F \in \text{pers\_recd}^*$ is a file of personnel records (as defined in Eq. 5.8).

a. Write an expression that computes the total hours worked of all employees in F.

b. Write an expression that computes the average hourly rate of all employees in F.

6.13 Constant Functions

To illustrate the use of constant functions, we derive an alternative definition of the length function. Since we want to "count one" for each element of the sequence, we can use the constant function $x \mapsto 1$. Then note that

$$
\begin{aligned}
\text{map } x \mapsto 1 <S_1, S_2, \ldots, S_n> \\
= <x \mapsto 1\ S_1, x \mapsto 1\ S_2, \ldots, x \mapsto 1\ S_n> \\
= <1, 1, \ldots, 1>
\end{aligned}
$$

where there are n ones in the preceding sequence. Thus the length of S is the sum of all the ones in that sequence. Hence

$$\text{length } S = \text{sum (map } x \mapsto 1\ S)$$

We can use composition to eliminate S from both sides of the equation:

$$\text{length} \equiv \text{sum} \circ \text{map } x \mapsto 1$$

Constant functions arise frequently in functional programming, suggesting that we define a functional for generating them.

Thus we define const k to be the constant function that always returns k:

$$\text{const } k\ x = k$$

Solving this equation by abstraction yields

$$\text{const } k \equiv x \mapsto k$$

With const the definition of length is

$$\text{length} \equiv \text{sum} \circ \text{map (const 1)}$$

Constant functions are especially useful when used with conditional construction (see Section 6.14). The archetype and prototype for constant functions are in Fig. 6.16. Note that there is a constant functional for each type.

Figure 6.16 Archetype and prototype for constant construction.

Archetype

Syntax:
    $\text{const}_T\colon S \to (T \to S)$

Semantics:
    $\text{const}_T\, k\, x\; =\; k$

Pragmatics:
    Takes constant time.

Prototype
    $\text{const}\, k \;\equiv\; x \mapsto k$

Exercise 6.99: Define the constant construction operation in LISP or Scheme.

Exercise 6.100: Suppose S is a sequence of characters representing a word. Write an expression for a sequence of blanks of the same length as S.

Exercise 6.101: Use the interval function and the answer to the previous exercise to define a function blanks n that returns a sequence of n blanks.

Exercise 6.102: The expression const $1\, x$ has the value 1 for all x. But consider the expression

const $1\,(1/0)$

Does it have a value? Discuss.

Exercise 6.103: Prove the following identities:

const $x \circ$ const $y \;=\;$ const x
$f \circ [, x] \circ$ const $y \;=\;$ const $[f\,(x,\,y)]$
(const x; const $y) \;=\;$ const $(x,\,y)$
$\mathbf{I} \circ$ const $k \;=\;$ const $k \;=\;$ const $k \circ \mathbf{I}$
$f \circ$ const $k \;=\;$ const $(f\,k)$
$f \circ ($const x; const $y) \;=\;$ const $[f\,(x,\,y)]$

Exercise 6.104: Is the identity const $k \circ f \;=\;$ const k generally true? What are the domains of the functions on each side of the equality?

Exercise 6.105: Show that

$$f \circ (\text{const } k; \text{I}) = f \circ [k,]$$
$$f \circ (\text{I}; \text{const } k) = f \circ [,k]$$

How would these equations look if mixed-level use of ';' is permitted?

Exercise 6.106: Explain and illustrate the following observation: An expression such as 'first + 1' can be thought of as either a *mixed-level* use of '+' or as a multilevel (lifted) use of the function '+' together with a lifted use of the object denotation '1'. *Hint:* To what function is '1' lifted?

6.14 Conditional Construction

Suppose we have a sequence W of all the distinct words in a given piece of text

$$W = <w_1, w_2, \ldots, w_n>$$

and that we want to generate a sequence

$$S = <(w_1, v_1), (w_2, v_2), \ldots, (w_n, v_n)>$$

in which the v_i are the frequencies of occurrence of the w_i in the text. It is convenient to start with a sequence of the form

$$S'' = <(w_1, 0), (w_2, 0), \ldots, (w_n, 0)>$$

That is, each element of W is paired with 0, the initial count. This sequence is generated by the following mapping:

$$S'' \equiv \text{map } [,0] \ W$$

Now suppose that we have a sequence of pairs in which the second element is the number of occurrences of that word found so far:

$$S = <(w_1, v_1), (w_2, v_2), \ldots, (w_n, v_n)>$$

To process a new word w, we must find the pair (w_i, v_i) in S for which $w = w_i$, and generate a new sequence in which this pair is replaced by $(w_i, 1 + v_i)$:

$$S' = <(w_1, v_1), (w_2, v_2), \ldots, (w_i, 1 + v_i), \ldots, (w_n, v_n)>$$

To compute S', notice that it is almost like S. In particular, for each pair in S, the corresponding pair in S' is either the same pair or is the result of incrementing the second element of the pair. Thus S' can be generated from S by mapping across S a function f that returns the (possibly modified) pair

$$S' \equiv \text{map } f\ S$$
$$\textbf{where } f\ (w_i, v_i) \equiv \begin{cases} (w_i, 1 + v_i), & \text{if } w = w_i \\ \textbf{else } (w_i, v_i) \end{cases}$$

Can we use functional-programming techniques to eliminate the explicit definition of f?

Consider the processing of a typical pair (w_i, v_i). There are two cases, depending on whether or not the first element of the pair is w. If not, then we return the pair unchanged; that is, we apply the identity function $\textbf{I}$. If w does equal the first element of the pair, then we apply to the pair the function g:

$$g\ (w_i, v_i) = (w_i, 1 + v_i)$$

We can solve for g by using functional product (Eq. 6.14):

$$\begin{aligned} g\ (w_i, v_i) &= (w_i, 1 + v_i) \\ &= (w_i, [1+]v_i) \\ &= (\textbf{I} \times [1+])\ (w_i, v_i) \end{aligned}$$

Thus we have $g \equiv \textbf{I} \times [1+]$, which makes clear that g passes the first element of its argument unchanged but increments the second element of its argument.

Returning to our original problem, the sequence S' is computed by mapping across S a function that is equivalent to $\textbf{I}$ if the first element of its argument is w, and equivalent to $\textbf{I} \times [1+]$ otherwise. Thus we must select between the functions $\textbf{I}$ and $\textbf{I} \times [1+]$ depending on a predicate P that tests for equality of the first element with w.

To handle the common situation of making this selection, we introduce a functional cond that selects between two functions F and G on the basis of a predicate P. The idea is that cond (P, F, G) applied to x is Fx if Px is true and Gx if Px is false. This can be visualized by the data-flow diagram in Fig. 6.17, in which the dotted lines indicate that the predicate selects one of the functions to be applied. The archetype and prototype appear in Fig. 6.18.

What is the predicate in this case? We want to test whether the left element of the argument pair is w. Hence, making use of a mixed-level '=',

$$Px = (w = \text{left } x) = (w = \text{left})x$$

Therefore $P \equiv w = \text{left}$. Combining these results, we have the formula for S':

Figure 6.17 Data-flow diagram for conditional construction.

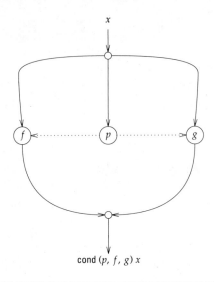

cond $(p, f, g) x$

$$S' \equiv \text{map [cond } (P, \mathbf{I}, g)] \, S$$
$$\textbf{where } P \equiv w = \text{left}$$
$$\textbf{and } g \equiv \mathbf{I} \times [1+]$$

Eliminating the bound identifiers P and g,

$$S' \equiv \text{map \{cond } (w = \text{left}, \mathbf{I}, \mathbf{I} \times [1+])\} \, S$$

Figure 6.18 Archetype and prototype for conditional construction.

Archetype

Syntax:
   cond: $(S \rightarrow \mathbb{B}) \times (S \rightarrow T) \times (S \rightarrow T) \rightarrow (S \rightarrow T)$

Semantics:
   cond $(P, F, G) x = Fx$, if $Px = \textbf{true}$
   cond $(P, F, G) x = Gx$, if $Px = \textbf{false}$

Pragmatics:
   Takes time which is the sum of that for P and either F or G.

Prototype

$$\text{cond } (P, F, G) = x \mapsto \begin{cases} Fx, & \text{if } Px \\ \textbf{else } Gx \end{cases}$$

Some functional languages such as that of Backus (1978) syntactically sugar the cond in some manner such as the following:

$$p \to f \mid g \Rightarrow \text{cond } (p, f, g)$$

This permits us to write

$$S' \equiv \text{map } \{w = \text{left} \to \mathbf{I} \mid \mathbf{I} \times [1+]\}\ S$$

We introduce an algebraically motivated variant of this notation in the next section.

Exercise 6.107: Show that the following completes the computation of the frequency table from T (the text) and W (the word list):

$$\text{freq } (T, W) \equiv \text{accl } (C, \text{map } [,0]\ W)\ T$$
where $C(S, w) \equiv \text{map } \{w = \text{left} \to \mathbf{I} \mid \mathbf{I} \times [1+]\}\ S$

Exercise 6.108: Define cond in LISP or Scheme.

Exercise 6.109: Define a function that takes a file of personnel records (Eq. 5.13) and returns a sequence containing the name of every present employee and every past employee who is alive.

The following exercises explore function-level definitions of functions similar to ones already defined (see Exercises 3.29, 3.31, 3.41, and 3.42).

Exercise 6.110: The function subst (x, y) substitutes x for y in an argument sequence. That is, subst (x, y) S is a sequence just like S except that every occurrence of y is replaced by x. Show that the following is a correct definition of subst:

$$\text{subst } (x, y) \equiv \text{map } ([=y] \to \text{const } x \mid \mathbf{I})$$

Note that we use the abbreviation for cond here.

Exercise 6.111: The function lsubst (X, y) substitutes the *sequence* X for every occurrence of y in an argument sequence. Note that X is grafted into the argument sequence and thus the resulting sequence may be longer than the argument. For example,

lsubst (<'the', 'king'>, 'S') <'S', 'is', 'dead', 'long', 'live', 'S'>
= <'the', 'king', 'is', 'dead', 'long', 'live', 'the', 'king'>

Show the following definition accomplishes this:

$$\mathsf{lsubst}\ (X,\ y)\ \equiv\ \mathsf{append} \circ \mathsf{map}\ \{[=y\,] \rightarrow \mathsf{const}\ X\ \mid\ [:\mathsf{nil}]\}$$

Exercise 6.112: The function sublis $<(x_1, y_1), \ldots, (x_n, y_n)>$ substitutes x_i for each occurrence of y_i in its argument sequence. Define sublis in terms of accr and subst.

Exercise 6.113: The function subpair $(<x_1, \ldots, x_n>, <y_1, \ldots, y_n>)$ substitutes x_i for each occurrence of y_i in its argument sequence. Define this using sublis and other (already defined) functions.

Exercise 6.114: Use the accumulation of a conditional construction to define fil.

6.15 Functional Summation

The conditional construction cond (p, f, g) diverts the data flow into one of two paths, f or g, depending on a Boolean condition p; it is thus a way to subdivide a function by cases. In the arithmetic-expression-processing problems in Chapter 5, we saw another way to break down a problem by cases by providing a case for each variant of a direct sum data type. This was an application of the Domain Structure Principle: the structure of a function is determined by the structure of its domain. Now we consider higher-order functions to break down into cases by variants.

Suppose that we are given a value x belonging to a direct sum type $S + T$; the goal is to apply one function f to x if it belongs to the S variant, and another function g if it belongs to the T variant. This can be done in two different ways. If f and g have the same range type, $f: S \rightarrow U$, $g: T \rightarrow U$, then the result is of type U no matter whether f or g is applied. On the other hand, if the range types are different, $f: S \rightarrow U$, $g: T \rightarrow V$, then the result will be of type $U + V$, with the variant depending on which function is applied. We investigate both forms of case analysis by variants.

The simplest way to program the case where f and g have the same range type is by using conditional construction and the discriminators (1st?, 2nd?):

$$\mathsf{cond}\ (\mathsf{1st?},\ f \circ \mathsf{1st}^{-1},\ g \circ \mathsf{2nd}^{-1})$$

For the case where they have different ranges (or even if they have the same range but we want to record which was applied), we simply tag the outputs:

$$\mathsf{cond}\ (\mathsf{1st?},\ \mathsf{1st} \circ f \circ \mathsf{1st}^{-1},\ \mathsf{2nd} \circ g \circ \mathsf{2nd}^{-1})$$

Figure 6.19 Archetype and prototype for functional direct sum and alternation.

Archetype

Syntax:

$[+]: [(S \rightarrow U) \times (T \rightarrow V)] \rightarrow [(S + T) \rightarrow (U + V)]$, for all $S, T, U, V \in$ **type**

$[\mid]: [(S \rightarrow U) \times (T \rightarrow U)] \rightarrow [(S + T) \rightarrow U]$, for all $S, T, U \in$ **type**

That is, $(f + g): S + T \rightarrow U + V$, for $f: S \rightarrow U, g: T \rightarrow V$

Also, $(f \mid g): S + T \rightarrow U$, for $f: S \rightarrow U$ and $g: T \rightarrow U$

Semantics:

$(f + g)\,(1\text{st } x) = 1\text{st }(fx),$ $(f + g)\,(2\text{nd } x) = 2\text{nd }(gx)$

$(f \mid g)\,(1\text{st } x) = fx,$ $(f \mid g)\,(2\text{nd } x) = gx$

Pragmatics:

Operations take the time of the selected summand.

Prototype

$f + g \equiv \text{cond } (1\text{st?, } 1\text{st} \circ f \circ 1\text{st}^{-1}, 2\text{nd} \circ g \circ 2\text{nd}^{-1})$

$f \mid g \equiv \text{cond } (1\text{st?, } f \circ 1\text{st}^{-1}, g \circ 2\text{nd}^{-1})$

Although the preceding solutions are adequate, we can learn more about functions by considering a more fundamental solution. In Section 6.9 we saw that for two functions $f: S \rightarrow U$ and $g: T \rightarrow V$ there is a *functional direct product* $f \times g$ between the product spaces:

$$(f \times g): S \times T \rightarrow U \times V$$

That is, the product of two functions maps the product of their domains into the product of their ranges. This suggests that we can define a *functional direct sum* $f + g$ so that the sum of two functions maps the sum of their domains into the sum of their ranges:

Figure 6.20 Type signature for functional direct sum.

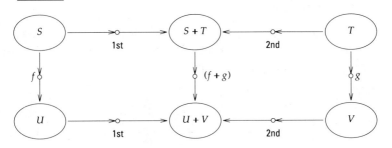

Figure 6.21 Type signature for functional alternation.

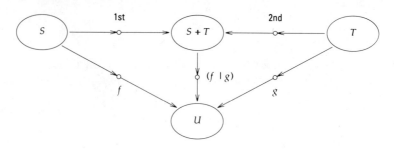

$$(f + g): S + T \rightarrow U + V$$

The definition is simple:

$$f + g \equiv \text{cond } (\text{1st?}, \text{1st} \circ f \circ \text{1st}^{-1}, \text{2nd} \circ g \circ \text{2nd}^{-1}) \qquad (6.34)$$

This handles the second of our variant case analyses. For the first we introduce the *functional alternation* $f \mid g$ with the signature

$$(f \mid g): S + T \rightarrow U$$

and the definition

$$f \mid g \equiv \text{cond } (\text{1st?}, f \circ \text{1st}^{-1}, g \circ \text{2nd}^{-1}) \qquad (6.35)$$

Archetypes and prototypes for these operations can be found in Fig. 6.19; their type signatures appear in Figs. 6.20 and 6.21.

Exercise 6.115: Prove the following identity:

$$f + g = (\text{1st} \circ f) \mid (\text{2nd} \circ g)$$

Exercise 6.116: Define the "untagging" operation $\nabla: T + T \rightarrow T$ so that $\nabla (\text{1st } x) = x$ and $\nabla (\text{2nd } x) = x$. Give a prototype implementation of ∇ in terms of the conditional. Then show the following identity:

$$\nabla = I \mid I$$

Exercise 6.117: Prove the following identity:

$$f \mid g \ = \ \nabla \circ (f + g)$$

for $f : R \to T$, $g : S \to T$.

Exercise 6.118: Prove that the prototypes in Fig. 6.19 satisfy the archetypes.

Exercise 6.119: Prove the following identity:

$$(f + g) \circ (h + k) \ = \ (f \circ h) + (g \circ k)$$

Exercise 6.120: Prove the following identity:

$$(f \mid g) \circ (h + k) \ = \ (f \circ h) \mid (g \circ k)$$

Exercise 6.121: Prove the following identity:

$$f \circ (g \mid h) \ = \ (f \circ g) \mid (f \circ h)$$

Exercise 6.122: Prove the following identity:

$$1\text{st}^{-1} \circ (f + g) \ = \ f \circ 1\text{st}^{-1}$$

Are there any situations in which one side is defined but the other is not? (The analogous identity, of course, holds for 2nd^{-1}.)

Exercise 6.123: Prove the following identities:

$$(f + g) \circ 1\text{st} \ = \ 1\text{st} \circ f, \quad (f \mid g) \circ 1\text{st} \ = \ f$$

Exercise 6.124: Suppose that $f: S \to U$ and $g: T \to U$. Prove that

$$f \mid g \ = \ (\text{I} \mid \text{I}) \circ (f + g)$$

Exercise 6.125: Prove the following identities:

$$\text{I} + \text{I} \ = \ \text{I}, \quad 1\text{st} \mid 2\text{nd} \ = \ \text{I}$$

Note that the 'I's (polymorphically) represent different identity functions, that is, identity functions over different domains. Show the signatures of the functions on both sides of these equations.

Exercise 6.126: Show that if $f: S + T \to U$, then

$$f \ = \ f \circ 1\text{st} \mid f \circ 2\text{nd}$$

Figure 6.22 Archetype and prototype for pretest conditional.

Archetype

Syntax:

$[\rightarrow]\colon (D \rightarrow A + B) \times (D{+}D \rightarrow R) \rightarrow (D \rightarrow R)$, for all A, B, D, $R \in$ **type**

That is, $(P \rightarrow Q)\colon D \rightarrow R$, for $P\colon D \rightarrow A + B$, $Q\colon D + D \rightarrow R$

Semantics:

$(P \rightarrow Q)x \;=\; Q(\text{1st } x)$, if 1st? (Px)

$(P \rightarrow Q)x \;=\; Q(\text{2nd } x)$, if 2nd? (Px)

Pragmatics:

$P \rightarrow Q$ takes time equal to the sum of times for P and Q.

Prototype

$P \rightarrow Q \;\equiv\; Q \circ \text{cond } (\text{1st? } \circ P,\ \text{1st},\ \text{2nd})$

In the last section we promised to introduce an algebraically motivated version of the conditional construction. Recall that the Boolean type can be defined as the direct sum

abstract structure $\mathbb{B} \equiv$ **true + false**

In other words, $\mathbb{B}$ is a direct sum of the trivial type with itself, $\mathbb{B} \cong \mathbf{1} + \mathbf{1}$. This close connection between Boolean values and direct sums suggests a way to use our functional sum and alternation operators to express conditional construction. Consider the application

cond $(P,\ F,\ G)x$

We want to pass x to either F or G, depending on whether Px is true or false. Note that $(F \mid G) \circ P$ will not do because it computes $F(Px)$ if $Px =$ **true** and $G(Px)$ if $Px =$ **false**. That is, it computes either $F(\textbf{true})$ or $G(\textbf{false})$; we lose the value x. The correct solution, however, is suggested. We must pass x to $F \mid G$, but "colored" to reflect the result of the test Px. That is, if $Px =$ **true**, then we color x "true"; otherwise we color it "false." Then we can compute either Fx or Gx depending on the color of x. To accomplish the coloring, we define a new functional, the *pretest conditional*, $P \rightarrow Q$, which colors its argument according to the predicate P and then passes the colored result to Q. That is,

$(P \rightarrow Q)x \;\equiv\; Q(\text{1st } x)$, if $Px =$ **true**

$(P \rightarrow Q)x \;\equiv\; Q(\text{2nd } x)$, if $Px =$ **false**

Now consider the expression $P \rightarrow (F \mid G)$; it is easy to show that this is equivalent to cond $(P,\ F,\ G)$ (see Exercise 6.129). Taking '$\rightarrow$' to be less binding than '$\mid$' gives us the notation $P \rightarrow F \mid G$ for conditional construction; it also suggests new possibilities. For example, if F and G have different ranges, we can still form a conditional construction if we write $P \rightarrow F + G$.

We can make the pretest conditional more useful by observing that the only thing significant about Px is the variant to which it belongs, **true** or **false**. Therefore, we can permit P to be any function whose range is a direct sum, $P: D \rightarrow A + B$, letting the variant of Px control the "coloring" of x. Hence we adopt the following more general definition:

$$(P \rightarrow Q)x \equiv Q(\text{1st } x), \quad \text{if 1st? } (Px) \tag{6.36}$$
$$(P \rightarrow Q)x \equiv Q(\text{2nd } x), \quad \text{if 2nd? } (Px)$$

The archetype and prototype for $\rightarrow$ are in Fig. 6.22.

Exercise 6.127: Explain the type signature for the pretest conditional (Fig. 6.22).

Exercise 6.128: Suppose E is a file of personnel records (as defined in Eq. 5.13). Write a formula to compute a file containing a pair for each employee that comprises:

a. the employee's name,

b. the hourly rate for present employees, or 0 for past employees.

Exercise 6.129: Show that the following identity holds:

$$\text{cond } (p, f, g) = p \rightarrow f \mid g$$

This provides an implementation of cond in terms of the pretest conditional and functional alternation.

Exercise 6.130: Prove the following identity:

$$(f \mid g) \circ (p \rightarrow h + k) = p \rightarrow (f \circ h) \mid (g \circ k)$$

Exercise 6.131: Prove the following identity:

$$f \circ (p \rightarrow g) = p \rightarrow (f \circ g)$$

Exercise 6.132: Prove the following identity:

$$(p \rightarrow f) \circ g = p \circ g \rightarrow f \circ (g + g)$$

Exercise 6.133: Prove the following identity:

$$(p \rightarrow f \mid g) \circ h = p \circ h \rightarrow f \circ h \mid g \circ h$$

Exercise 6.134:   Prove the following identity:

$$(p + q) \rightarrow f = f \circ (1\text{st} + 2\text{nd})$$

Hint: Write out the signatures of all functions.

Exercise 6.135:   Prove the following identity:

$$f \mid g = I \rightarrow f \circ 1\text{st}^{-1} \mid g \circ 2\text{nd}^{-1}$$

Hint: Write out the signatures of all functions.

Exercise 6.136:   Prove the following identity:

$$f + g = I \rightarrow f \circ 1\text{st}^{-1} + g \circ 2\text{nd}^{-1}$$

Hint: Write out the signatures of all functions.

6.16 Recursively Defined Functionals

The functional sum and alternation give us a viewpoint from which to understand a number of functionals more deeply. We begin by deriving a new version of map based on functional ideas. Since map $f: D^* \rightarrow R^*$, we can investigate map f by investigating its domain type D^*. That is, we apply the Domain Structure Principle.

Recall that in Section 5.3 we determined that sequence types are equivalent to recursively defined structure types:

$$D^* \cong D^0 + D \times D^* \tag{6.37}$$

Since D^* is the direct sum of two types, we can consider the behavior of map f on each of these variants. Since the only value in $D^0 = 1$ is (), we know the behavior of map f on this variant:

map f () = ()

Thus map f takes a value in D^0 into a value in R^0, both corresponding to the empty sequence. This agrees with the archetype, Eq. (6.3).

Now consider the other variant, $D \times D^*$. An arbitrary $S \in D \times D^*$ is a pair (ϕ, ρ), with $\phi \in D$ and $\rho \in D^*$, corresponding to a nonnull sequence whose first is ϕ and whose rest is ρ. The archetype for map (Eq. 6.4) tells us that

map f $(\phi, \rho) = (f\phi, \text{map } f\ \rho)$

We use the functional direct product to factor out the (ϕ, ρ):

$$\text{map } f \, (\phi, \rho) \; = \; (f \times \text{map } f) \, (\phi, \rho)$$

Hence we have an equation that defines map f on the second variant of D^*:

$$\text{map } f \, S \; = \; (f \times \text{map } f) \, S, \quad \text{for } S \in D \times D^*$$

Notice that map f takes a value of type $D \times D^*$ into a value of type $R \times R^*$. By defining map f on both variants of its domain, we have defined it completely. This leads directly to a recursive functional definition of map f:

$$\text{map } f \; \equiv \; \mathbf{I} + f \times \text{map } f \tag{6.38}$$

The functional direct sum is appropriate since $\mathbf{I}: D^0 \rightarrow R^0$ and $(f \times \text{map } f): D \times D^* \rightarrow R \times R^*$. Therefore,

$$\text{map } f : (D^0 + D \times D^*) \rightarrow (R^0 + R \times R^*)$$

We can learn a great deal about map by investigating Eq. (6.38). First, observe that since it is recursive it can be "unwound" once as follows:

$$\begin{aligned}
\text{map } f \; &= \; \mathbf{I} + (f \times \text{map } f) \\
&= \; \mathbf{I} + [f \times (\mathbf{I} + f \times \text{map } f)] \\
&\cong \; \mathbf{I} + (f \times \mathbf{I}) + (f \times f \times \text{map } f)
\end{aligned}$$

The last step follows from the identity

$$f \times (g + h) \; \cong \; (f \times g) + (f \times h) \tag{6.39}$$

where '$\cong$' denotes isomorphism (see Section 5.3).

Exercise 6.137: Show the identity of Eq. (6.39) by exhibiting one-to-one functions ϕ and ψ such that

$$\phi \circ [f \times (g + h)] \; = \; [(f \times g) + (f \times h)] \circ \psi$$

Continued unwinding of map f and application of Eq. (6.39) results in the infinite expansion

$$\text{map } f \; \cong \; \mathbf{I} + (f \times \mathbf{I}) + (f \times f \times \mathbf{I}) + (f \times f \times f \times \mathbf{I}) + \cdots \tag{6.40}$$

Thus we see map f as the infinite direct sum of all the finite direct products of f with itself. The structure is made more apparent by a little additional notation. Let $f^{<n>}$ represent the n-fold direct product of f:

$$f^{<0>} = I$$
$$f^{<n+1>} = f \times f^{<n>}, \quad n \geq 0$$

Then map f can be seen to be the sum of all the finite powers of f:

$$\text{map } f \cong f^{<0>} + f^{<1>} + f^{<2>} + f^{<3>} + \cdots \cong \sum_{n=0}^{\infty} f^{<n>}$$

This formula is easy to understand. Observe that $f^{<n>} : D^n \to R^n$ is the function that maps f across an n-element sequence (taken as a tuple). Thus map f is the sum of all the functions that map f across any finite sequence. This is in accord with our definition of D^* as the infinite direct sum of all the finite direct products of D:

$$D^* \cong D^0 + D^1 + D^2 + D^3 + \cdots \cong \sum_{n=0}^{\infty} D^n$$

In effect, the zero-element sequences are diverted through $f^{<0>}$, the one-element sequences through $f^{<1>}$, the two-element sequences through $f^{<2>}$, and so forth.

Note that $f^{<n>}$ represents the nth *horizontal* power of f; this must be carefully distinguished from the n-fold composition f^n, which is the nth *vertical* power of f. This suggests another functional that is the sum of all the finite vertical powers of f (see Exercise 6.147). For now simply observe that algebraic formulas such as Eq. (6.40) can suggest further generalizations.

We complete the investigation of map by relating Eq. (6.40) back to our original definition, Eq. (6.5). Recall that sequence types are not actually defined by Eq. (6.37); this would imply that they are weak types. Rather, as discussed in Section 5.3, we define sequences as the following recursively defined structures:

abstract structure $T^* \equiv$ nil + prefix (first $\in T$, rest $\in T^*$)   (5.21)

Given this definition, nil corresponds to 1st and prefix corresponds to 2nd (see Fig. 5.8). In Exercise (6.118) you proved the identity

$$f + g = \text{cond } (\text{1st?}, \text{1st} \circ f \circ \text{1st}^{-1}, \text{2nd} \circ g \circ \text{2nd}^{-1})$$

Using conditional notation and the constructors and discriminators for sequence types, we have

$$f + g = \text{nil?} \rightarrow \text{nil} \circ f \circ \text{nil}^{-1} \mid \text{prefix} \circ g \circ \text{prefix}^{-1}$$

Applying this to Eq. (6.38) yields the following equivalent definition of map f:

$$\text{map } f \equiv \text{nil?} \rightarrow \text{nil} \circ \mathbf{I} \circ \text{nil}^{-1} \mid \text{prefix} \circ (f \times \text{map } f) \circ \text{prefix}^{-1}$$

Since $\text{nil} \circ \text{nil}^{-1} = \mathbf{I}$ the consequent of the conditional can be simplified, yielding

$$\text{map } f \equiv \text{nil?} \rightarrow \mathbf{I} \mid \text{prefix} \circ (f \times \text{map } f) \circ \text{prefix}^{-1}$$

This formula says that map f is accomplished by the following operations: If the argument in null, then return it, otherwise (1) decompose it into its first and rest components, (2) apply f and map f to these components, and (3) recompose these components. It is easy to see that this is a purely functional definition of map, equivalent to the following:

$$\text{map } f \equiv S \mapsto \begin{cases} S, & \text{if null } S \\ \textbf{else } f \text{ (first } S) : \text{map } f \text{ (rest } S) \end{cases}$$

This is not quite the same as our original definition (Eq. 6.5), although they have the same effect.

Exercise 6.138: Develop a functional description of map f analogous to Eq. (6.38), but agreeing exactly with Eq. (6.5). *Hint:* Use functional operations to factor S out of the right-hand side of Eq. (6.4).

Exercise 6.139: Show that the following is a correct description of accr:

$$\text{accr } (f, z) \equiv \text{const } z \mid f \circ [\mathbf{I} \times \text{accr } (f, z)]$$

Exercise 6.140: Show that the following is a correct description of redl:

$$\text{redl } f = \text{null} \circ \text{rest} \rightarrow \text{first} \mid f \circ (\text{redl } f \circ \text{butlast} ; \text{last})$$

Exercise 6.141: Use functional alternation to derive an analogous formula for redr f.

Exercise 6.142: Use functional alternation to derive an analogous formula for accl (f, z).

Exercise 6.143: Use accl and functional alternation to define a function that evaluates postfix arithmetic sequences (without identifiers). *Hint:* The value passed along by the accumulation is the stack.

Exercise 6.144: Show that the following is a correct definition of pairs:

pairs ≡ null∘left ∧ null∘right → nil | (first × first) : pairs∘(rest × rest)

Note the use of multilevel functions.

Exercise 6.145: Backus (1978) defines a higher-order function **while** that is analogous to a **while**-loop in imperative languages. The function **while** (P, F) applies F iteratively as long as the predicate P returns **true**. That is,

$$\textbf{while}\,(P, F)\,x = x, \text{ if } \neg Px$$
$$\textbf{while}\,(P, F)\,x = \textbf{while}\,(P, F)\,(Fx), \text{ if } Px$$

a. Write the signature of **while**.

b. Define **while** recursively using conditional construction.

c. Expand the recursive definition of **while** into an infinite alternation of conditionals.

d. Use **while** to define map.

e. Use **while** to define fil.

f. Use **while** to define accr.

g. Use **while** to define accl.

h. Use **while** to define interval.

i. Use **while** to define pairs.

Exercise 6.146: The sequence generator gen is specified by

$$\text{gen}\,(F, x)\,n = \langle x, Fx, F^2x, \ldots, F^{n-1}x\rangle$$

where F^n denotes the n-fold composition of F with itself.

a. Write the signature of gen.

b. Use **while** to program gen.

c. Use gen and other functionals to define **while**.

d. Use gen to program interval.

Exercise 6.147: Define the functional rep by the following infinite direct sum:

$$\text{rep } f = f^0 + f^1 + f^2 + \cdots = \sum_{n=0}^{\infty} f^n$$

where $f^0 = I$.

a. What is rep's signature.

b. Give a recursive definition of rep f.

c. Implement length using rep.

d. Implement rep in terms of **while**.

Show that

$$\text{rep } f\, S\ =\ \text{last } [\text{gen} (f,\ S)\, (1 + \text{length } S)]$$

Exercise 6.148: The **while** functional is obviously very powerful; the other iterative functionals can be easily expressed in its terms. Discuss the pros and cons of eliminating maps, reductions, accumulations, and so forth, and replacing them with **while**.

Exercise 6.149: Suggest a *useful* sequence-processing functional. Define its meaning in a formal archetype, give several example applications, provide a prototype implementation, and prove that your prototype satisfies the archetype.

Exercise 6.150: Most of the functionals discussed in this chapter are for *sequence* processing. Design a library of functionals for *tree* processing. For example, you might try to define maps, reductions, and accumulations for trees. Use your functionals to program some of the functions discussed in Chapter 5. Some tree-oriented functionals are discussed in (Wile 1973), but try to come up with your own.

Exercise 6.151: Develop functionals for finite set and function processing.

Chapter 7

Infinite Data Structures

7.1 Introduction

In this chapter we investigate the manipulation of infinite data structures. An infinite data structure cannot be represented on a finite computer in the obvious way: by representing all its components *explicitly*. Rather, we must find some finite structure that represents its components *implicitly*. We faced a similar problem in discussing the definition of functions in Section 1.3, where we saw that functions with small, finite domains can be defined explicitly, by listing their input-output pairs but that functions with large or infinite domains must be defined implicitly by composition or recursion. That is, a finite formula (a function definition) can describe an infinite structure (the infinite set of input-output pairs). Here we use a similar approach, representing infinite data structures by functions that can be described finitely—computable functions. Since functional programming provides the means for manipulating these functions, it also provides the means for manipulating the infinite data structures they represent.

7.2 Recursive Sets

First we consider the manipulation of general (i.e., possibly infinite) sets. An infinite set can be represented by a computable function in two basic ways: *characteristic functions* and *enumeration functions*. We say that a predicate (Boolean-valued function) P is the characteristic function of a set S if it can be used to test for membership in S:

$$Px = \textbf{true} \Leftrightarrow x \in S \text{ and } Px = \textbf{false} \Leftrightarrow x \notin S$$

Since the technical term for a computable function is a *recursive* function, the sets that can be described by computable characteristic functions are called *recursive sets*.

The other way to represent an infinite set is by an enumeration function. We call F an enumeration function for S if $F1, F2, F3, \cdots$ enumerates all and only the elements of S. That is, for every element x of S we will eventually reach an n such that $x = Fn$. Conversely, every Fn is in S. The sets that can be enumerated by computable enumeration functions are known as the *recursively enumerable sets*. In this section we investigate characteristic functions; we investigate enumeration functions in the next section since they are closely related to infinite sequences.

Let's develop an archetype and a prototype for recursive sets (i.e., sets represented by characteristic functions). Clearly we want the set operations to satisfy the usual properties, for example, $x \in S \cap T = x \in S \wedge x \in T$. On the other hand, we have a particular representation in mind (i.e., characteristic functions), and it is not immediately apparent whether this representation will support all the usual operations. Indeed, we see shortly that certain well-known set operations, such as $\subseteq$, cannot be implemented for recursive sets. For this reason we alter our usual order and develop the prototype in tandem with the archetype. This will ensure that the prototype correctly implements the archetype but may leave us in doubt about whether the archetype specifies what we want. The only solution is to look at the resulting archetype and see whether it makes sense.

We use recset τ for the type of all recursive sets over the type τ. Since the recursive set type is so dependent on its representation, there is no point in making it an abstract type. We make it a *weak* type by the declaration:

type recset $\tau \equiv \tau \to \mathbb{B}$

(See Section 4.5 for the distinction between strong and weak typing.) That is, a recursive set of things of type τ is just a Boolean-valued function on τ.

We now investigate the usual set operations in terms of corresponding operations on characteristic functions. First consider intersection. We know $x \in S \cap T$ if and only if $x \in S$ and $x \in T$. Since S and T are represented by their characteristic functions, $x \in S$ and $x \in T$ return **true** if and only if both Sx and Tx return **true**. Therefore, since

$$(S \cap T)x = x \in S \cap T = x \in S \wedge x \in T = Sx \wedge Tx \tag{7.1}$$

we know that

$$S \cap T \equiv x \mapsto (Sx \wedge Tx) \qquad (7.2)$$

Observe that $\cap$ is *lifted* '$\wedge$' (see Section 6.10). This is more apparent if we eliminate the functional abstraction from Eq. (7.2):

$$S \cap T \equiv [\wedge] \circ (S; T) \qquad (7.3)$$

If we permit multilevel functions (Section 6.10), we can implement intersection directly by

$$S \cap T = S \wedge T \qquad (7.4)$$

Any one of Eqs. (7.2), (7.3), or (7.4) may serve as our prototype definition of intersection. The derivation (Eq. 7.1) shows that they satisfy the archetype. The remaining prototypes are just as easy; see Fig. 7.1.

The prototype implementation can easily be translated into functional languages such as Common LISP and Scheme. We show the Scheme versions first because they are closest. Here are recset←finset, $\in$, and $\cap$:

```
(define (recset-from-finset S)
  (lambda (x) (if (member x S) #t #f)))

(define (mem x S) (S x))

(define (inters S T)
  (lambda (x) (and (S x) (T x))))
```

The Common LISP definition is complicated slightly by the necessity of using funcall and a more complicated membership test:

```
(defun recset<-finset (S)
  #'(lambda (x) (if (member x S :test #'equal) t nil)))

(defun mem (x S) (funcall S x))

(defun inters (setS setT)
  #'(lambda (x) (and (funcall setS x) (funcall setT x))))
```

(We also rename the formals to avoid a collision with the LISP constant t for **true**.)

Exercise 7.1: Show that each of the prototype definitions in Fig. 7.1 satisfies the archetype in the figure.

Exercise 7.2: Translate the prototype implementation of Fig. 7.1 into Common LISP, Scheme, or some other functional language.

Using characteristic functions, the set that the mathematician would write

$$\{n \in \mathbb{Z} \mid n > 0 \land n \bmod 3 = 0\}$$

can be written in our functional language like this:

$$n \mapsto (n > 0 \land n \bmod 3 = 0)$$

Figure 7.1 Archetype and Prototype for recursive sets.

Archetype

Syntax:
> recset τ = $\tau \rightarrow \mathbb{B}$, for all $\tau \in$ **type**
> recset←finset: finset τ → recset τ
> ∩: recset τ × recset τ → recset τ
> ∪: recset τ × recset τ → recset τ
> \: recset τ × recset τ → recset τ
> ~: recset τ → recset τ
> $\varnothing \in$ recset τ
> $\bigcirc \in$ recset τ

Semantics:
> $x \in S = Sx$
> $x \in S \cap T = x \in S \land x \in T$
> $x \in S \cup T = x \in S \lor x \in T$
> $x \in S \setminus T = x \in S \land x \notin T$
> $x \in {\sim} S = x \notin S$
> $x \in \varnothing = $ **false**
> $x \in \bigcirc = $ **true**

Pragmatics:
> The cost of a membership test is the cost of the underlying characteristic function.
> All other operations take constant time (to construct the result set).

Prototype:
> **type** recset $\tau \equiv \tau \rightarrow \mathbb{B}$
> $x \in S \equiv Sx$
> ${\sim} S \equiv [\neg] \circ S$
> $S \cap T \equiv [\land] \circ (S; T)$
> $S \cup T \equiv {\sim}({\sim} S \cap {\sim} T)$
> $S \setminus T \equiv S \cap {\sim} T$
> $\varnothing \equiv $ const **false**
> $\bigcirc \equiv {\sim}\varnothing$
> recset←finset $S \equiv [\in S]$

Notice that in Fig. 7.1 we provide an operation recset←finset for converting finite sets into recursive sets. Thus a recursive set defined by explicit enumeration, such as {1, 3, 5, 7}, can be written

recset←finset {1, 3, 5, 7}

Fig. 7.1 also contains constants for the empty (∅) and universal (O) sets.

For a simple example application, we define Pos ∈ recset $\mathbb{Z}$ to be the set of all positive integers and Trips ∈ recset $\mathbb{Z}$ to be the set of all multiples of three:

$$Pos \equiv [> 0]$$
$$Trips \equiv n \mapsto (n \bmod 3 = 0)$$
$$\equiv [= 0] \circ [\bmod 3]$$

It is then easy to define PT to be all positive triples:

$$PT \equiv Pos \cap Trips$$

Exercise 7.3: Define an operation adjoin: $\tau \times$ recset $\tau \to$ recset τ analogous to the adjoin operation for finite sets. Note that, since recset τ is a weak type, adjoin can be defined either in terms of already defined recset operations or in terms of the underlying representation.

Exercise 7.4: Define the Cartesian product operation $S \times T$ on recursive sets.

Exercise 7.5: Write a formula for the recursive set of all x such that $\sin x \le 0$.

Exercise 7.6: Define the operation ⌃: (recset τ^*)$^2 \to$ recset τ^* such that $r \in S \wedge T$ if and only if for some $s \in S$ and $t \in T$, $r = s \wedge t$. *Hint:* This is not as easy as the other recursive set operations; you must define an auxiliary function.

Exercise 7.7: *Cofinite sets* are sets whose *complements* are finite (relative to some type). Define an archetype and prototype for cofinite sets. *Hint:* Use finite sets.

7.3 Extension and Intension

It is interesting to observe some of the differences between the archetypes for finite sets and recursive sets. For example, the complement operation (~) and the universal set (O) have no meaning for finite sets since they may not return finite sets. We say that the type finset τ is not *closed* under these operations. Conversely, card and the set relations and predicates (=, ≠, ⊂, ⊆, empty), while they can be implemented on finite sets, they are generally uncomputable on recursive sets.

To understand why the =, ≠, ⊆, ⊂ and empty operations aren't computable on recursive sets, think about what would be necessary to implement an equality test between recursive sets. By the Axiom of Extensionality, S and T are the same set if and only if, for all x, $x \in S = x \in T$. Thus we must determine whether for all x, $Sx = Tx$. In other words, we must determine whether S and T always have the same output for a given input. Equivalently, we must determine whether two programs S and T compute the same mathematical function.

Notice that it is not sufficient to compare the *formulas* representing the characteristic functions. For example, we could easily define a function that compared two formulas, say character by character, and told us whether or not they were the same. This is not, however, what we need—it would tell us that the formulas

$$'n \mapsto (n \bmod 3 = 0)', \quad 'n \mapsto (n \quad \bmod \quad 3 \quad = \quad 0)'$$

are different (there are extra blanks in the second formula), even though they represent the same set. Obviously we could avoid this problem by various means, such as representing the formulas by trees, as in Chapter 5. Nonetheless the problem remains since a tree comparison will not tell us that these two formulas represent the same set:

$$n \mapsto (n \bmod 3 = 0), \quad [=0] \circ [\bmod 3]$$

Clearly *syntactic* comparisons of the formulas will not do; we must analyze their *semantics* (meaning). One way to do this would be to write a program that proves or disproves the proposition that, for all x, $Sx = Tx$. Unfortunately, this is impossible.

It is a very deep and important result in computer science that no program can determine whether two other programs are equivalent. In fact, it is impossible to write a program to decide any of the properties we need to implement =, ≠, ⊆, ⊂, and empty. This is established by Rice's Theorem (Rice 1953), an extension of Turing's famous theorem proving the undecidability of termination (Turing 1936). We consider these results and their proofs in Section 9.9; for now it is sufficient to understand that they prevent the computation of operations that compare recursive sets.

You may be a little confused. There is obviously a sense in which recursive sets can be compared; we can write a program to compare (as strings or trees) formulas for them, and say whether those formulas are the same. On the other hand, we cannot write a formula to decide whether two formulas compute the same function. These conflicting notions of equality may be clarified by the notions of *intension* and *extension*.[1] The intension of a formula is its sense, whereas its extension is the object it denotes. For example, the intension of 'the morning star' includes 'a bright celestial object visible in the east just before sunrise'. Similarly, the intension of 'the evening star' includes 'a prominent celestial object visible in the west just after sunset'. The extension of both these terms is the same: the planet Venus. We have two different formulas with different intensions but the same extension.

Now let's apply these ideas to functional programming. We have already met with the extension of a set (Section 4.2)—the set's members, no matter how they're described. Thus

$$\text{'}\{5, 8, 16\}\text{'}, \qquad \text{'}\{8, 16, 5, 8\}\text{'}$$

are two different descriptions of the same (finite) set. In the finite case there is no difficulty in determining whether these two formulas denote the same set. On the other hand, the following two formulas

$$\text{'}n \mapsto (n + n)\text{'}, \qquad \text{'}n \mapsto (2 \times n)\text{'}$$

clearly have different intensions: The first describes 'the function that adds a number to itself'; the second, 'the function that multiplies a number by 2'. Only by (trivial) mathematical analysis can we show that these formulas denote the same function, that is, have the same extension. For an example where the mathematical analysis is not so trivial, consider the following recursive sets (in recset $\mathbb{Z}^3$):

$$\varnothing, \qquad (x, y, z) \mapsto (x^3 + y^3 = z^3 \ \wedge \ x \in \text{Pos} \ \wedge \ y \in \text{Pos} \ \wedge \ z \in \text{Pos})$$

These sets are equal if and only if Fermat's Last Theorem is true, an unsolved problem in mathematics for centuries.[2]

We summarize. The intension of 'the morning star' is different from that of 'the evening star'; the phrases have different senses. On the other hand, they have the same extension since they denote the same object. Similarly, the intension of '$n \mapsto (n + n)$' is different from the intension of '$n \mapsto (2 \times n)$'; they are different *programs*. Nevertheless their extensions are the same; they denote the same mathematical *function*. Comparing

---

1. These are terms from logic; for example (Jevons 1919, 37), "The meaning of a term in extension consists of the objects to which the term may be applied; its meaning in intension consists of the qualities which are necessarily possessed by objects bearing that name." See especially (Beth 1964, 466–467). Note that the word 'intension' contains an 's'.
2. This can be considered a "proof by intimidation" that we can't implement equality for recursive sets. If we could, then the truth of Fermat's Theorem could be easily decided.

the intensions of two formulas is generally easy since the intensions are usually the same just when the formulas are the same.[3] Comparing the extensions of infinite objects is generally uncomputable, however, since it would require the inspection of all the components of the object (as shown by Rice's and Turing's theorems). Since in mathematics, as in much of science, the description of a thing is less important than the thing itself, we are generally more interested in extensions than intensions. For this reason, we have not defined intensional equality tests on recursive sets and other functions. Unfortunately, we can't have what we really want: the extensional tests. In general, data structures that are represented intensionally (i.e., in terms of their properties rather than their members) will not have computable equality relations. This is the case for infinite data structures, which must be represented intensionally.[4]

On the subject of mathematical foundations, let's briefly investigate Russell's Paradox (Russell 1903, Chapter X). Recall that this paradox is based on the definition of the set of all sets that are not elements of themselves:

$$\{x \mid x \notin x\}$$

A contradiction arises from asking whether this set is a member of itself, for it is a member of itself if and only if it is not a member of itself. Let's see whether our definition of recursive sets sheds any light on this paradox. Define ω to be the set of all sets that are not members of themselves:

$$\omega \equiv x \mapsto (\neg\, x \in x)$$

Now we can evaluate the expression $\omega \in \omega$ as follows:

$$\begin{aligned} \omega \in \omega &\Rightarrow \omega\omega \\ &\Rightarrow x \mapsto (\neg\, x \in x)\, \omega \\ &\Rightarrow \neg\, \omega \in \omega \end{aligned}$$

In other words, $\omega \in \omega$ leads to the nonterminating computation

$$\omega \in \omega \;\Rightarrow\; \neg\, \omega \in \omega \;\Rightarrow\; \neg\,\neg\, \omega \in \omega \;\Rightarrow\; \cdots$$

3. We say 'generally' and 'usually' because there are many possible interpretations of the intension of a formula. Is its intension its literal description, character by character? Probably not, since that would include formatting details, such as blanks, in the sense of the formula. On the other hand, the order in which things are done (such as '$n+1$' versus '$1+n$') is almost certainly part of the sense of the formula. For most purposes abstract syntax (Chapter 10) can be taken to be isomorphic to intension.
4. Observe that this discussion applies to all functions, not just the characteristic functions of recursive sets. Extensional and intensional representations of functions, sets, and relations are contrasted in (MacLennan 1973).

Thus the contradiction results from the assumption that $\omega \in \omega$ has a truth value; since it is nonterminating, it has no value. These issues are discussed further in Sections 8.5 and 12.1.

We can gain additional insight by considering the type of ω. Let Ω represent the type of ω; we want to find a formula for Ω. For the application $\omega\omega$ to be legal, ω must be a member of the domain of ω. Thus the type of ω is $\Omega \to \mathbb{B}$. Since $\mathsf{recset}\,\tau = \tau \to \mathbb{B}$, the type of ω is defined by the recursive formula

$$\Omega \equiv \mathsf{recset}\ \Omega$$

That is, Ω is the type of all recursive sets whose members are of type Ω. This makes sense: Since ω is the set of all sets that are not members of themselves, and since ω is a potential member of itself, the type of the members of ω must be the same as the type of ω itself!

This is nonetheless an unusual type, one not permitted in many type systems. Indeed, Russell got around his paradox by defining a type theory that excludes self-referential types like Ω and thus indirectly rules out sets like ω. On the other hand, ω makes perfect computational sense. Although it may lead to a nonterminating computation, we know the computations it invokes. In fact, we can define ω in dynamically typed languages such as LISP and Scheme, since in these languages we can take Ω to be direct sum of all the types in the language (i.e., Ω is the *static* type of any LISP expression). Whether recursive types such as Ω should be permitted is an open question that we do not attempt to resolve in this book. Certainly ω has few (if any) applications. On the other hand, the paradoxes lurking in Ω should put us on our guard about other, more useful, recursive types.

Exercise 7.8: Define ω in LISP or Scheme. What is the result of evaluating

(mem omega omega)

Exercise 7.9: Define the recursive set ψ of all sets that *are* members of themselves. What is the result of evaluating $\psi \in \psi$? Give an intuitive explanation of its behavior.

7.4 An Application: Recognitive Grammars

In this section we illustrate the use of recursive sets by working through an example: the implementation of *recognitive grammars*, that is, grammars for recognizing strings as belonging to certain classes. The goal is use recursive set expressions as a way of defining infinite c' of strings. We already have part of what we need: The union $S \cup T$ contains all the strings that are in either S or T. Thus the set definition $R \equiv S \cup T$ is very much like the BNF definition $R ::= S \mid T$. For example, if letter is the recursive set of singleton letter sequences (<'a'>, <'b'>, and so on) and digit is the recursive set of singleton digits (<'0'>, <'1'>, and so on), then letter $\cup$ digit is the set of all singleton sequences of letters or digits (i.e., alphanumeric characters). We define the letter and digit classes as follows:

$$\text{letter} \equiv \#'a' \cup \#'b' \cup \cdots \cup \#'z' \qquad (7.5)$$
$$\text{digit} \equiv \#'0' \cup \#'1' \cup \cdots \cup \#'9'$$

Here we use $\#'a'$ for the recursive set containing just the sequence <'a'>:

$$\#k \equiv \text{recset} \leftarrow \text{finset} \{<k>\}$$

This example is not very interesting, however, since the resulting sets are finite.

Our next goal is to define an operation analogous to BNF catenation. If in BNF we define $R ::= ST$, then R is the class of all strings $s \wedge t$ obtainable by catenating strings s in S and t in T. We define an analogous operation $S \wedge T$ on recursive sets of sequences; note that we are overloading the '$\wedge$' operator. Thus if $S, T \in$ recset τ^*, then $S \wedge T$ is also in recset τ^* and has the following members:

$$r \in S \wedge T \text{ if and only if } r = s \wedge t \text{ for some } s \in S \text{ and } t \in T$$

For example, if <'b', 'o', 'o', 'k'> $\in S$ and <'k', 'e', 'e', 'p', 'e', 'r'> $\in T$, then <'b', 'o', 'o', 'k', 'k', 'e', 'e', 'p', 'e', 'r'> $\in S \wedge T$. We can read $S \wedge T$ as "S followed by T" or "S then T."

To evaluate $r \in S \wedge T$ we must consider all pairs of sequences s and t such that $r = s \wedge t$; if for one of these pairs we find $s \in S$ and $t \in T$, then we know $r \in S \wedge T$. The easiest way to accomplish this is to begin testing with $s = <>$ and $t = r$. If these fail, we try next $s = <r_1>$, $t = <r_2, \ldots, r_n>$, then $s = <r_1, r_2>$, $t = <r_3, \ldots, r_n>$, and so forth. If we reach $s = r$, $t = <>$ without a success, then we know $r \notin S \wedge T$. To perform the generate-and-test process we postulate an auxiliary function concataux:

$$S \wedge T \equiv r \mapsto \text{concataux (nil, } r, S, T)$$

The auxiliary function is simply defined by the following cases:

$$\text{concataux } (s, t, S, T) \equiv \textbf{true} \quad \text{if } s \in S \wedge t \in T \qquad (7.6)$$
$$\textbf{else concataux } (s, \text{nil}, S, T) \equiv \textbf{false}$$
$$\text{concataux } (s, x{:}t, S, T) \equiv \text{concataux [postfix } (s, x), t, S, T]$$

We can write letter ⌃ digit for the class of all sequences of a letter followed by a digit. Its members include <'a', '0'>, <'b', '7'>, and so forth, but it's still a finite set.

To get infinite sets from finite sets we need some sort of closure operation. One common operation is the *Kleene cross* or *transitive closure*, S^+— the set of all finite catenations of sequences from S. For example, digit$^+$ includes the following sequences:

$$<'3'>, \ <'2', '5', '6'>, <'4', '5'>, \ \cdots$$

In general, S^+ is the union of all finite catenations of S:

$$S^+ = S \cup S{⌃}S \cup S{⌃}S{⌃}S \cup S{⌃}S{⌃}S{⌃}S \cup \ \cdots \qquad (7.7)$$

Using the obvious identity $S{⌃}(T \cup U) = S{⌃}T \cup S{⌃}U$ allows Eq. (7.7) to be factored:

$$S^+ = S \cup S{⌃}(S \cup S{⌃}S \cup S{⌃}S{⌃}S \cup \ \cdots \ ) \qquad (7.8)$$

The parenthesized expression on the right of Eq. (7.8) is just S^+, so we get the recursive definition

$$S^+ = S \cup S ⌃ S^+ \qquad (7.9)$$

This makes sense: The set of all sequences of one or more Ss is the union of the set of sequences of one S together with the set of all sequences composed of an S followed by one or more Ss. Unfortunately, Eq. (7.9) cannot serve as a prototype definition of S^+.

Suppose that we are evaluating $r \in S^+$ and that $r \notin S$. We trace the evaluation according to Eq. (7.9):

$$
\begin{aligned}
r \in S^+ &= r \in (S \cup S ⌃ S^+) \\
&= r \in S \ \vee \ r \in S ⌃ S^+ \\
&= r \in S ⌃ S^+ \\
&= \textsf{concataux (nil, } r, S, S^+)
\end{aligned}
$$

If we look at the definition of concataux (Eq. 7.6 or Fig. 7.2), we can see that evaluating the preceding expression requires us to evaluate nil $\in S \wedge r \in S^+$. This in turn requires evaluating $r \in S^+$, but this is where we started, so we're in an infinite loop.[5] The problem arises because '⌃' begins its generate-and-test procedure with $s =$ nil. This is pointless in the

---

5. You may respond, "We wouldn't be in a loop if ⌃ were executed sequentially." In fact we still would, if nil happened to be in S. The issue is discussed further later in this section.

case of $r \in S^+$, since even if we determine that nil $\in S$ we must still determine whether $r \in S^+$. This also suggests a solution to the problem: Make the closure operation call concataux directly, but in such a way that it begins its generate-and-test with the pair $s = <r_1>$, $t = $ rest r:

$$r \in S^+ \equiv \textbf{true}, \quad \text{if } r \in S$$
$$r \in S^+ \equiv \text{concataux } (<r_1>, \text{rest } r, S, S^+), \text{ otherwise}$$

This will get us in trouble if $r = $ nil, so we must add the equation

$$\text{nil} \in S^+ \equiv \text{nil} \in S$$

The preceding definition can be simplified a little, as we'll see later.

The transitive closure allows the definition of some more interesting grammars. For example, if digit is as described in Eq. (7.5), we can define unsigned integers to be sequences of one or more digits by

$$\text{uns\_int} \equiv \text{digit}^+$$

How do we define signed integers? We would like to say that an integer is an unsigned integer optionally preceded by a '+' or '−'. One way to express this is

$$\text{int} \equiv (\# \text{'+'} \cup \# \text{'−'} \cup \varepsilon) \wedge \text{uns\_int}$$

Here we use ε for the recursive set containing just the null sequence:

$$\varepsilon \equiv \text{recset} \leftarrow \text{finset } \{<>\}$$

The combination $S \cup \varepsilon$, meaning "an optional S," occurs frequently enough that we give it a special notation:

$$S? \equiv \varepsilon \cup S$$

This (overloaded) use of '?' can be read "optional S." It permits the definition of int to be expressed more readably:

$$\text{int} \equiv (\# \text{'+'} \cup \# \text{'−'})? \wedge \text{uns\_int}$$

This is read, "An int is an optional '+' or '−' followed by an uns_int."

Finally, suppose we want to define an identifier as a letter followed by zero or more letters and digits. This can be easily expressed:

$$\text{id} \equiv \text{letter} \wedge [(\text{letter} \cup \text{digit})^+]?$$

That is, "An id is a letter followed by an optional string of one or more letters or digits." The combination "zero or more of . . ." occurs so frequently, however, that it is worthwhile to define the *reflexive transitive closure (Kleene star)*:

$$S^* \equiv (S^+)?$$

With it, identifiers can be defined:

$$id \equiv letter \wedge (letter \cup digit)^*$$

This is read: "An id is a letter followed by a sequence of zero or more letters or digits." The star notation is overloaded; in fact the Kleene star was the basis for our notation for sequence types. We now have all the operations typically found in extended BNF grammatical notations.

The Kleene star allows us to simplify our implementation of the Kleene cross. To see this, first observe that $S \wedge \varepsilon = S$ (Exercise 7.11). Then factor Eq. (7.9) to yield

$$S^+ = S \wedge (\varepsilon \cup S^+)$$

(You prove the legitimacy of this factoring in Exercise 7.10). The parenthesized expression is just S^*, so we have

$$S^+ = S \wedge S^*$$

We must still avoid infinite loops, but now two equations are sufficient:

$$nil \in S^+ \equiv nil \in S$$
$$x{:}r \in S^+ \equiv \text{concataux}(<x>, r, S, S^*)$$

The direct definition is in Fig. 7.2, the archetype and prototype for our recognitive grammar operations.

Exercise 7.10: Prove that $S \wedge T \cup S \wedge U = S \wedge (T \cup U)$.

Exercise 7.11: Prove that $S \wedge \varepsilon = S$.

Exercise 7.12: Translate the prototype definition in Fig. 7.2 into Common LISP, Scheme, or some other functional language. Test it on the arithmetic expression example described in the text (see Fig. 7.3).

Suppose we set about defining a recognitive grammar for integer arithmetic expressions. We have already defined integers and identifiers, so our next step might be to define primaries and factors:

$$\text{primary} \equiv \text{id} \cup \text{int} \cup \# \text{'('} \wedge \text{expr} \wedge \# \text{')'}$$
$$\text{factor} \equiv \text{factor} \wedge \text{mulop} \wedge \text{primary} \cup \text{primary}$$

This is the beginning of a typical recursive definition of an arithmetic expression hierarchy such as found in many BNF grammars of programming languages. Unfortunately it may lead to a nonterminating computation:

$$r \in \text{factor} = \text{concataux (nil, } r, \text{ factor, mulop} \wedge \text{primary)} \vee r \in \text{primary}$$

Figure 7.2 Archetype and Prototype for recognitive grammars.

Archetype

Syntax:

    $\varepsilon \in \text{recset } \tau^*$

    $\wedge: (\text{recset } \tau^*)^2 \to \text{recset } \tau^*$

    $\cdot^+: \text{recset } \tau^* \to \text{recset } \tau^*$

    $\cdot^*: \text{recset } \tau^* \to \text{recset } \tau^*$

    $\cdot?: \text{recset } \tau^* \to \text{recset } \tau^*$

    $\#: \tau \to \text{recset } \tau^*$

Semantics:

    $s \in \varepsilon = (s = <>)$

    $r \in S \wedge T$ if and only if $r = s \wedge t$ for some $s \in S, t \in T$

    $S^+ = S \wedge S^*$

    $S^* = (S^+)?$

    $S? = \varepsilon \cup S$

    $s \in \#k = (s = <k>)$

Prototype

    $\varepsilon \equiv \text{recset} \leftarrow \text{finset } \{<>\}$

    $\text{concataux}: \tau^* \times \tau^* \times \text{recset } \tau^* \times \text{recset } \tau^* \to \mathbb{B}$

    $\text{concataux } (s, t, S, T) \equiv \textbf{true}$, if $s \in S \wedge t \in T$

    else

        $\text{concataux } (s, \text{nil}, S, T) \equiv \textbf{false}$

        $\text{concataux } (s, x{:}t, S, T) \equiv \text{concataux } [\text{postfix } (s, x), t, S, T]$

    $S \wedge T \equiv r \mapsto \text{concataux (nil, } r, S, T)$

    $S^+ \equiv \text{null} \to [\varepsilon S] \mid s \mapsto \text{concataux } (<\text{first } s>, \text{rest } s, S, S^*)$

    $S^* = (S^+)?$

    $S? \equiv \varepsilon \cup S$

    $\#k = \text{recset} \leftarrow \text{finset } \{<k>\}$

Now, if $r \notin$ factor, this will eventually lead to an invocation in which $s = r$ and $t =$ nil:

concataux (r, nil, factor, mulop $\wedge$ primary)

If we look at the definition of concataux (Fig. 7.2), we see that this invocation requires evaluating the condition $s \in S \wedge t \in T$—in this case,

$r \in$ factor $\wedge$ nil $\in$ mulop $\wedge$ primary

Notice, the recursive invocation $r \in$ factor; we are again in an infinite loop!

The problem is that a *left-recursive* definition of the form

$$S \equiv S \wedge T \cup \cdots$$

may lead to a nonterminating invocation of S. Specifically, if in determining $r \in S$ we reach the pair $s = r$, $t =$ nil, we again face $r \in S$. It is also easy to see that a *right-recursive* definition of the form

$$S \equiv R \wedge S \cup \cdots$$

faces a nonterminating call right away, since it starts its search with $s =$ nil, $t = r$.

One way to avoid this potential nontermination altogether is by writing the definition of factor iteratively, using the Kleene star, rather then recursively (see Fig. 7.3). Another solution is to invent special recursive set operators for defining sets left and right recursively (see Exercise 7.13).

We pause to consider some of the pragmatics of using recursive sets as recognitive grammars. The operation $r \in S \wedge T$ iterates $n =$ length r times. Each iteration, however, performs a postfix operation, which takes $O(n)$

Figure 7.3 Example of recognitive grammar for arithmetic expressions.

```
expr ≡ term
term ≡ factor ∧ (addop ∧ factor)*
addop ≡ #'+' ∪ #'−'
factor ≡ primary ∧ (mulop ∧ primary)*
mulop ≡ #'×' ∪ #'÷'
primary = id ∪ int ∪ (#'(' ∧ expr ∧ #')')
id ≡ letter ∧ (letter ∪ digit)*
int ≡ (#'+' ∪ #'−')? ∧ digit⁺
letter ≡ #'a' ∪ #'b' ∪ ··· ∪ #'z'
digit ≡ #'0' ∪ #'1' ∪ ··· ∪ #'9'
```

time. Hence $r \in S \wedge T$ is overall $O(n^2)$. Things may be worse, however. Consider the expression $r \in S \wedge T \wedge U$, which iterates n times, but those inner iterations must determine membership in S and $T \wedge U$. The latter, as we've seen, is an $O(n^2)$ operation, so overall the performance will be $O(n^3)$. Clearly we do not want to use recursive sets to syntax-check programs! For classifying relatively short sequences according to relatively simple grammars, however, they are quite adequate.

Exercise 7.13: Define functions lrec and rrec that can be used for the left- and right-recursive definition of recursive sets of sequences. For example,

    factor ≡ lrec (primary, mulop ∧ primary)

is intended to define the same set as

    factor ≡ factor ∧ mulop ∧ primary ∪ primary

but not lead to nontermination.

Exercise 7.14: Show that the iterative definition of factor in Fig. 7.3 is equivalent to the left-recursive definition:

    factor ≡ factor ∧ mulop ∧ primary ∪ primary

Exercise 7.15: A useful grammatical operator is 'D || E', which matches a series of one or more Es separated by Ds; it can be thought of as a kind of grammatical reduction operator (MacLennan 1975). With it "a list of identifiers separated by commas" could be defined

    id_list ≡ ',' || id

Define this operator.

Exercise 7.16: Analyze in detail the amount of time (worst-case) necessary to evaluate $r \in S \wedge T$.

Exercise 7.17: Analyze the worst-case time complexity for $r \in S^+$.

Exercise 7.18: Write a recognitive grammar for a "path name" for some operating system with which you are familiar.

Exercise 7.19: Suppose $R \in$ recset **string*** is a set of *reserved words*. Write a recognitive grammar for any identifier (letter followed by letters or digits) that is not a reserved word.

Exercise 7.20: Our recognitive grammars based on recursive sets have a limitation: They may tell us that a sequence does not belong to a set, but not *why*. One way to improve error reporting ability is by use of an operation diode that allows the detection of syntactic errors. Specifically, diode (S, T) matches all strings r such that, for all $s \in S$, if for some t, $r = s \wedge t$, then $t \in T$. In effect diode (S, T) is like $S \wedge T$, but it cuts off backtracking when it has once found an $s \in S$. This allows us to return an error indication if the corresponding t is not in T. Define a new version of recognitive grammars based not on recursive sets, but on functions that return either a success indicator or a data structure indicating where the classification failed. Since the diode operation is the source of the error indicators, you might consider adding another parameter which is a diagnostic message to be issued when diode fails.

Exercise 7.21: *(Advanced)* Extend the solution to the previous exercise to an abstract data type for parsing. That is, your grammatical operators return either a parse tree or an indicator of why the parse failed.

7.5 Recursively Enumerable Sequences

Seeing some of the value of infinite sets suggests that we consider infinite extensions of other data structures, such as sequences and trees; we do this in the following sections. For infinite sequences, we have in mind data structures such as

$$\text{Naturals} \equiv <0, 1, 2, 3, 4, \cdots>$$
$$\text{Odds} \equiv <1, 3, 5, 7, \cdots>$$
$$\text{Triples} \equiv <3, 6, 9, 12, \cdots>$$
$$\text{Primes} \equiv <2, 3, 5, 7, 11, 13, \cdots>$$

Since it is not possible to represent an infinite sequence explicitly in the computer's memory, let's represent it implicitly by an enumeration function. We call F an *enumeration function* for the infinite sequence $<S_1, S_2, S_3, \cdots>$ if for any positive integer i, $Fi = S_i$. Since we restrict our attention to computable functions, and computable functions can be represented by a finite program, we can represent infinite sequences by finite programs. In particular, since functional programming permits us to manipulate functions as first-class citizens, it permits us to manipulate infinite sequences via their enumeration functions. A sequence that has a computable enumeration function is called a *recursively enumerable (RE)* sequence.

Fig. 7.4 shows an archetype for recursively enumerable sequences. Notice that most of the operations are simple extensions of the corresponding operations on finite sequences. Some operations, such as null, have been omitted since they are not useful on infinite sequences; others, such as length, have been omitted because they are not computable. On the other hand, we have added operations such as all, which wouldn't make sense on finite sequences. Informally, the purpose of the operations is as follows:

first $<S_1, S_2, S_3, \cdots> = S_1$
rest $<S_1, S_2, S_3, \cdots> = <S_2, S_3, \cdots>$
prefix $(S_0, <S_1, S_2, S_3, \cdots>) = <S_0, S_1, S_2, S_3, \cdots>$
$<S_1, S_2, S_3, \cdots>_k = S_k$
map $f <S_1, S_2, S_3, \cdots> = <fS_1, fS_2, fS_3, \cdots>$
all $k = <k, k, k, k, \cdots>$
Naturals $= <0, 1, 2, 3, 4, \cdots>$

In developing the prototype implementation, it is convenient to think of a recursively enumerable sequence as its enumeration function. Thus $S = <S(1), S(2), S(3), \cdots>$. Further, first $S = S1$ and, in general, $S_i = Si$. To derive the prototype definition for rest, start with its archetype (Fig. 7.4):

$(rest\ S)_i = S_{i+1}$

Figure 7.4 Archetype for recursively enumerable sequences.

Syntax:
reseq $\tau = \mathbb{N} \to \tau$, for all $\tau \in$ **type**
first: reseq $\tau \to \tau$
rest: reseq $\tau \to$ reseq τ
prefix: $\tau \times$ reseq $\tau \to$ reseq τ
map: $(\sigma \to \tau) \to ($reseq $\sigma \to$ reseq $\tau)$
all: $\tau \to$ reseq τ
Naturals $\in$ reseq $\mathbb{N}$

Semantics:
first $S = S_1$
$(rest\ S)_i = S_{i+1}$, $i \geq 1$
$[prefix\ (x, S)]_{i+1} = S_i$, $i \geq 1$
first $[prefix\ (x, S)] = x$
rest $[prefix\ (x, S)] = S$
prefix (first S, rest S) $= S$
$(map\ f\ S)_i = f(S_i)$
$(all\ k)_i = k$
Naturals$_i = i-1$

Pragmatics
All operations take constant time, except first and element selection, whose costs depend on the cost of the underlying enumeration function.

Replace selection by application of the enumeration function:

$$(\text{rest } S) \, i \; = \; S \, (i+1)$$

Now, to get an explicit definition for rest S, we must factor out i from the right-hand side so that it can be canceled from both sides:

$$(\text{rest } S) \, i \; = \; S \, ([1+] \, i) \; = \; (S \circ [1+]) \, i$$

Therefore

$$\text{rest } S \; \equiv \; S \circ [1+] \tag{7.10}$$

That is, the rest of S is S composed with the successor function. This is reasonable since the first element of rest S is the second element of S, and so forth.

Exercise 7.22: Note that the prototype definition of rest (Eq. 7.10) leads to the definition of $(\text{rest } S)_0$, which is probably not what we intended. Propose an alternative implementation of rest for which $(\text{rest } S)_i$ is defined only if $i \geq 1$.

The map functional is also quite easy. To derive it we start with its defining equation (Fig. 7.4), convert selection to function application, and cancel the index from both sides:

$$(\text{map } f \, S)_i \; = \; f \, (S_i)$$
$$(\text{map } f \, S) \, i \; = \; f \, (Si) \; = \; (f \circ S) \, i$$
$$\text{map } f \, S \; \equiv \; f \circ S$$

Thus the map of f on the recursively enumerable sequence S is just the composition of f with the enumeration function of S.

Consider next prefix. It must satisfy

$$[\text{prefix } (x, \, S)]_1 \; = \; x$$
$$[\text{prefix } (x, \, S)]_i \; = \; S_{i-1}, \quad i > 1$$

We combine the two cases by a conditional:

$$[\text{prefix } (x, \, S)]_i \; = \; \begin{cases} x, & \text{if } i = 1 \\ S(i-1), & \text{if } i > 1 \end{cases}$$

We can eliminate the i from the left-hand side by functional abstraction:

$$\text{prefix } (x, \, S) \; \equiv \; i \mapsto \begin{cases} x, & \text{if } i = 1 \\ S(i-1), & \text{if } i > 1 \end{cases}$$

Figure 7.5 Prototype for recursively enumerable sequences.

---

type reseq τ ≡ $\text{IN} \to \tau$
first S ≡ S_1
rest S ≡ $S \circ [1+]$
prefix (x, S) ≡ $[=1] \to$ const x | $S \circ [-1]$
map $f\,S$ ≡ $f \circ S$
all k ≡ const k
Naturals ≡ $[-1]$

This makes it obvious that prefix returns an enumeration function. Alternatively we can eliminate the functional abstraction by using conditional construction:

$$\text{prefix } (x, S) = [=1] \to \text{const } x \;|\; S \circ [-1]$$

The complete prototype is in Fig. 7.5.

It is straightforward to translate the prototype into functional languages such as Common LISP and Scheme. For example, in Scheme we define prefix for recursively enumerable sequences like this:

```
(define (prefix x S) (lambda (k) (if (= 1 k) x (S (- k 1)))))
```

Exercise 7.23:   Most of the properties in the archetype for RE sequences (Fig. 7.4) also apply to finite sequences (Fig. 2.5), and vice versa. What properties of finite sequences *do not* apply to RE sequences? What properties of RE sequences do not apply to finite sequences?

Exercise 7.24:   Prove that the prototype (Fig. 7.5) satisfies the archetype (Fig. 7.4).

Exercise 7.25:   Translate the prototype in Fig. 7.5 into Scheme or some other functional language.

Exercise 7.26:   Write a finite formula for the infinite sequence of squares <1, 4, 9, 16, $\cdots$>.

Exercise 7.27:   Write a finite formula for the infinite sequence of factorials <0!, 1!, 2!, 3!, 4!, $\cdots$>.

Exercise 7.28:   Suppose that expt $(x, n) = x^n$. Write a finite formula for the infinite sequence of powers of x, <1, x, x^2, x^3, $\cdots$>.

Exercise 7.29:   Define a function trans: reseq (reseq τ) $\to$ reseq (reseq τ) that computes the transpose of an infinite sequence of infinite sequences. That is,

$$\text{trans} <<S_{1,1}, S_{1,2}, S_{1,3}, \cdots >, <S_{2,1}, S_{2,2}, S_{2,3}, \cdots >, \cdots >$$
$$= <<S_{1,1}, S_{2,1}, S_{3,1}, \cdots >, <S_{1,2}, S_{2,2}, S_{3,2}, \cdots >, \cdots >$$

Exercise 7.30: We define a pairing function pairs: $(\text{reseq } \tau)^2 \to \text{reseq } (\tau^2)$ such that

$$\text{pairs } (S, T) \equiv <(S_1, T_1), (S_2, T_2), \cdots >$$

Note that this pairs function requires both arguments to be of the same type; a more general pairing function is defined in Section 7.7. Show that the following is a correct definition of pairs

$$\text{pairs } (S, T) \equiv \text{map (first; second) (trans} <S, T>)$$

where second $\equiv$ first $\circ$ rest.

Exercise 7.31: Suppose that S and T are two recursively enumerable sequences of numbers. Write a finite formula for the infinite sequence $<S_1 - T_1, S_2 - T_2, \cdots >$. *Hint:* Use pairs.

Exercise 7.32: Define a function psum: reseq $\mathbb{R} \to$ reseq $\mathbb{R}$ that computes the partial sums of a recursively enumerable sequence of numbers:

$$\text{psum } S = <0, S_1, S_1 + S_2, S_1 + S_2 + S_3, \cdots >$$

Exercise 7.33: Show that the following function computes the first differences of a recursively enumerable sequence of numbers:

$$\Delta \equiv (\text{map } [-]) \circ \text{pairs} \circ (\text{rest}; I)$$

Exercise 7.34: Investigate the formula Δ (psum S). Prove the appropriate identity.

Exercise 7.35: The exponential function is defined by the series

$$\exp z \equiv 1 + \frac{z}{1!} + \frac{z^2}{2!} + \frac{z^3}{3!} + \cdots$$

Define a function exp_series: $\mathbb{R} \to$ reseq $\mathbb{R}$ such that exp_series z is the infinite sequence of the finite series approximating exp z. That is, (exp_series $z)_k$ is a k-term approximation to exp z. *Hint:* Use answers to preceding exercises. There are several ways to do this, some neater than others. Try to find an elegant solution.

Exercise 7.36: Translate the preceding definition of exp_series into Common LISP, Scheme, or another functional language.

Exercise 7.37: The exp_series program suggests a way to implement *infinite precision* real numbers on a finite computer: Represent a real number by an infinite sequence of rational approximations to the real. Suppose we define a *computable real number* to be an infinite sequence of rationals (Exercise 5.9) satisfying the following convergence condition:

$$| x_m - x_n | \leq \frac{1}{m} + \frac{1}{n}$$

Implement the arithmetic operations $+$, $-$, and $\times$ on computable reals. Discuss ways to get around the uncomputability of the comparisons ($=$, $<$, etc.). *Hint:* Multiplication is quite hard. Think of approximations to the comparisons ("equal within . . ." etc.). This "computable real analysis" is worked out in detail, through the basic definitions of the calculus, in (MacLennan 1984b).

Exercise 7.38: Use map to define RE sequence operations corresponding to the finite sequence operations distl (Exercise 6.27), distr (Exercise 6.27), fmap (Exercise 6.31), smap (Exercise 6.32), subst (Exercise 6.110), and sublis P (Exercise 6.112; assume that P is finite).

Exercise 7.39: Define the functional gen: $(\tau \rightarrow \tau) \rightarrow (\tau \rightarrow$ reseq $\tau)$ so that

gen $F\ x\ =\ <x, Fx, F^2x, F^3x, \cdots >$

Does this functional simplify any of your answers to the preceding exercises?

Exercise 7.40: Define a function overl: reseq $\tau \times \mathbb{N} \times \tau \rightarrow$ reseq τ so that overl (S, k, x) is the RE sequence that results from replacing the kth element of S by x. That is,

[overl $(S, k, x)]_n\ =\ x$, if $k = n$
[overl $(S, k, x)]_n\ =\ S_n$, if $k \neq n$

Is there any reason to restrict overl to work on RE sequences, as opposed to arbitrary functions?

Exercise 7.41: Many of our functions on RE sequences will not work if the enumeration function is not defined for all natural numbers. On the other hand, it would be handy if RE sequences included finite sequences (just as recursive sets include finite sets). Develop an archetype and prototype for a variety of RE sequences that may have "ends" (i.e., for some sequences S, S_i may be undefined for all i greater than some number, the "length" of the sequence).

In Section 7.5 we explored *recognitive* grammars as an application of recursive sets. In the following exercises you use RE sequences to implement *generative* grammars. As suggested by the terms, a recognitive grammar *recognizes* all the sequences defined by the grammar, whereas a generative grammar *generates* all the sequences defined by the grammar. Most formal language theory concerns generative grammars.

The *language* (set of sequences) defined by a generative grammar is usually infinite, although it may be finite. Therefore we will represent these *recursively enumerable (RE) sets* by the possibly finite RE sequences defined in Exercise 7.41.

Exercise 7.42: Define the operation $S \cup T$ on RE sets S and T. Note that for each i there must be a j and k such that $S_i = (S \cup T)_j$ and $T_i = (S \cup T)_k$ (provided i is less than the "lengths" of S and T, respectively).

Exercise 7.43: Define the catenation operation $S \wedge T$ on RE sets. *Hint:* This is relatively difficult since every element must be generated for some finite index. That is, for every i and j there is a k such that $S_i \wedge T_j = (S \wedge T)_k$. Make sure you can prove this of your solution. One solution is to enumerate as follows:

$$S \wedge T = <S_1 \wedge T_1, S_2 \wedge T_1, S_1 \wedge T_2, S_3 \wedge T_1, S_2 \wedge T_2, S_1 \wedge T_3, \cdots >$$

That is, enumerate the $S_i \wedge T_j$ such that $i + j = 2$, then those such that $i + j = 3$, then $i + j = 4$, and so on.

Exercise 7.44: Define the operation #k on RE sets.

Exercise 7.45: Define the operation $S?$ on RE sets. *Hint:* This is very easy.

Exercise 7.46: Define the transitive closure S^+ on RE sets.

Exercise 7.47: Define the reflexive transitive closure S^* on RE sets.

Exercise 7.48: Can you define the difference operation $S \backslash T$ on RE sets? Explain.

Exercise 7.49: Translate your RE set operations into LISP or Scheme.

7.6 Evaluation Order and the Recursive Definition of Data Structures

Our recursively enumerable sequences satisfy a number of important identities. Consider the sequence Naturals, which represents the infinite sequence

$$\text{Naturals} = <0, 1, 2, 3, 4, \cdots >$$

If we map the successor function across this, we get

$$\text{map } [1+] \text{ Naturals} = <1, 2, 3, 4, 5, \cdots >$$

This is just Naturals with its first element deleted. That is, Naturals satisfies the identity

$$\text{rest Naturals } = \text{ map [1+] Naturals} \qquad (7.11)$$

By prefixing 0 onto both sides of Eq. (7.11), we see that it also satisfies

$$\text{Naturals } = 0 : \text{map [1+] Naturals} \qquad (7.12)$$

This equation looks like an explicit (albeit recursive) definition of Naturals. We have seen many recursive definitions of *functions,* and we've even seen recursive definitions of *data types,* but this is a recursive definition of a data *structure.* Is it legitimate?

If recursive data structure definitions are permitted, then a number of things become more convenient. For example, we can avoid recursively enumerable sequences by simply omitting from the finite sequence archetype (Fig. 2.5) the axiom that requires sequences to be finite. Infinite sequences can then be defined recursively. For example, we can define all k by

$$\text{all } k \equiv k : \text{all } k$$

Similarly, map is defined

$$\text{map } F \ (x{:}S) \equiv Fx : \text{map } F \ S \qquad (7.13)$$

For another example, we can define the infinite sequence of Fibonacci numbers by

$$F \equiv 1 : 1 : \text{map [+] [pairs } (F, \text{ rest } F)]$$

(Recall that pairs was defined in Exercise 7.30.) Once we see the idea of recursive data structures, other possibilities also become apparent. For example, consider the *infinite tree* of binary strings:

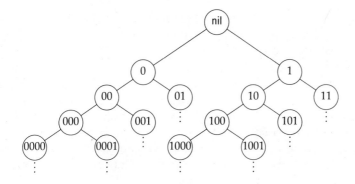

We can define this by the recursive equation

Binary ≡ (nil, treemap [0:] Binary, treemap [1:] Binary)

where we have made use of a functional for mapping a function across an infinite tree:

treemap f ≡ f × treemap f × treemap f

These examples suggest that the idea of recursive data definition is very powerful—if it makes sense.

To see why we should worry about its sensibleness, let's look at two ways of evaluating a simple expression involving Naturals, that is, first (rest Naturals). First observe that we have no equation that allows us to reduce rest Naturals. Therefore we appeal to Eq. (7.12) and write

first (rest {0 : map [1+] Naturals})

Since we have an equation for the rest of a prefix, we can reduce this to

first (map [1+] Naturals)

Expanding Naturals one step according to Eq. (7.12) and applying Eq. (7.13) once yields

first (1 : map [1+] Naturals)

Applying the reduction rules for first yields the intended answer, 1. This is sometimes called a *lazy* evaluation of the expression (Landin 1965, and Friedman and Wise 1976), since we evaluated an expression only when there was no other way to get a value. On the other hand, if we evaluate the expression *eagerly*, replacing Naturals by its definition (Eq. 7.12) whenever possible, then the result will be nontermination:

$$
\begin{aligned}
\text{first (rest Naturals)} &= \text{first (rest \{0 : map [1+] Naturals\})} \\
&= \text{first (rest \{0 : 1 : map [1+] Naturals\})} \\
&= \text{first (rest \{0 : 1 : 2 : map [1+] Naturals\})} \\
&\;\;\vdots
\end{aligned}
$$

Lazy evaluation avoids this nonterminating computation.

Don't the differing behaviors of 'first Naturals' contradict the statement in Chapter 1 that the value of an applicative expression is independent of its evaluation order? Not really. If an expression goes into an infinite loop, it doesn't have a value at all; we can't even discuss whether it is or isn't equal to some other value. What we can say (and will prove in Chapter 9) is that any evaluation order will always give a particular applicative expression the same value—if it gives it a value at all. Some evaluation orders may not even yield a value.

This situation should not be too surprising. Recall that fac (−1), as we have defined it, will go into an infinite loop. Now consider this expression:

rest {prefix [fac (−1), nil]}

If we begin our evaluation by attempting to evaluate fac (−1), then we will find ourselves in an infinite loop. Suppose, however, we do the prefix and rest before the fac:

rest {prefix [fac (−1), nil]} = rest <fac (−1)> = <>

The offending expression 'fac(−1)' was discarded before we even attempted to evaluate it.

The if function must work similarly. An expression like

if $(y = 0, 1, x/y)$

evaluates $y = 0$ before attempting to evaluate its other two arguments, 1 and x/y. This is necessary since if $y = 0$ then x/y is undefined. We say that if is *strict* in its first argument (since it always evaluates it), and *lenient* (or *nonstrict*) in its other two arguments (since it may not evaluate them). We treat these issues more systematically in Chapters 8 and 12; for now suffice it to say that evaluation order *can* affect the termination properties of applicative expressions, although not their values. In Section 7.7 we explore a way to control evaluation order.

Exercise 7.50: Prove from the archetype (Fig. 7.4) that Naturals satisfies Eq. (7.12).

Exercise 7.51: Prove from the archetype that all satisfies all $k = k$: all k.

Exercise 7.52: Prove inductively that the recursive definition of the infinite sequence of Fibonacci numbers is correct.

Exercise 7.53: What is the type of Binary? Write a signature for treemap. Comment on these.

Exercise 7.54: Prove that if P is any composition of lefts and rights, then P Binary is the reverse of the binary string we get from P by replacing left by 0 and right by 1. For example,

(right ∘ left ∘ left ∘ right ∘ right) Binary = <1, 1, 0, 0, 1>

Hint: Use induction on the length of the path P.

For another example of the use of recursive sequences, and to further explore the relation between evaluation order and termination, we consider *Hamming's Problem*[6]: Generate a sequence in ascending order, with no duplicates, of the numbers whose only factors are 2, 3, and 5. The sequence of Hamming Numbers begins as follows:

$$H = \;<2, 3, 4, 5, 6, 8, 9, 10, 12, 15, \cdots >$$

That is, H contains all the numbers of the form $2^l 3^m 5^n$ for l, m, $n \geq 0$.

The problem can be solved by making the following observations. If h is in H, then so are $2h$, $3h$, and $5h$. In fact, except for 2, 3, and 5 themselves, all members of H can be written as $2h$, $3h$, or $5h$, for some h in H. These observations provide the basis for a recursive definition of H. First let H2 be the RE sequence containing 2 and all numbers of the form $2h$ for $h \in H$:

$$H2 = \;<2, 4, 6, 8, 10, 12, \cdots >$$

This is defined

$$H2 \equiv 2 : \mathsf{map} \, [2\times] \, H \qquad (7.14)$$

Note that the elements of H2 are in ascending order provided the elements of H are in ascending order. We define H3 and H5 analogously:

$$H3 \equiv 3 : \mathsf{map} \, [3\times] \, H \qquad (7.15)$$
$$H5 \equiv 5 : \mathsf{map} \, [5\times] \, H$$

They begin like this:

$$H3 = \;<3, 6, 9, 12, 15, 18, \cdots >$$
$$H5 = \;<5, 10, 15, 20, 25, 30, \cdots >$$

Generating H is then simple; we simply merge H2, H3, and H5, eliminating all duplicates:

$$H \equiv \mathsf{merge} \, [H2, \mathsf{merge} \, (H3, H5)] \qquad (7.16)$$

Notice that all the definitions in Eqs. (7.14–7.16) are mutually recursive, but this is no problem.[7] We turn next to the merge function.

We must define a function merge that takes two sequences in ascending order with no duplicates and produces a sequence of the merged

6. See, for example, (Dijkstra 1976, 129–134); (Henderson 1980, 235–237); (Turner 1985a, 43–45); and (Abelson and Sussman 1985, 271). The original purpose of this problem was to show that far out in the sequence the multiples of 2, 3, and 5 are not very dense (i.e., there are big gaps).
7. Note that the recursion is based. Where are the bases?

elements in ascending order with duplicates removed. We can imagine doing this by hand, beginning with a finger pointed at the first element of each sequence. At each step we compare the two numbers at which we are pointing and write the smaller to the output sequence. Then we advance our finger over the number we just wrote out. But we must be careful, for if both fingers point at the same number, then we must advance both of them; otherwise we will have duplicates in the output sequence.

The next step is to turn this manual algorithm into a functional program. Consider the application merge (S, T). The first element of the result sequence will be the minimum of S_1 and T_1. What is the rest of the result sequence? There are several cases. If S_1 and T_1 are the same, then we must advance both sequences; the rest of the result is merge (rest S, rest T). If the first element of S is strictly less than the first element of T, then we want to advance S but not T; the rest of the result is merge (rest S, T). The case when T_1 is smaller is exactly analogous. Thus we can define merge as follows:

$$\text{merge } (S, T) \equiv \begin{cases} S_1 : \text{merge (rest } S, \text{ rest } T), & \text{if } S_1 = T_1 \\ S_1 : \text{merge (rest } S, T), & \text{if } S_1 < T_1 \\ T_1 : \text{merge } (S, \text{ rest } T), & \text{if } S_1 > T_1 \end{cases}$$

This definition, although mathematically correct, may lead to nontermination. Consider the behavior of merge: It compares the first two elements of S and T and calls itself recursively. This recursive instance will compare the first elements of the rests of S and/or T, and call itself recursively. We are in an infinite loop! Fortunately, if we are lazy in our evaluation, substituting the recursive call of merge into the definition of ':' before evaluating it, then we don't get into an infinite loop. For example,

$$H_2 = \left[\text{merge [H2, merge (H3, H5)]} \right]_2$$
$$= \left[\text{merge [H2, 3 : merge (rest H3, H5)]} \right]_2$$
$$= \left[2 : \text{merge [rest H2, 3 : merge (rest H3, H5)]} \right]_2$$
$$= \left[2 : 3 : \text{merge [rest H2, merge (rest H3, H5)]} \right]_2$$
$$= 3$$

We have used *lazy* evaluation to avoid applying merge to its arguments until absolutely necessary.

Once again, we see that evaluation order can affect termination (but not result). In previous chapters we usually were able to ignore evaluation order, but when dealing with infinite structures it becomes critical.

Based on the preceding considerations, we must ask whether there is an evaluation order that is always safe, that always terminates if any order terminates. There is such an order, called *normal order*. In brief, normal order works from the outside in, replacing formals by the corresponding actuals before the latter are evaluated. Normal order does this substitution, however, only when necessary to do so to get a result (i.e., it's just the *lazy* way to evaluate). We investigate in detail the properties of various evaluation orders in Chapter 12. For now, we need only say that each order has pros and cons, and that it's an unresolved research problem whether one order is desirable for all purposes. Thus in the next section we explore ways of controlling evaluation order.

Exercise 7.55:   Trace the computation of H_3.

Exercise 7.56:   Repeat Exercises 7.26–7.28 and Exercise 7.35 using recursive definitions of sequences rather than RE sequences.

The following exercises show how "fractal" structures can be represented by recursively defined data structures. See (Gleick 1987) for a nice introduction to fractals.

Exercise 7.57:   First we define a structure known as *Cantor's dust* or *Cantor's discontinuum* (Hausdorff 1957, 154–155), constructed as follows. Start with the interval [0, 1]. Subtract its middle third. Subtract from the two remaining pieces their middle thirds, and continue this process to infinity. Draw the first few steps in this process to make sure you understand it. Why do you suppose that in the limit this is called Cantor's dust? Now construct a recursive data structure that contains the coordinates of all the endpoints of the line segments in the limiting structure. Cantor's dust C is defined in terms of an auxiliary function f, where $f(x, y)$ returns all the structure between coordinates x and y. Thus

$$C \equiv f(0, 1)$$

Now $f(0, 1)$ is composed of $f(0, 1/3)$ and $f(2/3, 1)$, and so forth. Therefore the following structure is equivalent to the Cantor's dust:

$$f(x, y) \equiv (f[x, x + (y - x)/3], \; f[y - (y - x)/3, y])$$

We can't do much with the coordinates of the endpoints, which are not explicitly represented. Therefore we alter the definition of f to include the coordinates:

$$f(x, y) \equiv (x, f[x, a], a, b, f[b, y], y)$$

where $a \equiv x + (y - x)/3$
  and $b \equiv y - (y - x)/3$

Draw a tree diagram of the first few levels of C.

Exercise 7.58: Define a function $f(n)$ that returns a sequence of all the endpoints in the nth approximation of C. Notice that this is also an RE sequence of all the finite approximations of C.

Exercise 7.59: Define an infinite sequence λ such that λ_n is the length of the nth approximation of C. λ begins as follows:

$$\lambda = <2/3, 4/9, 8/27, \cdots >$$

What is the limit of this sequence?

Exercise 7.60: In this exercise you define a variant of the *Koch curve*, constructed as follows. Start with a unit square. On each side erect a square with sides equal to $1/4$. On each of the three outer sides of these squares erect squares with sides equal to $1/16$. And so forth to infinity. Show the first few steps of the construction.

Exercise 7.61: Define a recursive structure K that contains the coordinates of all the corners of this curve. *Hint:* Use an auxiliary function $f(x, y, x', y')$ that constructs the curve between (x, y) and (x', y').

Exercise 7.62: Define an infinite sequence of the finite approximations of K.

Exercise 7.63: Define an infinite sequence of the circumferences of the approximations of K. What is the limit of this sequence?

Exercise 7.64: Define an infinite sequence of the areas of the approximations of K. What is the limit of this sequence?

7.7 Delayed Evaluation and Streams

We have seen—especially when dealing with infinite structures—that termination may depend on evaluation order. In a sense, this is nothing new. Take the simplest recursive definition, one involving no infinite structures at all:

$$\text{fac } n \equiv \text{if } [n = 0, 1, n \times \text{fac } (n - 1)]$$

Now consider an "overly eager" evaluation of fac 3 in which we replace fac by its definition whenever possible:

$$\begin{aligned}
\text{fac } 3 &= \text{ if } [n = 0,\, 1,\, n \times \text{fac } (n-1)] \\
&= \text{ if } [n = 0,\, 1,\, n \times \text{if } [(n-1) = 0,\, 1,\, (n-1) \times \text{fac } ((n-1)-1)]] \\
&= \text{ if } [n = 0,\, 1,\, n \times \text{if } [(n-1) = 0,\, 1,\, (n-1) \times \\
&\qquad \text{if } [((n-1)-1) = 0,\, 1,\, ((n-1)-1) \times \text{fac } (((n-1)-1)-1)]]
\end{aligned}$$

$\vdots$

We are in an endless expansion. Why haven't we ever run into this problem before?

All our previous evaluations obeyed a restriction so familiar to you that you never noticed it:

> The Delayed Function Body Restriction: *Never evaluate the body of a function before it's been invoked.*

This restriction, which prevents the preceding overly eager evaluation,[8] is obeyed by virtually all programming languages, whether imperative or applicative. In programming terms, it simply says, Don't execute the body of a function or procedure until it is called. Stated this way it seems perfectly obvious. Realize, however, that this restriction is routinely violated in minor ways. For example, many compilers evaluate constant expressions at compile time, regardless of whether they occur in function or procedure bodies. This is usually safe because only simple expressions are optimized this way. For example, most compilers do not attempt to evaluate the constant expression 'fac (-1)'—a good thing, since attempting to do so would throw the compiler into an infinite loop.

If we assume the Delayed Function Body Restriction, then we can use functions as a way to control evaluation order. For example, consider the following recursive definition of an infinite tuple of ones:

Ones

Ones $\equiv$ (1, Ones)

---

8. It is also prevented by another restriction, obeyed by virtually all languages: *Don't evaluate an arm of a conditional until you know it's necessary to do so.*

This runs the risk of leading to a nonterminating evaluation. Suppose instead that we make Ones a function of one argument:

Ones $x \equiv$ (1, Ones)

Notice that the formal parameter x is not used in the definition of Ones. Nevertheless, an actual parameter must be provided to Ones before the body of the function, '(1, Ones)', is evaluated. Since the parameter doesn't matter, let's use 0 as a dummy actual.

To see that this solution works, observe that the Delayed Function Body Restriction prevents Ones from being evaluated unless it's applied. If we do apply it, then we get the tuple (1, Ones):

Ones 0 = (1, Ones)

There is no danger of a nonterminating computation because the embedded Ones is not applied to any argument. Whenever we want to look inside the infinite structure, we must apply the Ones function (thus forcing its body to be evaluated). For example,

left (Ones 0) = left (1, Ones) = 1
right (Ones 0) = right (1, Ones) = Ones
left [right (Ones 0) 0] = left [Ones 0] = 1
right [right (Ones 0) 0] = right [Ones 0] = Ones

And so forth. Thus we can walk as far as we want into the infinite structure, provided we apply it to an argument before we attempt to select a component. Applying to an argument has the effect of "unwinding" one coil of the potentially infinite structure. By unwinding the structure only when necessary, we avoid nontermination.

Having seen the general idea of using a function to delay evaluation, we can now approach the problem more systematically. To delay the evaluation of an expression E, we replace it by a functional abstraction $D = x \mapsto E$. We call D a *delayed expression*. If the type of E is τ, then the type of the delayed expression D is $\tau' \to \tau$ for some domain type τ'. We can *force* the evaluation of the delayed value D by applying it to any value a of type τ', that is, Da. Although τ' could be any type (in the preceding Ones example it was $\mathbb{Z}$), it makes sense to take τ' to be the trivial type **1**, since the value of the actual is irrelevant. Since the only value of type **1** is the empty tuple (), we can force the evaluation of D by $D()$. Similarly, we write the delayed version of E as () $\mapsto E$. Following these conventions we redefine Ones as follows:

Ones $\equiv$ () $\mapsto$ (1, Ones)

We can walk into the potentially infinite structure by expressions such as these:

left [Ones()],   left {right [Ones()] ()}, $\cdots$

These expressions are somewhat clearer if, as in some functional languages, we provide special syntactic sugar for delayed expressions and the operation of forcing them:

> **delayed** $\tau \Rightarrow \mathbf{1} \to \tau$ $\qquad\qquad\qquad\qquad$ (7.17)
> $\ll E \gg \Rightarrow () \mapsto E$
> force $E \Rightarrow E()$

The expression '$\ll E \gg$' is pronounced "delayed E." The definition of Ones becomes

Ones $\equiv \ll 1$, Ones$\gg$

Here we can *see* that Ones is a *delayed pair* of 1 and itself. Its type is defined by the recursive equation $\tau =$ **delayed** $(\mathbb{Z} \times \tau)$. Example expressions forcing evaluation of delayed expressions become

left (force Ones),   left {force [right (force Ones)]}

The analogous formulas in Scheme are[9]

```
(define Ones (delay (cons 1 Ones)))
(car (force Ones))
(car (force (cdr (force Ones))))
```

Note that although the operations in Eq. (7.17) satisfy the identity

force $\ll E \gg = E$

this doesn't tell the whole story. The key point is that $\ll E \gg$ can be manipulated successfully even though E might not have a value. We can't get in trouble until we force the evaluation.

A common use of delayed evaluation is as a way of implementing a kind of infinite sequence called a *stream* (Landin 1965, and Friedman and Wise 1976). You already saw an example, Ones. In general, a stream of type τ elements is a delayed pair representing a first element, which is of

---

9. Implementation of delay and force in Scheme is discussed in (Abelson and Sussman 1985, 264). Implementation in Common LISP is similar.

type τ, and a rest, which is a stream of τs. If we use τ^∞ for the type of a stream of τs, then we can define stream types by

$$\tau^\infty \equiv \textbf{delayed} \ (\tau \times \tau^\infty), \ \text{for all} \ \tau \in \textbf{type}$$

For example, Ones $\in \mathbb{Z}^\infty$. Stream-processing operations analogous to the sequence operations are easy to define. To prefix an element onto a stream we construct a delayed pair:

$$x :: S \ \Rightarrow \ \ll x, S \gg$$

To get the first or rest of a stream it must be forced:

first $S \equiv$ left (force S)
rest $S \equiv$ right (force S)

A complete archetype and prototype appear in Fig. 7.6.
   Consider a simple example of the use of streams, the stream of natural numbers:

Naturals $= 0 :: 1 :: 2 :: 3 :: \ \cdots$

Figure 7.6 Archetype and Prototype for streams.

Archetype

Syntax:
   $\tau^\infty \in \textbf{type}$, for all $\tau \in \textbf{type}$
   first: $\tau^\infty \rightarrow \tau$
   rest: $\tau^\infty \rightarrow \tau^\infty$
   [::]: $\tau \times \tau^\infty \rightarrow \tau^\infty$

Semantics:
   first $(x :: S) = x$,
   rest $(x :: S) = S$
   first $S ::$ rest $S = S$

Pragmatics:
   The prefixing operation delays evaluation of its arguments.
   The first and rest operations force evaluation of both stream components.

Prototype
   type $\tau^\infty \equiv \textbf{delayed} \ (\tau \times \tau^\infty)$
   first $\equiv$ left $\circ$ force
   rest $\equiv$ right $\circ$ force
   $x :: S \ \Rightarrow \ \ll x, S \gg$

If we had a map operation on streams, Naturals could be defined recursively (compare Eq. 7.12):

Naturals ≡ 0 :: map [1+] Naturals

Fortunately, map: $(D \to R) \to (D^\infty \to R^\infty)$ is easy to define:

$$\text{map } f \equiv S \mapsto [f(\text{first } S) :: \text{map } f \text{ (rest } S)] \tag{7.18}$$

These definitions can be directly translated into functional languages such as Scheme:

```
(define (map f)
  (lambda (S) (cons-stream (head S) ((map f) (tail S)))))

(define Naturals (cons-stream 0 (map (lambda (x) (+ 1 x))) Naturals))
```

Note that Scheme uses head, tail, and cons-stream for the stream selectors and constructors.[10]

Recall that our program for generating the sequence of Hamming numbers could get into trouble with some evaluation orders. By using streams we can avoid this problem and get a program that works with any order (provided it obeys the Delayed Function Body Restriction). The definition of merge is very much like our previous definition, but the stream prefix operation delays evaluation:

merge: $\mathbb{Z}^\infty \times \mathbb{Z}^\infty \to \mathbb{Z}^\infty$

$$\text{merge } (S, T) \equiv \begin{cases} \text{first } S :: \text{merge (rest } S, \text{ rest } T), & \text{if first } S = \text{first } T \\ \text{first } S :: \text{merge (rest } S, T), & \text{if first } S < \text{first } T \\ \text{first } T :: \text{merge } (S, \text{ rest } T), & \text{if first } S > \text{first } T \end{cases}$$

The definitions of H2, H3, and H5 are analogous.

Exercise 7.65: Show the evaluation of the expressions

left (force Ones),   left {force [right (force Ones)]}

Exercise 7.66: Remove the syntactic sugar for streams and delayed expressions from the definition of map (Eq. 7.18).

10. Cons-stream is not standard Scheme, but it is in the dialect used in (Abelson and Sussman 1985). See also Appendix C (Section C.11). The Common LISP programmer should be aware that the things called 'streams' in Common LISP have nothing to do with streams as defined here or in Scheme.

Exercise 7.67: Explain why there is no base case in the recursive definition of map (Eq. 7.18).

Exercise 7.68: Define H2, H3, and H5 as streams.

Streams provide a number of opportunities for improving the efficiency of applicative programs. To illustrate this, let's use the following program for computing the infinite stream of Fibonacci numbers:

$$F \equiv 1 :: 1 :: \text{map } [+] [\text{pairs } (F, \text{ rest } F)] \qquad (7.19)$$

We use pairs: $T^{\infty} \times U^{\infty} \to (T \times U)^{\infty}$, a function for merging a pair of streams into a stream of pairs:

$$\text{pairs } (S, T) \equiv (\text{first } S, \text{ first } T) :: \text{pairs } (\text{rest } S, \text{ rest } T) \qquad (7.20)$$

The Fibonacci program can be understood as follows:

$$
\begin{array}{lcccccc}
F = & 1 & 1 & 2 & 3 & 5 & \cdots \\
+ \text{ rest } F = & 1 & 2 & 3 & 5 & 8 & \cdots \\
\hline
F = 1::1:: & 2 & 3 & 5 & 8 & 13 & \cdots
\end{array}
$$

Let's consider a straightforward evaluation of several elements of this stream by making the delayed expressions in Eq. (7.19) explicit:

$$F \equiv \ll 1, \ll 1, \text{map } [+] [\text{pairs } (F, \text{ rest } F)] \gg\gg$$

Observe that, since first = left ∘ force,

$$
\begin{aligned}
F_1 &= \text{first } F \\
&= \text{left } \{\text{force} \ll 1, \ll 1, \text{map } [+] [\text{pairs } (F, \text{ rest } F)] \gg\gg\} \\
&= \text{left } (1, \ll 1, \text{map } [+] [\text{pairs } (F, \text{ rest } F)] \gg) \\
&= 1
\end{aligned}
$$

Similarly, since rest = right ∘ force,

$$
\begin{aligned}
F_2 &= \text{first } (\text{rest } F) \\
&= \text{first } (\text{right } \{\text{force} \ll 1, \ll 1, \text{map } [+] [\text{pairs } (F, \text{ rest } F)] \gg\gg\}) \\
&= \text{first } \{\text{right } (1, \ll 1, \text{map } [+] [\text{pairs } (F, \text{ rest } F)] \gg)\} \\
&= \text{first } \ll 1, \text{map } [+] [\text{pairs } (F, \text{ rest } F)] \gg \\
&= \text{left } \{\text{force} \ll 1, \text{map } [+] [\text{pairs } (F, \text{ rest } F)] \gg\} \\
&= \text{left } (1, \text{map } [+] [\text{pairs } (F, \text{ rest } F)]) \\
&= 1
\end{aligned}
$$

Notice how we evaluate only as much of the stream F as necessary to get the answer. In this sense streams are very efficient; the $\ll\cdot\gg$ brackets suppress evaluation until it is demanded by force. That is, we compute only as much as necessary to get the results we require. The efficiency of demand-driven evaluation is critical to the use of infinite data structures, since the attempt to compute the entire structure would lead to nontermination. Because in a finite amount of time we can ask to look at only a finite number of the components of a data structure, we force the evaluation of only these components. We can program as though the entire infinite data structure is there, but only as much as we try to look at is actually computed.

Although the demand-driven evaluation of stream expressions is potentially quite efficient, some potential inefficiencies must be avoided. Consider the following evaluation of F_3:

$$
\begin{aligned}
F_3 &= \text{first } [\text{rest } (\text{rest } F)] \\
&= \text{first } [\text{rest } (\text{right } \{\text{force} \ll 1, \ll 1, \text{map } [+] \; [\text{pairs } (F, \text{ rest } F)] \gg \gg \})] \\
&= \text{first } [\text{rest } (1, \ll 1, \text{map } [+] \; [\text{pairs } (F, \text{ rest } F)] \gg)] \\
&\;\;\vdots \\
&= \text{first } \{\text{map } [+] \; [\text{pairs } (F, \text{ rest } F)]\}
\end{aligned}
$$

Now we use the definition of map, but with the delayed expressions made explicit:

$$\text{map } f = S \mapsto \ll f \; (\text{first } S), \text{ map } f \; (\text{rest } S) \gg$$

The evaluation continues:

$$
\begin{aligned}
F_3 &= \text{left } \{\text{force} \ll [+][\text{first } \{\text{pairs } (F, \text{ rest } F)\}], \\
&\qquad\qquad \text{map } [+] \; [\text{rest } \{\text{pairs } (F, \text{ rest } F)\}] \gg \} \\
&= [+](\text{first } \{\text{pairs } (F, \text{ rest } F)\})
\end{aligned}
$$

The definition of pairs, with the delays and forces in Eq. (7.20) made explicit, is

$$\text{pairs } (x, y) \equiv \ll (\text{first } x, \text{ first } y), \text{ pairs } (\text{rest } x, \text{ rest } y) \gg$$

Continuing the evaluation:

$$
\begin{aligned}
F_3 &= [+] \; [\text{left } \{\text{force} \ll (\text{first } F, \text{ first } [\text{rest } F]), \text{ pairs } (\text{rest } F, \text{ rest } [\text{rest } F]) \gg \}] \\
&= [+] \; (\text{first } F, \text{ first } [\text{rest } F])
\end{aligned}
$$

Notice that the next step is to evaluate first F and first (rest F), that is, the first and second Fibonacci numbers, F_1 and F_2. Similarly, if we request F_4, then that will demand the evaluation of F_2 and F_3—the latter, as we've seen, demanding F_1 and F_2. Thus we have an exponential algorithm for accessing the elements of the stream of Fibonacci numbers.

Exercise 7.69: Explain in detail why the preceding algorithm is exponential.

We pause to analyze this situation. With normal (undelayed) data structures, we compute the values of the components in advance and store them in the structure, where they can be accessed repeatedly. With delayed structures, such as streams, no component is computed until actually required. This makes it much more efficient to build the structure, which is critical if the structure is infinite. On the other hand, when we attempt to access a component of such a structure, then we must pay the price for computing it. The real difficulty with our Fibonacci program, and with the prototype implementation of streams (Fig. 7.6), is that we unnecessarily recompute an element of a stream *every* time it is accessed.

The referential transparency property of applicative languages tells us that an expression can always be interchanged with its value. Therefore, if we know the value of an expression, it can be safely substituted everywhere that expression occurs. In particular, having once forced the evaluation of a component of a stream, there is no reason to ever evaluate that component again since we'll get the same answer every time. This solves the problem with our Fibonacci program. The first time we demand the value of a Fibonacci number we force the evaluation of all Fibonaccis less than that number. This computation takes place in linear time, however, since each Fibonacci is computed once.

The preceding observations apply to every kind of delayed expression. Having once forced a delayed expression, it can be replaced by its value so that all later demands for its value are immediately satisfied. This is true *lazy evaluation:* An expression is not evaluated until its value is needed, but once computed, the value is saved in case it's ever needed again.[11] A delayed expression with this property is said to be *memoized.*[12]

How can we implement memoized delayed expressions? This is a very basic evaluation mechanism that cannot be easily expressed in a purely applicative way. The reason is that, by intention, applicative languages are semantically (but not pragmatically) insensitive to the number of times a thing is evaluated. This is not such a problem—since memoization, if provided, is normally built into the applicative language interpreter or compiler, or even the computer hardware. Therefore let's define the memoization of delayed expressions in a sort of pidgin imperative language. For ≪E≫ we return a *procedural* (vice functional)

11. Of course there are many variations on this theme. Since the retained values consume space, we can consider discarding them (and "redelaying" the expression) when space becomes tight. The similarities to virtual memory systems are apparent.
12. "Memo-ized," not "memorized." Memoizing was apparently invented by Michie (1968).

abstraction that includes (1) the code for E, (2) an indication of whether E has been evaluated, and (3) its value if it has. Here is a typical implementation (assuming T is the type of E):

```
≪E≫ ⇒
  begin let var evaluated ∈ 𝔹 := false  and var value ∈ T;
    () ↦
      begin if not evaluated then value := E; evaluated := true; endif;
        return value  end;
  end;
```

The first time $≪E≫$ is forced, it evaluates E, saving its value in the local variable value and recording in evaluated the fact that the expression has been evaluated. Later attempts to force this expression simply return the value retained in value. (Note that the variables are local to the outer **begin** block, so they are instantiated for each textual instance of $≪E≫$, but that they are nonlocal to the delayed expression (the inner **begin** block), so that their values are retained across multiple forces of this expression.) From now on we use $≪·≫$ and force for *memoized* delayed expressions.

The foregoing observations and techniques apply to *all* expressions, not just delayed expressions. In an applicative language there is never any (semantic) reason to evaluate an expression more than once. For this reason, some implementations of applicative languages are *fully lazy*, in effect treating all expressions as though they are delayed. As we said before, it is still too soon to tell whether fully lazy evaluation is preferable to more eager evaluation strategies.[13]

Exercise 7.70:   Translate the Fibonacci program into Scheme or another functional language that supports streams.

Since we have introduced a new data type, streams, it is worthwhile to ask what higher-order functions are useful for stream processing. As we already saw, a map for streams is easy to define, and, as you'll discover in Exercise 7.71, fil is likewise easy. Next consider the reduction and accumulation functionals. Since the sequence operations must inspect the entire sequence before they can produce a result, they cannot be naively generalized to work on streams.

---

13. Fully lazy languages include KRC (Turner 1981) and Miranda (Turner 1985b). Abelson and Sussman (1985) distinguish between delay and force, which memoize, and freeze and thaw, which don't. They also memoize their streams. Standard Scheme provides memoizing delay and force.

We must avoid ever looking at all the elements of a stream. Any operation that depends on only a finite number of the streams elements is computable. For example, we can't ask for the sum of all the Fibonacci numbers, but we can ask for a stream whose nth element is the sum of the first n Fibonacci numbers:

$$S = <F_1, F_1 + F_2, F_1 + F_2 + F_3, \cdots >$$

The elements of this stream are the *partial sum-reductions* of the stream of Fibonaccis. Let predl be the functional that performs partial reductions from the left; thus $S = $ predl $[+]$ F. In general we can see that

$$(\text{predl } f \ S)_n = f \ (f\{ \ \cdots \ f \ [f \ (S_1, S_2), S_3], \cdots, S_{n-1}\}, S_n) \qquad (7.21)$$

To define predl, we search for a recursive reduction of this equation. Substituting $n - 1$ for n in Eq. 7.21 we get:

$$(\text{predl } f \ S)_{n-1} = f \ [f\{ \ \cdots \ f \ [f \ (S_1, S_2), S_3], \cdots, S_{n-2}\}, S_{n-1}] \qquad (7.22)$$

The right-hand side of Eq. (7.22) is part of the right-hand side of (7.21). Therefore we substitute the left-hand side of (7.22) for this in (7.21), yielding

$$(\text{predl } f \ S)_n = f \ [(\text{predl } f \ S)_{n-1}, S_n] \qquad (7.23)$$

This equation applies only for $n > 1$, but for $n = 1$ we have

$$(\text{predl } f \ S)_1 = S_1 \qquad (7.24)$$

Letting $R = $ predl $f \ S$, Eqs. (7.23) and (7.24) can be written

$$R_1 \equiv S_1$$
$$R_{n+1} \equiv f \ (R_n, S_{n+1}), \text{ for } n > 0$$

Lining up the elements of R,

$$R_1 = S_1$$
$$R_2 = f \ (R_1, S_2)$$
$$R_3 = f \ (R_2, S_3)$$
$$R_4 = f \ (R_3, S_4)$$
$$\vdots$$

Thus we can see that the rest of R is the result of mapping f across the stream:

$$(R_1, S_2) :: (R_2, S_3) :: (R_3, S_4) :: \ \cdots$$

The latter is just pairs $(R, \text{rest } S)$. Hence R is defined by the following recursive equation:

$$R \equiv S_1 :: \text{map } f \, [\text{pairs } (R, \text{rest } S)]$$

The formal definition of predl follows directly:

$$\text{predl } f \equiv S \mapsto \left[R \textbf{ where rec } R \equiv \text{first } S :: \text{map } f \, [\text{pairs } (R, \text{rest } S)] \right]$$

Exercise 7.71: Define the higher-order function fil: $(\tau \to \mathbb{B}) \to (\tau^\infty \to \tau^\infty)$ for filtering streams.

Exercise 7.72: Define a functional that performs *partial reductions from the right* on sequences. Can you define an analogous operation on streams?

Exercise 7.73: Define a functional that performs partial *accumulations* from the left on streams.

Exercise 7.74: Define a functional that performs partial accumulations from the left on *sequences.*

Exercise 7.75: Define a functional that performs partial accumulations from the *right* on sequences.

Exercise 7.76: Define a stream-generating operation gen analogous to that in Exercise (7.39).

7.8 Interactive and Real-time Applications

In this section we show how streams permit the use of functional languages for applications for which they are otherwise unsuited. In particular, we consider interactive programs, operating systems, database systems, and real-time systems. Their common characteristic is that they must respond to events taking place *in time*. Now the principal reason that applicative programming has abandoned the assignment statement is that assignment operations must be understood as events taking place at a certain time and as having temporal relations (such as before and after) with other events. Applicative languages have the Church-Rosser property, which means that the semantics of a program is largely independent of evaluation order. (We say "largely independent" because, as we've seen, evaluation order may affect termination.) It seems unlikely that the occurrence of events in time can be controlled by a language that strives to avoid all temporality. Yet, as we'll see, there is a very neat way to do this.

We can approach the problem of real-time input-output by considering the more general problem of input-output in functional languages. For our first example,[14] suppose we want a program lookup to look up the telephone numbers of a number of persons. We define

lookup ≡ map directory

Here we have assumed that directory ∈ finfunc (**string** → **string**) is a finite function mapping people's names into their phone numbers. We also assume that map has been overloaded to operate on finite as well as infinite functions—that is, map has been overloaded to include fmap (see Exercise 6.31). There is no problem in running lookup as a batch program; for example, suppose

directory ≡ ['Alice' ↦ '555-9090', 'JoAnn' ↦ '555-2718',
              'Bob' ↦ '555-0827', 'Ralph' ↦ '555-3142',
              'Tom' ↦ '555-3214', 'Sally' ↦ '555-7621']

We simply apply lookup to the sequence of input names and the corresponding phone numbers are returned:

→ lookup <'Tom', 'Alice', 'Ralph', 'JoAnn'>
        <'555-3214', '555-9090', '555-3142', '555-2718'>
→

For an interactive program, however, this will not do. We do not want to have to wait for all the input strings to be typed in before we see any of the output. In particular, we want the program to produce '555-3214' as soon as 'Tom' is typed in, '555-9090' as soon as 'Alice' is typed in, and so forth. Consider a text editor. You certainly wouldn't want to have to type in your entire editing session before seeing any of the editor's output.

We need some way that lookup can begin producing its output before all the input is typed in, a capability provided by streams. Since the rest of a stream is not evaluated until it's looked at, it doesn't have to exist until then. Think of a stream as a *promise* to get a sequence of values. A value doesn't *actually* have to be obtained until the corresponding element of the stream is forced. At that time the delayed stream element can return the value, if it's already been typed, or can wait for it to be typed, if not. The implementation of interactive streams is discussed in more detail later; for now just the idea is important.

Typically a functional programming system that permits interactive

---

14. Several of these examples derive ultimately from Peter Henderson; see (Darlington, Henderson, and Turner 1982).

streams will provide some way to connect streams to input-output channels. For example,

stream 'keyboard'

might represent the potentially infinite stream of strings (lines) that will be typed at the user's terminal. Thus lookup (**stream** 'keyboard') applies lookup to the stream of names typed by the user, returning a stream of the results. What do we do with the result stream? One solution is to pass it to a system function that displays the stream elements (as they are generated!) on the user's terminal:

display [lookup (**stream** 'keyboard')]

This has an imperative flavor since display is being executed for its side effect rather than its result. A cleaner solution, from an applicative standpoint, is to adopt the convention that whatever stream is bound to the file named 'display' will be used as the source of the information to be displayed at the user's terminal. Then our interactive program is expressed as follows:

stream 'display' $\equiv$ lookup (**stream** 'keyboard')

We are *defining* the output stream to be the result of applying lookup to the input stream.

There is one difficulty with the preceding program. Once it is in control of the keyboard it cannot be stopped. Since it expects an infinity of inputs, it will accept any string we type; since a stream is infinite it has no end. Of course, we could type in a name not in the directory, hoping that the resulting error aborts the program. Also, there is presumably some operating system command that permits runaway programs to be killed. All these solutions, however, are inelegant. A better approach is to define a "terminatable" stream—as opposed to our type τ^∞, which is the type of infinite (nonterminatable) streams of elements of type τ. A terminatable stream is one that *may* be infinite but may also be terminated (and hence made finite) at any time. The type is defined as follows:

tstream τ $\equiv$ empty + nonempty: **delayed** ($\tau \times$ tstream τ)

We must then redefine lookup: tstream **string** $\rightarrow$ tstream **string** so that it terminates and returns the empty stream whenever it encounters the empty stream as its input:

lookup: tstream **string** $\rightarrow$ tstream **string**
  lookup empty $\equiv$ empty
  lookup (nonempty S) $\equiv$ fapply (directory, first S) :: lookup (rest S)

Presumably the operating system's terminal-handling software provides some convention whereby the user can indicate the end of the input stream.

Exercise 7.77: Define a functional map: $(D \rightarrow R) \rightarrow ($tstream $D \rightarrow$ tstream $R)$ that maps a function across a terminatable stream.

We have seen how streams permit of interactive or real-time input-output to be implemented. Let's extend this example to implement an updatable database in a purely applicative way.

The lookup program looks up phone numbers in a fixed directory. It would be more practical if it permitted the directory to be modified, that is, if it permitted entries to be inserted, deleted, and replaced, as well as retrieved. To actually implement this system, we would have to accept commands as strings, parsing them to ensure that they are legal. To keep the example simple, however, we assume that this job has already been done and that we have a stream C containing the parsed commands. Since we will have three legal commands, find, define, and remove, we define the type command as a direct sum:

    command ≡ find: **string**
             + define (name ∈ **string**, pnumber ∈ **string**)
             + remove: **string**

Then we have $C \in$ command$^{\infty}$.[15] The ultimate output of the system is a stream of strings, comprising either phone numbers or acknowledgments of definitions and deletions.

As you know, in functional programming we never actually change a data structure, but instead usually compute a new data structure from an old one. We do the same here, defining a function execute that takes as input a command and an old directory, and returns as output a response string and a new directory. Thus its signature is

    execute: command ✕ directory → **string** ✕ directory

The cases are easy to define. If the command is find m, then we look up name m and return the phone number as a response; the directory remains unchanged:

    execute (find m, D) ≡ (Dm, D)

---

15. For the time being we use nonterminatable streams so that we need not deal with the issue of what happens to the directory when there's no more input.

If the command is define (m, n), then the name/number pair (m, n) must be put in the directory, possibly replacing a previous entry for m:

$$\text{execute } [\text{define } (m, n), D] \equiv ['OK', \text{overl } (D, m, n)]$$

Finally, if the command is remove m, then we return an acknowledgment and a directory with the entry for m removed:

$$\text{execute } (\text{remove } m, D) \equiv ['OK', \text{restr } (D, m)]$$

Notice that we have not done any error checking, such as ensuring that the requested name is in the directory (see Exercise 7.78).

For simplicity suppose that nihil is the initial directory and that C_1 is the first command. Then $(R_1, D_1) = \text{execute } (C_1, \text{nihil})$ is the first response and the first (noninitial) state of the directory. Similarly, the next response and directory state are $(R_2, D_2) = \text{execute } (C_2, D_1)$. In general,

$$(R_t, D_t) = \text{execute } (C_t, D_{t-1}), \quad t \geq 1 \tag{7.25}$$

where $D_0 = \text{nihil}$. Here we use the subscript t to emphasize that the stream elements are computed at successive *times*.

Equation 7.25 is in effect a *difference equation* that describes how the states of the streams change in time; it describes the difference between the states at times $t - 1$ and t. Our next step is to "integrate" this formula to get a timeless (i.e., applicative) equation for the directory system. Therefore we name the infinite streams:

$$C \equiv C_1 :: C_2 :: C_3 :: \cdots$$
$$R \equiv R_1 :: R_2 :: R_3 :: \cdots$$
$$D \equiv D_1 :: D_2 :: D_3 :: \cdots$$

According to Eq. (7.25) the pairs (R_t, D_t) can be generated by mapping execute across the pairs (C_t, D_{t-1}). This stream of pairs can be generated as follows:

$$(C_1, D_0) :: (C_2, D_1) :: (C_3, D_2) :: \cdots$$
$$= \text{pairs } (C_1 :: C_2 :: C_3 :: \cdots, \text{nihil} :: D_1 :: D_2 :: \cdots)$$
$$= \text{pairs } (C, \text{nihil} :: D)$$

Therefore

$$\text{map execute } [\text{pairs } (C, \text{nihil} :: D)] = (R_1, D_1) :: (R_2, D_2) :: (R_3, D_3) :: \cdots$$

We can see that the right-hand side of this equation is pairs (R, D). Hence map execute [pairs $(C,$ nihil $:: D)]$ = pairs (R, D)

This is a "timeless" equation for the system. We can separate out the streams R and D by use of an "unzipping" function:

pairs^{-1} $\equiv$ (map left; map right)

The result is a definition of the output stream R in terms of the input stream C:

(R, D) $\equiv$ pairs^{-1} {map execute [pairs $(C,$ nihil $:: D)]$}

Note that this definition is recursive through the stream of directory states D. The reason is apparent in the data-flow diagram for this system:

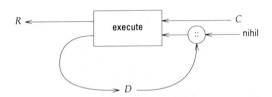

A real system would require a function parse: **string** $\rightarrow$ command for parsing input strings into commands. Thus a complete program for the phone directory manager (excluding the definition of execute) is

dirsys $\equiv$ pairs^{-1} ∘ map execute ∘ pairs
(**stream** 'display', D) $\equiv$ dirsys [map parse (**stream** 'keyboard'), nihil $:: D$]

Some unresolved issues remain, such as what parse should do when it detects an illegal command, but solving them is routine. Also note that since we have used nonterminatable streams, this system cannot be stopped (short of "pulling the plug").

Exercise 7.78: Redefine execute so that it returns an error message if a requested name is not in the directory. Also modify execute to return a warning if the user removes a nonexistent name.

Exercise 7.79: How should parse deal with illegal commands? One possibility is to return a special "error command" (thus requiring the definition of command to be extended); execute responds to an error command by printing a diagnostic message. Implement this solution. A more complicated approach is to change the structure of the streams so that diagnostic messages are passed directly from the parser to the response stream. Implement this solution also.

Exercise 7.80:   Redefine dirsys to be a terminatable program. It should take its initial directory from a file called "OldDirectory," run interactively until the user terminates the command stream, and then leave the final state of the directory in a file called "NewDirectory."

We have seen a purely functional implementation of a simple interactive system involving the interaction of one person with a system; this involved one input stream, one output stream, and one intermediate stream of directory states. The only ordering constraint on the computation of these streams is the functional dependency expressed in Eq. (7.25). This ensures, for example, that the response t depends on command t and directory state $t-1$. Thus output t will not be computed before input t; this seems reasonable enough. On the other hand, there is no guarantee that output t *will* be computed when it's possible to do so, that is, as soon as command t is entered. Unless this ordering of events can be guaranteed, it is not possible to execute our system interactively. We take a short digression to discuss the implementation of interactive streams.

First consider the interactive input stream **stream** 'keyboard', representing the potentially infinite stream of input lines that will be typed by the user. Clearly we cannot return an element of this stream whenever it's requested, since the user might not have typed it yet. Therefore, when a process requests an element of this stream that has not yet been typed, then the process must *suspend* itself until a line is typed. Therefore **stream** 'keyboard' can be implemented by a special version of the code we use for memoized streams:

```
stream 'keyboard' ≡ input_stream ()
  where rec  input_stream () ≡ ≪keyboard (), input_stream ()≫
    where  keyboard () ≡
      begin
        if not keyboard_input_available then suspend endif;
        return keyboard_input;
      end;
```

To see how this operates, notice that **stream** 'keyboard' is the result of calling input_stream, which returns a delayed pair. Nothing happens until this pair is forced by a first or rest. The first time it's forced, it calls keyboard, which determines (via keyboard_input_available) whether a line of text is available in the keyboard buffer (called keyboard_input). If input is available, it's paired up with the rest of the future input (i.e., input_stream ()) and returned as the value of input_stream. On the other hand, if no text is available in the keyboard buffer, this process suspends until keyboard input becomes available, at which time execution resumes and a pair is returned as before. Of course, once a particular element of the input stream is received, it's memoized so that it's never requested again.

The memoization of the input stream suggests that all the input ever typed is retained in the computer's memory in case it is accessed later. This certainly seems inefficient. On the other hand, we can't simply throw away an input value after it's been accessed once, since this violates referential transparency (Why?). The solution is to reclaim unused stream elements the same way other data structures are reclaimed: When a stream element is no longer accessible (as determined by a garbage collector or by reference counting, for example), then it can be destroyed. Thus a record of past input is kept only if the program can still use it; if the program, like most, never looks back, then the past input can be discarded as usual. In this sense, the use of streams in a functional language provides the best of both worlds: Past input is automatically available if we use it, but it is discarded if we don't.

Next we consider the implementation of the output stream, **stream** 'display'. We want an element of this stream to be printed as soon as it's available. This can be accomplished by passing the stream bound to **stream** 'display' to a procedure that loops, printing all its elements:

```
procedure display (output_stream ∈ string∞);
  begin let var S ∈ string∞ := output_stream;
  loop
    output first (S);
    S := rest (S);
  end loop;
  end;
```

Since streams are infinite, the body of display is an infinite loop. It will continue forever to request stream elements and output them to the display. In each case the first operation forces the computation of the next stream element, which may in turn force the computation of other streams. In the case of our phone directory system, this will ultimately cause the input stream to be forced, which may lead to the suspension of the entire process until another line of input is typed. When the input is available it permits computation of a stream element for the output stream, which is output to the display. The statement $S := \text{rest}(S)$ then discards the pointer to the first pair in the stream, thus allowing its storage to be reclaimed.

Exercise 7.81: Modify the display procedure to accept a terminatable stream.

Exercise 7.82:   Modify **stream** 'keyboard' to be a terminatable stream that is terminated when the user types a string equal to input_terminator.

We have investigated a simple interactive program involving a single input stream, a single output stream, and an intermediate stream of database versions. A more complicated situation occurs when a number of users simultaneously access the same database. This situation can be pictured as follows:

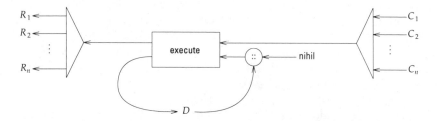

Here we have a sequence of input streams $<C_1, C_2, \cdots, C_n>$ and a sequence of output streams $<R_1, R_2, \cdots, R_n>$. The intent is that as commands arrive on the various input streams, the database is accessed, and the appropriate responses are sent out on the corresponding output streams. One obvious (but incorrect) solution is to use a merge procedure that combines two input streams into one:

merge (S, T) ≡ first S :: first T :: merge (rest S, rest T)

To understand the effect of merge, note that merge (S, T) is the infinite stream:

$$\text{merge } (S, T) = S_1 :: T_1 :: S_2 :: T_2 :: S_3 :: T_3 :: \cdots$$

Thus merge returns the first elements of both input streams, then the second elements, then the third, and so forth.

This solution, however, does not permit the users to interact *asynchronously* with the database. Before the second command of S, S_2, is processed, the first command of T, T_1, must be processed. Although very fair, this is too restrictive. It is not reasonable that the commands of S cannot be serviced just because T has not typed in a command. We would like the commands to be merged in the order (in real time) in which they're entered, ensuring that a response is generated as soon as possible, independent of the actions of the other users.

This is another situation in which the temporality of interactive programming conflicts with the atemporality of functional programming. A solution proposed by some authors is to build into the language a *non-*

deterministic merge, ndmerge. The only requirement placed on ndmerge (S, T) is that it preserve the order of elements in each stream. That is, if x occurs earlier than y in S, then x must also occur earlier than y in the merged stream. (Also, every member of S and T must eventually appear in the merged stream, and the merged stream must have no members other than the members of S and T.) The idea is that the order in which the elements are *actually* merged is the order in which they arrived in real time. Thus the nondeterminacy in the definition of the ndmerge operation is consistent with the dependence of its output on the temporal sequence of events.

The trouble with the nondeterministic merge is that it violates referential transparency and thus loses many of the advantages of functional programming. This situation arises whenever the output of a function is not completely determined by its input. Since ndmerge (S, T) may return many different streams, we cannot assume that two different occurrences of the expression 'ndmerge (S, T)' will have the same value; we cannot substitute equals for equals. We cannot even conclude something as simple as

first [ndmerge (S, T)] $=$ first [ndmerge (S, T)]

since the first call might return $S_1 :: T_1 :: \cdots$ whereas the second returns $T_1 :: S_1 :: \cdots$, or even $T_1 :: T_2 :: \cdots$. We are essentially back in the world of imperative programming, with the additional complication of nondeterminacy. This seems to be giving up too much.

How can nondeterminacy be avoided? The problem with the nondeterministic merge is that the output does not depend on the input. Specifically, the same input streams can lead to different output streams if the arrival times of stream elements differ. Thus one way to avoid this problem is to make the input streams themselves reflect the times at which the commands arrive. Then the merged stream can be completely determined by the input streams, and also reflect the order in which inputs arrive.

To see how this can be accomplished, suppose that each input stream has an element for the input entered in each second. (The time interval is not important, as will become apparent later.) Thus S_1 is the input typed in the next second, S_2 the input typed in the following second, and so forth. In general S_t is the input typed at time t in the future. If no input is typed on a stream in a given time interval, then the corresponding element of that stream is the empty string.

It is now easy to deterministically merge the two streams, preserving the time order of the inputs. Indeed, this can be accomplished with merge, our original deterministic merge, because the position of an input in its stream reflects the time at which it was entered. There is no indeterminacy, since different orders of events lead to different input streams. Of course, there will be many empty inputs in the merged stream, but these can be easily filtered out.[16]

Having seen that a deterministic solution to the merging problem is possible, let's consider how to make it more efficient. Generating a stream element at every time interval is in effect *polling*. That is, at every time interval we see whether any input has been typed, and return whatever is available—which may be nothing. If the polling interval is short (say a millisecond), then we generate many empty inputs, wasting storage. If the polling interval is long (say more than a second), then the system is unresponsive.

To avoid this characteristic problem of service by polling, we would like an element to be in the stream only when the user types something. This prevents flooding the system with empty strings. On the other hand, the streams must reflect the times at which inputs are provided, not just their arrival order. One way to accomplish this is to have each input stream *time stamp* its elements, with the time stamp reflecting the time at which the input was entered. For example, our input streams might look like this:

$$S = (2365, s_1) :: (2544, s_2) :: \cdots$$
$$T = (2455, t_1) :: (2501, t_2) :: \cdots$$

where s_i and t_i are the commands typed on the two streams. It's now easy to define a deterministic merge that combines the streams according to the time stamps:

$$\text{tmerge } [(t, x) :: S, (t', y) :: T] = \begin{cases} (t, x) :: (t', y) :: \text{tmerge } (S, T), & \text{if } t < t' \\ (t', y) :: (t, x) :: \text{tmerge } (S, T), & \text{if } t \geq t' \end{cases}$$

This seems to do the trick, but there's still a difficulty. To know which stream element to put first, tmerge must look at the first elements of *both* input streams. Hence it cannot return an element of the merged stream until elements are available for both the input streams. This is clearly unsatisfactory.

We can solve this problem by programming tmerge imperatively and giving it access to information unavailable to any other procedure. In particular, we assume that tmerge can perform the test ready (S) on a stream S; this determines whether the first element of S is available. Normal applicative programs cannot be permitted to perform this test, since the value returned depends on the time the test is done, so it is not referentially transparent. This referential opacity, however, can be hidden inside the tmerge procedure. With these assumptions tmerge can be defined as follows:

---

16. A similar approach is described in (Haynes and Friedman 1987).

```
tmerge (S, T) ≡
    «begin
        if not (ready(S) ∨ ready(T)) then
            suspend until ready(S) ∨ ready(T) endif;

        if ready(S) ∧ ready(T) then
            if time (first (S)) < time (first(T))
            then return (first(S), tmerge (rest(S), T));
            else return (first(T), tmerge (S, rest(T))) endif;
        elsif ready(S) then
            return (first(S), tmerge (rest(S), T));
        elsif ready(T) then
            return (first(T), tmerge (S, rest(T))); endif
    end»
```

Requesting an element of the merged stream forces the body of tmerge. This procedure suspends itself until an element is available from at least one of the input streams. If both streams have elements available, the earlier input is returned, along with the delayed remainder of the merged stream. If only one stream has an element available, then that element is returned, along with the delayed remainder.

There is another complication. Since tmerges are often used in combination, one tmerge must be able to test the readiness of the stream produced by another tmerge. Thus tmerge (S, T) has a ready attribute that is defined according to the following equation:

$$\text{ready } [\text{tmerge } (S, T)] \equiv \text{ready } (S) \vee \text{ready } (T)$$

The tmerge procedure is very imperative and certainly complicated, but at least we have avoided the referential opacity of the nondeterministic merge. Here the opacity is hidden in the body of tmerge.

Given the preceding definition of tmerge, we can complete the implementation of the multiuser directory system. We assume that we are given a sequence $C \in [(\mathbb{IN} \times \text{command})^\infty]^*$ of command input streams, and must generate a sequence $R \in (\textbf{string}^\infty)^*$ of response output streams. Note that we assume that the input streams are time stamped. Since the inputs are being merged into one command stream, and the response stream must be separated back out into multiple response streams, we need some way to keep track of the source of each time-stamped command. For example, if C_k is the command stream

$$C_k = (t_1, c_1) :: (t_2, c_2) :: (t_3, c_3) :: \cdots$$

then we want to convert it into the tagged stream

$$C'_k = (t_1, k - 1, c_1) :: (t_2, k - 1, c_2) :: (t_3, k - 1, c_3) :: \cdots$$

(We use $k - 1$ rather than k because it's more convenient if our tags begin with 0 rather than 1.) Note that we keep the time stamp as the first element of the tuple, where it is expected by tmerge. The tagged sequence C'_k is generated by mapping across C_k the tagging function $(t, c) \mapsto (t, k - 1, c)$. That is, $C'_k \equiv \text{map } (t, c) \mapsto (t, k - 1, c) \, C_k$. A formula for the sequence C' of tagged streams can be derived by

$$
\begin{aligned}
C' &= <C'_1, C'_2, \cdots, C'_n> \\
&= <\text{map } (t, c) \mapsto (t, 0, c) \, C_1, \ \text{map } (t, c) \mapsto (t, 1, c) \, C_2, \ldots, \\
&\quad \text{map } (t, c) \mapsto (t, n - 1, c) \, C_n> \\
&= <\text{tag } (0, C_1), \text{tag } (1, C_2), \ldots, \text{tag } (n - 1, C_n)>
\end{aligned}
$$

where $\text{tag } (k, S) \equiv \text{map } (t, c) \mapsto (t, k, c) \, S$. Hence

$$
\begin{aligned}
C' &= \text{map tag } <(0, C_1), (1, C_2), \ldots, (n - 1, C_n)> \\
&= \text{map tag } [\text{pairs } (<0, 1, \ldots, n - 1>, C)] \\
&= \text{map tag } \{\text{pairs } [\text{interval } (0, n), C]\}
\end{aligned}
$$

Now the commands streams $C'_1, \ldots, C'_k$ must be merged into one stream S according to their time stamps:

$$
\begin{aligned}
S &= \text{tmerge } \{C'_1, \text{tmerge } [C'_2, \cdots \text{tmerge } (C'_{n-1}, C'_n) \cdots]\} \\
&= \text{red tmerge } C'
\end{aligned}
$$

The stream S has the form

$$
S = (t_1, k_1, c_1) :: (t_2, k_2, c_2) :: (t_3, k_3, c_3) :: \cdots
$$

where the t_i are time stamps, the k_i are tags, and the c_i are commands. The time stamps must be stripped from S before the stream of (tagged) commands is passed to the directory manager proper; this can be accomplished by map right S. The tags must be retained to ensure that responses are routed to the correct output streams. We now have a stream of tagged commands T and a stream of directory states D:

$$
\begin{aligned}
T &= (k_1, c_1) :: (k_2, c_2) :: (k_3, c_3) :: \cdots \\
D &= D_0 :: D_1 :: D_2 :: \cdots
\end{aligned}
$$

Pairing the corresponding elements of these produces the stream of triples

$$
U = \text{pairs } (\text{nihil} :: D, T) = (D_0, k_1, c_1) :: (D_1, k_2, c_2) :: (D_2, k_3, c_3)
$$

Our goal is to produce an output stream V including the new directory states and the tagged responses:

$$V = (D_1, k_1, r_1) :: (D_2, k_2, r_2) :: (D_3, k_3, r_3) :: \cdots$$

Clearly, $V = \text{map } f \, U$ for some function f. We solve for f as follows:

$$
\begin{aligned}
V_i &= (D_i, k_i, r_i) \\
&= \text{rotl } (k_i, r_i, D_i)
\end{aligned}
$$

where rotl $(x, y, z) = (y, z, x)$. Continuing,

$$
\begin{aligned}
V_i &= \text{rotl } [k_i, (r_i, D_i)] \\
&= \text{rotl } [k_i, \text{execute } (c_i, D_{i-1})] \\
&= [\text{rotl} \circ (\mathbf{I} \times \text{execute})] \, (k_i, c_i, D_{i-1}) \\
&= [\text{rotl} \circ (\mathbf{I} \times \text{execute}) \circ \text{rotl}] \, (D_{i-1}, k_i, c_i) \\
&= [\text{rotl} \circ (\mathbf{I} \times \text{execute}) \circ \text{rotl}] \, U_i
\end{aligned}
$$

Hence $V = \text{map } [\text{rotl} \circ (\mathbf{I} \times \text{execute}) \circ \text{rotl}] \, U$. Now note that the streams of directory states and tagged responses can be separated from V by unpairing; that is, pairs$^{-1} V = (D, W)$, where

$$W = (k_1, r_1) :: (k_2, r_2) :: (k_3, r_3) :: \cdots$$

Next the kth response stream R_k can be obtained by filtering out of W all those responses whose tag is k: $R_k = \text{fil } [=k] \, W$. Therefore let get $W \, k \equiv \text{fil } [=k] \, W$. The sequence of response streams is then obtained by mapping get W across the sequence of tags:

$$
\begin{aligned}
R &= \text{map } (\text{get } W) \, [\text{interval } (0, n)] \\
&= \text{map } (\text{get } W) \, \text{tags}
\end{aligned}
$$

where $\text{tags} \equiv \text{interval } (0, n) = \text{interval } (0, \text{length } C)$. Assembling all the equations (and their types), we have

$$
\begin{array}{ll}
C' \equiv \text{map tag } [\text{pairs } (\text{tags}, C)] & C' \in [(\mathbb{N} \times \mathbb{N} \times \textbf{command})^\infty]^* \\
S \equiv \text{red tmerge } C' & S \in (\mathbb{N} \times \mathbb{N} \times \textbf{command})^\infty \\
T \equiv \text{map right } S & T \in (\mathbb{N} \times \textbf{command})^\infty \\
U \equiv \text{pairs } (\text{nihil} :: D, T) & U \in (\text{directory} \times \mathbb{N} \times \textbf{command})^\infty \\
V \equiv \text{map } [\text{rotl} \circ (\mathbf{I} \times \text{execute}) \circ \text{rotl}] \, U & V \in (\text{directory} \times \mathbb{N} \times \textbf{string})^\infty \\
(D, W) \equiv \text{pairs}^{-1} V & D \in \text{directory}^\infty, \; W \in (\mathbb{N} \times \textbf{string})^\infty \\
R \equiv \text{map } (\text{get } W) \, \text{tags} & R \in (\textbf{string}^\infty)^*
\end{array}
$$

Eliminating unnecessary variables yields

$$
\begin{aligned}
(D, W) \equiv{}& \text{dirsys } C \\
\textbf{where } \text{dirsys} \equiv{}& \text{pairs}^{-1} \circ \text{map } [\text{rotl} \circ (\mathbf{I} \times \text{execute}) \circ \text{rotl}] \\
&\circ \text{pairs} \circ [\text{nihil} :: D,] \circ \text{map right} \circ \text{red tmerge} \\
&\circ \text{map tag} \circ \text{pairs} \circ [\text{tags},]
\end{aligned}
$$

$$R \equiv \text{map } (\text{get } W) \, \text{tags}$$

Figure 7.7 Program for multiuser directory management system.

execute: command $\times$ directory $\rightarrow$ **string** $\times$ directory
execute (find m, D) $\equiv$ (Dm, D)
execute [define (m, n), D] $\equiv$ ['OK', overl (D, m, n)]
execute (remove m, D) $\equiv$ ['OK', restr (D, m)]

C $\equiv$ **file** 'input_streams'

file 'output_streams' $\equiv$ map (get W) tags

where rec (D, W) $\equiv$ dirsys C

and rec dirsys $\equiv$ pairs^{-1} $\circ$ map [rotl $\circ$ ($I \times$ execute) $\circ$ rotl]
 $\circ$ pairs $\circ$ [nihil :: D,] $\circ$ map right $\circ$ red tmerge
 $\circ$ map tag $\circ$ pairs $\circ$ [tags,]

 where tag (k, S) $\equiv$ map (t, c) $\mapsto$ (t, k, c) S
 and   get W $\equiv$ k $\mapsto$ (fil [=k] W)
 and   tags $\equiv$ interval (0, length C)
 and   rotl (x, y, z) $\equiv$ (y, z, x)

The complete program for the multiuser directory manager is shown in Fig. 7.7.

Exercise 7.83: Discuss the readability of the program in Fig. 7.7. Although there are no comments in the program text, all of the relevant discussion in this section can be considered the documentation of Fig. 7.7. How would you assess the readability of the figure *together with* the preceding discussion?

Part 2

Theory

Chapter 8

Completeness of the Lambda Calculus

8.1 Introduction

Part 2 of this book is devoted to the theoretical foundations of functional programming. As we have seen, many benefits of functional programming depend on properties such as referential transparency and evaluation order independence. We have tried to make a plausible case for these properties but have not proved that they hold in all cases; carrying out this proof is the task of Chapters 8 and 9. In addition, by investigating the foundations of functional programming, we reduce it to essentials, giving us important theoretical insights for implementing functional languages, in both software and hardware (see Chapters 11 and 12). Finally, our theoretical investigation will suggest some generalizations of both theoretical and practical value (Chapter 10).

Our theoretical investigation must center on the nature of *computable functions* because (1) the essence of functional programming is function definition and application (see Chapter 1) and (2) we cannot consider something to be programming unless its result can be executed on a computer. To facilitate this investigation, it is helpful to simplify as much as possible the notion of computable function application—the goal of the *lambda calculus.*[1]

A *calculus* is a notation that can be manipulated mechanically to achieve some end; 'calculus' is the Latin word for 'pebble', which is also the basis for words such as 'calculate', referring to the fact that people once did arithmetic by manipulating pebbles. For example, in the differential and integral calculi formulas can be manipulated according to the rules of integration and differentiation to get results that would otherwise have to be derived by solving complicated limits. Similarly, in the propositional and predicate calculi certain forms of deductive reasoning can be performed by manipulating symbols mechanically.

One reason for developing a calculus is that, by reducing some process to a set of simple mechanical rules, one decreases the chances of making an error. Also, since the rules of a calculus are mechanical and strictly defined, they are ideal for manipulation by computer. Anything that can be done by a calculus can be done by a computer. The converse also holds: Anything that can be done on a computer also be done by a calculus. Indeed, according to the commonly accepted definition of computability, several calculi are as powerful as any computer (see Section 1.9). These include Turing machines, Post productions, Markov algorithms, and—the lambda calculus. The importance of this calculus to us is that its computational engine is completely applicative—in contrast with other models of computation, such as Turing machines, which are imperative. In this chapter we attempt to convince you of the *computational completeness* of the lambda calculus, that is, that it can compute any computable function. First, however, we must look more carefully at bound identifiers.

8.2 Bound Identifiers

A central idea of programming languages, mathematical notation, and symbolic logic is the *bound identifier* (sometimes called a *dummy identifier*).[2] Bound identifiers are common in all mathematical notations. For instance, in the summation

---

1. The lambda calculus has been described thoroughly; see (Church 1936 and 1941) for early descriptions. A comprehensive presentation of lambda calculus theory, including copious references, is found in (Barendregt 1984).
2. Bound identifiers are often called bound *variables*. We avoid this usage because it conflicts with the programming language sense of "variable"—an updatable memory location. Nevertheless, be prepared to see the term "variable" used in functional programming as a synonym for "identifier." Rest assured that assignment statements are not being slipped back in.

$$\sum_{i=1}^{n} i^2 + 1$$

'i' is a bound identifier. It is a characteristic of bound identifiers that they can be systematically changed without altering the meaning of a formula. For example,

$$\sum_{k=1}^{n} k^2 + 1$$

means exactly the same thing as the previous summation. Similarly, the integral of $x^2 - 3x$ with respect to x

$$\int_{0}^{t} x^2 - 3x \, dx$$

is the same as the integral of $u^2 - 3u$ with respect to u:

$$\int_{0}^{t} u^2 - 3u \, du$$

In set theory, the set of all x such that $x \geq 0$ is the same as the set of all y such that $y \geq 0$:

$$\{x \mid x \geq 0\} = \{y \mid y \geq 0\}$$

Also, a proposition such as "for every x, $x + 1 > x$"

$$\forall x \, [x + 1 > x]$$

is the same as the proposition "for every y, $y + 1 > y$":

$$\forall y \, [y + 1 > y]$$

In the examples in Table 8.1 the bound identifiers are listed in the center column.

Two useful ideas are *bound occurrence* and *free occurrence*. Consider the expression

$$i \sum_{j=1}^{n} (j^2 + i - a) \tag{8.1}$$

In this expression the occurrence of 'j' in '$j^2 + i - a$' is called a bound occurrence of the identifier 'j'. It is bound by the summation operator ($\sum$), which is called the *binding site* (or just *binding*) of this occurrence of

Table 8.1. Use of bound identifiers.

Expression	Bound Identifier	In Words
$\displaystyle\sum_{i=1}^{n} A_i$	i	The sum for i from 1 to n of ...
$\displaystyle\prod_{j=1}^{m} f(j)$	j	The product for j from 1 to m of ...
$d(x^2 - 3x)/dx$	x	The derivative with respect to x of ...
$D_y(y^2 - 3y)$	y	The derivative with respect to y of ...
$\displaystyle\int_0^t x^2 - 3x \; dx$	x	The integral with respect to x of ...
$\{ x \mid x > 0 \}$	x	The set of all x such that ...
$\forall x [x + 1 > x]$	x	For all x, ...
$\exists y [2y = y]$	y	There exists a y such that ...
$\varepsilon x [x > y]$	x	Any x such that ...
$\iota y [2y = 1]$	y	The unique y such that ...

'j'. We see that 'j' is bound by noting that we can change it to any other identifier (except 'i') without changing the meaning of the expression. For example,

$$i \sum_{k=1}^{n} (k^2 + i - a) \qquad\qquad (8.2)$$

has exactly the same meaning as example (8.1). Any occurrence of an identifier that is not a bound occurrence is called a free occurrence. For example, 'i', 'n', and 'a' all occur free in expressions (8.1) and (8.2). Clearly, if we change a free identifier we have changed the meaning of the expression:

$$i \sum_{j=1}^{n} (j^2 + m - a)$$

Here we changed 'i' to 'm'.

Notice that when we say that an occurrence of an identifier is bound or free, we say this relative to some expression. For instance, 'j' is free in

'$j^2 + i - a$'

but is bound in

$$'\sum_{j=1}^{n} j^2 + i - a' \quad \text{and} \quad 'i! \sum_{j=1}^{n} ai^2 j^2'$$

Similarly, 'i' is free in the preceding expressions, but bound in

$$\sum_{i=1}^{m} \left[i! \sum_{j=1}^{n} j^2 + i - a \right]$$

The binding site of an identifier determines its *scope*, which is the region of the expression over which that identifier is bound. This region is usually indicated by some lexical convention such as brackets or parentheses.[3] To state things differently, all occurrences of an identifier which are in the scope of a binding of that identifier are bound occurrences of that identifier. The following figures exemplify these concepts:

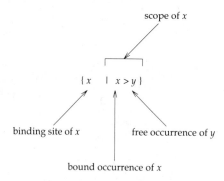

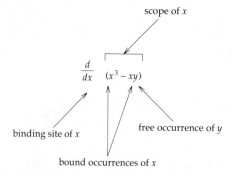

As already shown, it is perfectly meaningful for scopes to be nested within other scopes. Here are some examples of nested scopes (the brackets indicating scope are called *scoping lines*):

---

3. Hence the term *lexical scoping* (i.e., static scoping) in programming languages.

$$\sum_{i=1}^{m}\left[i\sum_{j=1}^{n}j^2+i-a\right]$$

```
        |_____|
        scope of j
    |_____|
        scope of i
```

$$\int_0^1 x \int_0^x y^2 + xy \; dy \; dx$$

```
        |_____|
      scope of y
    |_____|
      scope of x
```

We summarize these ideas as follows:

- The *binding site* of an identifier determines its *scope*.

- An occurrence of an identifier is *bound* if it is in the scope of a binding site of that identifier.

- An occurrence of an identifier is *free* otherwise.

- An expression is *closed* when it contains no free variables. (Open and closed expressions were introduced in Section 5.9.)

- An expression is *open* otherwise.

Exercise 8.1: For each identifier occurrence in the following expressions, indicate whether it is a binding site, a bound occurrence, or a free occurrence. Draw scoping lines to indicate the scope of each binding.

a. $\{ n \mid n > m \}$

b. $\int_0^1 x \; \sin(x/y) \; dx$

c. $\int_0^1 x \int_0^x \sin(yx) dy \; dx$

d. $\dfrac{\partial}{\partial x} \dfrac{\partial}{\partial y} \left[\dfrac{x^2 + y^2}{xy} \right]$

e. $\sum_{i=1}^{n} \sum_{j=1}^{i} ai^2 + jb - c$

f. $\forall x [x \in \mathbb{Z} \Rightarrow \exists y (y \in \mathbb{Z} \wedge x = y + 1)]$

g. $\{x \mid x > 0\} \cup \{x \mid x < 0\} = \{x \mid x \neq 0\}$

h. $\sinh(x) = \dfrac{e^x - e^{-x}}{2}$

As we have seen, bound identifiers are arbitrary. This is one reason they are often called *dummy* identifiers; they serve only to establish a connection between parts of an expression. Bound identifiers are the pronouns of mathematics.

Changing a bound identifier to another identifier usually does not change the meaning of an expression. For instance,

$$\sum_{i=1}^{m} A_{ij} \text{ and } \sum_{k=1}^{m} A_{kj}$$

both mean the sum of the jth column of the matrix A. Suppose we change the bound identifier to 'j':

$$\sum_{j=1}^{m} A_{jj}$$

This sums the *diagonal* of the matrix; we have altered the meaning of the expression! We got into this trouble because we changed the bound identifier 'i' to the identifier 'j', which already occurred free in the expression. Thus the occurrence of 'j' in A_{ij} became *accidently bound*. This is called a *collision of identifiers*. The following conclusion can be drawn: We can change a bound identifier, throughout its scope, to another identifier only if the latter identifier does not occur free in that scope.

Exercise 8.2: For each expression, determine whether the indicated change of identifier alters the meaning of the expression:

a. $\{x \mid x > y\}$; change $x \Rightarrow z$

b. $\{x \mid x > y\}$; change $x \Rightarrow y$

c. $\dfrac{d}{dx}(x^3 - xy)$; change $x \Rightarrow t$

d. $\dfrac{d}{dx}(x^3 - xy)$; change $x \Rightarrow y$

e. $\forall x [\exists y (y > x)]$; change $y \Rightarrow x$

f. $\dfrac{\partial}{\partial x} \dfrac{\partial}{\partial y} \left[\dfrac{x^2 + y^2}{xy} \right]$; change $y \Rightarrow x$

g. $\sinh(x) = \dfrac{e^x - e^{-x}}{2}$; change $x \Rightarrow u$

h. $\{m \mid m > e\} \cup \{e \mid \sin(e) = 0\}$; change $e \Rightarrow m$

i. $\{x \mid x > 0\} \cup \{y \mid y < 0\}$; change $y \Rightarrow x$

j. $\displaystyle\sum_{i=1}^{m} A_i + \sum_{j=1}^{n} B_j$; change $i \Rightarrow j$

k. $\displaystyle\sum_{i=1}^{m} i \cdot \sum_{j=1}^{n} V_j$; change $j \Rightarrow i$

8.3 Syntax of the Lambda Calculus

When bound identifiers are used in function definitions they are often called *formal parameters*. For example, in

$$f(x) \equiv x^2 - 3x$$

'x' is the bound identifier or formal parameter. We have previously seen functional abstractions such as

$$x \mapsto (x^2 - 3x)$$

The lambda calculus is simply a calculus of function application built on a variant of this notation. For example, in lambda notation this function is written

$$\lambda x(x^2 - 3x)$$

which can be read "that function which takes any x into $x^2 - 3x$." The Greek letter 'λ' (lambda) does not stand for anything; Church is said to have used it because of its similarity to a notation of Whitehead and Russell's (1970, p. 23).[4] The lambda notation is exactly equivalent to our previous notation

$$x \mapsto (x^2 - 3x)$$

In this chapter we use the lambda notation to emphasize that we are working in the pure lambda calculus.

In the lambda calculus, function application is just a substitution process. For example, suppose we have defined

$$f \equiv \lambda x(x^2 - 3x)$$

and want to know the value of '$f(5)$'; we can find it by substituting '5' for 'x' throughout its scope. More specifically, we start with

$$f(5)$$

---

4. The evolution was something like this: $\hat{x}(fx) \Rightarrow {\char`\~}x(fx) \Rightarrow \Lambda x(fx) \Rightarrow \lambda x(fx)$. This change of notation facilitated mechanical manipulation of bound variables.

Substituting '$\lambda x(x^2 - 3x)$' for 'f', we get

$$\lambda x(x^2 - 3x)\,(5)$$

Now we replace this expression by a copy of the *body* of f (i.e., '$x^2 - 3x$') in which every free occurrence of 'x' is replaced by '(5)':

$$(5)^2 - 3(5) \;\Rightarrow\; 25 - 15 \;\Rightarrow\; 10$$

This is called the *copy rule* for function application because the invocation '$f\,(5)$' is actually replaced by a copy of the body of the function with its parameter textually substituted, that is, '$(5)^2 - 3(5)$'.

The lambda calculus has a very simple syntax. Lambda expressions are composed of the symbols 'λ', '(', ')', and identifiers, put together according to the following four rules:

1. If x is an identifier, then it is an expression of the lambda calculus.

2. If x is an identifier and E is an expression of the lambda calculus, then (λxE) is an expression of the lambda calculus, called an *abstraction*. We call x the *binding* of the abstraction and E the *body* of the abstraction.

3. If F and E are expressions of the lambda calculus, then (FE) is an expression of the lambda calculus, called an *application*. We call F the *operator* of the application and E the *operand* of the application.

4. The only lambda expressions are those produced by finitely many applications of the rules $1 - 3$.

Thus the expressions of the lambda calculus are defined by this BNF grammar:

$$
\text{lambda\_exp} \equiv
\begin{cases}
(\;\lambda\ \text{identifier lambda\_exp}\;) \\
(\;\text{lambda\_exp lambda\_exp}\;) \\
\text{identifier}
\end{cases}
\tag{8.3}
$$

We assume a denumerably infinite set of identifiers.

To increase the readability of lambda expressions, let's introduce some syntactic sugar. First we also allow other kinds of brackets (e.g., [], {}) as alternatives to parentheses in expressions of all types. Second, to decrease the number of parentheses and brackets of all kinds we adopt the convention that all operators associate to the left. Thus '$((fx)y)$' can be abbreviated '(fxy)', which can be abbreviated 'fxy'. However, '$(f\,(gx))$' can be abbreviated '$f\,(gx)$' but not 'fgx'. Similarly, '$(\lambda x(fx))$' can be abbreviated '$\lambda x\,(fx)$' and '(λxx)' can be abbreviated 'λxx'.

To permit more meaningful examples, we sometimes allow additional types of expressions within our lambda expressions, such as conventional arithmetic expressions (e.g. '3 + x'). Keep in mind, however, that the *pure lambda calculus* has only the syntactic constructs described in Eq. (8.3).

The way in which we described the syntax of the lambda calculus forms a model for all later syntax descriptions. We enumerated a set of *primitives* (the basic symbols and identifiers) and described a set of *constructors* or formation rules, which will yield all the legal expressions of the language when applied recursively to the primitives finitely many times.

Exercise 8.3: Which of the following are legal lambda calculus expressions? That is, which of these are generated by the formal grammar (Eq. 8.3) without syntactic sugar?

a. x

b. $f(x)$

c. $\lambda x[f(x)]$

d. $(g)y$

e. $f(a)(b)$

f. $(f\,x)$

g. $\lambda x[f(x)](a)$

h. $\lambda x[f(x)](\lambda x[x])$

i. $(\lambda x(f\,x))$

j. $f\,g$

k. $[g(a)]$

l. $f[x]$

m. $f(\lambda x)$

Exercise 8.4: Which of the preceding are legal lambda expressions when the alternative brackets and rules for omitting brackets are allowed? In each case rewrite without syntactic sugar.

8.4 Semantics of the Lambda Calculus

As discussed in Chapter 4, *semantics* refers to the meaning of an expression. There are various senses, however, in which we can interpret the term 'meaning'. For example, the *mathematical* or *denotational* semantics of an expression is the mathematical object denoted by that expression. Thus the mathematical semantics of the lambda calculus expression '$\lambda x(x+x)$' is the mathematical function $x \mapsto 2x$. On the other hand, the *computational* semantics of an expression is the computation process(es) that it describes. Thus the computational semantics of '$[\lambda y(y \times y)]$ $[\lambda x(x+1)\,2]$' includes the evaluation sequences

$$[\lambda y(y \times y)][\lambda x(x+1)\,2] \Rightarrow [\lambda y(y \times y)]\,(2+1) \Rightarrow [\lambda y(y \times y)]\,3 \Rightarrow 3 \times 3 \Rightarrow 9$$
$$[\lambda y(y \times y)][\lambda x(x+1)\,2] \Rightarrow [\lambda x(x+1)\,2] \times [\lambda x(x+1)\,2]$$
$$\Rightarrow (2+1) \times (2+1) \Rightarrow 3 \times 3 \Rightarrow 9$$

The mathematical semantics of the lambda calculus has been investigated extensively,[5] but is beyond the scope of this book. We concentrate instead on the computational semantics, which has the advantage of being self-contained since it deals with computational processes and their results independently of their interpretation in any mathematical theory.

In the previous section we described informally the computational process of the lambda calculus by the copy rule. In this section this process is defined more exactly through two *reduction rules*:[6]

1. Renaming Rule: One expression may be reduced to another by changing a bound identifier throughout its scope to any other identifier that does not occur within that scope.

2. Substitution Rule: A subexpression of the form $((\lambda xE)A)$ may be reduced by replacing it by a copy of E in which all free occurrences of x are replaced by A, provided this does not result in any free identifier of A becoming bound.

We can restate the renaming rule as follows: An expression λxE may be reduced by renaming to an expression λyF, where F is obtained from E by replacing all free occurrences of x in E by y. This is allowed only if y does not occur in E. For example, to rename 'x' to 'u' in '$\lambda x(x^2 + 2x + 1)$', we change to 'u' all free occurrences of 'x' in '$x^2 + 2x + 1$', yielding '$\lambda u(u^2 + 2u + 1)$'. This reduction is symbolized as follows:

$$\lambda x(x^2 + 2x + 1) \;\Rightarrow\; \lambda u(u^2 + 2u + 1)$$

In general we use '$\Rightarrow$' for a reduction involving one or more applications of these rules. Some other reductions permitted by the renaming rule follow:

---

5. For a comprehensive overview with references, see (Barendregt 1984, Part V).
6. In the literature, the renaming rule is often known as α-*reduction* and the substitution rule as β-*reduction*. We will use the more descriptive names. These reduction rules are described more formally in Chapter 9.

$$\lambda xx \;\Rightarrow\; \lambda aa \;\Rightarrow\; \lambda gg \;\Rightarrow\; \lambda ff$$
$$\lambda x \,(\lambda y \,[x \,(y)]) \;\Rightarrow\; \lambda f \,(\lambda y \,[f \,(y)]) \;\Rightarrow\; \lambda f \,(\lambda a \,[f \,(a)])$$
$$\lambda x \,(x + 1) \;\Rightarrow\; \lambda u \,(u + 1)$$
$$\lambda x \,[\lambda y \,(x + y)] \;\Rightarrow\; \lambda a \,[\lambda y (a + y)] \;\Rightarrow\; \lambda a [\lambda b (a + b)]$$

To understand the restriction on the renaming rule, consider the following Algol-60 program skeleton:

```
begin real x;
      ⋮
      begin real z;

            ⋮

            print(x+z);

            ⋮
      end
      ⋮
end
```

The purpose of bound identifiers in programming languages, as in most notations, is to establish connections between remote portions of the program. For example, the two occurrences of the variable 'x' establish a connection between the declaration on the first line and the print invocation, telling us that the variable to be used in computing the value to print is the same variable that was declared in the outer block.

Of course, we can uniformly rename 'x' to 'y' without altering the meaning of the program:

```
begin real y;
      ⋮
      begin real z;

            ⋮

            print(y+z);

            ⋮
      end
      ⋮
end
```

That is, if we change 'x' to 'y' we have not altered the connections between the different parts of the program. Instead, suppose we decide to change 'x' to 'z'. We obtain

```
┌─ begin real z;
│     ⋮
│  ┌─ begin real z;
│  │     ⋮
│  │  print(z+z);
│  │     ⋮
│  └─ end
│     ⋮
└─ end
```

It is easy to see we have changed the meaning of the program by changing the structure of the connections between the parts of the program. In
particular, the first variable in the print invocation, which used to refer to
the real variable in the outer block, now refers to the real variable in the
inner block. The restriction on the renaming rule prevents this *collision of
identifiers*, since 'z' occurs in the scope of 'x'.

Let's consider an illegal application of the renaming rule in the lambda
calculus to understand the restriction better. Suppose we wish to apply
the renaming rule to

$$f = \lambda x \, [\lambda e \, (e \times x) \, 3]$$

Note that f is equivalent to $\lambda x \, (3 \times x)$. Changing 'x' to 'e' is not allowed
since 'e' occurs in 'e × x'. If we did the substitution anyway, we would
change the meaning of the expression:

$$f' = \lambda e \, [\lambda e \, (e \times e) \, 3] = \lambda e \, (3^2)$$

Note that $f(1) = 3$ while $f'(1) = 9$; f and f' are not the same function.
Renaming 'x' to 'y', however, would not change the meaning:

$$f'' = \lambda y \, [\lambda e \, (e \times y) \, 3]; \quad f''(1) = 3$$

The renaming rule is generally needed only to avoid identifier collisions,
as you'll see later.

Exercise 8.5: Apply the renaming rule as indicated, or state that its
application would be illegal:

a. λxx; change $x \Rightarrow y$

b. $\lambda x \, [\lambda y \, (x + y)]$; change $y \Rightarrow x$

c. $\lambda x \, (fx)$; change $f \Rightarrow g$

d. $\lambda d\,[d + e\,]$; change $d \Rightarrow e$

e. $\lambda x\,(\lambda y\,[x\,(y)])$; change $x \Rightarrow f$

Next we consider the substitution rule. The expression '$\lambda x\,(x + 1)\,3$' fits the form required by the substitution rule: It is an application whose operator is an abstraction. Hence we can reduce it by replacing all free occurrences of 'x' in '$x + 1$' by '3'. The result is '$3 + 1$'. Now consider

$$\lambda x\,[\lambda y\,(xy)]\,f$$

This is an application whose operator is the abstraction

$$\lambda x\,[\lambda y\,(xy)]$$

We can apply the substitution rule by replacing by 'f' all free occurrences of 'x' in '$\lambda y\,(xy)$'. This produces

$$\lambda y\,(fy)$$

To better understand the restriction on the substitution rule, first consider the following legal reduction:

$$\lambda y\,\{\lambda x\,[\lambda z\,(z + x)\,3]\,y\}1 \;\Rightarrow\; \lambda y\,\{\lambda z\,(z + y)\,3\}1 \qquad (8.4)$$
$$\Rightarrow\; \lambda z\,(z + 1)3$$
$$\Rightarrow\; 4$$

In the first step we replaced by 'y' all free occurrences of 'x' in '$\lambda z\,(z + x)3$'. Now let's look at a slightly different example:

$$\lambda y\,\{\lambda x\,[\lambda y\,(y + x)\,3]\,y\}1$$

This is the same expression as the previous one, with 'z' renamed to 'y'—which will create an identifier collision when we try to replace 'x' by 'y'. We start with the inner application:

$$\lambda x\,[\lambda y\,(y + x)\,3]y$$

To apply the substitution rule we must replace by 'y' all free occurrences of 'x' in '$\lambda y\,(y + x)3$'. This is only allowed, however, if it does not cause a free identifier of 'y' to become bound. In this case a collision does occur, since 'y' is free in 'y' but not in '$\lambda y\,(y + x)3$'. To see the reason for this restriction, let's perform the substitution; the result is '$\lambda y\,(y + y)3$'. This has changed the meaning of the expression, a fact we can see by continuing the evaluation:

$$\lambda y \{\lambda y\,(y+y)\,3\}1 \;\Rightarrow\; \lambda y\{6\}1 \;\Rightarrow\; 6$$

Hence this expression reduces to 6 although we know the answer should be 4.

To avoid this situation, we note that bound identifiers are arbitrary and simply rename the offending *bound* identifier. For instance, we can rename the inner 'y' to 'z' and then do the reduction as shown in Eq. (8.4). In fact, avoiding identifier collisions is the major use of the renaming rule.

Exercise 8.6: Determine whether the substitution rule is applicable to each of these expressions. If so, reduce the expression by the substitution rule, first applying the renaming rule if necessary.

a. $\lambda x\,[xy\,](f)$

b. $\lambda x\,[\lambda y\,(xy)](y)$

c. $f\,(3)$

d. $\lambda x\,[\lambda y\,(xy)]\,\lambda z\,(yz)$

e. $\lambda y\,[y \cdot y\,](3)$

f. $\lambda f\,[\,f\,(3)+f\,(4)\,](g)$

8.5 Normal Form

If and when an expression is reduced to the extent that the substitution rule can no longer be applied, it is said to be in *normal form* (sometimes *reduced* form). Intuitively, an expression is in normal form when it is an answer (i.e., it is done computing). The following table shows examples of both nonnormal and normal expressions:

Not Normal	Normal
$[\lambda xx\,](y)$	y
$\lambda y\,(fy)(a)$	fa
$\lambda x\,[\lambda y\,(xy)]f$	$\lambda y\,(fy)$
$(\lambda xx)(\lambda xx)$	λxx
$\lambda x\,(xx)y$	yy
$\lambda x\,(xy)[\lambda x\,(xx)]$	yy

In each of these cases, the expression on the right is the normal form resulting from the reduction of the expression on the left. For example,

$$\lambda x\,(xy)\,[\lambda x\,(xx)] \;\Rightarrow\; \lambda x\,(xx)y \;\Rightarrow\; yy$$

As usual, we write $X = Y$ if two formulas X and Y are interchangeable. In the lambda calculus the substitution and renaming rules tell us when one formula can be replaced by another. Therefore, if either $X \Rightarrow Y$ or $Y \Rightarrow X$, then $X = Y$ (i.e., equality is symmetric and reflexive). Since we also expect things equal to the same thing to be equal to each other (i.e., equality is transitive), we say that $X = Y$ just when there are formulas $X_1, \ldots, X_n$ such that $X = X_1$, $X_n = Y$, and for each i either $X_i \Rightarrow X_{i+1}$ or $X_{i+1} \Rightarrow X_i$. For example,

$$\lambda z\,(yz)y \;=\; \lambda x\,(xx)y$$

even though neither formula can be reduced to the other. To see the equality, note that

$$\lambda z\,(yz)y \;\Rightarrow\; yy \quad \text{and} \quad \lambda x\,(xx)y \;\Rightarrow\; yy$$

The foregoing shows us that two formulas with the same normal form are equal, since $X \Rightarrow N$ and $Y \Rightarrow N$ imply $X = Y$. Is the converse also true, that two equal formulas must have the same normal form? This is exactly what's guaranteed by the Church-Rosser Theorem (Chapter 9). Indeed, the theorem says that if $X = Y$, then—provided they have normal forms at all[7]—there is a *unique* (up to renaming) normal form N such that $X \Rightarrow N$ and $Y \Rightarrow N$. Combining these two results, if X and Y define terminating computations (have normal forms), then $X = Y$ if and only if they have the same normal form N, $X \Rightarrow N$ and $Y \Rightarrow N$. It thus makes sense to identify the *value* of a formula with its normal form.[8]

Exercise 8.7:   Decide whether each of the following expressions is in normal form. If not, reduce it to normal form.

---

7. We see shortly that some formulas do not have normal forms.
8. By 'value' we mean here the *computational value* of a formula, that is, the value defined by the computational semantics; the mathematical value (defined in terms of the mathematical semantics) is different. Also, as we will see, some formulas intuitively have a (computational) value even though they have no normal form (e.g., expressions returning a recursively defined function). For this reason, it is better to identify the value of an expression with its "head normal form" if it has one. Identifying head normal formulas with computational values is equivalent to obeying the Delayed Function Body Restriction (Section 7.7). Full discussion of this topic is beyond the scope of this book; see (Barendregt 1984, Chapter 2, Section 2).

a. $\lambda f\,[S\,(f\,3)\,(f\,4)]\,[\lambda y\,(Pyy)]$

b. $f\,[\,\lambda x\,(Sxx)]$

c. $\lambda x\,(Lx0)\,[\lambda x\,(Sx1)]$

d. $\lambda x\,(Lx0)\,[\lambda x\,(Sx1)\,2]$

> **Exercise 8.8:** Reduce the following to normal form:
>
> $\lambda f\{\text{succ}\,[S\,(f\,2)\,(f\,3)]\}\,\{\lambda x\,[S\,2\,(\text{square}\,x)]\}$
>
> **Exercise 8.9:** Suppose the following definitions are given:[9]
>
> Zero $\Rightarrow$ $\lambda f\,(\lambda cc)$
> One $\Rightarrow$ $\lambda f[\lambda c\,(fc)]$
> Two $\Rightarrow$ $\lambda f\{\lambda c\,[f\,(fc)]\}$
> Three $\Rightarrow$ $\lambda f(\lambda c\{f\,[f\,(fc)]\})$
>
> $\vdots$
>
> sum $\Rightarrow$ $\lambda M\Big[\lambda N\Big[\lambda f\{\lambda c\,[M\,f\,(N\,f\,c)]\}\Big]\Big]$

Reduce to normal form 'sum Two One'. What is this equal to? If you wonder about the motivation for these definitions, then try reducing 'Three succ 0' and 'Two succ 3', where 'succ' and '0' have the usual meanings.

Not all expressions have a normal form. Define Ω to be the expression $\omega\omega$, where ω is the expression $\lambda x\,(xx)$. We can apply the substitution rule to Ω to yield the reduction

$$\Omega \Rightarrow \omega\omega \Rightarrow \lambda x\,(xx)\,\omega \Rightarrow \omega\omega \Rightarrow \;\ldots$$

This is the lambda calculus equivalent of an infinite loop. The expression Ω has no normal form since the substitution rule always applies to it. The existence of lambda expressions without normal forms should not be too surprising. The lambda calculus is a model of computation, and the ability to write an infinite loop (or unending recursion) is fundamental to computation.

The formula Ω permits an unending reduction in which it repeatedly regenerates itself. It is also possible to have reductions that neither regenerate themselves nor terminate. Since they can neither stay the same size nor get smaller, such formulas must expand forever. We can get such a *divergent* formula by modifying ω. Since $\omega = \lambda x\,(xx)$, which when

---

9. See (Church 1941) for this definition of the numerals. We use $\Rightarrow$ here as a sign of abbreviation; see Section 8.6 for a fuller discussion.

applied to itself yields $\omega\omega$, we can get a diverging formula by using $W = \lambda x\,[F\,(xx)]$, which when applied to itself yields $F\,(WW)$:

$$WW \Rightarrow \lambda x\,[F\,(xx)]W \Rightarrow F\,(WW) \Rightarrow F\,(\lambda x\,[F\,(xx)]W) \Rightarrow \qquad (8.5)$$
$$F\,(F\,(WW)) \Rightarrow \;\ldots$$

The surprising thing is that formulas like WW have important applications, which we'll investigate in Section 8.12.

Since Ω permits an unending reduction, we may expect that an expression is undefined—that is, has no value—if it contains Ω or any other formula without a normal form. This is not the case, as can be seen by considering the example $(\lambda xa)\Omega$. If we attempt to reduce Ω before substituting it for x, then we indeed get a nonterminating reduction:

$$(\lambda xa)\,\Omega \Rightarrow (\lambda xa)\,(\omega\omega) \Rightarrow (\lambda xa)\,(\omega\omega) \Rightarrow \;\ldots$$

If we first perform the substitution for x, however, the reduction reaches normal form in one step:

$$(\lambda xa)\,\Omega \Rightarrow a$$

The reason, of course, is that the function (λxa) throws away its argument and always returns a; it is a constant function. In the terminology introduced in Section 7.6, the function (λxa) is lenient (nonstrict). Therefore in this case a lazy evaluation of the expression terminates, whereas an eager order does not. The issue of evaluation order is explored more formally in this chapter and most of the following ones.

We have seen that some lambda expressions do not have a normal form. We have also seen that, for those that do, reduction may or may not reach normal form depending on the order in which the rules are applied. As noted previously, however, different reduction orders cannot lead to *different* normal forms. This is guaranteed by the Church-Rosser Theorem, proved in Chapter 9. For now suffice it to say that this theorem tells us that our use of '=' is well-defined since it ensures that equal formulas have the same computational results (more accurately, the normal form is unique up to renaming of the bound identifiers). In the absence of this guarantee we could have the following situation: Suppose X has normal forms U and V, but that Y has only normal form U. Then, in spite of the fact that $X = Y$ (since $X \Rightarrow U$ and $Y \Rightarrow U$), we could have X and Y computing two different values: $X \Rightarrow V$, but $Y \Rightarrow U$. The Church-Rosser Theorem says that this situation can never happen, thus guaranteeing referential transparency and the consistency of our idea of equality.

8.6 Multiple Parameters and Abbreviations

In the rest of this chapter we argue that the lambda calculus is *computationally complete*, that is, that it can compute any computable function. In one sense this is trivial since the notion of computability is often defined in reference to the lambda calculus (Church 1936). On the other hand, it's certainly not intuitively obvious that the pure lambda calculus contains the necessary power to write all programs. Therefore in this section we define in the pure lambda calculus the data types used in the previous chapters: Booleans, integers, tuples, and sequences. That is, the primitive data types, previously described only by archetypes, will now be described by prototypes in the pure lambda calculus. By reducing the functional language to the pure lambda calculus, we will know that anything we prove about the pure lambda calculus (such as the Church-Rosser property) will also be true of the functional language.

Although the lambda expressions we have defined have only one parameter, as you remember from Section 6.6, we can get the effect of two parameters by nesting functional abstractions, a technique known as *currying*. For example,

$$\lambda x\,[\lambda y\,(x+y)]\,3\,1 \;\Rightarrow\; \lambda y\,(3+y)\,1 \;\Rightarrow\; 3+1 \;\Rightarrow\; 4$$

Because such curried functions are so common in the lambda calculus, we allow the following abbreviation (also using '$\Rightarrow$' as a sign of abbreviation):

$$\lambda xy.\,(x+y) \;\Rightarrow\; \lambda x\,[\lambda y\,(x+y)]$$

When the dot is used, the convention is that the body of the abstraction extends to the right as far as possible, consistent with being well-formed. Thus we can write $\lambda xy.x+y$ rather than $\lambda xy.\,(x+y)$. For convenience, the dot may be used even if there is only one parameter; thus $\lambda x.x^2+2x+1$ is the same as $\lambda x\,(x^2+2x+1)$.

Currying is the usual method of handling multi-argument functions in the lambda calculus. In Section 5.4 we saw the other method of converting multi-argument functions to single argument functions: The multiple arguments are made into a tuple. We cannot use this technique yet since we haven't shown how tuples can be represented in the pure lambda calculus.

Of course, normally it is unnecessary to think of curried functions as abbreviations; we just do the multiple parameter substitutions directly. For example, if $f = \lambda xy.\,x+y$, then

$$f\,3\,1 \;\Rightarrow\; (\lambda xy.\,x+y)\,3\,1 \;\Rightarrow\; 3+1 \;\Rightarrow\; 4$$

In exactly the same way, we allow substitutions involving any number of parameters:

$$(\lambda abc.\,ax^2+bx+c)\,9\,6\,1 \;\Rightarrow\; 9x^2+6x+1$$

In general, the multiple-parameter abbreviation is defined

$$\lambda x_1 x_2 \dots x_n . E \;\Rightarrow\; \lambda x_1 \{\lambda x_2 [\; \dots \; (\lambda x_n E) \dots]\}$$

Or, using the dot convention,

$$\lambda x_1 x_2 \dots x_n . E \;\Rightarrow\; \lambda x_1 . \lambda x_2 \dots \lambda x_n . E$$

As seen in some of the previous examples, lambda expressions can become quite large. To be able to program significant functions in the lambda calculus, it is convenient to have a way to attach names to lambda expressions. Therefore we allow rewrite rules of the following form:

$$
\begin{aligned}
\text{plusp} &\Rightarrow \lambda x.\, x \geq 0 \\
\text{minusp} &\Rightarrow \lambda x.\, x < 0 \\
\text{succ} &\Rightarrow \lambda x.\, x + 1 \\
\text{square} &\Rightarrow \lambda x.\, x \times x
\end{aligned}
\tag{8.6}
$$

These rules simply say, for example, that 'plusp' is an abbreviation for the lambda expression '$\lambda x.\, x \geq 0$'. It must be emphasized that these rewrite rules are not part of the lambda calculus, but simply abbreviations that *we* use for talking *about* lambda expressions. Abbreviations introduced in this way can always be eliminated by applying the rewrite rules until no abbreviations are left. For example,

$$\text{minusp (succ 2)} \Rightarrow (\lambda x.\, x < 0)\,(\text{succ } 2) \Rightarrow (\lambda x.\, x < 0)\,[(\lambda x.\, x + 1)\,2]$$

This means that these rules cannot be recursive; recursive definition must be accomplished differently (see Section 8.12).[10] As long as this is understood, however, there is no reason that we can't use rules such as (8.6) directly in reductions, as in the following example:

$$
\begin{aligned}
\text{minusp (succ 2)} &\Rightarrow (\lambda x.\, x < 0)\,(\text{succ } 2) \\
&\Rightarrow (\text{succ } 2) < 0 \\
&\Rightarrow (\lambda x.\, x + 1)2 < 0 \\
&\Rightarrow 2 + 1 < 0 \\
&\Rightarrow 3 < 0 \\
&\Rightarrow \textbf{false}
\end{aligned}
$$

Notice that we use the rewrite arrow '$\Rightarrow$' two ways: *prescriptively*, as a way to define abbreviations, and *descriptively*, as a way to describe reduction sequences.

---

10. Recall also the discussion of explicit and implicit definition in Section 1.8: Explicit definitions are unproblematical since they can always be eliminated; implicit definitions may or may not have solutions.

8.7 Typing in the Lambda Calculus

As seen previously, especially in Chapters 4 and 5, the *type* of an expression is important. In fact, in statically typed languages such as ours, programs that are type-inconsistent are considered *syntactically* incorrect. On the other hand, we have not mentioned any notion of typing in the lambda calculus; its notion of functions and function applications is completely *typeless*. Does this indicate that the lambda calculus is inadequate as a theoretical basis for functional programming?

It's quite easy to define a *typed* lambda calculus.[11] First define a set of *type identifiers*, which we can imagine includes symbols such as '$\mathbb{B}$', '$\mathbb{N}$', '$\mathbb{Z}$', and '$\mathbb{R}$'. This set is denumerable since the set of types (like everything else in a computer) is denumerable. Then we recursively define a set **type** to include the type identifiers and all *function types* ($\sigma \to \tau$) for $\sigma, \tau \in$ **type**. Next we stipulate that every identifier be tagged with a type (e.g., 'x_τ'), and that all typed lambda calculus formulas be type-consistent according to the following schemata (type tags are written as subscripts):

$$(F_{(\sigma \to \tau)} \, E_\sigma)_\tau$$

$$(\lambda x_\sigma \, M_\tau)_{(\sigma \to \tau)}$$

We require the renaming and substitution rules to maintain the type tags in the obvious way.

Although the typed lambda calculus might seem the appropriate theoretical foundation for functional programming, we continue to use the typeless calculus. The reason is that—in a statically typed language—once types have been checked, a syntactic process, the type information can be discarded without affecting the computational semantics of the program.[12] This is a familiar idea: In compiling a statically typed language such as Pascal, the type information need not be represented in the object code. Similarly here: The type information is not needed at run time. Thus there is little reason to abandon the simpler typeless calculus.

Exercise 8.10: Write out schemas for the renaming and substitution rules for the typed lambda calculus.

---

11. See, for example, (Barendregt 1984, Appendix A). Our formulation here is somewhat different from his.
12. The situation would be different if we were after the mathematical semantics, since typeless functions are very different mathematical objects from the usual typed functions. A principal goal of Scott's theory (Scott 1970–1977, Scott and Strachey 1971, Stoy 1977) is to legitimate the notion of a typeless function.

8.8 Booleans and Conditionals

In this section we develop a prototype implementation of the Boolean data type in the pure lambda calculus. Since all the lambda calculus can do is substitute actuals for formals, that must form the basis of our solution. We can get a handle on the problem by considering the uses to which Boolean values are put. The basic function of the truth values **true** and **false** is to select between alternatives. This selection is usually accomplished with the 'If' function: (If $c\ t\ f$) selects t if c is **true** and f if c is **false**.[13] That is, **true** selects t from the pair (t, f) and **false** selects f from the pair (t, f), suggesting that we view **true** and **false** as *selector functions:*

$$\textbf{true}\ t\ f \Rightarrow t$$
$$\textbf{false}\ t\ f \Rightarrow f$$

This leads immediately to the definitions

$$\textbf{true} \Rightarrow \lambda tf.t \qquad\qquad (8.7)$$
$$\textbf{false} \Rightarrow \lambda tf.f$$

Then, if c is an expression that returns **true** or **false**, we can use c to select between two alternatives by the application $(c\ t\ f)$. For example, suppose that we have defined (less $m\ n$) to compare m and n. The expression (less $m\ n$)mn will select the minimum of m and n, as shown by this example:

$$(\text{less } 2\ 6)\ 2\ 6 \Rightarrow \textbf{true}\ 2\ 6 \Rightarrow (\lambda tf.t)\ 2\ 6 \Rightarrow 2$$

Therefore we can see that

$$(\text{If } c\ t\ f) = ctf \qquad\qquad (8.8)$$

Next let's program the logical connectives: 'and', 'or', and 'not'. The 'not' function is the simplest since it just negates a truth value:

$$\text{not } \textbf{true} \Rightarrow \textbf{false}$$
$$\text{not } \textbf{false} \Rightarrow \textbf{true}$$

That is, if x is **true** then not x is **false**; otherwise not x is **true**. This can be directly translated to the lambda calculus using Eq. (8.8):

$$\text{not} \Rightarrow \lambda x.\text{If } x\ \textbf{false}\ \textbf{true}$$

---

13. We write (If $c\ t\ f$) rather than if (c, t, f) since the latter depends on the ability to construct the tuple (c, t, f). Thus we must use curried functions until lists are defined.

('If' can be omitted, but we retain it for clarity.) The 'and' function is defined so that (and x y) is **true** only if both x and y are **true**, as summarized in the following truth table:

and	true	false
true	true	false
false	false	false

We can see that if x is **true** then (and x y) has the same value as y, and that if x is **false** then (and x y) is **false** regardless of the value of y. We can translate this directly into the lambda calculus:

and $\Rightarrow \lambda xy.$ If x y **false**

A partial prototype implementation of Booleans is shown in Fig. 8.1.

Exercise 8.11:   Define or so that (or x y) is **true** if and only if x or y or both are **true**. That is, or must satisfy the following truth table:

or	true	false
true	true	true
false	true	false

Test whether your definition works by reducing (or **false true**).

Exercise 8.12: Define the equal function on Boolean values so that (equal x y) reduces to **true** if and only if the values are equal. Show a truth table for equal, prove your function satisfies the truth table, and test it on several pairs of Boolean values.

Of course, we must show that this prototype implementation satisfies the Boolean archetype in Figure 8.2. For example, to show if (**true**, a, b) = a, we derive

if (**true**, a, b) $\Rightarrow$ If **true** a b
$\Rightarrow$ ($\lambda ctf.ctf$) **true** a b
$\Rightarrow$ **true** a b
$\Rightarrow$ a

The last step is based on our already established property of **true**.

Figure 8.1 Partial prototype implementation of Boolean data type.

true $\Rightarrow$ $\lambda tf.t$
false $\Rightarrow$ $\lambda tf.f$
If $\Rightarrow$ $\lambda ctf.ctf$
not $\Rightarrow$ $\lambda x.$If x **false true**
and $\Rightarrow$ $\lambda xy.$If $x\ y$ **false**
or $\Rightarrow$ (exercise)
equal $\Rightarrow$ (exercise)

if $(c,\ t,\ f)$ $\Rightarrow$ (If $c\ t\ f$)
$\neg x$ $\Rightarrow$ not x
$x \wedge y$ $\Rightarrow$ and $x\ y$
$x \vee y$ $\Rightarrow$ or $x\ y$
$x = y$ $\Rightarrow$ equal $x\ y$
$x \neq y$ $\Rightarrow$ $\neg(x = y)$

Figure 8.2 Archetype for Boolean type.

Syntax:

$\mathbb{B} \in$ **type**
true, false $\in \mathbb{B}$
$\neg: \mathbb{B} \to \mathbb{B}$
$\wedge, \vee, =, \neq: \mathbb{B} \times \mathbb{B} \to \mathbb{B}$
if: $\mathbb{B} \times T \times T \to T$

Semantics:

$x \in \mathbb{B}$ if and only if $x =$ **true** or $x =$ **false**

$\neg$**true** = **false**
$\neg$**false** = **true**

true $\wedge$ **true** = **true**
false $\wedge y$ = **false**
$x \wedge$ **false** = **false**

$x \vee y = \neg(\neg x \wedge \neg y)$
$(x = y) = (x \wedge y) \vee (\neg x \wedge \neg y)$
$(x \neq y) = \neg(x = y)$

if (**true**, t, e) = t
if (**true**, t, $\bot$) = t

if (**false**, t, e) = e
if (**false**, $\bot$, e) = e

Pragmatics:

All operations take constant time.
The if operation is strict in its first parameter, but lenient in its second and third parameters.
The other operations are strict in their first parameters, and may be either strict or lenient in their other parameters.

Notice that although we can prove that the prototype satisfies all the *semantic* properties in Fig. 8.2, it does not satisfy the *syntactic properties*, since the multi-argument operators are specified to be uncurried. For example, ∧ is specified

$$\wedge:\ (\mathbb{B} \times \mathbb{B}) \to \mathbb{B}$$

whereas the prototype (Fig. 8.1) has the type[14]

$$\wedge:\ \mathbb{B} \to (\mathbb{B} \to \mathbb{B})$$

Therefore, the definitions of the multi-argument operators in Fig. 8.1 must be considered provisional until tuples are defined in the following section.

Exercise 8.13: Prove the remaining properties of Booleans described in Fig. 8.2.

8.9 Direct Product Types

We must find a way to represent tuples so that all the selectors and constructors of direct product data types can be implemented. Since the lambda calculus is a calculus of functions, tuples must ultimately be represented as functions of some form. Furthermore, our definition of tuples must be based on the facilities already defined: the pure lambda calculus and Booleans. How can these help us? Recall that the most basic property of the selectors and constructors of tuples is that they invert each other. Therefore letting pair $x\ y$ represent the (curried) operation that constructs the pair (x, y), we have

> left (pair $x\ y$) = x
> right (pair $x\ y$) = y

That is, pair must construct a pair in such a way that it is possible to recover each of the two elements that went into the pair. Thus we need a way to select either of these two elements. Our Boolean data type provides exactly this capability, since **true** $x\ y \Rightarrow x$ and **false** $x\ y \Rightarrow y$. That is, $(c\ x\ y)$ selects either x or y from the pair depending on whether c is **true** or **false**. Therefore let's define the pair returned by pair $x\ y$ to be a function

---

14. Of course, in a literal sense it has no type at all since it's expressed in the typeless lambda calculus. This signature expresses the function's *intended* type, given the specified representation for Boolean values.

Figure 8.3 Partial prototype implementation of direct product types.

pair $\Rightarrow$ $\lambda xy.\lambda c.cxy$
left $\Rightarrow$ $\lambda x.\ x$ **true**
right $\Rightarrow$ $\lambda x.\ x$ **false**

$(x,\ y)$ $\Rightarrow$ pair $x\ y$
equal $\Rightarrow$ (exercise)
$x = y$ $\Rightarrow$ equal $x\ y$
$x \neq y$ $\Rightarrow$ $\neg(x = y)$

that can return either x or y depending on whether it is applied to **true** or
to **false**:

pair $x\ y$ $\Rightarrow$ $\lambda c.cxy$

For example, the tuple (1, **true**) is represented by the lambda expression
'$\lambda c.\ c\ 1$ **true**'. Hence the prototype implementations of pair, left, and right
are

pair $\Rightarrow$ $\lambda xy.\lambda c.cxy$
left $\Rightarrow$ $\lambda x.\ x$ **true**
right $\Rightarrow$ $\lambda x.\ x$ **false**

For example, observe the reduction of 'left (pair $A\ B$)':

left (pair $A\ B$) $\Rightarrow$ left {$(\lambda xy.\lambda c.cxy)\ A\ B$}
                   $\Rightarrow$ left $(\lambda c.cAB)$
                   $\Rightarrow$ $(\lambda x.\ x$ **true**$)\ (\lambda c.cAB)$
                   $\Rightarrow$ $(\lambda c.cAB)$ **true**
                   $\Rightarrow$ **true** $A\ B$
                   $\Rightarrow$ A

Thus left (pair $A\ B$) $\Rightarrow$ A, as expected. A partial prototype implementation of direct product types is shown in Fig. 8.3.

Exercise 8.14: Show that right (pair $A\ B$) $\Rightarrow$ B.

Exercise 8.15: Develop a prototype implementation of the equal operation for tuples: equal $x\ y$ is **true** if and only if x and y are the same pairs. Assume
that you have operations $equal_\sigma$ and $equal_\tau$ applicable to the component types of
the tuple.

Exercise 8.16: Prove that the prototype implementation in Fig. 8.3
satisfies the direct product archetype (Fig. 5.2 or Fig. B.7).

Now that we have tuples, we can define the uncurried functions that we're used to. Consider, for example, the function

$$f \Rightarrow \lambda p.\text{square (left } p) + \text{right } p$$

Applying this to the pair (a, b) and reducing we get

$$
\begin{aligned}
f(a, b) &\Rightarrow [\lambda p.\text{square (left } p) + \text{right } p] \,(a, b) \\
&\Rightarrow \text{square [left } (a, b)] + \text{right } (a, b) \\
&\Rightarrow \text{square } a + b
\end{aligned}
$$

Thus we can get the effect of a multi-argument function by passing a tuple to the function and using left and right to select its components. This is simplified by the following syntactic sugar. If $E(x, y)$ is any expression involving (possibly many) occurrences of the identifiers x and y, then we take '$\lambda(x, y).E(x, y)$' to be an abbreviation for '$\lambda p.E(\text{left } p, \text{right } p)$', where '$E(\text{left } p, \text{right } p)$' represents E with its occurrences of x replaced by 'left p' and its occurrences of y by 'right p'. For example, our previous example becomes

$$f \Rightarrow \lambda(x, y).\ \text{square } x + y$$

This substitution of 'left p' for x and 'right p' for y can by accomplished by abstraction and application, so we formally define the uncurried function notation as follows:

$$\lambda(x, y).E \Rightarrow \lambda p.\,(\lambda xy.E)\,(\text{left } p)\,(\text{right } p)$$

This approach can be extended to handle any number of parameters. For example, for ternary functions,

$$\lambda(x, y, z).E \Rightarrow \lambda t.\,(\lambda xyz.E)\,(\text{left } t)\,[\text{left (right } t)]\,[\text{right (right } t)]$$

In general, define right^n to apply right n times by

$$
\begin{aligned}
\text{right}^0 &\Rightarrow \lambda xx \\
\text{right}^{n+1} &\Rightarrow \lambda x.\text{right (right}^n\ x)
\end{aligned}
$$

Then the following rule shows us how to reduce n-adic uncurried functions to the pure lambda calculus:

$$
\begin{aligned}
&\lambda(x_1, x_2, \ldots, x_{n-1}, x_n).E \hspace{3cm} (8.9) \\
&\Rightarrow \lambda t.\,(\lambda x_1 x_2 \ldots x_{n-1} x_n.E) \\
&\quad [\text{left (right}^0\ t)]\,[\text{left (right}^1\ t)]\,\ldots\,[\text{left (right}^{n-1}\ t)]\,(\text{right}^n\ t)
\end{aligned}
$$

Figure 8.4 Syntactic abbreviation for uncurried functions.

$\lambda(x).E \;\Rightarrow\; \lambda x.E$

$\lambda(x_1, x_2, \ldots, x_n).E \;\Rightarrow\; \lambda p.\,[\lambda x_1.\lambda(x_2, \ldots, x_n).E]\,(\text{left } p)\,(\text{right } p)$

$F \mapsto E \Rightarrow \lambda FE$

An alternative approach, shown in Fig. 8.4, depends on the fact that $(x_1, x_2, \ldots, x_n) = (x_1, (x_2, \ldots, x_n))$.

Exercise 8.17: Complete the prototype implementation of Booleans by redefining the multi-argument operators so that they're uncurried. For example,

$\wedge \;\Rightarrow\; \lambda(x, y)\,(\text{and } x\ y)$

Exercise 8.18: Prove the following property of uncurried functions:

$[\lambda(x, y).E\,(x, y)]\,(a, b) \;\Rightarrow\; E\,(a, b)$

Exercise 8.19: Prove that Eq. (8.9) defines the same function as Fig. 8.4.

8.10 Direct Sum Types and Sequences

In Section 5.2 we saw that the direct sum $T + U$ can be represented by the direct product $\mathbb{B} \times T \times U$. That is, an element of a direct sum type is represented by a triple (v, x, y) in which v is a discriminant telling us whether the value belongs to the first or second variant, and x and y hold the values of type T or U. Only one of x and y is in use in any given triple. Since the lambda calculus is typeless, we can use an even simpler representation here, using a single field to hold both variants. The resulting prototype implementation of direct sums is in Fig. 8.5. Note that we don't need a separate prototype definition of '=', since this is covered by the '=' operation for direct products.

Figure 8.5 Prototype implementation of direct sum types.

$\text{1st} \;\Rightarrow\; \lambda x\,(\textbf{true}, x)$

$\text{2nd} \;\Rightarrow\; \lambda y\,(\textbf{false}, y)$

$\text{1st}^{-1} \;\Rightarrow\; \lambda(v, x)x$

$\text{2nd}^{-1} \;\Rightarrow\; \lambda(v, y)y$

$\text{1st?} \;=\; \lambda(v, x)v$

$\text{2nd?} \;\Rightarrow\; \lambda x.\,\neg(\text{1st? } x)$

Exercise 8.20: Show that the prototype implementation in Fig. 8.5 satisfies the direct sum archetype (Fig. 5.5 or Fig. B.8).

In Section 5.3 we saw that the sequence data type can be defined by the following recursive structure declaration:

$$\textbf{abstract type} \ T^* \equiv \textbf{nil} + \textbf{prefix}(\textbf{first} \in T, \ \textbf{rest} \in T^*) \qquad (5.21)$$

In other words, sequences of type T^* can be represented by values belonging to the direct sum type $\mathbf{1} + T \times T^*$. This observation leads directly to the prototype implementation of sequences shown in Fig. 8.6. The definition of nil deserves some comment. We have tagged the value **true** to make nil, but any value with a defined equality operation would do (since we want nil = nil to be **true**). Also notice that we omitted the length operation, which requires the integer data type to be implemented; we postpone implementation of length until this has been accomplished in Section 8.13.[15]

We must, of course, prove that the prototype definition satisfies the archetype (Fig. 2.5 or Fig. B.4). Take, for example,

$$\text{null} \ [\text{prefix}(a, \ b)] = \textbf{false}$$

To do this we simply substitute definitions and reduce; in the derivation we use previously established results and omit several obvious steps:

$$
\begin{aligned}
\text{null} \ [\text{prefix}(a, \ b)] &\Rightarrow \text{null} \ [\text{2nd} \ (a, \ b)] \\
&\Rightarrow \text{1st?} \ [\text{2nd} \ (a, \ b)] \\
&\Rightarrow \textbf{false}
\end{aligned}
$$

Exercise 8.21: Prove the following properties of sequences:

a. first $< a, \ b > \ = a$

b. rest $< a, \ b > \ = \ < b >$

c. first (rest $< a, \ b >$) $= b$

Exercise 8.22: Prove the remaining properties of sequences described in Fig. 2.5 or Fig. B.4.

---

15. Note that we restrict our attention here to finite sequences. Since lambda calculus expressions must be finite, the representation in Fig. 8.6 will not work for infinite sequences. For the latter we can use any of the function-based representations discussed in Chapter 7 (recursive enumeration functions or delayed pairs).

Figure 8.6 Partial prototype implementation of sequence data types.

nil $\Rightarrow$ 1st **true**
null $\Rightarrow$ 1st?
prefix $\Rightarrow$ $\lambda(x, y)$.2nd (x, y)
first $\Rightarrow$ λx.left (2nd^{-1} x)
rest $\Rightarrow$ λx.right (2nd^{-1} x)

Exercise 8.23: We have not provided a prototype implementation of sequence equality; explain why.

Exercise 8.24: Suppose we have the following structure definition:

structure expr $\equiv$ leaf: IN
  + bind (tag $\in$ IN, body $\in$ expr)
  + couple (sinister $\in$ expr, dexter $\in$ expr)

Note that this is sugar for the recursive type declaration:

expr $\equiv$ IN + IN $\times$ expr + expr $\times$ expr

Reduce the following expressions to their lambda calculus equivalents:

a. 'leaf 2'

b. 'bind (5, leaf 3)'

c. 'couple [bind (5, leaf 3), couple (leaf 0, leaf 1)]'

d. 'bind? E'

e. 'couple? E'

f. 'body E'

g. 'dexter E'

Don't bother reducing numbers to the pure lambda calculus.

The remaining primitive data types are numbers and strings; to define these data types requires the use of recursion, which is the topic of Section 8.12.

8.11 Auxiliary Declarations

We saw in Section 5.9 that it makes no sense to ask the value of an *open* expression, that is, an expression containing free identifiers. Therefore any complete functional program must be *closed:* All its identifiers must be bound. In nontrivial programs this binding is accomplished with **let** and **where** declarations. To see how functional programs can be reduced to the pure lambda calculus, it's therefore necessary to investigate a prototype implementation of declarations. We first consider nonrecursive declarations; recursive ones are addressed in the next section.

Consider a simple nonrecursive auxiliary declaration 'E **where** $v \equiv x$'. This says that v is bound to x throughout E. By referential transparency, the meaning of 'E **where** $v \equiv x$' is the same as that of the expression that results from substituting x for every free occurrence of v in E. But this is exactly what the substitution rule of the lambda calculus accomplishes. Therefore the **where** notation can be defined as a "syntactic sugaring" of the function application

$$E \text{ where } v \equiv x \;\Rightarrow\; (\lambda v E)x$$

Reduction of $(\lambda v E)x$ results in substituting x for every free occurrence of v in E. For example, an expression such as

    if [success? C, synthesize C S, apply_rules (F, rest R)]
      where C ≡ match (A, F, nihil)

(taken from a functional program) is just syntactic sugar for

{λC. if [success? C, synthesize C S, apply_rules (F, rest R)]} [match (A, F, nihil)]

One application of the substitution rule reduces this to

    if {success? [match (A, F, nihil)], synthesize [match (A, F, nihil)] S,
      apply_rules (F, rest R)}

In analogy with functions of several arguments, we define *compound* **where** declarations:

$$E \text{ where } v_1 \equiv x_1 \text{ and } v_2 \equiv x_2 \text{ and } \ldots \text{ and } v_n \equiv x_n \Rightarrow \qquad (8.10)$$
$$[\lambda(v_1, v_2, \ldots, v_n).E]\,(x_1, x_2, \ldots, x_n)$$

For instance, the expression fragment

    eval [B, bindargs (X, V, C)]
      where C ≡ ep K
        and X ≡ formals (ip K)
        and B ≡ body (ip K)

is syntactic sugar for

{λ(C, X, B). eval [B, bindargs (X, V, C)]} [ep K, formals (ip K), body (ip K)]

Application of the substitution rule produces

eval {body (ip K), bindargs [formals (ip K), V, ep K]}

Similarly, **let** declarations are easily defined in the lambda calculus:

let $v \equiv x$ **in** $E \implies (\lambda v E)x$

Or, in general,

let $v_1 \equiv x_1$ **and** $v_2 \equiv x_2$ **and** ... **and** $v_n \equiv x_n$ **in** $E \implies$ $\qquad$ (8.11)
$[\lambda(v_1, v_2, \ldots, v_n).E] (x_1, x_2, \ldots, x_n)$

As an example of **let**, the expression fragment

let $A \equiv$ left (first R) $\qquad\qquad\qquad\qquad\qquad\qquad$ (8.12)
and $S \equiv$ right (first R) **in**
$\quad$ **let** $C \equiv$ match (A, F, nihil) **in**
$\qquad$ if [success? C, synthesize C S, apply_rules (F, rest R)]

is syntactic sugar for

$\lambda(A, S)$ {λC. if [success? C, synthesize C S, apply_rules (F, rest R)]
$\qquad\qquad\qquad$ [match (A, F, nihil)] }
$\quad$ [left (first R), right (first R)]

Abbreviations (8.10) and (8.11) show us how to express *nonrecursive* declarations in the lambda calculus. Recursive declarations, however, are not so easy. To understand the difficulty it's necessary to explore the scope of the identifiers bound in an auxiliary declaration.

Recall that in the abstraction '$\lambda x E$' the *scope* of 'x' is the expression 'E'. This determines the scope of the identifiers defined by a **let** or a **where**: In both 'E **where** $v \equiv x$' and '**let** $v \equiv x$ **in** E' the scope of x is E.[16] For example, in Eq. (8.12) the scopes of A and S are the expression

let $C \equiv$ match (A, F, nihil) **in**
$\quad$ if [success? C, synthesize C S, apply_rules (F, rest R)]

Put another way, the scope of an identifier is the region of an expression over which it has meaning, that is, the region throughout which the identifier is replaced by its value.

---

16. The actual boundaries of the scope are determined by the syntactic rules of the particular functional language. In this book we use indentation to make the scope clear, so formal rules should be unnecessary. The conventions used by the Φ language are in Appendix A.

Next we investigate the scope of compound declarations. Consider the two expressions

> **let** $v_1 \equiv e_1$ **in let** $v_2 \equiv e_2$ **in** B
>
> **let** $v_1 \equiv e_1$ **and** $v_2 \equiv e_2$ **in** B

Superficially they look very similar, but the second expression, which is called a *compound declaration*, is much more than merely a shorthand form of the first, which is simply two nested simple declarations. To see this, we reduce both to the lambda calculus:

> **let** $v_1 \equiv e_1$ **in let** $v_2 \equiv e_2$ **in** B $\Rightarrow$ $[\lambda v_1.(\lambda v_2 B)\, e_2]\, e_1$
>
> **let** $v_1 \equiv e_1$ **and** $v_2 \equiv e_2$ **in** B $\Rightarrow$ $[\lambda(v_1, v_2)B]\,(e_1, e_2)$

Observe that in the first expression e_2 is within the scope of v_1, whereas in the second the scope of both v_1 and v_2 is just B. On the one hand, the formula

> **let** $n \equiv 3$ **in let** $x \equiv 4 \times n + 1$ **in** $n \times (x + n)$ $\qquad$ (8.13)

is legal and has the same effect as

> **let** $x \equiv 4 \times 3 + 1$ **in** $3 \times (x + 3)$

On the other hand, the expression

> **let** $n \equiv 3$ **and** $x \equiv 4 \times n + 1$ **in** $n \times (x + n)$ $\qquad$ (8.14)

is illegal—unless, of course, 'n' is bound in some surrounding scope. This can be seen more clearly by translating the two expressions back to pure lambda notation. Equation (8.13) becomes

> $\{\lambda n.\,[\lambda x.n \times (x + n)]\,(4 \times n + 1)\}\, 3$

which is correct, and Eq. (8.14) becomes

> $[\lambda(n, x).n \times (x + n)]\,(3, 4 \times n + 1)$

which is not legal, since the use of n in the actual parameter list is not within the scope of the formal parameter n. This would seem to be a limitation of compound declarations, but we'll see their value in connection with recursive declarations, discussed next.

Exercise 8.25: Draw scoping lines to indicate the scopes of the bound identifiers in the following expressions:

a. **let** $x \equiv a$ **in let** $y \equiv b$ **and** $z \equiv c$ **in** $f\,(x,\ y,\ z)$

b. **let** $x \equiv ($**let** $y \equiv a$ **in** $f\,(x,\ y)) $ **in** $f\,(b,\ x)$

c. **let** $x \equiv a$ **in let** $y \equiv f\,(x)$ **and** $x \equiv g\,(b)$ **in** $h\,(x,\ y)$

8.12 Recursive Declarations

Our prototype definition of **let** and **where** does not permit recursive declarations. To see this, consider the following incorrect definition of the factorial function:

let fac $\equiv \lambda n.\,$if $[n = 0,\ 1,\ n \times$ fac $(n - 1)]$ **in** fac 4

The scope of 'fac' is 'fac 4', as can be seen by eliminating the syntactic sugar:

$(\lambda$ fac.fac 4$)\ \lambda n.\,$if $[n = 0,\ 1,\ n \times$ fac $(n - 1)]$

Therefore the occurrence of 'fac' in the body of its definition is unbound (i.e., free). This is made more obvious if we rename the *bound* identifier 'fac' to 'f' throughout its scope:

$(\lambda f.f\ 4)\ \lambda n.\,$if $[n = 0,\ 1,\ n \times$ fac $(n - 1)]$

Thus the **let** declaration does not permit us to define recursive functions because the right-hand side of the binding is evaluated in the environment surrounding the **let**—that is, the environment in existence before 'fac' is bound. We have a "chicken-and-egg" problem: 'fac' cannot be bound until we know the value of the expression on the right of the definition sign ($\equiv$). To permit recursive declarations, however, we must evaluate the expression on the right of the definition sign in an environment that includes the binding of 'fac'. This is a serious problem since most of our function definitions are recursive. To succeed in reducing the functional language to the lambda calculus, we must find some way to reduce recursive declarations to lambda expressions.

One solution is to use global rewrite rules, one for each recursive definition.[17] For example, fac could be defined

fac $\Rightarrow \lambda n.\,$if $[n = 0,\ 1,\ n \times$ fac $(n - 1)]$

Then, as long as we're careful about reduction order, we can evaluate fac 4 as follows:

---

17. This is in effect what is commonly done in Scheme and LISP; recursive functions are defined globally via define, rather than locally via let.

$$\begin{aligned} \text{fac } 4 &\Rightarrow \{\lambda n.\text{if } [n = 0, 1, n \times \text{fac } (n-1)]\}\ 4 \\ &\Rightarrow \text{if } [4 = 0, 1, 4 \times \text{fac } (4-1)] \\ &\Rightarrow 4 \times \text{fac } 3 \\ &\Rightarrow 4 \times \{\lambda n.\text{if } [n = 0, 1, n \times \text{fac } (n-1)]\}\ 3 \end{aligned}$$

And so forth. The main difficulty with this solution is that it requires us to extend the lambda calculus for each recursive function we need. In effect, we have not one lambda calculus, but a whole family of calculi, one for each set of global definitions. This creates a problem since crucial properties, in particular the Church-Rosser property, depend on the rules of the calculus. Thus, if we took this approach, instead of the categorical statement "the lambda calculus is Church-Rosser," the best we could get is a conditional statement of the form "an extended lambda calculus is Church-Rosser provided its global rules satisfy the following properties: ...." In fact, such a result can be proved for extended lambda calculi (see Chapter 10), but the properties are complicated to state. For these reasons we avoid global definitions for now (except nonrecursive abbreviations for our own convenience), directly addressing the issue of expressing recursive definitions in the pure lambda calculus.

Let's be more careful about what we need. We want to find a lambda calculus formula ϕ such that 'ϕ 4' reduces to 4!, that is, 24. We can attempt to derive ϕ from the definition of the factorial function. Since we want $\phi 0 \Rightarrow 1$ and $\phi n \Rightarrow n \times \phi(n-1)$ (for $n > 0$), let's try the following for a first guess:

$$\phi \equiv \lambda n.\text{if } [n = 0, 1, n \times \phi(n-1)]$$

This equation suggests that ϕ is a *self-embedding* formula, that is, a formula that contains itself. Since no finite formula can be self-embedding, ϕ must be an infinite formula. We can see this by trying to write out the formula for ϕ completely:

$$\begin{aligned} \phi \equiv \{\lambda n.\text{if } [n = 0, 1, n \times \\ \{\lambda n.\text{if } [n = 0, 1, n \times \\ \{\lambda n.\text{if } [n = 0, 1, n \times \ \ldots\ (n-1)]\}\ (n-1)]\}\ (n-1)]\} \end{aligned}$$

An infinite formula is not much use to us because we cannot write it down; we can only write down approximations of it. For example, the following are approximations of the formula ϕ:

$$\begin{aligned} \phi_0 &\equiv \bot \\ \phi_1 &\equiv \lambda n.\text{if } [n = 0, 1, n \times \phi_0(n-1)] \\ \phi_2 &\equiv \lambda n.\text{if } [n = 0, 1, n \times \phi_1(n-1)] \\ \phi_3 &\equiv \lambda n.\text{if } [n = 0, 1, n \times \phi_2(n-1)] \\ \phi_4 &\equiv \lambda n.\text{if } [n = 0, 1, n \times \phi_3(n-1)] \end{aligned}$$

$$\vdots$$

(We use '⊥' for an arbitrary "undefined" value.) Each ϕ_i includes ϕ_{i-1} as a subformula. Notice that ϕ_0 will not compute the factorial of anything; it is universally undefined. On the other hand, ϕ_1 will correctly compute the factorial of 0; ϕ_2 will correctly compute the factorial of 0 or 1; ϕ_3 will correctly compute the factorial of 0, 1, or 2; in general, ϕ_i will correctly compute the factorial of $0, 1, 2, \ldots, i-1$. None of these formulas, however, will compute the factorial of all natural numbers. To do this we again need the self-embedding formula that we now denote ϕ_∞:

$$\phi_\infty = \lambda n.\text{if } [n = 0, 1, n \times \phi_\infty(n-1)]$$

This ϕ_∞ is just the formula we previously called ϕ. We can think of ϕ_∞ as the limit of the sequence $\phi_0, \phi_1, \phi_2, \ldots$:

$$\phi_\infty = \lim_{i \to \infty} \phi_i$$

Does this limit exist? That is, is there a finite lambda calculus formula corresponding to ϕ_∞?

To answer this question, let's investigate a simpler problem. Consider the flowcharts in Fig. 8.7, in which we take ⊥ to be an "undefined statement," which always is an error. Thus flowchart F_1 executes statement S and then either exits normally if the condition is **true**, or is in error other-

---

Figure 8.7 A sequence of flowcharts.

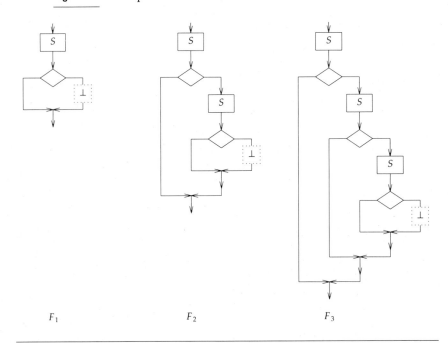

F_1 F_2 F_3

wise. Similarly, F_2 executes S and then either exits, or goes on to execute S again, and then to either exit or abort. Finally, F_3 executes S and then exits if the condition is **true**, or does the same as F_2 if the condition is **false**. It can be seen that each flowchart is embedded in the following one, and that this process can be continued to yield an infinite sequence of related flowcharts. In general F_i executes S at most i times. After each execution of S it tests the condition and exits if it is **true**, and goes on otherwise. If the condition has not become **true** after i executions of S, then the program aborts.

Does this sequence have a limit? If we imagine the infinite limit F_∞ of this sequence and consider its behavior, we can see that it will alternately evaluate S and the condition until the condition returns **true**, at which point it exits. The program can never reach the error statement $\bot$—that would require ∞ executions of S. But this is just the behavior of the trailing decision loop shown in Fig. 8.8. Therefore there is a finite flowchart that is equivalent in behavior to the limit of the sequence $F_1, F_2, F_3, \ldots$ and we are justified in saying

$$F_\infty = \lim_{i \to \infty} F_i$$

There is another way to look at these limits. Notice that flowchart F_i is derived from F_{i-1} by substituting F_{i-1} in an invariant *matrix*. This matrix, which we call ψ, is shown in Fig. 8.9. Our sequence of flowcharts is expressed in terms of ψ as follows:

$$F_0 = \bot$$
$$F_1 = \psi(F_0) = \psi(\bot)$$
$$F_2 = \psi(F_1) = \psi[\psi(\bot)]$$
$$F_3 = \psi(F_2) = \psi\{\psi[\psi(\bot)]\}$$
$$\vdots$$
$$F_i = \psi(F_{i-1}) = \psi^i(\bot)$$

Figure 8.8 Limit of a sequence of flowcharts.

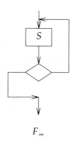

F_∞

Thus the limit F_∞ satisfies the equation

$$F_\infty = \psi(F_\infty)$$

Recall that any value x that satisfies $fx = x$ is called a *fixed point* of the function f. For example, 0 is a fixed point of the sine function. Some functions, such as the successor function, have no fixed point. Thus the problem of finding F_∞ can be restated as the problem of finding a fixed point for the function ψ.

Now let's attempt to apply these ideas to the problem of recursive definitions in the lambda calculus. Recall that we are seeking a finite formula ϕ that satisfies

$$\phi = \lambda n. \text{if } [n = 0, 1, n \times \phi(n - 1)]$$

This is the self-embedding limit of an infinite sequence of formulas in exactly the same way that F_∞ is the self-embedding limit of an infinite sequence of flowcharts. As before, we'll seek the matrix that is used to generate this infinite sequence—clearly,

$$\lambda n. \text{if } [n = 0, 1, n \times \ldots (n - 1)]$$

The formula ϕ_i is obtained from ϕ_{i-1} by embedding ϕ_{i-1} in the preceding matrix (in place of ' . . . '). Therefore we define the embedding function

$$\psi(f) = \lambda n. \text{if } [n = 0, 1, n \times f(n - 1)]$$

Figure 8.9 Matrix for flowchart sequence.

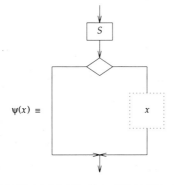

$\psi(x) \equiv$

Then we can see that

$$\phi_0 = \bot$$
$$\phi_1 = \psi(\phi_0) = \psi(\bot)$$
$$\phi_2 = \psi(\phi_1) = \psi[\psi(\bot)]$$
$$\phi_3 = \psi(\phi_2) = \psi\{\psi[\psi(\bot)]\}$$
$$\vdots$$
$$\phi_i = \psi(\phi_{i-1}) = \psi^i(\bot)$$

Clearly then what we seek is the fixed point of the function ψ:

$$\phi = \psi(\phi)$$

Since we know that no finite formula can be embedded in itself, what we really seek is a formula ϕ that *behaves the same* as the formula $\psi(\phi)$. We would have such a formula if ϕ were equal to $\psi(\phi)$ (recall the definition of equality for the lambda calculus in Section 8.5). Notice that this would permit the unending reduction

$$\phi \Rightarrow \psi(\phi) \Rightarrow \psi[\psi(\phi)] \Rightarrow \psi\{\psi[\psi(\phi)]\} \Rightarrow \cdots$$

Does this look familiar? It should, since it is similar to the behavior of the formula WW (see Eq. (8.5)):

$$WW \Rightarrow F(WW) \Rightarrow F(F(WW)) \Rightarrow F(F(F(WW))) \Rightarrow \cdots$$

Thus for any function F we can define a W

$$W \Rightarrow \lambda x [F(xx)]$$

such that $WW \Rightarrow F(WW)$, that is, such that WW is a fixed point of the function F. Now we want ϕ to be a fixed point of ψ, so we define

$$W \Rightarrow \lambda x.\psi(xx) \text{ and } \phi \Rightarrow WW$$

We now have the solution to our problem since

$$\phi \Rightarrow WW \Rightarrow [\lambda x.\psi(xx)]W \Rightarrow \psi(WW) = \psi(\phi)$$

and therefore $\phi = \psi(\phi)$.

To make our solution independent of the matrix ψ and therefore usable for arbitrary recursive definitions, we note that since

$$\phi = WW = [\lambda x.\psi(xx)] [\lambda x.\psi(xx)]$$

we can replace ψ by an arbitrary matrix f by writing

$$\mathbf{Y}f = [\lambda x.f\,(xx)]\,[\lambda x.f\,(xx)]$$

Therefore $\phi = \mathbf{Y}\psi$. We can see that

$$\mathbf{Y}f \Rightarrow f\,(\mathbf{Y}f) \Rightarrow f\,(f\,(\mathbf{Y}f)) \Rightarrow \ \cdots$$

For example,

$$\mathbf{Y}\ \text{not} \Rightarrow \text{not}\,(\mathbf{Y}\ \text{not}) \Rightarrow \text{not}\,(\text{not}\,(\mathbf{Y}\ \text{not})) \Rightarrow \ \cdots$$

For this reason, $\mathbf{Y}$ is called the *paradoxical combinator* (a *combinator* is any closed formula). Since $\mathbf{Y}f$ is a fixed point of f, $\mathbf{Y}$ is also called the *fixed-point-finding operation*. There are in fact infinitely many fixed-point-finding operations, but we need only $\mathbf{Y}$.[18]

Recall that we were seeking a formula ϕ such that ϕn reduces to the factorial of n. We have found this formula to be $\mathbf{Y}\psi$. Since

$$\psi \Rightarrow \lambda f.\lambda n.\text{if}\,[\,n = 0,\ 1,\ n \times f(n-1)\,]$$

we can write out ϕ as an explicit abbreviation:

$$\phi \Rightarrow \mathbf{Y}\,\lambda f.\lambda n.\text{if}\,[\,n = 0,\ 1,\ n \times f\,(n-1)\,]$$

That is, ϕ is the fixed point of

$$\lambda f.\lambda n.\text{if}\,[\,n = 0,\ 1,\ n \times f\,(n-1)]$$

that is, a function f such that

$$f = \lambda n.\text{if}\,[\,n = 0,\ 1,\ n \times f\,(n-1)]$$

This f is clearly the formula we sought for the factorial function.[19] Hence we can write

$$\text{fac} \Rightarrow \mathbf{Y}\,\lambda f.\lambda n.\text{if}\,[\,n = 0,\ 1,\ n \times f\,(n-1)]$$

18. Note the curious fact that every function in the lambda calculus has a fixed point (since for every f there is a corresponding $\mathbf{Y}f$). $\mathbf{Y}f$, however, doesn't have a normal form, so it's problematic whether it should be considered a *value*.
19. We have ignored several subtle mathematical issues. For example, is the fixed point unique? Some functions, such as $x + \sin x$, have an infinity of fixed points; others, such as the successor, have none. These issues are not relevant to our present purposes.

Note that this is a finite formula. It is not self-embedding, although it does permit an unending expansion. To see that this works, we can begin a reduction, replacing $\mathbf{Y}\psi$ by $\psi(\mathbf{Y}\psi)$ when necessary to continue:

$$
\begin{aligned}
\text{fac } 4 &\Rightarrow \mathbf{Y}\psi\, 4 \qquad\qquad\qquad\qquad\qquad\qquad\qquad\quad (8.15)\\
&\Rightarrow \psi(\mathbf{Y}\psi)\, 4\\
&\Rightarrow \{\lambda f.\lambda n.\text{if } [n = 0,\, 1,\, n \times f\, (n-1)]\}\, (\mathbf{Y}\psi)\, 4\\
&\Rightarrow \{\lambda n.\text{if } [n = 0,\, 1,\, n \times \mathbf{Y}\psi(n-1)]\}\, 4\\
&\Rightarrow 4 \times \mathbf{Y}\psi 3\\
&\Rightarrow 4 \times \psi(\mathbf{Y}\psi)3\\
&\ \ \vdots
\end{aligned}
$$

Exercise 8.26:   Complete the preceding reduction.

We can make our definition of 'fac' more readable by using 'fac' for the bound identifier of ψ; then the recursion is more obvious:

$$\text{fac} \ \Rightarrow\ \mathbf{Y}\,\lambda \text{fac}.\lambda n.\text{if } [n = 0,\, 1,\, n \times \text{fac } (n-1)]$$

Then we can write a closed lambda expression that computes fac 4:

let fac $\equiv \mathbf{Y}\,\lambda\text{fac}.\lambda n.\text{if } [n = 0,\, 1,\, n \times \text{fac } (n-1)]$ **in** fac 4

Haven't we missed something? Since the $\mathbf{Y}$ function leads to a nonterminating reduction, doesn't this mean that any definition that makes use of it, including fac, will be nonterminating? As shown in Eq. (8.15), we can reduce fac in such a way that the reduction terminates. Also, however, we can reduce fac in such a way that the reduction doesn't terminate:

$$\text{fac } 4 \ \Rightarrow\ \mathbf{Y}\psi\, 4 \ \Rightarrow\ \psi(\mathbf{Y}\psi)4 \ \Rightarrow\ \psi(\psi(\mathbf{Y}\psi))4 \ \Rightarrow\ \ \ldots$$

Again, the Church-Rosser Theorem states all reductions *that terminate* must produce the same normal form, not that if one reduction terminates, then so must all others.

One way to understand the operation of fac is to think of $\mathbf{Y}\psi$ as a formula that can replicate ψ any number of times. Therefore the proper way to execute fac is to push the reduction as far as possible until it is stopped by the need for a new copy of ψ. Then we let $\mathbf{Y}$ operate for one step to replicate ψ and continue with the reductions. This is called a *lazy* reduction order because we produce a copy of ψ only when it is needed. The alternative, allowing $\mathbf{Y}$ to produce as many copies of ψ as it can, is called an *eager* reduction order and leads to a nonterminating computation. The properties of various reduction orders are discussed in Chapter 12. (Recall also the "unwinding" of infinite data structures discussed in Sections 7.6 and 7.7.)

Since recursive declarations are so common we introduce the following syntactic sugar:

> **let rec** $f \equiv x$ **in** B $\Rightarrow$ **let** $f \equiv \mathbf{Y}(\lambda fx)$ **in** B
> B **where rec** $f \equiv x$ $\Rightarrow$ B **where** $f \equiv \mathbf{Y}(\lambda fx)$

This permits us to define and use fac conveniently:

> **let rec** fac $\equiv \lambda n.$if $[n = 0, 1, n \times$ fac $(n-1)]$ **in** fac 4

With another dash of sugar, we have

> **let rec** fac $n \equiv$ if $[n = 0, 1, n \times$ fac $(n-1)]$ **in** fac 4

Exercise 8.27: Discuss the reduction of *mutually recursive* definitions to the pure lambda calculus, that is, the reduction of definitions of the form

> **let rec** $f \equiv \ldots g \ldots h \ldots$
> **and rec** $g \equiv \ldots f \ldots h \ldots$
> **and rec** $h \equiv \ldots f \ldots g \ldots$ **in** $\ldots f \ldots$

Hint: Use tuples and deconstructing declarations.

Exercise 8.28: Define the equality relation for sequences.

8.13 Integers

Now let's return to our definition of the primitive data types. Our goal here is to define the type $\mathbb{Z}$ and to show that our definition satisfies the archetype in Fig. 8.10.

The problem we face is to find some way to represent integers so that the operations of the integer type are implementable in terms of the primitive types we already have (Booleans, tuples, sums, and sequences). In solving this problem we use our knowledge of number representation on computers; we know that any integer can be represented as a string of bits. Therefore one solution is to represent integers as strings of bits, that is, sequences of Boolean values.

Recall our goal, however, of attempting to show the computational completeness of the lambda calculus—in particular, that the primitives of the functional language Φ can be implemented in the lambda calculus.

Figure 8.10 Archetype for integers.

Syntax:

$0, 1, -1, 2, -2, \ldots \in \mathbb{Z}$

$+, -$ (*prefix*): $\mathbb{Z} \to \mathbb{Z}$

$+, -, \times, \div: \mathbb{Z} \times \mathbb{Z} \to \mathbb{Z}$

$=, \neq, <, >, \leq, \geq: \mathbb{Z} \times \mathbb{Z} \to \mathbb{B}$

Semantics:

$a \in \mathbb{Z}$ if and only if $a = 0$ or for some $b \in \mathbb{Z}, a = b + 1$ or $a = b - 1$

$a + 1 \neq a$

$a + b = b + a$

$a + (b + c) = (a + b) + c$

$a + 0 = a$

$a + (-a) = 0$

$a - b = a + (-b)$

$a \times 1 = a$

$a \times b = b \times a$

$a \times (b \times c) = (a \times b) \times c$

$a \times (b + c) = (a \times b) + (a \times c)$

$0 < 0 = $ **false**

$0 < 1 = $ **true**

$a < b = a + 1 < b + 1$

$a < b \wedge b < c = a < c$

$a \div 1 = a$

$a \div b = 0, \ 0 \leq a < b$

$a \div b = 1 + [(a - b) \div b], \ 0 \leq a, \ b \leq a$

$a \div b = -(-a \div b), \ a < 0$

$a \div b = -(a \div -b), \ b < 0$

$a > b = b < a$

$a \neq b = a > b \vee a < b$

$a \leq b = a < b \vee a = b$

$a \geq b = b \leq a$

$a = b = \neg(a \neq b)$

Pragmatics:

All operations take constant time.

There are maximum and minimum integer values, and the operations are undefined when either their arguments or their results are out of the allowed range.

For this purpose we do not need an efficient implementation; any correct implementation will do. Therefore, instead of representing numbers in binary notation, we represent them in *unary notation* since this will make our definitions easier.

Unary notation is the simplest number notation, since the number n is represented by n strokes. For example, the number five in unary notation is

$$| \; | \; | \; | \; |$$

Of course, there is nothing special about the stroke; any other symbol works as well:

$$* \; * \; * \; * \; *$$

The essence of unary notation is that a number is represented by example; to indicate five we show five things, with the understanding that the only relevant property is the number of things.

Since we have already defined sequences, we can translate these ideas directly into the lambda calculus. For example, the number five can be represented by a sequence of any five things. Just as in unary notation it doesn't really matter what these things are, so we can use any convenient value; here we use the value nil. Thus the number five is represented by a sequence of five nils:

<nil, nil, nil, nil, nil>

The number zero, of course, is represented by the sequence containing no nils, that is, the null sequence.

This method works well for the *natural numbers*—that is, the numbers 0 1, 2, 3, . . .—but will not work for negative integers; we can hardly represent the number –5 by a sequence containing negative five nils! There are several ways around this problem. For example, just as in a computer the sign of a number is represented by an extra bit, so we could represent an integer as a pair, the first element being a representation of the sign and the second element being a natural number. In Exercise 8.48 you work out the details of signed arithmetic; here we confine our attention to natural numbers.

Although the sequence representation works and is helpful in understanding unary notation, it is more complicated than necessary. We can get to the heart of the natural numbers through the recursive structure declaration:

$$\mathbb{N} \equiv 0 \; + \; \text{succ} \, (\text{pred} \in \mathbb{N}) \tag{8.16}$$

Don't be confused by the notation; succ is just a constructor and pred is just a field selector. Thus the values belonging to this type are 0, succ 0, succ (succ 0), succ [succ (succ 0)], and so forth. It is a typical unary representation since the number n is represented by a "stack" of n succs. The archetype for structure declarations (Fig. 5.3) tells us that values belonging to $\mathbb{N}$ satisfy the expected properties: pred (succ n) = n and succ (pred n) = n (for $n \neq 0$).

Exercise 8.29: Based on Eq. (8.16), show the lambda calculus formulas representing 0, 1, and 2. Show the lambda calculus formulas for the functions 0?, succ?, succ, and pred.

Exercise 8.30: Show that (0? 0) reduces to **true** and (0? 1) reduces to **false**.

Given the primitive operations in Eq. (8.16), it is straightforward to define the four arithmetic operations. For example, the definition of addition is based on the identities

$$m + 0 \equiv m$$
$$m + (\text{succ } n) \equiv \text{succ } (m + n)$$

Thus addition can be defined recursively in terms of successor:

$$\textbf{let rec } \text{sum } (m, n) \equiv \begin{cases} m, & \text{if } 0? \ n \\ \textbf{else } \text{succ } [\text{sum } (m, \text{ pred } n)] \end{cases}$$

This is easily translated into the lambda calculus.

Exercise 8.31: Work through sum (3, 2) to convince yourself that this definition is correct.

We show that this definition of addition is correct—that is, that the prototype satisfies the archetype. In particular, we must show the following properties:

Existence of Identity	sum $(a, 0)$ = a
Commutativity	sum (a, b) = sum (b, a)
Associativity	sum $[a, \text{sum } (b, c)]$ = sum $[\text{sum } (a, b), c]$

That 0 is an identity follows directly from the definition of sum. Now consider the commutative property; to prove this it is helpful if we first prove that

$$\text{sum } (m, n) = \text{succ}^n m$$

That is, sum (m, n) is the result of applying succ n times to m. This can be proved inductively. Second, we must prove that

$$m = \text{succ}^m 0$$

That is, m is the result of applying succ m times to 0. This is also easy to prove. Then we can prove commutativity by the following derivation:

$$
\begin{aligned}
\text{sum } (a, b) &= \text{succ}^b a \\
&= \text{succ}^b (\text{succ}^a 0) \\
&= \text{succ}^{b+a} 0 \\
&= \text{succ}^{a+b} 0 \\
&= \text{succ}^a (\text{succ}^b 0) \\
&= \text{succ}^a b \\
&= \text{sum } (b, a)
\end{aligned}
$$

Exercise 8.32: Carry out the proof of commutativity more rigorously. That is, prove inductively that sum $(m, n) = \text{succ}^n m$ and $m = \text{succ}^m 0$.

Exercise 8.33: Prove that our implementation of sum is associative.

Exercise 8.34: Define subtraction of natural numbers recursively.

Exercise 8.35: Prove that your definition of Exercise 8.34 satisfies these properties:

dif $(a, a) = 0$
dif $[a, \text{sum } (b, c)] = \text{dif } [\text{dif } (a, b), c]$

Exercise 8.36: Define multiplication of natural numbers recursively. The base of your recursion should be zero.

Exercise 8.37: Show that your definition of multiplication satisfies the following:

prod $(a, 1) = a$
prod $(a, b) = \text{prod } (b, a)$
prod $[a, \text{prod } (b, c)] = \text{prod } [\text{prod } (a, b), c]$
prod $[a, \text{sum } (b, c)] = \text{sum } [\text{prod } (a, b), \text{prod } (a, c)]$

Exercise 8.38: Discuss the recursive definition of division. Why is it more complicated than the other three arithmetic operations?

Exercise 8.39: Define recursively an equality test on natural numbers. *Hint:* Take the predecessor of both numbers until one or the other is zero. Can you think of an even simpler definition of equality?

Exercise 8.40:   Define recursively the less-than test on natural numbers.

Exercise 8.41: Prove the following properties of your less-than definition:

less $(0, 0)$ = **false**
less $(0, 1)$ = **true**
less (a, b) = less (succ a, succ b)

Exercise 8.42: Show that if less(a, b) = **true** and less (b, c) = **true**, then less (a, c) = **true**.

Exercise 8.43: The following function computes the quotient and remainder of the division of m by n:

$$
\textbf{let rec } \text{divide } (m, n) \equiv
\begin{cases}
(m, 0) & \text{if eq } (n, 1) \\
(0, m) & \text{if less } (m, n) \\
\textbf{else } (\text{succ } q, r) & \\
\quad \textbf{where } (q, r) \equiv \text{divide } [\text{dif } (m, n), n] &
\end{cases}
$$

Show that this definition satisfies the following:

divide $(a, 1)$ = $(a, 0)$
divide (a, b) = $(0, a)$, for $a < b$
right [divide (a, b)] = right [divide (dif [a, b], b)]
left [divide (a, b)] = succ (left {divide [dif (a, b), b]})

Exercise 8.44: Using properties of divide already established, show that if divide $(a, b) = (q, r)$, then

a = sum [prod $(b, q), r$]

Exercise 8.45: Using the divide function defined in the previous exercise, define quo (m, n) to be the quotient of m and n, and rem (m, n) to be the remainder of m and n.

Exercise 8.46: Using the functions on natural numbers already defined, but no conditionals (ifs) and no recursion, define the not-equal, greater-than, less-than-or-equal-to, and greater-than-or-equal-to relations.

Exercise 8.47: You have seen a definition of natural numbers based on a unary representation. Define natural number arithmetic in terms of a binary representation, such as sequences of Booleans. Define the four arithmetic operators, the comparison relations, and so forth.

Exercise 8.48: Using the facilities already provided, define integers in the lambda calculus. That is, pick a representation for integer numbers, and define the operations described in the integer archetype (Fig. 8.10). Show that your definitions satisfy the archetype.

Exercise 8.49: Discuss how you could define floating-point arithmetic in the lambda calculus.

Exercise 8.50: Define the string data type in the lambda calculus using the facilities already provided. *Hint:* Represent individual characters as natural numbers and represent strings as sequences of characters. Show that your definition satisfies the string archetype (Fig. B.3).

Chapter 9

Consistency of the Lambda Calculus

9.1 History

In the previous chapter we tried to convince you that the lambda calculus is *computationally complete*—that is, that it can be used to program anything that can be programmed at all. The basis for our argument was a demonstration that the primitive structures of functional languages can be expressed in the pure lambda calculus. If you think that the functional language is computationally complete, as supported by Part 1, then the preceding chapter should convince you that the lambda calculus is computationally complete. We cannot formally *prove*, however, that the lambda calculus is computationally complete: Computability is often defined in terms of the lambda calculus,[1] with the result that this calculus is computationally complete *by definition*. Although of course we could prove that the lambda calculus is equivalent to some other model of computation (e.g., Turing machines), this only begs the question. To convince ourselves that *any* of these models is computationally complete, we must appeal to informal arguments such as those in the preceding chapter.

---

1. See, for example, (Church 1936). This definition is commonly known as Church's Thesis, or sometimes the Church-Turing Thesis.

In this chapter we turn to the *computational consistency* of the lambda calculus. 'Consistency' means the compatability, agreement, or logical coherence of things; in this case we are concerned with the coherence of the computational processes defined by the lambda calculus. In particular, we want to know whether the result computed by a lambda calculus formula is well-defined, that is, whether there is a unique endpoint to the computational process—a question answered by the Church-Rosser Theorem.

The Church-Rosser Theorem has a long history: it was first proved by Alonzo Church and J. Barkley Rosser in 1936 (Church and Rosser 1936; Church 1941). This proof was very long and complicated, and much of the subsequent work on the theorem has aimed at simplifying it. Over the years the theorem has been proved in many different ways for many different calculi,[2] but the proofs have always been difficult. A trend toward shorter proofs began in 1972 with the work of W. Tait, P. Martin-Löf, and others. The proof we use is a new one developed and first presented by J. Barkley Rosser (1982). A more rigorous version is in (Barendregt 1984, Chapter 3).

9.2 Notation and Terminology

Since we are reasoning about substitutions, reductions, and other string operations on lambda calculus expressions, we must develop a notation to express these accurately. That is, we need a *metalanguage* for talking about the lambda calculus, our *object language*. To distinguish the object language from the metalanguage we adopt the convention that roman letters (e.g., x, y, z) are the identifiers used in lambda calculus expressions, but that italic letters (e.g., x, y, z, E, F) *stand for* expressions in the lambda calculus. The symbols 'λ', '(', and ')' stand for themselves. For example, if F stands for the expression '(λx(f x))' and E stands for the expression '(g a)', then the metalanguage notation $(F\ E)$ stands for the expression

$$((\lambda x(f\ x))\ (g\ a))$$

We adopt the further convention that lowercase italic letters (e.g., x, y, z) stand for lambda calculus identifiers (e.g., a, b, x, y); uppercase italic letters (e.g., A, E, F), for parenthesis-balanced lambda calculus expressions (e.g., '(f x)', 'f', '(λx(f x))'). Note that an uppercase italic letter may stand for a lambda calculus identifier since this is the simplest case of a parenthesis-balanced lambda calculus expression. Using these conventions we can describe the syntax of the pure (i.e., unextended) lambda

---

2. See, for example, (Newman 1942), (Curry, Feys, and Craig 1958), (Schroer 1965), (Hindley 1969), (Mitschke 1973), (Rosen 1973), (Hindley 1974), (Hindley, Lercher, and Selden 1972, Appendix 1), (Martin-Löf 1972), (Barendregt 1984), (Rosser 1982).

calculus as follows: A lambda expression has one of the three forms x, $(\lambda x B)$, or (FE).

We often wish to discuss lambda expressions embedded in larger lambda expressions. Thus we use the ellipsis '...' to represent an arbitrary sequence of characters. For example, '...$(\lambda x B)$...' represents any lambda expression containing an abstraction $(\lambda x B)$.

These notational conventions are *syntactic*, allowing us to describe lambda expressions having a given form. Next we introduce several *semantic* conventions, allowing us to describe transformations of lambda expressions.[3] The most fundamental transformation on lambda expressions is the substitution of an expression for a free identifier. Thus we use the notation $E[x = V]$ to represent the lambda expression that results from substituting V for all *free* occurrences of x in E. For example, if E is the expression

$$((\lambda a \ (f \ a)) \ ((g \ a) \ a))$$

and $x = $ 'a' and $V = $ '(h z)', then $E[x = V]$ is the expression

$$((\lambda a \ (f \ a)) \ ((g \ (h \ z)) \ (h \ z)))$$

The first two occurrences of 'a' were not replaced because they are not free occurrences.

We adopt the convention that the substitution operation applies to the immediately preceding metalinguistic variable. For example, $(F \ E[x = V])$ means that the substitution of V for x is performed in E but not F. To extend the scope of the substitution we use curly braces. For example, $\{(F \ E)\}[x = V]$ means that the substitution is to be performed in both F and E.

Using this substitution notation it is easy to define the semantics of the lambda calculus. There are two rules:

1. Renaming Rule: A subexpression $(\lambda x B)$ can be replaced by $(\lambda y \ B[x = y])$ provided y does not occur in B.

2. Substitution Rule: A subexpression $((\lambda x B)E)$ can be replaced by $B[x = E]$ provided no free identifier of E becomes bound as a result.

We must be able to describe the relation that holds between expressions when one results from the other by an application of the renaming or substitution rule. Thus we say E *reduces by renaming* to F whenever F results from an application of the renaming rule to E. That is,

---

3. Of course, we mean here the *computational* semantics, which refers to the computational process, not the *mathematical* semantics, which refers to the interpretation of lambda expressions as mathematical objects in some mathematical theory.

' ... (λxB) ... ' reduces by renaming to ' ... (λy B [x = y]) ... ', provided y does not occur in B. Notice that this relation is symmetric: If we can get from E to F by a renaming, then we can also get from F to E by a renaming. If F can be reached from E by *zero or more* renamings, we say that E and F are *equivalent up to renaming*.

Analogously, we say E *reduces by substitution* to F whenever F results from E by one application of the substitution rule. That is, ' ... ((λxB)V) ... ' reduces by substitution to ' ... B [x = V] ... ', provided no free identifier of V becomes bound as a result. Notice that this relation is *nonreflexive* and *antisymmetric*: If E reduces by substitution to F, then F does *not* reduce by substitution to E.

We write $E \Rightarrow F$, and say that E can be *reduced* to F, if F can be derived from E by a finite sequence of zero or more renamings and substitutions. This sequence of renamings and substitutions is called a *reduction* from E to F. We say that E is in *normal form* if the substitution rule cannot be applied to it; that is, there is no F (not equivalent to E up to renaming) such that $E \Rightarrow F$.

Finally, we say that E is *convertible* to F if E can be converted to F by a finite sequence of substitutions, reverse substitutions, or renamings.[4] That is, E is convertible to F if there are formulas $E_0, E_1, \ldots, E_n$ such that $E = E_0$, $E_n = F$, and, for each $1 \leq i \leq n$, $E_{i-1} \Rightarrow E_i$ or $E_i \Rightarrow E_{i-1}$. We then say that E *has a normal form* F if and only if F is in normal form and E is convertible to F. That is, E has a normal form F if and only if F can be reached from E by a finite sequence of substitutions, reverse substitutions and renamings. We said E has *a* normal form F rather than *the* normal form F because we have yet to show that the normal form is unique—which is precisely the purpose of the Church-Rosser Theorem.

Before stating and proving the theorem, we need one last definition. We say that a relation R *has the diamond property* if and only if the following holds for all well-formed formulas X, X_1 and X_2: If we have $X R X_1$ and $X R X_2$, then there is a well-formed formula X' such that $X_1 R X'$ and $X_2 R X'$. This can be represented by the following *confluence diagram*, in which the arrows represent the relation R:

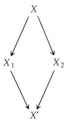

---

4. Note that convertibility is just the equality relation we defined in Section 8.5. Here we use the more precise technical term, reserving the symbol '=' for the identity of lambda expressions (as strings of symbols).

It is clear why Rosser (1982) and Barendregt (1984) call this the diamond property. The property is also called *confluence* (flowing together), especially in the context of abstract calculi (see Chapter 10).

Exercise 9.1: Suppose B is the expression (y (f y)). What expression does (λy B[y = x]) represent?

Exercise 9.2: Suppose M is the formula (λy (f y)) and N is the formula (λx (y (x y))). What formula does (M N)[y = a] represent?

Exercise 9.3: Are the following two formulas convertible?

((λf (f (f a))) (λx (g (g (g x)))))
((λh (h (h (h a)))) (λy (k (k y))))

Justify your answer.

9.3 Reachability and Uniqueness of Normal Form

The Church-Rosser Theorem can now be stated very simply:

The Church-Rosser Theorem: Reduction has the diamond property.

That is, if $X \Rightarrow X_1$ and $X \Rightarrow X_2$, then there is an X' such that $X_1 \Rightarrow X'$ and $X_2 \Rightarrow X'$. Before proving this, we must discuss the relevance of this theorem to evaluation order independence.

Notice that the Church-Rosser Theorem does *not* say anything about a formula's normal form being unique, but only asserts that two reduction sequences can eventually converge. Because uniqueness is an easy corollary of the main theorem, however, the two are commonly confused. To show this, also illustrating some of the techniques that will be used in the main proof, we state and prove this corollary.

Corollary If X has a normal form Y, then $X \Rightarrow Y$ and Y is unique (up to renaming). That is, if X has a normal form, then it is unique, and can be reached by reduction from X.

Proof:
We present an informal proof; you are asked to formalize it in Exercise 9.4. Since X has a normal form Y, X is convertible with Y. Therefore Y can be reached from X by a finite sequence of substitutions, reverse substitutions, and renamings. For example, a conversion of X into Y could be as follows:

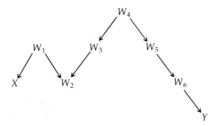

Here substitutions and renamings go downward, and reverse substitutions go upward.

Now, since reduction has the diamond property (remember that we assume the Church-Rosser Theorem), and since W_1 reduces to X and W_1 reduces to W_2, we know there is a W_7 such that X reduces to W_7 and W_2 reduces to W_7. Thus we can fill in the lower half of the first diamond:

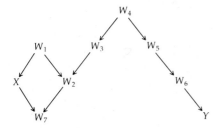

Since W_4 reduces to W_7 and W_4 reduces to Y, by the diamond property we can fill in W_8:

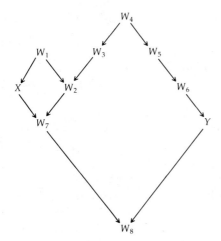

Hence there is a W (W_8 in this case) such that $X \Rightarrow W$ and $Y \Rightarrow W$. Now recall that (by hypothesis) Y is in normal form, which means that the substitution rule cannot be applied to Y. Therefore every step from Y to W must be a renaming step, which leads us to conclude Y is equivalent to W up to renaming. Since $X \Rightarrow W$ and W is equivalent to Y up to renaming, we have that $X \Rightarrow Y$. Thus we have shown that X can be reduced to its normal form. It remains to show that this normal form is unique.

Suppose X also has a normal form Z. Since (by the definition of having a normal form) Y is convertible into X and X is convertible into Z, we know Y is convertible into Z. Hence Y has a normal form Z. By the preceding reasoning, Y can reach its normal form, that is, $Y \Rightarrow Z$. Since Y is itself in normal form, however, renaming is the only reduction rule that applies. Therefore Y is equivalent to Z up to renaming; that is, Y is unique up to renaming. Q.E.D.

Exercise 9.4: Prove the preceding corollary more rigorously (i.e., by using induction on the number of steps in a conversion).

Exercise 9.5: If you look at your proof from the preceding exercise, you will see that it depends on only a few abstract properties of the '$\Rightarrow$' relation (such as transitivity and the diamond property). Determine what these properties are, and restate the theorem and proof as an abstract result about relations.

9.4 Walks

Our goal is to prove that reductions have the diamond property, but we do not prove this directly. As is often the case in mathematics, it is easier to prove a more specific result and then show that this implies the general result. Here we show that a very special kind of reduction, which Rosser calls a *walk*, has the diamond property. This is then the basis for showing that arbitrary reductions also have the diamond property.

We say that there is a *walk* from X to Y provided that $X \Rightarrow Y$, subject to the following *walk restriction*: If the reduction $X \Rightarrow Y$ contains substitutions for both $((\lambda x W)V)$ and $((\lambda y W')V')$, and the first is a proper subpart of the second, then the first substitution must be done before the second. This means that in a walk substitutions proceed from inside out; that is, inner substitutions are done before outer substitutions. It does *not* mean that a subformula must be reduced to normal form before it can be substituted, only that if it is to be reduced, then it must be reduced before it's substituted. For example, the following reduction is a walk:

$$((\lambda x(f\ x))\ ((\lambda y(g\ y))\ ((\lambda zz)\ a))) \qquad (9.1)$$
$$\Rightarrow ((\lambda x(f\ x))\ (g\ ((\lambda zz)\ a)))$$
$$\Rightarrow (f\ (g\ ((\lambda zz)\ a)))$$

The following reduction, however, is not a walk:

$$((\lambda x(f\ x))\ ((\lambda y(g\ y))\ ((\lambda zz)\ a)))$$
$$\Rightarrow\ (f\ ((\lambda y(g\ y))\ ((\lambda zz)\ a)))$$
$$\Rightarrow\ (f\ (g\ ((\lambda zz)\ a)))$$

This is because we performed the substitution $((\lambda y(g\ y))\ \ldots)$ after the substitution $((\lambda x(f\ x))\ \ldots)$, of which the former is a subpart. Notice that the subformula $((\lambda zz)\ a)$ is not a problem in either reduction since the substitution it represents is not done.

Note that the walk relation is *not* transitive: That is, just because we know there is a walk from X to Y and a walk from Y to Z, we cannot necessarily conclude that there is a walk from X to Z. More briefly, the catenation of two walks is not necessarily a walk. For example, if a walk from X to Y performs the substitution $((\lambda yW)V)$ and a walk from Y to Z performs the substitution $((\lambda xW')V')$, and if $((\lambda yW')V')$ is a proper part of $((\lambda xW)V)$, then the catenation of these walks will not be a walk.

Exercise 9.6:   Show that the following reduction is a walk

$$(f\ (g\ ((\lambda zz)\ a)))\ \Rightarrow\ (f\ (g\ a))$$

but that when it is catenated to the previous example of a walk (Eq. 9.1), it does not yield a walk.

9.5 Walks Are Substitutive

Next we prove a lemma that will be used several times in the proof of the theorem. This lemma says that if there is a walk from X to Y, then there is also a walk from $X[x = P]$ to $Y[x = P]$. That is, replacing in X and Y all the occurrences of a free identifier x by the same formula P does not affect the ability to walk from X to Y. We say that walks are *substitutive.*

The lemma can be visualized as follows. Suppose X is

$$X = {}' \ldots x \ldots x \ldots x \ldots{}'$$

That is, X is a string with some number (three in this example) free occurrences of x. The formula Y will also have zero or more free occurrences of x:

$$Y = {}' \ldots x \ldots x \ldots x \ldots x \ldots{}'$$

The steps in the walk from X to Y merely juggle these xs around, sometimes destroying an occurrence, sometimes making extra copies of it. If we replace all the free occurrences of x by P, we get

$$X[x = P] = ' \ldots P \ldots P \ldots P \ldots '$$

We can now apply to this formula exactly the same steps that got us from X to Y, except that now they will be juggling, destroying, and copying occurrences of P. Thus we will arrive by a walk at the formula

$$Y[x = P] = ' \ldots P \ldots P \ldots P \ldots P \ldots '$$

This lemma can be understood as stating the commutativity of two operations: a walk and a substitution. That is, suppose we walk from X to Y and then perform the substitution $[x = P]$; the result is $Y[x = P]$. The lemma says that if we *first* perform the substitution $[x = P]$ on X, yielding $X[x = P]$, then there will be a walk that takes this into the same result, $Y[x = P]$. In other words, we can perform the substitution either before or after the walk, and it will not affect the outcome.

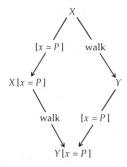

The lemma as proved has an additional restriction: None of the bound identifiers of X is a free identifier of X or P. This restriction eliminates the need for renaming steps in the walk from X to Y. The restriction is not important, however, since it can always be satisfied by first renaming the bound identifiers of X so that they are not the same as any of the free identifiers of X or P.

Lemma Suppose that X, Y, and P are well-formed formulas, that there is a walk from X to Y, and that none of the bound identifiers of X is a free identifier of X or P. Then there is a walk from $X[x = P]$ to $Y[x = P]$.

Proof:
If x does not occur free in X, then $X = X[x = P]$ and $Y = Y[x = P]$, so the

lemma is trivially true. Therefore suppose that x occurs free in X. The proof then proceeds by induction on the number of steps in the walk from X to Y. If this is zero, then $X = Y$, so $X[x = P] = Y[x = P]$, and there is thus a (length-zero) walk from $X[x = P]$ to $Y[x = P]$.

Now consider any walk from X to Y of length greater than zero. We can break this walk into two shorter walks, one from X to Z and another from Z to Y. Further suppose that Z is the last step in the walk from X to Y. Since the walk from X to Z is shorter than the walk from X to Y, we can apply the induction hypothesis and conclude that there is a walk from $X[x = P]$ to $Z[x = P]$. We must decide whether the catenation of this walk and the final step from $Z[x = P]$ to $Y[x = P]$ is also a walk.

This catenation could fail to be a walk only by failing to satisfy the walk restriction. That is, if the application reduced in going from $Z[x = P]$ to $Y[x = P]$ were a proper subpart of an application reduced in the walk from $X[x = P]$ to $Z[x = P]$, then the catenation of these reductions would not be a walk from $X[x = P]$ to $Y[x = P]$. To ensure that this is not the case, we make use of the fact that we have a walk from X to Y. Consider the last step in that walk. Since there is no overlap in the bound and free identifiers, there is no need for renamings in the walk from X to Y. Hence the step from Z to Y is a substitution:

$$Z = ' \ldots ((\lambda y W)V) \ldots ' \Rightarrow ' \ldots W[y = V] \ldots ' = Y$$

Since this is the last step in a walk from X to Y, we know that the application $((\lambda y W)V)$ is not a proper subpart of any application that was reduced earlier in the walk.

The walk from $X[x = P]$ to $Z[x = P]$ is exactly parallel to that from X to Z; that is, corresponding formulas are reduced at each step. The corresponding last step that takes $Z[x = P]$ into $Y[x = P]$ is

$$Z[x = P] = \{ \ldots ((\lambda y W)V) \ldots \}[x = P] \Rightarrow$$
$$\{ \ldots W[y = V] \ldots \}[x = P] = Y[x = P]$$

Therefore the formula in $Z[x = P]$ corresponding to $((\lambda y W)V)$ in Z—which we write $\{((\lambda y W)V)\}[x = P]$—will not be a proper subpart of any application already reduced in the walk from $X[x = P]$ to $Z[x = P]$. Therefore reducing the application $\{((\lambda y W)V)\}[x = P]$ will yield a legal walk, but will it yield $Y[x = P]$?

First consider an example. Note that $x \neq y$, since we have made the bound and free identifiers distinct. Since both x and y are identifiers (i.e., atomic symbols), and are in fact different identifiers, the occurrences of x and y in W cannot overlap. For example, suppose that

$$Z = ' \ldots x \ldots ((\lambda y(\ldots x \ldots y \ldots y \ldots))(\ldots x \ldots)) \ldots x \ldots '$$

Here $W = '(\ldots x \ldots y \ldots y \ldots)'$ and $V = '(\ldots x \ldots)'$. Since the xs and ys in W don't overlap, the xs and Vs in $W[y = V]$ will not overlap. For example,

$$Y = '\ldots x \ldots (\ldots x \ldots V \ldots V \ldots) \ldots x \ldots'$$

Here $W[y = V] = '(\ldots x \ldots V \ldots V \ldots)'$.
Now consider $Z[x = P]$:

$$Z[x = P] = '\ldots P \ldots ((\lambda y(\ldots P \ldots y \ldots y \ldots)) (\ldots P \ldots)) \ldots P \ldots'$$

It is easy to see that performing the substitution step yields the desired $Y[x = P]$:

$$Y[x = P] = '\ldots P \ldots (\ldots P \ldots (\ldots P \ldots) \ldots (\ldots P \ldots) \ldots) \ldots P \ldots'$$

Let's now show this more formally. We want to know whether

$$\{((\lambda y W)V)\}[x = P] \Rightarrow \{W[y = V]\}[x = P]$$

Note that

$$\{((\lambda y W)V)\}[x = P] = ((\lambda y W)[x = P] \, V[x = P])$$

Since x and y are distinct identifiers, we know $(\lambda y W)[x = P] = (\lambda y \, W[x = P])$. Now apply the substitution rule, obtaining:

$$((\lambda y \, W[x = P]) \, V[x = P]) \Rightarrow W[x = P][y = V[x = P]]$$

It is easy to see that $W[x = P][y = V[x = P]] = \{W[y = V]\}[x = P]$. That is, it doesn't make any difference whether we substitute P for x in V before or after V is substituted for y in W. This completes the proof of the lemma. Q.E.D.

9.6 Walks Have the Diamond Property

We now prove an important theorem that is the direct basis for proving the Church-Rosser Theorem.

Theorem Walks have the diamond property. That is, if there is a walk from X to X_1, and a walk from X to X_2, then there is an X' such that there is a walk from X_1 to X', and a walk from X_2 to X':

Proof:
The proof is by induction on the size of the formula X. Recall that there are exactly three legal forms for lambda expressions:

1. Identifiers: x

2. Abstractions: $(\lambda x M)$

3. Applications: (MN)

The proof is divided into three cases corresponding to these three kinds of lambda expressions.

Case 1: The first case forms the base of the induction, since the only lambda expressions of size 1 are the identifiers. Therefore suppose that X is a single identifier. Since no reduction rules can be applied to a free identifier, we have $X = X_1 = X_2$. Hence if we take $X' = X$ the theorem is true for formulas of size 1.

Case 2: Next we consider abstractions; suppose that $X = (\lambda x M)$. Notice that neither renaming nor reduction will remove the '$(\lambda \ldots)$' from around M.[5] Therefore the walk from X to X_1 can operate only on the body M of the abstraction. Thus X_1 must be of the form $(\lambda x M_1)$, where M_1 can be reached by a walk from M. The same reasoning shows us that X_2 has the form $(\lambda x M_2)$, where M_2 can be reached by a walk from M.

Since M is smaller than X we can apply the inductive hypothesis, which tells us that there is an M' that can be reached by walks from M_1 and M_2:

---

5. Actually, renaming could change the bound variable x, but this trivial change does not affect the following argument.

Clearly, if there is a walk from M_1 to M', then there is also a walk from $(\lambda x M_1)$ to $(\lambda x M')$. The same applies to M_2, so we have

$$(\lambda x M) \swarrow \searrow (\lambda x M_1) \quad (\lambda x M_2) \searrow \swarrow (\lambda x M')$$

Thus we take $X' = (\lambda x M')$, and we have established the theorem for the case of abstractions.

Case 3: Finally we consider the case in which X is an application, (MN). This case is not as easy as the previous one since we cannot assume that X_1 has the form $(M_1 N_1)$ or that X_2 has the form $(M_2 N_2)$. This is because the walk from X to X_1 might have performed the substitution implied by the application (MN). The same applies to the walk to X_2. Thus we have four subcases depending on whether or not the outermost application was reduced in either of the two walks:

	Applications Reduced	
	X to X_1	X to X_2
Subcase 1	No	No
Subcase 2	Yes	No
Subcase 3	No	Yes
Subcase 4	Yes	Yes

Subcase 1: In the simplest subcase, when neither application is reduced, we know that X_1 has the form $(M_1 N_1)$ and X_2 has the form $(M_2 N_2)$. As a result we can proceed as for case 2 (abstractions). Since there is a walk from (MN) to $(M_1 N_1)$, we can disentangle the steps that apply to M from those that apply to N and conclude that there is a walk from M to M_1 and a walk from N to N_1. Similar reasoning tells us that there is a walk from M to M_2 and a walk from N to N_2. Since M is smaller that X, we can apply the inductive hypothesis and conclude that there is an M' such that M_1 and M_2 both walk to M'. Similarly we conclude that there is an N' such that N_1 and N_2 both walk to N'.

Now, since we have a walk from M_1 to M' and a walk from N_1 to N', and since M and N do not overlap, we can catenate these two walks to yield a walk from $(M_1 N_1)$ to $(M'N')$. Similar reasoning shows us there is a walk from $(M_2 N_2)$ to $(M'N')$. Therefore we let $X' = (M'N')$ and we have proved subcase 1:

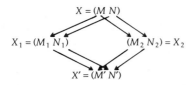

Subcase 2: Next we consider the case in which the application is reduced in the walk from X to X_1 but not in the walk from X to X_2. First consider the reduction from $X = (MN)$ to X_1. Since this reduction is a walk, inner substitutions must be performed before outer substitutions. Since the application (MN) is outermost, the resulting substitution must be the last substitution in the walk. Hence the last step in the walk from X to X_1 is a reduction of a string of the form $((\lambda y W_1)N_1)$ to a string of the form $W_1[y = N_1]$. Let $M_1 = (\lambda y W_1)$ and observe that there are walks from M to M_1 and from N to N_1 (extracted from the walk from X to X_1).

Now consider the walk from X to X_2. Since the outermost application is not performed in this walk, X_2 must still have the form $(M_2 N_2)$, where there are walks from M to M_2 and from N to N_2. We apply the inductive hypothesis to M and conclude that there is an M' reachable by walks from M_1 and M_2. But recall that M_1 is $(\lambda y W_1)$. Since none of the steps in the walk from M_1 to M' can remove the surrounding $(\lambda y \ldots)$ from M_1, M' must also have the form $(\lambda y W')$. Therefore there is a walk from M_2 to $(\lambda y W')$, and hence a walk from X_2 to $((\lambda y W')N_2)$. We can diagram this as follows:

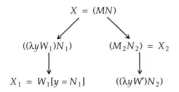

By the inductive hypothesis, there is an N' reachable by walks from both N_1 and N_2. Therefore let X' be $W'[y = N']$, which we must now show can be reached by walks from X_1 and X_2.

We have already shown that there is a walk from X_2 to $((\lambda y W')N_2)$. Since there is a walk from N_2 to N', we can walk from $((\lambda y W')N_2)$ to $((\lambda y W')N')$. Since M_2 and N_2 do not overlap, we can catenate these two walks to yield a walk from X_2 to $((\lambda y W')N')$. Since this application is outermost, we can perform it without violating the walk restriction to yield $W'[y = N']$. Thus X' can be reached from X_2 by a walk.

Now consider X_1; we must show that there is a walk from $X_1 = W_1[y = N_1]$ to $X' = W'[y = N']$. Since we have a walk from N_1 to N', we can perform the steps of this walk on each copy of N_1 in $W_1[y = N_1]$, yielding $W_1[y = N']$. Since these copies of N_1 are disjoint, the catenation of these walks is a walk. Thus there is a walk from X_1 to $W_1[y = N']$.

Now we must show that there is a walk from $W_1[y = N']$ to $W'[y = N']$.

But we know this is true by our lemma since there is a walk from W_1 to W', implying a walk from $W_1[y = N']$ to $W'[y = N']$. Hence we know that there is a walk from $W_1[y = N']$ to X'.

We have walks from X_1 to $W_1[y = N']$ and from $W_1[y = N']$ to X'. We cannot immediately conclude, however, that there is a walk from X_1 to X'. To do this we must observe that we first operated on the copies of N_1, which are subformulas of $W_1[y = N_1]$. Therefore we did not violate the walk restriction by doing these first. Hence there is a walk from X_1 to X', and we have proved subcase 2.

Subcase 3: In this subcase, the application is reduced in the second walk (from X to X_2) but not in the first. The proof is exactly analogous to the previous subcase.

Subcase 4: In this subcase, the indicated application is performed in both of the walks. By the same reasoning as in subcase 2, we know that the last step in the walk from X to X_1 is the reduction of $((\lambda y W_1)N_1)$ to $W_1[y = N_1]$. Similarly, the last step in the walk from X to X_2 is the reduction of $((\lambda y W_2)N_2)$ to $W_2[y = N_2]$. As before, W_1 and W_2 can be reached by walks from W, and N_1 and N_2 are reachable by walks from N. Therefore we apply the induction hypothesis to get W' and N' such that W' is reachable from W_1 and W_2 by walks, and N' from N_1 and N_2 by walks.

The obvious choice for X' is $W'[y = N']$, but we must show that this can be reached from X_1 and X_2 by walks. Let's reduce $X_1 = W_1[y = N_1]$ to $W_1[y = N']$, and then reduce this to $W'[y = N'] = X'$, using the steps in the walk from N_1 to N' to operate individually on each copy of N_1 in $W_1[y = N_1]$. Because these copies do not overlap, this sequence of operations is a walk, yielding $W_1[y = N']$. Now by the lemma, since there is a walk from W_1 to W', we know there is a walk from $W_1[y = N']$ to $W'[y = N']$. The catenation of this walk with the previous one is also a walk because the copies of N_1 are proper subformulas of $W_1[y = N_1]$.

Hence we have a walk from X_1 to X'. Exactly analogous reasoning shows that there is a walk from X_2 to X', which proves this subcase. This completes the last subcase of the last case. Q.E.D.

9.7 Reduction Has the Diamond Property

We have shown that the walk relation has the diamond property. Next we show that any finite sequence of walks has the diamond property. Since a single renaming or substitution step is a walk, the Church-Rosser Theorem then follows easily.

Lemma Finite sequences of walks have the diamond property. That is, if X reduces to X_1 by a finite sequence of walks, and X reduces to X_2 by a finite sequence of walks, then there is an X' such that X_1 and X_2 each reduce to X' by a finite sequence of walks.

Proof:
Rather than prove the lemma rigorously, we use an informal demonstration. The formal proof is left as an exercise.

Suppose that X reduces to X_1 by a sequence of three walks. That is, there is a walk from X to W_1, a walk from W_1 to W_2, and a walk from W_2 to X_1. Similarly, suppose that X reaches X_2 by two walks, from X to W_3 and from W_3 to X_2. This can be diagrammed as follows:

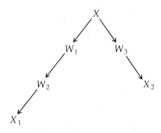

Now, by the diamond property of walks, we can fill in a W_4 such that there are walks from W_1 and W_3 to W_4. This process can be continued until all the diamonds are filled in:

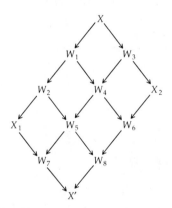

We can see that there is an X' that can be reached by a finite sequence of walks from both X_1 and X_2. This completes our informal demonstration. *Q.E.D.*

Exercise 9.7: Make the preceding proof more rigorous by using induction.

Church-Rosser Theorem Reduction has the diamond property. That is, if $X \Rightarrow X_1$ and $X \Rightarrow X_2$ then there is an X' such that $X_1 \Rightarrow X'$ and $X_2 \Rightarrow X'$.

Proof:
Note that a single renaming or substitution step is a legal walk. Thus, since a reduction is a finite sequence of renamings and substitutions, a reduction is a finite sequence of walks. Since finite sequences of walks have the diamond property, so also do reductions. *Q.E.D.*

The Church-Rosser Theorem shows that reductions that diverge from each other can eventually be brought back together, that is, they are *confluent*. This implies (by the corollary in Section 9.3) that normal forms are unique. Thus the computational consistency of the lambda calculus is established.

9.8 Introduction to the Halting Problem

The Church-Rosser Theorem implies that if a formula has a normal form, then that normal form is unique. How can we determine whether a formula has a normal form? In particular, can we write a program that will determine whether a given lambda calculus expression has a normal form? A related problem is whether *all* reduction sequences lead to the normal form of a formula, that is, whether the formula does not permit nonterminating reductions. In this section we address the existence of *decision procedures* for answering questions such as these.

The *halting problem* addresses the question of whether there is an algorithm that will decide whether a given formula has a normal form. The problem was first addressed and answered (in the negative) by Alan Turing in 1936 (Turing 1936). Turing's proof is long and complicated because he used Turing machines as a model of computation. Our use of the lambda calculus as a model of computation and our prior reduction of Φ to the lambda calculus (Chapter 8) greatly simplify the proof.

The goal is to be able to decide for any given lambda expression whether that lambda expression has a normal form. Notice, however, that for lambda expressions to be operated on by algorithms they must be represented as data structures. In this case we assume that lambda expressions are represented in the obvious way as trees:

> **abstract structure** lamexp $\equiv$ id: **string**   (9.2)
> $+$ lambda (bv $\in$ **string**, body $\in$ lamexp)
> $+$ appl (rator $\in$ lamexp, rand $\in$ lamexp)

We use $\overline{E}$ (pronounced "the representation of E" or "E's representation") to denote the tree corresponding to the lambda expression E. For example, if E is the expression '$(\lambda x(f\,x))$', then

$$\overline{E} = \text{lambda ['x', appl (id 'f', id 'x')]}$$

Exercise 9.8:   For each of the following lambda expressions E, give the corresponding representation $\bar{E}$:

a. '(λx (y (x y)))'

b. '((λx (f x)) (g a))'

c. 'λtf.t'

d. 'λc.cxy'

e. 'λf. [λx.f(xx)] [λx.f(xx)]'

Exercise 9.9:   Reduce each of the following formulas in Φ to a formula E in the pure lambda calculus (see Chapter 8 for reductions), and then give the corresponding representation $\bar{E}$. For example, given '(a, b)' you should first reduce as follows:

$$(a, b) \Rightarrow \text{pair } a\ b \qquad\qquad (9.3)$$
$$\Rightarrow (\lambda xy.\ \lambda c.cxy)ab$$
$$\Rightarrow \lambda c.cab$$

This is represented by the data structure

$$\overline{(a, b)} = \text{lambda } \{\text{'c', appl [appl (id 'c', } \bar{a}), \bar{b}]\} \qquad\qquad (9.4)$$

where $\bar{a}$ and $\bar{b}$ are the trees representing the lambda expressions a and b.

a. nil

b. **false**

c. prefix (x, S)

d. 1st S

e. 2 (i.e., the natural number 2; see Section 8.13)

f. succ n

Exercise 9.10:   In this exercise you define functions that construct the trees representing the pure lambda calculus equivalents of various data structures. For example, you saw in Eq. (9.3) that the pair (a, b) is represented by the lambda expression $\lambda c.cab$, which is represented by the tree in Eq. (9.4). Hence the following function $\overrightarrow{\text{pair}}$: lamexp$^2 \to$ lamexp constructs the tree corresponding to (a, b) from the trees $\bar{a}$ and $\bar{b}$:

$$\overrightarrow{\text{pair}}\ (\bar{a}, \bar{b}) \equiv \text{lambda } \{\text{'c', appl [appl (id 'c', } \bar{a}), \bar{b}]\}$$

Define the following analogous functions:

a. $\overrightarrow{1st}$ and $\overrightarrow{2nd}$.

b. $\overrightarrow{prefix}$

c. $\overrightarrow{succ}$

Hint: Keep your answers simple by first defining **true** and $\overline{\text{false}}$, the trees representing **true** and **false**.

Exercise 9.11: This exercise is exactly like the preceding, but may be more confusing. The goal is to define the functions $\overrightarrow{id}$, lambda, and $\overrightarrow{appl}$ that convert lamexp trees into the lamexp trees that represent the pure lambda expressions to which the input trees are reduced.[6] To this end, note that Eq. (9.2) is equivalent to

lamexp ≡ **string** + (**string** × lamexp + lamexp × lamexp)

Therefore

appl (F, E) = 2nd [2nd (F, E)] = 2nd [2nd (pair F E)]

This permits the definition of the constructor for trees representing applications:

$\overrightarrow{appl}$ $(\bar{F}, \bar{E})$ = $\overrightarrow{2nd}$ {$\overrightarrow{2nd}$ [$\overrightarrow{pair}$ $(\bar{F}, \bar{E})$]}

a. Define $\overrightarrow{id}$; assume that you have conv: **string** → lamexp so that conv s converts a string s into the corresponding lambda expression tree.

b. Define $\overrightarrow{lambda}$, given conv: **string** → lamexp.

Exercise 9.12: In this exercise you define functions that convert various data structures into the trees representing their pure lambda calculus equivalents. For example, to define an operation conv: $\mathbb{B}$ → lamexp that converts a Boolean to the tree representing its lambda calculus equivalent,

conv **true** ≡ $\overline{\text{true}}$
conv **false** ≡ $\overline{\text{false}}$

Based on answers to preceding exercises, define the following conversion functions:

6. Note that a data type is being used to represent itself. An analogy may make this clear. ASCII strings such as 'ABC' may be represented by sequences of natural numbers, such as 65, 66, 67. But sequences of natural numbers can be represented by ASCII strings of decimal digits, such as '656667'. Thus the ASCII string '656667' represents (indirectly) the ASCII string 'ABC'.

a. conv: $S \times T \to$ lamexp, for any types S, T

b. conv: $S + T \to$ lamexp, for any types S, T

c. conv: $T^* \to$ lamexp, for any type T

d. conv: lamexp $\to$ lamexp. Of course the intent of this function is that, for example,

$$\text{conv } [\text{appl } (F, E)] = \overrightarrow{\text{appl}} \, (\text{conv } F, \text{ conv } E)]$$

9.9 Undecidability of the Halting Problem

Now let's state the halting problem more precisely. The halting problem is to determine whether or not there exists a functional program Halts that, given a tree $\bar{E} \in$ lamexp representing a lambda expression E, will determine whether E has a normal form. That is, we want Halts $\bar{E} = $ **true** if E has a normal form, and Halts $\bar{E} = $ **false** if it doesn't. Notice that Halts returns either **true** or **false**, and hence halts itself, for any tree representing a lambda calculus expression. Mathematically, Halts: lamexp $\to \mathbb{B}$ is a *total* function. The function Halts is called a *decision procedure* for the halting problem for the lambda calculus.

Theorem (Turing) There is no decision procedure for the halting problem for the lambda calculus.

Proof:
The only way to prove the nonexistence of something is to show that its existence would contradict other assertions whose truth we do not doubt. Hence we prove the theorem by assuming the existence of a decision procedure and showing that this leads to a contradiction.

Therefore suppose that we have a definition in Φ of a program Halts defined so that Halts $\bar{E} = $ **true** or **false** depending on whether or not the lambda expression E has a normal form. Following Turing, we derive a contradiction from this supposition by a diagonalization argument similar to that used by Cantor to show that the real numbers are not countable. You will recall that Cantor's argument proceeds by assuming that we have an enumeration of the reals, and then constructing a real number that is guaranteed to be different from every real in the enumeration, thus contradicting the assumption that the reals could be enumerated. Turing's proof has a similar structure.

Consider all the possible function applications FL in which a function F: lamexp $\to \mathbb{N}$ is applied to a tree $L \in$ lamexp. Let's define a function

Terminates: lamexp $\times$ lamexp $\to \mathbb{B}$

so that Terminates $(\bar{F}, L)$ is **true** if FL halts, and **false** otherwise.[7] Notice that we pass to Terminates the tree $\bar{F}$ representing F rather than the function F itself.

Clearly we will use Halts to define Terminates, but Halts requires the program to be represented as a tree. Therefore we compute the tree representing FL:

$$\overline{FL} = \text{appl}\,(\bar{F}, \bar{L})$$

where $\bar{L} \in$ lamexp is the tree representing the pure lambda expression corresponding to L (which also happens to be of type lamexp; recall Exercise 9.11). Then Terminates satisifes the identity:

$$\text{Terminates}\,(\bar{F}, L) = \text{Halts}\,[\text{appl}\,(\bar{F}, \bar{L})]$$

Notice that we have L on the left but $\bar{L}$ on the right. To complete the definition we need a function to convert L to its representation. This is routine to define, as you saw in Exercise (9.12). Therefore, letting $\bar{L} = \text{conv}\,L$, we have defined Terminates as follows:

$$\text{Terminates}\,(\bar{F}, L) \equiv \text{Halts}\,[\text{appl}\,(\bar{F}, \text{conv}\,L)]$$

Since Halts (by hypothesis) is computable, so is Terminates. That is, it is total on lamexp $\times$ lamexp.

To perform the diagonalization, we consider the value of Terminates $(\bar{F_i}, \bar{F_j})$ for all possible pairs of trees representing lambda expressions, $(\bar{F_i}, \bar{F_j}) \in$ lamexp $\times$ lamexp. We can imagine these values arranged as an infinite table:

Terminates	$\bar{F_1}$	$\bar{F_2}$	$\bar{F_3}$	$\ldots$
$\bar{F_1}$	true	false	false	$\ldots$
$\bar{F_2}$	false	false	false	$\ldots$
$\bar{F_3}$	false	true	true	$\ldots$
$\vdots$	$\vdots$	$\vdots$	$\vdots$	

Thus the (i, j) entry of this table is **true** or **false** depending on whether or not the application $F_i\bar{F_j}$ halts.

By hypothesis (since Terminates works on all members of lamexp) every lambda calculus function has a representation appearing somewhere among the $\bar{F_i}$. Our goal is to reach a contradiction by constructing a

---

7. In fact, we define Terminates so that it works on any pairs of lambda expression trees, not just those pairs representing functions lamexp $\rightarrow$ IN and arguments in lamexp.

function that cannot appear among the F_i. Thus we need a function Q: lamexp $\rightarrow$ IN whose behavior differs from each F_i on at least one input value. We do this by going down the diagonal of the preceding table and negating each entry, thus defining a halting behavior for Q that differs from every other entry in the table. In particular, if $F_i\overline{F_j}$ halts, then $Q\overline{F_j}$ will not halt; and if $F_i\overline{F_j}$ doesn't halt, then $Q\overline{F_j}$ will halt:

Terminates	$\overline{F_1}$	$\overline{F_2}$	$\overline{F_3}$	$\ldots$
$\overline{Q}$	false	true	false	$\ldots$

Such a Q is easy to define:

$$Q\overline{F} \equiv \begin{cases} \Omega, \text{ if Terminates } (\overline{F}, \overline{F}) \\ \textbf{else } 0 \end{cases}$$

Recall (Section 8.5) that the formula Ω leads to a nonterminating reduction. Hence $Q\overline{F_i}$ halts if and only if $F_i\overline{F_i}$ doesn't halt. Thus Q cannot be F_i, for any of the F_i.

We have now reached a contradiction. Q is defined in terms of Terminates, and Terminates is defined in terms of Halts. Thus, if Halts is definable in Φ, then so is Q. But, since every Φ program can be reduced to a pure lambda calculus expression, the definition of Q can be reduced to a pure lambda calculus expression with a representation $\overline{Q}$. But by hypothesis, the $\overline{F_i}$ are all the lambda expressions, so for some q, $\overline{Q} = \overline{F_q}$. The contradiction arises from the construction of Q, which differs in its halting behavior from each F_i on at least one input (i.e., $\overline{F_i}$). But the F_i include all functions.

We can see an even simpler contradiction by asking whether $Q\overline{Q}$ terminates. By the definition of Q, $Q\overline{F}$ terminates if and only if $\overline{FF}$ doesn't terminate. Hence, substituting Q for F, $Q\overline{Q}$ terminates if and only if $Q\overline{Q}$ doesn't terminate, which is a contradiction. Hence we must reject at least one of our hypotheses. Since the only hypothesis open to question is the assumption that Halts exists, this is the hypothesis we reject. $Q.E.D.$

It is important to notice that the same proof technique shows that there do not exist decision procedures for any nontrivial properties of the lambda calculus—a generalization of Turing's result known as *Rice's Theorem* (Rice 1953). Suppose that we had a procedure Decide_P for deciding whether or not a given lambda expression does or does not do P. Then we can define a function (analogous to Terminates) that determines whether a function F does P when applied to a tree L:

Does_P $(\overline{F}, L) \equiv$ Decide_P [appl $(\overline{F}$, conv $L)$]

Next, assuming that we can explicitly control the doing or not doing of P (in the way we controlled halting by computing either Ω or 0), we can define Q as follows:

$$Q\bar{F} \equiv \begin{cases} \textit{don't do } P, & \text{if } \texttt{Does\_P}\ (\bar{F}, \bar{F}) \\ \textbf{else } \textit{do } P \end{cases}$$

Then considering whether or not $Q\bar{Q}$ does P leads directly to a contradiction.[8]

Exercise 9.13: Carry this argument through in detail by showing that there cannot be a decision procedure for determining whether an expression reduces to 0 (or any other chosen value).

On the other hand, not all properties P are under direct control. For example, if P is "halts within 10 minutes," then we might not be able to define a suitable Q. Consider the following definition:

$$Q\bar{F} \equiv \begin{cases} \textit{run for at least 10 minutes}, & \text{if } \texttt{Halts\_in\_10}\ (\bar{F}, \bar{F}) \\ \textbf{else } \textit{stop immediately} \end{cases}$$

This does not lead to a contradiction since if 'Halts_in_10 $(\bar{F}, \bar{F})$' requires 10 or more minutes to run, then $Q\bar{F}$ always requires at least 10 minutes to run, regardless of $\bar{F}$. Hence no contradiction arises, even from the self-application $Q\bar{Q}$. This does not mean, of course, that the decision procedure Halts_in_10 exists, but only that the diagonalization process does not show its nonexistence. In general the diagonalization proof works for unlimited properties (e.g., halts eventually), but not for limited properties (e.g., halts in 10 minutes).

Exercise 9.14: Show in detail that no contradiction arises from the application $Q\bar{Q}$, where Q is defined in terms of Halts_in_10 as just shown.

Exercise 9.15: Is there a decision procedure for the property of halting within 10 minutes? Explain.

Exercise 9.16: Give three examples of properties of algorithms for which there are no decision procedures. Give three examples of properties for which there might be decision procedures (i.e., the diagonalization process does not lead to a contradiction).

---

8. The similarity to Russell's paradox (Section 7.3) should be apparent. One difference here is that by using the representation $\bar{Q}$ rather than the function Q, the formula $Q\bar{Q}$ avoids problematic self-applications like $\Omega = \omega\omega$ (Section 8.5).

Chapter 10

Abstract Calculi

It is manifest that if we could find characters or signs appropriate to the expression of all our thoughts as definitely and as exactly as numbers are expressed by arithmetic . . . [then] all inquiries that depend on reasoning would be performed by the transposition of characters and by a kind of calculus that would directly assist the discovery of elegant results.

Gottfried Wilhelm von Leibniz,
On Method, Preface to the General Science (1677)

10.1 Advantages and Disadvantages of Calculi

A *calculus* is a notation that can be manipulated mechanically to achieve some end. In our investigation of the completeness of the lambda calculus in Chapter 8, you saw that calculi can be very powerful. The lambda calculus, defined by three formation rules and two transformation rules, can compute any computable function; in a sense this simple system is as powerful as any computer. Clearly the mechanical rearrangement of symbols has a lot of potential, which we investigate in this chapter.

You might object that although the lambda calculus can compute any computable function, it does this very inefficiently—certainly the definition of arithmetic in terms of the successor function is not very economical. In fact the inefficiency of the lambda calculus partly results from the fact that it tries to do so much with so little. In this chapter we will investigate more specialized and therefore more efficient calculi.

One advantage of calculi is that, by reducing a process to a set of mechanical rules, we decrease the chances of making an error in that process. This is the purpose of the arithmetical algorithms that we all learned as children. By mechanically applying the rules for copying digits, adding digits, carrying, borrowing, and so forth we can perform arithmetic operations reliably.

The benefits of reducing various thought processes to mechanical symbol manipulation have long been recognized. For example, Leibniz[1] urged the development of a calculus of reasoning that would permit all disputes to be settled by a process of calculation. In a letter to Johann Friedrich, Duke of Hanover, in 1679, he said that, rather than argue, rational men would simply "take their pencils in their hands, sit down to their slates, and say to each other . . . *'calculemus'* [let us calculate]."

Another advantage of calculi is more recent: If the mechanical rules of a calculus are computable, then the calculus can be implemented on a computer and the application of the rules automated. Thus, by developing a calculus for a process, we are well on the way to automating it. Indeed a computer can be viewed as a device for carrying out the symbol-manipulation rules of a calculus.

Calculi are purely *formal*, dealing solely with the arrangement and rearrangement of symbols, but completely disregarding the meaning of those symbols.[2] The symbols of a calculus are treated as meaningless tokens (i.e., pebbles—*calculi*) that are manipulated according to mechanical rules. Any meaning we might attach to the symbols is irrelevant to their manipulation—which is what makes them ideal bases for computer processing.

The formal character of a calculus is both an advantage and a disadvantage. By ignoring the meaning or interpretation of symbols and concentrating on their form, calculi are amenable to automated processing—certainly an advantage. The disadvantage, however, is that a calculus can deal with meaning only to the extent to which that meaning can be embodied in the arrangement—the syntax—of the symbols. The individual symbols have no meaning, which is what ultimately prevents us from reaching Leibniz's goal.

If we are concerned with the meaning of the arrangements of the symbols, then we must take care that the rules of the calculus preserve this meaning as they rearrange the symbols. Starting with an arrangement of symbols that has meaning, by the rules of the calculus we might change it into a meaningless arrangement—a trap if we are concerned with *interpreting* a calculus, that is, attaching a meaning to the symbols and their arrangements.

---

1. Gottfried Wilhelm von Leibniz (1646–1716), German philosopher and mathematician, co-inventor of the integral and differential calculi. Leibniz also experimented with calculi for knowledge representation and inference; see (Parkinson 1966).
2. In this sense calculi are entirely *syntactic;* they have no *semantics.* Here of course 'semantics' refers to some external interpretation of the formulas of the calculus, perhaps in a mathematical theory. Note, however, that since calculi define a computational process, they do have a computational semantics. See Section 8.4 for more on mathematical versus computational semantics.

When we presented the lambda calculus, we freely interpreted its formulas as functions, applications, and so forth. This is valid as motivation, but we must be cautious if we want to take this interpretation seriously. It is not obvious that every lambda calculus formula describes a mathematically meaningful object. For example, this calculus permits functions that can be applied to themselves, which are generally rejected by mathematicians. Fortunately Dana Scott (Scott 1970, 1974; Milne and Strachey 1976) has developed an elegant mathematical theory that defines the exact conditions under which lambda calculus formulas can be interpreted as generally recognized mathematical objects. This theory, however, uses sophisticated mathematical techniques that are beyond the scope of this book. Since we interpret calculi only for motivational purposes we do not need it.

Exercise 10.1:   List at least three calculi (other than the lambda calculus) with which you are familiar; they need not have the word 'calculus' in their names. For each calculus, identify the process that is reduced to mechanical rules, and discuss limitations or dangers in the strictly syntactic manipulation of symbols.

10.2 Definition of Calculi

Let's now consider how calculi are defined, using the lambda calculus as a case from which to abstract some general principles. Recall that we defined the lambda calculus in two steps. First, we defined all the arrangements of symbols that are to be allowed as lambda calculus formulas, by stating three *formation rules* that define the ways in which the individual symbols can be assembled into well-formed formulas. In the case of the lambda calculus we said that if x was a symbol and E and F were well-formed formulas, then x, (λxE), and (FE) were to be counted as well-formed formulas. The formation rules can be more briefly expressed in a context-free grammar in a notation such as BNF:

$$\text{lambda\_exp} \equiv \begin{cases} \text{identifier} \\ (\lambda \text{ identifier lambda\_exp}) \\ (\text{lambda\_exp lambda\_exp}) \end{cases} \qquad (8.3)$$

$$\text{identifier} \equiv \text{a} \mid \text{b} \mid \cdots$$

To complete the definition of a calculus, we must define the permitted means for *rearranging* the symbols; this is done by stating one or more *transformation rules* (also known as *rewrite rules*). For example, the allowable rearrangements of lambda calculus formulas are defined by two transformation rules, renaming and substitution:

1. $(\lambda x\ E) \Rightarrow (\lambda y\ E[x = y])$, if y does not occur in E.

2. $((\lambda xE)\ V) \Rightarrow E[x = V]$, if the bound variables of E are distinct from the free variables of V.

Notice that there may be constraints on transformation rules that limit their applicability.[3] Also notice that these transformation rules for the lambda calculus presuppose the substitution process: '$-[-=-]$'. In Section 10.8 we investigate the definition of this process.

10.3 Transformation Rules

As we have seen, the formation rules of a calculus can be described by a context-free grammar in a notation such as BNF. How can the transformation rules of a calculus be defined? In particular, can they be defined in a way that allows them to be executed on a computer? Since the purpose of the transformation rules is to show the permitted rearrangements of symbols, the simplest way to describe them is by showing the arrangement of symbols before and after the transformation.

We have in fact been using transformation rules all along—to introduce syntactic sugar. Consider the following example, similar to one we saw in Section 8.11:

$$E\ \textbf{where}\ v \equiv X\ \Rightarrow\ (\lambda vE)X$$

This means that whenever we see an arrangement of symbols matching the pattern 'E **where** $v \equiv X$' we can replace it by the arrangement '$(\lambda vE)X$', thus eliminating the syntactic sugar. For example, this transformation rule permits the string

$$\text{'sin}[(a - 1) \times (a - 2)\ \textbf{where}\ a \equiv x \times y]\text{'}$$

to be rearranged into

$$\text{'sin}[\lambda a\ [(a - 1) \times (a - 2)]\ (x \times y)]\text{'}$$

The pattern on the left of the transformation rule matches the original arrangement when $E = \text{'}(a - 1) \times (a - 2)\text{'}$, $v = \text{'}a\text{'}$ and $X = \text{'}x \times y\text{'}$. These

---

3. In this case we have not stated the constraints rigorously; see Section 11.3. Obviously, to be executed on a computer, a calculus must be specified with complete formality.

values are then substituted in the template on the right of the rule to yield the new arrangement that replaces the original.[4]

Thus the general form of a transformation rule is

analysis $\Rightarrow$ *synthesis*

where *analysis* is a pattern describing the *a priori* arrangement of symbols, and *synthesis* is a template describing the *a posteriori* arrangement of symbols.

Both parts of a transformation rule are composed of the same elements: constants and variables. Constants—symbols such as 'sin', ']', and '**let**'—stand for themselves. In the analysis part of a rule this means that they match themselves. Variables—symbols such as '*v*' and '*E*'—stand for arbitrary strings (arrangements of symbols), possibly a different string each time the rule is applied. Let's adopt the convention that within an application of a rule the same variable always stands for the same string. For example, if X stands for '$x \times y$' during the analysis, then it stands for the same string during the synthesis. Further, if the same variable appears more than once in the analysis part, then each occurrence must match the same string in any given application of the rule.

Exercise 10.2: Show how the transformation rules for **let rec**, **let**, and **Y** will transform a recursive declaration into a pure lambda calculus formula (see Sections 8.11 and 8.12).

Exercise 10.3: Investigate either the propositional or the predicate calculus. Write a context-free grammar for the formation rules for this calculus. Write transformation rules expressing the rules of inference of this calculus.

10.4 Disadvantages of Concrete Calculi

The calculi we have discussed are based on strings of symbols; the formation rules describe sets of well-formed strings, while the transformation rules rearrange the symbols constituting these strings. These calculi are called *concrete calculi* because they deal with specific syntactic representations of information structures. To motivate an investigation of *abstract calculi* later in this chapter, we must first explore concrete calculi further.

The string-transformation rules discussed so far have several important limitations, which we illustrate using a definition of arithmetic based

---

4. The binding of the variables in a pattern is clearly related to the unification process described in Section 5.10; the exact connection is discussed in Section 10.12.

on unary notation similar to that in Section 8.13. Recall, for example, that the number five is represented by the string

'succ (succ (succ (succ (succ (0)))))'

This notation, while very suggestive, cannot be taken too literally. Remember that a calculus is completely formal: The transformation rules operate independently of the meaning of the symbols. Thus, although the preceding string is obviously *intended* to represent a composition of five applications of the successor function to zero, in fact it is simply a string of characters, a data structure, that can be used to represent a natural number. Although it would be less readable, we could as easily represent five by the string

'* * * * *!'

It is only important that at least one string represent each natural number. As long as this is kept in mind, there is no harm, and considerable advantage, in using symbols that suggest their intended meaning. Clearly, however, the transformation rules have no knowledge of this intended meaning; that exists only in our heads.

To make effective use of calculi—that is, computers—it is valuable to be able to shift between the syntactic and semantic viewpoints. When we consider a calculus from the semantic viewpoint, we pay attention to the intended meaning of the symbols. This viewpoint has great motivational value since it helps us understand the *purpose* of the calculus. On the other hand, when we view a calculus from the syntactic viewpoint, then we ignore the intended meaning of the symbols, viewing the formulas as formal arrangements of arbitrary tokens—we then take a machine's view of the calculus. This is useful in understanding the way a calculus actually works, for example, when debugging it. There is, however, an even more important benefit of the syntactic viewpoint. By freeing ourselves of the intended interpretation, we can often see formal transformations of the symbol structures that make no sense semantically yet help us achieve the goals of the calculus. Examples of the syntactic (or purely formal) approach abound in mathematics; the use of differentials and generating functions are two cases that allow the manipulation of symbols that are apparently meaningless, and yet achieve correct results.

Let's now define the formation rules of our arithmetic calculus. We want to allow initial strings such as '$2 + 3 \times 5$', intermediate strings such as '$2 + \text{succ} (\text{succ} (1)) \times 5$', and final (normal forms) strings such as

'succ (succ (succ (0)))'

These considerations lead to the following grammar for arithmetic expressions, including their intermediate and final forms:

$$
\text{arith\_expr} \equiv \left\{
\begin{array}{l}
\text{arith\_expr} + \text{arith\_expr} \\
\text{arith\_expr} - \text{arith\_expr} \\
\text{arith\_expr} \times \text{arith\_expr} \\
\text{arith\_expr} \div \text{arith\_expr} \\
\text{succ (arith\_expr)} \\
\text{digit}
\end{array}
\right\}
$$

digit $\equiv$ 0 | 1 | 2 | 3 | 4 | 5 | 6 | 7 | 8 | 9

To keep the presentation simple, we define only single-digit numerals; you will define decimal notation in Exercise (10.10).

Next we consider transformation rules that describe unary arithmetic on these strings. The first transformation rules define the numerals $1-9$ by reducing them to unary form:

(1) $1 \Rightarrow \text{succ}\,(0)$
(2) $2 \Rightarrow \text{succ}\,(1)$
(3) $3 \Rightarrow \text{succ}\,(2)$
(4) $4 \Rightarrow \text{succ}\,(3)$
(5) $5 \Rightarrow \text{succ}\,(4)$
(6) $6 \Rightarrow \text{succ}\,(5)$
(7) $7 \Rightarrow \text{succ}\,(6)$
(8) $8 \Rightarrow \text{succ}\,(7)$
(9) $9 \Rightarrow \text{succ}\,(8)$

Each rule is labeled with a number, (1)–(9), for later reference. The following rules, also labeled, define addition and multiplication recursively:

$(+_1)$ $\text{succ}\,(m) + n \Rightarrow \text{succ}\,(m+n)$
$(+_2)$ $0 + n \Rightarrow n$
$(\times_1)$ $\text{succ}\,(m) \times n \Rightarrow n + m \times n$
$(\times_2)$ $0 \times n \Rightarrow 0$

Using these rules we can reduce an arithmetic expression to the normal form representing its value. For example, we can reduce the string '2 + 3' by applying the rules as follows:

$2 + 3$
$(2) \Rightarrow \text{succ}\,(1) + 3$
$(+_1) \Rightarrow \text{succ}\,(1 + 3)$
$(1) \Rightarrow \text{succ}\,(\text{succ}\,(0) + 3)$
$(+_1) \Rightarrow \text{succ}\,(\text{succ}\,(0 + 3))$
$(+_2) \Rightarrow \text{succ}\,(\text{succ}\,(3))$
$(3) \Rightarrow \text{succ}\,(\text{succ}\,(\text{succ}\,(2)))$
$(2) \Rightarrow \text{succ}\,(\text{succ}\,(\text{succ}\,(\text{succ}\,(1))))$
$(1) \Rightarrow \text{succ}\,(\text{succ}\,(\text{succ}\,(\text{succ}\,(\text{succ}\,(0)))))$

The expression on the right of the last line is in *normal form* because no more transformation rules can be applied to it. As expected, this expression is the normal form representing the number five.

Does the order in which the rules are applied make a difference? Consider the reduction of a more complicated expression, '$2 + 3 \times 5$'.

$$
\begin{aligned}
2 + 3 \times 5 & \\
(3) & \Rightarrow 2 + \operatorname{succ}(2) \times 5 \\
(\times_1) & \Rightarrow 2 + 5 + 2 \times 5 \\
(2) & \Rightarrow 2 + 5 + \operatorname{succ}(1) \times 5 \\
(\times_1) & \Rightarrow 2 + 5 + 5 + 1 \times 5 \\
(1) & \Rightarrow 2 + 5 + 5 + \operatorname{succ}(0) \times 5 \\
(\times_1) & \Rightarrow 2 + 5 + 5 + 5 + 0 \times 5 \\
(\times_2) & \Rightarrow 2 + 5 + 5 + 5 + 0 \\
& \vdots
\end{aligned}
$$

You can see that, as intended, the reduction is progressing to the normal form representing 17. Since there are no constraints on the order in which rules are applied, however, the following is also a legal reduction:

$$
\begin{aligned}
2 + 3 \times 5 & \\
(2) & \Rightarrow \operatorname{succ}(1) + 3 \times 5 \\
(+_1) & \Rightarrow \operatorname{succ}(1 + 3) \times 5 \\
(1) & \Rightarrow \operatorname{succ}(\operatorname{succ}(0) + 3) \times 5 \\
(+_1) & \Rightarrow \operatorname{succ}(\operatorname{succ}(0 + 3)) \times 5 \\
(+_2) & \Rightarrow \operatorname{succ}(\operatorname{succ}(3)) \times 5
\end{aligned}
$$

This produces a different answer, 25, which is incorrect according to our intended purpose! Here we have a case in which we can say the calculus is *wrong*—its operation does not agree with its intended meaning.

The problem with the last reduction, of course, is that we began reducing the addition before the multiplication, whereas the usual precedence rules for the arithmetic operators require multiplication to be reduced before addition. The transformation rules, however, know nothing about precedence; they are simply string-matching and substitution rules—the second reduction is as legal as the first. In other words this calculus is *inconsistent*: Its computational result is not well-defined. In the preceding chapter we proved that the lambda calculus is consistent—an important result, since there are inconsistent calculi. Since we will design calculi for many specific purposes, it is critical to find general conditions for their consistency, a topic addressed in Section 10.11.

One way to make our arithmetic calculus consistent would be to build into our rules some knowledge of the precedence of arithmetic operators. This solution would not be very general, however, since it would not work for other calculi. A better alternative is to alter our calculus so that it allows only fully parenthesized expressions. Thus we state new formation rules:

$$
\text{arith\_expr} \equiv \begin{cases} (\text{arith\_expr} + \text{arith\_expr}) \\ (\text{arith\_expr} - \text{arith\_expr}) \\ (\text{arith\_expr} \times \text{arith\_expr}) \\ (\text{arith\_expr} \div \text{arith\_expr}) \\ (\text{succ arith\_expr}) \\ \text{digit} \end{cases} \qquad (10.1)
$$

digit ≡ 0 | 1 | 2 | 3 | 4 | 5 | 6 | 7 | 8 | 9

This change in representation necessitates new rules for the numerals:

(1) $1 \Rightarrow (\text{succ } 0)$
(2) $2 \Rightarrow (\text{succ } 1)$
(3) $3 \Rightarrow (\text{succ } 2)$
     $\vdots$

We must also make minor adjustments to the arithmetic rules:

$(+_1)$ $((\text{succ } m) + n) \Rightarrow (\text{succ } (m + n))$
$(+_2)$ $(0 + n) \Rightarrow n$
$(\times_1)$ $((\text{succ } m) \times n) \Rightarrow (n + (m \times n))$
$(\times_2)$ $(0 \times n) \Rightarrow 0$

This seems to solve the problem with the previous calculus. Since expressions are fully parenthesized, there is now no doubt about which operator should be evaluated first. We will see, however, there are problems (bugs) in this new calculus.

To understand the problems, we must consider in some detail a reduction of '$((2 + 1) \times 4)$'. The substring '2' matches the left-hand side of rule (2), so we can replace '2' by '(succ 1)' to yield

$(((\text{succ } 1) + 1) \times 4)$

Next, the substring '$((\text{succ } 1) + 1)$' matches the left-hand side of $(+_1)$, with $m = $ '1' and $n = $ '1'. This substring is replaced by (succ $(m + n)$)—that is, '(succ $(1 + 1)$)'—yielding the string

$((\text{succ } (1 + 1)) \times 4)$

Now the entire string can match the left-hand side of $(\times_1)$, with $m = {'}(1+1){'}$ and $n = {'}4{'}$. Thus the string is replaced by $(n + (m \times n))$, yielding

$$(4 + ((1 + 1) \times 4))$$

You can see that the reduction is proceeding as intended.

The preceding reductions were described in detail so that you can understand the following, less-intuitive reductions. We start with the same initial string, ${'}((2 + 1) \times 4){'}$. As before, we apply rule (2) to yield

$$(((\mathsf{succ}\ 1) + 1) \times 4)$$

Now notice that if $m = {'}1) + 1{'}$ and $n = {'}4{'}$, then

$$
\begin{aligned}
&{'}((\mathsf{succ}{'} \wedge m \wedge {'}) \times {'} \wedge n \wedge {'}){'} \\
&= {'}((\mathsf{succ}{'} \wedge {'}1) + 1{'} \wedge {'}) \times {'} \wedge {'}4{'} \wedge {'}){'} \\
&= {'}((\mathsf{succ}\ 1) + 1) \times 4){'}
\end{aligned}
$$

Hence, if $m = {'}1) + 1{'}$ and $n = {'}4{'}$, then the pattern on the left of $(\times_1)$ matches the substring after the first open parenthesis of ${'}(((\mathsf{succ}\ 1) + 1) \times 4){'}$. The right-hand side of $(\times_1)$ is the template $(n + (m \times n))$. If we substitute these values of m and n into the template, we get the result of applying rule $(\times_1)$:

$$
\begin{aligned}
&{'}({'} \wedge n \wedge {'}+({'} \wedge m \wedge {'}\times{'} \wedge n \wedge {'})){'} \\
&= {'}({'} \wedge {'}4{'} \wedge {'}+({'} \wedge {'}1) + 1{'} \wedge {'}\times{'} \wedge {'}4{'} \wedge {'})){'} \\
&= {'}(4 + (1) + 1 \times 4)){'}
\end{aligned}
$$

Substituting this for the substring after the first open parenthesis, we get

$$({'}(4 + (1) + 1 \times 4)){'}$$

This is gibberish; given our decision to fully parenthesize expressions, it is not even a legal expression according to the grammar (Eq. 10.1). You can see that the transformation rules have generated a string that is not permitted by the formation rules. Since the transformation rules were designed to operate only on the strings described by the formation rules, we cannot expect them to operate correctly from now on. Thus the reduction can only get worse.

The problem, of course, is that m matched the substring ${'}1) + 1{'}$, which is not the sort of string we intended m to match in rule $(\times_1)$. We intended m and n to match only those strings that stand for numbers in our intended interpretation of the symbols. The string ${'}1) + 1{'}$ does not stand for a number in this interpretation; it has no meaning. For the rules to work correctly, it is necessary that the variables match only *well-formed substrings*—in our case, substrings that are properly balanced with respect to parentheses.

Both of our attempts to describe arithmetic by means of string-transformation rules have failed. What is the source of the difficulty? Simple string-transformation rules do not preserve the *structure* of the expression. Substrings like '1) + 1' and '3) + (1' do not represent meaningful subexpressions. One way to solve this problem would be to require the variables in patterns to match only parenthesis-balanced expressions. Although not very general, this will work. In the next section we explore a more direct solution to the problems of string-transformation rules.

Exercise 10.4: Show that the rules (4) and $(+_1)$, when applied in succession to '$((4 + (1) + 1 \times 4))$', yield

$$((\text{succ}\,(3) + (1 + 1 \times 4)))$$

Exercise 10.5: Investigate the programming language SNOBOL 4. Write a SNOBOL 4 program to evaluate fully parenthesized arithmetic expressions by string transformation. What facilities does SNOBOL provide to simplify this task?

10.5 Expression Trees

As we saw, the problem with using string-transformation rules to express computations is that these rules ignore the intended structure of the strings. In this section we consider calculi that deal with trees, which are objects that have more structure than strings. You will recall that in Sections 5.5–5.7 we used *expression trees* to represent arithmetic expressions. For example, the expression '$(2 \times a \times x + b)$', given the usual precedence rules, is equivalent to the tree

The tree is called the *abstract structure* of the expression because it reflects the structure of the expression explicitly and independently of syntactic details. The string '$(2 \times a \times x + b)$', called a *concrete structure* for the expression, is one of several concrete representations of the same abstract structure; others include '$((2 \times a) \times x + b)$' and '$(2 \times a \times x) + b$'.

One reason trees are often used to represent expressions is that they make the structure of the expression explicit. That is, it is easy to identify the operands of an operator: They are the immediate descendents of the operator node. To identify an operator's operands in an expression in concrete form requires a parsing process; the operands are not immediately accessible. Parsing is essentially a process of discovering structure; in an abstract expression the structure need not be discovered because it is explicit.

This suggests that we can avoid the problems with string-transformation rules by considering tree-transformation rules. Such rules are more commonly known as *abstract transformation rules,* as opposed to the *concrete transformation rules* investigated in the previous section. (Abstract transformation rules are also called *term-rewrite rules,* and abstract calculi are also called *term-rewriting systems.*)

We write abstract transformation rules in the same way as concrete transformation rules—*analysis* ⇒ *synthesis*—except that now the analysis part is a *tree* pattern, and the synthesis part is a *tree* template. For example, corresponding to the concrete rule

$$((\text{succ } m) + n) \;\Rightarrow\; \text{succ } (m + n)$$

we have the abstract rule

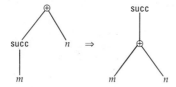

This says that if we see a subtree matching the pattern on the left of the arrow, then we can replace it by a subtree constructed according to the template on the right. Thus, if we have the tree

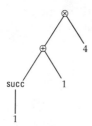

then we can apply this rule to the subtree rooted at the '+' node to yield the tree

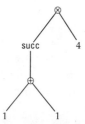

Since each variable in the abstract transformation rules matches a subtree of the abstract structure, there is no possibility that variables will be bound to ill-formed parts of the structure. Thus we avoid the problems of the previous section.

Exercise 10.6: Write the abstract transformation rules corresponding to the concrete rules (1), (2), (3), ($+_1$), ($+_2$), ($\times_1$), and ($\times_2$).

10.6 Abstract Syntax

We have seen that there are important advantages to dealing with *abstract structures* as opposed to the usual *concrete structures*. Therefore we wish to consider abstract calculi, analogous to concrete calculi. The two kinds of calculi are described in the same way: by stating *formation* and *transformation* rules. In the previous section we saw examples of abstract transformation rules; here we investigate abstract formation rules.

The formation rules of a concrete calculus can be described with a notation such as BNF; the formation rules of abstract calculi can be described by structure declarations. For example, corresponding to the concrete grammar (Eq. 10.1), we can define an abstract language of arithmetic expressions:

abstract structure expr $\equiv$ const: digit
$\qquad\qquad\qquad\qquad$ + succ: expr
$\qquad\qquad\qquad\qquad$ + dyadic (dyop $\in$ dyad, arg1 $\in$ expr, arg2 $\in$ expr)

abstract structure dyad $\equiv$ plus + minus + times + divide
abstract structure digit $\equiv$ 0 + 1 + 2 + 3 + 4 + 5 + 6 + 7 + 8 + 9

(For convenience we use the digits as names of the variants of digit. Do not confuse them with the natural numbers; they are only symbols.)

Let's make abstract syntax descriptions more readable by adopting some syntactic sugar. First, we stack direct sums in curly braces. Second, we omit selector names since selection is accomplished by pattern matching. Third, we omit the colons after variant names. The result is that the curly braces contain *schematic examples* of the allowed structures, in much the same way that BNF grammars describe the allowed strings through schematic examples. Thus the formation rules of expr can be expressed in this abstract grammar:

$$
\text{expr} \equiv
\begin{cases}
\text{const digit} \\
\text{succ expr} \\
\text{dyadic (dyad, expr, expr)}
\end{cases}
$$

The next step in defining the calculus of abstract arithmetic expressions is to state the transformation rules. For example, addition is defined by these rules:

$(+_1)$ dyadic (plus, succ m, n) $\Rightarrow$ succ [dyadic (plus, m, n)]
$(+_2)$ dyadic (plus, 0, n) $\Rightarrow$ n

Single-digit numerals are defined by the following transformations:

(1) 1 $\Rightarrow$ succ 0
(2) 2 $\Rightarrow$ succ 1
(3) 3 $\Rightarrow$ succ 2

$\vdots$

(9) 9 $\Rightarrow$ succ 8

To see how these rules operate, let's reduce a simple expression, the abstract equivalent of '$(2 + 1) \times 4$':

dyadic (times, dyadic (plus, 2, 1), 4)
  (2) $\Rightarrow$ dyadic (times, dyadic (plus, succ 1, 1), 4)
 $(+_1)$ $\Rightarrow$ dyadic (times, succ (dyadic (plus, 1, 1)), 4)
  (1) $\Rightarrow$ dyadic (times, succ (dyadic (plus, succ 0, 1)), 4)
 $(+_1)$ $\Rightarrow$ dyadic (times, succ (succ (dyadic (plus, 0, 1))), 4)
 $(+_2)$ $\Rightarrow$ dyadic (times, succ (succ 1), 4)
 $(\times_1)$ $\Rightarrow$ dyadic (plus, 4, dyadic (times, succ 1, 4))

$\vdots$

Because the variables in the abstract transformation rules match *trees*, that is, well-defined substructures of the expression, we do not encounter the problems we had with concrete transformation rules.

Exercise 10.7: Write out the abstract transformation rules for multiplication and subtraction.

Exercise 10.8: Translate the following expressions to abstract form:

a. succ 2

b. 1 + (succ 0)

c. [succ (1 + 1)] $\times$ 4

d. 3 $\times$ 2

e. (2 $-$ 1) $\times$ 3

Exercise 10.9: Reduce the abstract structures of Exercise 10.8 to normal form using reduction rules for addition, subtraction, and multiplication.

Exercise 10.10: Consider the following definition of decimal numerals:

$$\text{decimal} \equiv \left\{ \begin{array}{l} \text{dec (digit, decimal)} \\ \text{nil} \end{array} \right\}$$

abstract structure digit $\equiv 0 + 1 + 2 + 3 + 4 + 5 + 6 + 7 + 8 + 9$

Write a revised abstract grammar for expr that includes decimal numerals, and write additional transformation rules that reduce decimal numerals to unary form.

10.7 Equations and Transformation Rules

At this point you may have some doubt about the usefulness of calculi, abstract or otherwise. The only application you've seen is unary arithmetic, which is not very useful. All computers provide built-in arithmetic facilities that perform the arithmetic operations much more efficiently than possible using this calculus. We used the unary arithmetic example, however, to illustrate the ideas of an abstract calculus and to show how even the most basic operations can be described in terms of simple symbol manipulation operations. In the remainder of the section we investigate some more practical applications of abstract calculi; each application illustrates an important characteristic of such calculi.

Our first application, sequence processing, is familiar. Recall from the discussion in Section 5.3 the essence of sequences: prefix constructs a pair in such a way that first and rest can extract its components. To take a direct approach to solving this problem with an abstract calculus, we represent these pairs by structures of the form prefix (f, r), where f is the first element of the sequence and r is the rest of the sequence. We now express the first and rest rules directly in terms of prefix:

$$\begin{aligned} &\text{first [prefix } (f, r)] \Rightarrow f \\ &\text{rest [prefix } (f, r)] \Rightarrow r \end{aligned} \qquad (10.2)$$

To see how these transformation rules work, consider the reduction:

first (rest {prefix [A, prefix (B, nil)]})
$\Rightarrow$ first [prefix (B, nil)]
$\Rightarrow$ B

The preceding observations lead us to formation rules for a calculus of sequence expressions:

$$\text{seqexp} \equiv \left\{ \begin{array}{l} \text{nil} \\ \text{prefix (seqexp, seqexp)} \\ \text{first seqexp} \\ \text{rest seqexp} \\ \text{member (seqexp, seqexp)} \\ \text{cat (seqexp, seqexp)} \\ \textbf{true} \\ \textbf{false} \\ \text{atom} \end{array} \right\}$$

$$\text{atom} \equiv A + B + C + \cdots$$

We have included cat and member variants to give us some examples of recursive algorithms. For example, member is defined by the transformation rules

$$\text{member } (x, \text{ nil}) \Rightarrow \textbf{false} \qquad (10.3)$$
$$\text{member } [x, \text{ prefix } (x, z)] \Rightarrow \textbf{true}$$
$$\textbf{else } \text{member } [x, \text{ prefix } (y, z)] \Rightarrow \text{member } (x, z)$$

The 'else' in the last line means that that rule should be applied to a structure only if the previous rules cannot be applied to that structure, that is, only if $x \neq y$.

Exercise 10.11: Reduce the formula

member (C, prefix (A, prefix (B, prefix (C, nil))))

Exercise 10.12: Write transformation rules that reduce formulas of the form cat (S, T) to the result of catenating S and T.

Let's make several observations about this calculus of sequences. First, the distinction between functions and data is not as clear as we are used to. Formulas of the form prefix (f, r) can be thought of either as function applications or as data structures. Indeed, they are both, since they represent function applications but are manipulated symbolically, like data. This blurring of functions and data is characteristic of many functional programming systems, especially *logic programming languages* such as Prolog.[5]

---

5. Clearly, rules of inference are the abstract transformation rules of a logical calculus. On the other hand, a logic programming language must be able to *backtrack* the transformation process since it must explore many chains of inference. See (Clocksin and Mellish 1981) or (MacLennan 1987b, Chapter 13).

Second, the transformation rules are similar to the equations defining the algebraic properties of the operators. Consider the transformation rules (10.2) for defining the sequence operations and compare them to the equations from the archetype for sequences in Chapter 2 (Fig. 2.5):

Transformation Rules	Equations
first [prefix (x, y)] $\Rightarrow x$	first [prefix (x, y)] $= x$
rest [prefix (x, y)] $\Rightarrow y$	rest [prefix (x, y)] $= y$

The rules and the equations are the same except that the transformations have '$\Rightarrow$' where the equations have '$=$'. Thus we see that the transformation rules often follow directly from the equations specifying the properties of the operations, a situation exploited in *equational programming languages* (Hoffman and O'Donnell 1984). Notice, however, that while equations can be applied in either direction, transformation rules go only one way. Many so-called equational programming languages are actually transformational programming languages (O'Donnell 1985). This is an important distinction: It's much easier to reason about equations than transformation rules.

The third thing to notice about this calculus is the similarity of the transformation rules to function definitions. Consider the rules that define member

$$member (x, nil) \Rightarrow \textbf{false} \qquad\qquad (10.3)$$
$$member [x, prefix (x, z)] \Rightarrow \textbf{true}$$
$$\textbf{else } member [x, prefix (y, z)] \Rightarrow member (x, z)$$

and compare them with our definition of the member function in Section 3.3 (Exercise 3.17):

$$member (x, nil) \equiv \textbf{false}$$
$$member [x, prefix (x, z)] \equiv \textbf{true}$$
$$\textbf{else } member [x, prefix (y, z)] \equiv member (x, z)$$

There is obviously a close similarity.

There is an important consequence of the similarity of algebraic specifications to abstract transformation rules, and the similarity of abstract transformation rules to functional programs. The algebraic specification is the archetype of the function, describing in abstract form the intended properties of the function, and thus represents the goal to be achieved. Often, as reflected in the close connections between equational programming systems and abstract calculi, the algebraic equations can be easily converted into abstract transformation rules. Since the abstract transformation rules can be applied mechanically, we have in effect derived a prototype implementation from the specification, thus ensuring that our specifications are satisfiable (and hence consistent; Section 4.1). Indeed the abstract calculus can often be viewed as an *executable specification* since it is both close to the original specification and amenable to automatic processing.

Of course, the pattern-matching and replacement operations implicit in the abstract transformation rules might not be a very efficient implementation of the specifications. The close connection between abstract transformation rules and functional programs, however, facilitates translating the possibly inefficient transformation rules into potentially more efficient function definitions; you'll see an example of this translation in Chapter 11. For a wide class of transformation rules this translation can be automated, providing a way to compile abstract calculi into functional programs. We have here the rudiments of a methodology for moving from specifications to programs in small, well-defined steps.

Exercise 10.13:   Define an abstract calculus to convert arithmetic expression trees into postfix form (see Section 5.8).

Exercise 10.14:   Define an abstract calculus for converting postfix sequences into arithmetic expression trees.

10.8 The Abstract Lambda Calculus

For another example of an abstract language, let's take the *abstract lambda calculus*. First recall the syntax of the *concrete lambda calculus*:

$$\text{lambda\_exp} \equiv \begin{cases} \text{identifier} \\ (\ \lambda \text{ identifier lambda\_exp }) \\ (\text{ lambda\_exp lambda\_exp }) \end{cases} \tag{8.3}$$

Here identifier denotes a countably infinite set of identifiers:

$$\text{identifier} \equiv \{'a', 'b', \dots, 'aa', 'ab', \dots, 'fac', \dots\}$$

We have already developed an abstract grammar for the lambda calculus (see Section 9.8):

abstract structure lamexp ≡ id: **string**   (9.2)
        + lambda (bv ∈ **string**, body ∈ lamexp)
        + appl (rator ∈ lamexp, rand ∈ lamexp)

Corresponding to a concrete lambda expression such as '$f[\lambda x(gx)]$', we have the abstract structure

$$\text{appl } \{\text{id 'f', lambda ['x', appl (id 'g', id 'x')]}\} \qquad (10.4)$$

Since this is a bit cumbersome, let's abbreviate the abstract lambda calculus constructors as follows:

$$\text{appl } (F, E) \Rightarrow (F\ E) \qquad (10.5)$$
$$\text{lambda } (x, E) \Rightarrow (\lambda x\ E)$$
$$\text{id 'x'} \Rightarrow x$$

Thus (10.4) can be rewritten

$$(f\ (\lambda x\ (g\ x))) \qquad (10.6)$$

which happens to be identical to the corresponding concrete formula. Do not forget, however, that (10.6) describes a tree, not a string.

We record both the structure (9.2) and the abbreviations (10.5) in the following abstract grammar:

$$\text{lamexp} \equiv \left\{ \begin{array}{l} \text{identifier} \\ (\lambda \text{ identifier lamexp}) \\ (\text{lamexp lamexp}) \end{array} \right\} \qquad (10.7)$$

$$\text{identifier} \equiv \textbf{string}$$

Note the similarity of the concrete (8.3) and abstract (10.7) grammars. This is why we had no problem in using concrete transformation rules on the lambda calculus: Its concrete syntax is essentially the same as its abstract syntax. That is, although the lambda calculus as originally formulated is a concrete calculus, its structure is as explicit as that of an abstract calculus.[6]

Exercise 10.15:   Translate the following concrete lambda expressions into the equivalent abstract lambda expressions:

a. $(fx)y$

b. $\lambda x [f (x)](a)$

---

6. We also assumed that the variables in the renaming and substitution rules matched only well-formed substrings, that is, only intact structural units.

c. $\lambda x [f (x)](\lambda x [x])$

d. $(\lambda x (fx))$

e. $f [\lambda x (gx)]$

Now let's consider the transformation rules for the abstract lambda calculus. Recall the transformation rules of the concrete lambda calculus:

1. $(\lambda x E) \Rightarrow (\lambda y E [x = y])$, provided y does not occur in E.

2. $((\lambda x E) V) \Rightarrow E [x = V]$, provided the bound variables of E are distinct from the free variables of V.

Because of the similarity of the concrete and abstract lambda calculi, these are also the (informal) transformation rules of the abstract lambda calculus.

Although these rules are perfectly adequate for performing reductions by hand, they are not adequate for automatic (i.e., computer) reductions. There are two problems. First, we haven't defined the substitution process denoted by the '$-[-=-]$' notation; we will do so shortly. Second, we haven't incorporated the constraints into the transformation rules. This problem is harder to solve; we postpone it until Section 11.3.

How can we formally describe the substitution process? In the preceding statement of the transformation rules of the lambda calculus, we used $E [x = V]$ as a *metalinguistic* notation to describe a substitution process to be applied by hand. To mechanize this process, however, we must alter the calculus to include expressions of this form. Because the transformation rules can operate on only those things that are represented in the structures of the calculus, we must design an abstract structure analogous to the notation $E [x = V]$. For this purpose we can use tuples of the form $(\Sigma E x V)$, with the Σ representing the substitution operation. This leads to new formation rules:

$$
\text{lamexp} \equiv \left\{
\begin{array}{l}
\text{identifier} \\
(\lambda \text{ identifier lamexp}) \\
(\text{lamexp lamexp}) \\
(\Sigma \text{ lamexp identifier lamexp})
\end{array}
\right\} \tag{10.8}
$$

We must now design the transformation rules so that, for example, the following reduction is allowed:

$$[\Sigma (f (g a)) a (h 0)] \Rightarrow (f (g (h 0)))$$

That is, '(f (g (h 0)))' is the result of substituting '(h 0)' for all free occurrences of 'a' in '(f (g a))'. Following the Domain Structure Principle, we define substitution process recursively by considering each kind of abstract lambda expression. (Compare with the substitution function defined in Section 5.10.)

The simplest kinds of lambda expressions are identifiers. If x and y are identifiers, the result of substituting V for all free occurrences of y in x is V if $x = y$, and x otherwise. That is,

$$(\Sigma\, x\, x\, V) \Rightarrow V$$
$$(\Sigma\, x\, y\, V) \Rightarrow x, \ \text{if } x \neq y$$

We can omit the constraint $x \neq y$ by imposing an ordering on the transformation rules:

$$(\Sigma\, x\, x\, V) \Rightarrow V$$
$$\textbf{else}\ (\Sigma\, x\, y\, V) \Rightarrow x$$

Next consider applications. The result of replacing by V all free occurrences of x in $(F\, E)$ is the application formed from the result of doing this substitution in F and E individually:

$$[\Sigma\, (F\, E)\, x\, V] \Rightarrow ([\Sigma\, F\, x\, V]\, [\Sigma\, E\, x\, V])$$

Finally we come to abstractions, $(\lambda\, y\, E)$. There are two cases depending on whether or not y is the variable being replaced. Suppose that $x = y$. Now $[\Sigma\, (\lambda\, x\, E)\, x\, V]$ is supposed to replace by V all *free* occurrences of x in $(\lambda\, x\, E)$, but since x is bound by the lambda, there are no free occurrences of x in this expression. Hence

$$[\Sigma\, (\lambda\, x\, E)\, x\, V] \Rightarrow (\lambda\, x\, E)$$

If $x \neq y$, then we can apply the substitution process to the body of the

---

Figure 10.1 Example of free variable substitution.

$\{\Sigma\, ([\lambda\, x\, (f\, x)]\, [\lambda\, y\, (y\, x)])\ x\ (h\, a)\}$
$\Rightarrow (\{\Sigma\, [\lambda\, x\, (f\, x)]\ x\ (h\, a)\}\ \{\Sigma\, [\lambda\, y\, (y\, x)]\ x\ (h\, a)\})$
$\Rightarrow ([\lambda\, x\, (f\, x)]\ \{\Sigma\, [\lambda\, y\, (y\, x)]\ x\ (h\, a)\})$
$\Rightarrow ([\lambda\, x\, (f\, x)]\ [\lambda\, y\, \{\Sigma\, (y\, x)\ x\ (h\, a)\}])$
$\Rightarrow ([\lambda\, x\, (f\, x)]\ [\lambda\, y\, (\{\Sigma\, y\, x\, (h\, a)\}\ \{\Sigma\, x\, x\, (h\, a)\}\,)])$
$\Rightarrow ([\lambda\, x\, (f\, x)]\ [\lambda\, y\, (y\, \{\Sigma\, x\, x\, (h\, a)\})])$
$\Rightarrow ([\lambda\, x\, (f\, x)]\ [\lambda\, y\, (y\, (h\, a))])$

abstraction:

$$[\Sigma\,(\lambda\,y\,E)\,x\,V] \;\Rightarrow\; (\lambda\,y\,[\Sigma\,E\,x\,V])$$

An example substitution using all these rules can be found in Fig. 10.1. Notice how the Σ node "sweeps" down from the root of the tree, replacing free occurrences of 'x' in the process.

Exercise 10.16: Explain why we do not need a transformation rule describing the application of a Σ to a Σ—for example, $[\Sigma\,(\Sigma\,E\,x\,U)\,y\,V]$.

Exercise 10.17: Complete the following definition of a function for performing free identifier substitution on abstract lambda calculus formulas:

subst: lamexp × identifier × lamexp → lamexp
subst (id x, x, V) ≡ V

  ⋮

Show that, when applied to an abstract lambda calculus expression, the subst function produces the same results as the Σ transformation rules.

Exercise 10.18: Define an abstract calculus to evaluate arithmetic expressions in a context (see Section 5.9). Assume that you already have rules that evaluate constant expressions.

Exercise 10.19: Define an abstract calculus to unify arithmetic expressions as in Section 5.10.

10.9 The SKI Calculus

Curry, Feys, and Craig (1958) define a number of *combinators* (closed formulas),[7] among them the following:

$$
\begin{aligned}
\mathbf{S} &\equiv \lambda fgx.fx(gx) \\
\mathbf{K} &\equiv \lambda xy.x \\
\mathbf{I} &\equiv \lambda x.x
\end{aligned}
\tag{10.9}
$$

The **I** combinator is just the identity function, $\mathbf{I}x = x$, discussed in Section 6.9; the **K** combinator is the constant functional, $\mathbf{K}xy = x$, called const in Section 6.13. The **S** functional, which is harder to understand, can be described as *lifted application* (Section 6.10). The utility of this combinator will become more apparent later in this section.

---

7. In Section 8.12 you saw another of their combinators, **Y**.

Exercise 10.20:   Show that **S** is lifted application. *Hint:* Consider the relation between normal and lifted addition, then ask yourself what lifted application would be.

Exercise 10.21:   Write formation rules for the abstract language of formulas composed entirely of applications of the **S**, **K**, and **I** combinators. For example, a legal formula is (((**S**(**KK**))**I**)**S**).

Exercise 10.22:   Write transformation rules corresponding to Eqs. 10.9. These rules should permit, for example, the reduction

$$(((\mathbf{S}(\mathbf{KK}))\mathbf{I})\mathbf{S}) \ \Rightarrow \ (((\mathbf{KK})\mathbf{S})(\mathbf{IS}))$$
$$\Rightarrow \ (((\mathbf{KK})\mathbf{S})\mathbf{S})$$
$$\Rightarrow \ (\mathbf{KS})$$

Exercise 10.23:   Apply your transformation rules from Exercise 10.22 to (((**SI**)**I**)X), where X is any **SKI** formula.

Exercise 10.24:   Let $E \equiv$ (**S**(**K**F)(**SII**)), where F is any **SKI** formula. Note that, because we've suppressed left-associative parentheses, $E \equiv$ ((**S**(**K**F))((**SI**)**I**)). Apply your transformation rules from Exercise 10.22 to EX. *Hint:* Use results from preceding exercises.

Exercise 10.25:   Let E be defined as in the preceding exercise, and apply your transformation rules to EE. Discuss the result. *Hint:* Use results from the preceding exercises, and don't expand the second E.

Exercise 10.26:   Write in an imperative language an interpreter for reducing formulas in the **SKI** calculus. Try to make your implementation as efficient as possible. *Hint:* Use a stack for keeping track of pending reductions.

It is remarkable that the **SKI** calculus is computationally complete; that is, these three simple symbol-manipulation operations are sufficient to implement any operation that can be programmed on any digital computer! Rather than demonstrating this directly, let's show it indirectly by presenting an algorithm for translating lambda calculus formulas into formulas in the **SKI** calculus. Since we are already convinced of the completeness of the lambda calculus, this will establish the completeness of **SKI**.

The completeness of **SKI** may have important implications for computer architecture. Since functional languages can be compiled into the lambda calculus, and the lambda calculus can be compiled into **SKI**, it follows that any functional language can be implemented on a computer

providing just the **SKI** operations![8] Why would anyone want to do this?
As you probably know, function application is relatively expensive on
conventional computers; a principal reason is the complexity of maintain-
ing the data structures that support access to the bound identifiers. The
problems are especially severe when higher-order functions are permitted, since then a simple stack discipline is inadequate (MacLennan 1987b,
Chapter 6). Because a formula of the **SKI** calculus contains no bound
identifiers, its reduction rules can be implemented as simple data structure manipulations (see Exercise 10.26). Further, since the **SKI** calculus is
Church-Rosser (see Section 10.11), the reduction rules can be applied in
any order, or in parallel. Thus it seems possible to design a massively
parallel computer that executes functional languages very efficiently. For
more information on these *graph reduction machines* see (Fasel and Keller
1987) and the proceedings of the ACM Functional Languages and Computer Architecture Conferences.

   The lambda calculus is translated to the **SKI** calculus by eliminating all
bound variables in the formula. Thus we want to replace each formula
λxE by an equivalent formula F that does not contain the bound variable
x. By 'equivalent' we mean that the formulas have the same *extension* (see
Section 7.3)—that is, for all V, $(\lambda xE)V = FV$. The operation for converting
λxE into F, called *bracket abstraction*, is represented by $(\Lambda x E)$; thus
$F = (\Lambda x E)$. Given the bracket-abstraction operator, we can eliminate all
bound variables from a formula by replacing every abstraction λxE by the
"abstract" $(\Lambda x E)$. The following bracket-abstraction rules are based on
(Curry, Feys, and Craig 1958, pages 188ff.):

$$(\Lambda x\, x) \Rightarrow \mathbf{I} \tag{10.10}$$
$$\textbf{else } (\Lambda x\, y) \Rightarrow (\mathbf{K}\, y)$$
$$(\Lambda x\, (F\, E)) \Rightarrow ((\mathbf{S}\, (\Lambda x\, F))\, (\Lambda x\, E))$$

Exercise 10.27: Explain why Eqs. (10.10) do not contain rules of the form
$'(\Lambda x\, (\lambda yE)) \Rightarrow \cdots'$.

Exercise 10.28: Apply by hand the bracket-abstraction rules (Eqs. 10.10)
to $(\lambda n((\text{minus } n)\, 1)))$. Notice that the free variable 'minus' is left untouched; in a
practical **SKI** computer it would be a built-in operation.

Exercise 10.29: Use Eqs. (10.10) to eliminate n from

$$\lambda n(\text{If (equal } n\ 0)\ 1\ (\text{times } n\ (\text{fac (minus } n\ 1)))) \tag{10.11}$$

8. Turner and others have noted that, although the **SKI** combinators are sufficient, much
more efficient representations are obtained by including a few additional combinators;
see (Turner 1979a, 1979b) and (Abdali 1976a) for examples.

Note that we have suppressed parentheses by assuming that application is left-associative.

Exercise 10.30: Apply Eqs. (10.10) to eliminate the bound variable from $\lambda x(F(xx))$. Does the result look familiar? Explain.

Exercise 10.31: Write the formation rules for an abstract language that will accommodate the lambda and **SKI** calculi and the bracket-abstraction rules (Eqs. 10.10).

Exercise 10.32: Show that the bracket-abstraction rules (Eqs. 10.10) are semantics preserving, that is, that λxE is extensionally equivalent to $(\Lambda\ x\ E)$.

Exercise 10.33: Apply the bracket-abstraction rules (Eqs. 10.10) to $\lambda x.\lambda y.xy$. Check your answer by reducing both $(\lambda x.\lambda y.xy)ab$ and $(\Lambda\ x\ (\Lambda\ y\ (xy)))ab$.

Exercise 10.34: Notice that the size of the abstracts grows rapidly (in fact quadratically) in the number of bound variables. This is a problem since the combinator code is essentially the machine code for an **SKI** computer. Therefore Turner (1979b) has suggested that, in addition to **SKI**, the following combinators be included in the machine's instruction set:

$$\mathbf{B}fgx \Rightarrow f(gx)$$
$$\mathbf{C}fxy \Rightarrow fyx$$

(Note that **B** is curried composition and **C** is curried rev.) Turner adds the following optimization rules:

$$\mathbf{S}(KE)(KF) \Rightarrow K(EF)$$
$$\mathbf{S}(KE)\mathbf{I} \Rightarrow E$$
$$\mathbf{else}\ \mathbf{S}(KE)F \Rightarrow BEF$$
$$\mathbf{else}\ SE(KF) \Rightarrow CEF$$

These rules recognize special cases that can be handled by the **B** and **C** combinators. Show that these optimizations are correctness preserving.

Exercise 10.35: Apply Turner's improved algorithm to Eq. (10.11) and compare with the result in Exercise 10.29.

Exercise 10.36: Apply Turner's improved algorithm to $\lambda x.\lambda y.xy$ and compare with the result in Exercise 10.33.

Exercise 10.37: Compare the original and improved bracket-abstraction algorithms on the formulas $(\Lambda\ x\ (fxy))$ and $(\Lambda\ y\ (fxy))$.

10.10 The Wang Algorithm for the Propositional Calculus

Let's now consider a significant application of abstract calculi: Hao Wang's algorithm for proving theorems in the propositional calculus (Wang 1960). This algorithm is based on some simple observations about the propositional calculus. After discussing the algorithm informally, we present a calculus for performing it.

First recall the definition of the propositional calculus. Well-formed formulas in the propositional calculus are built up from *atomic propositions,* such as P, Q, R, by finite recursive application of the *connectives* $\wedge$, $\vee$, $\supset$, $\equiv$, and $\sim$. For example, the following are well-formed formulas of the propositional calculus:

$$[\sim(P \vee Q)] \supset \sim P$$
$$(\sim P \wedge \sim Q) \supset (P \equiv Q)$$
$$\sim(P \wedge Q) \equiv (\sim P \vee \sim Q)$$

All of the preceding formulas happen to be true; they are *tautologies.*

To arrive at the Wang Algorithm, let η and ζ be two well-formed formulas of the propositional calculus. Then we will use $\eta \rightarrow \zeta$ to mean that ζ is derivable from η. Such a formula is called a *sequent.*

Under what conditions can we conclude that the sequent $\eta \rightarrow \zeta$ is true? Consider first the case where η and ζ are atomic. Clearly $P \rightarrow P$ is true; that is, any atomic formula implies itself. Also, $(P \wedge Q) \rightarrow P$ is true, since we have just strengthened the hypothesis, and $P \rightarrow (P \vee Q)$ is true, since we have just weakened the conclusion. In general, we see that

$$P_1 \wedge P_2 \wedge \cdots \wedge P_m \rightarrow Q_1 \vee Q_2 \vee \cdots \vee Q_n$$

is true if and only if at least one of the atomic formulas P_i is the same as one of the atomic formulas Q_j. For example,

$$R \wedge P \rightarrow Q \vee P \vee Q$$

is true, but

$$R \wedge Q \rightarrow P$$

is not. Thus, if we can reduce a formula to the form $\alpha \rightarrow \beta$, where α is a *conjunction* of atomic propositions and β is a *disjunction* of atomic propositions, then we can decide the truth of the formula by seeing whether any of the atomic propositions on the left also appears on the right. For this reason we adopt this form as our normal form.

To reduce an arbitrary formula to this normal form, we must eliminate from the left all connectives except conjunctions, and from the right all connectives except disjunctions. For example, suppose that we have a negation on the left:

$$(\sim \phi \wedge \eta) \rightarrow \zeta$$

Note that $\eta \rightarrow \zeta$ is true when either η is false or ζ is true—that is, $\eta \rightarrow \zeta$ behaves just like the material implication $\eta \supset \zeta$. Hence we can eliminate the not-sign by rewriting the sequent as a disjunction, applying DeMorgan's laws, and converting the disjunction back to a sequent:

$$(\sim \phi \wedge \eta) \rightarrow \zeta$$
$$\Leftrightarrow \sim(\sim \phi \wedge \eta) \vee \zeta$$
$$\Leftrightarrow \phi \vee \sim\eta \vee \zeta$$
$$\Leftrightarrow \sim\eta \vee (\phi \vee \zeta)$$
$$\Leftrightarrow \eta \rightarrow (\phi \vee \zeta)$$

We have moved the formula ϕ from the left side to the right side and in the process eliminated a not-sign, and are thus one step closer to our normal form. The process can be summarized in the following transformation rule:

$$(\sim \phi \wedge \eta) \rightarrow \zeta \Rightarrow \eta \rightarrow (\phi \vee \zeta) \qquad (10.12)$$

Exercise 10.38: Write the transformation rule for eliminating not-signs from the *right* side of a sequent.

Next consider the elimination of a conjunction on the right:

$$\zeta \rightarrow [(\phi \wedge \psi) \vee \eta]$$

Again we replace the sequent by a disjunction:

$$\sim\zeta \vee [(\phi \wedge \psi) \vee \eta]$$

Next we distribute the second disjunction over $\phi \wedge \psi$:

$$\sim\zeta \vee [(\phi \vee \eta) \wedge (\psi \vee \eta)]$$

The first disjunction also distributes over the conjunction:

$$(\sim\zeta \vee \phi \vee \eta) \wedge (\sim\zeta \vee \psi \vee \eta)$$

Finally, we replace the sequents:

$$[\zeta \rightarrow (\phi \vee \eta)] \wedge [\zeta \rightarrow (\psi \vee \eta)]$$

This does not look very helpful! We didn't get rid of the and-sign, and we have a considerably more complicated formula. Notice, however, that, taken individually, each sequent is closer to normal form. We can continue to work on each of the sequents individually to reduce them to normal form. The original formula will be true if and only if both of the resulting normal-form sequents are true. Thus our transformation rule for eliminating conjunctions on the right is

$$\zeta \rightarrow [(\phi \wedge \psi) \vee \eta] \;\Rightarrow\; [\zeta \rightarrow (\phi \vee \eta)] \wedge [\zeta \rightarrow (\psi \vee \eta)] \qquad (10.13)$$

This rule is easy to understand: If ζ leads to either ϕ and ψ or to η, then ζ leads to ϕ or η and ζ leads to ψ or η. The other logical connectives can be eliminated by similar transformation rules.

Exercise 10.39: Write the transformation rule for eliminating conjunctions from the left side of a sequent.

Exercise 10.40: Show that this transformation is a correct elimination of an implication from the right side of a sequent:

$$\zeta \rightarrow [(\phi \supset \psi) \vee \eta] \;\Rightarrow\; (\phi \wedge \zeta) \rightarrow (\psi \vee \eta)$$

Exercise 10.41: Write the transformation rule for eliminating an implication from the left side of a sequent.

Exercise 10.42: Show that this transformation rule is a correct elimination of equivalences from the right sides of sequents:

$$\zeta \rightarrow [(\phi \equiv \psi) \vee \eta] \;\Rightarrow\; [(\phi \wedge \zeta) \rightarrow (\psi \vee \eta)] \wedge [(\psi \wedge \zeta) \rightarrow (\phi \vee \eta)]$$

Exercise 10.43: Write the transformation rule for eliminating equivalences from the left sides of sequents.

We now have an informal algorithm that tells us whether or not a sequent is true: We use the elimination rules to reduce the sequent to one or more sequents in normal form, and then we check the truth of the normal-form sequents by seeing whether any of the atomic propositions on the left sides also appear on the right sides. Thus, if we can find a way to express a propositional calculus formula as a sequent, then we can decide its truth. Now notice that

$$\zeta \Leftrightarrow \textbf{false} \vee \zeta \Leftrightarrow \sim\!\textbf{true} \vee \zeta \Leftrightarrow \textbf{true} \rightarrow \zeta$$

Thus, to prove or disprove a formula ζ, we express it in the form **true** $\rightarrow \zeta$, and then apply the Wang Algorithm. To make this clear let's work through a simple example. We want to prove or disprove

$$(\sim P \wedge Q) \supset [(P \wedge R) \vee Q]$$

We rewrite it as a sequent and reduce:

$$
\begin{aligned}
\textbf{true} &\to (\sim P \wedge Q) \supset [(P \wedge R) \vee Q] \\
&\Rightarrow \sim P \wedge Q \wedge \textbf{true} \to (P \wedge R) \vee Q \\
&\Rightarrow Q \wedge \textbf{true} \to P \vee (P \wedge R) \vee Q \\
&\Rightarrow Q \wedge \textbf{true} \to (P \wedge R) \vee P \vee Q \\
&\Rightarrow (Q \wedge \textbf{true} \to P \vee P \vee Q) \wedge (Q \wedge \textbf{true} \to R \vee P \vee Q) \\
&\Rightarrow \textbf{true} \wedge \textbf{true} \\
&\Rightarrow \textbf{true}
\end{aligned}
$$

Thus the formula is a theorem of the propositional calculus. The Wang algorithm is probably the closest we have ever come to Leibniz's *calculemus*. Given the Gödel incompleteness result, it is perhaps as close as we can come.

Exercise 10.44:   Use the Wang Algorithm to decide the validity of the following formulas:

a. $\sim P \vee P$

b. $P \wedge \sim P$

c. $\sim (P \vee Q) \supset \sim P$

d. $(\sim P \wedge \sim Q) \supset (P \equiv Q)$

It is fairly easy to see that the Wang Algorithm will decide any formula of the propositional calculus. For example, if we define the *degree* of a sequent to be the number of nonconjunction connectives on the left plus the number of nondisjunction connectives on the right, we can then observe that applying any of the elimination rules to a sequent produces one or more sequents of lower degree. Eventually we reach one or more sequents of degree 0, that is, sequents in normal form. Also observe that we can decide a normal-form sequent by seeing whether any of the atomic propositions on the left also appear on the right.

Exercise 10.45:   Prove the Wang Algorithm more rigorously. *Hint:* Use induction on the degree of the sequents.

We can now define an abstract calculus for automating the Wang Algorithm. Clearly, we will need abstract structures representing atomic propositions. To make them easily distinguishable as a class from nonatomic propositions, we use the variant tag **atm**. For example, the tuples (**atm P**) and (**atm Q**) represent the atomic propositions P and Q. Nonatomic propositions are represented by tuples containing a connective and either one or two tuples representing propositions. Rather than representing these in prefix form, such as $(\wedge\, p\; q)$, let's represent them in infix form, such as $(p \wedge q)$, since the latter is more readable. The following table shows several example propositions in both their conventional concrete form and their abstract form:

Concrete	Abstract
$[\sim(P \vee Q)] \supset \sim P$	$(\{\sim[(\mathbf{atm\ P}) \vee (\mathbf{atm\ Q})]\} \supset [\sim(\mathbf{atm\ P})])$
$[\sim P \wedge \sim Q] \supset (P \equiv Q)$	$(\{[\sim(\mathbf{atm\ P})] \wedge [\sim(\mathbf{atm\ Q})]\} \supset [(\mathbf{atm\ P}) \equiv (\mathbf{atm\ Q})])$
$\sim(P \wedge Q) \equiv [\sim P \vee \sim Q]$	$(\{\sim[(\mathbf{atm\ P}) \wedge (\mathbf{atm\ Q})]\} \equiv \{[\sim(\mathbf{atm\ P})] \vee [\sim(\mathbf{atm\ Q})]\})$

What other abstract structures do we need? Clearly we must represent sequents; the obvious way to do this is by tuples of the form $(\eta \to \zeta)$. Notice however, that we must be able to recognize when a sequent is in normal form. To do this it is convenient to keep the atomic propositions separate from the nonatomic, an approach suggested by McCarthy et al. (1969). Therefore let's represent a sequent by a tuple of the form

$$(\eta \wedge \alpha \to \zeta \vee \beta)$$

in which α is a conjunction of atomic propositions, β is a disjunction of atomic propositions, η is a conjunction of arbitrary propositions, and ζ is a disjunction of arbitrary propositions. Our goal is to use the transformation rules to move propositions from η and ζ to α and β, since when η and ζ become empty we know the sequent is in normal form. Note that the $\wedge$ and $\vee$ are included in sequent tuples for readability only; they are otherwise unnecessary.

We can now state the formation rules; they are shown in Fig. 10.2. Notice that we added **true** and **false** to denote the results of the proof process; **imp**, **member**, and **prove** are discussed later.

Now let's consider the transformation rules for performing the Wang Algorithm. Because the atomic propositions are kept separate from the propositions not known to be atomic or nonatomic, wherever in our informal transformations we had a formula of the form $(\eta \to \zeta)$ we now have a formula of the form

$$(\eta \wedge \alpha \to \zeta \vee \beta)$$

For example, our informal transformation for eliminating a not-sign from the left of a sequent was

$$(\sim\phi \wedge \eta) \to \zeta \;\Rightarrow\; \eta \to (\phi \vee \zeta) \qquad\qquad (10.12)$$

Correspondingly, we have the formal transformation

$$\{[(\sim\phi) \wedge \eta] \wedge \alpha \to \zeta \vee \beta\} \;\Rightarrow\; \{\eta \wedge \alpha \to [\phi \vee \zeta] \vee \beta\} \qquad\qquad (10.14)$$

Now we must systematically investigate the reduction of all the different kinds of propositions in each place they can occur. Therefore consider the following sequent:

$$(\eta \wedge \alpha \to \zeta \vee \beta)$$

We require the formula η to be a (possibly empty) conjunction of arbitrary propositions. Thus it has the form

$$\eta = (\phi_1 \wedge (\phi_2 \wedge \cdots (\phi_{n-1} \wedge (\phi_n \wedge \textbf{true})) \cdots))$$

An empty conjunction of formulas is represented by the single atom **true**. If the conjunction is not empty, then the *lead proposition* of the conjunction, ϕ_1, can be of any of the forms defined in Fig. 10.2—that is:

Figure 10.2 Formation rules for Wang algorithm.

$$\text{proposition} \equiv \begin{cases} (\textbf{atm } identifier) \\ (\sim proposition) \\ (proposition \wedge proposition) \\ (proposition \vee proposition) \\ (proposition \supset proposition) \\ (proposition \equiv proposition) \end{cases}$$

$$\text{expr} \equiv \begin{cases} \textbf{true} \\ \textbf{false} \\ (proposition \wedge proposition \to proposition \vee proposition) \\ (expr \wedge expr) \\ (\textbf{prove } proposition) \\ (proposition \textbf{ imp } proposition) \\ (proposition \textbf{ member } proposition) \end{cases}$$

$$\text{identifier} \equiv P + Q + R + \cdots$$

$$(\textbf{atm } p), \ (\sim\phi), \ (\phi \wedge \psi), \ (\phi \vee \psi), \ (\phi \supset \psi), \ (\phi \equiv \psi)$$

Let's consider each of these in turn.

If we find an atomic proposition as the lead proposition, then we can transfer it directly to the conjunction of atomic propositions. The rule for this is

$$\{[(\textbf{atm } p) \wedge \eta] \wedge \alpha \ \rightarrow \ \zeta \vee \beta\} \ \Rightarrow \ \{\eta \wedge [(\textbf{atm } p) \wedge \alpha] \ \rightarrow \ \zeta \vee \beta\}$$

Thus we copy atomic propositions from η to α.

The next kind of proposition is a negation; we have already seen its elimination rule:

$$\{[(\sim\phi) \wedge \eta] \wedge \alpha \ \rightarrow \ \zeta \vee \beta\} \ \Rightarrow \ \{\eta \wedge \alpha \ \rightarrow \ [\phi \vee \zeta] \vee \beta\} \qquad (10.14)$$

Suppose that the lead proposition on the left is a conjunction:

$$\{[(\phi \wedge \psi) \wedge \eta] \wedge \alpha \ \rightarrow \ \zeta \wedge \beta\}$$

We must do something with it; otherwise it will stop the reductions. We can't transfer ϕ and ψ to α, however, because we don't know whether they're atomic. But since we know that

$$(\phi \wedge \psi) \wedge \eta \ \Leftrightarrow \ \phi \wedge (\psi \wedge \eta)$$

we know that it's safe to transform the sequent to

$$\{[\phi \wedge (\psi \wedge \eta)] \wedge \alpha \ \rightarrow \ \zeta \wedge \beta\}$$

Now ϕ is the lead proposition and reduction can proceed with it. After ϕ is processed, the rules will begin to operate on ψ, and so on. The remaining transformation rules for operating on the left of sequents are similar.

Exercise 10.46: Write the transformation rules for eliminating $\vee$, $\supset$, and $\equiv$ from the left sides of sequents.

We have seen how abstract transformation rules can be used to break down nonatomic propositions on the left of a sequent; we now consider analogous rules for the right. Recall our informal rule for eliminating conjunctions on the right:

$$\zeta \rightarrow [(\phi \wedge \psi) \vee \eta] \ \Rightarrow \ [\zeta \rightarrow (\phi \vee \eta)] \wedge [\zeta \rightarrow (\psi \vee \eta)] \qquad (10.13)$$

To convert this into the formal transformation rule, we need only carry along the sequences of atomic propositions α and β:

$$\{\zeta \wedge \alpha \rightarrow [(\phi \wedge \psi) \vee \eta] \vee \beta\}$$
$$\Rightarrow \{[\zeta \wedge \alpha \rightarrow (\phi \vee \eta) \vee \beta] \wedge [\zeta \wedge \alpha \rightarrow (\psi \vee \eta) \vee \beta]\}$$

The remaining rules for processing the right-hand side of sequents are similar.

Exercise 10.47:   Write the transformation rule for handling atomic propositions on the right side of a sequent.

Exercise 10.48:   Write the transformation rules for eliminating not, $\vee$, $\supset$, and $\equiv$ from the right sides of sequents.

How does this elimination process get started? For convenience we assume that we wish to prove a proposition η, which is presented in a tuple of the form (**prove** η). We use the following transformation rule to place this proposition in a sequent as discussed earlier in this section.

(**prove** η) $\Rightarrow$ [**true** $\wedge$ **true** $\rightarrow$ ($\eta \vee$ **false**) $\vee$ **false**]

Notice that we have in effect used **true** to represent a null conjunction of propositions and **false** to represent a null disjunction of propositions. As the transformation rules proceed, propositions are broken out of η and added to these initially null sequences. For example, to prove $\sim P \vee P$ we have the following reduction:

(**prove** {[$\sim$ (**atm** P)] $\vee$ (**atm** P)})
    $\Rightarrow$ (**true** $\wedge$ **true** $\rightarrow$ ({[$\sim$ (**atm** P)] $\vee$ (**atm** P)} $\vee$ **false**) $\vee$ **false**)
    $\Rightarrow$ (**true** $\wedge$ **true** $\rightarrow$ ([$\sim$ (**atm** P)] $\vee$ {(**atm** P) $\vee$ **false**}) $\vee$ **false**)
    $\Rightarrow$ ([(**atm** P) $\wedge$ **true**] $\wedge$ **true** $\rightarrow$ {(**atm** P) $\vee$ **false**} $\vee$ **false**)
    $\Rightarrow$ (**true** $\wedge$ [(**atm** P) $\wedge$ **true**] $\rightarrow$ {(**atm** P) $\vee$ **false**} $\vee$ **false**)
    $\Rightarrow$ (**true** $\wedge$ [(**atm** P) $\wedge$ **true**] $\rightarrow$ **false** $\vee$ [(**atm** P) $\vee$ **false**])

We see that this reduction has produced a sequent

(**true** $\wedge$ α $\rightarrow$ **false** $\vee$ β)

in which α is a conjunction of atomic propositions and β is a disjunction of atomic propositions. It remains to determine whether any of the atomic propositions in α are also in β. Thus we rewrite the preceding sequent as the tuple (α **imp** β) to perform this test.

Now consider a tuple of the form (α **imp** β). The formula α is a conjunction of atomic propositions, which is either empty or nonempty. If it is empty, α = **true**, then the **imp** expression is **false**:

(**true imp** β) $\Rightarrow$ **false**

If it is nonempty, then it has the form $(\phi \wedge \alpha)$, so the **imp** will be **true** either if ϕ is a member of β, or if $(\alpha$ **imp** $\beta)$ is **true**. This gives us the transformation rule:

$$[(\phi \wedge \alpha) \text{ imp } \beta] \Rightarrow [(\phi \text{ member } \beta) \vee (\alpha \text{ imp } \beta)]$$

This rule and the previous one handle all legal tuples of the form $(\alpha$ **imp** $\beta)$.

The membership test is routine; the rules for implementing it are shown in Fig. 10.3, as are the rules for reducing $\wedge$ and $\vee$.

Figure 10.3 Transformation rules for Wang algorithm.

$(((\text{atm } \pi) \wedge \lambda) \wedge \alpha \to \zeta \vee \beta) \Rightarrow (\lambda \wedge ((\text{atm } \pi) \wedge \alpha) \to \zeta \vee \beta)$
$(\zeta \wedge \alpha \to ((\text{atm } \pi) \vee \lambda) \vee \beta) \Rightarrow (\zeta \wedge \alpha \to \lambda \vee ((\text{atm } \pi) \vee \beta))$

$(\zeta \wedge \alpha \to ((\sim \phi) \vee \lambda) \vee \beta) \Rightarrow ((\phi \wedge \zeta) \wedge \alpha \to \lambda \vee \beta)$
$(((\sim \phi) \wedge \lambda) \wedge \alpha \to \zeta \vee \beta) \Rightarrow (\lambda \wedge \alpha \to (\phi \vee \zeta) \vee \beta)$

$(\zeta \wedge \alpha \to ((\phi \wedge \psi) \vee \lambda) \vee \beta) \Rightarrow ((\zeta \wedge \alpha \to (\phi \vee \lambda) \vee \beta) \wedge (\zeta \wedge \alpha \to (\psi \vee \lambda) \vee \beta))$
$(((\phi \wedge \psi) \wedge \lambda) \wedge \alpha \to \zeta \vee \beta) \Rightarrow ((\phi \wedge (\psi \wedge \lambda)) \wedge \alpha \to \zeta \vee \beta)$

$(\zeta \wedge \alpha \to ((\phi \vee \psi) \vee \lambda) \vee \beta) \Rightarrow (\zeta \wedge \alpha \to (\phi \vee (\psi \vee \lambda)) \vee \beta)$
$(((\phi \vee \psi) \wedge \lambda) \wedge \alpha \to \zeta \vee \beta) \Rightarrow (((\phi \wedge \lambda) \wedge \alpha \to \zeta \vee \beta) \wedge ((\psi \wedge \lambda) \wedge \alpha \to \zeta \vee \beta))$

$(\zeta \wedge \alpha \to ((\phi \supset \psi) \vee \lambda) \vee \beta) \Rightarrow ((\phi \wedge \zeta) \wedge \alpha \to (\psi \vee \lambda) \vee \beta)$
$(((\phi \supset \psi) \wedge \lambda) \wedge \alpha \to \zeta \vee \beta) \Rightarrow (((\psi \wedge \lambda) \wedge \alpha \to \zeta \vee \beta) \wedge (\lambda \wedge \alpha \to (\phi \vee \zeta) \vee \beta))$

$(\zeta \wedge \alpha \to ((\phi \equiv \psi) \vee \lambda) \vee \beta)$
$\quad \Rightarrow (((\phi \wedge \zeta) \wedge \alpha \to (\psi \vee \lambda) \vee \beta) \wedge ((\psi \wedge \zeta) \wedge \alpha \to (\phi \vee \lambda) \vee \beta))$
$(((\phi \equiv \psi) \wedge \lambda) \wedge \alpha \to \zeta \vee \beta)$
$\quad \Rightarrow (((\phi \wedge (\psi \wedge \lambda)) \wedge \alpha \to \zeta \vee \beta) \wedge (\lambda \wedge \alpha \to (\phi \vee (\psi \vee \zeta)) \vee \beta))$

$(\text{true} \wedge \alpha \to \text{false} \vee \beta) \Rightarrow (\alpha \text{ imp } \beta)$

$((p \wedge \alpha) \text{ imp } \beta) \Rightarrow ((p \text{ member } \beta) \vee (\alpha \text{ imp } \beta))$
$(\text{true imp } \beta) \Rightarrow \text{false}$

$(\phi \text{ member } (\phi \vee \beta)) \Rightarrow \text{true}$
else $(\phi \text{ member } (\psi \vee \beta)) \Rightarrow (\phi \text{ member } \beta)$
$(\phi \text{ member false}) \Rightarrow \text{false}$

$(\text{true} \wedge \text{true}) \Rightarrow \text{true}$
$(\text{false} \wedge p) \Rightarrow \text{false}$
$(p \wedge \text{false}) \Rightarrow \text{false}$

$(\text{false} \vee \text{false}) \Rightarrow \text{false}$
$(\text{true} \vee p) \Rightarrow \text{true}$
$(p \vee \text{true}) \Rightarrow \text{true}$

$(\text{prove } \lambda) \Rightarrow (\text{true} \wedge \text{true} \to (\lambda \vee \text{false}) \vee \text{false})$

Figure 10.4 Example proof by Wang algorithm.

(**prove**((~ ((atm P) ∨ (atm Q))) ⊃ (~ (atm P))))
(**true** ∧ **true** → (((~ ((atm P) ∨ (atm Q))) ⊃ (~ (atm P))) ∨ **false**) ∨ **false**)
(((~ ((atm P) ∨ (atm Q))) ∧ **true**) ∧ **true** → ((~ (atm P)) ∨ **false**) ∨ **false**)
(((atm P) ∧ ((~ ((atm P) ∨ (atm Q))) ∧ **true**)) ∧ **true** → **false** ∨ **false**)
(((~ ((atm P) ∨ (atm Q))) ∧ **true**) ∧ ((atm P) ∧ **true**) → **false** ∨ **false**)
(**true** ∧ ((atm P) ∧ **true**) → (((atm P) ∨ (atm Q)) ∨ **false**) ∨ **false**)
(**true** ∧ ((atm P) ∧ **true**) → ((atm P) ∨ ((atm Q) ∨ **false**)) ∨ **false**)
(**true** ∧ ((atm P) ∧ **true**) → ((atm Q) ∨ **false**) ∨ ((atm P) ∨ **false**))
(**true** ∧ ((atm P) ∧ **true**) → **false** ∨ ((atm Q) ∨ ((atm P) ∨ **false**)))
(((atm P) ∧ **true**) **imp** ((atm Q) ∨ ((atm P) ∨ **false**)))
(((atm P) **member** ((atm Q) ∨ ((atm P) ∨ **false**)))
   ∨ (**true imp** ((atm Q) ∨ ((atm P) ∨ **false**))))
(((atm P) **member** ((atm P) ∨ **false**))
   ∨ (**true imp** ((atm Q) ∨ ((atm P) ∨ **false**))))
(**true** ∨ (**true imp** ((atm Q) ∨ ((atm P) ∨ **false**))))
true

In Fig. 10.4 we show a formal reduction of the formula

$$(\textbf{prove } ((\text{\textasciitilde} ((\textbf{atm P}) \vee (\textbf{atm Q}))) \supset (\text{\textasciitilde} (\textbf{atm P}))))$$

Exercise 10.49: Translate the Wang Algorithm into a functional programming language.

Exercise 10.50: Define an abstract calculus for performing symbolic differentiation of algebraic formulas. Consider transformation rules for performing obvious simplifications, such as $1 - 1$, x^0, and $1 \times x$.

10.11 Computational Consistency

We have seen how abstract calculi, often the simplest and most direct descriptions of computational processes,[9] can be defined for many purposes. Thus, although the lambda calculus is complete and computationally consistent, as we learned by proving the Church-Rosser Theorem, it may be more convenient to use a special-purpose calculus. There is a

---

9. This is especially true for language processing applications, accounting in part for the popularity of *transformational grammars* in linguistics. See also (MacLennan 1975) for the use of abstract calculi and transformation rules to specify the syntax and semantics of programming languages.

disadvantage to dealing with a variety of calculi, however, since we have no guarantee that they are computationally consistent. (In particular, recall the inconsistent concrete calculi in Section 10.4.)

A few examples may convince you of the possibility of inconsistent calculi. In the simplest case, we have two or more rules with the same left-hand side, but different right-hand sides:

$$1 \Rightarrow \mathsf{succ}\,0, \quad 1 \Rightarrow 0 \tag{10.15}$$

In this case we can reduce '1' to two different formulas, '0' and 'succ 0'—not a very interesting case of inconsistency since we are unlikely to write such blatantly *ambiguous* rules, and in any case they are easy to detect. A less obviously inconsistent calculus is the following:

$$f(0, y) \Rightarrow 0, \quad f(x, 1) \Rightarrow 1 \tag{10.16}$$

We may use these *conflicting* rules to reduce the formula '$f(0, 1)$' to either '0' or '1'. We could of course look for rules that may apply to the same formula, but still this will not eliminate all inconsistencies. Consider the following:

$$f(g(x)) \Rightarrow a, \quad g(h(x)) \Rightarrow b \tag{10.17}$$

We may apply either rule to '$f(g(h(x)))$', yielding the inconsistent results 'a' and '$f(b)$'.[10] Now we could continue like this, generating examples of rules that lead to inconsistency, and attempting thereby to discover the conditions for the consistency of calculi. Unless we can *prove* that the conditions are sufficient, however, we will never be confident that we've got them all. A better approach is to start with an outline for a consistency proof, then determine the conditions we need to make the proof go through.[11] We can do this by beginning with the proof of the Church-Rosser Theorem in Chapter 9 and seeing what steps depend on the particular transformation rules of the lambda calculus; these are the steps we must modify to accommodate other calculi. (It might be worthwhile to review the proof of the Church-Rosser Theorem now.)

To begin, recall that the notion of a *walk* was crucial in establishing the Church-Rosser property. We therefore define an analogous notion for

---

10. Of course, these rules wouldn't be inconsistent if we had a rule such as $f(x) \Rightarrow a$ that brought the reductions back together. The restrictions we will place on rules guarantee consistency without the need for considering such complicated interactions.
11. Such *proof-generated theorems* are very common in mathematics; for an insightful discussion see (Lakatos 1976). There have been many proofs of Church-Rosser theorems for abstract calculi, some for larger classes of rules than admitted here; see, for example, (Rosen 1973). The present proof is based on (MacLennan 1984a).

arbitrary calculi. It is convenient to have some notation. Consider a transformation rule $A \Rightarrow S$, and let the variables in its analysis part be $v_1, \ldots, v_m$; these variables also appear in its synthesis part. By saying that a formula X *matches* A we mean that there are some formulas $M_1, \ldots, M_m$ that when substituted for the variables of A yield X. That is,

$$X = A[v_1 = M_1, \ldots, v_m = M_m]$$

The result Y of the rule is synthesized by substituting the formulas $M_1, \ldots, M_m$ for the variables in the template S:

$$Y = S[v_1 = M_1, \ldots, v_m = M_m]$$

The effect of a rule can also be expressed through two functions, the analyzer α and the synthesizer σ, defined as follows:

$$\alpha(v_1, \ldots, v_m) \equiv A$$
$$\sigma(v_1, \ldots, v_m) \equiv S$$

Note that any tree matched by A can be written $\alpha(M_1, \ldots, M_m)$ for some trees $M_1, \ldots, M_m$. The tree synthesized as a result of such a match is $\sigma(M_1, \ldots, M_m)$.

Since we will write many lists of variables and trees, we use a more compact "vector notation." The notation $\vec{v}$ represents the variables $v_1, \ldots, v_m$; the notation $\vec{M}$, the trees $M_1, \ldots, M_m$. Hence the analyzer and synthesizer functions are defined $\alpha(\vec{v}) \equiv A$ and $\sigma(\vec{v}) \equiv S$. The rule $A \Rightarrow S$ can apply to a tree X if and only if $X = \alpha(\vec{M})$ for some trees $\vec{M}$, the result of this application is $\sigma(\vec{M})$. Thus $A \Rightarrow S$ corresponds to the function

$$\alpha(\vec{v}) \mapsto \sigma(\vec{v})$$

The copy rule for function application allows us to relate the analyzer to the analysis pattern and the synthesizer to the synthesis template:

$$\alpha(\vec{M}) = A[v_1 = M_1, \ldots, v_m = M_m] = A[\vec{v} = \vec{M}]$$
$$\sigma(\vec{M}) = S[v_1 = M_1, \ldots, v_m = M_m] = S[\vec{v} = \vec{M}]$$

Next we introduce a way of talking about the place in a tree where a rule is applied. First note that, if a tree X contains a tree Y, then X can be written $X = T[w = Y]$, where the "template" T is a tree containing a single instance of the variable w. Now suppose that a tree X is transformed into a tree Y by applying the rule $A \Rightarrow S$ to a node within X. We express this by writing

$$X = T[w = \alpha(\vec{M})] \text{ and } Y = T[w = \sigma(\vec{M})]$$

We say that the transformation has *applied at location* T and has *transformed all the nodes in* $\sigma(\vec{M})$.

We can now define a walk. Informally, a walk is a reduction sequence that never "goes inward." Thus each step in the sequence must affect a portion of the tree that was not affected previously. Thus that part must either be nonoverlapping or be above previously modified parts. Formally, a reduction sequence is a *walk* if and only if it satisfies the following *walk restriction:* Whenever a rule $A \Rightarrow S$ applies at a location T, $X = T[w = \alpha(\vec{M})]$, then all previously transformed nodes are in either T or $M_1, \ldots, M_m$ (i.e., they are not in the structure corresponding to the non-variable part of A). Nodes in T are nonoverlapping; nodes in $\vec{M}$ are below the level at which $A \Rightarrow S$ is operating.

As proved in the following lemma, the walk restriction means that a structure matched by a rule must have been present from the beginning of the walk.

Lemma 1   Suppose the last step in a walk from $X \Rightarrow Y$ applies the rule $A \Rightarrow S$ to the root. Then there are trees $U_1, \ldots, U_m$ such that $X = \alpha(\vec{U})$.

Proof:
Let Z be the second to the last step in the walk. Since $A \Rightarrow S$ applies at the root,

$$Z = w[w = \alpha(\vec{M})] = \alpha(\vec{M})$$

By the walk restriction, all previously transformed nodes are in $\vec{M}$. Hence X must also have the form $\alpha(\vec{U})$. *Q.E.D.*

It is clear from Eqs. (10.15–10.17) that the Church-Rosser property will not hold unless restrictions are placed on the rules. As a start, we state restrictions that prohibit Eqs. (10.15–10.17); the proof will show us whether these restrictions are sufficient.

We want to disallow rules whose left-hand sides can match the same formulas (as in Eqs. 10.15 and 10.16), and rules whose left-hand sides can match overlapping formulas (Eq. 10.17). Because the former case is just a special case of the latter, we can cover both in a single formal definition: We say a rule $A' \Rightarrow S'$ *conflicts* with a rule $A \Rightarrow S$ if there is a B, not a variable, such that for some T, $A = T[w = B]$ and

$$A'[\vec{u} = \vec{M}] = B[\vec{v} = \vec{N}] \tag{10.18}$$

for some formulas $M_1, \ldots, M_m, N_1, \ldots, N_n$. (Here $u_1, \ldots, u_m$ are the variables of A and $v_1, \ldots, v_n$ are the variables of B.) Note that Eq. (10.18) can also be expressed

$$\alpha'(\vec{M}) = \beta(\vec{N}) \tag{10.19}$$

where α' is the analyzer of A' and β is the analyzer of B. Note that a rule may conflict with itself if, for example, $A = A'$ (but $T \neq w$); see Exercise 10.52. (Of course, the case $T = w$ (ambiguity) is not considered a case of a rule conflicting with itself.)

Exercise 10.51: Show that Eqs. (10.15–10.17) are examples of conflicting rules.

Exercise 10.52: Consider the rule

$$f(x, f(y, z)) \Rightarrow z$$

Show that, by the preceding definition, this rule conflicts with itself. Exhibit a specific inconsistency by finding a formula to which this rule can be applied in two different ways so that it reduces to two different formulas.

We can now prove a result that is a dual to the preceding lemma: An A structure will be preserved by a walk that does not apply $A \Rightarrow S$, as long as the rules are nonconflicting.

Lemma 2 Suppose $X = \alpha(\vec{U})$ and the reduction sequence $X \Rightarrow Y$ does not apply $A \Rightarrow S$ at the root. Then, if the rules are nonconflicting, there is a $\vec{V}$ such that $Y = \alpha(\vec{V})$.

Proof:
We will show that if there is any step that alters the A structure, then the rules are conflicting. Therefore suppose that the A structure is altered by a reduction $\alpha(\vec{N}) \Rightarrow Z$ and that $A' \Rightarrow S'$ is the rule applied at this step. Suppose $A' \Rightarrow S'$ applies to a part B of the A structure; thus we can write $A = T[w = B]$, where there is only one occurrence of w in T. Now note that

$$\begin{aligned}
\alpha(\vec{N}) &= A[\vec{v} = \vec{N}] \\
&= T[w = B][\vec{v} = \vec{N}] \\
&= T[\vec{v} = \vec{N}][w = B[\vec{v} = \vec{N}]]
\end{aligned}$$

(The last step is an obvious property of the substitution operator.) Therefore the B part of $\alpha(\vec{N})$ is $B[\vec{v} = \vec{N}]$. Since A' matches the B part of $\alpha(\vec{N})$, we know that, for some $\vec{M}$,

$$A'[\vec{u} = \vec{M}] = B[\vec{v} = \vec{N}]$$

where $\vec{u}$ are the variables of A'. But this is exactly the definition of conflicting rules (Eq. 10.18). Therefore, if conflicting rules are not allowed, the A structure must be preserved. *Q.E.D.*

We are now ready to attack the main part of the proof, establishing that walks have the diamond property. The proof has the same structure as the corresponding proof for the lambda calculus (Section 9.6).

Theorem Walks of nonconflicting rules have the diamond property. That is, if there are walks $X \Rightarrow X_1$ and $X \Rightarrow X_2$, then there is an X' such that there are walks $X_1 \Rightarrow X'$ and $X_2 \Rightarrow X'$.

Proof:

The proof is by induction on the size of (number of constructors in) X.

Case 1: If the size of X is 1, then it is an atom a. Only one rule can apply (otherwise we would have conflicting rules). Furthermore, since this rule transforms the root of X, it must be the last step in the walks $X \Rightarrow X_1$ and $X \Rightarrow X_2$. Hence $X_1 = X_2$ and the base of the induction is established by letting $X' = X_1 = X_2$.

Case 2: Here we suppose the size of X is greater than 1. As in the proof for the lambda calculus, there are four subcases depending on whether or not the root is transformed in each of the two walks.

Subcase 1: The root is untransformed in both walks. Since the size of X is greater than 1, we can write $X = \phi(U_1, \ldots, U_n)$ for some constructor ϕ. Since the root is untransformed we can also write $X_1 = \phi(V_1, \ldots, V_n)$ and $X_2 = \phi(W_1, \ldots, W_n)$. Thus

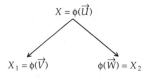

Therefore separate out of the walk $X \Rightarrow X_1$ the individual walks $U_i \Rightarrow V_i$, and out of the walk $X \Rightarrow X_2$ the walks $U_i \Rightarrow W_i$. By the inductive

hypothesis there are Y_i such that there are walks $V_i \Rightarrow Y_i$ and $W_i \Rightarrow Y_i$. Let $X' = \phi(Y_1, \ldots, Y_n)$. Since the walks from $V_i \Rightarrow Y_i$ are nonoverlapping, they can be combined into a walk $X_1 \Rightarrow X'$; likewise for $X_2 \Rightarrow X'$:

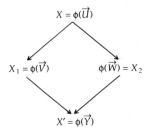

Hence subcase 1 is proved.

Subcase 2: In subcase 2 the root is transformed in the walk $X \Rightarrow X_1$ but not in the walk $X \Rightarrow X_2$. First consider the walk $X \Rightarrow X_1$ and suppose the rule $A \Rightarrow S$ is applied in the last step. By Lemma 1, we can write $X = \alpha(\vec{U})$, for some formulas $\vec{U}$. Suppose Z is the formula to which $A \Rightarrow S$ is applied in the last step to yield X_1. By Lemma 2 we know $Z = \alpha(\vec{V})$ for some formulas $\vec{V}$. Applying the rule $A \Rightarrow S$ at the root then yields $X_1 = \sigma(\vec{V})$.

Next consider the walk $X \Rightarrow X_2$. Since this walk does not apply $A \Rightarrow S$ at the root, we can apply Lemma 2 directly and conclude that $X_2 = \alpha(\vec{W})$, for some formulas $\vec{W}$. Thus we have the following incomplete confluence diagram:

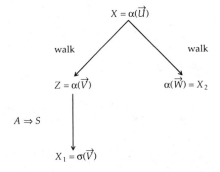

As in the lambda calculus proof, we can separate the walks $U_i \Rightarrow V_i$ from the walk $X \Rightarrow Z$; similarly we can separate the walks $U_i \Rightarrow W_i$. Next apply the inductive hypothesis and conclude that there are $Y_1, \ldots, Y_m$ such that there are walks $V_i \Rightarrow Y_i$ and $W_i \Rightarrow Y_i$. By filling in the missing parts in the following confluence diagram we can walk both X_1 and X_2 to $X' = \sigma(\vec{Y})$:

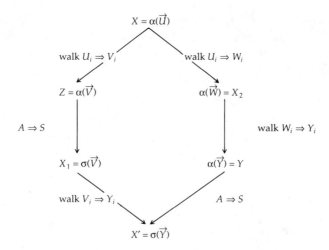

It is necessary, of course, to show that the diagram can be completed as indicated and that the resulting reductions $X_1 \Rightarrow X'$ and $X_2 \Rightarrow X'$ are walks. First consider $X_1 \Rightarrow X'$. Since each occurrence of V_i in $\sigma(\vec{V})$ corresponds to a variable in S, the formulas V_i must be nonoverlapping. Thus the individual walks $V_i \Rightarrow Y_i$ can be combined into a walk $X_1 \Rightarrow X'$.

Now consider the reduction $X_2 \Rightarrow X'$. For the same reasons, the walks $W_i \Rightarrow Y_i$ can be combined into a walk $X_2 \Rightarrow Y = \alpha(\vec{Y})$. These walks leave the A structure (represented by α) untransformed, so it does not violate the walk restriction to apply $A \Rightarrow S$ at the root of Y to obtain X'. This completes the proof of subcase 2.

Subcase 3: This subcase is symmetric with subcase 2.

Subcase 4: In this subcase the top node is transformed in both reductions, $X \Rightarrow X_1$ and $X \Rightarrow X_2$. The basic approach is similar to subcase 2, and is left to the reader. This covers all the cases and subcases, and completes the proof that walks have the diamond property. *Q.E.D.*

Exercise 10.53: Complete subcase 4 in the preceding proof that walks have the diamond property. *Hint:* Use Lemma 1 to show that $X = \alpha(\vec{U})$, where $A \Rightarrow S$ is the rule applied in the last step of $X \Rightarrow X_1$. Then show that the appropriate confluence diagram can be completed.

From the diamond property of walks, we can prove the diamond property of reduction sequences, just as we did for the lambda calculus (Section 9.7). Indeed, the proof is correct as stated in Chapter 9. We summarize the conditions we have found that are sufficient for an abstract calculus to be Church-Rosser:

Theorem (Generalized Church-Rosser) *An abstract calculus is Church-Rosser if its rules are nonconflicting.*

These are not the most general conditions under which a Church-Rosser result can be obtained, but they allow a broad class of rules that are adequate for expressing functional programs. See (Rosen 1973) for more general results.

Exercise 10.54: Show that the arithmetic calculus defined in Section 10.6 is Church-Rosser.

Exercise 10.55: Show that the **SKI** calculus (Exercise 10.22) is Church-Rosser.

Exercise 10.56: Our proof assumes that there are no ordering constraints among the transformation rules of the calculus (i.e., no **else** clauses). If **else** clauses are allowed, then certain conflicting rules become permissible without losing the Church-Rosser property. Prove a Church-Rosser Theorem for abstract calculi with ordering constraints among the rules.

Exercise 10.57: Show that the sequence calculus defined in Section 10.7 is Church-Rosser.

Exercise 10.58: Show that the variable elimination rules (Eqs. 10.10) are Church-Rosser.

Exercise 10.59: The Wang calculus (Fig. 10.3) is Church-Rosser, but we cannot use the theorem in Ex. 10.56 to prove that. Why? What simple modification can you make to the rules in Fig. 10.3 so that the theorem applies?

10.12 Implementation

You have seen a number of applications of abstract calculi, as well as how it is often straightforward to translate an algebraic specification of a problem into an abstract calculus for solving it. You have also seen how abstract calculi can often be converted into functional programs. In this section we complete this discussion by investigating a functional implementation of a system to apply abstract transformation rules.

Let's be clearer about our goal. We want to define a function reduce so that reduce $C\,F$ is the result of reducing the formula F according to the abstract calculus C. Note that we have made reduce a *curried* function (see Section 6.6), making it more convenient to use reduce C, the function implemented by the abstract calculus C.

Since reduce must be able to determine the structure of the formula, we define a type list (patterned after LISP lists) that represents an arbitrary formula (tree):

structure list ≡ atom: **string** + nonatom: list*

For example, the tree

dyadic (plus, const 2, const 1)

will be represented by the data structure

nonatom <atom 'dyadic', atom 'plus', nonatom <atom 'const', atom '2'>,
nonatom <atom 'const', atom '1'>>

Suppressing the injectors for clarity, we have

<'dyadic', 'plus', <'const', '2'>, <'const', '1'>>

Our goal is to define a function reduce: abscalc → list → list such that (in this case)

reduce C <'dyadic', 'plus', <'const', '2'>, <'const', '1'>>
= <'succ', <'succ', <'succ', '0'>>>

(We define abscalc, the type of abstract calculi, later.)

We develop our implementation from the top down. Suppose we have a function reduce_once: abscalc × list → step_result, defined so that reduce_once (C, F) attempts one application of the transformation rules of C to F. This function returns a value of type step_result, which indicates whether or not the reduction step was successful:

abstract structure step_result ≡ failure + success: list

If the rules are applicable, then this invocation returns the result of one application (tagged by success); otherwise it returns the special value failure. Thus reduce recursively applies reduce_once[C,] to F until the latter returns failure. More specifically,

reduce C F = F, if reduce_once (C, F) = failure
reduce C F = reduce C F', if reduce_once (C, F) = success F'

Next we define reduce_once. The effect of reduce_once (C, F) must be to search through the formula F, finding at least one place where a rule of

C can be applied. In particular, if F is nonatomic, then a rule might be applicable to F itself, to one of the sublists of F, to one of the sublists of these sublists, and so forth. Therefore suppose that we have a function transform: abscalc × list → step_result, defined so that transform (C, F) attempts to apply the rules of C directly to F. If one of these rules can be applied, then transform (C, F) returns the result of that application (tagged by success); otherwise it returns failure.

We can now define reduce_once in terms of transform. If transform (C, F) succeeds, then the result of transform is the result of reduce_once:

$$\text{reduce\_once } (C, F) \equiv \text{transform } (C, F), \text{ if success? [transform } (C, F)]$$

On the other hand, if transform (C, F) = failure, then we must search the sublists of F. If F is atomic, however, then it has no sublists, so reduce_once fails:

$$\text{reduce\_once } (C, \text{atom } a) \equiv \text{failure, if failure? [transform } (C, \text{atom } a)]$$

If F is not atomic, then we apply reduce_once to each element of F, which is accomplished by reduce_seq (C, F), with signature reduce_seq: abscalc × list* → step_result. The resulting definition of reduce_once is

reduce_once$(C, F) \equiv$
   let $r \equiv$ transform (C, F) **in**

$$\begin{cases} r, \text{ if success? } r \\ \textbf{else } \text{failure, if atom? } F \\ \textbf{else } \text{reduce\_seq } (C, \text{nonatom}^{-1} F) \end{cases}$$

The application reduce_seq (C, F) fails only if it cannot find a member of F to which a rule can be applied. If it does find such an element, however, the application must return a list like F, except that a reduction step has been performed on one of its elements. More precisely, if F_i is the first element of F for which reduce_once $(C, F_i) \neq$ failure, then

reduce_seq $(C, F) = $ success (nonatom $<F_1, \ldots, F_{i-1}, F_i', F_{i+1}, \ldots, F_n>$)
   where $F_i' \equiv$ success^{-1} [reduce_once (C, F_i)]

To express this as a functional program, we must consider the possible cases for F. If F is null, then we cannot perform any reductions on the elements of F (it hasn't any), so reduce_seq fails:

$$\text{reduce\_seq } (C, \text{nil}) \equiv \text{failure} \qquad\qquad (10.20)$$

If F is nonnull, then we try to reduce the first element of F. If this succeeds, then we return F with a transformed first element:

$$\text{reduce\_seq } (C, \, x:y) \equiv \text{success } (\text{success}^{-1}h:y), \text{ if success? } h \qquad (10.21)$$
$$\textbf{where } h \equiv \text{reduce\_once } (C, \, x)$$

If we cannot apply a rule to the first element of F, then we must continue trying on the rest of F, which we do with the recursive application reduce_seq $(C, \, y)$. If this succeeds, then its value is the transformation of y, yielding

$$\text{reduce\_seq}(C, \, x:y) \equiv \text{success } (x:\text{success}^{-1}t), \text{ if success? } t \qquad (10.22)$$
$$\textbf{where } t \equiv \text{reduce\_seq } (C, \, y)$$

If the recursive invocation of reduce_seq fails, then we must return failure, because we have been unable to apply a rule to any of the elements of F:

$$\text{reduce\_seq } (C, \, x:y) \equiv \text{failure, if failure? } [\text{reduce\_seq } (C, \, y)] \quad (10.23)$$

We assemble these cases (Eqs. 10.20–10.23) into a formal definition of reduce_seq:

$$\text{reduce\_seq } (C, \, \text{nil}) \equiv \text{failure}$$

$$\text{reduce\_seq } (C, \, x:y) \equiv$$
$$\textbf{let } h \equiv \text{reduce\_once } (C, \, x) \textbf{ in}$$

$$\left\{ \begin{array}{l} \text{success } (\text{success}^{-1}h:y), \text{ if success? } h \\ \textbf{else let } t \equiv \text{reduce\_seq } (C, \, y) \textbf{ in} \\ \quad \left\{ \begin{array}{l} \text{success } (x:\text{success}^{-1}t), \text{ if success? } t \\ \text{failure, if failure? } t \end{array} \right. \end{array} \right.$$

Next we must consider transform: abscalc $\times$ list $\rightarrow$ step_result. The goal of transform $(C, \, F)$ is to transform the formula F by one of the rules in C, which is assumed to be a sequence of transformation rules. Thus

$$\textbf{type } \text{abscalc} \equiv \text{rule}^*$$

How can we define transform $(C, \, F)$? If the sequence of rules is empty, then we cannot apply any of them to F, so the invocation must fail:

$$\text{transform } (\text{nil}, \, F) \equiv \text{failure}$$

On the other hand, if the sequence of rules is nonnull, then we must try applying the first rule to F. To program this we must decide on the representation of rules.

Let's assume that each rule $r = C_i$ is a tuple, $r = \text{rl}(A, S)$, in which A, the *analysis part*, is a pattern to be matched against F, and S, the *synthesis part*, is a template to be used to transform F. Thus

abstract structure rule $\equiv$ rl (analysis $\in$ pattern, synthesis $\in$ pattern)

A pattern is like a list except that it allows variables as the leaves of trees:

structure pattern $\equiv$ var: **string** + atom: **string** + nonatom: pattern

For example, the abstract transformation rule

dyadic (plus, succ m, n) $\Rightarrow$ succ [dyadic (plus, m, n)]

is represented by the tuple

rl (<'dyadic', 'plus', <'succ', m >, n >, <'succ', <'dyadic', 'plus', m, n >>)

Both pattern variables and pattern constants are represented by strings. For convenience we leave the quotation marks off the variables and put them in italics.

We now return to the development of transform. Suppose rl (A, S) is the first transformation rule in C. Application of this rule to F occurs in two steps: analysis and synthesis. First we must match pattern A against F, which we assume is accomplished by match (A, F, nihil).[12] The nihil argument represents an initially empty list of bindings of pattern variables. If this match succeeds, then the invocation returns a finite function containing the bindings of the pattern variables bound by the matching process. Thus the signature of match is

match: pattern $\times$ list $\times$ bindings $\rightarrow$ match_result.
abstract structure match_result $\equiv$ failure + success: bindings
type bindings $\equiv$ finfunc (**string** $\rightarrow$ list)

The bindings returned by a successful match are used by a function synthesize, which constructs the transformed F according to the template S. If the match fails, then we try to apply the rest of the rules to F. The resulting definition of transform is

---

12. Compare and contrast the match function to the unification function described in Section 5.10, which is very similar.

$$\text{transform (nil, } F) \equiv \text{failure}$$

transform [rl $(A, S) : C, F$] $\equiv$
let $r \equiv$ match (A, F, nihil) **in**

$$\begin{cases} \text{synthesize (success}^{-1} \ r) \ S, & \text{if success? } r \\ \text{transform } (C, F), & \text{if failure? } r \end{cases}$$

Note that we take synthesize to be curried:

$$\text{synthesize: bindings} \rightarrow \text{pattern} \rightarrow \text{list}$$

As we'll see later, this simplifies the definition of synthesize.

We now come to the heart of the abstract transformation system: the pattern matcher. We define match (P, F, C) to match the pattern P against the formula F in the context (set of bindings) C. The result of this matching process is either failure, or, if the match succeeded, an augmented context success C' containing the additional bindings added by the match.

Following the Domain Structure Principle, let's break the problem down into easy-to-solve subproblems. The pattern P is an atom, a nonatom, or a variable. If P is a nonatom, then the match can succeed only if F is also a nonatom and P and F match element for element. The latter test is performed by an auxiliary function, match_seq: pattern* $\times$ list* $\times$ bindings $\rightarrow$ match_result. Thus we have the following cases:

$$\begin{aligned} &\text{match (nonatom } P, \text{ atom } a, C) \equiv \text{failure} &\quad (10.24)\\ &\text{match (nonatom } P, \text{ nonatom } F, C) \equiv \text{match\_seq } (P, F, C) \end{aligned}$$

If P is an atom, then the match succeeds only if F is that very same symbol. Thus we have the following cases:

$$\begin{aligned} &\text{match (atom } a, \text{ atom } a, C) \equiv \text{success } C &\quad (10.25)\\ &\textbf{else } \text{match (atom } a, F, C) \equiv \text{failure} \end{aligned}$$

If P is a pattern variable, then there are two subcases, depending on whether or not P is already bound: If it is bound, F must equal its bound value; if not bound, it matches anything and becomes bound to it. This leads to the following cases:

match (var a, F, C) $\equiv$ compare F to bound value of a, if a is bound
match (var a, F, C) $\equiv$ new context with a bound to F, if a is unbound

If a is already bound, then its binding is in the finite function C. Hence we can determine whether a is bound by the test $a \in \text{dom } C$, and can access its bound value by Ca. Therefore

$$\text{match (var } a, F, C) \equiv \text{success [exten } (C, a, F)], \text{ if } a \notin \text{dom } C \quad (10.26)$$

handles the case in which a is not bound. If it is bound, then we can compare F to the bound value of a by a recursive invocation of match:

$$\text{match } (\text{var } a, F, C) \equiv \text{match } [\text{2nd } (Ca), F, C] \qquad (10.27)$$

Note that we must inject the list Ca into the type pattern; this is allowed since list and pattern are weak types.

We assemble all these cases (Eqs. 10.24–10.27) into a definition of match:

match (nonatom P, atom a, C) $\equiv$ failure

match (nonatom P, nonatom F, C) $\equiv$ match_seq (P, F, C)

match (atom a, atom a, C) $\equiv$ success C

else match (atom a, F, C) $\equiv$ failure

else match (var a, F, C) $\equiv \begin{cases} \text{success } [\text{exten } (C, a, F)], & \text{if } a \notin \text{dom } C \\ \textbf{else } \text{match } [\text{2nd } (Ca), F, C] \end{cases}$

The definition of match_seq is a routine breakdown into cases. The pattern sequence S is either null or nonnull. If S is null, then match_seq (nil, F, C) succeeds, returning success C, if and only if F is also null. If S is nonnull, then F must also be nonnull for match_seq to succeed. Further, if S is nonnull, then the first elements of S and F must match, and the rests of S and F must match. Note, however, that matching the first elements might have bound some pattern variables that are used in matching the rests of the lists. Thus the context constructed by the match of the first elements must be passed as the context for the matching of the rests. That is, if

$$\text{success } C' = \text{match } (\text{first } P, \text{first } F, C)$$

then

$$\text{match\_seq } (P, F, C) = \text{match\_seq } (\text{rest } P, \text{rest } F, C')$$

Exercise 10.60: Based on the preceding analysis, define the match_seq function.

To complete our definition of this system for performing abstract reductions, we require only one more function: synthesize. Compared with analysis, synthesis is very simple. There are three cases, depending on whether the template is an atom, a nonatom, or a variable. If the template is a nonatom, then we recursively perform the synthesis on each element of the template. Thus

$$\text{synthesize } C \text{ (nonatom} <S_1, \ldots, S_n>) =$$
$$\text{nonatom} <\text{synthesize } C \ S_1, \ldots, \text{synthesize } C \ S_n>$$

Clearly this can be accomplished by mapping.

Finally, if $S = \text{var } a$ we replace S by Ca; otherwise we leave it alone. The resulting definition of synthesize is straightforward:

synthesize C (nonatom S) $\equiv$ nonatom [map (synthesize C) S]

synthesize C (atom a) $\equiv$ atom a

synthesize C (var a) $\equiv$ Ca

This completes the definition of reduce and its auxiliary functions.

Exercise 10.61: Translate the abstract calculus interpreter into LISP or Scheme. Test it on the examples in this chapter (e.g., the Wang Algorithm).

Exercise 10.62: Characterize the order in which this program does reductions. Do inner or outer formulas tend to be reduced first? Is the order from right to left, or from left to right?

Exercise 10.63: Modify this program to do reductions in a different order.

Exercise 10.64: Discuss the efficiency of this system. Can you think of ways to improve it?

Exercise 10.65: How could imperative features, such as the ability to modify list structures, allow a more efficient implementation?

Exercise 10.66: The preceding program (specifically the transform function) tries to apply each transformation rule to each subformula. Suggest heuristics that would allow us to try only those rules that are likely to match a given subformula. *Hint:* The first element of a list is usually an atom representing the variant tag of a tree.

Exercise 10.67: Suggest restrictions to the class of allowable abstract grammars that would permit more efficient execution.

Exercise 10.68: Write a program to test abstract calculi to determine whether their rules are nonconflicting. *Hint:* Think about match and the unification algorithm of Chapter 5. See also the Knuth-Bendix Algorithm (Knuth and Bendix 1970).

Chapter 11

Universal Functions

11.1 The Utility of Universal Functions

A *universal function* for a language L is a program that can interpret any program in L. For example, a universal function for Pascal is a program that can read in any Pascal program and simulate its actions on given inputs. Since a universal function for a language L is just a program, it can be written in L itself.

One reason we are concerned with universal functions is that they simplify the investigation of certain problems in programming languages. For example, suppose that we can program in language M a universal function for language L. Then anything that we can do with an L program we can also do with an M program: We just take the L program for the task and use it as input to the universal function for L written in M. In a sense we have shown that M is at least as powerful as L, since anything that can be done in L can also be done in M, albeit indirectly. Conversely, if we can write in L a universal function for M, then we know that L is at least as powerful as M. Combined with the previous result, this tells us that L and M are equally powerful.

In the first half of this century many formalizations of the notion of computability (then known as *effective calculability*) were developed, including the lambda calculus, Turing machines, Markov algorithms, and recursive functions. All have been shown to be equally powerful; that is, a universal function for any one of them can be programmed in any of the others. As Church (1936) noted,

> The fact, however, that ... such widely different and (in the opinion of the author) equally natural definitions of effective calculability turn out to be equivalent adds to the strength of the reasons ... for believing that they constitute as general a characterization of this notion as is consistent with the usual intuitive understanding of it.

The hypothesis that these definitions are equivalent is known as *Church's Thesis:*

> A function of positive integers shall be called effectively calculable if it is λ-definable. ...

In Sections 8.6 – 8.13, we showed how to reduce programs in the functional programming language Φ to pure lambda expressions. Hence the lambda calculus is at least as powerful as Φ. This chapter develops a universal function for the lambda calculus in Φ, thus showing that Φ and the lambda calculus are equally powerful. In particular, since by definition the lambda calculus can compute any computable function, so can Φ. Alternatively, if you think it more likely that Φ can compute any computable function than can the lambda calculus, then you can conclude from the reduction of Φ to the lambda calculus that the lambda calculus can compute any computable function.

Further, the approach we use to program a universal function for the lambda calculus in Φ makes it clear that this function could be programmed about as easily in any practical programming language. Hence any programming language that can express a universal function for the lambda calculus—which is any practical programming language—is at least as powerful as the lambda calculus, and thus can compute any computable function.

As will become clear, we can program in Φ a universal function for any computer. Since any programming language must run on a computer, we indirectly have a universal function for any programming language. Since Φ can be reduced to the lambda calculus, we can conclude that the lambda calculus is at least as powerful as any programming language— that is, no programming language can compute more than the computable functions. This leads us to the result that all practical programming languages (i.e., all languages powerful enough to express a lambda calculus universal function) are equally powerful. Of course, this result ignores important issues such as efficiency.

We have argued that universal functions are useful theoretically, but they also have practical applications. A universal function for L is essentially an *interpreter* for L. But since universal functions are usually developed for theoretical purposes—it is generally adequate to know that a universal function exists—they are usually not designed to be efficient. Often, however, we can apply correctness-preserving transformations to a universal function that improve its performance, thus obtaining a practical interpreter. We demonstrate this process by converting the universal function for the lambda calculus into a practical interpreter for the functional programming language Φ.

Just as universal functions can be used as a basis for the design of interpreters, they can also form the basis of a family of related language processors, including code generators, unparsers, type checkers, and macroprocessors. With this motivation let's investigate a universal function for the lambda calculus.

11.2 Mechanical Reduction

The obvious approach to programming a universal function for the lambda calculus is to write a program that duplicates our manual reduction procedures, but this is easier said than done.

To see the difficulties, let's consider how to automate the reduction process. We reduce a lambda expression by applying the substitution rule again and again, until we are forced to stop by an imminent collision of identifiers. We then use the renaming rule to change the offending bound identifier to one that won't cause a collision, and continue with our substitutions. Except on very complex lambda expressions, it is generally easy for a person—but not a computer—to see whether a collision of identifiers will occur. A person can see the collision at a glance, while a computer must do the check with an exhaustive search. That is, in order for a computer to determine whether it is legal to substitute an actual parameter for a particular (free) occurrence of an identifier, it must first compute a list of the free identifiers in the actual parameter. This requires scanning the expression and noting all the binding sites and their scopes. It must then compute all the identifiers whose scopes contain the prospective substitution site and determine whether any of these identifiers are the same as free identifiers of the actual parameter, that is, compute the intersection of these sets. This check is expensive to perform and intricate and tricky to program.[1]

A mechanical implementation of the reduction procedure is also slow. As you've probably observed in your own reductions, this process involves a lot of recopying of the formulas, something that most computers don't do efficiently. For these reasons let's investigate an implementa-

---

1. Avoiding the complicated rules of bound identifiers is a major motivation for the combinator-based lambda calculus implementations discussed in Section 10.9.

tion that involves neither textual substitution nor a complicated collision-of-identifiers test.

To see how to accomplish this, we take another look at the way people use identifiers. Suppose someone reads a phrase such as 'let $\theta = 2\pi ft$' and later reads a formula such as '2 sin θ cos θ'. Does the reader mentally transform the latter into

$$2 \sin (2\pi ft) \cos (2\pi ft)$$

by performing the substitutions? Of course not. Having been told 'Let $\theta = 2\pi ft$', readers remember this fact and in their minds associate 'θ' with $2\pi ft$. We say that the readers have *bound* 'θ' to $2\pi ft$. When they read the formula '2 sin θ cos θ' they interpret it contextually, that is, in the *context* of the relevant meanings of '2', 'sin', 'cos', and 'θ'. They need not make a textual substitution.

As you'll remember, the reason for the collision-of-identifiers restriction on the substitution rule was to prevent altering the meaning of an expression by changing the context of its interpretation. In this case the context is just a set of *bindings,* that is, associations between identifiers and their values. The next section shows how to keep track of the context of a formula in such a way that it can be evaluated without the use of substitution, renaming, or collision tests.

11.3 Context

What is the point of the collision-of-identifiers test? Recall our discussion in Section 8.4, where we said that violating the restriction on the substitution rule could change the intended meaning of a formula. By moving an actual parameter containing a free identifier into a context in which that identifier was bound, we changed its intended meaning. This is the essence of the problem. Hence we investigate free variables and ways to preserve the intended meaning of formulas containing them.

First we introduce some terminology. A formula is *open* if it contains one or more free identifiers; *closed,* if it has no free identifiers. For example, the arithmetic expression '$2 \times a + 1$' is open because 'a' is a free identifier. (Technically constants are also free, but we ignore them for the sake of our examples.) Similarly, the lambda expression '$[\lambda f\ (fa)]$' is open because it contains the free identifier 'a'. An example of a closed arithmetic formula is '$2 \times 3 + 1$'. Another, containing a bound identifier, is

$$\text{'}2 \times a + 1\ \textbf{where}\ a = 2 + 1\text{'}$$

An example of a closed formula in the lambda calculus is

$$\text{'}\{\lambda a\ [\lambda f(fa)]\ (\lambda xx)\}\text{'}$$

Open formulas are in a way *incomplete;* we can't say which number (if any) the formula '$2 \times a + 1$' denotes until we know what 'a' denotes. Hence the meaning of this formula is *context-dependent,* that is, dependent on the context in which it is used, since different contexts may give different meanings to 'a'. On the other hand, closed formulas are *complete,* denoting a value as they stand.[2] Hence their meaning is *context-independent,* that is, independent of the contexts in which they occur. For this reason, most functional programming languages require a program to be closed, that is, complete. You certainly find this familiar, since most programming languages do not permit undeclared identifiers, which is exactly what an identifier would be if it were free in the entire program.[3] Hence for now we restrict our attention to the reduction of closed lambda calculus formulas.

We can always convert an open formula to a closed formula by providing *bindings* (i.e., meanings) for its free identifiers. For example,

$$(2 \times a + 1)\,[a=3] \;\Rightarrow\; (2 \times 3 + 1)$$

This transformation can be read in two different ways. First, by substituting '3' for the free identifier 'a' we can convert the open formula '$(2 \times a + 1)$' into the closed formula '$(2 \times 3 + 1)$'. Second, the value of the expression '$(2 \times a + 1)$' in the context $a = 3$ is the same as the value of '$(2 \times 3 + 1)$'. As we show later, these two readings are equivalent.

We define the process of *closing* an open formula more precisely. If F is an open formula with free variables $x_1, \ldots, x_n$, and if $V_1, \ldots, V_n$ are closed formulas, then $F[x_1 = V_1, \ldots, x_n = V_n]$ is a closed formula, called the *closure* of F in the context $x_1 = V_1, \ldots, x_n = V_n$.[4] An open formula is incomplete because its meaning depends on an unspecified context. Closing a formula completes it by specifying a context in which to interpret it. In other words, a closure makes a context-dependent formula context-independent by attaching to the formula a context.

Based on the preceding observations, we develop revised transformation rules for the lambda calculus. To avoid the collision-of-identifiers test, it is important to note that if V is closed then it is always legal to perform the reduction:

$$((\lambda x B)\, V) \;\Rightarrow\; B\,[x = V]$$

---

2. This is not quite correct. The formula '$1/0$' is closed yet does not denote a value. In any case, the formula has a definite meaning, the division of 1 by 0.
3. Of course most languages permit the use of identifiers that are free in *your* program, for instance, the standard mathematical functions (sin, cos, tan, and so forth). In effect, your program is embedded in a larger program, provided by the system, which provides bindings for these "built-in" identifiers. Hence this larger program must still be closed.
4. In case the x_i are not distinct, the bindings are assumed to be done from left to right. Thus earlier bindings take precedence over later ones.

This is because the restriction on the substitution rule applies only to the free identifiers of V, and V has no free variables. Put another way, since V is closed, its meaning is context-independent, and thus it is safe to move it from its position as an actual parameter into B, the body of the abstraction. Hence, if we can arrange it so that we have to substitute only closed formulas, then we can perform the substitution safely without the collision test.

Recall that the entire formula that is to be reduced is required to be closed. Hence any identifier that is free in any subformula of the entire formula is bound in some more inclusive subformula. This implies that we can close any open subformula by substituting closed formulas for its free variables. In particular, we can close an actual parameter by reducing it to a closed form. Then it can be safely substituted for its corresponding formal parameter.

Since it is safe to perform a substitution when we know the actual parameter is closed, we need a way to know when a formula is closed. Thus we need a way to mark those formulas that are known to be closed so we can distinguish them from those not known to be closed. Since we know that closures are closed, we adopt the convention of representing as closures all formulas known to be closed. In essence, the square brackets of the substitution notation are our mark that we are dealing with a known closed formula. Thus if we see a formula $F[x_1 = V_1, \ldots, x_n = V_n]$ we assume that it is closed by the substitutions in the square brackets. For uniformity, we adopt the convention that if F is already closed then we mark this fact by $F[]$; that is, *no* substitutions are required in order to close F. In particular, suppose that F is a formula representing a complete program. Since we are currently assuming that the entire formula to be reduced (i.e., the program) is closed, we can begin our reduction process by marking this fact by $F[]$. The reduction process proceeds by passing the mark of closure to the subformulas of F.

We now develop reduction rules for the lambda calculus based on the transformation of closures into closures. Suppose we are reducing a closure $X[C]$, in which X is a lambda calculus formula and C is a list of identifier bindings (i.e., substitutions). There are only three possible cases for X: identifiers, applications, and abstractions. We consider each in turn.

Suppose that X is an identifier. Since $[C]$ closes X we know that X must be one of the identifiers bound in the context C, as expressed by the following transformation rule:

$$x_i[x_1 = V_1, \ldots, x_i = V_i, \ldots, x_n = V_n] \Rightarrow V_i \qquad (11.1)$$

Next we consider the case in which X is an application $(F\ A)$. Since an application introduces no free identifiers, and we know that $[C]$ closes $(F\ A)$, we also know the $[C]$ closes F and A individually. That is, if all the free identifiers of $(F\ A)$ can be found in C, then all the free identifiers of F

can be found in C, and all the free identifiers of A can be found in C. Thus we can transfer the mark of closure from the formula $(F\ A)$ to its subformulas F and A:

$$(F\ A)[C] \Rightarrow (F[C]\ A[C]) \tag{11.2}$$

This is our second transformation rule.

Finally we consider the case in which X is an abstraction $(\lambda x B)$. Clearly we cannot have the transformation $(\lambda x B)[C] \Rightarrow (\lambda x\ B[C])$, since x might be one of the identifiers bound in C. This would effectively violate the collision-of-identifiers restriction on substitution. One solution is to eliminate such collisions with a rule like this one:

$$(\lambda x_i\ B)[x_1 = V_1, \ldots, x_n = V_n] \Rightarrow$$
$$(\lambda x_i\ B[x_1 = V_1, \ldots, x_{i-1} = V_{i-1}, x_{i+1} = V_{i+1}, \ldots, x_n = V_n])$$
$$\textbf{else}\ (\lambda x B)[C] \Rightarrow (\lambda x\ B[C])$$

That is, we have eliminated the binding for x_i from the context. There is, however, another solution: We can just leave a closed abstraction in the form $(\lambda x B)[C]$ and not attempt to push the $[C]$ into the body. We will apply $[C]$ to B later, when and if the abstraction is applied to an actual parameter, a subject to which we now turn.

Consider the substitution rule. The effect of our previous rules was to push the mark of closure to lower and lower levels, thus flagging subformulas of the original formula as closed; the goal was to identify actual parameters that were closed and hence eligible for substitution. Therefore suppose we have an abstraction in which both the operator and the operand are closed: $((\lambda x B)[C]\ A[D])$. We know that the operator $(\lambda x B)[C]$ and the operand $A[D]$ are closed because both are represented as closures.

To find the result of this substitution, we apply the usual lambda calculus substitution rule:

$$((\lambda x B)[C]\ A[D]) = ((\lambda x\ B[C'])\ A[D]) \Rightarrow B[C'][x = A[D]]$$

Here we use C' to stand for the context C with bindings of x, if any, deleted.[5] Now consider the formula $B[C'][x = A[D]]$, which means to first perform the substitutions $[C']$ on B, and then to substitute $A[D]$ for x in the result. Notice, however, that since $A[D]$ is closed and C' does not bind x, we get the same result if we first substitute $A[D]$ for x and then perform the substitutions $[C']$ on this result. Hence we have the identity

$$B[C'][x = A[D]] = B[x = A[D]][C']$$

---

5. Hence $B[C']$ is not necessarily closed; it is open if B contains a free occurrence of x.

Now we observe that, if there are any free occurrences of x in B, they will be bound by the first substitution $[x = A[D]]$. Hence it doesn't matter whether or not any later substitutions bind x. Therefore we can replace C' by C without altering the preceding formula:

$$B[x = A[D]][C'] = B[x = A[D]][C]$$

But the right-hand side of this equation is just what we have been writing: $B[x = A[D], C]$, which is a closure. This justifies the following new substitution rule for the lambda calculus:

$$((\lambda xB)[C] A[D]) \Rightarrow B[x = A[D], C] \tag{11.3}$$

This rule can always be applied safely since it requires that the actual parameter be a closure and hence context-independent.

We can simplify this rule somewhat. Recall that in the transformation rule for applications (Eq. 11.2), $(F A)[C] \Rightarrow (F[C] A[C])$, we close the operator and the operand at the same time. Therefore we know that if the operator is closed then so is the operand. We can thus write the following substitution rule:

$$((\lambda xB)[C] V) \Rightarrow B[x = V, C] \tag{11.4}$$

We know that V is closed because $(\lambda xB)[C]$ is closed.

This new substitution rule is really quite intuitive: To apply $(\lambda xB)[C]$ to V we merely add the binding $x = V$ to the front of the list of bindings C, which constitutes the context of definition of the abstraction. To state this in terms of conventional programming language implementation, C is essentially the static chain of bindings defining the environment of definition of the function (λxB). Function application proceeds by "stacking" the new binding $x = V$ on this chain. This connection, which is more than coincidental, is explored in depth in Section 11.9.

We have thus derived a new set of transformation rules for the lambda calculus, summarized in Fig. 11.1. Let's call the process described by the new rules *reduction by closure* to distinguish it from *reduction by renaming*

Figure 11.1 Rules for reduction by closure of closed formulas.

$(F A)[C] \Rightarrow (F[C] A[C])$

$((\lambda xB)[C] V) \Rightarrow B[x = V, C]$

$x[x = V, C] \Rightarrow V$

else $x[y = V, C] \Rightarrow x[C]$

Figure 11.2 Example reduction by closure of closed formulas.

$((\lambda xx)\,(\lambda xx))\,[]$
  $\Rightarrow ((\lambda xx)\,[]\,(\lambda xx)\,[])$
  $\Rightarrow x\,[x=(\lambda xx)\,[]]$
  $\Rightarrow (\lambda xx)\,[]$

$((\lambda x\,(x\,(\lambda xx)))\,(\lambda x\,(x\,x)))\,[]$
  $\Rightarrow ((\lambda x\,(x\,(\lambda xx)))\,[]\,(\lambda x\,(x\,x))\,[])$
  $\Rightarrow (x\,(\lambda xx))\,[x=(\lambda x\,(x\,x))\,[]]$
  $\Rightarrow (\,x\,[x=(\lambda x\,(x\,x))\,[]]\,(\lambda xx)\,[x=(\lambda x\,(x\,x))\,[]]\,)$
  $\Rightarrow (\,(\lambda x\,(x\,x))\,[]\,(\lambda xx)\,[x=(\lambda x\,(x\,x))\,[]]\,)$
  $\Rightarrow (x\,x)\,[x=(\lambda xx)\,[x=(\lambda x\,(x\,x))\,[]]]$
  $\Rightarrow (\,x\,[x=(\lambda xx)\,[x=(\lambda x\,(x\,x))\,[]]]\,x\,[x=(\lambda xx)\,[x=(\lambda x\,(x\,x))\,[]]]\,)$
  $\Rightarrow (\,(\lambda xx)\,[x=(\lambda x\,(x\,x))\,[]]\,(\lambda xx)\,[x=(\lambda x\,(x\,x))\,[]]\,)$
  $\Rightarrow x\,[\,x=(\lambda xx)\,[x=(\lambda x\,(x\,x))\,[]],\,x=(\lambda x\,(x\,x))\,[]]\,]$
  $\Rightarrow (\lambda xx)\,[x=(\lambda x\,(x\,x))\,[]]$

and substitution process described by the usual rules. In Fig. 11.2 we show two example reductions by closure, equivalent to the following reductions by renaming and substitution:

$$((\lambda xx)\,(\lambda xx)) \;\Rightarrow\; (\lambda xx)$$

$$((\lambda x\,(x\,(\lambda xx)))\,(\lambda x\,(x\,x))) \;\Rightarrow\; ((\lambda x\,(x\,x))\,(\lambda xx))$$
$$\Rightarrow\; ((\lambda xx)\,(\lambda xx))$$
$$\Rightarrow\; (\lambda xx)$$

Notice that the reduction-by-closure rules leave abstractions in the form of closures. They also require more steps since the mark of closure must be propagated down to the identifiers.

11.4 Free Identifiers

The last two rules in Fig. 11.1 make it explicit that later ("more to the left") bindings take precedence over earlier ("more to the right") bindings. In effect these rules constitute a recursive, left-to-right search of the context, not unlike the **assoc** function in Ex. 3.20. If this search fails to find a match, we eventually reach a formula of the form $x\,[]$—an identifier in a context that doesn't bind that identifier, that is, a unbound identifier. This can occur only if x is free in the entire formula to be reduced, a condition we have disallowed.

Now we consider lifting this restriction, that is, allowing the reduction of open formulas. Note that the rules for reduction by renaming and substitution leave free variables untouched: Although they may survive into the normal form or be discarded along the way, the restrictions on the renaming and substitution rules do not permit them to become accidently bound. Consider the following legal reduction by renaming and substitution. Note that the rightmost occurrence of 'y' is free in the entire formula, and would become bound if directly substituted for x. Therefore the first step avoids this collision by renaming the bound y to z.

$$(\{\lambda x\,[\lambda y\,(x\ y)]\ y\}\ a) \;\Rightarrow\; (\{\lambda x\,[\lambda z\,(x\ z)]\ y\}\ a) \tag{11.5}$$
$$\Rightarrow\; (\lambda z\,(y\ z)\ a)$$
$$\Rightarrow\; (y\ a)$$

Notice that the free identifiers y and a have been moved around but have not become bound. Of course, if we omit the renaming step we get the wrong result:

$$(\{\lambda x\,[\lambda y\,(x\ y)]\ y\}\ a) \;\Rightarrow\; (\lambda y\,(y\ y)]\ a)$$
$$\Rightarrow\; (a\ a)$$

Here the free y became bound by being moved into the scope of the bound y.

The simplest way to handle free identifiers in the reduction-by-closure process is to observe that if an identifier is not bound in its associated closure, then it must be free. That is, if we have a subformula $F[C]$, then we know that C binds all identifiers in F that are not free in the entire formula. This is because any identifier in F that is not free in the entire formula must be bound in some formula surrounding F, and that binding will be reflected in C. Thus we can reduce a formula of the form $x[C]$ in which x is not bound in C to the formula x. We detect that x is not bound in C by eliminating the bindings from C one by one until none is left. Hence our reduction rule is $x[] \Rightarrow x$. Figure 11.3 shows the revised rules for reduction by closure that accommodate free identifiers. Figure 11.4 shows several example reductions, including the one with the potential collision of identifiers discussed earlier (Eq. 11.5).

Figure 11.3 Reduction by closure rules for arbitrary formulas.

$$(F\ A)[C] \;\Rightarrow\; (F[C]\ A[C])$$
$$((\lambda x B)[C]\ V) \;\Rightarrow\; B[x = V,\ C]$$
$$x[] \;\Rightarrow\; x$$
$$x[x = V,\ C] \;\Rightarrow\; V$$
$$\mathbf{else}\ \ x[y = V,\ C] \;\Rightarrow\; x[C]$$

Figure 11.4 Example reduction by closure of open formula.

$$(\{\lambda x\,[\lambda y\,(x\ y)]\ y\}\ a)\,[\,]$$
$$\Rightarrow (\{\lambda x\,[\lambda y\,(x\ y)]\ y\}[\,]\ a\,[\,])$$
$$\Rightarrow (\{\lambda x\,[\lambda y\,(x\ y)]\,[\,]\ y\,[\,]\}\ a)$$
$$\Rightarrow (\{\lambda x\,[\lambda y\,(x\ y)]\,[\,]\ y\}\ a)$$
$$\Rightarrow ([\lambda y\,(x\ y)]\,[x = y]\ a)$$
$$\Rightarrow (x\ y)\,[y = a,\ x = y]$$
$$\Rightarrow (x\,[y = a,\ x = y]\ y\,[y = a,\ x = y])$$
$$\Rightarrow (x\,[x = y]\ a)$$
$$\Rightarrow (y\ a)$$

11.5 Automating Reduction

Now let's automate the reduction process described in the previous section by first defining an abstract calculus for performing lambda calculus reductions, and then writing a functional program equivalent to this calculus.

First we consider the formation rules of our calculus. We need structures representing the three kinds of lambda expressions—identifiers, abstractions, and applications—which we defined in Section 9.8. For example, the lambda expression '$\lambda x(f\ x)$' is represented by the structure

lambda ['x', appl (id 'f', id 'x')]

These rules describe the static, program structures; we also need rules that define the dynamic structures that occur during reduction, especially

Figure 11.5 Formation rules for closure-reduction calculus.

$$\text{expr} \equiv \begin{cases} \text{id identifier} \\ \text{lambda (identifier, expr)} \\ \text{appl (expr, expr)} \\ \text{closure (expr, context)} \end{cases}$$

$$\text{context} \equiv \begin{cases} \textbf{nihil} \\ \text{bind (identifier, expr, context)} \end{cases}$$

identifier $\equiv$ **string**

Figure 11.6 Transformation rules for closure-reduction calculus.

closure [appl $(F, A), C$] $\Rightarrow$ appl [closure (F, C), closure (A, C)]
appl {closure [lambda $(x, B), C$], V} $\Rightarrow$ closure [B, bind (x, V, C)]
closure [id x, **nihil**] $\Rightarrow$ id x
closure [id x, bind (x, V, C)] $\Rightarrow$ V
else closure [id x, bind (y, V, C)] $\Rightarrow$ closure (id x, C)

---

closures and contexts. The closure of F by context $[C]$, which we have been writing $F[C]$, is now represented by the structure closure (F, C). We represent contexts recursively, essentially as lists of pairs. Thus the empty context is represented by the atom **nihil**,[6] whereas the context $[x = V, C]$ is represented by bind (x, V, C). For example, the closure '$y [x = \lambda xx, y = \lambda x (x\ x)]$' is represented by

---

Figure 11.7 Example reduction by closure-reduction calculus.

closure (appl (appl (lambda $(x$, lambda $(y$, appl (id x, id y))), id y), id a), **nihil**)
appl (closure (appl (lambda $(x$, lambda $(y$, (appl (id x, id y)))),
  id y), **nihil**), closure (id a, **nihil**))
appl (appl (closure (lambda $(x$, lambda $(y$, appl (id x, id y))), **nihil**),
  closure (id y, **nihil**)), closure (id a, **nihil**))
appl (closure (lambda $(y$, appl (id x, id y)), bind $(x$, closure (id y, **nihil**), **nihil**)),
  closure (id a, **nihil**))
appl (closure (lambda $(y$, appl (id x, id y)), bind $(x$, id y, **nihil**)),
  closure (id a, **nihil**))
closure (appl (id x, id y), bind $(y$, closure (id a, **nihil**), bind $(x$, id y, **nihil**)))
appl (closure (id x, bind $(y$, closure (id a, **nihil**), bind $(x$, id y, **nihil**))),
  closure (id y, bind $(y$, closure (id a, **nihil**), bind $(x$, id y, **nihil**))))
appl (closure (id x, bind $(x$, id y, **nihil**)),
  closure (id y, bind $(y$, closure (id a, **nihil**), bind $(x$, id y, **nihil**))))
appl (id y, closure (id y, bind $(y$, closure (id a, **nihil**), bind $(x$, id y, **nihil**))))
appl (id y, closure (id a, **nihil**))
appl (id y, id a)

---

6. Don't confuse this **nihil** with the empty finite function; this is just a trivial variant of the type of contexts. We use the name because an empty context is conceptually an empty finite function. See also Section 11.9.

closure (id 'y', bind ['x', lambda ('x', id 'x'),
                    bind {'y', lambda ['x', appl (id 'x', id 'x')], **nihil**})

The formation rules of our calculus are stated in Fig. 11.5.

Next we must consider the transformation rules for reduction by closure. Essentially transcriptions of our informal rules, these rules are shown in Fig. 11.6. The automatic reduction in Fig. 11.7 corresponds to the manual reduction in Fig. 11.4.

11.6 A Functional Program for Lambda Calculus Reduction

Our abstract calculus for reduction by closure gives us an automatic process for performing lambda calculus reductions. In this section we translate this abstract calculus into a functional program that constitutes a universal function for the lambda calculus.

We define a function called reduce so that if F is any tree representing a lambda calculus expression, then reduce F will be the tree representing its normal form (if it has one). Thus the type of reduce is

reduce: expr → expr

where expr is as defined in Fig. 11.5.

We derive reduce by considering each of the allowable lambda expressions from Fig. 11.5, applying the Domain Structure Principle. To determine what reduce should return for a given kind of lambda expression, we consult the transformation rules in Fig. 11.6.

First let's consider the simplest lambda expressions, identifiers. If reduce is applied to a tree of the form

closure [id x, bind (x, V, C)]

the transformation rules tell us it must return V. This is expressed by the equation

reduce {closure [id x, bind (x, V, C)]} ≡ V (11.6)

In this case reduce returns a formula in normal form.

On the other hand, if reduce is applied to a tree of the form

closure [id x, bind (y, V, C)]

in which $x \neq y$, then its value is the same as that of reduce [closure (id x, C)]. We express this by the equation

$$\text{reduce \{closure [id } x, \text{ bind } (y, V, C)]\} \equiv \qquad (11.7)$$
$$\text{reduce [closure (id } x, C)], \text{ if } x \neq y$$

In this case the call of reduce does not directly return a formula in normal form; rather reduce calls itself recursively to continue searching for a binding for the identifier.

Eventually this search will either find such a binding (Eq. 11.6) or will have reduced the context to the empty context, **nihil**. This leads us to the equation for free variables:

$$\text{reduce [closure (id } x, \textbf{nihil})] \equiv \text{ id } x \qquad (11.8)$$

This invocation of reduce returns a formula in normal form.

Having completed our consideration of identifiers, we now consider abstractions. What should be the effect of reduce applied to a list of the following form?

$$\text{closure [lambda } (x, B), C]$$

The transformation rules do not operate directly on closures of abstractions, but leave them unchanged until they come to be applied to an argument. Hence the appropriate equation is

$$\text{reduce \{closure [lambda } (x, B), C]\} \equiv \text{ closure [lambda } (x, B), C] \qquad (11.9)$$

Here again reduce returns a formula in normal form.[7]

Next we consider the transformation rules for applications. The first rule specifies the reduction of the operator and the operand:

$$\text{closure [appl } (F, A), C] \Rightarrow \text{ appl [closure } (F, C), \text{ closure } (A, C)]$$

The two closures on the right eventually cause the expressions F and A to be reduced to normal form. That is, if the normal form of closure (F, C) is K and the normal form of closure (A, C) is V, then the transformation rule for applications will eventually lead to the expression appl (K, V). Even after this occurs, however, we might not be done with the application: The rule

$$\text{appl \{closure [lambda } (x, B), C], V\} \Rightarrow \text{ closure [} B, \text{ bind } (x, V, C)]$$

---

7. Technically this is incorrect, since the body of the abstraction might not be in normal form. We can consider it to be in normal form, however, if we follow the Delayed Function Body Restriction (see Section 7.7).

is actually responsible for reducing the abstraction body in the case that K is a closure of an abstraction. Thus the application must be passed back to reduce for further reduction:

reduce {closure [appl (F, A), C]}   (11.10)

$\equiv$ reduce $\Big[$ appl {reduce [closure (F, C)], reduce [closure (A, C)]} $\Big]$

The case in which the operator reduces to the closure of an abstraction is defined by the following equation:

reduce $\Big[$ appl {closure [lambda (x, B), C], V} $\Big]$ $\equiv$ (11.11)

    reduce {closure [B, bind (x, V, C)]}

If the operator does not reduce to a closed abstraction, the normal form of the application is the application itself. Since the only lambda calculus expressions that are not closed abstractions (i.e., closures) are identifiers and applications, we have the remaining two equations for reduce:

    reduce [appl (id f, V)] $\equiv$ appl (id f, V)   (11.12)
    reduce {appl [appl (M, N), V]} $\equiv$ appl [appl (M, N), V]

More briefly, if F is not a closure, then

    reduce [appl (F, V)] $\equiv$ appl (F, V) (11.13)

We now have all the equations defining the reduce function. Clearly they could be assembled into an explicit definition of reduce; they are summarized in Fig. 11.8.

Figure 11.8 Equations defining reduce.

reduce {closure [id x, **nihil**]} $\equiv$ id x
reduce {closure [id x, bind (x, V, C)]} $\equiv$ V
reduce {closure [id x, bind (y, V, C)]} $\equiv$ reduce [closure (id x, C)], if $x \neq y$

reduce {closure [lambda (x, B), C]} $\equiv$ closure [lambda (x, B), C]

reduce {closure [appl (F, A), C]} $\equiv$
    reduce (appl [reduce {closure (F, C)}, reduce {closure (A, C)}])

---

reduce (appl {closure [lambda (x, B), C], V}) $\equiv$
    reduce {closure [B, bind (x, V, C)]}
else reduce [appl (F, V)] $\equiv$ appl (F, V)

Notice, however, that all the equations above the line in the figure have the form

> reduce [closure (E, C)] $\equiv$ $\cdots$

This suggests that the closure constructor serves little purpose, allowing us to make the following simplification:

> reduce [closure (E, C)] $\Rightarrow$ eval (E, C) (11.14)

where eval is a new function. Observe that 'eval (E, C)' means "evaluate the expression E in the context C." The signature of eval is clearly

> eval: expr $\times$ context $\rightarrow$ expr

Performing transformation (11.14) on the first four equations defining reduce yields the following equations defining eval:

> eval [id x, **nihil**] $\equiv$ id x (11.15)
> eval [id x, bind (x, V, C)] $\equiv$ V
> eval [id x, bind (y, V, C)] $\equiv$ eval (id x, C), if $x \neq y$
> eval [lambda (x, B), C] $\equiv$ closure [lambda (x, B), C]

Similarly, the equations below the line in Fig. 11.8 have the form

> reduce [appl (F, V)] $\equiv$ $\cdots$

We simplify these equations by replacing them with a call to a new function apply:

> reduce [appl (F, V)] $\Rightarrow$ apply (F, V) (11.16)

The apply function applies an evaluated function to an evaluated argument; its signature is

> apply: expr $\times$ expr $\rightarrow$ expr

After making these substitutions, we have a new final equation for eval and two equations defining apply:

> eval [appl (F, A), C] $\equiv$ apply [eval (F, C), eval (A, C)] (11.17)
> apply {closure [lambda (x, B) C], V} $\equiv$ eval [B, bind (x, V, C)]
> **else** apply (F, V) $\equiv$ appl (F, V)

Figure 11.9 Basic evaluator for pure lambda calculus.

eval [id x, **nihil**] ≡ id x
eval [id x, bind (x, V, C)] ≡ V
eval [id x, bind (y, V, C)] ≡ eval (id x, C), if $x \neq y$
eval [lambda $(x, B), C$] ≡ closure [lambda $(x, B), C$]
eval [appl $(F, A), C$] ≡ apply [eval (F, C), eval (A, C)]

---

apply {closure [lambda $(x, B), C$], V} ≡ eval [B, bind (x, V, C)]
else apply (F, V) ≡ appl (F, V)

The second equation for apply is used when F is not a closure. The resulting definition is shown in Fig. 11.9.

By a formal process of correctness-preserving transformations, we have converted the lambda calculus reduction rules into an interpreter quite similar to the pure LISP interpreter described in (McCarthy 1960). In the remainder of this chapter we continue this process, using formal transformations to produce a practical interpreter.

Having defined the evaluator, we can type in the expression

eval {appl [appl (lambda {'x', lambda ['y', appl (id 'x', id 'y')]},   (11.18)
     id 'y'), id 'a'], **nihil** }

and get the response

    appl (id 'y', id 'a')

which is equivalent to reduction (11.5); see also Figs. 11.4 and 11.7. It would be inconvenient, of course, to have to type in lambda expressions to be reduced in their abstract form as we've done here, but to do otherwise requires a parser for converting concrete lambda expressions into abstract lambda expressions.

Exercise 11.1:   Trace the steps in the invocation of eval in Eq. (11.18).

Exercise 11.2:   Translate the reduce interpreter in Fig. 11.8 into Scheme or LISP.

Exercise 11.3:   Translate the eval interpreter in Fig. 11.9 into Scheme or LISP.

11.7 An Imperative Program for Lambda Calculus Reduction

To demonstrate how the ideas we've discussed can be transferred to other languages, let's translate our *functional* program for lambda calculus reduction to a corresponding *imperative* program. We use Pascal as a typical imperative language, although it will become apparent that almost any imperative language could be used, as long as it supports recursion.

First we must design appropriate data structures. In particular, we must be able to represent the abstract programs described by the grammar in Fig. 11.5. The obvious way to do this in Pascal is a variant record; Fig. 11.10 shows the data type declarations corresponding to the abstract grammar in Fig. 11.5.

It is now straightforward to translate the evaluator in Fig. 11.9 into Pascal (see Figs. 11.11 and 11.12). We are confident of the correctness of this Pascal program because it is derived from the functional program by simple translation; we are confident of the correctness of the functional program because it is derived by simple correctness-preserving transformations from the formal semantics of the lambda calculus.

Exercise 11.4:   To have a complete interpreter for the lambda calculus, we need procedures for reading in abstract structures in some concrete form, and

---

Figure 11.10 Pascal data structure for closure reduction calculus.

```
type
  expr = ↑exprecord;
  context = ↑contextrecord;

  identifier = array [1..10] of char;

  exprkind = (id, appl, lambda, closure);

  exprecord = record
    case kind: exprkind of
      id: (ident: identifier);
      lambda: (bv: identifier; body: expr);
      appl: (rator, rand: expr);
      closure: (ip: expr; ep: context)
    end;
  contextkind = (nihil, bind);

  contextrecord = record
    case kind: contextkind of
      nihil: ();
      bind: (formal: identifier; actual: expr; nonlocal: context)
    end;
```

Figure 11.11 eval function programmed in Pascal.

```
function eval (E: expr; C: context): expr;
  var newexpr: expr;
begin
  case E↑.kind of
    id:
      If C↑.kind = nihil then eval := E
      else if C↑.formal = E↑.ident then eval := C↑.actual
      else eval := eval (E, C↑.nonlocal);

    lambda:  begin new (newexpr, closure);
      with newexpr↑ do
        begin kind := closure; ip := E; ep := C end;
      eval := newexpr  end;

    appl:  eval := apply (eval (E↑.rator, C), eval (E↑.rand, C) );
  end;
end;
```

for printing out the results of a reduction. Implement these procedures and combine them with the evaluator in Figs. 11.11 and 11.12 to produce a complete
lambda calculus interpreter.

Figure 11.12 apply function programmed in Pascal.

```
function apply (K: expr; V: expr): expr;
  var newexpr: expr;  newcontext: context;
begin
  if K↑.kind = closure then
    begin new (newcontext, bind);
      with newcontext↑ do begin
        kind := bind;
        formal := K↑.ip↑.bv;
        actual := V;
        nonlocal := K↑.ep
      end;
      apply := eval (K↑.ip↑.body, newcontext)
    end;
  else
    begin new (newexpr, appl);
      with newexpr↑ do
        begin kind := appl; rator := K; rand := V end;
      apply := newexpr
    end
end;
```

11.8 Functional Language Interpreters

In the remainder of this chapter we improve the performance of our lambda calculus evaluator by applying several correctness-preserving transformations. The result will be a practical interpreter for the functional language Φ (although the same basic interpreter will handle almost any functional language).

Our goal is to produce an interpreter for Φ written in Φ, that is, a universal function for Φ in Φ. Why would anyone want an interpreter for a language written in the same language? For example, to use a Pascal interpreter written in Pascal, it seems necessary to already have a working Pascal system, in which case there's not much point in using the interpreter. There are, however, some important reasons for studying a Φ interpreter written in Φ.

First, since the subject of this book is functional programming, we should investigate how an important software tool—an interpreter—is programmed functionally. Second, to fully understand functional programming languages, we should investigate the implementation of these languages, especially their implementation by interpreters. We can satisfy both goals at once by investigating a functional program for interpreting a functional programming language.

Another reason is that the techniques we investigate are seminal. Although the interpreter we present is for a particular functional language, Φ, it can be easily adapted to other functional languages and even to imperative languages. In addition, although the interpreter we present is written in Φ, it can be translated fairly easily into other languages, a process we illustrate by translating it into Pascal.

11.9 Representation of Contexts

A typical program contains more identifiers than any other single language construct; hence the accessing of the value bound to an identifier is one of the most frequent operations performed by an interpreter. We can often improve the performance of an interpreter by finding a representation for contexts that accelerates identifier lookup.

Our lambda calculus interpreter certainly stands in need of improvement in this area. Contexts are represented by nested bind nodes. For example, the context making the bindings $x_1 = V_1, x_2 = V_2, \ldots, x_n = V_n$ is represented by the tree

$$\text{bind} (x_1, V_1, \text{bind} (x_2, V_2, \ldots, \text{bind} (x_n, V_n, \textbf{nihil}) \cdots))$$

This representation is inefficient: The bind tags serve no useful purpose. One immediate improvement would be to represent this context by the sequence

Figure 11.13 Interpreter with finite function contexts.

eval: expr × context → expr

eval (id x, C) ≡ Cx, if $x \in$ dom C
else eval (id x, C) ≡ id x
eval [lambda (x, B), C] ≡ closure [lambda (x, B), C]
eval [appl (F, A), C] ≡ apply [eval (F, C), eval (A, C)]

---

apply: expr × expr → expr

apply {closure [lambda (x, B), C], V} ≡ eval [B, overl (C, x, V)]
else apply (F, V) ≡ appl (F, V)

$$<(x_1, V_1), (x_2, V_2), \ldots, (x_n, V_n)>$$

This is still not very good, however, since looking up the kth identifier in the context requires eval to call itself recursively k times. This makes it very inefficient to access global identifiers (especially free identifiers) from deeply nested expressions. It would be better to represent a context as some kind of *table* that facilitates fast searches.

Recall that in Sections 4.9–4.11 we introduced finite functions for exactly this purpose. The archetype for finite functions permits them to be implemented in many ways. Some of these implementations, for example those using hashing, can do table lookups in constant time. Hence let's represent a context C by a finite function so that $Cx_i =$ fapply (C, x_i) = V_i:

type context ≡ finfunc (identifier → expr)

We can determine whether x is bound in C by the test $x \in$ dom C, and can add the pair (x, V) to C by overl(C, x, V). When these changes are made, we get the eval interpreter shown in Fig. 11.13.

Exercise 11.5: Modify your Scheme or LISP interpreter to make use of *association lists*. (Association lists are more efficient than the recursive calls of eval but are still linear time.)

Exercise 11.6: LISP includes hash tables as a built-in data type; modify your LISP implementation of eval to use hash tables.

Exercise 11.7: Define in Pascal (or another imperative language) a function 'fapply (C, x)' that efficiently looks up the identifier x in the context C.

Exercise 11.8:   Define a function 'overl (C, x, V)', compatible with the fapply defined in the previous exercise, that returns the context resulting from adding the pair (x, V) to the context C. Modify the Pascal definitions of eval and apply to make use of fapply and overl.

Exercise 11.9:   Discuss the implementation in Pascal of a hash-coding scheme for representing contexts.

11.10 Multiple-Argument Functions

Look again at Fig. 11.5, which contains the formation rules for the language accepted by our interpreter; this language permits abstractions and applications with only a single argument. How can we handle multiple-argument functions?

In Section 6.6 we showed that theoretically only single-argument functions are necessary, since every multiple-argument function can be converted into a single-argument function by *currying*. In particular, the multiple-argument abstraction $\lambda(x_1, x_2, \ldots, x_n)B$ can be curried to

$$\lambda x_1[\lambda x_2(\cdots \lambda x_n B \cdots)]$$

which involves only single-argument abstractions. For consistency, we must curry multiple-argument applications $f(a_1, a_2, \ldots, a_n)$ to

$$\{[(fa_1)a_2] \cdots a_n\}$$

Although currying demonstrates the theoretical reducibility of multiple-argument functions to single-argument functions (and some functional languages provide only single-argument functions for exactly this reason), in a practical sense it is preferable that our interpreter directly support parameter lists. Therefore we extend our language to permit a list of bound variables in an abstraction, and to include a linguistic mechanism for constructing actual parameter lists (tuples).[8] These changes are reflected in the formation rules in Fig. 11.14. For example, the multiple-argument abstraction $\lambda(x, y)[f(y, x)]$ is represented by the tree

lambda {multi ('x', single 'y'), appl [id 'f', tuple (id 'y', id 'x')]}

Longer actual and formal parameter lists are represented by nested tuples. For example, $\lambda(x, y, z)[f(z, y, x)]$ is represented by

---

8. Thus we are building into the language a limited form of the parameter binding mechanisms discussed in Section 5.4. The full form is addressed in Ex. 11.31.

Figure 11.14 Abstract syntax including multiple-argument functions.

$$\text{expr} \equiv \left\{ \begin{array}{l} \text{id identifier} \\ \text{lambda (formals, expr)} \\ \text{appl (expr, expr)} \\ \text{tuple (expr, expr)} \\ \text{closure (expr, context)} \end{array} \right\}$$

$$\text{formals} \equiv \left\{ \begin{array}{l} \text{multi (identifier, formals)} \\ \text{single identifier} \end{array} \right\}$$

context ≡ finfunc (identifier → expr)
identifier ≡ **string**

---

lambda (multi ['x', multi ('y', single 'z')],
          appl {id 'f', tuple [id 'z', tuple (id 'y', id 'x')]})

We next extend our interpreter to handle these new constructs. Consider first the argument tuple constructor tuple (A, B); how is this evaluated? The result should be a structure tuple (V, W) in which the values V and W result from evaluating the corresponding expressions A and B in the current context. Hence

$$\text{eval [tuple } (A, B), C] \equiv \text{tuple [eval } (A, C), \text{eval } (B, C)] \qquad (11.19)$$

Next we consider abstractions with multiple formal parameters. Therefore, suppose that the first argument to apply is a closure containing an abstraction with a list of formal parameters:

$$K \equiv \text{closure \{lambda [multi } (x_1, \ldots, \text{single } x_n), B], C\}$$

Furthermore, suppose that V is a corresponding tuple of evaluated actual parameters:

$$V \equiv \text{tuple \{}v_1, \text{tuple } [v_2, \ldots, \text{tuple } (v_{n-1}, v_n) \cdots]\}$$

(For simplicity we ignore the check that ensures the number of formals and actuals is the same.) The body B of the abstraction is to be evaluated in a context C' resulting from overlaying the pairs (x_i, v_i) on the context of definition C. Hence

$$C' = \text{overl \{} \cdots \text{overl [overl } (C, x_1, v_1), x_2, v_2] \cdots, x_n, v_n\}$$

Figure 11.15 Interpreter with multiple-arguments.

eval: expr ✕ context → expr

eval (id x, C) ≡ Cx, if x ∈ dom C
else eval (id x, C) ≡ id x
eval [lambda (x, B), C] ≡ closure [lambda (x, B), C]
eval [appl (F, A), C] ≡ apply [eval (F, C), eval (A, C)]
eval [tuple (A, B), C] ≡ tuple [eval (A, C), eval (B, C)]

---

apply: expr ✕ expr → expr

apply {closure [lambda (X, B), C], V} ≡ eval [B, bindargs (X, V, C)]
else apply (F, V) ≡ appl (F, V)

---

bindargs: formals ✕ expr → context

bindargs [multi (x, Y), tuple (v, W), C] ≡ overl [bindargs (Y, W, C), x, v]
bindargs (single x, v, C) ≡ overl (C, x, v)

This can be accomplished by recursively walking the formal and actual trees. We can handle the case of either single- or multiple-parameter bindings of formals to actuals by a new auxiliary function bindargs:

$$\text{bindargs [multi } (x, Y), \text{ tuple } (v, W), C] \equiv \qquad (11.20)$$
$$\text{overl [bindargs } (Y, W, C), x, v]$$
$$\text{bindargs (single } x, v, C) \equiv \text{overl } (C, x, v)$$

The complete multiple-argument interpreter is shown in Fig. 11.15.

Exercise 11.10: Trace the execution of the following eval call:

eval (appl {lambda [multi ('x', single 'y'), appl (id 'x', id 'y')], tuple (id 'y', id 'a')}, nihil)

Exercise 11.11: Some functional languages (including Φ, see Section 5.4) permit *formal patterns* in definitions. For example, in such a language, if we had defined the function f by

$$f(K, (L, x, B), C) \equiv \cdots$$

then we could invoke f with any actual parameter that returned a list of the form $(V_1, (V_2, V_3, V_4), V_5)$. The body of the function would see the bindings $K = V_1$, $L = V_2$, $x = V_3$, $B = V_4$, and $C = V_5$. Extend the abstract syntax of Fig. 11.14 and the interpreter of Fig. 11.15 to permit formal patterns.

Exercise 11.12:   Modify your Scheme or LISP interpreter to accommodate the tuple construct and multiple-argument abstractions.

Exercise 11.13:   Modify the Pascal type declarations in FIg. 11.10 to incorporate the tuple construct and multiple-argument abstractions.

Exercise 11.14:   Modify the Pascal eval and apply functions (Figs. 11.11 and 11.12) and define a Pascal bindargs function so the the interpreter in Figs. 11.11 and 11.12 accommodates multiple-argument functions.

11.11 Constants

In Section 11.3 we said that complete functional programs are normally required to be closed, that is, to contain no unbound identifiers. Yet our interpreter, following the reduction rules of the lambda calculus, permits programs to contain free identifiers. Indeed it treats them very much like constant data values, since it passes them around without altering them. For example, if we evaluate the abstract equivalent of $[\lambda(x, y)x]\,(2, 3)$,

eval (appl {lambda [multi ('x', single 'y'), id 'x'], tuple (id '2', id '3')}, nihil)

we get the result id '2'.

Thus a program passed to our interpreter could contain free variables for two different reasons: they could be acting as constant values or they could be errors (e.g., misspelled identifiers). To distinguish these two cases, let's incorporate a new construct into our language to represent constant data values; we can then make free identifiers illegal. We extend the definition of expr to include constants belonging to a given type D, called the *data domain:*

$$
\text{expr } D \equiv \left\{
\begin{array}{l}
\text{con } D \\
\text{id identifier} \\
\text{lambda (formals, expr } D) \\
\text{tuple (expr } D, \text{ expr } D) \\
\text{appl (expr } D, \text{ expr } D) \\
\text{closure (expr } D, \text{ context } D)
\end{array}
\right\} \qquad (11.21)
$$

Since we have parameterized expr by D we will have different types of expressions depending on the domain of constant values that we presuppose. Similarly, we must parameterize context by the data domain:

type context D ≡ finfunc (identifier → expr D)   (11.22)

A typical data domain is a direct sum of other types, perhaps recursively defined.

The principal change necessary to our interpreter is to alter the first two clauses in the definition of eval to

$$\text{eval (con } k, C) \equiv \text{con } k \tag{11.23}$$
$$\text{eval (id } x, C) \equiv Cx$$

In the second equation, if x is not in the domain of C, the application of eval will be in error (although we have not bothered to write the equations for error handling). Another change, in the definition of apply, is necessary, since the case

$$\text{apply } (F, V) \equiv \text{appl } (F, V)$$

occurs only when F is not a closure; in other words, when it is a free identifier, or something that cannot legally be applied, such as a tuple. Since we have eliminated free identifiers, we eliminate this clause from apply. The resulting evaluator is shown in Fig. 11.16.

Consider the signature of that function:

$$\text{eval: expr } D \times \text{context } D \rightarrow \text{expr } D$$

Notice that eval returns something of the same type that it takes—expr D. This is to be expected since we derived eval from the reduction rules in Fig. 11.6, which map the abstract domain of closed expressions into itself.

Figure 11.16 Interpreter with constants over a data domain.

eval: expr D × context D → expr D

eval (con k, C) ≡ con k
eval (id x, C) ≡ Cx
eval [lambda (x, B), C] ≡ closure [lambda (x, B), C]
eval [appl (F, A), C] ≡ apply [eval (F, C), eval (A, C)]
eval [tuple (A, B), C] ≡ tuple [eval (A, C), eval (B, C)]

---

apply: expr D × expr D → expr D

apply {closure [lambda (X, B), C], V} ≡ eval [B, bindargs (X, V, C)]

---

bindargs: formals × expr D → context D

bindargs [multi (x, Y), tuple (v, W), C] ≡ overl [bindargs (Y, W, C), x, v]
bindargs (single x, v, C) ≡ overl (C, x, v)

On the other hand, this evaluator is different from our evaluator for arithmetic expressions in Section 5.9, which took expression trees as input but returned numeric values as output:

value←tree: tree × context → ℝ

The latter is more what we expect of an *evaluation* function: We expect it to return a value rather than an expression. This fundamental distinction between values and expressions should be accommodated in our syntax.

What sort of values can our interpreter return? Consider each clause of eval in turn. The clause

eval (con k, C) ≡ con k

says that eval may return an expression of the form con k, where k is of type D. Thus eval may return constants in the data domain. The clause

eval (id x, C) ≡ Cx

says that eval may return anything to which an identifier may be bound. Identifiers, however, are bound only to the values of actual parameters, and these are evaluated by eval, so this equation tells us nothing new about values returned by eval. Next consider the clause

eval [lambda (x, B), C] ≡ closure [lambda (x, B), C]

This tells us that eval may return a closure, so we have two kinds of things (so far) that may be results of evaluation: constants in the data domain and closures. Consider the next equation:

eval [appl (F, A), C] ≡ apply [eval (F, C), eval (A, C)]

This tells us that eval returns the same sorts of things that apply returns. To determine what these are, we look at the equation for apply:

apply {closure [lambda (X, B), C], V} ≡ eval [B, bindargs (X, V, C)]

We see that apply returns the same sorts of things as eval, so we have learned nothing new. The last equation adds a third kind of value, tuples:

eval [tuple (A, B), C] ≡ tuple [eval (A, C), eval (B, C)]

Thus the results of evaluation may only be constants in the data domain, closures, or tuples.

The preceding analysis suggests that we can divide our abstract structures into two kinds: *expressions* (constants, identifiers, tuples, abstractions, and applications) and *values* (data domain values, tuples, and closures). This leads to the abstract syntax shown in Fig. 11.17, in which we have included a *typical* definition of the data domain D.[9] As explained earlier, it's necessary to include tuples and closures among the data values since they may be results of evaluation. Now that we have separated the expression (program) domain and the data domain we can give eval a more familiar signature:

$$\text{eval: expr } D \times \text{context } D \rightarrow D$$

The necessary changes to the interpreter are minor, and can be found in Fig. 11.18. Indeed they are simplifications.

Figure 11.17 Abstract syntax for expressions and values.

$$\text{expr } D \equiv \left\{ \begin{array}{l} \text{con } D \\ \text{id identifier} \\ \text{lambda (formals, expr } D) \\ \text{appl (expr } D, \text{ expr } D) \\ \text{tuple (expr } D, \text{ expr } D) \end{array} \right\}$$

$$\text{formals} \equiv \left\{ \begin{array}{l} \text{multi (identifier, formals)} \\ \text{single identifier} \end{array} \right\}$$

$$D \equiv \left\{ \begin{array}{l} \text{Boolean } \mathbb{B} \\ \text{number } \mathbb{R} \\ \text{str } \textbf{string} \\ \text{tuple } (D, D) \\ \text{sequence } D^* \\ \text{closure (expr } D, \text{ context } D) \end{array} \right\}$$

context $D \equiv$ finfunc (identifier $\rightarrow D$)
identifier $\equiv$ **string**

9. Notice that making D a direct sum causes the interpreter to implement dynamic typing (since every data value carries its tag). The ultimate reason for this is our decision, in Section 8.7, to use the untyped lambda calculus. Providing dynamic typing is not a problem since static typing is more restrictive. Therefore this interpreter will work for a statically typed language such as Φ as well as for a dynamically typed language. In a statically typed language, type checking is typically done by the compiler rather than the interpreter.

Figure 11.18 Interpreter with different expression and data domains.

eval: expr D × context D → D

eval (con k, C) ≡ k
eval (id x, C) ≡ Cx
eval [lambda (x, B), C] ≡ closure [lambda (x, B), C]
eval [appl (F, A), C] ≡ apply [eval (F, C), eval (A, C)]
eval [tuple (A, B), C] ≡ tuple [eval (A, C), eval (B, C)]

apply: D × D → D

apply {closure [lambda (X, B), C], V} ≡ eval [B, bindargs (X, V, C)]

bindargs: formals × D → context D

bindargs [multi (x, Y), tuple (v, W), C] ≡ overl [bindargs (Y, W, C), x, v]
bindargs (single x, v, C) ≡ overl (C, x, v)

Exercise 11.15: Trace the execution of the following invocation of eval:

eval (appl {lambda [multi ('x', single 'y'), appl (id 'x', id 'y')],
        tuple [con (str 'f'), con (number 3)]}, nihil)

Exercise 11.16: The interpreter as described does not check for unbound identifiers. Alter it so that it returns a special error value if we attempt to evaluate an unbound identifier. *Hint:* You must alter the definition of D.

Exercise 11.17: Modify your Scheme or LISP interpreter to incorporate constants.

Exercise 11.18: Modify your previous Pascal definition of eval to incorporate constants. Note that since Pascal does not have polymorphic types, you must define a particular data domain D for the expressions.

11.12 Intrinsic Identifiers

Beyond the two reasons discussed in the previous section, there is a third reason why we might have free identifiers in a program: We might assume they are *predefined* or *intrinsic* to the language. Many languages include such predefined identifiers, for example, for mathematical constants (e.g., 'pi'), for built-in types (e.g., **'string'**), for standard input and standard output files (e.g., 'stand-in'), and for built-in functions (e.g., 'sin').

These are often considered to be bound in a *standard prelude* of **let** declarations that are appended by the system to the beginning of every program.

Alternatively, the intrinsic identifiers can be considered to be bound in a standard context that is used to evaluate every program. For example, when a user types in an expression E to be evaluated, instead of executing eval $(E,$ nihil$)$, we execute eval $(E,$ Intrinsics$)$, in which Intrinsics is the name of a context (finite function) that binds all the intrinsic identifiers. For example,

Intrinsics $\equiv$ ['pi' $\mapsto$ number 3.141592653589, 'nil' $\mapsto$ sequence <>, $\cdots$]

The important topic of intrinsic functions is discussed next.

Our interpreter now handles many of the constructs one would expect in a practical programming language: constants, user-defined and intrinsic identifiers, and user-defined functions. It still, however, lacks something very important: built-in or *intrinsic* functions. You know from Sections 8.8–8.13 that in a theoretical sense the primitive types ($\mathbb{B}$, $\mathbb{Z}$, T^*, and so forth), including their operators, can be defined in terms of the pure lambda calculus. Thus they are not strictly necessary. On the other hand, representing integers in unary notation by tuples, and tuples in turn by abstractions, is very inefficient, and efficiency is our main concern in the last part of this chapter.

One reason why this definition of arithmetic is so inefficient is inherent in the use of unary notation: The time to perform arithmetic operations tends to be proportional to the magnitudes of the operands, rather than to the logarithms of these magnitudes, as in binary notation. The more fundamental reason, however, is that most computers provide hardware instructions that perform the arithmetic operations very efficiently— usually in constant time. Thus it is good engineering for the implementation of the interpreted language to make use of these hardware-provided facilities.

It is not necessary to program in machine language, however, to make use of these facilities. Just as we used function calls in the *interpreting* language to describe function calls in the *interpreted* language, we can use the primitive functions of the interpreting language to describe the primitive functions of the interpreted language. That might seem a bit odd in this case, since the interpreting and interpreted languages are the same (i.e., Φ), but it is true nonetheless. Thus we use the '+' operator of Φ (as the interpreting language) to implement the '+' operator of Φ (as the interpreted language).

Although this may seem to be mysterious, or even a vicious circle, it is easy to understand if we consider writing a desk calculator program in a conventional language such as Pascal. Surely we would use the numeric types and arithmetic operators of Pascal to implement the corresponding operations in the desk calculator. Similarly, to write a Φ interpreter in

Pascal, we would use the numerical facilities of Pascal to implement the numerical facilities of Φ, and the pointer facilities of Pascal to implement the sequences of Φ. The same situation holds if we write our Φ interpreter in Φ.

To see how to modify our interpreter to handle intrinsic functions, consider an application such as '[+] (2, 3)', which is represented by the tuple

appl {id '[+]', tuple [con (number 2), con (number 3)]}

Evaluating the actual parameter list yields tuple (number 2, number 3), which becomes the second argument to apply. What is the result of evaluating the operator, id '[+]'?

If '[+]' were a user-defined function—that is, if '[+]' were bound to an abstraction—then this evaluation would yield a closure, which would be handled by apply in the usual way.

On the other hand, if '[+]' is an intrinsic function, then it is not defined in the interpreted language; it is not bound to an abstraction. It must be bound to something that tells apply to perform an intrinsic operation. For example, we could introduce a new referent for bound identifiers denoting intrinsic functions; the resulting syntax is shown in Fig. 11.19.

Figure 11.19 Abstract syntax including intrinsic functions.

$$\text{expr } D \equiv \left\{ \begin{array}{l} \text{con } D \\ \text{id identifier} \\ \text{lambda (formals, expr } D) \\ \text{appl (expr } D, \text{ expr } D) \\ \text{tuple (expr } D, \text{ expr } D) \end{array} \right.$$

$$\text{formals} \equiv \left\{ \begin{array}{l} \text{multi (identifier, formals)} \\ \text{single identifier} \end{array} \right.$$

$$D \equiv \left\{ \begin{array}{l} \text{Boolean } \mathbb{B} \\ \text{number } \mathbb{R} \\ \text{str string} \\ \text{tuple } (D, D) \\ \text{sequence } D^* \\ \text{closure (expr } D, \text{ context } D) \\ \text{intrinsic identifier} \end{array} \right.$$

context $D \equiv$ finfunc (identifier $\rightarrow D$)
identifier $\equiv$ string

Then, if the first argument of apply were intrinsic '+', it would know to do a + operation; if it were intrinsic 'first', a first operation, and so forth. An appropriate definition of apply is shown in Fig. 11.20. The structure of this definition shows that the only things that can be applied are closures and intrinsics (i.e., user-defined functions and built-in functions).

We have also used an auxiliary definition, apply_intrinsic, to handle intrinsic function applications. Note that for single-argument functions V is the argument, whereas for multiple-argument functions the argument list has the form of a tuple tuple $(V_1, \text{tuple } (V_2, \cdots, V_n) \cdots)$, so V_1, $V_2, \cdots$ are the actual arguments. Also notice that the type checking of the arguments of the intrinsic functions is implicit in the cases of apply_intrinsic.

Exercise 11.19: Explain each of the tags in the definition of apply_intrinsic in Fig. 11.20.

Of course the definition of apply can be extended to include whatever functions it is useful and economical to build into the language. To make these intrinsic functions available to the programmer, it is necessary to bind names to them in the standard prelude. This is accomplished by a definition such as

$$\text{Intrinsics} \equiv ['[+]' \mapsto \text{intrinsic '+',}$$
$$'[-]' \mapsto \text{intrinsic '-',}$$
$$'[=]' \mapsto \text{intrinsic '=', } \cdots]$$

Here we use the same string for both the name of the function and the code passed to apply_intrinsic, that is, for operator s, fapply (Intrinsics, '[s]') = intrinsic 's'. This is certainly not necessary; if we wanted the standard

---

Figure 11.20 apply function that handles intrinsic functions.

apply: $D \times D \rightarrow D$

apply {closure [lambda $(X, B), C$], V} $\equiv$ eval [B, bindargs (X, V, C)]
apply (intrinsic f, V) $\equiv$ apply_intrinsic (f, V)

where   apply_intrinsic ['+', tuple (number U, number W)] $\equiv$ number $(U + W)$
apply_intrinsic ['-', tuple (number U, number W)] $\equiv$ number $(U - W)$
apply_intrinsic ['=', tuple (number U, number W)] $\equiv$ Boolean $(U = W)$
apply_intrinsic ['prefix', tuple $(U$, sequence $W)$] $\equiv$ sequence $(U : W)$
apply_intrinsic ('first', sequence V) $\equiv$ first V
apply_intrinsic ('rest', sequence V) $\equiv$ sequence (rest V)

$\vdots$

names for addition, subtraction, and equality to be 'plus', 'minus', and 'equal', we could use the standard prelude

Intrinsics ≡ ['plus' ↦ intrinsic '+',
              'minus' ↦ intrinsic '−',
              'equal' ↦ intrinsic '=', · · ·]

Hence the design of the interpreter is independent of the names chosen for the intrinsic functions.

With these extensions it is now possible to evaluate an expression such as '2 × 3 + 1', that is, '[+] {[×] (2, 3), 1}', by the invocation

eval {appl (id '[+]', tuple [appl {id '[×]', tuple [con (number 2),
                          con (number 3)]}, con (number 1)], Intrinsics}

(supposing that Intrinsics included bindings for '[+]' and '[×]'). This invocation would return number 7.

Exercise 11.20: Translate the following expression to abstract form and trace the execution of its evaluation in the Intrinsics context:

{λf. [+] (f3, f5)} {λx. [−] (x, 1)}

Exercise 11.21: Do the same for the expression

let i ≡ 3 **in**
  let fx ≡ [−] (x, i) **in**
    let i ≡ 2 **in**
      $f\,i$

Note that you must first convert the **let**s into abstractions and applications (Section 8.11).

Exercise 11.22: Modify your Scheme or LISP interpreter to incorporate intrinsic functions.

Exercise 11.23: Modify the Pascal type declaration for expr to incorporate intrinsic identifiers.

Exercise 11.24: Define an appropriate apply_intrinsic for the Pascal implementation of eval.

Notice that the definition of apply_intrinsic is highly regular; this regularity can be made more apparent by writing the applications in prefix form. For example, the case

$$\text{apply\_intrinsic } ['+', \text{ tuple (number } U, \text{ number } W)] \equiv \text{number } (U + W)$$

can be written

apply_intrinsic $('+', V) \equiv$
   $(\text{number} \circ [+]) \, [(\text{number}^{-1} \circ \text{left} \circ \text{tuple}^{-1}) \, V, \, (\text{number}^{-1} \circ \text{right} \circ \text{tuple}^{-1}) \, V \,]$

The right-hand side can be written

$$[\text{number} \circ [+] \circ (\text{number}^{-1} \times \text{number}^{-1}) \circ \text{tuple}^{-1}] \, V$$

Notice that, reading from *right to left*, we first find tuple^{-1}, which defines the structure of the argument V; next we find (number^{-1} × number^{-1}), which restricts the types of its components; next is [+], which executes the operation; and finally we find number, which defines the type of the result. All the cases of apply_intrinsic can be similarly expressed:

apply_intrinsic $('+', V) \equiv [\text{number} \circ [+] \circ (\text{number}^{-1} \times \text{number}^{-1}) \circ \text{tuple}^{-1}] \, V$
apply_intrinsic $('-', V) \equiv [\text{number} \circ [-] \circ (\text{number}^{-1} \times \text{number}^{-1}) \circ \text{tuple}^{-1}] \, V$
apply_intrinsic $('=', V) \equiv [\text{Boolean} \circ [=] \circ (\text{number}^{-1} \times \text{number}^{-1}) \circ \text{tuple}^{-1}] \, V$
apply_intrinsic $('\text{prefix}', V) \equiv [\text{sequence} \circ \text{prefix} \circ (\mathbf{I} \times \text{sequence}^{-1}) \circ \text{tuple}^{-1}] \, V$
apply_intrinsic $('\text{first}', V) \equiv [\text{first} \circ \text{sequence}^{-1}] \, V$
apply_intrinsic $('\text{rest}', V) \equiv [\text{sequence} \circ \text{rest} \circ \text{sequence}^{-1}] \, V$

In general, if p is the string that names operator P, as '+' names

$$\text{number} \circ [+] \circ (\text{number}^{-1} \times \text{number}^{-1}) \circ \text{tuple}^{-1}$$

then each case has the form 'apply_intrinsic $(p, V) \equiv PV$'. Thus, if we had a table Meaning that bound p directly to P, we could write apply_intrinsic as

$$\text{apply\_intrinsic } (f, V) \equiv (\text{Meaning } f) \, V$$

That is, we apply the intrinsic function named f to V by looking up the name f in Meaning and applying the function obtained to V. The definition of the finite function Meaning is very simple:

Meaning $\equiv ['+' \mapsto \text{number} \circ [+] \circ (\text{number}^{-1} \times \text{number}^{-1}) \circ \text{tuple}^{-1},$
   $'-' \mapsto \text{number} \circ [-] \circ (\text{number}^{-1} \times \text{number}^{-1}) \circ \text{tuple}^{-1},$
   $'=' \mapsto \text{Boolean} \circ [=] \circ (\text{number}^{-1} \times \text{number}^{-1}) \circ \text{tuple}^{-1}, \cdots]$

This approach simplifies the definition so much that we can eliminate the auxiliary function apply_intrinsic altogether; the resulting interpreter is shown in Fig. 11.21.

Notice that the design of the interpreter is now completely independent of the intrinsic functions. The available intrinsic functions are determined by Meaning, and their names, by which they are known in

---

Figure 11.21 Interpreter with functionally implemented intrinsics.

---

eval: expr D × context D → D

eval (con k, C) ≡ k
eval (id x, C) ≡ Cx
eval ˙lambda $(x, B), C$] ≡ closure [lambda $(x, B), C$]
eval [appl $(F, A), C$] ≡ apply [eval (F, C), eval (A, C)]
eval [tuple $(A, B), C$] ≡ tuple [eval (A, C), eval (B, C)]

---

apply: D × D → D

apply {closure [lambda $(X, B), C$], V} ≡ eval [B, bindargs (X, V, C)]
apply (intrinsic f, V) ≡ Meaning f V

---

bindargs: formals × D → context D

bindargs [multi (x, Y), tuple $(v, W), C$] ≡ overl [bindargs (Y, W, C), x, v]
bindargs (single x, v, C) ≡ overl (C, x, v)

---

programs, are defined by Intrinsics. Thus the interpreter defines an application-independent *language framework*, while the data structures Intrinsics and Meaning particularize this framework by providing a set of application-oriented primitives. Thus we can have a family of closely related application-oriented languages.[10]

The Meaning data structure is somewhat unusual. It is a table (finite function), but the table entries contain functions, that is, code. Such *functional data structures* are perfectly acceptable in a functional programming language since functions are first-class citizens. They are not, however, acceptable in most nonfunctional languages (e.g., Pascal and Ada). In these languages it would be necessary to use the earlier, nonfunctional definition of apply_intrinsic. The nonfunctional definition does not separate the application-oriented intrinsics from the application-independent framework as well as the functional definition does.

Exercise 11.25: Discuss the pros and cons of using data structures, such as Meaning, that contain code.

Exercise 11.26: Using this new interpreter, redo the previous exercises that asked you to trace the evaluation of expressions involving intrinsic functions.

Exercise 11.27: Modify your Scheme or LISP interpreter to use the Meaning structure.

---

10. See (Landin 1966) and (Backus 1978) for a fuller discussion of these ideas. See also Section 2.1.

11.13 Auxiliary Declarations

We next consider the implementation of auxiliary declarations (i.e., **lets** and **where**s). Recall from Section 8.11 that auxiliary declarations are formally defined in terms of function application. In particular, '**let** $x \equiv V$ **in** B' and 'B **where** $x \equiv V$' are both considered syntactic sugarings of '$(\lambda xB)V$'. Thus the simplest way to implement auxiliary declarations is to translate them into the corresponding applications. An expression like '**let** $a \equiv 2$ **in** $a + 1$' is translated into the abstract structure

> appl [lambda (single 'a', appl {id '[+]', tuple [id 'a', con (number 1)]}),
>   con (number 2)]

If we take this approach, then the interpreter need not even be aware of the existence of auxiliary declarations.

Although auxiliary declarations can be implemented in this way, it is a little inefficient. Consider the steps in evaluating the expression $(\lambda xB)V$. Since this is an application, the interpreter must evaluate the operator (λxB) and the operand V. Evaluation of the operator, which is an abstraction, results in the construction of a closure, which is passed to apply along with the value of V. The apply procedure immediately breaks this closure down into its components, and constructs the environment of evaluation for the body B. Thus we go to the trouble to assemble a closure even though we will disassemble it as our very next action. This seems a bit wasteful.

In fact it is easy to see that it's not necessary to construct the closure at all. The purpose of the closure is to record the context of definition of the abstraction, allowing it to be used as the nonlocal context for the body of the abstraction. This is because a call is performed in the context of the definition of the function, rather than in the context of the call. In the case of the application $(\lambda xB)V$ resulting from a auxiliary declaration, however, the context of definition and the context of call are the same. Hence there is no need to save the context of definition in a closure.

The preceding discussion may have left you a bit confused. If we attempt to improve the implementation of auxiliary declarations by avoiding closure construction, can we be sure that our implementation is correct? Fortunately, a functional programming technique allows us to prove that our optimized implementation has the same effect as the formal definition.

To illustrate the technique, we begin with a simple example: noncompound auxiliary declarations (i.e., **lets** and **where**s without **and**s). Let's add to the abstract syntax of our language new abstract structures of the form let (x, V, B), which correspond to the concrete structures '**let** $x \equiv V$ **in** B' and 'B **where** $x \equiv V$'. Next we *derive* the correct implementation of this construct from its formal definition. The evaluation of an expression let (x, V, B) in a context C must be the same as the evaluation of

appl [lambda $(x, B), V$]

in C. Applying the single-argument definition of eval (Fig. 11.13) we derive

$$
\begin{aligned}
\text{eval } [\text{let } (x, V, B), C] &= \text{eval } \{\text{appl } [\text{lambda } (x, B), V], C\} \\
&= \text{apply } \{\text{eval } [\text{lambda } (x, B), C], \text{eval } (V, C)\} \\
&= \text{apply } \{\text{closure } [\text{lambda } (x, B), C], \text{eval } (V, C)\} \\
&= \text{eval } \{B, \text{overl } [C, x, \text{eval } (V, C)]\}
\end{aligned}
$$

This result is very plausible: To evaluate 'let $x \equiv V$ in B' we evaluate B in the context that results from adding to the current context the binding of x to the value of V. Hence we can incorporate noncompound auxiliary declarations into our interpreter by adding this clause to eval:

$$
\text{eval } [\text{let } (x, V, B), C] \equiv \text{eval } \{B, \text{overl } [C, x, \text{eval } (V, C)]\} \qquad (11.24)
$$

We can now address the general case of compound auxiliary declarations. Recall from Section 8.11 that compound declarations

$$
\text{let } x_1 \equiv V_1 \text{ and } x_2 \equiv V_2 \text{ and } \cdots \text{ and } x_n \equiv V_n \text{ in } B
$$
$$
B \text{ where } x_1 \equiv V_1 \text{ and } x_2 \equiv V_2 \text{ and } \cdots \text{ and } x_n \equiv V_n
$$

are formally defined by the application

$$
[\lambda(x_1, x_2, \ldots, x_n) B] (V_1, V_2, \ldots, V_n)
$$

which is represented by the abstract structure

appl (lambda [multi $\{x_1,$ multi $[x_2, \ldots,$ multi $(x_{n-1}, \text{single } x_n) \cdots]\}, B],$
    tuple $\{V_1,$ tuple $[V_2, \ldots,$ tuple $(V_{n-1}, V_n) \cdots]\})$

Therefore we take an analogous form for the abstract structure representing compound auxiliary declarations:

let (multi $\{x_1,$ multi $[x_2, \ldots,$ multi $(x_{n-1}, \text{single } x_n) \cdots]\},$
    tuple $\{V_1,$ tuple $[V_2, \ldots,$ tuple $(V_{n-1}, V_n) \cdots]\}, B)$

This is reflected in the abstract syntax in Fig. 11.22.

Figure 11.22 Abstract syntax including auxiliary declarations.

$$\text{expr } D \equiv \left\{ \begin{array}{l} \text{con } D \\ \text{id identifier} \\ \text{lambda (formals, expr } D) \\ \text{appl (expr } D, \text{ expr } D) \\ \text{tuple (expr } D, \text{ expr } D) \\ \text{let (formals, expr } D, \text{ expr } D) \end{array} \right\}$$

$$\text{formals } \equiv \left\{ \begin{array}{l} \text{multi (identifier, formals)} \\ \text{single identifier} \end{array} \right\}$$

$$D \equiv \left\{ \begin{array}{l} \text{Boolean } \mathbb{B} \\ \text{number } \mathbb{R} \\ \text{str } \textbf{string} \\ \text{tuple } (D, D) \\ \text{sequence } D^* \\ \text{closure (expr } D, \text{ context } D) \\ \text{intrinsic identifier} \end{array} \right\}$$

context $D \equiv$ finfunc (identifier $\rightarrow D$)
identifier $\equiv$ **string**

It is now a simple matter to derive the implementation from the formal definition:

$$\begin{aligned} \text{eval [let } (X, V, B), C] &= \text{eval \{appl [lambda } (X, B), V], C\} \\ &= \text{apply \{eval [lambda } (X, B), C], \text{ eval } (V, C)\} \\ &= \text{apply \{closure [lambda } (X, B), C], \text{ eval } (V, C)\} \\ &= \text{eval \{} B, \text{ bindargs } [X, \text{ eval } (V, C), C]\} \end{aligned}$$

Hence general auxiliary declarations can be handled by adding this clause to the interpreter:

$$\text{eval [let } (X, V, B), C] \equiv \text{eval \{} B, \text{ bindargs } [X, \text{ eval } (V, C), C]\} \qquad (11.25)$$

The resulting interpreter is shown in Fig. 11.23. In a sense the interpreter is complete, and in a sense incomplete. We have not included conditional expressions or recursive declarations. You know from Sections 8.8 and 8.12, however, that these can be defined in terms of the constructs that we've already implemented. We'll see that these definitions work correctly only if the interpreter implements a certain evaluation order. These important issues are the subject of the next chapter.

Figure 11.23 Interpreter with auxiliary declarations.

eval: expr D X context D → D

eval (con k, C) ≡ k
eval (id x, C) ≡ Cx
eval [lambda (x, B), C] ≡ closure [lambda (x, B), C]
eval [appl (F, A), C] ≡ apply [eval (F, C), eval (A, C)]
eval [tuple (A, B), C] ≡ tuple [eval (A, C), eval (B, C)]
eval [let (X, V, B), C] ≡ eval {B, bindargs [X, eval (V, C), C]}

---

apply: D X D → D

apply {closure [lambda (X, B), C], V} ≡ eval [B, bindargs (X, V, C)]
apply (intrinsic f, V) ≡ Meaning f V

---

bindargs: formals X D X context D → context D

bindargs [multi (x, Y), tuple (v, W), C] ≡ overl [bindargs (Y, W, C), x, v]
bindargs (single x, v, C) ≡ overl (C, x, v)

Exercise 11.28: Modify your Scheme or LISP interpreter to incorporate auxiliary declarations.

Exercise 11.29: Alter the Pascal type declarations for **expr** to incorporate auxiliary declarations.

Exercise 11.30: Alter the Pascal implementation of **eval** to incorporate auxiliary declarations.

Exercise 11.31: Alter the interpreter to incorporate deconstructing auxiliary declarations (see Section 5.4). For example, if Fx returns a list of the form $(u, (v, w), x)$, then

let $(a, (b, c), d) \equiv Fx$ **in** $\cdots$

binds a, b, c and d to the elements u, v, w and x. *Hint:* This can be accomplished by *simplifying* both the abstract syntax and the interpreter.

Chapter 12

Evaluation Order and Recursion

12.1 Pass-by-Value or Pass-by-Name?

In the last chapter we derived an interpreter from the transformation rules of the lambda calculus. Since this derivation was accomplished by correctness-preserving transformations, we know—barring mistakes in our application of the transformations—that the resulting interpreter is correct. In this case, 'correct' means that the interpreter will produce the same value as the lambda calculus transformation rules. This is not all there is to correctness, however, because the transformation rules can be applied in many different orders. Even though the Church-Rosser Theorem says that the value (normal form) is unique, we know that some reduction orders do not terminate. Although our interpreter might seem to implement a particular reduction order, this is not the case: Because our interpreter is a functional program, and functional programs are independent of evaluation order, different implementations of the functional language might pick different evaluation orders.[1] Therefore the

---

1. Of course, the definitions of some functional languages constrain the permissible evaluation orders. We have chosen not to do this in Φ so that evaluation order can be discussed as an issue.

evaluation order implemented by our interpreter might be influenced by the evaluation order of the language in which it's written. Although desirable in some cases, in most cases we wish to *decouple* the evaluation orders, allowing us to control the implemented evaluation order. The topic of this chapter is the effects of evaluation order and the means to control it.

Suppose that f is the constant 1 function: $f \equiv x \mapsto 1$. Then $fa = 1$, for all values a; the value of a does not matter. Consider now the application f (**YY**), supposing as usual that **YY** leads to a nonterminating computation:

$$\mathbf{YY} \Rightarrow \mathbf{Y(YY)} \Rightarrow \mathbf{Y(Y(YY))} \Rightarrow \cdots$$

What is the value of the application f (**YY**)? On the one hand, we've said that $fa = 1$ for all a; and seemingly this includes $a = \mathbf{YY}$, so we could conclude that f (**YY**) = 1. On the other hand, if in attempting to reduce f (**YY**) we begin with its argument, we are led to the nonterminating reduction

$$f\,(\mathbf{YY}) \Rightarrow f\,(\mathbf{Y(YY)}) \Rightarrow f\,(\mathbf{Y(Y(YY))}) \Rightarrow \cdots$$

We will never find out that f is a constant function because we will never finish evaluating its actual parameter.

It seems that f (**YY**) = 1 and that f (**YY**) is nonterminating. Is this a contradiction? It depends on what we mean by a *value*. We said that $fa = 1$ for all *values a*. If we say that *value* denotes any expression whatsoever, including **YY**, we can conclude that f (**YY**) = 1. On the other hand, we can say that *value* denotes the result of evaluating (i.e., reducing) an expression. Since **YY** has no normal form, we can conclude that it has no value. Hence we *cannot* conclude that f (**YY**) = 1, since the equation $fa = 1$ applies only when a is a value and **YY** is not a value.

This illustrates two different semantic interpretations of functions. A function is said to have *strict* semantics if an application of that function is undefined whenever at least one of its arguments is undefined. A function is said to have *lenient* semantics if an application of that function may be defined even though one or more of its arguments is undefined. Thus there are two interpretations of the constant function $f \equiv x \mapsto 1$. The strict interpretation says that f (**YY**) is undefined; the lenient interpretation, that f (**YY**) = 1.

Both interpretations reflect legal reductions; which is correct? Consider the lambda calculus expression $(\lambda x\,1)\,(\mathbf{YY})$. If we first reduce the *outermost* application, the one whose operator is '$(\lambda x\,1)$', we get the terminating reduction

$$(\lambda x\,1)\,(\mathbf{YY}) \Rightarrow 1[x = \mathbf{YY}] \Rightarrow 1$$

This is because there are *no* free occurrences of 'x' in '1', the body of the abstraction, so we discard the dangerous formula '**YY**'. On the other hand, if we reduce the *innermost* application—**YY**—first, then we get a nonterminating reduction:

$$(\lambda x\, 1)\, (\mathbf{YY}) \;\Rightarrow\; (\lambda x\, 1)\, (\mathbf{Y(YY)}) \;\Rightarrow\; (\lambda x\, 1)\, (\mathbf{Y(Y(YY))}) \;\Rightarrow\; \cdots$$

The outcome is different depending on the evaluation order. Of course, this does not contradict the Church-Rosser Theorem, since the theorem states only that *terminating* reductions yield the same normal forms; it says nothing about *nonterminating* reductions.

We can gain some further insight by considering an analogous problem in conventional imperative languages. Consider an Algol 60 procedure corresponding to *f*:

```
integer procedure f (x);
value x; integer x;
begin f := 1 end;
```

In Algol 60 the *value specification*, '**value** x', requests that the parameter 'x' be *passed-by-value*, which means that it is evaluated once, at call time, and that the resulting value is used throughout the invocation of the procedure.

What is the result of the function invocation 'f (1/0)'? Attempting to evaluate the actual parameter '1/0' will result in an error (the practical equivalent of a nonterminating reduction), so the function 'f' will never be invoked. Thus pass-by-value corresponds to the *innermost* reduction order.

Algol 60 has another parameter-passing mode, *pass-by-name*, which is not found in most other programming languages. The programmer requests that a parameter be passed by name by omitting the value specification:

```
integer procedure f (x);
integer x;
begin f := 1 end;
```

Thus pass-by-name is the default parameter-passing mode in Algol 60.

A parameter passed by name is *not* evaluated at the time of the call, but rather every time the parameter is used during the execution of the procedure. If used more than once, it will be evaluated more than once. Since imperative languages do not have referential transparency this reevaluation may affect the outcome of the program—each evaluation can yield a different value. Indeed the confusions resulting from the interaction of pass-by-name and the "referential opacity" of imperative languages are the main reason why pass-by-name has been dropped from most languages designed after Algol 60. These confusions are discussed in more detail in (MacLennan 1987b, Chapter 3).

A parameter passed by name is evaluated just as many times as it is used; if the parameter is never used, it will never be evaluated. This is the situation with the function 'f'; because it never references the parameter 'x', we will never attempt the erroneous division '1/0'. The invocation 'f (1/0)' proceeds by entering 'f' (without evaluating the parameter), executing the assignment 'f := 1' and returning the value 1. The expression '1/0' causes no trouble because it is never executed. You can see that pass-by-name corresponds to an *outermost* reduction order.

A similar situation is found in Pascal. Suppose the array 'A' has been declared by

```
var  A: array [1..100] of integer;
```

A common mistake is to write code such as the following to search the array:

```
i := 1;
while (i ≤ 100) and (A[i] ≠ key) do i := i+1;
```

What is wrong with this? If the value 'key' is not in the array, then the entire array will be searched and on the last iteration 'i' will be 101. Thus, in the process of evaluating the expression

```
(i ≤ 100) and (A[i] ≠ key)
```

we must evaluate 'A[101]', which violates the bounds on the array 'A'. The problem is that in Pascal the arguments of the and operator are passed by value; thus both 'i ≤ 100' and 'A[i] ≠ key' must be evaluated before they can be passed to the and operator. In this case the second argument has no value.

To avoid this problem some languages, such as Scheme and LISP, define the logical connectives so that their arguments are passed by name. In the Scheme or LISP expression

```
(and E_1 E_2 ··· E_n)
```

the expressions E_i are evaluated in order from left to right. As soon as one of them returns false, the entire and returns false, since false and anything is false. Similarly, Ada has the **'and then'** operator, which allows the array search loop to be written in the obvious way:

```
I := 1;
while I <= 100 and then A[I] /= KEY loop
  I := I+1;
end loop;
```

The 'and then' terminology explicitly reflects the fact that the second relation should be evaluated only if necessary, that is, only if the first relation
is true. This is called the *sequential* or *conditional* interpretation of the logical connectives: The second argument is evaluated only if necessary to
determine the result of the connective.

Exercise 12.1: How are the logical connectives defined in the programming languages that you use? Does the language definition say they are strict or
lenient, or does it neglect to say at all? Often programmers write programs that
depend on a lenient semantics even though the language definition may not
require that the operators be implemented leniently. Such programs are not port-
able.

12.2 Strict or Lenient Semantics?

There are several equivalent ways to view the most common evaluation
orders. First, they can be viewed as different parameter-passing modes:
pass-by-value if the parameter is evaluated once at call time; *pass-by-name*,
if evaluated just as many times as it is used. Second, evaluation orders
can be viewed as different reduction orders: *standard order* (or *applicative
order*) if reduction begins with the *innermost* applications; *normal order* if it
begins with the *outermost* application. Third, they can be viewed as different semantic interpretations of functions: *strict* if the value of a function
is defined only if its argument is defined; *lenient* if the value may
be defined even if its argument is undefined. These are summarized in
Table 12.1.

The preceding discussion leads to an obvious question: Does the functional language Φ use pass-by-value or pass-by-name semantics? More
generally, which semantics *should* be used in functional languages?

It has seemed preferable to avoid the issue of evaluation order in Φ
since this order does not affect the outcome of most functional programs.[2]
Furthermore, since different functional languages use different evaluation
orders, it seemed best to discuss functional programming independently

---

Table 12.1. Evaluation orders compared.

Reduction Order	Starting Place	Function Semantics	Parameter Passing Mode
Standard	Innermost	Strict	Value
Normal	Outermost	Lenient	Name

---

2. Of course, evaluation order is crucial to some programs, such as those using recursive
   data structures (see Section 7.6). Implementation of recursive data structures is the subject of Section 12.11.

of evaluation order. Thus Φ programs, like the lambda calculus expressions to which they correspond, can be evaluated in a variety of orders. This gives implementations the flexibility to implement Φ programs efficiently, for example, by parallel evaluation.

As we've seen, however, although evaluation order cannot affect *what* value we get, it can affect *whether* we get a value. The time has come to investigate in more detail the properties of various evaluation orders.

Exercise 12.2: Discuss the advantages and disadvantages of strict and lenient function semantics. Which do you think is better for functional programming?

12.3 Inheritance of Evaluation Order

Can we tell which evaluation order is used in a language by inspecting a universal function for that language? Consider the interpretation by the eval interpreter (Fig. 11.23) of the tree representation of the Φ program '$(x \mapsto 1)(1/0)$':

```
eval [appl (lambda [single 'x', con (number 1)],
            appl {id '[/]', tuple [con (number 1), con (number 0)]}),
      Intrinsics]
```

Let F be the tree representation of the function $x \mapsto 1$ and U be the tree representation of the undefined expression (1/0). Then, to consider the evaluation of

```
eval [appl (F, U), Intrinsics]
```

we simply follow the definition of eval:

```
eval [appl (F, U), Intrinsics]
= apply [eval (F, Intrinsics), eval (U, Intrinsics)]
```

What happens next? If Φ uses pass-by-value, then we will attempt to evaluate the arguments of apply, allowing their values to be passed to apply. Evaluating 'eval (U, Intrinsics)', however, will result in an error, preventing proper termination of the program. On the other hand, suppose that Φ uses pass-by-name. Then the arguments to apply will be substituted into the body of apply:

```
apply [eval (F, Intrinsics), eval (U, Intrinsics)]
= eval {B, bindargs [X, eval (U, Intrinsics), C]}
    where closure [lambda (X, B), C] ≡ eval (F, Intrinsics)
```

Once again the actual parameter 'eval (U, Intrinsics)' will be passed by name (i.e., without being evaluated), this time to bindargs, which in turn will overlay the pair (X, eval (U, Intrinsics)) onto Intrinsics. Notice that the offending expression U has still not been evaluated; it will be placed into the context in safely unevaluated form. Later the body of F—con (number 1)—will be evaluated to yield the value number 1. Since the body of F does not reference the formal parameter x, the dangerous expression eval (U, Intrinsics) will never be retrieved from the context, and hence never evaluated. Thus 'eval [appl (L, U), Intrinsics]' will terminate and return number 1.

Now let's look at the issue of evaluation order in a slightly more general context. Consider a formula in the interpreted language representing a nested function application, such as $f(ga)$. This is represented by the structure

appl [F, appl (G, A)]

where F, G, and A are the structures representing f, g, and a. Next consider the interpretation by eval of this structure in a context C:

eval {appl [F, appl (G, A)], C}
    $\Rightarrow$ apply {eval (F, C), eval [appl (G, A), C]}
    $\Rightarrow$ apply {eval (F, C), apply [eval (G, C), eval (A, C)]}

If the interpreting language uses an innermost order, then the inner application of apply will be performed before the outer; this is pass-by-value. The effect in the interpreted language is that g is applied before f. If the interpreting language uses an outermost order, however, then the outer application of apply will be performed before the inner; this is pass-by-name. The effect in the interpreted language is that f is applied before g.

This difference in evaluation orders can make a difference in the result only if one of the evaluation orders is nonterminating. Suppose that the interpreting language uses strict function semantics (innermost order). Then the outer application of apply is defined only if the inner one is defined. That is, $f(gx)$ is defined only if gx is defined, which means that the interpreted language also has strict function semantics. If the interpreting language uses lenient function semantics (outermost order), then the outer application of apply could be defined even if the inner one is not. That is, $f(gx)$ could be defined even if gx is not, which means that the interpreted language also has lenient function semantics.

Let's summarize. We have seen that if the interpreting language (the language in which the eval is written) uses pass-by-value, then the interpreted language will also use pass-by-value; if the interpreting language uses pass-by-name, then so will the interpreted language. Similarly, if the interpreting language uses strict semantics, then so does the interpreted language, and likewise for lenient semantics. We can say that eval passes on to the interpreted language the evaluation order of the interpreting language, or that the interpreted language *inherits* the evaluation order of the interpreting language.

Since in this case the interpreted and interpreting languages are the same—both Φ—we cannot learn anything about the evaluation order of either language by this approach. If, however, the interpreting language were Pascal, which uses pass-by-value, we could conclude that the interpreted language, Φ, also uses pass-by-value.

This inheritance of evaluation order from the interpreter is unsatisfactory; we should have whatever order we want, regardless of the language used to write the interpreter. That is, we wish to *decouple* the evaluation orders of the interpreted and interpreting languages. This is possible because it is eval that passes on to the interpreted language the evaluation strategy of the interpreting language. In the following sections we investigate how different definitions of eval can decouple the evaluation strategies of the two languages.

Exercise 12.3: What evaluation order is implemented by the eval interpreter that you wrote in Scheme or LISP?

Exercise 12.4: What evaluation order is implemented by the eval interpreter that you wrote in Pascal?

Exercise 12.5: Translate the following program into abstract form and run it on your eval interpreter:

let true $(t, f) \equiv t$
and false $(t, f) \equiv f$
and if $(b, t, f) \equiv b(t, f)$
in if {**true**, 0, [/] (1, 0)}

Explain the results.

12.4 Conditionals

We turn now to the interpretation of the conditional construct, which as you'll see bears on the topic of the previous section: the control of evaluation order. Consider the conditional expression

if $(a = 0, 1, 1/a)$

Clearly the intent of this conditional is to avoid a division by zero when $a = 0$. If the arguments to if are passed by value, then we will attempt to evaluate '$1/a$' even when its value is not needed, thus defeating the intended purpose of the conditional.

For this reason, the last two arguments of a conditional (the consequent and alternate) must be passed by name, even in a language that generally passes parameters by value. The intent of a conditional is to delay evaluation of its consequent and alternate until it has determined which to evaluate. This will not be accomplished if these are passed by value. To put it another way, no matter whether a language uses, in general, strict or lenient function semantics, the if function *must* have lenient semantics (at least with respect to its last two arguments).

How can we implement the conditional construct of Φ? If Φ used pass-by-name semantics, then there would be no problem, for we could define the Boolean values and if as in Section 8.8:

$$\textbf{true } (t, f) \equiv t$$
$$\textbf{false } (t, f) \equiv f$$
$$\text{if } (b, t, f) \equiv b(t, f)$$

(Here we use the uncurried version of the conditional; it would make no difference if we used the curried version.) This wouldn't work if Φ used pass-by-value semantics because we would attempt to evaluate t and f before substituting them into the body of if. Since we are not commiting ourselves to a particular evaluation order for Φ, we would like to define eval in such a way that it works under either evaluation strategy.

To solve this problem, let's make use of our observation that the conditional must be lenient with regard to its consequent and alternate. We can define eval in such a way that it passes on to the conditional of the interpreted language the leniency of the conditional of the interpreting language. Thus, if cond (b, t, f) is the structure representing a Φ conditional, then we want

$$\text{eval } [\text{cond } (b, t, f), C] \equiv \begin{cases} \text{eval } (t, C), & \text{if Boolean}^{-1}[\text{eval } (b, C)] \qquad (12.1) \\ \textbf{else } \text{eval } (f, C) \end{cases}$$

(Recall that Boolean is the tag for the Boolean variant of the data domain (Fig. 11.17)). Here we use the fact that the Φ conditional on the right will evaluate 'eval (t, C)' only if eval $(b, C) =$ Boolean **true**, and will evaluate 'eval (f, C)' only if eval $(b, C) =$ Boolean **false**. We can accomplish this by incorporating Eq. (12.1) as an additional case into the definition of eval.

It would seem that we have succeeded in decoupling the evaluation strategies of the interpreted and interpreting languages. The conditional in the interpreted language is lenient, regardless of whether the interpreting language is generally lenient or strict. To accomplish this, however, we have made use of the fact that in any useful language the conditional must be lenient, regardless of the general evaluation order. Thus the conditional of the interpreted language inherits the leniency of the conditional of the interpreting language. True decoupling still eludes us.

Exercise 12.6: Modify the abstract syntax specification of Fig. 11.22 to include conditional expressions.

Exercise 12.7: Write out the complete definition of eval including this new clause (Eq. 12.1).

Exercise 12.8: Make the corresponding changes to the Pascal type declaration of expr.

Exercise 12.9: Modify the Pascal implementation of eval to handle conditional expressions.

Exercise 12.10: Modify your Scheme or LISP implementation of eval to incorporate conditional expressions.

Exercise 12.11: Test one of your implementations of eval with conditionals on the abstract form of this program:

if true then 0 **else** [/] (1, 0) **endif**

12.5 Recursive Declarations with Normal-Order Languages

Next we consider recursive declarations, that is, declarations of the form

let rec $f \equiv \cdots f \cdots$ **in** B

Initially we restrict our attention to simple (noncompound) recursive declarations—those without **and** clauses. We saw in Section 8.12 how a recursive declaration could be reduced to a nonrecursive declaration through the use of the **Y** combinator:

let rec $f \equiv E$ **in** $B \implies$ **let** $f \equiv Y(f \mapsto E)$ **in** B

This would seem to solve our problem, since we have already implemented nonrecursive **let**s, and **Y** is easily defined:

$$\mathbf{Y}f \equiv [x \mapsto f\,(xx)]\,[x \mapsto f\,(xx)]$$

This approach works if the interpreting language is normal order (that is, outermost first), but if the interpreting language is standard order (innermost first), then the evaluation of '$\mathbf{Y}(f \mapsto E)$' is nonterminating:

$$\mathbf{Y}(f \mapsto E) \implies (f \mapsto E)\,[\mathbf{Y}(f \mapsto E)] \implies (f \mapsto E)\,\{(f \mapsto E)\,[\mathbf{Y}(f \mapsto E)]\} \implies \cdots$$

This is another case in which the evaluation order of the interpreted language is inherited from the interpreting language. Thus we must find a way to decouple their evaluation orders.

Exercise 12.12:   Write out the tree representation of

let Y $\equiv [x \mapsto f(xx)] [x \mapsto f(xx)]$
in let $f \equiv \mathbf{Y}(f \mapsto E)$
    in B

Exercise 12.13:   Trace the interpretation by eval of this structure. Show that if the interpreting language is standard order, then this tree causes eval to loop.

12.6 Recursive Declarations with Recursive Data Structures

As we just saw, if the interpreting language is lenient, then there is no difficulty implementing recursive declarations, but this solution does not work if the interpreting language is strict. We solved a similar problem with the conditional by introducing a new construct into the abstract syntax. Let's try the same approach here by defining a structure to represent recursive declarations:

let rec $f \equiv E$ **in** $B \implies$ letrec (f, E, B)

Then we can consider the result of evaluating letrec (f, E, B) in a context C. Clearly the goal is to evaluate the body B of the declaration in a new context C' that results from binding 'f' to the value v of E:

$$\text{eval } [\text{letrec } (f, E, B), C] = \text{eval } (B, C') \qquad (12.2)$$
$$\textbf{where } C' \equiv \text{overl } (C, f, v)$$

We are not done, however, since C' is defined in terms of v, which is not yet defined.

We have said that v is the value of E, but this is incomplete; we can speak only of the value of an expression *in some context*. In what context is E evaluated? The point of a recursive declaration is that the expression E be able to "see" the binding of 'f'. This means that E must be evaluated in the environment C':

$$v \equiv \text{eval } (E, C') \qquad (12.3)$$

Substituting this into the previous definition of C' (Eq. 12.2) yields

$$C' \equiv \text{overl } [C, f, \text{eval } (E, C')] \qquad (12.4)$$

The definition of C' is itself recursive!

This recursiveness is easy to understand. Our goal is to evaluate the body of the declaration in the context that results from binding the name f to the result of evaluating the expression E in the context that results from binding the name f to the result of evaluating the expression E in the context that results from . . . . We have a self-embedding expression—to be expected, since that is the result of the **Y** combinator. Thus, for languages that permit recursive data declarations, the following additional clause in eval will handle recursive declarations in the interpreted language:

$$\text{eval [letrec } (f,\ E,\ B),\ C] \equiv \text{eval } (B,\ C') \tag{12.5}$$
$$\textbf{where rec } C' \equiv \text{bindargs [single } f,\ \text{eval } (E,\ C'),\ C\,]$$

Here we substitute bindargs for overl for consistency with the rest of the interpreter, and in anticipation of handling compound recursive declarations.

12.7 Recursive Declarations with Delayed Expressions

We have seen that some functional languages permit recursive data structure declarations like Eq. (12.4). Unfortunately, these languages usually use normal reduction order, whereas our difficulties with recursive declarations arise only with standard-order languages. The attentive reader may ask "why we don't simply use delayed expressions (see Section 7.7)." Let's consider this approach.

To make use of delayed expressions, we must make sure that they are in our data domain:

$$D \equiv \left\{ \begin{array}{c} \vdots \\ \text{delay (\textbf{delayed} } D) \\ \vdots \end{array} \right\}$$

(The tag 'delay' indicates a delayed value.) We can then replace Eq. 12.4 by a definition that binds f to a delayed expression:

$$C' \equiv \text{bindargs [single } f,\ \text{delay } \ll\text{eval}\,(E,\ C')\gg,\ C\,] \tag{12.6}$$

Because the recursive use of C' is delayed, the definition will not lead to nontermination, even in a standard-order language.

We now, however, have identifiers bound to both delayed and undelayed values. Before we can use an identifier bound to a delayed value, we must force the evaluation of that value. On the other hand, we don't want to force evaluation whenever such an identifier is accessed (see Exercise 12.14). Therefore we must force evaluation only when necessary—for example, when the delayed value is used as an operator, since we can't apply the operator unless we know the closure or intrinsic that will be produced by the delayed value. This can be accomplished by passing the operator to a function actual, whose purpose is to get the actual value of the operator:

$$\text{eval } [\text{appl } (F, A)] \equiv \text{apply } \{\text{actual } [\text{eval } (F, C)], \text{eval } (A, C)\} \qquad (12.7)$$

The actual function is tolerant; it will force a delayed (potential) value, but leave an actual value unchanged:

$$\text{actual } (\text{delay } E) \equiv \text{actual } (\text{force } E)$$
$$\textbf{else } \text{actual } E \equiv E$$

Notice that we feed the result of force back into actual, since we may have delayed values that produce delayed values and so forth.

We've seen that it's necessary to actualize a delayed expression used as an operator. Are there other situations in which this must be done? Certainly recursive *functions* must be actualized only when they're applied, but what about recursive *data structures*? These must be actualized whenever their actual structure is required, which occurs only when they're used as arguments to intrinsic functions. Hence the actualization of recursive data structures can be ensured by changing the equation for applying intrinsic functions:

$$\text{apply } (\text{intrinsic } f, V) \equiv \text{Meaning } f (\text{actual } V) \qquad (12.8)$$

We have not entirely succeeded in decoupling the evaluation orders of the interpreting and interpreted languages. Recall from Section 7.7 that delayed expressions work because of the Delayed Function Body Restriction. In other words, even standard-order languages delay evaluating the body of a function until the function is called. Thus the delay in evaluating of the interpreted language is inherited from the delay in the interpreting language.

A further difficulty with the present solution is that it requires the interpreting language to permit *functional data structures*, that is, data structures that contain functions. The reason is that contexts bind identifiers to delayed expressions, and delayed expressions are really functions; recall from Section 7.7 that

$$\textbf{type delayed } D \equiv \textbf{1} \rightarrow D$$

This is not a problem in functional languages such as Scheme and LISP, but it's not permitted in languages such as Pascal that do not allow code to be mixed with data. We'll see in Section 12.9 that there is a way to avoid the need for functional data structures.

Exercise 12.14: Suppose we actualize an identifier whenever it's retrieved:

eval (id x, C) ≡ actual (Cx)

What's wrong with this apparently simpler solution?

Exercise 12.15: Is the following a correct implementation of simple recursive declarations by delayed expressions?

eval [letrec (f, E, B), C] ≡ eval (B, force C')
   where C' ≡ «bindargs [single f, eval (E, force C'), C]»

Justify your answer.

Exercise 12.16: Modify your Scheme or LISP version of eval to implement simple recursive declarations by delayed expressions. Note that you must define your own delay/force operations if your Scheme/LISP dialect doesn't provide them (see Section 7.7).

12.8 Recursive Function Declarations with Imperative Features

As we've seen, if the interpreting language allows general recursive declarations, including recursive data structure declarations, then we can implement general recursive declarations in the interpreted language. Unfortunately, many languages, especially many standard-order languages, do not allow recursive data structures. On the other hand, virtually all programming languages, whether normal or standard order, permit recursive function declarations. Therefore it is reasonable to ask whether we can use recursive functions in the interpreting language to implement recursive functions in the interpreted language, much as we used conditionals in the interpreting language to implement conditionals in the interpreted language. In particular, perhaps we can directly construct the value v, the result of evaluating E, without recourse to self-embedding structures.

To investigate this possibility, we restrict our attention to simple (non-compound) recursive *function* declarations:

let rec $f x \equiv E$ **in** B ⇒ letrec [f, lambda (x, E), B]

Substituting into the definition of eval yields

eval {letrec [f, lambda (x, E), B], C} ≡ eval (B, C')
   where C' ≡ bindargs (single f, v, C)
        where v ≡ eval [lambda (x, E), C']

Since v results from the evaluation of an abstraction, it is easy to see that it must be a closure:

$$v = \text{closure [lambda } (x, E), C']$$

Unfortunately, this still leads to a recursive data structure:

$$C' = \text{bindargs \{single } f, \text{closure [lambda } (x, E), C'], C\}$$

The context C' binds f to a closure, but that closure refers back to the context C'.

Although this solution will not work in standard-order *applicative* languages, it suggests an approach that will, at least in standard-order *imperative* languages. The purpose of **Y** is to embed a structure in itself— or more to the point, to create a cyclic structure. In particular, recursive declarations, whether of functions or data structures, are used to allow structures to refer (point) back to themselves. In other words, recursive declarations create cyclic structures.

In imperative languages cyclic structures can be created by the assignment operation. For example, in an imperative language, f could be bound to a closure constructed with a null context part. Then a pointer to the resulting context could be assigned to the context part of the closure, thus creating the required cyclic structure (see Fig. 12.1). This could be accomplished in an imperative implementation of eval by code such as this:

```
eval [letrec (f, L, B), C] ≡ begin  K := closure (L, nil);
                                     C' := bindargs (single f, K, C);
                                     ep K := C';
                                     eval (B, C') end
```

Figure 12.1 Creation of self-referential context.

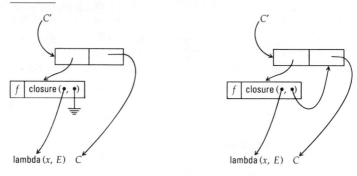

We have assumed that ep is the name of the environment part of the closure:

closure (ip ∈ expr D, ep ∈ context D)

Exercise 12.17:   Implement these ideas in the Pascal implementation of eval, including the appropriate changes to the type declaration for expr.

Exercise 12.18:   Test your Pascal interpreter on the following program:

let rec fac n ≡ **if** $n = 0$ **then** 1 **else** $n \times$ fac $(n - 1)$ **endif**
in fac 3

12.9 Recursive Function Declarations with Y-Closures

We have seen how imperative features can be used to create the self-referential structures needed for implementing recursive declarations. We must still see, however, how recursive declarations can be interpreted in a purely functional way. Consider again the formal definition of a recursive declaration in terms of the **Y** combinator:

let rec $f \equiv E$ **in** B $\Rightarrow$ **let** $f \equiv \mathbf{Y}(f \mapsto E)$ **in** B

A standard-order evaluation of '$\mathbf{Y}(f \mapsto E)$' leads to a nonterminating process. Is there any way to avoid this and still take advantage of the self-embedding effect of **Y**?

In Section 8.12 we saw that a self-embedding structure can be viewed as an infinite structure that is the limit of an infinite sequence of finite structures. This infinite structure provides the copies of a recursive function that are needed in a series of recursive calls. Thus a self-referential structure can be thought of as an infinite supply of something—data in the case of recursive data structures, function bindings in the case of recursive function declarations. Since a terminating computer program must execute in a finite amount of time, however, only a finite number of things from this infinite reservoir can ever be obtained. Thus, as discussed in Chapter 7, we must think of a self-referential structure as a *potentially* infinite structure—there's as much there as we need, but we can ask only for a finite amount.

The trouble with a standard-order evaluation of '$\mathbf{Y}(f \mapsto E)$' is that it attempts to obtain from the **Y** combinator all of its infinite supply of structures. To avoid this, we can make a special case of **Y** (as we did of if) so that structures are drawn from this infinite supply only when needed. The problem is to determine when a structure is needed.

We can see how to do this by restricting our attention to recursive functions (vice data structures), since a copy is needed just when the function is applied. Consider again a recursive function declaration:

let rec $f \equiv F$ **in** B

Here we assume that F is a functional abstraction $x \mapsto E$. We eliminate syntactic sugar in two steps, replacing **let rec** by **let** and **Y**, then replacing **let** by function application:

$$\textbf{let rec } f \equiv F \textbf{ in } B \;\Rightarrow\; \textbf{let } f \equiv \textbf{Y}(f \mapsto F) \textbf{ in } B \;\Rightarrow\; (f \mapsto B)\,[\textbf{Y}(f \mapsto F)] \qquad (12.9)$$

The basic approach is to leave the formula '$\textbf{Y}(f \mapsto F)$' unevaluated until it comes to be applied to an argument: '$\textbf{Y}(f \mapsto F)\,A$'. When this occurs, we unwind just one structure from **Y** for use in the application.

Y applications of the form $\textbf{Y}(f \mapsto F)$ are passed around in unevaluated form until they come to be applied to an argument, which will be detected by apply. This is analogous to the way a functional abstraction $x \mapsto E$ is passed around until it comes to be applied to an argument. Recall, however, that in the case of functional abstractions it is necessary to preserve the context of the function, for which purpose we introduced closures. The same arguments apply to the **Y** applications: To preserve their meaning, we must keep track of their context. Thus the closure K of the formula $\textbf{Y}(f \mapsto F)$ in a context C will be an expression of the form

$$K = \{\textbf{Y}(f \mapsto F)\}\,[C] \qquad (12.10)$$

We call such a structure a **Y**-*closure*.

Now consider the evaluation of a recursive declaration in a context C. By eliminating syntactic sugar (according to Eq. 12.9) we obtain

$$\{\textbf{let rec } f \equiv F \textbf{ in } B\}\,[C] \;\Rightarrow\; \{(f \mapsto B)\;\{\textbf{Y}(f \mapsto F)\}\}\,[C]$$

We can now move the mark of closure $[C]$ into the application (Eq. 11.2), closing both the operator and the operand:

$$\{(f \mapsto B)\,[C]\;\{\textbf{Y}(f \mapsto F)\}\,[C]\}$$

But we have defined $K \equiv \{\textbf{Y}(f \mapsto F)\}\,[C]$, so the preceding is equivalent to

$$\{(f \mapsto B)\,[C]\;K\}$$

The substitution rule (Eq. 11.4) can now be applied, yielding $B\,[f = K, C]$.

The formula $B\,[f = K, C]$ is easy to understand. It instructs us to evaluate the body B of the declaration in a context $C' \equiv [f = K, C]$ formed by binding f to the **Y** closure K in the nonlocal context C. This works because we delay unwinding K until it comes to be applied to an argument.

To see how this unwinding occurs, recall from the definition of **Y** that

$$
\begin{aligned}
K &= \{\mathbf{Y}\,(f \mapsto F)\}\,[C] \\
  &\Rightarrow \mathbf{Y}\,\{(f \mapsto F)\,[C]\} \\
  &\Rightarrow (f \mapsto F)\,[C]\,\{\mathbf{Y}(f \mapsto F)\,[C]\}
\end{aligned}
$$

But the operand (in braces) of the application on the right is just K. Thus one step of this unwinding is

$$
K \Rightarrow (f \mapsto F)\,[C]\,K
$$

Now consider the application of f to an argument A in a context D that binds f to K. We further assume that $A\,[D] \Rightarrow V$:

$$
\begin{aligned}
(f\,A)\,[D] &\Rightarrow (f\,[D]\,A\,[D]) \\
            &\Rightarrow (K\,V)
\end{aligned}
$$

Unwinding K once and performing the function application, we have

$$
\begin{aligned}
(K\,V) &\Rightarrow (f \mapsto F)\,[C]\,K\,V \\
       &\Rightarrow F[f = K,\,C]\,V
\end{aligned}
$$

In the first step we unwind one copy of $f \mapsto F$ from K. In the second we use this copy to bind f to K so that K is available for further recursive calls in F, the recursive function.

Let's pause to consider the meaning of the formula $F[f = K,\,C]$. Recall that F is a functional abstraction $x \mapsto E$ constituting the body of the recursive function. The formula $F[f = K,\,C]$ closes F in a context that binds f to K—the same context C' in which the body of the declaration B is evaluated. Therefore evaluating E is similar to evaluating B: If we must call f again (i.e., recursively), we need only look up f to get the **Y** closure K. We can then unwind from K another copy of $f \mapsto F$.

How can we apply these ideas to the eval interpreter? Since **Y** is to be treated as a special function, we use expressions of the form letrec (f, F, B). Notice that, for the time being at least, we are trying to handle only recursive functions, not recursive data structures. Thus F must be a lambda structure.

We need structures to represent **Y** closures. Look again at the definition of K:

$$
K \equiv \mathbf{Y}(f \mapsto F)\,[C] \tag{12.10}
$$

It contains only three pieces of information: f, F, and C. Let's use the Yclosure structure to represent this information:

Yclosure (f, F, C)

Here f is the name of the recursive function, F is its body (i.e., an abstraction such as lambda (x, E)), and C is its context of definition.

To extend eval to accommodate noncompound recursive declarations, we look again at the reduction rule:

$$\{\textbf{let rec } f \equiv F \textbf{ in } B\}\,[C] \;\Rightarrow\; B\,[f = K, C] \qquad\qquad (12.11)$$

This yields directly the corresponding equation for eval:

$$\text{eval } [\text{letrec } (f, F, B), C] = \text{eval } (B, C') \qquad\qquad (12.12)$$
$$\textbf{where } C' \equiv \text{bindargs (single } f, K, C)]$$
$$\textbf{where } K \equiv \text{Yclosure } (f, F, C)$$

We have used bindargs to bind f to K in anticipation of later extensions to compound recursive declarations. Notice also that the definition of C' is not recursive (neither directly nor indirectly through K).

To see what apply must do when passed a Yclosure, we look again at the unwinding process:

Figure 12.2 Abstract syntax including conditionals and recursive functions.

$$\text{expr } D \equiv \left\{ \begin{array}{l} \text{con } D \\ \text{id identifier} \\ \text{abstraction } D \\ \text{appl (expr } D, \text{ expr } D) \\ \text{tuple (expr } D, \text{ expr } D) \\ \text{let (formals, expr } D, \text{ expr } D) \\ \text{letrec (identifier, abstraction } D, \text{ expr } D) \\ \text{cond (expr } D, \text{ expr } D, \text{ expr } D) \end{array} \right\}$$

$$\text{abstraction } D \equiv \text{lambda (formals, expr } D)$$

$$\text{formals} \equiv \left\{ \begin{array}{l} \text{multi (identifier, formals)} \\ \text{single identifier} \end{array} \right\}$$

$$D \equiv \left\{ \begin{array}{l} \text{Boolean } \mathbb{B} \\ \text{number } \mathbb{R} \\ \text{str } \textbf{string} \\ \text{tuple } (D, D) \\ \text{sequence } D^* \\ \text{closure (abstraction } D, \text{ context } D) \\ \text{Yclosure (identifier, abstraction } D, \text{ context } D) \\ \text{intrinsic identifier} \end{array} \right\}$$

$$\text{context } D \equiv \text{finfunc (identifier} \rightarrow D)$$
$$\text{identifier} \equiv \textbf{string}$$

Figure 12.3 Interpreter with conditionals and recursive functions.

eval: expr D × context D → D

eval (con k, C) ≡ k
eval (id x, C) ≡ Cx
eval [lambda $(x, B), C$] ≡ closure [lambda $(x, B), C$]
eval [appl $(F, A), C$] ≡ apply [eval (F, C), eval (A, C)]
eval [tuple $(A, B), C$] ≡ tuple [eval (A, C), eval (B, C)]
eval [let $(X, V, B), C$] ≡ eval {B, bindargs [X, eval $(V, C), C$]}
eval [letrec $(f, F, B), C$] = eval [B, reccontext (f, F, C)]

$$
\text{eval [cond } (b, t, f), C] \equiv \begin{cases} \text{eval } (t, C), & \text{if Boolean}^{-1}[\text{eval } (b, C)] \\ \textbf{else eval } (f, C) \end{cases}
$$

---

apply: D × D → D
apply {closure [lambda $(X, B), C$], V} ≡ eval [B, bindargs (X, V, C)]
apply [Yclosure $(f, F, C), V$] = apply {eval [F, reccontext (f, F, C)], V}
apply (intrinsic f, V) ≡ Meaning f V

---

bindargs: formals × D → context D
bindargs [multi (x, Y), tuple $(v, W), C$] ≡ overl [bindargs $(Y, W, C), x, v$]
bindargs (single x, v, C) ≡ overl (C, x, v)

---

reccontext: identifier × abstraction D × context D → context D
reccontext (f, F, C) ≡ bindargs [single f, Yclosure $(f, F, C), C$]

$$KV \Rightarrow F[f = K, C] \, V \tag{12.13}$$

The expression on the right is a normal application of the (normal) closure $F[f = K, C]$ to V. This closure results from evaluating the abstraction F in the context $[f = K, C]$. Therefore the equation for apply of a Yclosure is

$$\text{apply [Yclosure } (f, F, C), V] \equiv \text{apply [eval } (F, C'), V] \tag{12.14}$$
$\qquad$ **where** $C' \equiv$ bindargs (single f, K, C)
$\qquad$ **where** $K \equiv$ Yclosure (f, F, C)

Of course the same C' appears in the equations for both eval and apply (Eqs. 12.12 and 12.14). Therefore we factor out the recurring pattern by defining a new function:

$$\text{reccontext } (f, F, C) \equiv \text{bindargs [single } f, \text{ Yclosure } (f, F, C), C] \tag{12.15}$$

In this one formula we can see both the *actual* binding of f to K in C, reflected by the application of bindargs, and the *potential* binding of f to K

in C, reflected by the Yclosure. The resulting abstract syntax for Φ is shown in Fig. 12.2; the corresponding definition of eval, in Fig. 12.3.

Let's summarize what we've learned about the implementation of recursive declarations.

1. As long as the interpreted language is normal order (outermost first), we can reduce a recursive declaration to an application of the **Y** combinator. This works because a outermost reduction order unwinds the **Y** application only as far as necessary to reach normal form.

2. If the interpreted language is not normal order, then we cannot use the **Y** combinator. If the *interpreting* language permits recursive data structures, however, we can construct the self-referential context required for implementing recursive declarations. The problem with this approach is that recursive data structures are usually permitted only in normal-order languages; as we've seen, this definition of eval passes on to the interpreted language the evaluation order of the interpreting language. Thus it is unlikely that we will have recursive data structures in the interpreting language unless the interpreted language is normal order, in which case solution (1) can be applied.

3. We saw that the recursive structure can be constructed in a standard-order language by means of delayed expressions. On the other hand, this approach requires functional data structures, which are not permitted in some languages.[3]

4. Next we restricted our attention to recursive *function* declarations, concluding that recursive data structures and delayed expressions could be avoided if the interpreting language is imperative, since an assignment operation can be used to create a self-referential closure. This solution works regardless of whether the interpreting language is normal- or standard-order, although virtually all imperative languages are standard-order.

5. Finally, we discussed an implementation of recursive functions that works for both normal-order and standard-order interpreting languages. This solution handles **Y** as a special case, in much the same way if was handled. In effect, **Y** is treated as a pass-by-name function that is expanded only when necessary.

Note that solutions (4) and (5) do not address the issue of recursive data structures in the *interpreted* language. We return to this issue in Section 12.11.

---

3. Also notice that the interpreted language will be standard order if the interpreting language is standard order. In this case we must be very careful using recursive data structures in the interpreted language, since, as we saw in Section 7.6, that combination often leads to nontermination.

12.10 Compound Recursive Function Declarations

We turn now to compound recursive declarations. As shown in Section
8.12, a compound recursive declaration of the form

let rec $x_1 \equiv E_1$ **and rec** $x_2 \equiv E_2$ **and** $\cdots$ **and rec** $x_n \equiv E_n$ **in** B

is equivalent to the following nonrecursive declaration using the **Y** combinator:

let $(x_1, x_2, \ldots, x_n) \equiv \mathbf{Y}[(x_1, x_2, \ldots, x_n) \mapsto (E_1, E_2, \ldots, E_n)]$ **in** B

If the interpreted language is normal order, then, as in the case of noncompound recursive declarations, this reduction provides us with a perfectly correct implementation of recursive declarations of both functions
and data structures. This is the simplest solution.

Now consider the case where the interpreted language is not normal
order. We saw in Section 12.6 that recursive declarations can be implemented if we can construct their self-referential context. If the interpreting language provides recursive data structures, then we can use them to
construct this self-referential context, as for the noncompound declarations. If the interpreting language permits functional data structures,
then we can use delayed expressions to achieve the effect of recursive
data structures (as in Section 12.7). If the interpreting language is imperative, then the self-referential structure can be constructed by the assignment operation (Section 12.8). But recall that these self-referential
contexts solve the problem for recursive functions but not recursive data
structures in the interpreted language (see Section 12.11).

Exercise 12.24: Extend your Scheme or LISP implementation of eval to include compound (mutually) recursive declarations.

Exercise 12.25: Extend the Pascal implementation of eval to include compound (mutually) recursive declarations.

Now we turn to the case where the interpreting language is standard order and permits neither recursive nor functional data structures. To implement a pass-by-name version of the **Y** combinator, just as in the non-compound case, reduce the compound recursive function declarations to the **Y** combinator, eliminate syntactic sugar, introduce a few useful abbreviations, and follow the execution.

Consider a compound recursive declaration:

$$\textbf{let rec } f_1 \equiv F_1 \textbf{ and } \cdots \textbf{ and rec } f_n \equiv F_n \textbf{ in } B \tag{12.16}$$

We begin by assuming the F_i to be functional abstractions, since then we know to unwind the **Y** when it is found in the operator position of an application. The compound recursive declaration (12.16) can be reduced as before to a recursive deconstructing declaration:

$$\textbf{let rec } (f_1, \ldots, f_n) \equiv (F_1, \ldots, F_n) \textbf{ in } B$$

By writing F for the list of functions $(F_1, \ldots, F_n)$, we have

$$\textbf{let rec } (f_1, \ldots, f_n) \equiv F \textbf{ in } B$$

Eliminating the recursion by inserting the implicit **Y** yields

$$\textbf{let } (f_1, \ldots, f_n) \equiv \textbf{Y}[(f_1, \ldots, f_n) \mapsto F] \textbf{ in } B$$

Eliminating the **let** sugar, we have

$$[(f_1, \ldots, f_n) \mapsto B] \ \{\textbf{Y}[(f_1, \ldots, f_n) \mapsto F]\}$$

Finally, by writing

$$\Phi \equiv (f_1, \ldots, f_n) \mapsto F \tag{12.17}$$

we find that the **let rec** (Eq. 12.16) is equivalent to the application

$$[(f_1, \ldots, f_n) \mapsto B] \ (\textbf{Y}\Phi)$$

Consider the evaluation of this expression in an arbitrary context C:

$$\{[(f_1, \ldots, f_n) \mapsto B] \ (\textbf{Y}\Phi)\} [C] \Rightarrow \{[(f_1, \ldots, f_n) \mapsto B][C] \ (\textbf{Y}\Phi)[C]\} \tag{12.18}$$

As in the noncompound case, we write K for the closure of $\mathbf{Y}\Phi$ in C

$$K \equiv (\mathbf{Y}\Phi)[C] \tag{12.19}$$

and call this expression a $\mathbf{Y}$-*closure*. Substituting Eq. (12.19) in Eq. (12.18) produces the following expression:

$$\{[(f_1, \ldots, f_n) \mapsto B][C]K\}$$

By the substitution rule this is

$$B[f_1 = K_1, \ldots, f_n = K_n, C]$$

Let's pause to interpret this formula. It says that we should evaluate the body B of the declaration in a context resulting from binding the names f_i of the recursive functions to the subscripted $\mathbf{Y}$ closures K_i. The $\mathbf{Y}$ closure K will be unwound when a recursive function is applied.

Since we'll use it again, let's abbreviate the context of evaluation of the declaration body B:

$$C' \equiv [f_1 = K_1, \ldots, f_n = K_n, C] \tag{12.20}$$

Hence the compound recursive declaration (12.16) reduces to $B[C']$; as can be seen, C' is the context in which the body is to be evaluated. C' comprises the bindings of the f_i and the nonlocal context C.

In the course of evaluating the body B of the declaration, recursive applications $(f_i\ A)$ may be encountered. We know from our analysis of noncompound recursive declarations (Section 12.9) that in this situation we can safely unwind the $\mathbf{Y}$ closure K. Therefore we consider the evaluation of the application $(f_i\ A)$ in some context D that binds f_i to K_i:

$$\{f_i\ A\}[D] \implies \{f_i[D]\ A[D]\}$$

Since $f_i[D] \implies K_i$ and $A[D] \implies V$, the preceding formula reduces to $(K_i\ V)$, corresponding to the arguments that are passed to apply. Instead of a simple closure or a $\mathbf{Y}$ closure for the first argument, we now have the more complex expression K_i, which selects an element from a $\mathbf{Y}$ closure. To make this selection we must, of course, unwind K.

By the definition of $\mathbf{Y}$ we have $\mathbf{Y}\Phi \implies \Phi(\mathbf{Y}\Phi)$, so

$$K \implies (\mathbf{Y}\Phi)[C] \implies \{\Phi\ (\mathbf{Y}\Phi)\}[C]$$

Moving the mark of closure $[C]$ into the application and using the abbreviation K (Eq. 12.19) yields

$$\{\Phi[C]\ (\mathbf{Y}\Phi)[C]\} = \{\Phi[C]\ K\}$$

Replacing Φ by its definition (Eq. 12.17) allows us to perform the substitution:

$$\Phi[C]\, K \;\Rightarrow\; \{(f_1, \ldots, f_n) \mapsto F\}[C]\; K \;\Rightarrow\; F[f_1 = K_1, \ldots, f_n = K_n, C] \;=\; F[C']$$

As expected, the list of functions F is evaluated in the same context C' used to evaluate the body B.

We can further reduce the operator of this application by expanding F and moving the mark of closure $[C']$ into the list brackets:

$$F[C'] \;\Rightarrow\; (F_1, \ldots, F_n)[C'] \;\Rightarrow\; (F_1[C'], \ldots, F_n[C'])$$

Therefore K_i reduces to $F_i[C']$. Hence our recursive application $(f_i\ A)$ reduces to the simple application $\{F_i[C']\, V\}$. Since F_i is a common abstraction (function denotation), $F_i[C']$ is a simple function closure. Hence the application $\{F_i[C']\, V\}$ can be performed by the apply already defined for nonrecursive functions.

We summarize the results. The compound recursive declaration is evaluated by the rule

$$\{\textbf{let rec } f_1 \equiv F_1 \textbf{ and } \cdots \textbf{ and rec } f_n \equiv F_n \textbf{ in } B\}[C] \;\Rightarrow\; B[C'] \qquad (12.21)$$
$$\textbf{where } C' \equiv [f_1 = K_1, \ldots, f_n = K_n, C],$$
$$\textbf{where } K \equiv \mathbf{Y}\{(f_1, \ldots, f_n) \mapsto F\}[C].$$

Notice that we have written K in the unreduced form rather than as $F[C']$, since the latter would make C' and K mutually recursive—exactly what we are trying to avoid. Therefore we leave $\mathbf{Y}$ unapplied until the appropriate time, the application of a recursive function. We have seen that the rule for this is

$$\{K_i\, V\} \;\Rightarrow\; \{F_i[C']\, V\} \qquad (12.22)$$

where K and C' are as defined in Eq. (12.21).

Before applying our analysis to the eval interpreter, we define an abstract syntax for compound recursive declarations:

$$\textbf{let rec } f_1 \equiv F_1 \textbf{ and } \cdots \textbf{ and rec } f_n \equiv F_n \textbf{ in } B \qquad (12.23)$$
$$\Rightarrow \text{letrec } \{\text{multi } [f_1, \ldots, \text{ multi } (f_{n-1}, \text{ single } f_n) \cdots],$$
$$\text{tuple } [F_1, \ldots, \text{ tuple } (F_{n-1}, F_n) \cdots], B\}$$

Thus we consider applications of eval such as

$$\text{eval } [\text{letrec } (f, F, B), C]$$

where f and F represent a list (formal tree) of function names and a list (tuple tree) of function bodies, respectively.

Clearly a central issue is the data structure corresponding to the **Y** closure K. As shown by its definition (Eq. 12.19),

$$K \equiv \mathbf{Y}\{(f_1, \ldots, f_n) \mapsto F\}[C] \tag{12.24}$$

K is composed of three other structures: the list of function names $f = (f_1, \ldots, f_n)$, the list of function bodies F, and the nonlocal context C. This leads us to define a **Y**closure as a three-element structure

$$K \equiv \mathbf{Y}\text{closure }(f, F, C) \tag{12.25}$$

containing the necessary information. Thus K can be computed as a function of f, F, and C, which can be obtained from the arguments supplied to eval, that is, letrec (f, F, B) and C.

Now we consider recursive applications. Corresponding to the subscripted **Y** closure K_i is the abstract structure

recelem (K, i)

Notice that the **Y**closure K is part of this structure. A typical invocation of apply is

apply [recelem (K, i), V]

The applicable reduction rule is

$$\{K_i\, V\} \Rightarrow \{F_i[C']\, V\} \tag{12.22}$$

Thus we compute the closure $F_i[C']$ from K_i by evaluating the abstraction F_i in the context C'. Accessing the abstraction F_i is easy since it is part of the **Y**closure:

recelem (K, i) = recelem [**Y**closure (f, F, C), i]

The context of evaluation

$$C' = [f_1 = K_1, \ldots, f_n = K_n,\ C] \tag{12.20}$$

is seen to be composed of f, K, and C. But, as we saw in Eq. (12.25), K is a function of f, F, and C, so we have that C' is a function of f, F, and C, say $C' \equiv$ reccontext (f, F, C).

We can now sketch the necessary equations for eval and apply. The formula for eval makes use of reccontext for computing C':

$$\text{eval } [\text{letrec } (f, F, B), C] \equiv \text{eval } [B, \text{reccontext } (f, F, C)] \qquad (12.26)$$

The equation for apply is

$$\begin{aligned} &\text{apply } \{\text{recelem } [\text{Yclosure } (f, F, C), i], V\} \equiv \qquad (12.27)\\ &\quad \text{apply } \{\text{eval } [F_i, \text{reccontext } (f, F, C)], V\} \end{aligned}$$

where F_i is the ith element of the list (tuple tree) F. It remains to define the function reccontext (see Exercise 12.26).

Exercise 12.26: Define the function reccontext. Recall that reccontext (f, F, C) must overlay the pairs $(f_i, \text{recelem } [K, i])$ on the context C, where K is the Yclosure of f, F, and C.

Exercise 12.27: Write out an abstract syntax for Φ that supports compound recursive declarations.

Exercise 12.28: Write out a complete definition for eval and apply that supports compound recursive function declarations via **Y**-closures.

Exercise 12.29: Modify your Scheme or LISP interpreter to implement compound recursive function declarations by means of **Y**-closures.

Exercise 12.30: Modify your Pascal interpreter to implement compound recursive function declarations by means of **Y**-closures.

Let's summarize what we've accomplished. As before, we've found that there is no problem implementing compound recursive declarations, provided that at least one of the following applies:

1. The interpreted language is normal order.

2. The interpreting language provides recursive data structures.

3. The interpreting language provides functional data structures.

4. The interpreting language is imperative, and so permits self-referencing data structures (although this works only for *function* declarations).

If none of these conditions applies, then, for function declarations, we use the technique of the controlled unwinding of the **Y** combinator. In brief this technique is to bind the recursive names to structures (Yclosures) that contain an unevaluated expression tree and the recursive context in *poten-*

tial form. The attempted use of these structures in function applications leads to the evaluation of the contained expression in the *actualization* of the recursive context. This technique works regardless of the evaluation order of the interpreting language, and is thus always safe.

Incidently, we have also seen how algebraic methods can be used to accomplish subtle programming with confidence. By deriving the definitions of eval and apply from equations based on the formal reduction process, we are much more confident that they are correct then if we had tried to program them without this aid. Part of the ease of converting the transformations into equations derives from the close relationship between transformational programming and functional programming (see Section 10.7).

12.11 Recursive Data Structures

The solution we developed in Section 12.10 implements recursive functions but not recursive data structures. We now readdress recursive data structures to see whether our solution can be extended. Consider the recursive declaration

$$\textbf{let rec } x_1 \equiv E_1 \textbf{ and } \cdots \textbf{ and rec } x_n \equiv E_n \textbf{ in } B \tag{12.28}$$

where now we impose no restrictions on the expressions E_i; they may be expressions of any type, including functions. By eliminating syntactic sugar, declaration (12.28) reduces to

$$[(x_1, \ldots, x_n) \mapsto B] \ (\textbf{Y}\Phi) \tag{12.29}$$

where $\Phi \equiv (x_1, \ldots, x_n) \mapsto E$ and where $E \equiv (E_1, \ldots, E_n)$.

Exercise 12.31: Show in detail how the recursive declaration (12.28) reduces to the expression (12.29).

As with recursive functions, we consider the evaluation of the preceding application in an arbitrary context C:

$$\{[(x_1, \ldots, x_n) \mapsto B] \ (\textbf{Y}\Phi)\} [C] \Rightarrow B[C'] \tag{12.30}$$

where $C' \equiv [x_1 = K_1, \ldots, x_n = K_n, C]$ and where $K \equiv (\textbf{Y}\Phi) [C]$.

Exercise 12.32: Show the steps in the reduction of Eq. (12.30).

Figure 12.4 Interpreter with full recursive declarations.

eval: expr D X context D → D

eval (con k, C) ≡ k
eval (id x, C) ≡ Cx
eval [lambda (x, B), C] ≡ closure [lambda (x, B), C]
eval [appl (F, A), C] ≡ apply {actual [eval (F, C)], eval (A, C)}
eval [tuple (A, B), C] ≡ tuple [eval (A, C), eval (B, C)]
eval [let (X, V, B), C] ≡ eval {B, bindargs [X, eval (V, C), C]}
eval [letrec (X, E, B), C] = eval [B, reccontext (X, E, C)]
eval [cond (b, t, f), C] ≡ $\begin{cases} \text{eval } (t, C), & \text{if Boolean}^{-1}[\text{eval } (b, C)] \\ \textbf{else } \text{eval } (f, C) \end{cases}$

apply: D X D → D
apply {closure [lambda (X, B), C], V} ≡ eval [B, bindargs (X, V, C)]
apply (intrinsic f, V) ≡ Meaning f (actual V)

bindargs: formals X D → context D
bindargs [multi (x, Y), tuple (v, W), C] ≡ overl [bindargs (Y, W, C), x, v]
bindargs (single x, v, C) ≡ overl (C, x, v)

reccontext: formals X expr D X context D → context D
reccontext (X, E, C) ≡ bindargs [X, recelems $(X, E, C, 1)$, C]

recelems: formals X expr D X context D X $\mathbb{N}$ → D
recelems [multi (x, Y), E, C, i] = [Yclose i, recelems $(Y, E, C, i+1)$]
else recelems (single x, E, C, i) = Yclose i
    where Yclose i = recelem [Yclosure (x, E, C), i]

actual: D → D
actual {recelem [Yclosure (X, E, C), i]} ≡
    actual {eval [select (X, E, i), reccontext (X, E, C)]}
else actual V ≡ V

select: formals X expr D X $\mathbb{N}$ → expr D
select (single x, e, 1) ≡ e
select [multi (x, Y), tuple (e, F), 1] ≡ e
else select [multi (x, Y), tuple (e, F), i] ≡ select $(Y, F, i-1)$

Thus the binding of the recursive names x_i to the subscripted **Y** closures K_i proceeds exactly as for recursive functions. To see how these closures are actualized, consider the application of an intrinsic function f to x_i in a context D that binds f to F and x_i to K_i:

$$(f\, x_i)\, [C] \;\Rightarrow\; (F\; K_i) \tag{12.31}$$

Performing the operation F requires unwinding (actualizing) the subscripted **Y** closure K_i:

$$K_i \;\Rightarrow\; E_i[C'] \tag{12.32}$$

where C' is as defined in Eq. (12.30). It can be seen that our previous analysis applies exactly, provided we can determine when the subscripted **Y** closure must be unwound.

Exercise 12.33:   Show the reduction $K_i \Rightarrow E_i[C']$ in detail.

Thus the problem is when to unwind the K_i. We saw in Section 12.7 that a potential value must be actualized when it's passed to an intrinsic function. This can be accomplished by the same equation (12.8) if we define the actual function as follows:

$$\begin{aligned}
&\textsf{actual \{recelem [Yclosure } (X,\, E,\, C),\; i\,]\} \;\equiv\; &(12.33)\\
&\quad \textsf{actual \{eval } [E_i,\; \textsf{reccontext } (X,\, E,\, C)]\}\\
&\textbf{else } \textsf{actual } E \;\equiv\; E
\end{aligned}$$

where E_i is the ith element of the list (tuple tree) E. The resulting definitions of eval and apply follow easily (see Fig. 12.4). (Note that we've added an auxiliary function select for extracting E_i from the tuple tree E.) We've seen how recursive function declarations and recursive data structure declarations can be implemented, even in a standard-order interpreting language. We still, however, have not decoupled the evaluation orders in general. Fortunately, we have all the ingredients we need; you are asked to fill in the details in Exercises 12.38–12.41.

Exercise 12.34:   Why do we pass X to select (in Fig. 12.4) when the purpose of select is simply to compute E_i?

Exercise 12.35:   Modify your Scheme or LISP implementation of eval to accommodate full recursive declarations (i.e., compound recursive declarations of both functions and data).

Exercise 12.36: Modify your Pascal implementation of eval to accommodate full recursive declarations (i.e., compound recursive declarations of both functions and data).

Exercise 12.37: Trace the evaluation of the program

let rec ones ≡ 1 : ones **in** first (rest ones)

Exercise 12.38: In a normal-order language, all parameters are in effect passed by name, which means that their evaluation is delayed until it's required. Show how a normal-order interpreted language can be implemented in a standard-order language by means of delayed expressions. *Hint:* See Section 12.7.

Exercise 12.39: Repeat the preceding exercise, but assume that the interpreting language does not permit delayed expressions. *Hint:* Use a structure similar to Yclosure.

Exercise 12.40: Suppose we want to implement a standard-order language by means of a normal-order interpreting language. This is difficult because the interpreting language will avoid diverging if possible, whereas we want the interpreted language to diverge whenever possible. To simplify the problem assume that the interpreting language provides an intrinsic function strictly: $T \rightarrow T$ that is a strict identity function. That is,

strictly $\perp$ = $\perp$
else strictly x = x

(Here '$\perp$' denotes a potentially divergent computation.) Show that strictly can be used to implement strict function semantics in the interpreted language.

Exercise 12.41: Prove or disprove that it's possible to implement a standard-order interpreted language using an interpreting language that is entirely normal order (i.e., has no special features such as strictly). *Hint:* Think about your answers to Exercises 10.62 and 10.63.

Exercise 12.42: In Section 7.8 we discussed the use of streams to represent input/output operations. Discuss how the ideas of potential and actual values could be applied to implement practical input/output by means of streams in a functional programming language.

Exercise 12.43: Modify the abstract language accepted by eval to include imperative features (such as assignments to identifiers). Make appropriate modifications to eval to interpret this language. Notice that since expressions will now have side effects, you must be aware of the order in which expressions are evaluated, and make arrangements to return (possibly altered) contexts from evaluations.

Chapter 13

Whither Functional Programming?

It has been a decade since Backus presented the virtues of functional programming in his Turing Award lecture (Backus 1978). Two decades have passed since Landin defined many of the central issues of applicative programming (Landin 1964, 1966). Two decades is a long time in the history of computer science. Is functional programming at the beginning or the end of its life?

Three considerations suggest that functional programming will be of increasing importance in computer science: the role of mathematics, the advantages of functions, and the power of higher-order functions. Let's discuss each consideration in turn.

As should be apparent from Chapter 10, computation is the mechanical manipulation of symbolic structures. Therefore mathematics, our principal tool for symbolic manipulation, must retain a central role in the science of computation. Here is the first advantage of functional programming: Since functional programming is essentially programming in mathematics, mathematical tools are especially applicable to functional programs. You have seen examples throughout this book.

On the other hand, there are problems in using mathematics in computation. At least in some applications, computation is *temporal*, whereas mathematics is *atemporal* (MacLennan 1983a, 1983b, 1983d, 1985). That is, some applications (e.g., interactive, real-time, database, and graphics programs) must be understood as executing in time and therefore the relationships and truths that hold in these systems may change in time. (This is the reason it's so important to identify *invariants,*—relations and truths that don't change.) In contrast, mathematics is timeless; if 2 < 3 now, then 2 < 3 later; if 2 + 2 = 4 in the future, then 2 + 2 = 4 in the past.[1]

The sciences have developed many techniques for dealing with time mathematically, the most common of which treats time as a dimension analogous to a spatial dimension. This "geometrical" approach to temporal reasoning embeds the flow of time in the "atemporal instant" of mathematics. As you saw in Section 7.8, the same approach can be used in functional programming, where a process that generates values is modeled as an (atemporal) infinite stream of those values.

The sciences have also developed specialized tools, such as the differential and integral calculi, for reasoning mathematically about change. It's likely that the science of computation will require its own specialized tools.[2]

Even if mathematics will play a central role in programming, it does not follow that programming should be based on the mathematical idea of a function; many other mathematical structures could be used instead. For example, logic programming views relations as more basic than functions. Also, as argued elsewhere (MacLennan 1973, 1975, 1981, 1983b, 1983c, 1983d, 1988), relations are more flexible than functions since they facilitate reasoning about nondeterminism.

Nevertheless there are significant advantages to the use of functions, stemming from the fact that applicative (pure) expressions are *referentially unambiguous;* they have a unique *referent.* You know the reason: An applicative expression is built up from (unambiguous) constants by the recursive application of single-valued functions. Thus an applicative expression refers to a unique value—if it refers to a value at all.[3] As a result, applicative expressions can be thought of as *complex names* for their values. Names can be manipulated much more reliably than other symbolic structures. In particular, their referential unambiguity leads to other important properties, such as referential transparency. You have seen how referential transparency permits the use of the familiar and powerful tools of algebraic and equational reasoning. These advantages are likely to give functional programming a permanent edge over relational programming styles.

The arguments made by Backus in 1978 for the use of higher-order functions still apply: To get more mileage from our finite cognitive capac-

---

1. This is not to deny that mathematics as a science changes, but such historical changes are too slow to be relevant to the issues being discussed.
2. See, for example, (MacLennan 1986, 1987a, 1989). Another example of such a tool is *temporal logic,* which has been investigated extensively.
3. Indeed, the latter condition can be dropped by using strictly algebraic reasoning, which takes all functions to be total. For examples, see (MacLennan 1987a, 1989).

ities, we must think in larger units. We have seen analogous developments in the sciences, for example, in the progression from the mechanics of a few simple bodies to the mathematics of fields and waves. The latter—built, it should be noted, on higher-order functions—are tools of great sophistication and power.

Functional programming has made a start in this direction, but only a start. The higher-order functions most discussed in the functional programming literature (including this book) go barely beyond the operators provided by APL, a language designed in 1960. The innovative proposals of David Wile's (1973) thesis do not appear to have been pursued. New directions must be explored, and many alternatives tried. This was the case in the development of vector analysis (Crowe 1969), and we can expect it to be the case in functional programming. Without variation there is no evolution.

Exercise 13.1: Do you agree that mathematics must play an increasing role in programming? Defend your position.

Exercise 13.2: Discuss the various methods by which the sciences have dealt with time mathematically. Which method(s) may apply to functional programming?

Exercise 13.3: What is the proper relation between temporal programming and functional programming? Is functional programming unsuited to temporal applications? If it is suitable, how can time be best incorporated in a functional framework?

Exercise 13.4: Investigate temporal logic and write an essay on its practicality as a tool for temporal reasoning.

Exercise 13.5: Compare functional programming with logic programming and other relational styles of programming. Which has the greatest promise for the future?

Exercise 13.6: What *kinds* of higher-order functions do we need? (Don't try to design specific functionals, just discuss the kinds of operations that should be provided.)

Exercise 13.7: Evaluate the higher-order functions proposed in Wile (1973). Which should be included in future functional languages? Can you suggest additional functionals?

Exercise 13.8: Write an essay on the future of functional programming. Try to separate the pros and cons of functional programming *methodology* from those of functional programming *languages*.

Exercise 13.9: Write an essay discussing the prospects of designing special architectures for functional programming.

References

Abdali, S. K. (1976a) An Abstraction Algorithm for Combinatory Logic, *Journal of Symbolic Logic 41*, 1 (March): 222–224.

Abdali, S. K. (1976b) A Lambda-Calculus Model of Programming Languages—I. Simple Constructs, *Journal of Computer Languages 1*: 287–301.

Abelson, Harold, and Sussman, Gerald Jay, with Sussman, Julie (1985) *Structure and Interpretation of Computer Programs*, The MIT Press, Cambridge.

Asimow, Morris (1962) *Introduction to Design*, Prentice-Hall, Englewood Cliffs, N.J.

Backus, John (1978) Can Programming Be Liberated from the von Neumann Style? A Functional Style and Its Algebra of Programs, *Communications of the ACM 21*, 8 (August): 613–641.

Backus, John (1981) Function Level Programs as Mathematical Objects, *Proceedings of the 1981 Conference on Functional Programming Languages and Computer Architecture* (October 18–22), ACM Order No. 556810, pp. 1–10.

Backus, John; Williams, John H.; and Wimmers, Edward L. (1986) *FL Language Manual (Preliminary Version)*, IBM Research Report RJ 5339 (54809) (November 7).

Barendregt, H. P. (1984) *The Lambda Calculus: Its Syntax and Semantics*, revised edition, North-Holland, Amsterdam.

Barron, D. W. (1968) *Recursive Techniques in Programming,* McDonald, London and American Elsevier, Amsterdam.

Beth, Evert W. (1964) *The Foundations of Mathematics: A Study in the Philosophy of Science,* revised edition, Harper & Row, New York.

Burge, W. H. (1975) *Recursive Programming Techniques,* Addison-Wesley, Reading, Mass.

Burstall, R. M.; Collins, J. S.; and Popplestone, R. J. (1971) *Programming in POP-2,* Edinburgh University Press, Edinburgh.

Cartwright, Robert (1980) A Constructive Alternative to Axiomatic Data Type Definitions, *Conference Record of the 1980 LISP Conference,* The LISP Conference, Redwood Estates, pp. 46–55.

Cartwright, Robert, and Donahue, James (1982) The Semantics of Lazy (and Industrious) Evaluation, *Conference Record of the 1982 ACM Symposium on LISP and Functional Programming,* ACM Order No. 552820, pp. 253–264.

Church, A. (1936) An Unsolvable Problem of Elementary Number Theory, *American Journal of Mathematics 58:* 345–363.

Church, A. (1941) The Calculi of Lambda-Conversion, *Annals of Mathematics Studies,* No. 6, Princeton University Press, Princeton, N.J. (reprinted 1951).

Church, A., and Rosser, J. B. (1936) Some Properties of Conversion, *Transactions of the American Mathematical Society 39:* 472–482.

Churchman, C. West, and Ratoosh, Philburn (1959) *Measurement, Definitions and Theories,* Wiley, New York.

Clocksin, W., and Mellish, C. (1981) *Programming in Prolog,* Springer-Verlag, Berlin.

Crowe, Michael J. (1969) *A History of Vector Analysis: The Evolution of the Idea of a Vectorial System,* University of Notre Dame Press, Notre Dame, Ind.

Curry, H. B.; Feys, R.; and Craig, W. (1958) *Combinatory Logic, Vol. I,* Studies in Logic and the Foundations of Mathematics, North-Holland, Amsterdam.

Dahl, O.-J.; Dijkstra, E. W.; and Hoare, C. A. R. (1972) *Structured Programming,* Academic Press, London.

Darlington, J.; Henderson, P.; and Turner, D. A. (1982), eds., *Functional Programming and Its Applications: An Advanced Course,* Cambridge University Press, Cambridge.

Davis, Martin (1965), ed., *The Undecidable: Basic Papers on Undecidable Propositions, Unsolvable Problems and Computable Functions,* Raven Press, Hewlett, N.Y.

DeRemer, F., and Kron, H. (1976) Programming-in-the-Large versus Programming-in-the-Small, *IEEE Transactions on Software Engineering SE-2* (June): 80–86.

Dijkstra, E. W. (1968) Go To Statement Considered Harmful, *Communications of the ACM 11,* 3 (March): 147–148.

Dijkstra, E. W. (1976) *A Discipline of Programming,* Prentice-Hall, Englewood Cliffs, N.J.

Fasel, J. H., and Keller, R. M. (1987) *Graph Reduction,* Lecture Notes in Computer Science 279, Springer-Verlag, Berlin.

Foster, J. M. (1967) *List Processing*, McDonald, London, and American Elsevier, Amsterdam.

Fox, L. (1966), ed., *Advances in Programming and Non-numerical Computation*, Pergamon Press, London.

Friedman, Daniel P., and Wise, David S. (1976) CONS Should Not Evaluate Its Arguments, *Automata, Languages, and Programming: Third International Colloquium*, eds., R. Michaelson and R. Milner, Edinburgh University Press, pp. 257–284.

Gleick, James (1987) *Chaos: Making a New Science*, Viking, New York.

Goguen, J. A.; Thatcher, J. W.; and Wagner, E. G. (1978) An Initial Algebra Approach to the Specification, Correctness, and Implementation of Abstract Data Types, *Current Trends in Programming Methodology*, ed., R. Yeh, Prentice-Hall, Englewood Cliffs, N.J.

Gordon, M. (1979) *The Denotational Description of Programming Languages*, Springer-Verlag, Berlin.

Gordon M.; Milner, R.; and Wadsworth, C., (1979) *Edinburgh LCF. A Mechanical Logic of Computation*, Lecture Notes in Computer Science 78, Springer-Verlag, Berlin.

Gorn, S. (1961) Some Basic Terminology Connected with Mechanical Languages and Their Translators, *Communications of the ACM 4*, 8 (August): 336–339.

Guttag, J. V. (1977) Abstract Data Types and the Development of Data Structures, *Communications of the ACM 20*, 6 (June): 396–404.

Guttag, J. V. (1980) Notes on Data Abstraction (Version 2), *IEEE Transactions on Software Engineering SE-6*, 1 (January): 13–23.

Hall, Cordelia V., and O'Donnell, John T. (1985) Debugging in a Side Effect Free Programming Environment, *Proceedings of the ACM SIGPLAN 85 Symposium on Language Issues in Programming Environments, SIGPLAN Notices 20*, 7 (July): 60–68.

Hausdorff, Felix (1957) *Set Theory*, translated by John R. Aumann et al., Chelsea, New York.

Haynes, C. T., and Friedman, D. P. (1987) Abstracting Timed Preemption with Engines, *Computer Languages 12*, 2: 109–121.

Henderson, Peter (1980) *Functional Programming: Application and Implementation*, Prentice-Hall International, Englewood Cliffs, N.J.

Hindley, J. Roger (1969) An Abstract Form of the Church-Rosser Theorem, Part I, *Journal of Symbolic Logic 14*: 545–560.

Hindley, J. R. (1974) An Abstract Form of the Church-Rosser Theorem, Part II: Applications, *Journal of Symbolic Logic 19*: 1–21.

Hindley, J. R.; Lercher, B.; and Selden, J. P. (1972) *Introduction to Combinatory Logic*, London Mathematics Society Lecture Note Series 7, Cambridge University Press, Cambridge.

Hoare, C. A. R. (1969) An Axiomatic Basis for Computer Programming, *Communications of the ACM 12*, 10 (October): 576–580, 583.

Hoare, C. A. R. (1972) Notes on Data Structuring, in Dahl, Dijkstra, and Hoare (1972), pp. 83–174.

Hoare, C. A. R. (1973) *Hints on Programming Language Design*, Stanford Universtiy Computer Science Department Technical Report STAN-CS-73-403 (December): 16

Hoare, C. A. R., and Shepherdson, J. C. (1985), eds., *Mathematical Logic and Programming Languages*, Prentice-Hall International, Englewood Cliffs, N.J.

Hoffman, C. M., and O'Donnell, M. J. (1984) Implementation of an Interpreter for Abstract Equations, *Conference Record of the Eleventh Annual ACM Symposium on Principles of Programming Languages* (January 15–18).

Hudak, P., and Bloss, A. (1985) The Aggregate Update Problem in Functional Programming Systems, *Conference Record of the Twelfth Annual ACM Symposium on Principles of Programming Languages* (January 14–16).

Iverson, K. E. (1962) *A Programming Language*, Wiley, New York.

Iverson, K. E. (1980) Notation as a Tool of Thought, *Communications of the ACM 23*, 8 (August): 444–465.

Iyanaga, S., and Kawada, Y. (1977), eds., *Encyclopedic Dictionary of Mathematics*, MIT Press, Cambridge.

Jevons, W. Stanley (1919) *Elementary Lessons in Logic: Deductive and Inductive*, Macmillan, New York.

Jouannaud, J.-P. (1985), ed., *Functional Programming Languages and Computer Architecture*, Lecture Notes in Computer Science 201, Springer-Verlag, Berlin.

Kamin, S. (1983), Final Data Types and Their Specification, *ACM Transactions on Programming Languages and Systems 5*, 1 (January): 97–121.

Knuth, D. E., and Bendix, P. (1970) Simple Word Problems in Universal Algebras, in *Computational Problems in Abstract Algebra*, ed. J. Leech, Pergamon Press, Oxford, pp. 263–297.

Lakatos, Imre (1976) *Proofs and Refutations: The Logic of Mathematical Discovery*, Cambridge University Press, Cambridge.

Landin, P. J. (1964) The Mechanical Evaluation of Expressions, *Computer Journal 6*, 4 (January): 308–320.

Landin, P. J. (1965) A Correspondence between Algol 60 and Church's Lambda-Notation, *Communications of the ACM 8*, 2 (February): 89–101, and 3 (March): 158–165.

Landin, P. J. (1966) The Next 700 Programming Languages, *Communications of the ACM 9*, 3 (March): 157–166.

Landin, P. J. (1971) A Formal Description of ALGOL 60, in *Formal Language Description Languages for Computer Programming*, ed. T. B. Steel, Jr., North-Holland, Amsterdam.

Lehman, M. M. (1980) Programs, Life Cycles and Laws of Software Evolution, *Proceedings of the IEEE Special Issue on Software Engineering* (Sept. 1980), pp. 1060–1076.

Lehman, M. M. (1981), The Environment of Program Development and Maintenance—Programs, Programming and Program Support, *Proceedings of the 1981 International Computing Symposium*, IPC Business Press (1981), pp. 1–12; reprinted in *Tutorial: Software Development Environments*, ed. A. I. Wasserman, IEEE Computer Society Press, pp. 3–14.

MacLane, S., and Birkhoff, G. (1967) *Algebra*, Macmillan, New York.

MacLennan, B. J. (1973) Fen—An Axiomatic Basis for Program Semantics, *Communications of the ACM 16*, 8 (August) 468–474.

MacLennan, B. J. (1975) *Semantic and Syntactic Specification and Extension of Languages*, Ph.D. dissertation, Purdue University, West Lafayette, Ind.

MacLennan, B. J. (1981) Introduction to Relational Programming, *Proceedings of the 1981 Conference on Functional Programming Languages and Computer Architecture*, (October 18–22), ACM Order No. 556810, pp. 213–220.

MacLennan, B. J. (1983a) Abstraction in the Intel iAPX-432 Prototype Systems Implementation Language, *SIGPLAN Notices 18*, 12 (December): 86–95.

MacLennan, B. J. (1983b) A View of Object-oriented Programming, Naval Postgraduate School Computer Science Department Technical Report NPS52-83-001 (February).

MacLennan, B. J. (1983c) Overview of Relational Programming, *SIGPLAN Notices 18*, 3 (March): 36–45.

MacLennan, B. J. (1983d) Relational Programming, Naval Postgraduate School Computer Science Department Technical Report NPS52-83-012 (September).

MacLennan, B. J. (1983e) Values and Objects in Programming Languages, *SIGPLAN Notices 17*, 12 (December): 70–79. Reprinted in *Object-Oriented Computing, Volume 1: Concepts*, ed., Gerald E. Peterson, IEEE Computer Society Press, 1987, pp. 9–14.

MacLennan, B. J. (1984a) A Simple Proof of a Generalized Church-Rosser Theorem, Naval Postgraduate School Computer Science Department Technical Report NPS52-84-007 (June).

MacLennan, B. J. (1984b) Computable Real Analysis, Naval Postgraduate School Computer Science Department Technical Report NPS52-84-024 (December).

MacLennan, B. J. (1985) A Simple Software Environment Based on Objects and Relations, *Proceedings of the ACM SIGPLAN 85 Symposium on Language Issues in Programming Environments, SIGPLAN Notices 20*, 7 (July): 199–207.

MacLennan, B. J. (1986) Preliminary Investigation of a Calculus of Functional Differences: Fixed Differences, Naval Postgraduate School Computer Science Department Technical Report NPS52-86-010 (February).

MacLennan, B. J. (1987a) An Algebraic Approach to a Calculus of Functional Differences: Fixed Differences and Integrals, Naval Postgraduate School Computer Science Department Technical Report NPS52-87-041 (September).

MacLennan, B. J. (1987b) *Principles of Programming Languages: Design, Evaluation, and Implementation*, second edition, Holt, Rinehart & Winston, New York.

MacLennan, B. J. (1988) Four Relational Programs, *SIGPLAN Notices 23*, 1 (January): 109–119.

MacLennan, B. J. (1989) The Calculus of Functional Differences and Integrals, University of Tennessee, Knoxville, Computer Science Department Technical Report CS-89-80.

MacQueen, David B. (1984) Modules for Standard ML, *Proceedings of the Third International Conference on LISP and Functional Programming*, Austin, Texas (August), pp. 198–207.

Martin-Löf, P. (1972) *An Intuitionistic Theory of Types,* manuscript, University of Stockholm.

Manna, Zohar, and Waldinger, Richard (1985) *The Logical Basis for Computer Programming, Volume I, Deductive Reasoning,* Addison-Wesley, Reading, Mass.

McCarthy, J. (1960) Recursive Functions of Symbolic Expressions and Their Computation by Machine, Part I, *Communications of the ACM 3,* 4 (April): 184–195.

McCarthy, J. (1978) History of LISP, in *Preprints: ACM SIGPLAN History of Programming Languages Conference, SIGPLAN Notices 13,* 8 (August): 217–223.

McCarthy, J.; Abrahams, P. W.; Edwards, D. J.; Hart, T. P.; and Levin, M. I. (1969) *LISP 1.5 Programmer's Manual,* second edition, The MIT Press, Cambridge.

Menger, Karl (1944) Algebra of Analysis, *Notre Dame Mathematical Lectures 3.*

Menger, Karl (1953) The Idea of Variable and Function, *Proceedings of the National Academy of Sciences 39:* 956–961.

Menger, Karl (1954) On Variables in Mathematics and in Natural Science, *British Journal for the Philosophy of Science 5:* 134–152.

Menger, Karl (1955) *Calculus: A Modern Approach,* Ginn, Lexington, Mass.

Menger, Karl (1959) Mensuration and Other Mathematical Connections of Observable Material, in Churchman and Ratoosh (1959), pp. 97–128.

Michie, D. (1968) 'Memo' Functions and Machine Learning, *Nature 218* (April): 19–22.

Milne, Robert, and Strachey, Christopher (1976) *Theory of Programming Language Semantics,* Halsted Press, London.

Mitschke, G. (1973) Ein algebraischer Beweis für das Church-Rosser Theorem, *Archiv für mathematische Logik und Grundlagenforschung 15:* 146–157.

Morris, Charles (1938) *Foundations of the Theory of Signs, International Encyclopedia of Unified Science, Volume 1, Number 2,* University of Chicago Press, Chicago.

Morris, J. H. (1973) Protection in Programming Languages, *Communications of the ACM 16,* 1 (January): 15–21.

Newman, M. H. A. (1942) On Theories with a Combinatorial Definition of "Equivalence," *Annals of Mathematics (2), 43:* 223–243.

O'Donnell, John T. (1985) Dialogues: A Basis for Constructing Programming Environments, *Proceedings of the ACM SIGPLAN 85 Symposium on Language Issues in Programming Environments, SIGPLAN Notices 20,* 7 (July): 19–27.

O'Donnell, Michael J. (1985) *Equational Logic as a Programming Language,* The MIT Press, Cambridge.

Pakin, S. (1972) *APL/360 Reference Manual,* second edition, Science Research Associates, Inc, Chicago.

Parkinson, G. H. R. (1966) *Leibniz Logical Papers,* Clarendon Press, Oxford.

Quine, W. V. O. (1960) *Word and Object,* Technology Press, Cambridge, Mass., and Wiley, New York.

Rees, J., and Clinger, W., (1986), eds., Revised[3] Report on the Algorithmic Language Scheme, *SIGPLAN Notices 21,* 12 (December): 37–43.

Reynolds, John C. (1981) *The Craft of Programming,* Prentice-Hall, Englewood Cliffs, N.J.

Rice, H. G. (1953) Classes of Recursively Enumerable Sets and Their Decision

Problems, *Transactions of the American Mathematical Society 74:* 358–366.

Robinson, J. A. (1965) A Machine-oriented Logic Based on the Resolution Principle, *Journal of the ACM 12,* 1 (January): 23–41.

Rosen, B. K. (1973) Tree Manipulation Systems and Church-Rosser Theorems, *Journal of the ACM 20,* 1 (January): 160–187.

Rosser, J. Barkley (1982) Highlights of the History of the Lambda-Calculus, *Conference Record of the 1982 ACM Symposium on LISP and Functional Programming* (August 15–18), pp. 216–225.

Russell, Bertrand (1903) *The Principles of Mathematics,* second edition, Norton, New York.

Schönfinkel, Moses (1924) Über die Bausteine der mathematischen Logik, *Mathematische Annalen 92:* 305–316.

Schroer, David E. (1965) The Church-Rosser Theorem, Ph.D. thesis, Cornell University, Ithaca, N.Y.; University Microfilms 66-41.

Scott, D. S. (1970) Outline of a Mathematical Theory of Computation, *Proceedings of the Fourth Annual Princeton Conference on Information Sciences and Systems,* Department of Electrical Engineering, Princeton University, Princeton, N.J., pp. 160–176; also Technical Monograph PRG-2, Programming Research Group, University of Oxford, Oxford.

Scott, D. S. (1971) The Lattice of Flow Diagrams, *Symposium on the Semantics of Algorithmic Languages,* ed. E. Engeler, Springer-Verlag, Berlin, pp. 311–366; also Technical Monograph PRG-3, Programming Research Group, University of Oxford, Oxford.

Scott, D. S. (1972) Continuous Lattices, *Toposes, Algebraic Geometry and Logic,* ed. F. W. Lawvere, Springer-Verlag, Berlin, pp. 97-136; also Technical Monograph PRG-7, Programming Research Group, University of Oxford, Oxford.

Scott, D. S. (1973) Lattice-Theoretic Models for Various Type-Free Calculi, *Logic, Methodology and Philosophy of Science IV,* eds. P. Suppes; L. Henkin; A. Joja; and G. C. Moisil, North-Holland, Amsterdam, pp. 157–187.

Scott, D. S. (1976) Data Types as Lattices, *Proceedings of the 1974 Colloquium in Mathematical Logic, Kiel,* Springer-Verlag, Berlin, pp. 579–650.

Scott, D. S. (1977) Logic and Programming Languages, *Communications of the ACM 20,* 9 (September): 634–641.

Scott, D. S., and Strachey, C. (1971) Towards a Mathematical Semantics for Computer Languages, *Proceedings of the Symposium on Computers and Automata,* ed. J. Fox, Polytechnic Institute of Brooklyn Press, New York, pp. 19–46; also Technical Monograph PRG-6, Programming Research Group, University of Oxford, Oxford.

Sintzoff, Michel (1972) Calculating Properties of Programs by Valuations on Specific Models, *Proceedings of ACM Conference on Proving Assertions about Programs, SIGPLAN Notices 7,* 1, and *SIGACT News,* No. 14 (January): 203–207.

Steele, Guy L., Jr. (1984) *Common LISP: The Language,* Digital Press, Burlington, Mass.

Stoy, J. E. (1977) *Denotational Semantics: The Scott-Strachey Approach to Programming Language Theory,* The MIT Press, Cambridge.

Turing, A. M. (1936) On Computable Numbers, with an Application to the Entscheidungsproblem, *Proceedings of the London Mathematical Society, Series 2, 42* (1936): 230–265; corrections, *Proceedings of the London Mathematical Society, Series 2, 43* (1937): 544–546.

Turner, D. A. (1979a) Another Algorithm for Bracket Abstraction, *Journal of Symbolic Logic 44*, 2 (June): 267–270.

Turner, D. A. (1979b) A New Implementation Technique for Applicative Languages, *Software—Practice and Experience 9:* 31–49.

Turner, D. A. (1981) *KRC Language Manual*, University of Kent, Kent.

Turner, D. A. (1985a) Functional Programs as Executable Specifications, in Hoare and Shepherdson (1985), pp. 29–50.

Turner, D. A. (1985b) Miranda: A Non-strict Functional Language with Polymorphic Types, in Jouannaud (1985), pp. 1–16.

Wand, Mitchell (1980) *Induction, Recursion, and Programming*, North-Holland, New York.

Wang, Hao. (1960) Towards Mechanical Mathematics, *IBM Journal of Research and Development 4*, 1 (January).

Whitehead, Alfred North, and Russell, Bertrand (1970) *Principia Mathematica to *56*, Cambridge University Press, Cambridge.

Wile, David S. (1973) *A Generative Nested-Sequential Basis for General Purpose Programming Languages*, Ph.D. dissertation, Department of Computer Science, Carnegie-Mellon University, Pittsburgh.

Zemanek, H. (1966) Semiotics and Programming Languages, *Communications of the ACM 9*, 3 (March): 139–141.

Appendix A

The Functional Language Φ

A.1 **Grammatical Notation**

Both '$\{C_1 \mid C_2 \mid \ldots \mid C_n\}$' and $\left\{\begin{array}{c} C_1 \\ C_2 \\ \vdots \\ C_n \end{array}\right\}$ mean *exactly one* of $C_1, C_2, \ldots, C_n$.

Similarly, '$[C_1 \mid \ldots \mid C_n]$' and $\left[\begin{array}{c} C_1 \\ \vdots \\ C_n \end{array}\right]$ mean *at most one* of $C_1, \ldots, C_n$.

The notation 'C^*' means *zero* or more Cs; 'C^+' means *one* or more Cs; '$CD \ldots$' means a list of one or more Cs separated by Ds. Terminal symbols appear in quotation marks when they could be confused with metasymbols.

The brackets ⁅ and ⁆ surround material that is considered a structural unit and is hence indented. A structure editor indents this material automatically; text- or batch-oriented implementations require the user to use indenting or some other lexical convention to denote such units. Similarly, the symbol □ represents a required newline; this is provided automatically by structure editors, but must be typed by the user in text- or batch-oriented implementations. Finally, note that there are some ambiguities in the grammar; these will not bother structure editors. For text-oriented systems the ambiguities can be avoided by routine lexical changes (e.g., writing **less** and **greater** for < and > when they are used as relational operators).

A.2 Grammar

$$
def \ = \ \left\{
\begin{array}{l}
packdef \\
datadef \\
typedef \\
strucdef \\
signature \\
funcdef
\end{array}
\right\}
$$

packdef = [typeparams] **package** id, ... **is**: ⟨ def^+ ⟩
datadef = [**rec**] formals ≡ qualexp □
typedef = [typeparams] [**rec**] [**abstract**] **type** id [formals] ≡ typeexp [qualifier] □
strucdef = [typeparams] [**rec**] [**abstract**] **structure** id [formals] ≡ strucexp [qualifier] □
signature = id : typeexp [qualifier] □
funcdef = $clause^+$ [**else** ⟨ funcdef ⟩]
clause = id formal ≡ arm

$$
formals \ = \ \left\{
\begin{array}{l}
id \\
(\ formals\ ,\ \ldots\ ) \\
formals : formals \\
id\ formals \\
denotation
\end{array}
\right\}
$$

typeparams = **for all** id, ...
qualexp = expression [qualifier]
qualifier = ⟨ **where** def **and** ... ⟩ [qualifier]
expression = [expression ∨] conjunction
conjunction = [conjunction ∧] negation
negation = [¬] relation
relation = [funcexp relator] funcexp
relator = { = | ≠ | < | > | ≤ | ≥ | ∈ | ∉ }
funcexp = simplexp [functional funcexp]
functional = { : | :: | + | '|' | ∘ | ; | × | → }
simplexp = [simplexp addop] term
addop = { + | − | ^ | ∪ | \ }
term = [term mulop] factor

$$mulop = \{ \times \mid / \mid \div \mid \cap \}$$

$$factor = \begin{bmatrix} + \\ - \end{bmatrix} primary$$

$$primary = \left\{ \begin{array}{l} application \\ primary_{application} \end{array} \right\}$$

$$application = [application]\, actual$$

$$actual = \left\{ \begin{array}{l} id\,[\,\$(\,typeexp,\,\ldots\,)\,] \\ denotation \\ conditional \\ compound \\ section \\ block \\ \{\,\textbf{file}\,\mid\,\textbf{stream}\,\}\,'char^{+\,'} \end{array} \right\}$$

$$denotation = \left\{ \begin{array}{l} 'char^{*\,'} \\ digit^{+}\,[\,.\,digit^{+}] \\ nil \\ \varnothing \\ nihil \\ formals \mapsto actual \end{array} \right\}$$

$$conditional = '\{\,'\,arms$$

$$arms = \blacktriangleleft arm^{+}\,[\,\textbf{else}\,arms\,]\,\blacktriangleright$$
$$arm = expression\,[guard]\,[qualifier]\,\square$$
$$guard = \{\,[,]\,\textbf{if}\,\mid\,,\,\}\,expression$$

$$compound = \left\{ \begin{array}{l} (\,elements\,) \\ '[\,'\,elements\,']\,' \\ '\{\,'\,elements\,'\}\,' \\ <\,elements\,> \\ \ll elements \gg \\ '[\,'pair,\,\ldots\,']\,' \end{array} \right\}$$

$$elements = [\,expression,\,\ldots\,]$$
$$pair = primary \mapsto primary$$

$$section = '[\,'\left\{ \begin{array}{l} op\,actual \\ op \\ actual\,op \end{array} \right\}']\,'$$

$op = \{ , \mid relator \mid functional \mid addop \mid mulop \mid \textbf{sub} \}$

$block = \textbf{begin}\ blockbody\ \textbf{end}$

$blockbody = \{ \textbf{let}\ defs \}^+ qualexp$

$defs = \langle\!\langle def\ \textbf{and} \ldots \rangle\!\rangle$

$typeexp = typedom\ [\rightarrow typeexp]$

$typedom = typeterm\ [+ typedom]$

$typeterm = typefac\ [\times typeterm]$

$typefac = \left\{ \begin{array}{l} typeprimary\ {}^{'*'} \\ typeprimary^{\infty} \\ id\ [actual] \\ typeprimary \end{array} \right\}$

$typeprimary = \left\{ \begin{array}{l} id \\ primtype \\ (\ typeexp\ ) \end{array} \right\}$

$primtype = \{ \mathbb{R} \mid \mathbb{Z} \mid \mathbb{N} \mid \mathbb{B} \mid \textbf{1} \mid \textbf{type} \}$

$strucexp = variant + \ldots$

$variant = id \left[\begin{array}{l} : typeterm \\ (field , \ldots) \end{array} \right]$

$field = id , \ldots \in strucexp$

For batch use, a program is considered a *blockbody*; for interactive use it is considered a *Session*:

$Session = command^+$

$command = \left\{ \begin{array}{l} \textbf{let}\ defs \\ qualexp\ \square \end{array} \right\}$

A.3 ASCII Representation of Φ

The following table shows how the functional language Φ is represented in ASCII.

Reference	ASCII
$\equiv$	==
$\vee$	\/
$\wedge$	/\
$\neg$	~
$\leq$	<=
$\geq$	>=

Table (continued)

≠	<>
∈	in
∉	notin
\	\
∪	union
∩	inters
∧	^
×	*
/	/
÷	%
∘	o (lowercase oh)
′ ′	` ´
↦	|->
{	either
A_i	A sub i
T^*	T*
T^∞	T**
→	->
+	#
×	$X ><
∅	{}
ℝ	$R
ℤ	$Z
ℕ	$N
𝔹	$B
1	$1

For text-oriented systems, lexical conventions such as the following are required for nonambiguity:

Name	Reference Symbol	Text-Oriented Symbol
Sequences	< >	< >
Relators	< >	less greater
Compounds	[ ]	[ ]
Sections	[ ]	$[ ]
Indent	⊣	tab character
Outdent	⊁	nothing, or require end of line
Newline	□	nothing, or require end of line

Symbols can be printed in their reference forms.

Appendix B

Collected Archetypes

Figure B.1 Archetype for Boolean type.

Syntax:

$\mathbb{B} \in$ **type**

true, false $\in \mathbb{B}$

$\neg: \mathbb{B} \to \mathbb{B}$

$\wedge, \vee, =, \neq: \mathbb{B} \times \mathbb{B} \to \mathbb{B}$

if: $\mathbb{B} \times T \times T \to T$

Semantics:

$x \in \mathbb{B}$ if and only if $x =$ **true** or $x =$ **false**

true $\neq$ **false**

$\neg$**true** $=$ **false**
$\neg$**false** $=$ **true**

true $\wedge$ **true** $=$ **true**
false $\wedge y =$ **false**
$x \wedge$ **false** $=$ **false**

$x \vee y = \neg(\neg x \wedge \neg y)$
$(x = y) = (x \wedge y) \vee (\neg x \wedge \neg y)$
$(x \neq y) = \neg(x = y)$

Figure B.1 (continued)

if (**true**, t, e) = t
if (**true**, t, $\perp$) = t

if (**false**, t, e) = e
if (**false**, $\perp$, e) = e

Pragmatics:

All operations take constant time.

The if operation is strict in its first parameter, but lenient in its second and third parameters.

The other operations are strict in their first parameters, and may be either strict or lenient in their other parameters.

Figure B.2 Archetype for integer type.

Syntax:

$0, 1, 2, \cdots \in \mathbb{Z}$
$+, - (prefix): \mathbb{Z} \to \mathbb{Z}$
$+, -, \times, \div: \mathbb{Z} \times \mathbb{Z} \to \mathbb{Z}$
$=, \neq, <, >, \leq, \geq: \mathbb{Z} \times \mathbb{Z} \to \mathbb{B}$

Semantics:

$a \in \mathbb{Z}$ if and only if $a = 0$ or for some $b \in \mathbb{Z}$, $a = b + 1$ or $a = b - 1$

$a + 1 \neq a$

$a + b = b + a$
$a + (b + c) = (a + b) + c$
$a + 0 = a$
$a + (-a) = 0$

$a - b = a + (-b)$

$a \times 1 = a$
$a \times b = b \times a$
$a \times (b \times c) = (a \times b) \times c$
$a \times (b + c) = (a \times b) + (a \times c)$

$0 < 0 = $ **false**
$0 < 1 = $ **true**
$a < b = a + 1 < b + 1$
$a < b \wedge b < c = a < c$

$a \div 1 = a$
$a \div b = 0, \quad 0 \leq a < b$
$a \div b = 1 + [(a - b) \div b], \quad 0 \leq a, \ b \leq a$
$a \div b = -(-a \div b), \quad a < 0$
$a \div b = -(a \div -b), \quad b < 0$

$$a > b = b < a$$
$$a \neq b = a > b \vee a < b$$
$$a \leq b = a < b \vee a = b$$
$$a \geq b = b \leq a$$
$$a = b = \neg(a \neq b)$$

Pragmatics:

All operations take constant time.

There are maximum and minimum integer values, and the operations are undefined when either their arguments or their results are out of the allowed range.

Figure B.3 Archetype for string type.

Syntax:

$'c_1 c_2 \cdots c_n' \in$ **string**

$=, \neq:$ **string** $\times$ **string** $\to \mathbb{B}$

seqn$\leftarrow$string: **string** $\to$ **string***

string$\leftarrow$seqn: **string*** $\to$ **string**

Semantics:

$x \in$ **string** if and only if for some characters $c_1, c_2, \ldots, c_n, x = 'c_1 c_2 \cdots c_n'$

$$'c_1 c_2 \cdots c_m' = 'd_1 d_2 \cdots d_n' = \begin{cases} \textbf{true,} & \text{if } m = n \text{ and each } c_i = d_i \\ \textbf{false,} & \text{otherwise} \end{cases}$$

$x \neq y = \sim(x = y)$

seqn$\leftarrow$string (string$\leftarrow$seqn L) $= L$

string$\leftarrow$seqn (seqn$\leftarrow$string s) $= s$

seqn$\leftarrow$string $'c_1 c_2 \cdots c_n' = <'c_1', 'c_2', \ldots, 'c_n'>$

Pragmatics:

The 'string$\leftarrow$seqn' and 'seqn$\leftarrow$string' operations take time proportional to the length of the string or sequence.

The '=' and '$\neq$' operations take time at most proportional to the length of the larger string, although on some implementations they may take constant time.

Figure B.4 Archetype for sequence types.

Syntax:

$\tau^* \in$ **type**, for all $\tau \in$ **type**

nil $\in \tau^*$

null: $\tau^* \to \mathbb{B}$

first: $\tau^* \to \tau$

rest: $\tau^* \to \tau^*$

prefix: $\tau \times \tau^* \to \tau^*$

length: $\tau^* \to \mathbb{N}$

Figure B.4 (continued)

$x : S \Rightarrow$ prefix (x, S)

$<> \Rightarrow$ nil

$<x_1, x_2, \ldots, x_n> \Rightarrow x_1 : <x_2, \ldots, x_n>$

Semantics:

nil $\in \tau^*$ $x : S \in \tau^*$

$z \notin \tau^*$, otherwise

null nil $=$ **true**   null $(x:S) =$ **false**

first nil $\neq x$ first $(x:S) = x$

rest nil $\neq S$ rest $(x:S) = S$

length nil $= 0$ length $(x:S) = 1 +$ length S

length is a total function on τ^*

Pragmatics:

The first, rest, prefix, and null operations all take constant time.
The prefix operation is significantly slower than the others.
The length operation takes time at most proportional to the length of
its argument.

Figure B.5 Archetype for finite set types.

Syntax:

finset $\tau \in$ **type**, for all $\tau \in$ **type**

$\varnothing \in$ finset τ

adjoin: $\tau \times$ finset $\tau \rightarrow$ finset τ

empty: finset $\tau \rightarrow \mathbb{B}$

$\in, \notin : \tau \times$ finset $\tau \rightarrow \mathbb{B}$

card: finset $\tau \rightarrow \mathbb{N}$

$\cap, \cup, \backslash$: finset $\tau \times$ finset $\tau \rightarrow$ finset τ

$\subset, \subseteq, =, \neq$: finset $\tau \times$ finset $\tau \rightarrow \mathbb{B}$

$\{\} \Rightarrow \varnothing$

$\{x_1, x_2, \ldots, x_n\} \Rightarrow$ adjoin $(x_1, \{x_2, \ldots, x_n\})$

Semantics:

$\varnothing \in$ finset τ

adjoin $(x, S) \in$ finset τ

$z \notin$ finset τ otherwise

empty $\varnothing =$ **true**

empty $[$adjoin $(x, S)] =$ **false**

$x \in \varnothing =$ **false**

$x \in$ adjoin $(y, S) = (x = y \lor x \in S)$

$\varnothing \subseteq S =$ **true**

adjoin $(x, S) \subseteq T = x \in T \land S \subseteq T$

card $\varnothing$ = 0
card [adjoin (x, S)] = card S, if $x \in S$
card [adjoin (x, S)] = $1 +$ card S, if $x \notin S$
card is a total function on finset τ

$S = T$ if and only if for all $x, x \in S = x \in T$

$x \in S \cap T = x \in S \wedge x \in T$
$x \in S \cup T = x \in S \vee x \in T$
$x \in S \setminus T = x \in S \wedge x \notin T$

$x \notin S = \neg (x \in S)$
$S = T = S \subseteq T \wedge T \subseteq S$
$S \neq T = \neg (S = T)$
$S \subset T = S \subseteq T \wedge S \neq T$

Figure B.6 Archetype for finite function types.

Syntax:

finfunc $(D \rightarrow R) \in$ **type** for all $D, R \in$ **type**

nihil $\in$ finfunc $(D \rightarrow R)$
fapply: finfunc $(D \rightarrow R) \times D \rightarrow R$
dom: finfunc $(D \rightarrow R) \rightarrow$ finset D
restr: finfunc $(D \rightarrow R) \times D \rightarrow$ finfunc $(D \rightarrow R)$
exten: finfunc $(D \rightarrow R) \times D \times R \rightarrow$ finfunc $(D \rightarrow R)$
overl: finfunc $(D \rightarrow R) \times D \times R \rightarrow$ finfunc $(D \rightarrow R)$
$=, \neq$: finfunc $(D \rightarrow R) \times$ finfunc $(D \rightarrow R) \rightarrow \mathbb{B}$

$Fx \Rightarrow$ fapply (F, x)
$[\,] \Rightarrow$ nihil
$[x_1 \mapsto y_1, x_2 \mapsto y_2, \ldots, x_n \mapsto y_n] \Rightarrow$ exten $([x_2 \mapsto y_2, \ldots, x_n \mapsto y_n], x_1, y_1)$

Semantics:

nihil $\in$ finfunc $(D \rightarrow R)$
exten $(F, x, y) \in$ finfunc $(D \rightarrow R)$, if $x \notin$ dom F
$z \notin$ finfunc $(D \rightarrow R)$ otherwise

fapply $(nihil, x) \neq y$
fapply [exten $(F, x, y), x$] $= y$
fapply [exten $(F, x, y), z$] $=$ fapply (F, z), if $x \neq z$

restr $(nihil, x) = nihil$
restr [exten $(F, x, y), x$] $= F$
restr [exten $(F, x, y), z$] $=$ exten [restr $(F, z), x, y$], if $x \neq z$

dom nihil $= \varnothing$
dom [exten (F, x, y)] $=$ dom $F \cup \{x\}$
dom is a total function on finfunc $(D \rightarrow R)$

overl $(F, x, y) =$ exten [restr $(F, x), x, y$]

$F = G$ if and only if dom $F =$ dom G,
  and for all $x \in$ dom $F, Fx = Gx$

Figure B.6 (continued)

$(F = G) = $ **true** if $F = G$
$(F = G) = $ **false** if $F \neq G$
$(F \neq F) = \neg(F = G)$

Pragmatics:

The fapply, dom, exten, restr, and overl operations take time at most proportional to the number of pairs in the finite function.

Figure B.7 Archetype for direct product types.

Syntax:

$T \times U \in$ **type**, for all $T, U \in$ **type**
left: $T \times U \rightarrow T$
right: $T \times U \rightarrow U$
$=, \neq: (T \times U)^2 \rightarrow \mathbb{B}$

$T_1 \times T_2 \times \cdots \times T_n \Rightarrow T_1 \times (T_2 \times \cdots \times T_n)$
$T^1 \Rightarrow T$
$T^n \Rightarrow T \times T^{n-1}$, for $n > 1$
$(x_1, x_2, \ldots, x_n) \Rightarrow (x_1, (x_2, \ldots, x_n))$

Semantics:

$(x, y) \in T \times U$
$z \notin T \times U$ otherwise

left $(x, y) = x$
right $(x, y) = y$
$(x, y) = (x', y')$ if and only if $x = x'$ and $y = y'$
$(p = p') = $ **true**, if $p = p'$
$(p = p') = $ **false**, if $p \neq p'$
$p \neq p' = \neg(p = p')$

Pragmatics:

All operations except '=' and '≠' take constant time.
The time complexity of '=' and '≠' depends on that of the '=' operations of the base types.

Figure B.8 Archetype generated by structure declarations for direct products.

Declaration:

abstract structure $T \equiv C(\phi_1 \in T_1, \phi_2 \in T_2, \ldots, \phi_n \in T_n)$

Syntax:

$T \in$ **type**
$C: T_1 \times T_2 \times \cdots \times T_n \rightarrow T$

$$\phi_i: T \to T_i$$
$$\phi_i!: T_i \times T \to T$$
$$=, \neq: T^2 \to \mathbb{B}$$

Semantics:

$$C(x_1, \ldots, x_n) \in T$$
$$z \notin T \text{ otherwise}$$
$$\phi_i[C(x_1, x_2, \ldots, x_n)] = x_i$$
$$\phi_i[\phi_i! (x, t)] = x$$
$$\phi_i[\phi_j! (x, t)] = \phi_i t, \text{ if } i \neq j$$
$$C(x_1, \ldots, x_n) = C(y_1, \ldots, y_n) \text{ if and only if } x_1 = y_1, \ldots, x_n = y_n$$
$$(t = t') = \textbf{true}, \text{ if } t = t'$$
$$(t = t') = \textbf{false}, \text{ if } t \neq t'$$
$$t \neq t' = \neg (t = t')$$

Pragmatics:

All operations except '=' and '≠' take constant time.
The time complexity of '=' and '≠' depends on that of the '=' operations of the base types.

Figure B.9 Archetype for direct sum types.

$$T + U \in \textbf{type}, \text{ for all } T, U \in \textbf{type}$$

1st: $T \to T + U$	2nd: $U \to T + U$
$1st^{-1}: T + U \to T$	$2nd^{-1}: T + U \to U$
1st?: $T + U \to \mathbb{B}$	2nd?: $T + U \to \mathbb{B}$

$$=, \neq: (T + U)^2 \to \mathbb{B}$$
$$T_1 + T_2 + \cdots T_n \Rightarrow T_1 + (T_2 + \cdots + T_n)$$

Semantics:

1st $x \in T + U$	2nd $x \in T + U$

$$z \notin T + U \text{ otherwise}$$

$1st^{-1} (1st\ x) = x$	$2nd^{-1} (2nd\ x) = x$
$1st^{-1} (2nd\ x) \neq y$	$2nd^{-1} (1st\ x) \neq y$
1st? (1st x) = **true**	2nd? (2nd x) = **true**
1st? (2nd x) = **false**	2nd? (1st x) = **false**
1st x = 1st y if and only if $x = y$	2nd x = 2nd y if and only if $x = y$

$$1st\ x \neq 2nd\ y$$

$(x = y) = \textbf{true}, \text{ if } x = y$	$(x = y) = \textbf{false}, \text{ if } x \neq y$

$$(x \neq y) = \neg (x = y)$$

Pragmatics:

All operations except '=' and '≠' take constant time.
The time complexity of '=' and '≠' depends on that of the '=' operations of the base types.

Figure B.10 Archetype generated by structure declarations for direct sums.

Declaration:
>**abstract structure** $T \equiv v_1 \colon T_1 + v_2 \colon T_2 + \cdots + v_n \colon T_n$

Syntax:
>$T \in$ **type**
>
>$v_i \colon T_i \to T$
>
>$v_i^{-1} \colon T \to T_i$
>
>$v_i? \colon T \to \mathbb{B}$
>
>$=, \neq \colon T^2 \to \mathbb{B}$

Semantics:
>$v_i x \in T$
>
>$z \notin T$ otherwise
>
>$v_i^{-1}(v_i\, x) = x$
>
>$v_i^{-1}(v_j\, x) \neq y$, if $i \neq j$
>
>$v_i?\,(v_i\, x) =$ **true**
>
>$v_i?\,(v_j\, x) =$ **false**, if $i \neq j$
>
>$v_i\, x = v_i\, y$ if and only if $x = y$
>
>$v_i\, x \neq v_j\, y$, if $i \neq j$
>
>$(x = y) =$ **true**, if $x = y$
>
>$(x = y) =$ **false**, if $x \neq y$
>
>$(x \neq y) = \neg\,(x = y)$

Pragmatics:
>All operations except '=' and '≠' take constant time.
>The time complexity of '=' and '≠' depends on that of the '=' operations of the base types.

Figure B.11 Archetype for trivial type.

Syntax:
>$\mathbf{1} \in$ **type**
>
>$() \in \mathbf{1}$
>
>$=, \neq \colon \mathbf{1}^2 \to \mathbb{B}$

Semantics:
>$() \in \mathbf{1}$
>
>$z \notin \mathbf{1}$ otherwise
>
>$[() = ()] =$ **true**
>
>$[() \neq ()] =$ **false**

Pragmatics:
>Both operations take constant time.

Figure B.12 Archetypes of map and filter functionals.

Syntax:
map: $(T \to U) \to (T^* \to U^*)$, for all $T,\ U \in$ **type**
fil: $(T \to \mathbb{B}) \to (T^* \to T^*)$, for all $T \in$ **type**

Semantics:
map f nil $=$ nil
map $f\ (x : S) = fx\ :\ $ map $f\ S$

fil P nil $=$ nil
fil $P\ (x : S) = x\ :\ $ fil $P\ S$, if $Px =$ **true**
fil $P\ (x : S) = $ fil $P\ S$, if $Px =$ **false**

Pragmatics:
With sequential implementations these take linear time.
With some parallel implementations they take constant time.

Figure B.13 Archetype for composition.

Syntax:
$\circ : [(S \to T) \times (R \to S)] \to (R \to T)$, for all $R,\ S,\ T \in$ **type**
That is, $(f \circ g): R \to T$ for $f: S \to T$ and $g: R \to S$

Semantics:
$(f \circ g)\,x = f\,(gx)$

Pragmatics:
Composition takes constant time.

Figure B.14 Archetype for functional construction.

Syntax:
$[;]: [(S \to T) \times (S \to U)] \to [S \to (T \times U)]$, for all $S,\ T,\ U \in$ **type**
That is, $(f ; g): S \to (T \times U)$, for $f: S \to T$ and $g: S \to U$.
$(f_1; f_2; \cdots ; f_{n-1}; f_n) \Rightarrow (f_1; (f_2; \cdots ; f_{n-1}; f_n))$

Semantics:
$(f ; g)\,x = (fx, gx)$

Pragmatics:
Binary construction takes constant time.
With sequential implementations, n-ary construction takes linear time.
With some parallel implementations it takes constant time.

Figure B.15 Archetype of reduction and accumulation functionals.

Syntax:

redr, redl, red: $(T \times T \to T) \to (T^* \to T)$, for all $T \in$ **type**

accr: $\{[(S \times T) \to T] \times T\} \to (S^* \to T)$, for all $S, T \in$ **type**

accl: $\{[(S \times T) \to S] \times S\} \to (T^* \to S)$, for all $S, T \in$ **type**

Semantics:

redr $f <x> = x$

redr $f (x : S) = f (x,$ redr $f S)$, if f is associative

redl $f <x> = x$

redl f [postfix (S, x)] $= f ($ redl $f S, x)$

red $f <x> = x$, if f is associative

red $f (S {\wedge} T) = f ($red $f S,$ red $f T)$, if f is associative

red $f S \neq y$, if f isn't associative

accr (f, z) nil $= z$

accr $(f, z) (x : Y) = f [x,$ accr $(f, z) Y]$

accl (f, z) nil $= z$

accl (f, z) [postfix (X, y)] $= f [$accl $(f, z) X, y]$

Pragmatics:

With a sequential implementation all reductions and accumulations take linear time.

With some parallel implementations 'red' takes logarithmic time.

Figure B.16 Archetype for constant construction.

Syntax:

$\mathrm{const}_T: S \to (T \to S)$, for all $S, T \in$ **type**

Semantics:

$\mathrm{const}_T k x = k$

Pragmatics:

Takes constant time.

Figure B.17 Archetype for conditional construction.

Syntax:

cond: $(S \to \mathbb{B}) \times (S \to T) \times (S \to T) \to (S \to T)$

Semantics:

cond $(P, F, G) x = Fx$, if $Px =$ **true**

cond $(P, F, G) x = Gx$, if $Px =$ **false**

Pragmatics:

Takes time which is the sum of that for P and either F or G.

Figure B.18 Archetype for functional direct sum and alternation.

Syntax:

$[+]: [(S \to U) \times (T \to V)] \to [(S + T) \to (U + V)]$, for all $S, T, U, V \in$ **type**

$[|]: [(S \to U) \times (T \to U)] \to [(S + T) \to U]$, for all $S, T, U \in$ **type**

That is, $(f + g): S + T \to U + V$, for $f : S \to U, g : T \to V$

Also, $(f | g): S + T \to U$, for $f : S \to U$ and $g : T \to U$

Semantics:

$(f + g) \,(1st\ x) = 1st\ (fx),$ $\qquad\qquad (f + g) \,(2nd\ x) = 2nd\ (gx)$

$(f | g) \,(1st\ x) = fx,$ $\qquad\qquad\qquad (f | g) \,(2nd\ x) = gx$

Pragmatics:

Operations take the time of the selected summand.

Figure B.19 Archetype for pretest conditional.

Syntax:

$[\to]: (D \to A + B) \times (D+D \to R) \to (D \to R)$, for all $A, B, D, R \in$ **type**

That is, $(P \to Q): D \to R$, for $P: D \to A + B,\ \ Q: D + D \to R$

Semantics:

$(P \to Q)x = Q\,(1st\ x),$ if $1st?\ (Px)$

$(P \to Q)x = Q\,(2nd\ x),$ if $2nd?\ (Px)$

Pragmatics:

$P \to Q$ takes time equal to the sum of times for P and Q.

Figure B.20 Archetype for recursive set types.

Syntax:

recset $\tau = \tau \to \mathbb{B}$, for all $\tau \in$ **type**

recset$\leftarrow$finset: finset $\tau \to$ recset τ

$\cap$: recset $\tau \times$ recset $\tau \to$ recset τ

$\cup$: recset $\tau \times$ recset $\tau \to$ recset τ

$\setminus$: recset $\tau \times$ recset $\tau \to$ recset τ

$\sim$: recset $\tau \to$ recset τ

$\varnothing \in$ recset τ

$O \in$ recset τ

Semantics:

$x \in S = Sx$

$x \in S \cap T = x \in S \wedge x \in T$

$x \in S \cup T = x \in S \vee x \in T$

$x \in S \setminus T = x \in S \wedge x \notin T$

$x \in {\sim} S = x \notin S$

$x \in \varnothing =$ **false**

$x \in O =$ **true**

Pragmatics:
> The cost of a membership test is the cost of the underlying characteristic function.
>
> All other operations take constant time (to construct the result set).

Figure B.21 Archetype for recursively enumerable sequence types.

Syntax:
> reseq τ = $\mathbb{N} \to \tau$, for all $\tau \in$ **type**
> first: reseq $\tau \to \tau$
> rest: reseq $\tau \to$ reseq τ
> prefix: $\tau \times$ reseq $\tau \to$ reseq τ
> map: $(\sigma \to \tau) \to$ (reseq $\sigma \to$ reseq τ)
> all: $\tau \to$ reseq τ
> Naturals $\in$ reseq $\mathbb{N}$

Semantics:
> first $S = S_1$
> $(\text{rest } S)_i = S_{i+1}$ $i \geq 1$
> $[\text{prefix } (x, S)]_{i+1} = S_i$, $i \geq 1$
>
> first $[\text{prefix } (x, S)] = x$
> rest $[\text{prefix } (x, S)] = S$
> prefix (first S, rest S) = S
>
> $(\text{map } f\ S)_i = f(S_i)$
> $(\text{all } k)_i = k$
> $\text{Naturals}_i = i - 1$

Pragmatics:
> All operations take constant time, except first and element selection, whose costs depend on the cost of the underlying enumeration function.

Figure B.22 Archetype for stream types.

Syntax:
> $\tau^{\infty} \in$ **type**, for all $\tau \in$ **type**
> first: $\tau^{\infty} \to \tau$
> rest: $\tau^{\infty} \to \tau^{\infty}$
> [::]: $\tau \times \tau^{\infty} \to \tau^{\infty}$

Semantics:
> first $(x :: S) = x$,
> rest $(x :: S) = S$
> first $S ::$ rest $S = S$

Pragmatics:
> The prefixing operation delays evaluation of its arguments.
>
> The first and rest operations force evaluation of both stream components.

Appendix C

Functional Programming in Scheme and LISP

C.1 General

Because it is rare that constructs in different languages are exactly equivalent, the following correspondences must be treated cautiously. Although the correspondences are adequate for most purposes, the programmer should consult the standard Scheme and Common LISP definitions for detailed semantics. By 'standard Scheme' we mean the dialect described in (Rees and Clinger 1986); the source for Common LISP is (Steele 1984). Both languages, however, continue to evolve.

Scheme, like LISP, is an imperative language, but in Scheme all the imperative procedures end their names with an exclamation point (often pronounced "bang"), for example, 'set!' and 'set-cdr!'. Therefore, to program applicatively in Scheme, simply avoid all procedures whose names end with an exclamation point. Scheme has all the facilities required for true functional programming (i.e., programming with higher-order functions). It uses an eager evaluation strategy, however, so caution must be exercised in the use of infinite data structures.

C.2 Declarations

Φ	Scheme	Common LISP
$x \equiv E$	(define x E)	(defconstant x E)
$f x \equiv E$	(define (f x) E)	(defun f (x) E)
$f(x_1, \ldots, x_n) \equiv E$	(define (f x_1 $\ldots$ x_n) E)	(defun f $(x_1 \ldots x_n)$ E)
let $x_1 \equiv E_1$ **and** $x_2 \equiv E_2$ $\vdots$ **and** $x_n \equiv E_n$ **in** E	(let ((x_1 E_1) (x_2 E_2) $\vdots$ (x_n E_n)) E)	(let ((x_1 E_1) (x_2 E_2) $\vdots$ (x_n E_n)) E)
let rec $x_1 \equiv E_1$ **and rec** $x_2 \equiv E_2$ $\vdots$ **and rec** $x_n \equiv E_n$ **in** E	(letrec ((x_1 E_1) (x_2 E_2) $\vdots$ (x_n E_n)) E)	
let rec $f_1(p_1) \equiv E_1$ **and rec** $f_2(p_2) \equiv E_2$ $\vdots$ **and rec** $f_n(p_n) \equiv E_n$ **in** E	(letrec ((f_1 (lambda (p_1) E_1)) (f_2 (lambda (p_2) E_2)) $\vdots$ (f_n (lambda (p_n) E_n))) E)	(labels ((f_1 (p_1) E_1) (f_2 (p_2) E_2) $\vdots$ (f_n (p_n) E_n)) E)
E **where** $x_1 \equiv E_1$ **and** $\ldots$	(let ((x_1 E_1) $\ldots$) E)	(let ((x_1 E_1) $\ldots$) E)
E **where rec** $x_1 \equiv E_1$ **and rec** $\ldots$	(letrec ((x_1 E_1) $\ldots$) E)	
E **where rec** $f_1(p_1) \equiv E_1$ **and rec** $\ldots$	(letrec ((f_1 (lambda (p_1) E_1)) $\ldots$) E)	(labels ((f_1 (p_1) E_1) $\ldots$) E)

Notes

1. Scheme and LISP distinguish between multiple-argument functions and single-argument functions that happen to expect a list. For ways around this, see Section C.3.

2. The 'labels' construct in LISP can be used to define mutually recursive functions, but not data structures. The notation p_i refers to a list of one or more parameters (separated by commas in Φ, separated by spaces in Scheme and LISP).

C.3 Applications and Abstractions

Φ	Scheme	Common LISP
$f\,E$	$(f\ E)$	$(f\ E)$
$f\,(E_1, E_2, \ldots, E_n)$	$(f\ E_1\ E_2\ \ldots\ E_n)$	$(f\ E_1\ E_2\ \ldots\ E_n)$
$F\,(E_1, E_2, \ldots, E_n)$	$(F\ E_1\ E_2\ \ldots\ E_n)$	$(\text{funcall}\ F\ E_1\ E_2\ \ldots\ E_n)$
$F\,E$	$(\text{apply}\ F\ E)$	$(\text{apply}\ F\ E)$
$x \mapsto E$	$(\text{lambda}\ (x)\ E)$	$\#'(\text{lambda}\ (x)\ E)$
$(x_1, \ldots, x_n) \mapsto E$	$(\text{lambda}\ (x_1\ \ldots\ x_n)\ E)$	$\#'(\text{lambda}\ (x_1\ \ldots\ x_n)\ E)$

Notes

1. Scheme and LISP distinguish between multi-argument and single-argument functions that happen to expect a list. If f expects one argument, it is invoked '$(f\ E)$'. If f expects an argument list that is computed by the expression E, then it must be invoked '$(\text{apply}\ f\ E)$'.

2. In the preceding equivalences, f represents a function name, whereas F represents an expression that returns a function value.

3. In Common LISP a function name f used as an actual parameter must be written $\#'f$. For example, $(\text{map}\ \#'\text{sin}\ S)$.

C.4 Booleans

Φ	Scheme	Common LISP
true, false	#t, #f	t, nil
$\neg E$	$(\text{not}\ E)$	$(\text{not}\ E)$
$E \wedge E'$	$(\text{and}\ E\ E')$	$(\text{and}\ E\ E')$
$E \vee E'$	$(\text{or}\ E\ E')$	$(\text{or}\ E\ E')$
$E = E'$	$(\text{eq}\ E\ E')$	$(\text{eq}\ E\ E')$
$E \neq E'$	$(\text{not}\ (\text{eq}\ E\ E'))$	$(\text{not}\ (\text{eq}\ E\ E'))$
and, or		every, some
if B	$(\text{if}\ B$	$(\text{if}\ B$
then T	T	T
else F **endif**	$F)$	$F)$
if B **then** T	$(\text{cond}\ (B\quad T)$	$(\text{cond}\ (B\quad T)$
elsif B' **then** T'	$(B'\quad T')$	$(B'\quad T')$
$\vdots$	$\vdots$	$\vdots$
else F **endif**	$(\text{else}\ F))$	$(\text{t}\ F))$

C.5 Numbers

Φ	Scheme	Common LISP
$E_1 + E_2 + \ldots + E_n$	$(+\ E_1\ E_2\ \ldots\ E_n)$	$(+\ E_1\ E_2\ \ldots\ E_n)$
$E_1 \times E_2 \times \ldots \times E_n$	$(*\ E_1\ E_2\ \ldots\ E_n)$	$(*\ E_1\ E_2\ \ldots\ E_n)$
$+E, -E$	$(+\ E), (-\ E)$	$(+\ E), (-\ E)$
$+, -, \times, /$	$+, -, *, /$	$+, -, *, /$
$E \div E'$	(truncate ($/\ E\ E'$))	(truncate $E\ E'$)
$E \uparrow E'$	(expt $E\ E'$)	(expt $E\ E'$)
$<, \leq, =, \geq, >$	$<, <=, =, >=, >$	$<, <=, =, >=, >$
$E \neq E'$	(not (= $E\ E'$))	($/=\ E\ E'$)

Notes

1. The multi-argument forms of + and * are not provided in some Scheme implementations. Also, expt is not available in some implementations.

2. Scheme provides integer, rational, real, and complex numbers, although some implementations may not provide all of these. Some Scheme implementations provide arbitrary precision integers.

3. The numerical system of Common LISP is very similar to that of Scheme.

4. Some Scheme implementations don't have truncate, in which case use (quotient $E\ E'$), which is number theoretic division.

C.6 Strings

Φ	Scheme	Common LISP
'$ccc \ldots ccc$'	"$ccc \ldots ccc$"	"$ccc \ldots ccc$"
$E = E'$	(string=? $E\ E'$)	(string= $E\ E'$)
$E \neq E'$	(not (string=? $E\ E'$))	(not (string= $E\ E'$))
string←seqn E	(list->string E)	(coerce E 'string)
seqn←string E	(string->list E)	(coerce E 'list)

C.7 Sequences

Φ	Scheme	Common LISP
$<k_1, k_2, \ldots, k_n>$	'$(k_1\ k_2\ \ldots\ k_n)$	'$(k_1\ k_2\ \ldots\ k_n)$
$<E_1, E_2, \ldots, E_n>$	(list $E_1\ E_2\ \ldots\ E_n$)	(list $E_1\ E_2\ \ldots\ E_n$)
nil, <>	'()	nil, '()
first	car	first, car
rest	cdr	rest, cdr
prefix	cons	cons

null, nil?	null?	null
length	length	length
member	member	member
reverse	reverse	reverse
second	cadr	cadr
elt (E, E'), $E_{E'}$	(list-ref E $(- E'$ 1))	(elt E $(1- E'$))
$E_1 \wedge E_2 \wedge \ldots \wedge E_n$	(append E_1 E_2 $\ldots$ E_n)	(append E_1 E_2 $\ldots$ E_n)

Notes

1. In the preceding table, k_i represents a constant denotation and E_i represents an arbitrary expression.

2. Some Scheme implementations may provide 'nil' as a synonym for '().

3. Note that Scheme and Common LISP index sequences from 0, whereas Φ indexes from 1. Some other LISP dialects also index from 1.

4. Some Scheme implementations may not permit $n \neq 2$ in append applications.

C.8 Finite Sets

Φ	Common LISP
$\{k_1, \ldots, k_n\}$	'(k_1 $\ldots$ k_n)
$\{E_1, \ldots, E_n\}$	(list E_1 $\ldots$ E_n)
$\varnothing$	nil, '()
adjoin	adjoin
empty	null
$E \in E'$	(member E E')
$E \notin E'$	(not (member E E'))
card	length
$E \cap E'$	(intersection E E')
$E \cup E'$	(union E E')
$E \setminus E'$	(set-difference E E')
$E \subseteq E'$	(subsetp E E')
$E \subset E'$	
$E = E'$	(null (set-exclusive-or E E'))
$E \neq E'$	(not (null (set-exclusive-or E E')))

Notes

1. In Common LISP, finite sets are just lists. Thus the programmer must be careful not to introduce duplicates into the lists representing sets. One way to accomplish this is to use the function 'remove-duplicates'.

2. Scheme does not provide any functions (except member) for treating lists as sets.

C.9 Finite Functions

Φ	Scheme	Common LISP
$[x_1 \mapsto y_1, \ldots, x_n \mapsto y_n]$	$'((x_1\ y_1)\ \ldots\ (x_n\ y_n))$	$'((x_1 . y_1)\ \ldots\ (x_n . y_n))$
$[E_1 \mapsto F_1, \ldots, E_n \mapsto F_n]$	(list (list E_1 F_1) ... (list E_n F_n))	(list (cons E_1 F_1) ... (cons E_n F_n))
nihil	'()	nil, '()
fapply (F, x), Fx	(cadr (assoc x F))	(cdr (assoc x F :test #'equal))
dom F	(map car F)	(mapcar #'car F)
overl (F, x, y)		(acons x y F)
restr, exten		
$E = E'$		(null (set-exclusive-or E E'))
$E \neq E'$		(not (null (set-exclusive-or E E')))

Notes

1. In Scheme and Common LISP, finite functions are represented by *association lists*, that is, lists of pairs.

C.10 Direct Products, Sums, and Structures

Φ	Scheme	Common LISP
(k, k')	$'(k . k')$	$'(k . k')$
(E, E')	(cons E E')	(cons E E')
left, right	car, cdr	car, cdr
$E = E'$	(equal? E E')	(equal E E')
$E \neq E'$	(not (equal? E E'))	(not (equal E E'))
structure $S \equiv$	(define-structure	(defstruc (S
$C\ (\phi_1 \in t_1, \ldots, \phi_n \in t_n)$	$S\ \phi_1\ \ldots\ \phi_n$)	(:constructor C ($\phi_1\ \ldots\ \phi_n$)))
		$\phi_1\ \ldots\ \phi_n$)
$C(E_1, \ldots, E_n)$	(make-S E_1 ... E_n)	(C E_1 ... E_n)
$\phi_k\ E$	(S-ϕ_k E)	(S-ϕ_k E)
$C?\ E$	($S?$ E)	(S-p E)
$C^{-1}\ E$		

Notes

1. The correspondence is only approximate, since Φ is statically typed, whereas Scheme and LISP are dynamically typed.

2. Standard Scheme does not have structures; the syntax shown in the preceding table is provided in some dialects, such as Texas Instrument's PC-Scheme.

3. Direct sums are implemented by declaring a structure for each variant. In this case the filters are implemented by using the appropriate field selectors.

C.11 Streams

Φ	Scheme
$E :: E'$	(cons E (delay E')), (cons-stream E E')
first, rest	head, tail
$\ll E \gg$	(delay E)
force E	(force E)

Notes

1. Standard Scheme does not provide cons-stream, which is part of the Scheme dialect used in (Abelson and Sussman 1985).

2. Some Scheme dialects may omit delay and force.

3. Common LISP does not have streams in this sense at all. What it calls streams are IO ports.

C.12 Functionals

Φ	Scheme	Common LISP
map F E	(map F E)	(mapcar F E), (map 'list F E)
fil P E		(remove-if-not P E)
redl F E		(reduce F E)
redr F E		(reduce F E :from-end t)
accl (F, D) E		(reduce F E :initial-value D)
accr (F, D) E		(reduce F E :from-end t :initial-value D)
red		
const k	(lambda (x) k)	#'(lambda (x) k)
cond		
$F \circ G$		
$F ; G$		
$F + G$		
$F \mid G$		
$F \rightarrow G$		

Notes

1. Functionals not provided in Scheme or LISP (such as cond, ∘) can be expressed as abstractions, as done in the preceding table for const. Another solution is to simply implement these functionals.

Index of Notation

Symbol	Name*
″	Quotation marks
( )	Parentheses
[ ]	Square brackets
{ }	Curly braces
< >	Angle brackets
≪ ≫	Delay brackets
Φ	Phi language
≡	Definition
=	Equality
≠	Inequality
∈	Membership
∉	Nonmembership
←	From
→	To
$.^n$	Superscripts
$._n$	Subscripts
:	Colon

* Name under which the symbol can be found in the index.

$\Rightarrow$	Rewrites
$\mathbf{T}[\![\,]\!]$	Time of
$\bot$	Undefined
λ	Lambda
$\mathbb{B}$	Boolean type
$\mathbb{N}$	Natural type
$\mathbb{R}$	Real type
$\mathbb{Z}$	Integer type
$\mathbf{1}$	Trivial type
$\neg$	Not sign
$\wedge$	And sign
$\vee$	Or sign
$+$	Addition
$-$	Subtraction
$\times$	Multiplication
$/$	Division
$\div$	Truncating division
$<$	Less than
$>$	Greater than
$\leq$	Less than or equal
$\geq$	Greater than or equal
$.^{*}$	Sequence type
$<x_1, \ldots, x_n>$	Sequence denotation
$\wedge$	Catenation
$\{x_1, \ldots, x_n\}$	Set denotation
$\varnothing$	Empty set
$\cap$	Intersection
$\cup$	Union
$\setminus$	Set difference
$\subseteq$	(Improper) subset
$\subset$	Proper subset
$[x_1 \mapsto y_1, \ldots, x_n \mapsto y_n]$	Finite function denotation
$(x_1, \ldots, x_n)$	Tuple denotation; tuple constructor
$\times$	Direct product type
$+$	Direct sum type; summation, functional
$!$	Substitution
$?$	Discriminator
$.^{-1}$	Injector
$()$	Trivial value
ω_T	Irrelevant value
$\cong$	Isomorphism
$.^{+}$	Nonnull sequence type

↦	Maps to
○	Arbitrary operator; universal set
,	Tuple constructor
∘	Composition
;	Construction
|	Alternation
Σ	Summation
.\<n\>	Direct product, *n*-fold
~	Complement
∧	Language catenation
#	Singleton language
ε	Empty language
?	Language optionality
::	Delayed prefix
.∞	Stream
→	Vector
∓	Representation
·[·=·]	Substitution context
Σ	Substitution operator
Λ	Abstraction operator

Index

Prefix notation, 195
Prefix representation, 196–198
Presection, 241
Pretest conditional, 286–288
prf (function), 244
Primitive operation, 38
Principle, *see* Abstraction
    Principle; Domain Structure
    Principle; Induction
    recapitulates recursion;
    Method of Differences
prod (function), 82
Product, Cartesian, 298
Programming in the large, 223
PROLOG, 4, 436
Proof
    difficult for iterative proof,
      109–110
    theorem based on, 456
    see also Correctness proof;
      Inductive proof
Proper subset, 115, 123
Propositional Calculus, Wang
    algorithm, 446–455
Prototype
    vs. archetype, 114–115
    Boolean, 375
    definition, 114–115
    direct product type, 375
    direct sum, 179–180, 377
    direct sum type, 377
    efficiency, 115
    establishes computability, 115
    establishes consistency, 115
    finite function, 159–161
    finite set, 129–133
    implementations, 4–5
    proof of finite set, 138–143
    reduction, 271
    sequence, 184–186, 377, 379
Pseudo-interpretation, 209
Pseudofunction, 11
psum (function), 274, 314
Pure expression, 8, 15–17
    properties, 15
Pure function, 15–17

Question mark, *see* Discriminator;
    Language optionality
Quotation marks, 5
    string denotations, 38
Quotes, *see* Quotation marks

rand (selector), 414
Rational type, 171
rator (selector), 414
RE sequence, *see* Recursively
    enumerable sequence
ready (pseudofunction), 345
Real number
    computable, 314–315
    infinite precision, 314–315

Real-time program, 334–348,
    541–542
Real type, 38
    infinite precision, 315–516
    operations, 38
rec (keyword), 391, 520
reccontext (function), 529, 533
recelem (variant), 535
Recognitive grammars, 302–309
    archetype and prototype, 307
    for arithmetic grammar, 308
    vs. generative, 315–316
Record, 160
    vs. array, 162
    variant, 177–180
    variant flattening, 180
    see also Personnel record
recset (type constructor), 295, 297
    see also Recursive set
recset←finset (function), 298
Recurrence relation, 98
Recursion
    broken by pointer, 185
    finite expression of infinite
      structure, 289–290
    and induction, 71
    and infinite formulas, 18–19,
      182–183
    left vs. right, 309
    performance compared with
      iteration, 108
    and performance equation, 99
    see also Tail recursion
Recursive
    structure of expressions, 14
    see also Recursive data
      structure; Recursive
      declaration; Recursive
      definition; Recursively
      enumerable; Recursive
      function; Recursive set;
      Recursive type
Recursive data structure
    and evaluation order, 316–323
    fractals, 322–323
    to implement recursive
      declaration, 520
    implementation, 537–539
Recursive declaration
    compound, implementation,
      531–537
    with delayed expressions,
      521–523
    with imperative features, 523
    implementation, 519–539
    in normal order language,
      519–520
    mutual, 391
    with recursive data structures,
      520–521
    reduction to lambda calculus,
      532
    by rewrite rule, 383–384
    syntactic sugar, 391

Recursive definition
    developing, 68–69, 73–76
    of functionals, 288–291
    are implicit, 22
    as infinity of cases, 19
    stopping condition, 75
    of types, *see* Recursive type
Recursive function, 295
    in theory of computation, 24
Recursive function declaration
    with **Y** closures, 525–530
Recursive set
    archetype, 297
    Cartesian product, 298
    extension vs. intension,
      298–301
    from finite set, 297–298
    intersection, 295–296
    prototype, 297
    recognitive grammar, 302–309
    recset, 295, 297
    vs. recursively enumerable set,
      295
    Russell's paradox, 301–302
    type definition, 295
    unimplementable operations
      295, 298–302
Recursive type, 180–181
    Russell's paradox, 302
    sequence as, 181–187
Recursively enumerable set, 295,
    316
Recursively enumerable
    sequence, 310–316
    archetype, 311
    enumeration function, 310
    generative grammar, 315–316
    prototype, 313
    reseq, 311, 313
    terminatable, 315
red (functional), 269–272
redl (functional), 267–269, 271
    as a recursive functional, 291
redr (functional), 266–267, 271
reduce (function)
    abstract calculi, 463–464
    eval derived from, 486–487
    lambda calculus, 483–486
Reduced form, *see* Normal form
Reduces
    by renaming, 400–401
    by substitution, 401
Reduction, 80–84
    vs. accumulation, 273
    and, 83, 266, 272, 274
    append, 83, 266, 272, 274
    by closure, 478, 480
    by renaming and substitution,
      360, 424, 440–442
    closure reduction calculus,
      481–483
    closure reduction program,
      483–486
    definition, 401